THE MYTHIC MIND

The History and Philosophy of Psychology

———————————

THE MYTHIC MIND

THE HISTORY AND PHILOSOPHY OF PSYCHOLOGY

By Neil Alan Soggie

THE MYTHIC MIND: The History and Philosophy of Psychology

Neil Alan Soggie

Copyright © 2004 by Neil Alan Soggie

ALL RIGHTS RESERVED

International Standard Book Number

1-894928-41-5

All scripture quotations, unless otherwise indicated, are taken from the
HOLY BIBLE, NEW INTERNATIONAL VERSION®. NIV®.
Copyright ©1973, 1978, 1984 by International Bible Society.
Used by permission of Zondervan. All rights reserved.

Individual orders of this text are available through Amazon.com and Barnes & Noble.com

For bookstore & university orders please contact:

Word Alive Press
131 Cordite Road
Winnipeg, Manitoba Canada
R3W 1S1
1-800-665-1468 ext.203

Printed in the United States of America

It is my hope that the general theme of this book (the way we make meaning in life) will allow you to not only learn about the history of psychology but also reflect upon your own life and its meaning. Throughout this book I trust that you will ponder what makes up your own *personal story* and thereby gain greater self-awareness. I trust that you will peel away the layers of your *public story* and begin to reflect upon the *transformational* and *sacred* stories that give your life meaning.

- Neil Soggie

TABLE OF CONTENTS:

SECTION 1 – ANCIENT PSYCHOLOGY

Chapter 1 – In the Beginning 3

Chapter 2 – Mythopoeics and Wellness 13
 The Torah (22)

Chapter 3 – Ancient Models of Meaning and Being............................47
 Quoheleth (Ecclesiastes) (56)
 Proverbs (59)
 Job (68)

SECTION 2 – EASTERN AND WESTERN FOUNDATIONS

Chapter 4 – An Oriental Model..95
 Teachings of Buddah (99)
 Sayings of Confucius (102)

Chapter 5 – The Greek Tradition..103
 Myth of the Cave - Plato (109)
 On the Sacred Disease - Hippocrates (113)
 On Dreams – Aristotle (123)

Chapter 6 – Christian & Islamic Models...131
 Romans /1 Corinthians (136)
 Augustine's Confessions (148)

Chapter 7 – Middle Ages and the Renaissance 165
 In Praise of Folly – Erasmus of Rotterdam (170)
 Descartes' Meditations on First Philosophy (189)
 Baruch Spinoza (198)
 John Locke (213)
 The Critique of Practical Reason – Immanuel Kant (220)

SECTION 3 – THE FOUR HEADED MONSTER

Chapter 8 – Cognitive Psychology 243
 Eugenics: Its Definition, Scope and Aims –Galton (246)
 Hereditary Talent and Character – Galton (250)
 New Methods/Diagnosis of Intellectual Subnormals – Binet (272)

Chapter 9 – Behaviorism 297
    Lecture on the Work of the Cerebral Hemisphere – Pavlov (301)
    Conflicting Psychologies of Learning – Hull (311)
    Psychology as the Behaviourist Views It – Watson (335)
    Two Types of Conditioned Reflex/Pseudo Type – Skinner (348)

Chapter 10 – Psychoanalysis 357
    What Life Should Mean to You – Adler (362)
    A Philosophy of Life – Freud (376)
    Essay on Psychological Types – Jung (392)

Chapter 11 – Humanistic Psychology 449
    Significant Aspects of Client-Centered Therapy – Rogers (451)
    A Theory of Human Motivation – Maslow (462)

SECTION 4 – THE FLAVOURING MOVEMENTS

Chapter 12 – Phenomenological Existential Psychology 483
    The Crisis of European Sciences – Husserl (489)
    The Basic Problems of Phenomenology – Heidegger (501)
    Sartre's Existential View (519)
    Excerpts from Victor Frankl (520)
    Quotations from Rollo May (522)
    Existential Development of James Fowler (526)

Chapter 13 – Rediscovering a Lost Heritage: Understanding the Value of a Traditional Christian Approach 535

POST-SCRIPT

Post-Script – Perversions of Psychology 559

References 567

Appendix A – The Greek Alphabet 573

Appendix B – History Timeline 579

SECTION ONE

ANCIENT PSYCHOLOGY

Chapter One:

IN THE BEGINNING

DISCOVERING OUR NEED FOR MYTHS

EDEN IS ...

That old-fashioned House
We dwell in every day
Without suspecting our abode
Until we drive away.

How fair on looking back, the Day
We sauntered from the Door –
Unconscious our returning
But discover it no more.

Emily Dickenson

Truth is of concern to everyone. As the Roman Governor Pilate stood in front of Jesus he leaned forward to posit this question, "What is Truth?"[1] At times we may feel the frustration of Pilate for there is no response that comes forth on this issue. Jesus stood silent, and so too do philosophy and science as we look at *truth* and *the mind*. Oftentimes we search for an ultimate answer to questions like, "What do I need to be happy?" or "What is the meaning of life?" yet we are met with silence.

Could it be that we are asking the wrong questions? Perhaps the way we work, where we come from and how we make life meaningful are entirely subjective. Perhaps what is important is people's attitudes toward their circumstances and their orientation towards the cosmos. Perhaps one's mythic story and overall belief structure holds the key to all of these questions.

---

[1] In contrast to traditional systemic or individual therapies, the mythopoeic perspective of psychology brings in the recognition that knowledge is individually, socially and consensually constructed. That is, when we say that something is "true" or "factual", we can understand this as saying that a sufficient community currently accepts this information as "true" or "factual" within their story or meaning structure for organizing the complex phenomenon of existence.

4   THE MEANING OF LIFE

The basic issues of life and love and meaning are issues central to both psychology and existentialism. Since the existential is in many ways the earliest form of psychology we shall use it as a guide through our historical survey of the mind. Since the whole existential approach rails against the dogmatic categorization of people and the rigid doctrine of narrow therapeutic approaches but does esteem the appraisal of orientation, it is the natural springboard for our survey of the history of the mind.

The Importance of Existentialism

It is clear that an understanding of personal experience and interpretation is often missing from the modern medical/bio-behavioural model of psychology (Sacks, 1998). In contrast to this model the existential approach to psychology is one that emphasizes that the therapist must always consider the constructed, interpretive aspect of experience (Spinelli, 2003). However it is important to recognize that an existential view does not deny that there are some aspects of our identities and experiences that are part of our existence and not simply a psychological construct. As Corrie suggests, gender is an example of this form of experience. While gender is a relational and psychological construct, it is also a personal experience of embodiment. Therefore, the existential approach helps us to recognize that there is a difference between the *interpretation*[2] of experiences and the fact of *embodied experience* available to each individual (Keijzer, 2000).

According to existentialism, the cognitive construct is part of the package—not the entire parcel[3]. To this end the first quality of consciousness, self-awareness, is implicitly one of the founding assumptions of existentialism; that we are capable of being aware of our existence (May, 1958). It is this essential quality that allows us to assess value and meaning to our existence and state of being (Williams, 1994). It is this self-awareness then that helps us monitor our oneness with the world and to assess and guide ourselves through the *infinite number of possibilities* (May, 1958).

However, it is not as simple as mere awareness of being. Consciousness is much more complex than this, as it is the awareness of the aspects of the self. This means at a basic level being aware of one's individual narrative and the context of this narrative within the mythic structure of the community (Williams, 1994). This mythic story of self is the organizing function of one's self, including one's existence, thought processes, and memories. This narrative form of consciousness is sometimes labelled *metacognition* because it is considered in some aspects of

---

2 Fred Keijzer's article (2000) notes that while other researchers claim to provide neural-network models of important aspects of subjective human experience such claims are false and that any model of interpretive experience must include an aspect of the body-centered interpretation of experience, drawn from the work of Merleau-Ponty.

3 Anthony Williams' article (1994) notes that living social systems also have a place in forming the environment of human existence. Williams contends that social themes for construction of meaning, time and space all influence the formation of human stories and their time/spatial relationships. *Clinical sociometry to define space in family systems.* Journal of Group Psychotherapy, Psychodrama and Sociometry. 47 (3): 126-144.

cognitive psychology to be a rostral activity above and beyond the mechanical psychological functions of environmental input. While it is true that this *mythic structure* of the self, or *metacognition* (Hamel, LeClerc, & LeFrancois, 2003), can be categorized into awareness and executive functions, it expands to form the basis of all human experience[4].

The second aspect of the human experience, then, is the capacity to will and make choices. Personal will is an offspring of the basic meta-cognition processes that occur within the individual. This will is formed in large part to feed the needs of the biological structures, but also to interact with the mythic story of the community. The role of personal story is placed within the community story, tempered by the emotional conditioning associated with the personal interaction with the community narrative. This full interaction process is essential for navigating through the human experience. It is through this navigation that we experience "becoming" (Yalom, 1980) in the very fluid process of being an individual. As Yalom (1980) terms it, the *present-becoming-future* is central to the human experience and is also vital in the existential approach to psychology.

The Mythopoeic Foundation of Existentialism

While some fixed embodied experiences are acknowledged, existentialism is quick to point out that even within these phenomenological experiences there are a wide variety of responses to these experiences based upon stance and identity factors. In this view then, it is not the particular acts that are of major significance, but the ways in which we make personal and social sense of them (Penticoff, 2002). Such a view harkens back to the oldest ideas of humanity and its integration with the "real" physical world.[5]

The wisdom of ancient cultures is that they understood (if only intuitively) the role of public myth and legend in the formation of the individual. Since psychology has emerged as a discipline into the world of mass media, its basic structures often do not acknowledge the importance of myth. In contrast, cultures of strong oral tradition still have as a central tenet *the story* as key to developing the individual. Indeed, even the modern North American aboriginal nations still perform the *vision quest* and other essential rites of forming the individual's story within the mythic structure of the community.

In order to understand the nature of humanity it is essential to begin with the most basic theme that connects us to the most ancient of ancients. In this sense the foundational component

---

4 Hamel et al's (2003) article notes that some of the leading existential psychotherapists of the mid 20th century viewed the idea of social meaning within a mythic structure (what they termed the transcendent) is essential for experiencing "meaning" in life.

5 Judith Penticoff (2002) notes that metacognition is an intricate process used to activate prior learning and provide a sense of personal journey in situations like reading literature. In essence ,metacognition is part of the autonoetic process of personal narrative and interaction with the mythic structure set before someone.

6   THE MEANING OF LIFE

of humanity that we can draw from the ancients is that of mythology. The assertion that myth making is the most natural of human activities is not of course limited to the individual but is part and parcel of community and culture (Eakin).[6] However, in order to appreciate the nature of myth it is important to break it down to its smallest parts and its function within the individual. Without an understanding of the function of myth within the person we will not be able to fully appreciate the impact of great legends (Shotter 1989).[7]

Myth is in many ways the cornerstone of individual identity and autobiography. While memory is important in much of human functioning, the fact is that story creation is a greater force from a neuropsychological perspective than is factual memory (Shotter, 1989). In speaking in such terms it is the "stories" that are formed, shaped and invented that both reflect and influence our functioning and ways of making meaning. Certainly this does not mean that memory does not play a part in a person's functioning, yet it is relived as a "story", "myth" or "legend". Indeed, in many ways the core of human experience is found in the stories that are used to understand reality. They are what make us "human" (Squire, 1989).[8]

Myth and humanity seem to begin together in civilization, and with myth, humanity enters into a new and unique dimension of existence (Sartorius, 2003). For the evolutionary scientist storytelling is seen as the new agency of recreating reality that gives expression to the muteness of our animal existence within evolutionary history. Indeed, if one surveys the most ancient Sumerian cultures it is as if, in a moment, humanity emerged from being lithic brutes to virtuosos of mythical music. For those who are of a religious persuasion the power of story is obvious, as it frames the understanding of history, present meaning and future redemption.

Understanding this fascinating subject of humanity's mythical past must constitute the first step in gaining a broad historical perspective and a deeper knowledge of the human mind. Although fraught with exegetical difficulties, the dividends gained for professional counselling makes the attempt eminently worthwhile. In this book we shall explore the universal nature and

---

6 In the book *Touching the World: Reference in Autobiography,* Paul Eakin argues that autobiography is governed by a referential aesthetic that points to a mythical context beyond the story told. Eakin contends that this is the most natural of human activities.

7 The psychologist John Shotter's article in the book *Texts of Identity* (London: Sage Books, 1989): 137; argues that a healthy sense of self-hood is found in the context of myth and experience. The myth provides the meaning for the experience and it is then through this experience that one's personal identity is formed.

8 As Larry Squire in his article "Biological foundations of accuracy and inaccuracy in memory" in the book by Schacter, *Memory Distortion: How Minds, Mbrains, and Societies Reconstruct the Past* (Cambridge, Mass., Harvard University Press, 1995): 197-224. Squire argues that memory is not a single faculty but consists of different systems that depend on different brain structures and connections. Since the body changes and the consciousness alters in a very true neurological sense, the past can never be recovered, only the myths of the past are accessible.

IN THE BEGINNING **7**

significance of mythopoeic[9] thought; in other words, the content and function of narrative thought in life. It is this common skein that connects the epochs of history that have sought to discover the basic answers about the mind.

Perhaps the most general view of mythmaking is that it is a mode of apprehending reality by means of stories that serve as explanations of natural and cosmic events. Among some of the more specific views are those, such as can be seen in Freud, that consider myths to be the collective counterparts of individual dreams. Further along the line of the Vienna schools, Jung views myths as a projection on nature by the forces in humanity's collective unconscious. Some reflection on these views suggests that they may indeed be complementary to one another.

Like names and stories, myth seems to be the key to opening the door to the forms of the human consciousness (Dorsa, 1995)[10] (Montana, 2002). The magic of myth must lie in the fact that at some point in time, humanity began to tell stories. Like the stories of children, these tales must have been reflections of the wishes and unconscious psychic processes of ancient cultures and at the same time attempts to explain the natural surroundings which literally supported them, not merely metaphorically, but for their bio psychosocial needs (Mageo, 2002). Yet it was more than a simple biological urge, but a way to organize one's existence. Stories play the eminent role of telling us who we are, where we came from, what is important in life, how we are to function and what is the hope we have to give us energy each day.

In its best expression a human being is an existential creature. This existential creature shares and communicates its existential frameworks through mythopoeic thought which may be best summarized as a concrete, personal, subjective and participatory mode of apprehending existence in a dynamic cosmos (Barton, 2000). It is in this context where the whole person confronts a living and dynamic world. Thus mythopoeic thought orders the images and facts of the world and explains the events of nature by means of stories in which individuals are personally involved with the cosmos (Cenkner, 1997). This participation in the life of nature is through what we call ritual, and it is at this juncture that religion emerges as a corporate expression of the larger cosmic drama[11]. Myth is, therefore, a form of poetry that transcends poetry and proclaims both social and subjective personal truth.

---

9 This term refers to how the human mind creates myths and then how these personal myths eventually form societal myths that then become the context for personal myths. This basic mythic structure and the myth making process are naturally related to existential analysis and counselling as these are the psychological schemas in which individuals process and interpret reality. Μψτηοσ (Greek: Mythos) plus Ποιειν (Greek: Poiein) gives us the term Μψτηοποειχ meaning 'Myth-making' or 'Myth-creation'.

10 Deanna Dorsa's dissertation (1995) *The Importance of Ritual to Children* notes that rituals support life narratives, and these life narratives are essential for coping with the key issues of life such as marriage, death, puberty, sexuality, etc.

11 The book *Evil and the Response of World Religions* (Cenkner 1997) notes that the mythic construct of cosmos has always defined how religions define and respond to "evil". The notion of a mythic construct is essential for

8   THE MEANING OF LIFE

Throughout the history of the world the way that people have interpreted "who they are", "where they come from", and "to whom they are accountable" has been from stories. Specifically in the Western World, such modes of interpreting nature, the self, and society all stem from a very basic story of Creation. This story does much to frame our conscious self and organize our most basic unconscious experiences.

Genesis 1 & 2 (Author's translation/paraphrase)

Time came through the door of existence in the act of God's creation of the entire universe and the earth. The earth itself was at first a formless mass of darkness, but even then God was there with the formless elements. God called into existence light, so there was light and darkness on the first day. The second day God called into existence the oceans and sky. The third day God brought up the land and formed vegetation upon it. The fourth day God caused the stars in the sky to appear. The fifth day God called into existence the creatures of the earth.

Then on the sixth day God made a caretaker for the earth, one creature with more authority and responsibility than all the others. Like God who rules over the cosmos, caring for and nurturing it, so God made people to rule over and care for the birds of the air, over the animals of the earth and the creatures of the waters. Making the caretakers male and female God gave them permission to use the earth which they were to care for to fulfill all of their needs.

After all of this God rested from the creative work, and it was the seventh day. God gave this day to the caretaker as a special day to remember the Creator and how even the Creator rested upon the seventh day.

Again we may tell the story of how we came to be. God created the cosmos but it was empty of life, yet as life emerged from the stuff of the earth, God also formed a man to live in and care for this place. This place was full of trees and beauty and was called Eden and the role of the man was to care for this place. The man was told not to eat of one particular tree, for it contained a deadly knowledge.

Yet God recognized that the man was not yet complete, so God formed from the man a helper[12] that was suitable for him. Since a man and woman are made for each other to help one another, from then on they have had sexual relationships and formed special bonds in family. They were both naked and they enjoyed their existence.

In addition to telling us where we come from, stories also allow us to form value judgments about things and describe why we like or do not like certain things. The fact is that everything in our experience must be incorporated into our personal process of storytelling if it is to have value

---

understanding such a notion as "good" or "bad" and responding to the natural experiences imposed upon us by the cosmos.

12 The literal term does not indicate a level of importance, since it is used throughout Hebrew Literature for God.

IN THE BEGINNING **9**

or meaning. As I sit at my desk I see before me a pen and a lamp, but that does not really describe what they are so much as describe how they fit into a person's personal story, if only on a very basic level. For example, the pen may be a fine stainless steel weighted roller pen, or a $0.29 bic, yet you know that it is for writing on paper. Since you know basically what it does you do not worry about the details because it has meaning for you.

The same basic idea can be said about likes and dislikes, or to some extent about good and bad. We may, for example, go to a modern art gallery and view some abstract piece of art that is full of random lines. We may say we dislike it, that it is a bad painting or even dispute whether or not it is art. The reason we do this is simple—all the colours and shapes have no meaning for us. Due to the anxiety and irritation that this meaningless experience evokes, you will likely declare that this art is in some way less acceptable or less worthy than other forms of art. However, if you look at your own process closely you will discover that in coming to the conclusion that this is bad art you have formed a meaningful explanation of the random lines and if you accept that conclusion within yourself, you have succeeded in removing or reducing the tension that you experienced about the painting.

Forming meaning within our own storied structure and interacting with the dynamic forces of life mythopoeically is therefore implicit in our experience of reality. We cannot tolerate meaninglessness. It is, of course, this same process that forms what is bad and good within our experience and all of this is based upon our basic mythic structures and how we form stories in our own lives. Philip Booth provides us with a good example of the basic foundational story we have about goodness and badness and the values we use to make sense of our environment and our own bodily experiences.

Time was the apple Adam ate.
Eve bit, gave seconds to his mouth,
And then they had no minute left to lose.
Eyes opened ... in mid-kiss,
They saw, for once, raw nakedness,
And hid that sudden consequence
Behind an hour's stripped leaves.
... fell, an old brown core, at God's stopped feet.
He reached, and wound the clock.

■ Philip Booth[13]

Within this little illustration Philip Booth has incorporated very ancient notions of goodness and evil and added a touch of meaning for the modern reader. I encourage you to reflect upon this

---

13 Booth, P. from "Letter from a Distant Land" (1957). Used by permission of The Viking Press Inc.

10   THE MEANING OF LIFE

little poem and see what kinds of meaning you form from it. Undoubtedly you will initially find that it creates an uncomfortable level of anxiety within you, but as you slowly form a meaning for Booth's words reflect upon how that anxiety subsides.

Upon completing the task reflecting upon Booth's words, read my paraphrase of Genesis 3-4 and take some time to write out your reflection on this piece of literature.

Genesis 3 – 4 *(Author's translation/paraphrase)*

While the man and woman worked as the caretakers, God made other creatures that were also intelligent and crafty. The greatest of these creatures, a snake, spoke to the woman one day and questioned her about the meaning of the command not to eat of the tree that held a deadly knowledge. The woman was swept up in this question and longed to taste the fruit, which she did, along with her husband.

No sooner had they bit the fruit than they felt exposed and were no longer happy with their existence, feeling shame. In an attempt to appease this new feeling of dissatisfaction they sewed fig leaves together and covered themselves. They also hid from God as he moved through the garden where they worked.

Upon questioning them on their disobedience the man blamed the woman, and the woman blamed the crafty creature. The master told each of them the consequences of this action beginning with hatred between the creatures and the human caretakers. To the woman the master foretold of physical and emotional pain and injustice at the core of relationships. To the man God foretold of the existential frustration of working but not achieving.

Adam, the man, and Eve, the woman, were clothed by God and placed in a changed world, where life was difficult and in the end they would die. In this new place they made a family and taught their children about God. Yet one of their sons, Cain, became jealous of another son, Abel, and murdered him. God called Cain to account for his brother's life, but still God protected Cain.

Adam and Eve's family grew and they had many children and grandchildren.

Creation Myths from Egypt

In the earliest Egyptian creation story the world began as a formless watery void, entombed in darkness. When this primeval "water-stuff" subsided, the first mound of earth appeared. On this first island the creator-god Atum brought into being all other creatures and things. How he did this varies in the versions. According to one account, he masturbated (since he was male and had no mate) and brought the lesser male and female deities into existence. From their mating came the populated earth. According to another version, Atum named his own body parts and, as it were, out of himself came other separate beings.

Another creation story later emerged, called the Memphis theology of creation. Dating to the earliest dynastic period in Egypt (third millennium B.C.E.), this story supported the superiority of Memphis and its patron god Ptah over the previous capital. It states that Ptah was the heart and tongue, which is to say he was divine mind and speech. Ptah conceived the idea of the universe, ordered it, and called it into being with a command. Because of this Ptah existed prior to Atum as the principle and mechanism through which the world came into being. In positing the priority of the divine word, this theology of creation has a notable similarity to the Priestly account of creation in Genesis.

Compare the following quotations from the 1st Century C.E. with your reading of the Primeval Story and the creation of woman found in Genesis:

Woman, says the Law, is in all things inferior to man. Let her accordingly be submissive, not for humiliation, but that she may be directed; for authority has been given by God to man.

■ Josephus, Against Apion, ii. 24

I permit no woman to teach or to have authority over a man; she is to keep silent. For Adam was formed first, then Eve; and Adam was not deceived, but the woman was deceived and became a transgressor.

■ St. Paul, First Letter to Timothy, 2:12-14

<u>Do you think these views would be supported or undermined by Genesis 2-3?</u>

CHAPTER 2

MYTHOPOEICS AND THE WELLNESS MODEL

The Latest Decalogue – by Arthur H. Clough

1. Thou shalt have one God only; who would be at the expense of two?
2. No graven images may be worshipped, except the currency.
3. Swear not at all; for, for thy curse thine enemy is none the worse.
4. At church on Sunday to attend will serve to keep the world thy friend.
5. Honour thy parents; that is, all from whom advancement may befall.
6. Thou shalt not kill; but need'st not strive officiously to keep alive.
7. Do not adultery commit; advantage rarely comes of it.
8. Thou shalt not steal; an empty feat when it's so lucrative to cheat.
9. Bear not false witness; let the lie have time on its own wings to fly.
10. Thou shalt not covet, but tradition approves all forms of competition.

14 THE MEANING OF LIFE

Stories are the human method of transmitting meaning and giving value. It is the most natural teaching tool and it can be easily argued that myth may well have been a language for preserving and perpetuating a complex body of knowledge, not only astronomically but also socially, historically and psychologically. The universality of mythical themes of heroism, trickery, and rebirth strongly suggests that myths represent permanent features and forces of the human psyche (Campbell, 1989). It is such that the mythic imagery may allow psychologists to better chart the inner cosmos (Jung). Therefore to reject or ignore the importance of the mythopoeic perspective signifies the utter failure of the science of psychology[14].

For indeed, myth, not only in its content but in its structure and methodological motivations, is essential to the personal narrative and normal human functioning. In psychology the professional terms are "personal history", "biography" and "case study", in psychometrics it is "personality projection", but the essential content is the same. However, it can be recognized that the mythopoeic thought pattern is much deeper. This ancient thought pattern not only incorporates the public and shallowest stories of an individual, but the private and sacred story levels of the individual, where most psychological research ends. The mythical thought pattern and its existential structure goes deeper still, to the third level of personal story and its transformational existence[15]. Indeed it is true that the ancient myths provide a deeper meaning structure to all of existence by providing form and content to the sacred story of the individual which is widely considered the deepest of all psychic structures (Jung).

While at first myth likely only sustained life in its evolutionary history, its creative function continued to be a supporting force of all the narrative functions of humanity from the earliest society down through time. A survey of myth makes it clear that the human experience is at its core "mythmaking". Even psychology as a science is in a sense expressed by myth, for as each person's mythopoeic processes interact with others, they become socially and culturally conditioned[16] (McDowell, 2001), and even psychology as a science itself has taken upon a kind of mythic structure.

---

14 Clare Montana's (2002) dissertation notes that the mythopoeic process may indeed be the key to understanding the functioning of people, particularly those with mental illnesses like schizophrenia. She notes that the intricate incorporation of one myth within another can provide key self-awareness for an individual to develop meaning in the midst of suffering with a mental illness.

15 The nature and function of transformational stories can be observed in that people predictably rate their past functioning and behavior as "below average" when one considers all actions. Yet when that same individual is asked to rate their current level of functioning there is inevitably an increase in the rating of functioning of "self". The current personal myth tends to be superior to the past myth of the personal, suggesting a living within the context of myth of personal transformation and growth.

16 Maxon's article (2001) notes that virtually all social and psychological systems are an incorporation of social and personal myths organized and mediated through ritual and belief.

> **Torah – As a basis of mythic continuation and social order**
>
> In the thousands of years since the giving of the *Law of Moses* some great traditions have grown out of this historically instructive document. The basic principles of the Torah, "Love your neighbour as yourself" and "Walk in the ways of God", express themselves in the simple act of kindness. According to Rabbinical tradition this is expressed best through three means of human interaction: 1. Sharing of knowledge 2. Sharing of physical assistance 3. Sharing of resources (financial). The first act of kindness in sharing is of the most important from our perspective because it enacts the principle of social interaction and the continuation of the mythopoeic structure.
>
> As one individual is inspired by the Torah story to act in the sharing of knowledge and the giving of advice, undoubtedly that knowledge message will be informed with concepts from the Torah, which enables transmission of the story and incorporates this individual into the larger societal mythopoeic construct. As such, the simple act of giving then motivates the next individual to also give as they are touched by the stories of the Torah and its message of love.

Since the mythopoeic process is the basis of existentialism's contribution to scientific psychology, it is important to evaluate whether modern science confirms this notion. For in being true to the existential eclectic approach, this book must also draw from modern neuroscience and glean what benefits it may contribute to this approach. In so doing we will be on a better footing when it comes to professional psychology and helping people within the psychotherapeutic setting.

In entering an analysis of mythopoeic functioning within the individual it is also important to evaluate how environment plays a role. This investigation will therefore employ the insights of modern neuroscience to unlock some basics of the nature and function of memory in its different forms and how this clarifies the developments of human mythopoeics. At the outset, as we consider human society and the formation of societal myths, we are concerned primarily with the verbal declaration and direct expression of experiences, which we commonly call memory (Lord 1968). This type of memory is what is termed in neuropsychology as *declarative memory* (Eichenbaum 1997), and it is this type of memory that is mediated through the hippocampus, though the content of memory is stored in the cerebral cortex.[17] This key function of declarative memory is based, at least partially, upon a relational representation encoding of memories,

---

17 The work of H. Eichenbaum 1997 "Declarative memory: Insights from cognitive neuro-biology" *Annual Review of Psychology* 48: 548-572; gives a clear picture of how studies upon forms of human amnesia have clarified the nature of declarative memory.

16   THE MEANING OF LIFE

developing a relationship among all the various items (Eichenbaum 1997).[18] Simply put, the person's personal mythic structure will dictate the schema of memory encoding.

The simplest example is the telling of an event that one experienced during the day. In all likelihood the story will change depending upon the relationship the teller has with the listener. This is indicative of the strong association between declarative memory and its foundation in the association zones within the brain. While the mythopoeic process is logically founded in actual events, the natural function of this declarative memory is that stories will continue to grow and change through the natural process of the storyteller's transitive conjecture and relative prejudice (Eichenbaum 1997). Moreover, you will note that the story is told and the facts are often fluid, indicating the importance of *story* over *factual reality* in human experience.

Another simple example is the everyday experience of how a story, when it is told and retold by one teller, eventually takes upon a specific form. No longer is there the subtle editing of the story to suit the audience and the mood of the teller. Through this process it becomes very clear that the line between the memory of the event (which is fluid) and the belief of the event (which is rigid) quickly becomes blurred. For as the factual encoding of the event based upon a basic personal schema can be called memory (though it is actually a fluid personal story/myth)(Stein, 1987)[19], the very relational inferential nature of declaring that memory reworks that memory (Eichenbaum 1997). As that memory transmission process occurs in the sharing of the story beliefs then start to form and are reinforced by the memory and the schema that supports it. Therefore it becomes clear that mythopoeics is the foundation of belief as memories are beliefs about what happened, and beliefs are constructed from, and reinforced by, mythic reconstruction known as "memories" (Schacter 2001).

Further, the transition to the "belief" of the story also means that the form of the story will tend not to change based upon the context (De Andrade, 2000). Indeed as "belief" emerges it is essentially a rigid myth. It is important to recognize the form and function of this type of mythopoeic memory in the overall mythopoeic process[20], for it provides cues in counselling as to the nature of the client's socio-mythic context. Simply put, we can start with a schema that shapes a memory, but as the mythic memory is reworked into a belief, the schema reforms within the individual. This type of experience means that the source monitoring accuracy of a mythic

---

18 It is important to recognize that the key foundational aspect of declarative memory is its reliance upon representational flexibility that is very different from the inflexible memories that are encoded in a single isolated location within the brain. This means that declarative memory is flexible and can naturally make transitive inferences.

[19] Stein (1987) notes that archetypes play a significant role in self-identity and interpretation of one's past and the meaning of one's life. Mythic structures/archetypes are therefore the basic foundation for thinking of one historically or autobiographically.

[20] De Andrade's dissertation (2000) notes that the use of positive archetypes is an important part of the counselling/psychotherapeutic process, especially for dealing with life transition issues.

MYTHOPOEICS AND WELLNESS   17

memory is influenced by internal mental associations that vary the qualitative features of mythopoeic memories through things like perceptual details and semantic associations and overall mythic schemas/beliefs (Markham 1993). [21] Evidence of this is seen when every time a story of a real event is retold there are elements brought into the story that are confabulations of the person's mental organization and associations. In a sense, then, it is impossible to truly remember anything and most human experience is mythopoeic interpretation.

As such, the existential human experience is a very fluid interaction between internal and external mythic cues that form and reform our interpretation of phenomenologically factual events, for what we call memories are simply initially constructed perceptions, thoughts, beliefs, and goals active together at the time. Subsequently they are reconstructed, often differently, in the context of different social myths and different activated information, with the result that they may be reactivated incompletely with different features active at different times, conflated with similar memories from other events and embellished or otherwise changed by additional perceptual or reflective processing (Eisenbaum 1993).[22]

Understanding this process is of course essential to understanding the formation of the religious stories that form the basis of ancient man's view of himself and the world.

Since neuroscience does a good job affirming the mythopoeic nature of humanity, let us examine the basic neurological structures that form the basis of this process. It is also important to remember that the very nature of declarative memory (and therefore societal myths) is based upon neurological association zones (as this thesis has already mentioned). This means that key cues are required in order to maintain the structure of the story, and these cues are always blurred with other aspects associated with them (Keeler & Swanson, 2001). One of the most common ways of understanding this blurring process is found in the confusion of semantic associates that accompany the nature of memory. As individuals encode information it is placed with other information that is associated with it, either through the interpretive meaning of the individual or through semantic association (Campion & Rossi, 2001). Later, when the memory is recalled, the various ranges of interpretive and semantic associations will often resurface, sometimes resulting in a shift of the meaning of the memory or the confabulation of additional information based upon the associated encoded information.[23]

---

21 R. Markham and L. Hynes (1993) in their article "The Effect of Vividness of Imagery on Reality Monitoring" *Journal of Mental Imagery* 17: 160-170; provide a good example of how this qualitative association is central to memory and changes the nature of the memory/belief. Other studies have also shown that visual imagery during the reading of an account of the event leads people to say they saw in a picture what they only read about in text.

22 Clancy's article (2000) suggests that natural associative functions of recreating the past can actually result in the utter fabrication of "memories" of events that never actually occurred. In "False Recognition in Women Reporting Recovered Memories of Sexual Abuse." *Psychological Science.* 11: 26-31.

23 In the author's neuroscience class a simple example of this type of associative function of meaning and semantics is given and here is illustrative. If you quickly flash words across a screen and then ask people to recall as many words from the list, there will be common constructed confabulations. An example of this is if the list contains the following

18 THE MEANING OF LIFE

The assertion that myth making is the most natural of human activities is not of course limited to the individual (Eakin 1997), but is part and parcel of social existence (Nidditch 1996).[24] However, in order to appreciate the nature of myth it is important to break it down to its smallest parts and its function within the individual. Without an understanding of how stories form the person we will not be able to fully appreciate the impact of mythopoeics upon psychology.[25]

Myth is in many ways the cornerstone of individual identity and autobiography. While memory is important in much of human functioning, the fact is, from a neuropsychological perspective, that myth is a greater force than memory. Speaking in such terms, it is the *stories* that are formed, shaped and invented. To put it simply, the myth forms the schema for the organization of memories. Certainly this does not mean that memory does not play a part in a person's functioning, yet it is relived as a "story", "myth" or "legend" (Shotter 1989). The latest developments in cognitive neuroscience confirm the extent to which memory re-constructs the materials from the past rather than simply retrieving information that is merely stored (Shotter 1989).[26]

The simple fact is that the self is continually evolving, becoming different (as Yalom points out), and revising history in the individual's mythic memory (Squire 1995). However, it must be remembered that memory's frailty and appetite for redefining history is paradoxically helpful, for it is just this type of mythical memory that is essential for the formation of an individual's identity and the constant editing and revising necessary to adapt to ever changing situations.[27] A mythic past (and a clear social mythic context) is essential in order for a person to cope with the

---

words: "silver, gray, sewing, thin, long, hospital, poke, pain, nurse, dentist, drugs, blood, old, white". And you ask the audience to write out as many words as they remember, approximately 70% will respond with the common constructed confabulation of "needle" (though needle was not in the list).

24 In the book *Touching the World: Reference in Autobiography,* Paul Eakin argues that autobiography is governed by a referential aesthetic that points to a mythical context beyond the story told. Eakin contends that this is the most natural of human activities.

25 The psychologist John Shotter's article in the book: *Texts of Identity* (London: Sage Books, 1989): 137; argues that a healthy sense of self-hood is found in the context of myth and experience. The myth then provided the meaning for the experience and it is then through this experience that one's personal identity is formed.

26 As Larry Squire in his article "Biological Foundations of Accuracy and Inaccuracy in Memory" in the book: Schacter ed. 1995. ***Memory Distortion: How Minds, Brains, and Societies Reconstruct the Past*** (Cambridge: Harvard University Press: 197-224) Squire argues that memory is not a single faculty but consists of different systems that depend on different brain structures and connections. Since the body changes and the consciousness alters in a very true neurological sense, the past can never be recovered, only the myths of the past are accessible.

27 Jerome Brunner and other "narrative psychologists" have made a very persuasive case for the decisive role played by narrative in identity formation. In addition, philosophers like Anthony Kerby claim that "self narration" is the defining act of the human subject, an act which is not only "descriptive of self" but "fundamental to the emergence of reality of that subject".

needs and requirements of the present. As such, it is clear that societal myths grow and form out of the attempt to also meet the needs and requirements of the community (or even scientific discipline) in interacting with the present. These myths form out of the culturally available narrative forms for recounting the past mixed with the needs and meanings of the present (Squire 1995).[28]

It is therefore evident that mythopoeics is the core foundational function of the human mind, and essential to human existence. Meaning making is largely the result of the mythopoeic process, as are will, motivation, joy and suffering. Experiences are interpreted and our very human mode of interpretation and meaning making is through narrative. A wonderful example of this is how moral and existential teachings were transmitted within the proto-Israelite culture. This process is best expressed in the book of Deuteronomy as it reads:

These are the commands, decrees and laws the master, your God, wanted you to observe in the land. So be sure to tell your children the stories and teach them to both fear and love God, always following the instruction given by God for your lives. By doing this your life will be long. So hear this most important message. Love God with all your heart and all your essence and all your strength. Take the stories and teachings given to you and make them a part of your very being and the inspiration of your life.

Be sure to impress these stories upon your children. Talk about them when you are sitting at home and in your everyday activities let them be the theme of conversation. They ought to be the first thing you talk about in the morning and what you talk about at night. In fact, decorate your home with reminders of these stories and let the symbols on your clothes reflect this as well. Even let your lawn ornaments be reminders of the stories of God's goodness and decrees.

In the future, when your children ask you what the meaning of the instructions and rules of the Lord are, tell them the stories about how God saved you from slavery and gave you this new land to live in. The instruction was given so that we may thrive and live a good long life within this land, and this will be our righteousness.

■ (Author's paraphrase of Deuteronomy 6)

---

28 Fivush (1988), in the book by Neisser: *Remembering Reconsidered: Ecological and Traditional Approaches to the Study of Memory*, argues that the self-concept and memories of past experiences develop dialectically and begin to form a life history. The life history, in turn, helps organize both memories of past experiences and the self-concept. The life history is essentially what is called the extended time-line. It is only with the construction of the life history that we truly have a mythical memory. This format can also be seen when we examine the history of Israel and the deep impact of myth relating to the life history of Israel, particularly the birth of the nation.

20   THE MEANING OF LIFE

In the story of Moses we find a man raised by the ruling family of the most powerful empire of its time. Moses, being undoubtedly trained in the best tradition of law and conduct like Hummurabi's law code, brought the "instruction" for life that is later framed into the great exodus story. The term *Torah*, which is often translated as 'law', is better thought of as "instruction". In this we see the merging of practical advice for physical care along with a clear mythic structure about how the universe is ordered and what place people have within this world.

Within this model of instruction is a clear concept of *good and evil*, all of which is incorporated into a clear mythic structure and then summarized. The summary of this can be clearly found in Exodus 20 and is commonly called the Ten Commandments. This Torah is in many senses groundbreaking because it recognizes the incorporation of all the aspects of human existence in the health of the individual and society. The mythic was important, the social was important, the physical was important and the mental was important. Any one would invariably influence the wellness of the whole person. The Mosaic Law can be considered one of the first psychosocial wellness models, and as such, a history of psychology must include an understanding of this outline.

The whole idea behind wellness is to care for the whole existence of the person and in so doing improve the quality and quantity of life for people. This, too, is an overarching goal of psychology. The ancient people had a word for this, *Haya*, a term that can be best translated 'being' ('in the world'). So, if someone asked you how you were doing you would express it as a *state of being*. It was a way of describing the many facets of the quality of life in one simple concept. In more modern psychological terms it can be seen as roughly equivalent to the Global Assessment of Functioning.

This ancient concept is also something that God wanted the proto-Israelite people to learn. At the essence of the Ten Commandments we see this, "Honour your Father and Mother so that you may live life well and live long in the land the Lord your God has given you" (Exodus 20:12). Notice there was a mythic existential construct with a relational theme and a wellness consequence. This overall theme is clear and unmistakable throughout the Mosaic literature, for there are instructions about everything from how to cook food, to how to raise children, to how to control disease within a community, with the overall goal being wellness:

Rest and remember that I am God. If you follow my decrees and instructions then the environment will work as it should, and you will be blessed with plenty of food. Treat others with love and you will live in a land of peace. I will look on you with favour and dwell with you and that relationship will give meaning to you.

But if you will not listen to me and my instructions for wellness and the decrees for cleanliness and fairness and love, then you will be overtaken with both terror and disease. You will work and those you have wronged will eat your crops and your arrogance will be broken. When you suffer from these things, if you return to my instructions life will return to goodness for you.

However, if you persist in your own stupid ways then your health will dissolve, your countryside will be ravaged with war and you will lose your mind.

■ (author's paraphrase of Leviticus 26 with insights from Deuteronomy 28).

Torah and the Jewish Psyche

Historically, Jews have been persecuted so often that they tend to be on their guard, anticipating attack while privately reassuring themselves that they are "God's chosen people." The Jewish communal mind tends to focus upon this issue of suffering and spirituality, held together by its core as the chosen people of God central to the story of the Moses. In more recent history the centrality of suffering as a community event has been highlighted as the children of survivors of the Nazi Holocaust have become public figures and leaders in the media.

As the issue of mythic storytelling and finding meaning in suffering has long been central to the Jewish family, the natural cultural correlate of this is the cultural tendency toward emotional verbalization. That is, verbal expression of feelings has historically been considered the path to education and health and holiness. This value has been carried down through history in the study of the Talmud and Torah as students must verbally evaluate and work through issues.

It is not surprising therefore that the modern father of Psychoanalysis, Sigmund Freud, drew upon this cultural value of his Jewish heritage to define the "talking cure" of modern psychology. In many ways Freud's perspective on the basics of developing a healthy mind harkens back to the thousands of years of Jewish culture that focused on self-expression, high achievement and verbal skills of interaction with the willingness to express pain and anger and thereby to form a pattern of mental health.

---

22 THE MEANING OF LIFE

> ## READ THE FOLLOWING PASSAGES FROM THE TORAH
> ## AND DRAW YOUR OWN CONCLUSIONS:

Exodus 20

The Ten Commandments

[1] And God spoke all these words:

[2] "I am the LORD your God, who brought you out of Egypt, out of the land of slavery.

[3] "You shall have no other gods before me.

[4] "You shall not make for yourself an idol in the form of anything in heaven above or on the earth beneath or in the waters below. [5] You shall not bow down to them or worship them; for I, the LORD your God, am a jealous God, punishing the children for the sin of the fathers to the third and fourth generation of those who hate me, [6] but showing love to a thousand {generations} of those who love me and keep my commandments.

[7] "You shall not misuse the name of the LORD your God, for the LORD will not hold anyone guiltless who misuses his name.

[8] "Remember the Sabbath day by keeping it holy. [9] Six days you shall labor and do all your work, [10] but the seventh day is a Sabbath to the LORD your God. On it you shall not do any work, neither you, nor your son or daughter, nor your manservant or maidservant, nor your animals, nor the alien within your gates. [11] For in six days the LORD made the heavens and the earth, the sea, and all that is in them, but he rested on the seventh day. Therefore the LORD blessed the Sabbath day and made it holy.

[12] "Honor your father and your mother, so that you may live long in the land the LORD your God is giving you.

[13] "You shall not murder.

[14] "You shall not commit adultery.

[15] "You shall not steal.

[16] "You shall not give false testimony against your neighbor.

[17] "You shall not covet your neighbor's house. You shall not covet your neighbor's wife, or his manservant or maidservant, his ox or donkey, or anything that belongs to your neighbor."

[18] When the people saw the thunder and lightning and heard the trumpet and saw the mountain in smoke, they trembled with fear. They stayed at a distance [19] and said to Moses, "Speak to us yourself and we will listen. But do not have God speak to us or we will die."

20 Moses said to the people, "Do not be afraid. God has come to test you, so that the fear of God will be with you to keep you from sinning."
21 The people remained at a distance, while Moses approached the thick darkness where God was.

Idols and Altars

22 Then the LORD said to Moses, "Tell the Israelites this: 'You have seen for yourselves that I have spoken to you from heaven: 23 Do not make any gods to be alongside me; do not make for yourselves gods of silver or gods of gold.
24 " 'Make an altar of earth for me and sacrifice on it your burnt offerings and fellowship offerings, your sheep and goats and your cattle. Wherever I cause my name to be honored, I will come to you and bless you. 25 If you make an altar of stones for me, do not build it with dressed stones, for you will defile it if you use a tool on it. 26 And do not go up to my altar on steps, lest your nakedness be exposed on it.'

Exodus 21

1 "These are the laws you are to set before them:

Hebrew Servants

2 "If you buy a Hebrew servant, he is to serve you for six years. But in the seventh year, he shall go free, without paying anything. 3 If he comes alone, he is to go free alone; but if he has a wife when he comes, she is to go with him. 4 If his master gives him a wife and she bears him sons or daughters, the woman and her children shall belong to her master, and only the man shall go free.
5 "But if the servant declares, 'I love my master and my wife and children and do not want to go free,' 6 then his master must take him before the judges. He shall take him to the door or the doorpost and pierce his ear with an awl. Then he will be his servant for life.
7 "If a man sells his daughter as a servant, she is not to go free as menservants do. 8 If she does not please the master who has selected her for himself, he must let her be redeemed. He has no right to sell her to foreigners, because he has broken faith with her. 9 If he selects her for his son, he must grant her the rights of a daughter. 10 If he marries another woman, he must not deprive the first one of her food, clothing and marital rights. 11 If he does not provide her with these three things, she is to go free, without any payment of money.

Personal Injuries

12 "Anyone who strikes a man and kills him shall surely be put to death. 13 However, if he does not do it intentionally, but God lets it happen, he is to flee to a place I will designate. 14 But if a man schemes and kills another man deliberately, take him away from my altar and put him to

24 THE MEANING OF LIFE

death.

[15] "Anyone who attacks his father or his mother must be put to death.

[16] "Anyone who kidnaps another and either sells him or still has him when he is caught must be put to death.

[17] "Anyone who curses his father or mother must be put to death.

[18] "If men quarrel and one hits the other with a stone or with his fist and he does not die but is confined to bed, [19] the one who struck the blow will not be held responsible if the other gets up and walks around outside with his staff; however, he must pay the injured man for the loss of his time and see that he is completely healed.

[20] "If a man beats his male or female slave with a rod and the slave dies as a direct result, he must be punished, [21] but he is not to be punished if the slave gets up after a day or two, since the slave is his property.

[22] "If men who are fighting hit a pregnant woman and she gives birth prematurely but there is no serious injury, the offender must be fined whatever the woman's husband demands and the court allows. [23] But if there is serious injury, you are to take life for life, [24] eye for eye, tooth for tooth, hand for hand, foot for foot, [25] burn for burn, wound for wound, bruise for bruise.

[26] "If a man hits a manservant or maidservant in the eye and destroys it, he must let the servant go free to compensate for the eye. [27] And if he knocks out the tooth of a manservant or maidservant, he must let the servant go free to compensate for the tooth.

[28] "If a bull gores a man or a woman to death, the bull must be stoned to death, and its meat must not be eaten. But the owner of the bull will not be held responsible. [29] If, however, the bull has had the habit of goring and the owner has been warned but has not kept it penned up and it kills a man or woman, the bull must be stoned and the owner also must be put to death. [30] However, if payment is demanded of him, he may redeem his life by paying whatever is demanded. [31] This law also applies if the bull gores a son or daughter. [32] If the bull gores a male or female slave, the owner must pay thirty shekels of silver to the master of the slave, and the bull must be stoned.

[33] "If a man uncovers a pit or digs one and fails to cover it and an ox or a donkey falls into it, [34] the owner of the pit must pay for the loss; he must pay its owner, and the dead animal will be his.

[35] "If a man's bull injures the bull of another and it dies, they are to sell the live one and divide both the money and the dead animal equally. [36] However, if it was known that the bull had the habit of goring, yet the owner did not keep it penned up, the owner must pay, animal for animal, and the dead animal will be his.

Exodus 22

Protection of Property

[1] "If a man steals an ox or a sheep and slaughters it or sells it, he must pay back five head of cattle for the ox and four sheep for the sheep.

[2] "If a thief is caught breaking in and is struck so that he dies, the defender is not guilty of

bloodshed; [3] but if it happens after sunrise, he is guilty of bloodshed.
"A thief must certainly make restitution, but if he has nothing, he must be sold to pay for his theft.
[4] "If the stolen animal is found alive in his possession-whether ox or donkey or sheep-he must pay back double.
[5] "If a man grazes his livestock in a field or vineyard and lets them stray and they graze in another man's field, he must make restitution from the best of his own field or vineyard.
[6] "If a fire breaks out and spreads into thorn bushes so that it burns shocks of grain or standing grain or the whole field, the one who started the fire must make restitution.
[7] "If a man gives his neighbor silver or goods for safekeeping and they are stolen from the neighbor's house, the thief, if he is caught, must pay back double. [8] But if the thief is not found, the owner of the house must appear before the judges to determine whether he has laid his hands on the other man's property. [9] In all cases of illegal possession of an ox, a donkey, a sheep, a garment, or any other lost property about which somebody says, 'This is mine,' both parties are to bring their cases before the judges. The one whom the judges declare guilty must pay back double to his neighbor.
[10] "If a man gives a donkey, an ox, a sheep or any other animal to his neighbor for safekeeping and it dies or is injured or is taken away while no one is looking, [11] the issue between them will be settled by the taking of an oath before the LORD that the neighbor did not lay hands on the other person's property. The owner is to accept this, and no restitution is required. [12] But if the animal was stolen from the neighbor, he must make restitution to the owner. [13] If it was torn to pieces by a wild animal, he shall bring in the remains, as evidence and he will not be required to pay for the torn animal.
[14] "If a man borrows an animal from his neighbor and it is injured or dies while the owner is not present, he must make restitution. [15] But if the owner is with the animal, the borrower will not have to pay. If the animal was hired, the money paid for the hire covers the loss.

Social Responsibility

[16] "If a man seduces a virgin who is not pledged to be married and sleeps with her, he must pay the bride-price, and she shall be his wife. [17] If her father absolutely refuses to give her to him, he must still pay the bride-price for virgins.
[18] "Do not allow a sorceress to live.
[19] "Anyone who has sexual relations with an animal must be put to death.
[20] "Whoever sacrifices to any god other than the LORD must be destroyed.
[21] "Do not mistreat an alien or oppress him, for you were aliens in Egypt.
[22] "Do not take advantage of a widow or an orphan. [23] If you do and they cry out to me, I will certainly hear their cry. [24] My anger will be aroused, and I will kill you with the sword; your wives will become widows and your children fatherless.
[25] "If you lend money to one of my people among you who is needy, do not be like a moneylender; charge him no interest. [26] If you take your neighbor's cloak as a pledge, return it to

26   THE MEANING OF LIFE

him by sunset, [27] because his cloak is the only covering he has for his body. What else will he sleep in? When he cries out to me, I will hear, for I am compassionate.
[28] "Do not blaspheme God or curse the ruler of your people.
[29] "Do not hold back offerings from your granaries or your vats.
"You must give me the firstborn of your sons. [30] Do the same with your cattle and your sheep. Let them stay with their mothers for seven days, but give them to me on the eighth day.
[31] "You are to be my holy people. So do not eat the meat of an animal torn by wild beasts; throw it to the dogs.

Exodus 23

Laws of Justice and Mercy

[1] "Do not spread false reports. Do not help a wicked man by being a malicious witness.
[2] "Do not follow the crowd in doing wrong. When you give testimony in a lawsuit, do not pervert justice by siding with the crowd, [3] and do not show favoritism to a poor man in his lawsuit.
[4] "If you come across your enemy's ox or donkey wandering off, be sure to take it back to him. [5] If you see the donkey of someone who hates you fallen down under its load, do not leave it there; be sure you help him with it.
[6] "Do not deny justice to your poor people in their lawsuits. [7] Have nothing to do with a false charge and do not put an innocent or honest person to death, for I will not acquit the guilty.
[8] "Do not accept a bribe, for a bribe blinds those who see and twists the words of the righteous.
[9] "Do not oppress an alien; you yourselves know how it feels to be aliens, because you were aliens in Egypt.

Sabbath Laws

[10] "For six years you are to sow your fields and harvest the crops, [11] but during the seventh year let the land lie unplowed and unused. Then the poor among your people may get food from it, and the wild animals may eat what they leave. Do the same with your vineyard and your olive grove.
[12] "Six days do your work, but on the seventh day do not work, so that your ox and your donkey may rest and the slave born in your household, and the alien as well, may be refreshed.
[13] "Be careful to do everything I have said to you. Do not invoke the names of other gods; do not let them be heard on your lips.

The Three Annual Festivals

[14] "Three times a year you are to celebrate a festival to me.
[15] "Celebrate the Feast of Unleavened Bread; for seven days eat bread made without yeast, as I commanded you. Do this at the appointed time in the month of Abib, for in that month you came

out of Egypt.

"No one is to appear before me empty-handed.

[16] "Celebrate the Feast of Harvest with the firstfruits of the crops you sow in your field.

"Celebrate the Feast of Ingathering at the end of the year, when you gather in your crops from the field.

[17] "Three times a year all the men are to appear before the Sovereign LORD .

[18] "Do not offer the blood of a sacrifice to me along with anything containing yeast.

"The fat of my festival offerings must not be kept until morning.

[19] "Bring the best of the firstfruits of your soil to the house of the LORD your God.

"Do not cook a young goat in its mother's milk.

God's Angel to Prepare the Way

[20] "See, I am sending an angel ahead of you to guard you along the way and to bring you to the place I have prepared. [21] Pay attention to him and listen to what he says. Do not rebel against him; he will not forgive your rebellion, since my Name is in him. [22] If you listen carefully to what he says and do all that I say, I will be an enemy to your enemies and will oppose those who oppose you. [23] My angel will go ahead of you and bring you into the land of the Amorites, Hittites, Perizzites, Canaanites, Hivites and Jebusites, and I will wipe them out. [24] Do not bow down before their gods or worship them or follow their practices. You must demolish them and break their sacred stones to pieces. [25] Worship the LORD your God, and his blessing will be on your food and water. I will take away sickness from among you, [26] and none will miscarry or be barren in your land. I will give you a full life span.

[27] "I will send my terror ahead of you and throw into confusion every nation you encounter. I will make all your enemies turn their backs and run. [28] I will send the hornet ahead of you to drive the Hivites, Canaanites and Hittites out of your way. [29] But I will not drive them out in a single year, because the land would become desolate and the wild animals too numerous for you. [30] Little by little I will drive them out before you, until you have increased enough to take possession of the land.

[31] "I will establish your borders from the Red Sea to the Sea of the Philistines, and from the desert to the River. I will hand over to you the people who live in the land and you will drive them out before you. [32] Do not make a covenant with them or with their gods. [33] Do not let them live in your land, or they will cause you to sin against me, because the worship of their gods will certainly be a snare to you."

Exodus 24

The Covenant Confirmed

[1] Then he said to Moses, "Come up to the LORD , you and Aaron, Nadab and Abihu, and seventy

28 THE MEANING OF LIFE

of the elders of Israel. You are to worship at a distance, [2] but Moses alone is to approach the LORD ; the others must not come near. And the people may not come up with him."
[3] When Moses went and told the people all the LORD's words and laws, they responded with one voice, "Everything the LORD has said we will do." [4] Moses then wrote down everything the LORD had said.
He got up early the next morning and built an altar at the foot of the mountain and set up twelve stone pillars representing the twelve tribes of Israel. [5] Then he sent young Israelite men, and they offered burnt offerings and sacrificed young bulls as fellowship offerings to the LORD . [6] Moses took half of the blood and put it in bowls, and the other half he sprinkled on the altar. [7] Then he took the Book of the Covenant and read it to the people. They responded, "We will do everything the LORD has said; we will obey."
[8] Moses then took the blood, sprinkled it on the people and said, "This is the blood of the covenant that the LORD has made with you in accordance with all these words."
[9] Moses and Aaron, Nadab and Abihu, and the seventy elders of Israel went up [10] and saw the God of Israel. Under his feet was something like a pavement made of sapphire, clear as the sky itself. [11] But God did not raise his hand against these leaders of the Israelites; they saw God, and they ate and drank.
[12] The LORD said to Moses, "Come up to me on the mountain and stay here, and I will give you the tablets of stone, with the law and commands I have written for their instruction."
[13] Then Moses set out with Joshua his aide, and Moses went up on the mountain of God. [14] He said to the elders, "Wait here for us until we come back to you. Aaron and Hur are with you, and anyone involved in a dispute can go to them."
[15] When Moses went up on the mountain, the cloud covered it, [16] and the glory of the LORD settled on Mount Sinai. For six days the cloud covered the mountain, and on the seventh day the LORD called to Moses from within the cloud. [17] To the Israelites the glory of the LORD looked like a consuming fire on top of the mountain. [18] Then Moses entered the cloud as he went on up the mountain. And he stayed on the mountain forty days and forty nights.

Exodus 25

Offerings for the Tabernacle

[1] The LORD said to Moses, [2] "Tell the Israelites to bring me an offering. You are to receive the offering for me from each man whose heart prompts him to give. [3] These are the offerings you are to receive from them: gold, silver and bronze; [4] blue, purple and scarlet yarn and fine linen; goat hair; [5] ram skins dyed red and hides of sea cows ; acacia wood; [6] olive oil for the light; spices for the anointing oil and for the fragrant incense; [7] and onyx stones and other gems to be mounted on the ephod and breastpiece.
[8] "Then have them make a sanctuary for me, and I will dwell among them. [9] Make this tabernacle and all its furnishings exactly like the pattern I will show you.

MYTHOPOEICS AND WELLNESS **29**

The Ark

[10] "Have them make a chest of acacia wood-two and a half cubits long, a cubit and a half wide, and a cubit and a half high. [11] Overlay it with pure gold, both inside and out, and make a gold molding around it. [12] Cast four gold rings for it and fasten them to its four feet, with two rings on one side and two rings on the other. [13] Then make poles of acacia wood and overlay them with gold. [14] Insert the poles into the rings on the sides of the chest to carry it. [15] The poles are to remain in the rings of this ark; they are not to be removed. [16] Then put in the ark the Testimony, which I will give you.

[17] "Make an atonement cover of pure gold-two and a half cubits long and a cubit and a half wide. [18] And make two cherubim out of hammered gold at the ends of the cover. [19] Make one cherub on one end and the second cherub on the other; make the cherubim of one piece with the cover, at the two ends. [20] The cherubim are to have their wings spread upward, overshadowing the cover with them. The cherubim are to face each other, looking toward the cover. [21] Place the cover on top of the ark and put in the ark the Testimony, which I will give you. [22] There, above the cover between the two cherubim that are over the ark of the Testimony, I will meet with you and give you all my commands for the Israelites.

The Table

[23] "Make a table of acacia wood-two cubits long, a cubit wide and a cubit and a half high. [24] Overlay it with pure gold and make a gold molding around it. [25] Also make around it a rim a handbreadth wide and put a gold molding on the rim. [26] Make four gold rings for the table and fasten them to the four corners, where the four legs are. [27] The rings are to be close to the rim to hold the poles used in carrying the table. [28] Make the poles of acacia wood, overlay them with gold and carry the table with them. [29] And make its plates and dishes of pure gold, as well as its pitchers and bowls for the pouring out of offerings. [30] Put the bread of the Presence on this table to be before me at all times.

The Lampstand

[31] "Make a lampstand of pure gold and hammer it out, base and shaft; its flowerlike cups, buds and blossoms shall be of one piece with it. [32] Six branches are to extend from the sides of the lampstand-three on one side and three on the other. [33] Three cups shaped like almond flowers with buds and blossoms are to be on one branch, three on the next branch, and the same for all six branches extending from the lampstand. [34] And on the lampstand there are to be four cups shaped like almond flowers with buds and blossoms. [35] One bud shall be under the first pair of branches extending from the lampstand, a second bud under the second pair, and a third bud under the third pair-six branches in all. [36] The buds and branches shall all be of one piece with the lampstand,

30   THE MEANING OF LIFE

hammered out of pure gold.
[37] "Then make its seven lamps and set them up on it so that they light the space in front of it. [38] Its wick trimmers and trays are to be of pure gold. [39] A talent of pure gold is to be used for the lampstand and all these accessories. [40] See that you make them according to the pattern shown you on the mountain.

Leviticus 15

Discharges Causing Uncleanness

[1] The LORD said to Moses and Aaron, [2] "Speak to the Israelites and say to them: 'When any man has a bodily discharge, the discharge is unclean. [3] Whether it continues flowing from his body or is blocked, it will make him unclean. This is how his discharge will bring about uncleanness:
[4] " 'Any bed the man with a discharge lies on will be unclean, and anything he sits on will be unclean. [5] Anyone who touches his bed must wash his clothes and bathe with water, and he will be unclean till evening. [6] Whoever sits on anything that the man with a discharge sat on must wash his clothes and bathe with water, and he will be unclean till evening.
[7] " 'Whoever touches the man who has a discharge must wash his clothes and bathe with water, and he will be unclean till evening.
[8] " 'If the man with the discharge spits on someone who is clean, that person must wash his clothes and bathe with water, and he will be unclean till evening.
[9] " 'Everything the man sits on when riding will be unclean, [10] and whoever touches any of the things that were under him will be unclean till evening; whoever picks up those things must wash his clothes and bathe with water, and he will be unclean till evening.
[11] " 'Anyone the man with a discharge touches without rinsing his hands with water must wash his clothes and bathe with water, and he will be unclean till evening.
[12] " 'A clay pot that the man touches must be broken, and any wooden article is to be rinsed with water.
[13] " 'When a man is cleansed from his discharge, he is to count off seven days for his ceremonial cleansing; he must wash his clothes and bathe himself with fresh water, and he will be clean. [14] On the eighth day he must take two doves or two young pigeons and come before the LORD to the entrance to the Tent of Meeting and give them to the priest. [15] The priest is to sacrifice them, the one for a sin offering and the other for a burnt offering. In this way he will make atonement before the LORD for the man because of his discharge.
[16] " 'When a man has an emission of semen, he must bathe his whole body with water, and he will be unclean till evening. [17] Any clothing or leather that has semen on it must be washed with water, and it will be unclean till evening. [18] When a man lies with a woman and there is an emission of semen, both must bathe with water, and they will be unclean till evening.
[19] " 'When a woman has her regular flow of blood, the impurity of her monthly period will last seven days, and anyone who touches her will be unclean till evening.

MYTHOPOEICS AND WELLNESS 31

[20] " 'Anything she lies on during her period will be unclean, and anything she sits on will be unclean. [21] Whoever touches her bed must wash his clothes and bathe with water, and he will be unclean till evening. [22] Whoever touches anything she sits on must wash his clothes and bathe with water, and he will be unclean till evening. [23] Whether it is the bed or anything she was sitting on, when anyone touches it, he will be unclean till evening.

[24] " 'If a man lies with her and her monthly flow touches him, he will be unclean for seven days; any bed he lies on will be unclean.

[25] " 'When a woman has a discharge of blood for many days at a time other than her monthly period or has a discharge that continues beyond her period, she will be unclean as long as she has the discharge, just as in the days of her period. [26] Any bed she lies on while her discharge continues will be unclean, as is her bed during her monthly period, and anything she sits on will be unclean, as during her period. [27] Whoever touches them will be unclean; he must wash his clothes and bathe with water, and he will be unclean till evening.

[28] " 'When she is cleansed from her discharge, she must count off seven days, and after that she will be ceremonially clean. [29] On the eighth day she must take two doves or two young pigeons and bring them to the priest at the entrance to the Tent of Meeting. [30] The priest is to sacrifice one for a sin offering and the other for a burnt offering. In this way he will make atonement for her before the LORD for the uncleanness of her discharge.

[31] " 'You must keep the Israelites separate from things that make them unclean, so they will not die in their uncleanness for defiling my dwelling place, which is among them.' "

[32] These are the regulations for a man with a discharge, for anyone made unclean by an emission of semen, [33] for a woman in her monthly period, for a man or a woman with a discharge, and for a man who lies with a woman who is ceremonially unclean.

Leviticus 16

The Day of Atonement

[1] The LORD spoke to Moses after the death of the two sons of Aaron who died when they approached the LORD . [2] The LORD said to Moses: "Tell your brother Aaron not to come whenever he chooses into the Most Holy Place behind the curtain in front of the atonement cover on the ark, or else he will die, because I appear in the cloud over the atonement cover.

[3] "This is how Aaron is to enter the sanctuary area: with a young bull for a sin offering and a ram for a burnt offering. [4] He is to put on the sacred linen tunic, with linen undergarments next to his body; he is to tie the linen sash around him and put on the linen turban. These are sacred garments; so he must bathe himself with water before he puts them on. [5] From the Israelite community he is to take two male goats for a sin offering and a ram for a burnt offering.

[6] "Aaron is to offer the bull for his own sin offering to make atonement for himself and his household. [7] Then he is to take the two goats and present them before the LORD at the entrance to the Tent of Meeting. [8] He is to cast lots for the two goats-one lot for the LORD and the other

32 THE MEANING OF LIFE

for the scapegoat. [9] Aaron shall bring the goat whose lot falls to the LORD and sacrifice it for a sin offering. [10] But the goat chosen by lot as the scapegoat shall be presented alive before the LORD to be used for making atonement by sending it into the desert as a scapegoat.

[11] "Aaron shall bring the bull for his own sin offering to make atonement for himself and his household, and he is to slaughter the bull for his own sin offering. [12] He is to take a censer full of burning coals from the altar before the LORD and two handfuls of finely ground fragrant incense and take them behind the curtain. [13] He is to put the incense on the fire before the LORD , and the smoke of the incense will conceal the atonement cover above the Testimony, so that he will not die. [14] He is to take some of the bull's blood and with his finger sprinkle it on the front of the atonement cover; then he shall sprinkle some of it with his finger seven times before the atonement cover.

[15] "He shall then slaughter the goat for the sin offering for the people and take its blood behind the curtain and do with it as he did with the bull's blood: He shall sprinkle it on the atonement cover and in front of it. [16] In this way he will make atonement for the Most Holy Place because of the uncleanness and rebellion of the Israelites, whatever their sins have been. He is to do the same for the Tent of Meeting, which is among them in the midst of their uncleanness. [17] No one is to be in the Tent of Meeting from the time Aaron goes in to make atonement in the Most Holy Place until he comes out, having made atonement for himself, his household and the whole community of Israel.

[18] "Then he shall come out to the altar that is before the LORD and make atonement for it. He shall take some of the bull's blood and some of the goat's blood and put it on all the horns of the altar. [19] He shall sprinkle some of the blood on it with his finger seven times to cleanse it and to consecrate it from the uncleanness of the Israelites.

[20] "When Aaron has finished making atonement for the Most Holy Place, the Tent of Meeting and the altar, he shall bring forward the live goat. [21] He is to lay both hands on the head of the live goat and confess over it all the wickedness and rebellion of the Israelites-all their sins-and put them on the goat's head. He shall send the goat away into the desert in the care of a man appointed for the task. [22] The goat will carry on itself all their sins to a solitary place; and the man shall release it in the desert.

[23] "Then Aaron is to go into the Tent of Meeting and take off the linen garments he put on before he entered the Most Holy Place, and he is to leave them there. [24] He shall bathe himself with water in a holy place and put on his regular garments. Then he shall come out and sacrifice the burnt offering for himself and the burnt offering for the people, to make atonement for himself and for the people. [25] He shall also burn the fat of the sin offering on the altar.

[26] "The man who releases the goat as a scapegoat must wash his clothes and bathe himself with water; afterward he may come into the camp. [27] The bull and the goat for the sin offerings, whose blood was brought into the Most Holy Place to make atonement, must be taken outside the camp; their hides, flesh and offal are to be burned up. [28] The man who burns them must wash his clothes and bathe himself with water; afterward he may come into the camp.

[29] "This is to be a lasting ordinance for you: On the tenth day of the seventh month you must deny

yourselves and not do any work-whether native-born or an alien living among you- [30] because on this day atonement will be made for you, to cleanse you. Then, before the LORD , you will be clean from all your sins. [31] It is a sabbath of rest, and you must deny yourselves; it is a lasting ordinance. [32] The priest who is anointed and ordained to succeed his father as high priest is to make atonement. He is to put on the sacred linen garments [33] and make atonement for the Most Holy Place, for the Tent of Meeting and the altar, and for the priests and all the people of the community.

[34] "This is to be a lasting ordinance for you: Atonement is to be made once a year for all the sins of the Israelites."

And it was done, as the LORD commanded Moses.

Leviticus 17

Eating Blood Forbidden

[1] The LORD said to Moses, [2] "Speak to Aaron and his sons and to all the Israelites and say to them: 'This is what the LORD has commanded: [3] Any Israelite who sacrifices an ox, a lamb or a goat in the camp or outside of it [4] instead of bringing it to the entrance to the Tent of Meeting to present it as an offering to the LORD in front of the tabernacle of the LORD -that man shall be considered guilty of bloodshed; he has shed blood and must be cut off from his people. [5] This is so the Israelites will bring to the LORD the sacrifices they are now making in the open fields. They must bring them to the priest, that is, to the LORD , at the entrance to the Tent of Meeting and sacrifice them as fellowship offerings. [6] The priest is to sprinkle the blood against the altar of the LORD at the entrance to the Tent of Meeting and burn the fat as an aroma pleasing to the LORD . [7] They must no longer offer any of their sacrifices to the goat idols to whom they prostitute themselves. This is to be a lasting ordinance for them and for the generations to come.'

[8] "Say to them: 'Any Israelite or any alien living among them who offers a burnt offering or sacrifice [9] and does not bring it to the entrance to the Tent of Meeting to sacrifice it to the LORD -that man must be cut off from his people.

[10] " 'Any Israelite or any alien living among them who eats any blood-I will set my face against that person who eats blood and will cut him off from his people. [11] For the life of a creature is in the blood, and I have given it to you to make atonement for yourselves on the altar; it is the blood that makes atonement for one's life. [12] Therefore I say to the Israelites, "None of you may eat blood, nor may an alien living among you eat blood."

[13] " 'Any Israelite or any alien living among you who hunts any animal or bird that may be eaten must drain out the blood and cover it with earth, [14] because the life of every creature is its blood. That is why I have said to the Israelites, "You must not eat the blood of any creature, because the life of every creature is its blood; anyone who eats it must be cut off."

[15] " 'Anyone, whether native-born or alien, who eats anything found dead or torn by wild animals must wash his clothes and bathe with water, and he will be ceremonially unclean till evening;

34 THE MEANING OF LIFE

then he will be clean. [16] But if he does not wash his clothes and bathe himself, he will be held responsible.' "

Leviticus 18

Unlawful Sexual Relations

[1] The LORD said to Moses, [2] "Speak to the Israelites and say to them: 'I am the LORD your God. [3] You must not do as they do in Egypt, where you used to live, and you must not do as they do in the land of Canaan, where I am bringing you. Do not follow their practices. [4] You must obey my laws and be careful to follow my decrees. I am the LORD your God. [5] Keep my decrees and laws, for the man who obeys them will live by them. I am the LORD .
[6] " 'No one is to approach any close relative to have sexual relations. I am the LORD .
[7] " 'Do not dishonor your father by having sexual relations with your mother. She is your mother; do not have relations with her.
[8] " 'Do not have sexual relations with your father's wife; that would dishonor your father.
[9] " 'Do not have sexual relations with your sister, either your father's daughter or your mother's daughter, whether she was born in the same home or elsewhere.
[10] " 'Do not have sexual relations with your son's daughter or your daughter's daughter; that would dishonor you.
[11] " 'Do not have sexual relations with the daughter of your father's wife, born to your father; she is your sister.
[12] " 'Do not have sexual relations with your father's sister; she is your father's close relative.
[13] " 'Do not have sexual relations with your mother's sister, because she is your mother's close relative.
[14] " 'Do not dishonor your father's brother by approaching his wife to have sexual relations; she is your aunt.
[15] " 'Do not have sexual relations with your daughter-in-law. She is your son's wife; do not have relations with her.
[16] " 'Do not have sexual relations with your brother's wife; that would dishonor your brother.
[17] " 'Do not have sexual relations with both a woman and her daughter. Do not have sexual relations with either her son's daughter or her daughter's daughter; they are her close relatives. That is wickedness.
[18] " 'Do not take your wife's sister as a rival wife and have sexual relations with her while your wife is living.
[19] " 'Do not approach a woman to have sexual relations during the uncleanness of her monthly period.
[20] " 'Do not have sexual relations with your neighbor's wife and defile yourself with her.
[21] " 'Do not give any of your children to be sacrificed to Molech, for you must not profane the name of your God. I am the LORD .

MYTHOPOEICS AND WELLNESS **35**

[22] " 'Do not lie with a man as one lies with a woman; that is detestable.

[23] " 'Do not have sexual relations with an animal and defile yourself with it. A woman must not present herself to an animal to have sexual relations with it; that is a perversion.

[24] " 'Do not defile yourselves in any of these ways, because this is how the nations that I am going to drive out before you became defiled. [25] Even the land was defiled; so I punished it for its sin, and the land vomited out its inhabitants. [26] But you must keep my decrees and my laws. The native-born and the aliens living among you must not do any of these detestable things, [27] for all these things were done by the people who lived in the land before you, and the land became defiled. [28] And if you defile the land, it will vomit you out as it vomited out the nations that were before you.

[29] " 'Everyone who does any of these detestable things-such persons must be cut off from their people. [30] Keep my requirements and do not follow any of the detestable customs that were practiced before you came and do not defile yourselves with them. I am the LORD your God.' "

Leviticus 19

Various Laws

[1] The LORD said to Moses, [2] "Speak to the entire assembly of Israel and say to them: 'Be holy because I, the LORD your God, am holy.

[3] " 'Each of you must respect his mother and father, and you must observe my Sabbaths. I am the LORD your God.

[4] " 'Do not turn to idols or make gods of cast metal for yourselves. I am the LORD your God.

[5] " 'When you sacrifice a fellowship offering to the LORD , sacrifice it in such a way that it will be accepted on your behalf. [6] It shall be eaten on the day you sacrifice it or on the next day; anything left over until the third day must be burned up. [7] If any of it is eaten on the third day, it is impure and will not be accepted. [8] Whoever eats it will be held responsible because he has desecrated what is holy to the LORD ; that person must be cut off from his people.

[9] " 'When you reap the harvest of your land, do not reap to the very edges of your field or gather the gleanings of your harvest. [10] Do not go over your vineyard a second time or pick up the grapes that have fallen. Leave them for the poor and the alien. I am the LORD your God.

[11] " 'Do not steal.

" 'Do not lie.

" 'Do not deceive one another.

[12] " 'Do not swear falsely by my name and so profane the name of your God. I am the LORD .

[13] " 'Do not defraud your neighbor or rob him.

" 'Do not hold back the wages of a hired man overnight.

[14] " 'Do not curse the deaf or put a stumbling block in front of the blind, but fear your God. I am the LORD .

[15] " 'Do not pervert justice; do not show partiality to the poor or favoritism to the great, but judge

36   THE MEANING OF LIFE

your neighbor fairly.

16 " 'Do not go about spreading slander among your people.

" 'Do not do anything that endangers your neighbor's life. I am the LORD .

17 " 'Do not hate your brother in your heart. Rebuke your neighbor frankly so you will not share in his guilt.

18 " 'Do not seek revenge or bear a grudge against one of your people, but love your neighbor as yourself. I am the LORD .

19 " 'Keep my decrees.

" 'Do not mate different kinds of animals.

" 'Do not plant your field with two kinds of seed.

" 'Do not wear clothing woven of two kinds of material.

20 " 'If a man sleeps with a woman who is a slave girl promised to another man but who has not been ransomed or given her freedom, there must be due punishment. Yet they are not to be put to death, because she had not been freed. 21 The man, however, must bring a ram to the entrance to the Tent of Meeting for a guilt offering to the LORD . 22 With the ram of the guilt offering the priest is to make atonement for him before the LORD for the sin he has committed, and his sin will be forgiven.

23 " 'When you enter the land and plant any kind of fruit tree, regard its fruit as forbidden. For three years you are to consider it forbidden ; it must not be eaten. 24 In the fourth year all its fruit will be holy, an offering of praise to the LORD . 25 But in the fifth year you may eat its fruit. In this way your harvest will be increased. I am the LORD your God.

26 " 'Do not eat any meat with the blood still in it.

" 'Do not practice divination or sorcery.

27 " 'Do not cut the hair at the sides of your head or clip off the edges of your beard.

28 " 'Do not cut your bodies for the dead or put tattoo marks on yourselves. I am the LORD .

29 " 'Do not degrade your daughter by making her a prostitute, or the land will turn to prostitution and be filled with wickedness.

30 " 'Observe my Sabbaths and have reverence for my sanctuary. I am the LORD .

31 " 'Do not turn to mediums or seek out spiritists, for you will be defiled by them. I am the LORD your God.

32 " 'Rise in the presence of the aged, show respect for the elderly and revere your God. I am the LORD .

33 " 'When an alien lives with you in your land, do not mistreat him. 34 The alien living with you must be treated as one of your native-born. Love him as yourself, for you were aliens in Egypt. I am the LORD your God.

35 " 'Do not use dishonest standards when measuring length, weight or quantity. 36 Use honest scales and honest weights, an honest ephah and an honest hin. I am the LORD your God, who brought you out of Egypt.

37 " 'Keep all my decrees and all my laws and follow them. I am the LORD .' "

Leviticus 20

Punishments for Sin

[1] The LORD said to Moses, [2] "Say to the Israelites: 'Any Israelite or any alien living in Israel who gives any of his children to Molech must be put to death. The people of the community are to stone him. [3] I will set my face against that man and I will cut him off from his people; for by giving his children to Molech, he has defiled my sanctuary and profaned my holy name. [4] If the people of the community close their eyes when that man gives one of his children to Molech and they fail to put him to death, [5] I will set my face against that man and his family and will cut off from their people both him and all who follow him in prostituting themselves to Molech.
[6] " 'I will set my face against the person who turns to mediums and spiritists to prostitute himself by following them, and I will cut him off from his people.
[7] " 'Consecrate yourselves and be holy, because I am the LORD your God. [8] Keep my decrees and follow them. I am the LORD , who makes you holy.
[9] " 'If anyone curses his father or mother, he must be put to death. He has cursed his father or his mother, and his blood will be on his own head.
[10] " 'If a man commits adultery with another man's wife-with the wife of his neighbor-both the adulterer and the adulteress must be put to death.
[11] " 'If a man sleeps with his father's wife, he has dishonored his father. Both the man and the woman must be put to death; their blood will be on their own heads.
[12] " 'If a man sleeps with his daughter-in-law, both of them must be put to death. What they have done is a perversion; their blood will be on their own heads.
[13] " 'If a man lies with a man as one lies with a woman, both of them have done what is detestable. They must be put to death; their blood will be on their own heads.
[14] " 'If a man marries both a woman and her mother, it is wicked. Both he and they must be burned in the fire, so that no wickedness will be among you.
[15] " 'If a man has sexual relations with an animal, he must be put to death, and you must kill the animal.
[16] " 'If a woman approaches an animal to have sexual relations with it, kill both the woman and the animal. They must be put to death; their blood will be on their own heads.
[17] " 'If a man marries his sister, the daughter of either his father or his mother, and they have sexual relations, it is a disgrace. They must be cut off before the eyes of their people. He has dishonored his sister and will be held responsible.
[18] " 'If a man lies with a woman during her monthly period and has sexual relations with her, he has exposed the source of her flow, and she has also uncovered it. Both of them must be cut off from their people.
[19] " 'Do not have sexual relations with the sister of either your mother or your father, for that would dishonor a close relative; both of you would be held responsible.
[20] " 'If a man sleeps with his aunt, he has dishonored his uncle. They will be held responsible;

38   THE MEANING OF LIFE

they will die childless.

21 " 'If a man marries his brother's wife, it is an act of impurity; he has dishonored his brother. They will be childless.

22 " 'Keep all my decrees and laws and follow them, so that the land where I am bringing you to live may not vomit you out. 23 You must not live according to the customs of the nations I am going to drive out before you. Because they did all these things, I abhorred them. 24 But I said to you, "You will possess their land; I will give it to you as an inheritance, a land flowing with milk and honey." I am the LORD your God, who has set you apart from the nations.

25 " 'You must therefore make a distinction between clean and unclean animals and between unclean and clean birds. Do not defile yourselves by any animal or bird or anything that moves along the ground-those which I have set apart as unclean for you. 26 You are to be holy to me because I, the LORD , am holy, and I have set you apart from the nations to be my own.

27 " 'A man or woman who is a medium or spiritist among you must be put to death. You are to stone them; their blood will be on their own heads.' "

Deuteronomy 27

The Altar on Mount Ebal

1 Moses and the elders of Israel commanded the people: "Keep all these commands that I give you today. 2 When you have crossed the Jordan into the land the LORD your God is giving you, set up some large stones and coat them with plaster. 3 Write on them all the words of this law when you have crossed over to enter the land the LORD your God is giving you, a land flowing with milk and honey, just as the LORD , the God of your fathers, promised you. 4 And when you have crossed the Jordan, set up these stones on Mount Ebal, as I command you today, and coat them with plaster. 5 Build there an altar to the LORD your God, an altar of stones. Do not use any iron tool upon them. 6 Build the altar of the LORD your God with fieldstones and offer burnt offerings on it to the LORD your God. 7 Sacrifice fellowship offerings there, eating them and rejoicing in the presence of the LORD your God. 8 And you shall write very clearly all the words of this law on these stones you have set up."

Curses From Mount Ebal

9 Then Moses and the priests, who are Levites, said to all Israel, "Be silent, O Israel, and listen! You have now become the people of the LORD your God. 10 Obey the LORD your God and follow his commands and decrees that I give you today."

11 On the same day Moses commanded the people:

12 When you have crossed the Jordan, these tribes shall stand on Mount Gerizim to bless the people: Simeon, Levi, Judah, Issachar, Joseph and Benjamin. 13 And these tribes shall stand on Mount Ebal to pronounce curses: Reuben, Gad, Asher, Zebulun, Dan and Naphtali.

[14] The Levites shall recite to all the people of Israel in a loud voice:

[15] "Cursed is the man who carves an image or casts an idol-a thing detestable to the LORD , the work of the craftsman's hands-and sets it up in secret."
Then all the people shall say, "Amen!"
[16] "Cursed is the man who dishonors his father or his mother."
Then all the people shall say, "Amen!"
[17] "Cursed is the man who moves his neighbor's boundary stone."
Then all the people shall say, "Amen!"
[18] "Cursed is the man who leads the blind astray on the road."
Then all the people shall say, "Amen!"
[19] "Cursed is the man who withholds justice from the alien, the fatherless or the widow."
Then all the people shall say, "Amen!"
[20] "Cursed is the man who sleeps with his father's wife, for he dishonors his father's bed."
Then all the people shall say, "Amen!"
[21] "Cursed is the man who has sexual relations with any animal."
Then all the people shall say, "Amen!"
[22] "Cursed is the man who sleeps with his sister, the daughter of his father or the daughter of his mother."
Then all the people shall say, "Amen!"
[23] "Cursed is the man who sleeps with his mother-in-law."
Then all the people shall say, "Amen!"
[24] "Cursed is the man who kills his neighbor secretly."
Then all the people shall say, "Amen!"
[25] "Cursed is the man who accepts a bribe to kill an innocent person."
Then all the people shall say, "Amen!"
[26] "Cursed is the man who does not uphold the words of this law by carrying them out."
Then all the people shall say, "Amen!"

Deuteronomy 28

Blessings for Obedience

[1] If you fully obey the LORD your God and carefully follow all his commands I give you today, the LORD your God will set you high above all the nations on earth. [2] All these blessings will come upon you and accompany you if you obey the LORD your God:

[3] You will be blessed in the city and blessed in the country.
[4] The fruit of your womb will be blessed, and the crops of your land and the young of your livestock-the calves of your herds and the lambs of your flocks.

40 THE MEANING OF LIFE

⁵ Your basket and your kneading trough will be blessed.
⁶ You will be blessed when you come in and blessed when you go out.

⁷ The LORD will grant that the enemies who rise up against you will be defeated before you. They will come at you from one direction but flee from you in seven.
⁸ The LORD will send a blessing on your barns and on everything you put your hand to. The LORD your God will bless you in the land he is giving you.
⁹ The LORD will establish you as his holy people, as he promised you on oath, if you keep the commands of the LORD your God and walk in his ways. ¹⁰ Then all the peoples on earth will see that you are called by the name of the LORD , and they will fear you. ¹¹ The LORD will grant you abundant prosperity-in the fruit of your womb, the young of your livestock and the crops of your ground-in the land he swore to your forefathers to give you.
¹² The LORD will open the heavens, the storehouse of his bounty, to send rain on your land in season and to bless all the work of your hands. You will lend to many nations but will borrow from none. ¹³ The LORD will make you the head, not the tail. If you pay attention to the commands of the LORD your God that I give you this day and carefully follow them, you will always be at the top, never at the bottom. ¹⁴ Do not turn aside from any of the commands I give you today, to the right or to the left, following other gods and serving them.

Curses for Disobedience

¹⁵ However, if you do not obey the LORD your God and do not carefully follow all his commands and decrees I am giving you today, all these curses will come upon you and overtake you:

¹⁶ You will be cursed in the city and cursed in the country.
¹⁷ Your basket and your kneading trough will be cursed.
¹⁸ The fruit of your womb will be cursed, and the crops of your land, and the calves of your herds and the lambs of your flocks.
¹⁹ You will be cursed when you come in and cursed when you go out.

²⁰ The LORD will send on you curses, confusion and rebuke in everything you put your hand to, until you are destroyed and come to sudden ruin because of the evil you have done in forsaking him. ²¹ The LORD will plague you with diseases until he has destroyed you from the land you are entering to possess. ²² The LORD will strike you with wasting disease, with fever and inflammation, with scorching heat and drought, with blight and mildew, which will plague you until you perish. ²³ The sky over your head will be bronze, the ground beneath you iron. ²⁴ The LORD will turn the rain of your country into dust and powder; it will come down from the skies until you are destroyed.
²⁵ The LORD will cause you to be defeated before your enemies. You will come at them from one direction but flee from them in seven, and you will become a thing of horror to all the kingdoms

on earth. [26] Your carcasses will be food for all the birds of the air and the beasts of the earth, and there will be no one to frighten them away. [27] The LORD will afflict you with the boils of Egypt and with tumors, festering sores and the itch, from which you cannot be cured. [28] The LORD will afflict you with madness, blindness and confusion of mind. [29] At midday you will grope about like a blind man in the dark. You will be unsuccessful in everything you do; day after day you will be oppressed and robbed, with no one to rescue you.

[30] You will be pledged to be married to a woman, but another will take her and ravish her. You will build a house, but you will not live in it. You will plant a vineyard, but you will not even begin to enjoy its fruit. [31] Your ox will be slaughtered before your eyes, but you will eat none of it. Your donkey will be forcibly taken from you and will not be returned. Your sheep will be given to your enemies, and no one will rescue them. [32] Your sons and daughters will be given to another nation, and you will wear out your eyes watching for them day after day, powerless to lift a hand. [33] A people that you do not know will eat what your land and labor produce, and you will have nothing but cruel oppression all your days. [34] The sights you see will drive you mad. [35] The LORD will afflict your knees and legs with painful boils that cannot be cured, spreading from the soles of your feet to the top of your head.

[36] The LORD will drive you and the king you set over you to a nation unknown to you or your fathers. There you will worship other gods, gods of wood and stone. [37] You will become a thing of horror and an object of scorn and ridicule to all the nations where the LORD will drive you.

[38] You will sow much seed in the field but you will harvest little, because locusts will devour it. [39] You will plant vineyards and cultivate them but you will not drink the wine or gather the grapes, because worms will eat them. [40] You will have olive trees throughout your country but you will not use the oil, because the olives will drop off. [41] You will have sons and daughters but you will not keep them, because they will go into captivity. [42] Swarms of locusts will take over all your trees and the crops of your land.

[43] The alien who lives among you will rise above you higher and higher, but you will sink lower and lower. [44] He will lend to you, but you will not lend to him. He will be the head, but you will be the tail.

[45] All these curses will come upon you. They will pursue you and overtake you until you are destroyed, because you did not obey the LORD your God and observe the commands and decrees he gave you. [46] They will be a sign and a wonder to you and your descendants forever. [47] Because you did not serve the LORD your God joyfully and gladly in the time of prosperity, [48] therefore in hunger and thirst, in nakedness and dire poverty, you will serve the enemies the LORD sends against you. He will put an iron yoke on your neck until he has destroyed you.

[49] The LORD will bring a nation against you from far away, from the ends of the earth, like an eagle swooping down, a nation whose language you will not understand, [50] a fierce-looking nation without respect for the old or pity for the young. [51] They will devour the young of your livestock and the crops of your land until you are destroyed. They will leave you no grain, new wine or oil, nor any calves of your herds or lambs of your flocks until you are ruined. [52] They will lay siege to all the cities throughout your land until the high fortified walls in which you trust fall

42   THE MEANING OF LIFE

down. They will besiege all the cities throughout the land the LORD your God is giving you.
[53] Because of the suffering that your enemy will inflict on you during the siege, you will eat the fruit of the womb, the flesh of the sons and daughters the LORD your God has given you. [54] Even the most gentle and sensitive man among you will have no compassion on his own brother or the wife he loves or his surviving children, [55] and he will not give to one of them any of the flesh of his children that he is eating. It will be all he has left because of the suffering your enemy will inflict on you during the siege of all your cities. [56] The most gentle and sensitive woman among you-so sensitive and gentle that she would not venture to touch the ground with the sole of her foot-will begrudge the husband she loves and her own son or daughter [57] the afterbirth from her womb and the children she bears. For she intends to eat them secretly during the siege and in the distress that your enemy will inflict on you in your cities.
[58] If you do not carefully follow all the words of this law, which are written in this book, and do not revere this glorious and awesome name-the LORD your God- [59] the LORD will send fearful plagues on you and your descendants, harsh and prolonged disasters, and severe and lingering illnesses. [60] He will bring upon you all the diseases of Egypt that you dreaded, and they will cling to you. [61] The LORD will also bring on you every kind of sickness and disaster not recorded in this Book of the Law, until you are destroyed. [62] You who were as numerous as the stars in the sky will be left but few in number, because you did not obey the LORD your God. [63] Just as it pleased the LORD to make you prosper and increase in number, so it will please him to ruin and destroy you. You will be uprooted from the land you are entering to possess.
[64] Then the LORD will scatter you among all nations, from one end of the earth to the other. There you will worship other gods-gods of wood and stone, which neither you nor your fathers have known. [65] Among those nations you will find no repose, no resting place for the sole of your foot. There the LORD will give you an anxious mind, eyes weary with longing, and a despairing heart. [66] You will live in constant suspense, filled with dread both night and day, never sure of your life. [67] In the morning you will say, "If only it were evening!" and in the evening, "If only it were morning!"-because of the terror that will fill your hearts and the sights that your eyes will see. [68] The LORD will send you back in ships to Egypt on a journey I said you should never make again. There you will offer yourselves for sale to your enemies as male and female slaves, but no one will buy you.

Deuteronomy 29

Renewal of the Covenant

[1] These are the terms of the covenant the LORD commanded Moses to make with the Israelites in Moab, in addition to the covenant he had made with them at Horeb.
[2] Moses summoned all the Israelites and said to them:

Your eyes have seen all that the LORD did in Egypt to Pharaoh, to all his officials and to all his land. [3] With your own eyes you saw those great trials, those miraculous signs and great wonders. [4] But to this day the LORD has not given you a mind that understands or eyes that see or ears that hear. [5] During the forty years that I led you through the desert, your clothes did not wear out, nor did the sandals on your feet. [6] You ate no bread and drank no wine or other fermented drink. I did this so that you might know that I am the LORD your God.

[7] When you reached this place, Sihon king of Heshbon and Og king of Bashan came out to fight against us, but we defeated them. [8] We took their land and gave it as an inheritance to the Reubenites, the Gadites and the half-tribe of Manasseh.

[9] Carefully follow the terms of this covenant, so that you may prosper in everything you do. [10] All of you are standing today in the presence of the LORD your God-your leaders and chief men, your elders and officials, and all the other men of Israel, [11] together with your children and your wives, and the aliens living in your camps who chop your wood and carry your water. [12] You are standing here in order to enter into a covenant with the LORD your God, a covenant the LORD is making with you this day and sealing with an oath, [13] to confirm you this day as his people, that he may be your God as he promised you and as he swore to your fathers, Abraham, Isaac and Jacob. [14] I am making this covenant, with its oath, not only with you [15] who are standing here with us today in the presence of the LORD our God but also with those who are not here today.

[16] You yourselves know how we lived in Egypt and how we passed through the countries on the way here. [17] You saw among them their detestable images and idols of wood and stone, of silver and gold. [18] Make sure there is no man or woman, clan or tribe among you today whose heart turns away from the LORD our God to go and worship the gods of those nations; make sure there is no root among you that produces such bitter poison.

[19] When such a person hears the words of this oath, he invokes a blessing on himself and therefore thinks, "I will be safe, even though I persist in going my own way." This will bring disaster on the watered land as well as the dry. [20] The LORD will never be willing to forgive him; his wrath and zeal will burn against that man. All the curses written in this book will fall upon him, and the LORD will blot out his name from under heaven. [21] The LORD will single him out from all the tribes of Israel for disaster, according to all the curses of the covenant written in this Book of the Law.

[22] Your children who follow you in later generations and foreigners who come from distant lands will see the calamities that have fallen on the land and the diseases with which the LORD has afflicted it. [23] The whole land will be a burning waste of salt and sulfur-nothing planted, nothing sprouting, no vegetation growing on it. It will be like the destruction of Sodom and Gomorrah, Admah and Zeboiim, which the LORD overthrew in fierce anger. [24] All the nations will ask: "Why has the LORD done this to this land? Why this fierce, burning anger?"

[25] And the answer will be: "It is because this people abandoned the covenant of the LORD , the God of their fathers, the covenant he made with them when he brought them out of Egypt. [26] They went off and worshiped other gods and bowed down to them, gods they did not know, gods he had not given them. [27] Therefore the LORD's anger burned against this land, so that he brought on it all the curses written in this book. [28] In furious anger and in great wrath the LORD uprooted

44   THE MEANING OF LIFE

them from their land and thrust them into another land, as it is now."
[29] The secret things belong to the LORD our God, but the things revealed belong to us and to our children forever, that we may follow all the words of this law.

Deuteronomy 30

Prosperity After Turning to the LORD

[1] When all these blessings and curses I have set before you come upon you and you take them to heart wherever the LORD your God disperses you among the nations, [2] and when you and your children return to the LORD your God and obey him with all your heart and with all your soul according to everything I command you today, [3] then the LORD your God will restore your fortunes and have compassion on you and gather you again from all the nations where he scattered you. [4] Even if you have been banished to the most distant land under the heavens, from there the LORD your God will gather you and bring you back. [5] He will bring you to the land that belonged to your fathers, and you will take possession of it. He will make you more prosperous and numerous than your fathers. [6] The LORD your God will circumcise your hearts and the hearts of your descendants, so that you may love him with all your heart and with all your soul, and live. [7] The LORD your God will put all these curses on your enemies who hate and persecute you. [8] You will again obey the LORD and follow all his commands I am giving you today. [9] Then the LORD your God will make you most prosperous in all the work of your hands and in the fruit of your womb, the young of your livestock and the crops of your land. The LORD will again delight in you and make you prosperous, just as he delighted in your fathers, [10] if you obey the LORD your God and keep his commands and decrees that are written in this Book of the Law and turn to the LORD your God with all your heart and with all your soul.
The Offer of Life or Death
[11] Now what I am commanding you today is not too difficult for you or beyond your reach. [12] It is not up in heaven, so that you have to ask, "Who will ascend into heaven to get it and proclaim it to us so we may obey it?" [13] Nor is it beyond the sea, so that you have to ask, "Who will cross the sea to get it and proclaim it to us so we may obey it?" [14] No, the word is very near you; it is in your mouth and in your heart so you may obey it.
[15] See, I set before you today life and prosperity, death and destruction. [16] For I command you today to love the LORD your God, to walk in his ways, and to keep his commands, decrees and laws; then you will live and increase, and the LORD your God will bless you in the land you are entering to possess.
[17] But if your heart turns away and you are not obedient, and if you are drawn away to bow down to other gods and worship them, [18] I declare to you this day that you will certainly be destroyed. You will not live long in the land you are crossing the Jordan to enter and possess.
[19] This day I call heaven and earth as witnesses against you that I have set before you life and death, blessings and curses. Now choose life, so that you and your children may live [20] and that

you may love the LORD your God, listen to his voice, and hold fast to him. For the LORD is your life, and he will give you many years in the land he swore to give to your fathers, Abraham, Isaac and Jacob

CHAPTER 3

ANCIENT MODELS OF MEANING AND BEING

"Let's talk of graves, of worms and epitaphs;
Make dust our paper and with rainy eyes write sorrow on the bosom of the earth.

For God's sake, let us sit upon the ground and tell sad stories of the death of kings.
How some have been deposed; some slain in war;
some poisoned by their wives; some sleeping killed;
All murdered: for within the hollow crown that rounds the mortal's temples of a king
Keep Death his court and there the antic sits, scoffing he state and grinning at his pomp.
Allowing him a breath, a little scene, To monarchize, be fear'd and kill with looks,
As if this flesh which walls about our life were brass impregnable, and humour'd thus
Comes at the last and with a little pin, Bores through his castle wall, and farewell king."

Richard II, Act 3, Scene 2 – William Shakespeare

The meaning of existence and the ability to find meaning in the fleeting moment of human life has been an issue that has haunted humanity since the beginning of time itself. More recently psychology has taken up the issue of meaning and has floundered with the issue as it tries to keep a firm grasp upon its scientific moorings. Yet in the end a step must be made past science, to the land of myth and history in order to engage this issue. The indispensable contribution of history to psychology is that it begins to help the discipline recover from the amnesia that it seems to be suffering from (Tamas, 2002), for at the heart of psychology are the teachings and narrative structures that have supported humanity for at least three millennia (Olson, 1977)[29]. It is precisely for this reason that modern academic psychology has so little to offer by way of an essential understanding of human nature and why the rebirth of existential approaches are becoming so popular in the 21st century. There has been much time and energy spent on maintaining the posture of science while simultaneously ignoring the fact that scientific methodology is a means

---

29 Olson (1977) notes that existential reorientation and the narratives and societal/ religious structures that support a person's existential, social, and universal narratives have always been a central part of function of society. In particular, Olson notes how the ancient Hindu initiation (Upanayana) ceremony was crucial for an individual, as it provided an occasion to actively reorient oneself to the changing situations evident in the seasons of life.

48   THE MEANING OF LIFE

and not an end (Adams, 1999). The burden of reminding the discipline of psychology of what we are all about has fallen upon the ancient philosophers and religious thinkers. As such, this book cannot properly speak of psychology until we first form an adequate mythic structure from the perspective of the ancients. Only then can we proceed to examining the process and outcome components of psychology and develop new approaches for the counselling profession.

With psychology slowly forming its own self-narrative, settling into scientism and becoming narrow as an understanding of human nature, it is clear that it must discover the breadth of the ancient narratives. [30] Psychology's amnesia of the classics is so self-evident that this book must draw out the great historical themes of existentialism that are central to a full understanding of human nature.[31] Recovering from such amnesia requires connection both with the ethos of the ancients but also the larger historical context of the scientific method. It is imperative to reclaim the knowledge and perspectives on human existence that have developed over the past three millennia (MacHovec, 1984). In reclaiming this larger narrative (and use of narrative) we can identify the universal frameworks and structures for restoring meaning to the realm of human experience.

Gleaning the wisdom of the ancients means respect for the ancients and their formative approaches to meaning and human existence. This does not mean peering at them as remote objects of curiosity and veneration, but as contemporaries with whose thoughts we must grasp in order that we may understand the very structure and categories of our own thoughts. There is an art and science to forming the intellectual and meaning worlds of people and societies. In many of the ancient cultures the depth of this formation and mythical narrative process far outweighs our modern understanding of human nature. Beholding the power and wisdom of ancient thought is in itself a humbling experience—worth cultivating for its value in maintaining a balanced and informed intellectual perspective.[32]

---

30 By thus sterilizing itself with a misunderstood scientific methodology, psychology has succeeded only in creating a conceptual anarchy. As Sigmund Kock noted, the pooled pseudo-knowledge that is much of psychology can be seen as an array of exceedingly simple images with a dense cluster of scholarly support circling each image. The point was that the broader understanding is lacking and largely ignored as the discipline "Misses the forest for all the trees". IN: "Psychology cannot be a Coherent Science," *Psychology Today*, 1969: 14.

31 Clearly these statements are not directed towards the more "humanistic" approaches to psychology or the philosophical psychoanalysis schools. However, the general trend with quantitative research and behavioral analysis, as well as much of the biologically based neurosciences, is towards such a narrow focus that attachment to the normal human functioning of life is lost. That is to say, the attachment to issues like meaning and freedom are often replaced with a reductionism and determinism that often belies the experience of most people. In essence, the contribution of these science to those individuals simply searching for "meaning" and "happiness" is minimal. Therefore, this project will place a deliberate emphasis upon the ancients in order to affirm their ability to help the "helping profession" of psychoanalysis.

32 Philip Rieff in his book *Fellow Teachers* (New York, Dell Publishing, 1973): 39; observes that the role of leaders in a field is to first develop a personal protection of older wisdom which may help stave off arrogant stupidities parading as originality, modernization, revolution and of course, values.

ANCIENT MODELS OF MEANING AND BEING   49

Indeed, the modern father of counselling professions, Sigmund Freud, began his historical legacy by drawing from the past. This legacy was an expression of Freud's Jewish heritage of overt expression of feelings and the intellectual literary wealth of his age that carried with it the Socratic mission of self-knowledge. Therefore one of the most important parts of Freud's legacy was not his theories, but the fact that his theories sprang from experience in the lives and mythic narratives of people, not in a laboratory.[33]

However, unlike the legendary Oedipus, psychology as a professional discipline began to fear self-knowledge and as a result repressed its historical connectedness (Bernstein, 2001). Of course, we must acknowledge that the historical ignorance was not limited to psychology as a discipline, but was reflected in the societies in which psychology flourished as well. Ironically, the work of the Vienna school, with all of its richness and connectedness to history, was deemed too subjective to be acknowledged as a real "science" and was therefore sidelined for something shallower and narrower in focus.

Nevertheless, the major divisions of psychology continue to feel the impact of the Freudian paradigm. Indeed the psychoanalytic ideas found within the Vienna schools continue to find their way into "new schools" under various guises. Thus almost every aspect of modern psychological thought that is of any significance in our understanding of human nature bears an imprint of the ideas of previous thinkers who in turn were imbedded in historical wisdom. Therefore, echoing Whitehead's comment on philosophy being "a series of footnotes on Plato" (Solomon, 1972), we may also say of modern psychology that it, to a large extent, is a series of footnotes on Freud. Of course, Freud and others of the Vienna schools, like Jung, were themselves cradled in a larger perspective of philosophy, history and literature.[34] This massive corpus of wisdom far outweighs the combined output of all the psychological laboratories and clinics of the twelve decades in which Psychology has been an independent science.

It is therefore essential within this book to study the long past of humanity and defining humanness to make it abundantly clear that the central themes throughout history relating to human nature and functioning are "meaning" and "story"[35] (MacHovec, 1984). This is the

---

[33] The major contribution of Freud's daughter Anna is also important to note. With her collaborator E. Erikson, who later taught at Harvard, some of the best models for understanding human development have been derived.

[34] The great insight of Freud and his drawing upon Greek thought clearly formed the basis of modern psychoanalysis. Carl Gustaf Jung's interest with the literature and philosophical constructs of the east (along with his deep understanding of western thought and religion) clearly provided a basis for his elucidation of the notion of archetypes. While this project does not wish to diminish the contribution of neuroscience, the fact is that the functional understanding of psychological wellness as it relates to the average individual has come largely from the Vienna schools.

[35] MacHovec (1984)contends that the seeds of virtually all of the modern individual and family therapies can be found in the ancient world. Whether Gestalt, existential, psychoanalytical etc. they have find their roots in the ancient near-

50 THE MEANING OF LIFE

weakness of much of modern psychology for it is clear to all that there is much more in the depths of human nature than is ever dreamt of by a science and its reductionism. It is clear at this point, at least intuitively, that psychology historically has been expressed as ancient philosophy, mythology, literature and even at times in religious structures. Therefore it is only in the comprehensive vision of humanity in its essential existence that any discipline can hope to engage in a truly honest and unified science of human nature.

A modern understanding of psychology must therefore be informed by the historical and the existential. However, in order for that to occur psychology must loosen its grip upon the rigid structuralism of its narrow reductionist ways and become grounded in its human past of mythology, religion, philosophy and literature. Such works tend to centre on the primitive queries relating to the nature of humanity, society, and the universe, as well as intra-psychic and interpersonal relationships.

As such, while myth holds a mirror to the thought of ancient humanity, mythic history provides a reasonably well-documented record of the origin of the self-conscious quest for knowledge and therefore can be called the birth of psychology. In a sense, the idea of the mythopoeic process is the most natural psychological function. Therefore psychology in history is expressed through the great mythic constructs of a living cosmos and the kinship of all life that is common to all ancient mythical structures from the ancient Egyptian and Sumerian cultures to Greeks and is again emerging in the ecological sciences (Caveny, 2003).

In reviewing the nature of humanity and the essence of what it means to be human, it is clear that the existential perspective is crucial.[36] In many ways the existentialist asserts that there is no real "essence" in humanness (Lasky, 1975) and that all meaning and purpose is found in the living of life and in the process of existence rather than being apart from the existence (Sartre, 1956). It is fascinating to note that this existential perspective is not only a concept that is unique to philosophy but it is also the thread that ties together virtually any study of humanness. Indeed, the evolutionary model of human history also affirms this perspective, for while humanity is driven along, emerging out of the distant past by its genetic structure, the genes are concerned only with their own propagation and in many ways wholly ignore the human experience of finding meaning (Barash, 2000).

---

eastern or eastern teachers like Quoheleth or LoaTse. Central to most of these "seeds" was the notion of maturing and meaning through the seasons of life.

36 The framework of a mythic structure for defining existence has been recognized as the defining core of human existence down through history. Existential philosophy, and particularly Phenomenological Existentialism as a general movement, therefore focuses upon the logic of this long accepted foundation of human existence.

ANCIENT MODELS OF MEANING AND BEING 51

As evolutionary biosocial theorists like Barash (2000) note, existence is a form into which we have been thrown.[37] The meaning of life is therefore whatever we make of it. We may be both driven and constrained by our genes, but genes care nothing of meaning, only of perpetuating the form of existence. Therefore the idea of meaning is found only in our human freedom expressed in shaping the very fluid form of existence that is set out by our evolutionary history.

In the 3rd Millenium B.C.E. with the emergence of Sumerian cuneiform[38] literature we see these two great themes of "existence" intermingle as the source of meaning is tied with the evolutionary genetic drive of "continuing existence". The prime example of this is the ancient Babylonian Epic of Gilgamesh, when Siduru tells Gilgamesh that his search for everlasting life is hopeless:

"Gilgamesh, where are you hurrying to? You will never find that life for which you are looking. When the gods created man they allotted to him death, but life they retained in their own keeping. As for you Gilgamesh, fill your belly with good things; day and night, dance and be merry, feast and rejoice. Let your clothes be fresh, bathe yourself in water, cherish the little child that holds your hand, and make your wife happy in your embrace; for this too is the lot of man."

■ Sanders (1987)

For some scholars the meaning of our internal desire for immortality is simply an expression of our evolutionary history; that somehow we are genetically and biologically driven to "continue" the survival of the species. For others, this longing for immortality is a spiritual quest that can only be expressed in terms of a religious search and an eventual "salvation" from death. However, as the story of Gilgamesh makes clear, at times it is not the source of this longing that is important. What is important is how we use this longing to orient ourselves to our present life circumstances and what meaning we make of this present life.

It seems that even at the dawn of time bar tenders were giving advice on the meaning of life (Siduru was a young lady that owned a tavern). In the case of Gilgamesh we see a pattern for how we are to psychologically orient ourselves in life and how this provides a structure for us to engage life (even in the face of our own death). This predictable pattern is best expressed in the

---

37 Barash (2000) warns, and rightly so, that we must be careful not to draw too many guidelines from existence, for "mere existence" does not necessarily imply "meaning". Rather, meaning is likely something that must be created, and is separate to some extent from mere existence in the evolutionary sense.

38 The very generic term Cuneiform refers to mode of writing in clay tablets by pressing the end of a reed or bone stylus into the wet clay; the resulting wedge-shaped marks are "cuneiform" (Latin *cuneus,* "Wedge"), a name for all such scripts in whatever language they occur. Of particular concern in this reference is the literature written in Akkadian and epic stories of creation *Enuma Elish* and of searching for eternal life *The Gilgamesh Epic.* Chambers, M.; Grew, R.; Herlihy, D.; Rabb, T.; Woloch, I. (1987) *The Western Experience.* New York: Knopf.

52 THE MEANING OF LIFE

Latin phrase: 'Existo fontis; Existo opus; Existo Mortalitus'. In basic terms this phrase means that the meaning in life is found in defining ourselves, in relation to our source (God), in our actions (Work), and in our approach to death (and what comes after death—salvation).

Structurally, the advice given by Siduru on how to deal with this emotional issue of life and death is the precursor to every historical existential philosophy to follow. Siduru's first observation is that we do not understand everything so there are those mysteries that we must relegate to the gods (or God). In believing in and trusting in the divine we are then able to have a narrative that allows us to "fill in the gaps" of our own knowledge about everyday life. This allows us to then engage life, work and relationships with a guiding narrative (that helps us create meaning in our own lives). In the end, this trust in the divine and the personal narrative that we draw from this trust allows us to approach death with authenticity.

What is important about the Siduru conversation with Gilgamesh is that it makes some basic issues clear. First, without a mythic structure that includes the divine our everyday lives will lack meaning (because in death all is lost). Secondly, the only way we as individuals discover and experience meaning in life is through engaging the world and defining ourselves in both relationships and actions because of death the human life is an active and organic process of continually defining ourselves in relationship to others. Finally, the "faith" or "trust" that we have in the divine allows us to not be overcome by the inevitable and deeply personal experience of our own death.

Going down through history this basic mythic structure also forms the skeleton of the ancient Egyptian notion of how to psychologically manage the stresses of life. The ancient Egyptians (Chambers et al, 1987) believed their ultimate source of existence was from the gods. This basic belief in this divine/human relationship gave them a reason for their actions and work (and of course religion). In addition, the natural psychological anxiety about the meaning of life and the inevitability of death was managed as the ancient Egyptians viewed death as an extension of life and its actions. Therefore it was the responsibility of an individual to engage in life and its activities, and from this define his/her place and meaning in eternity (a farmer in life would be a farmer in death—after he or she was resurrected by the gods). For the ancient Egyptians there was no difference between "meaning" and "existence"; the two were intricately bound together and provided a great way to manage the psychological stresses associated with death and the difficulties of life.

The ancient Egyptians drew upon this twofold drive, but their narrative structure dictated that it be expressed in a somewhat different form. For the ancient Egyptian, the notion of eternal life was a given (finding an expression for the genetic drive). The power of the existential portion of human expression was found in the construct of this eternal life. It was essentially an extension of the current life and its actions (Chambers et al, 1987). Therefore it was the responsibility of an individual to be engaged in life and its activities, and from this to define their place and meaning in eternity. For the ancient Egyptian there was no separation of some type of "meaning" from "existence", the two were intricately bound together.

ANCIENT MODELS OF MEANING AND BEING   53

This existential expression of life is articulated within the second millennium B.C.E. in the term *Maat*. This term is in essence translated as "the right order' (Teeter, 1997)[39]. The expression means that life is pleasant and existence is meaningful when the function of all things is in its proper place fulfilling its proper task (Chambers et al 1987). The logical extension of this is that when an individual finds "where they fit in" and can express themselves within the larger societal and mythic structures, they experience meaning. In this we see the expression of essential existentialism.

Similarly within the west-Semitic regions under Egyptian control following the Old Kingdom the term *Shal'm* [40] comes into use as it expresses not only an emotional state of contentment but also the organizational sense of the Egyptian term *Maat*. Due to the crosspollination that the west-Semitic colonies received from trade between the Assyrian and Egyptian empires it is not surprising to find such a similar existential expression of mental health. However, as Egyptian influence waned within this region following the reign of Rameses II the emerging Semitic kingdoms began extending this existential philosophy through their own mythic construction.

The first obvious feature within the literature of this time (1000 – 600 B.C.E.) is its continuation of the existential thought that there is not "meaning in life", but meaning is to be experienced in the interacting with the form of life (Kushner, 1986). As the book *Quoheleth*[41] (Ecclesiastes) makes clear, the ceaseless cycle of life is itself meaningless (literally "as elusive as air") (Kaiser, 1979). Human existence is only bearable when a specific constructed formula is followed, for meaning and purpose are only found in "engaging in a mythic structure for life" and "engaging in the actions of life/finding one's particular place". Yet, in the midst of that mythic structure[42] and working, one must remember that there is still a mystery of existence that will never be grasped by us, and one must accept this fact. At the end of the book it is clear that the role of a mythic structure is important practical advice, lest the enigmas of life discourage people from experiencing the joy to be found in interacting with one's own "existence" (Kaiser 1987).

---

39 Teeters (1997) notes that this concept was the form and basis of meaning and personal piety within Egypt during the Old Kingdom and through the New Kingdom until the time of Ramesses. During the development of the Empire under Ramesses and the post-Ramesses decline, the idea and the rituals associated with the idea of Maat saw a decline in influence.

40 מ.אָיש (SHALOM) is often translated as 'complete', 'safe', 'at peace', 'whole', 'a mind at peace with', a 'perfect relationship' In. Brown, F. *A Hebrew and English Lexicon*. Oxford: Clarendon.

41 While this book has many names, often after a Greek or Latin translation, the original west-Semitic title of the book is "The Teacher" and this title best expresses the purpose of the book, "To teach about life".

42 Quoheleth does not clearly define what this mythic structure is, though given the west-semitic cultural context of the book such a structure is assumed to be a form of monotheistic religion.

54   THE MEANING OF LIFE

This full existential perspective of humanness is also embedded within the language of ancient near-eastern wisdom literature. The term itself, "wisdom"[43] had a broad range of meaning that expressed that the "wise person" was one who was engaged in all the existential functions of life. The word described someone who lived life within a defined mythic structure that allowed for a judgment of "good" and "bad"(Johnson, 1975). The meaning of the word is not limited to this however, but the person who was *Hokmah* (wise) was also well informed with an encyclopaedic knowledge (Johnson). Yet simple knowledge did not allow one to reach the level of wisdom unless one could have the functional cleverness to use it in differing situations. Finally, one also had to have the skill of a *craftsmanship* to interact with the physical world (and manipulate it). This full range of humanness was the basis of a "good life". In this way ancient Near-Eastern wisdom literature incorporated a full range of human experiences into its existential understanding of human psychology (MacHovec, 1984).

The ancient Indo-Aryan beliefs also reflect the process of "engaging life" (Richards, 1978) within a mythic framework harkening back to the 2nd millennia B.C.E. Sumerian literature, the Vedic existential structure drawing from a primordial mythic story (Jacob, 1999). This story defines and shapes the existence within which an individual must find meaning[44]. The interplay between the present experience and the eternal cosmological perspective is so intricate that the two are almost indistinguishable (Jacob). It is clear, again, that the great themes of a mythic structure and a "place to find meaning in existence" sustained the people within the Indo-Aryan societies.

Following this great age of existential awareness we also have the emergence of the great Greek civilization and its insights into existence. With the clear influence of Babylonian culture upon Greece, and vice versa, especially following Alexander's conquest, one would expect to find similar structures about human existence. In addition, with Philo of Alexandria's claim that the west-Semitic cultures were a major font of Greek thought, one would expect teachings about existence (Najman, 2000).

---

43 The Semitic term εημΘη(Hokmah) is the source of this discussion. (Brown et al 1988).

44 Richards (1978) notes that meaning was intricately linked with social structure, not within "clans" but in a wider societal structure that provided a specific place within which the individual was expected to exist. This early structure eventually formed into the caste system of modernity and is obviously formed by the mythic story structures of Vedic literature.

READ AND DECIDE FOR YOURSELF

Excerpts from:

QUOHELETH *(ECCLESIASTES)*

PROVERBS

JOB

QUOHELETH (ECCLESIASTES)

Author's Paraphrase:

Chapter 1

These are the words of the Preacher, the son of David, king in Jerusalem: "Ultimately meaningless," says the Preacher, "Everything is ultimately meaningless!"

What good comes of all of the work that a man does in his life? One generation after another, people come and people go – only the earth itself remains constant. The sun rises in the morning, then sets in the evening – only to return and do it all over the next day. The wind blows to the south, then again to the north, swirling around back to where it started from. All of the rivers flow into the sea, but the sea never fills up. The waters return to their source to flow again. It makes me weary just to think about it!

The eye is never satisfied that it has seen enough, nor is the ear satisfied that it has heard enough. Everything repeats itself – if it existed before it will exist again and if it happened before it will happen again. There really isn't anything new under the sun. What significant things in life can you look at and really say "This is new"? Whatever it is has actually been around for ages – since before you and I existed. We don't remember things past very well, and future generations won't remember the things of our generation.

I, the Preacher, have been king over Israel in Jerusalem. I determined in my mind that I was going to use my wisdom to seek and explore everything that happens in life. This is perhaps the most difficult task God has given man to wrestle with. I have looked at every thing man does and decided that, when it comes right down to it, everything is ultimately meaningless – about as useless as trying to catch the wind. You can spend your whole life righting wrongs, but there will always be more wrongs to be righted. Recognize that your comprehension is limited, so don't be discouraged by not being able to make everything fit into nice, neat little boxes. In my moments of honest self-evaluation I recognize that I have more wisdom than any of my predecessors. I have stored up a wealth of wisdom and knowledge. I decided to identify what constitutes wisdom and what just leads to foolishness – then I realized that even this was an ultimately meaningless endeavor. Even wisdom doesn't keep us from grief and knowledge just leads to more intelligent heartaches.

Chapter 5

Consider your attitude carefully as you prepare to worship God. Approach as a humble student ready to learn – it would be very wrong to be arrogant before God. In God's presence you shouldn't be flippant or careless in what you choose to say or even think. Remember who God is

ANCIENT MODELS OF MEANING AND BEING 57

and who you are – it's not like you know anything that He doesn't. Being involved in too many activities will keep you awake at night, and too many words will keep you from hearing God's voice. Don't make a commitment to God unless you know you can keep it; He takes no pleasure in your careless words. Follow through with your promises! It is better not to promise than to make a promise and not live up to it. Don't let your mouth get you into trouble and then try to get out of it by saying, "It was all a mistake." Do you want God's anger at your words to cause Him to take His blessing away from the things that you do? Don't be caught up in the emptiness of your own dreams and endless rambling. Better to show God respect and seek to know His heart.

Don't be surprised when you see the poor being oppressed, justice being denied, and blatant unrighteousness in the land. Governments are made up of many layers of officials, and some corruption is likely to be found in such bureaucracies. A government leader who serves well will bring blessing to the nation.

Anyone who loves money will never be satisfied with it, and anyone seeking wealth will never be happy with whatever they acquire. What a useless waste of life! Needs always increase to consume anything extra, so all we can do is stand by and watch the flow – in one hand and out the other. Of course a man who works hard sleeps well; while the rich man's full stomach keeps him awake at night.

And here's another detestable situation: When a rich man hoards his wealth to his own detriment. He eventually loses his wealth to a bad investment and then can't feed his own children. He was born with nothing and he'll die with nothing. He has nothing left to show for all the wealth he once had. This is futile also, that a man will take to the grave exactly what he brought from the womb. So, what do you get as a result of constantly striving for "success"? A life of depression, frustration, stress, and despair.

So here's what I've found to be worthwhile: to eat, drink, and enjoy your work during the few years God gives you, for the ability to enjoy life is your reward. If God grants you riches and wealth, recognize the gift God has given you in the ability to provide for your own needs and enjoy your work. Keep this perspective and the joy God provides will keep you from wallowing in the memories of the difficult times.

Chapter 11

Give to others at every opportunity, and you will find others will be willing to give back when you need it. The more widespread your giving, the better your chances that one of those you've given to, or someone they know, will be able to help in your time of need. The clouds rain when they get full of moisture; trees fall in the wilderness and lie whichever way they fall; you have no control over any of this. Don't let yourself be paralyzed by waiting for perfect conditions or you'll never accomplish anything. You don't know where the wind will blow or how bones are formed in the womb, or any of God's other mysterious ways. So don't be lazy, but invest your energies in several things – you don't know which ones will pay off and which ones won't.

58   THE MEANING OF LIFE

Being alive is an experience we should savor. Even if you live a long life, enjoy each day, and appreciate even the hard times – you will experience many of them. Don't get too wrapped up in your circumstances, they are insignificant in the long run. Don't try to grow up too quick – enjoy your youth and stay light-hearted about life as long as you can. Don't be afraid to be impulsive and pursue the things you desire, but remember that God is watching and will hold you accountable for your actions. So don't let yourself be buried in sorrow and pain. Childhood quickly turns to manhood, and even manhood is a fleeting thing.

Chapter 12

Make God a vital part of your life while you are young, before you become burdened with the challenges of old age – before just finding pleasure in life becomes difficult. The day will come when even the good times won't seem so exciting any more, and you'll just barely get over one ailment when another will strike. Your hands will tremble and your back will no longer be straight. You'll have few teeth left and your eyesight will fade. Even your lips won't open as readily as they used to, but then you won't have enough teeth to chew anything anyway. You'll rise as the first birds begin to sing in the morning, but you'll have a hard time hearing them. Falling will become a major fear and you'll think twice before even risking going out of your house. Your hair will turn gray, and nothing will excite your passions any more. You'll know that your own death is approaching as you watch others mourning for your friends.

So get to know God now – before your senses are dull and your mind is weak; before your organs give out and your heart becomes unreliable; before you return to the dust from which we all came and your spirit returns to God who gave it to you. Life, in itself, is futile – absolutely meaningless!

Here is the key to finding meaning in life: Respect God and be obedient to his commands, for this is the only thing that will really bring any value and meaning to your life. For in death there is only God and only in God is there hope for meaning.

PROVERBS

Proverbs 1

Prologue: Purpose and Theme

[1] The proverbs of Solomon son of David, king of Israel:

[2] for attaining wisdom and discipline;
for understanding words of insight;
[3] for acquiring a disciplined and prudent life,
doing what is right and just and fair;
[4] for giving prudence to the simple,
knowledge and discretion to the young-
[5] let the wise listen and add to their learning,
and let the discerning get guidance-
[6] for understanding proverbs and parables,
the sayings and riddles of the wise.

[7] The fear of the Lord is the beginning of knowledge,
but fools despise wisdom and discipline.

Exhortations to Embrace Wisdom

Warning Against Enticement

[8] Listen, my son, to your father's instruction
and do not forsake your mother's teaching.
[9] They will be a garland to grace your head
and a chain to adorn your neck.

[10] My son, if sinners entice you,
do not give in to them.
[11] If they say, "Come along with us;
let's lie in wait for someone's blood,
let's waylay some harmless soul;
[12] let's swallow them alive, like the grave,
and whole, like those who go down to the pit;

60 THE MEANING OF LIFE

[13] we will get all sorts of valuable things
and fill our houses with plunder;
[14] throw in your lot with us,
and we will share a common purse"-
[15] my son, do not go along with them,
do not set foot on their paths;
[16] for their feet rush into sin,
they are swift to shed blood.
[17] How useless to spread a net
in full view of all the birds!
[18] These men lie in wait for their own blood;
they waylay only themselves!
[19] Such is the end of all who go after ill-gotten gain;
it takes away the lives of those who get it.

Warning Against Rejecting Wisdom

[20] Wisdom calls aloud in the street,
she raises her voice in the public squares;
[21] at the head of the noisy streets she cries out,
in the gateways of the city she makes her speech:

[22] "How long will you simple ones love your simple ways?
How long will mockers delight in mockery
and fools hate knowledge?
[23] If you had responded to my rebuke,
I would have poured out my heart to you
and made my thoughts known to you.
[24] But since you rejected me when I called
and no one gave heed when I stretched out my hand,
[25] since you ignored all my advice
and would not accept my rebuke,
[26] I in turn will laugh at your disaster;
I will mock when calamity overtakes you-
[27] when calamity overtakes you like a storm,
when disaster sweeps over you like a whirlwind,
when distress and trouble overwhelm you.

[28] "Then they will call to me but I will not answer;

they will look for me but will not find me.
[29] Since they hated knowledge
and did not choose to fear the LORD ,
[30] since they would not accept my advice
and spurned my rebuke,
[31] they will eat the fruit of their ways
and be filled with the fruit of their schemes.
[32] For the waywardness of the simple will kill them,
and the complacency of fools will destroy them;
[33] but whoever listens to me will live in safety
and be at ease, without fear of harm."

Proverbs 2

Moral Benefits of Wisdom

[1] My son, if you accept my words
and store up my commands within you,
[2] turning your ear to wisdom
and applying your heart to understanding,
[3] and if you call out for insight
and cry aloud for understanding,
[4] and if you look for it as for silver
and search for it as for hidden treasure,
[5] then you will understand the fear of the LORD
and find the knowledge of God.
[6] For the LORD gives wisdom,
and from his mouth come knowledge and understanding.
[7] He holds victory in store for the upright,
he is a shield to those whose walk is blameless,
[8] for he guards the course of the just
and protects the way of his faithful ones.
[9] Then you will understand what is right and just
and fair-every good path.
[10] For wisdom will enter your heart,
and knowledge will be pleasant to your soul.
[11] Discretion will protect you,
and understanding will guard you.

[12] Wisdom will save you from the ways of wicked men,

62   THE MEANING OF LIFE

from men whose words are perverse,
[13] who leave the straight paths
to walk in dark ways,
[14] who delight in doing wrong
and rejoice in the perverseness of evil,
[15] whose paths are crooked
and who are devious in their ways.

[16] It will save you also from the adulteress,
from the wayward wife with her seductive words,
[17] who has left the partner of her youth
and ignored the covenant she made before God.
[18] For her house leads down to death
and her paths to the spirits of the dead.
[19] None who go to her return
or attain the paths of life.

[20] Thus you will walk in the ways of good men
and keep to the paths of the righteous.
[21] For the upright will live in the land,
and the blameless will remain in it;
[22] but the wicked will be cut off from the land,
and the unfaithful will be torn from it.

Proverbs 3

Further Benefits of Wisdom
[1] My son, do not forget my teaching,
but keep my commands in your heart,
[2] for they will prolong your life many years
and bring you prosperity.

[3] Let love and faithfulness never leave you;
bind them around your neck,
write them on the tablet of your heart.
[4] Then you will win favor and a good name
in the sight of God and man.

[5] Trust in the LORD with all your heart
and lean not on your own understanding;

^{6} in all your ways acknowledge him,
and he will make your paths straight.

^{7} Do not be wise in your own eyes;
fear the LORD and shun evil.
^{8} This will bring health to your body
and nourishment to your bones.

^{9} Honor the LORD with your wealth,
with the firstfruits of all your crops;
^{10} then your barns will be filled to overflowing,
and your vats will brim over with new wine.

^{11} My son, do not despise the LORD's discipline
and do not resent his rebuke,
^{12} because the LORD disciplines those he loves,
as a father the son he delights in.

^{13} Blessed is the man who finds wisdom,
the man who gains understanding,
^{14} for she is more profitable than silver
and yields better returns than gold.
^{15} She is more precious than rubies;
nothing you desire can compare with her.
^{16} Long life is in her right hand;
in her left hand are riches and honor.
^{17} Her ways are pleasant ways,
and all her paths are peace.
^{18} She is a tree of life to those who embrace her;
those who lay hold of her will be blessed.

^{19} By wisdom the LORD laid the earth's foundations,
by understanding he set the heavens in place;
^{20} by his knowledge the deeps were divided,
and the clouds let drop the dew.

^{21} My son, preserve sound judgment and discernment,
do not let them out of your sight;
^{22} they will be life for you,
an ornament to grace your neck.

64   THE MEANING OF LIFE

23 Then you will go on your way in safety,
and your foot will not stumble;
24 when you lie down, you will not be afraid;
when you lie down, your sleep will be sweet.
25 Have no fear of sudden disaster
or of the ruin that overtakes the wicked,
26 for the LORD will be your confidence
and will keep your foot from being snared.

27 Do not withhold good from those who deserve it,
when it is in your power to act.
28 Do not say to your neighbor,
"Come back later; I'll give it tomorrow"-
when you now have it with you.

29 Do not plot harm against your neighbor,
who lives trustfully near you.
30 Do not accuse a man for no reason-
when he has done you no harm.

31 Do not envy a violent man
or choose any of his ways,
32 for the LORD detests a perverse man
but takes the upright into his confidence.

33 The LORD's curse is on the house of the wicked,
but he blesses the home of the righteous.
34 He mocks proud mockers
but gives grace to the humble.
35 The wise inherit honor,
but fools he holds up to shame.

Proverbs 4

Wisdom Is Supreme

1 Listen, my sons, to a father's instruction;
pay attention and gain understanding.
2 I give you sound learning,
so do not forsake my teaching.

ANCIENT MODELS OF MEANING AND BEING   **65**

[3] When I was a boy in my father's house,
still tender, and an only child of my mother,
[4] he taught me and said,
"Lay hold of my words with all your heart;
keep my commands and you will live.
[5] Get wisdom, get understanding;
do not forget my words or swerve from them.
[6] Do not forsake wisdom, and she will protect you;
love her, and she will watch over you.
[7] Wisdom is supreme; therefore get wisdom.
Though it cost all you have, get understanding.
[8] Esteem her, and she will exalt you;
embrace her, and she will honor you.
[9] She will set a garland of grace on your head
and present you with a crown of splendor."

[10] Listen, my son, accept what I say,
and the years of your life will be many.
[11] I guide you in the way of wisdom
and lead you along straight paths.
[12] When you walk, your steps will not be hampered;
when you run, you will not stumble.
[13] Hold on to instruction, do not let it go;
guard it well, for it is your life.
[14] Do not set foot on the path of the wicked
or walk in the way of evil men.
[15] Avoid it, do not travel on it;
turn from it and go on your way.
[16] For they cannot sleep till they do evil;
they are robbed of slumber till they make someone fall.
[17] They eat the bread of wickedness
and drink the wine of violence.

[18] The path of the righteous is like the first gleam of dawn,
shining ever brighter till the full light of day.
[19] But the way of the wicked is like deep darkness;
they do not know what makes them stumble.

[20] My son, pay attention to what I say;
listen closely to my words.

66 THE MEANING OF LIFE

21 Do not let them out of your sight,
keep them within your heart;
22 for they are life to those who find them
and health to a man's whole body.
23 Above all else, guard your heart,
for it is the wellspring of life.
24 Put away perversity from your mouth;
keep corrupt talk far from your lips.
25 Let your eyes look straight ahead,
fix your gaze directly before you.
26 Make level paths for your feet
and take only ways that are firm.
27 Do not swerve to the right or the left;
keep your foot from evil.

Proverbs 5

Warning Against Adultery

1 My son, pay attention to my wisdom,
listen well to my words of insight,
2 that you may maintain discretion
and your lips may preserve knowledge.
3 For the lips of an adulteress drip honey,
and her speech is smoother than oil;
4 but in the end she is bitter as gall,
sharp as a double-edged sword.
5 Her feet go down to death;
her steps lead straight to the grave.
6 She gives no thought to the way of life;
her paths are crooked, but she knows it not.

7 Now then, my sons, listen to me;
do not turn aside from what I say.
8 Keep to a path far from her,
do not go near the door of her house,
9 lest you give your best strength to others
and your years to one who is cruel,
10 lest strangers feast on your wealth
and your toil enrich another man's house.

[11] At the end of your life you will groan,
when your flesh and body are spent.
[12] You will say, "How I hated discipline!
How my heart spurned correction!
[13] I would not obey my teachers
or listen to my instructors.
[14] I have come to the brink of utter ruin
in the midst of the whole assembly."

[15] Drink water from your own cistern,
running water from your own well.
[16] Should your springs overflow in the streets,
your streams of water in the public squares?
[17] Let them be yours alone,
never to be shared with strangers.
[18] May your fountain be blessed,
and may you rejoice in the wife of your youth.
[19] A loving doe, a graceful deer-
may her breasts satisfy you always,
may you ever be captivated by her love.
[20] Why be captivated, my son, by an adulteress?
Why embrace the bosom of another man's wife?

[21] For a man's ways are in full view of the LORD ,
and he examines all his paths.
[22] The evil deeds of a wicked man ensnare him;
the cords of his sin hold him fast.
[23] He will die for lack of discipline,
led astray by his own great folly.

68   THE MEANING OF LIFE

JOB

Job 1

Prologue

[1] In the land of Uz there lived a man whose name was Job. This man was blameless and upright; he feared God and shunned evil. [2] He had seven sons and three daughters, [3] and he owned seven thousand sheep, three thousand camels, five hundred yoke of oxen and five hundred donkeys, and had a large number of servants. He was the greatest man among all the people of the East.
[4] His sons used to take turns holding feasts in their homes, and they would invite their three sisters to eat and drink with them. [5] When a period of feasting had run its course, Job would send and have them purified. Early in the morning he would sacrifice a burnt offering for each of them, thinking, "Perhaps my children have sinned and cursed God in their hearts." This was Job's regular custom.

Job's First Test

[6] One day the angels came to present themselves before the LORD , and Satan also came with them. [7] The LORD said to Satan, "Where have you come from?"
Satan answered the LORD , "From roaming through the earth and going back and forth in it."
[8] Then the LORD said to Satan, "Have you considered my servant Job? There is no one on earth like him; he is blameless and upright, a man who fears God and shuns evil."
[9] "Does Job fear God for nothing?" Satan replied. [10] "Have you not put a hedge around him and his household and everything he has? You have blessed the work of his hands, so that his flocks and herds are spread throughout the land. [11] But stretch out your hand and strike everything he has, and he will surely curse you to your face."
[12] The LORD said to Satan, "Very well, then, everything he has is in your hands, but on the man himself do not lay a finger."
Then Satan went out from the presence of the LORD .
[13] One day when Job's sons and daughters were feasting and drinking wine at the oldest brother's house, [14] a messenger came to Job and said, "The oxen were plowing and the donkeys were grazing nearby, [15] and the Sabeans attacked and carried them off. They put the servants to the sword, and I am the only one who has escaped to tell you!"
[16] While he was still speaking, another messenger came and said, "The fire of God fell from the sky and burned up the sheep and the servants, and I am the only one who has escaped to tell you!"
[17] While he was still speaking, another messenger came and said, "The Chaldeans formed three

ANCIENT MODELS OF MEANING AND BEING **69**

raiding parties and swept down on your camels and carried them off. They put the servants to the sword, and I am the only one who has escaped to tell you!"

[18] While he was still speaking, yet another messenger came and said, "Your sons and daughters were feasting and drinking wine at the oldest brother's house, [19] when suddenly a mighty wind swept in from the desert and struck the four corners of the house. It collapsed on them and they are dead, and I am the only one who has escaped to tell you!"

[20] At this, Job got up and tore his robe and shaved his head. Then he fell to the ground in worship [21] and said:

"Naked I came from my mother's womb,
and naked I will depart.
The LORD gave and the LORD has taken away;
may the name of the LORD be praised."

[22] In all this, Job did not sin by charging God with wrongdoing.

Job 2

Job's Second Test

[1] On another day the angels came to present themselves before the LORD , and Satan also came with them to present himself before him. [2] And the LORD said to Satan, "Where have you come from?"

Satan answered the LORD , "From roaming through the earth and going back and forth in it."

[3] Then the LORD said to Satan, "Have you considered my servant Job? There is no one on earth like him; he is blameless and upright, a man who fears God and shuns evil. And he still maintains his integrity, though you incited me against him to ruin him without any reason."

[4] "Skin for skin!" Satan replied. "A man will give all he has for his own life. [5] But stretch out your hand and strike his flesh and bones, and he will surely curse you to your face."

[6] The LORD said to Satan, "Very well, then, he is in your hands; but you must spare his life."

[7] So Satan went out from the presence of the LORD and afflicted Job with painful sores from the soles of his feet to the top of his head. [8] Then Job took a piece of broken pottery and scraped himself with it as he sat among the ashes.

[9] His wife said to him, "Are you still holding on to your integrity? Curse God and die!"

[10] He replied, "You are talking like a foolish woman. Shall we accept good from God, and not trouble?"

In all this, Job did not sin in what he said.

Job's Three Friends

70   THE MEANING OF LIFE

[11] When Job's three friends, Eliphaz the Temanite, Bildad the Shuhite and Zophar the Naamathite, heard about all the troubles that had come upon him, they set out from their homes and met together by agreement to go and sympathize with him and comfort him. [12] When they saw him from a distance, they could hardly recognize him; they began to weep aloud, and they tore their robes and sprinkled dust on their heads. [13] Then they sat on the ground with him for seven days and seven nights. No one said a word to him, because they saw how great his suffering was.

Job 3

Job Speaks

[1] After this, Job opened his mouth and cursed the day of his birth.
[2] He said:

[3] "May the day of my birth perish,
and the night it was said, 'A boy is born!'
[4] That day-may it turn to darkness;
may God above not care about it;
may no light shine upon it.
[5] May darkness and deep shadow claim it once more;
may a cloud settle over it;
may blackness overwhelm its light.
[6] That night-may thick darkness seize it;
may it not be included among the days of the year
nor be entered in any of the months.
[7] May that night be barren;
may no shout of joy be heard in it.
[8] May those who curse days curse that day,
those who are ready to rouse Leviathan.
[9] May its morning stars become dark;
may it wait for daylight in vain
and not see the first rays of dawn,
[10] for it did not shut the doors of the womb on me
to hide trouble from my eyes.

[11] "Why did I not perish at birth,
and die as I came from the womb?
[12] Why were there knees to receive me
and breasts that I might be nursed?

ANCIENT MODELS OF MEANING AND BEING **71**

[13] For now I would be lying down in peace;
I would be asleep and at rest
[14] with kings and counselors of the earth,
who built for themselves places now lying in ruins,
[15] with rulers who had gold,
who filled their houses with silver.
[16] Or why was I not hidden in the ground like a stillborn child,
like an infant who never saw the light of day?
[17] There the wicked cease from turmoil,
and there the weary are at rest.
[18] Captives also enjoy their ease;
they no longer hear the slave driver's shout.
[19] The small and the great are there,
and the slave is freed from his master.

[20] "Why is light given to those in misery,
and life to the bitter of soul,
[21] to those who long for death that does not come,
who search for it more than for hidden treasure,
[22] who are filled with gladness
and rejoice when they reach the grave?
[23] Why is life given to a man
whose way is hidden,
whom God has hedged in?
[24] For sighing comes to me instead of food;
my groans pour out like water.
[25] What I feared has come upon me;
what I dreaded has happened to me.
[26] I have no peace, no quietness;
I have no rest, but only turmoil."

Job 4

Eliphaz

[1] Then Eliphaz the Temanite replied:

[2] "If someone ventures a word with you, will you be impatient?
But who can keep from speaking?
[3] Think how you have instructed many,

72   THE MEANING OF LIFE

how you have strengthened feeble hands.
[4] Your words have supported those who stumbled;
you have strengthened faltering knees.
[5] But now trouble comes to you, and you are discouraged;
it strikes you, and you are dismayed.
[6] Should not your piety be your confidence
and your blameless ways your hope?

[7] "Consider now: Who, being innocent, has ever perished?
Where were the upright ever destroyed?
[8] As I have observed, those who plow evil
and those who sow trouble reap it.
[9] At the breath of God they are destroyed;
at the blast of his anger they perish.
[10] The lions may roar and growl,
yet the teeth of the great lions are broken.
[11] The lion perishes for lack of prey,
and the cubs of the lioness are scattered.

[12] "A word was secretly brought to me,
my ears caught a whisper of it.
[13] Amid disquieting dreams in the night,
when deep sleep falls on men,
[14] fear and trembling seized me
and made all my bones shake.
[15] A spirit glided past my face,
and the hair on my body stood on end.
[16] It stopped,
but I could not tell what it was.
A form stood before my eyes,
and I heard a hushed voice:
[17] 'Can a mortal be more righteous than God?
Can a man be more pure than his Maker?
[18] If God places no trust in his servants,
if he charges his angels with error,
[19] how much more those who live in houses of clay,
whose foundations are in the dust,
who are crushed more readily than a moth!
[20] Between dawn and dusk they are broken to pieces;
unnoticed, they perish forever.

ANCIENT MODELS OF MEANING AND BEING   **73**

[21] Are not the cords of their tent pulled up,
so that they die without wisdom?'

Job 5

[1] "Call if you will, but who will answer you?
To which of the holy ones will you turn?
[2] Resentment kills a fool,
and envy slays the simple.
[3] I myself have seen a fool taking root,
but suddenly his house was cursed.
[4] His children are far from safety,
crushed in court without a defender.
[5] The hungry consume his harvest,
taking it even from among thorns,
and the thirsty pant after his wealth.
[6] For hardship does not spring from the soil,
nor does trouble sprout from the ground.
[7] Yet man is born to trouble
as surely as sparks fly upward.

[8] "But if it were I, I would appeal to God;
I would lay my cause before him.
[9] He performs wonders that cannot be fathomed,
miracles that cannot be counted.
[10] He bestows rain on the earth;
he sends water upon the countryside.
[11] The lowly he sets on high,
and those who mourn are lifted to safety.
[12] He thwarts the plans of the crafty,
so that their hands achieve no success.
[13] He catches the wise in their craftiness,
and the schemes of the wily are swept away.
[14] Darkness comes upon them in the daytime;
at noon they grope as in the night.
[15] He saves the needy from the sword in their mouth;
he saves them from the clutches of the powerful.
[16] So the poor have hope,
and injustice shuts its mouth.

74   THE MEANING OF LIFE

[17] "Blessed is the man whom God corrects;
so do not despise the discipline of the Almighty.
[18] For he wounds, but he also binds up;
he injures, but his hands also heal.
[19] From six calamities he will rescue you;
in seven no harm will befall you.
[20] In famine he will ransom you from death,
and in battle from the stroke of the sword.
[21] You will be protected from the lash of the tongue,
and need not fear when destruction comes.
[22] You will laugh at destruction and famine,
and need not fear the beasts of the earth.
[23] For you will have a covenant with the stones of the field,
and the wild animals will be at peace with you.
[24] You will know that your tent is secure;
you will take stock of your property and find nothing missing.
[25] You will know that your children will be many,
and your descendants like the grass of the earth.
[26] You will come to the grave in full vigor,
like sheaves gathered in season.

[27] "We have examined this, and it is true.
So hear it and apply it to yourself."

Job 6

Job

[1] Then Job replied:

[2] "If only my anguish could be weighed
and all my misery be placed on the scales!
[3] It would surely outweigh the sand of the seas—
no wonder my words have been impetuous.
[4] The arrows of the Almighty are in me,
my spirit drinks in their poison;
God's terrors are marshaled against me.
[5] Does a wild donkey bray when it has grass,
or an ox bellow when it has fodder?
[6] Is tasteless food eaten without salt,

or is there flavor in the white of an egg ?
[7] I refuse to touch it;
such food makes me ill.

[8] "Oh, that I might have my request,
that God would grant what I hope for,
[9] that God would be willing to crush me,
to let loose his hand and cut me off!
[10] Then I would still have this consolation-
my joy in unrelenting pain-
that I had not denied the words of the Holy One.

[11] "What strength do I have, that I should still hope?
What prospects, that I should be patient?
[12] Do I have the strength of stone?
Is my flesh bronze?
[13] Do I have any power to help myself,
now that success has been driven from me?

[14] "A despairing man should have the devotion of his friends,
even though he forsakes the fear of the Almighty.
[15] But my brothers are as undependable as intermittent streams,
as the streams that overflow
[16] when darkened by thawing ice
and swollen with melting snow,
[17] but that cease to flow in the dry season,
and in the heat vanish from their channels.
[18] Caravans turn aside from their routes;
they go up into the wasteland and perish.
[19] The caravans of Tema look for water,
the traveling merchants of Sheba look in hope.
[20] They are distressed, because they had been confident;
they arrive there, only to be disappointed.
[21] Now you too have proved to be of no help;
you see something dreadful and are afraid.
[22] Have I ever said, 'Give something on my behalf,
pay a ransom for me from your wealth,
[23] deliver me from the hand of the enemy,
ransom me from the clutches of the ruthless'?

76   THE MEANING OF LIFE

24 "Teach me, and I will be quiet;
show me where I have been wrong.
25 How painful are honest words!
But what do your arguments prove?
26 Do you mean to correct what I say,
and treat the words of a despairing man as wind?
27 You would even cast lots for the fatherless
and barter away your friend.

28 "But now be so kind as to look at me.
Would I lie to your face?
29 Relent, do not be unjust;
reconsider, for my integrity is at stake.
30 Is there any wickedness on my lips?
Can my mouth not discern malice?

Job 7

1 "Does not man have hard service on earth?
Are not his days like those of a hired man?
2 Like a slave longing for the evening shadows,
or a hired man waiting eagerly for his wages,
3 so I have been allotted months of futility,
and nights of misery have been assigned to me.
4 When I lie down I think, 'How long before I get up?'
The night drags on, and I toss till dawn.
5 My body is clothed with worms and scabs,
my skin is broken and festering.

6 "My days are swifter than a weaver's shuttle,
and they come to an end without hope.
7 Remember, O God, that my life is but a breath;
my eyes will never see happiness again.
8 The eye that now sees me will see me no longer;
you will look for me, but I will be no more.
9 As a cloud vanishes and is gone,
so he who goes down to the grave does not return.
10 He will never come to his house again;
his place will know him no more.

ANCIENT MODELS OF MEANING AND BEING **77**

[11] "Therefore I will not keep silent;
I will speak out in the anguish of my spirit,
I will complain in the bitterness of my soul.
[12] Am I the sea, or the monster of the deep,
that you put me under guard?
[13] When I think my bed will comfort me
and my couch will ease my complaint,
[14] even then you frighten me with dreams
and terrify me with visions,
[15] so that I prefer strangling and death,
rather than this body of mine.
[16] I despise my life; I would not live forever.
Let me alone; my days have no meaning.

[17] "What is man that you make so much of him,
that you give him so much attention,
[18] that you examine him every morning
and test him every moment?
[19] Will you never look away from me,
or let me alone even for an instant?
[20] If I have sinned, what have I done to you,
O watcher of men?
Why have you made me your target?
Have I become a burden to you?
[21] Why do you not pardon my offenses
and forgive my sins?
For I will soon lie down in the dust;
you will search for me, but I will be no more."

Job 38

The LORD Speaks

[1] Then the LORD answered Job out of the storm. He said:

[2] "Who is this that darkens my counsel
with words without knowledge?
[3] Brace yourself like a man;
I will question you,
and you shall answer me.

78   THE MEANING OF LIFE

4 "Where were you when I laid the earth's foundation?
Tell me, if you understand.
5 Who marked off its dimensions? Surely you know!
Who stretched a measuring line across it?
6 On what were its footings set,
or who laid its cornerstone-
7 while the morning stars sang together
and all the angels shouted for joy?

8 "Who shut up the sea behind doors
when it burst forth from the womb,
9 when I made the clouds its garment
and wrapped it in thick darkness,
10 when I fixed limits for it
and set its doors and bars in place,
11 when I said, 'This far you may come and no farther;
here is where your proud waves halt'?

12 "Have you ever given orders to the morning,
or shown the dawn its place,
13 that it might take the earth by the edges
and shake the wicked out of it?
14 The earth takes shape like clay under a seal;
its features stand out like those of a garment.
15 The wicked are denied their light,
and their upraised arm is broken.

16 "Have you journeyed to the springs of the sea
or walked in the recesses of the deep?
17 Have the gates of death been shown to you?
Have you seen the gates of the shadow of death ?
18 Have you comprehended the vast expanses of the earth?
Tell me, if you know all this.

19 "What is the way to the abode of light?
And where does darkness reside?
20 Can you take them to their places?
Do you know the paths to their dwellings?
21 Surely you know, for you were already born!

You have lived so many years!

[22] "Have you entered the storehouses of the snow
or seen the storehouses of the hail,
[23] which I reserve for times of trouble,
for days of war and battle?
[24] What is the way to the place where the lightning is dispersed,
or the place where the east winds are scattered over the earth?
[25] Who cuts a channel for the torrents of rain,
and a path for the thunderstorm,
[26] to water a land where no man lives,
a desert with no one in it,
[27] to satisfy a desolate wasteland
and make it sprout with grass?
[28] Does the rain have a father?
Who fathers the drops of dew?
[29] From whose womb comes the ice?
Who gives birth to the frost from the heavens
[30] when the waters become hard as stone,
when the surface of the deep is frozen?

[31] "Can you bind the beautiful Pleiades?
Can you loose the cords of Orion?
[32] Can you bring forth the constellations in their seasons
or lead out the Bear with its cubs?
[33] Do you know the laws of the heavens?
Can you set up God's dominion over the earth?

[34] "Can you raise your voice to the clouds
and cover yourself with a flood of water?
[35] Do you send the lightning bolts on their way?
Do they report to you, 'Here we are'?
[36] Who endowed the heart with wisdom
or gave understanding to the mind ?
[37] Who has the wisdom to count the clouds?
Who can tip over the water jars of the heavens
[38] when the dust becomes hard
and the clods of earth stick together?

[39] "Do you hunt the prey for the lioness

80 THE MEANING OF LIFE

and satisfy the hunger of the lions
[40] when they crouch in their dens
or lie in wait in a thicket?
[41] Who provides food for the raven
when its young cry out to God
and wander about for lack of food?

Job 39

[1] "Do you know when the mountain goats give birth?
Do you watch when the doe bears her fawn?
[2] Do you count the months till they bear?
Do you know the time they give birth?
[3] They crouch down and bring forth their young;
their labor pains are ended.
[4] Their young thrive and grow strong in the wilds;
they leave and do not return.

[5] "Who let the wild donkey go free?
Who untied his ropes?
[6] I gave him the wasteland as his home,
the salt flats as his habitat.
[7] He laughs at the commotion in the town;
he does not hear a driver's shout.
[8] He ranges the hills for his pasture
and searches for any green thing.

[9] "Will the wild ox consent to serve you?
Will he stay by your manger at night?
[10] Can you hold him to the furrow with a harness?
Will he till the valleys behind you?
[11] Will you rely on him for his great strength?
Will you leave your heavy work to him?
[12] Can you trust him to bring in your grain
and gather it to your threshing floor?

[13] "The wings of the ostrich flap joyfully,
but they cannot compare with the pinions and feathers of the stork.
[14] She lays her eggs on the ground
and lets them warm in the sand,

ANCIENT MODELS OF MEANING AND BEING **81**

[15] unmindful that a foot may crush them,
that some wild animal may trample them.
[16] She treats her young harshly, as if they were not hers;
she cares not that her labor was in vain,
[17] for God did not endow her with wisdom
or give her a share of good sense.
[18] Yet when she spreads her feathers to run,
she laughs at horse and rider.

[19] "Do you give the horse his strength
or clothe his neck with a flowing mane?
[20] Do you make him leap like a locust,
striking terror with his proud snorting?
[21] He paws fiercely, rejoicing in his strength,
and charges into the fray.
[22] He laughs at fear, afraid of nothing;
he does not shy away from the sword.
[23] The quiver rattles against his side,
along with the flashing spear and lance.
[24] In frenzied excitement he eats up the ground;
he cannot stand still when the trumpet sounds.
[25] At the blast of the trumpet he snorts, 'Aha!'
He catches the scent of battle from afar,
the shout of commanders and the battle cry.

[26] "Does the hawk take flight by your wisdom
and spread his wings toward the south?
[27] Does the eagle soar at your command
and build his nest on high?
[28] He dwells on a cliff and stays there at night;
a rocky crag is his stronghold.
[29] From there he seeks out his food;
his eyes detect it from afar.
[30] His young ones feast on blood,
and where the slain are, there is he."

Job 40

[1] The LORD said to Job:

82 THE MEANING OF LIFE

[2] "Will the one who contends with the Almighty correct him?
Let him who accuses God answer him!"

[3] Then Job answered the LORD :

[4] "I am unworthy-how can I reply to you?
I put my hand over my mouth.
[5] I spoke once, but I have no answer-
twice, but I will say no more."

[6] Then the LORD spoke to Job out of the storm:

[7] "Brace yourself like a man;
I will question you,
and you shall answer me.

[8] "Would you discredit my justice?
Would you condemn me to justify yourself?
[9] Do you have an arm like God's,
and can your voice thunder like his?
[10] Then adorn yourself with glory and splendor,
and clothe yourself in honor and majesty.
[11] Unleash the fury of your wrath,
look at every proud man and bring him low,
[12] look at every proud man and humble him,
crush the wicked where they stand.
[13] Bury them all in the dust together;
shroud their faces in the grave.
[14] Then I myself will admit to you
that your own right hand can save you.

[15] "Look at the behemoth,
which I made along with you
and which feeds on grass like an ox.
[16] What strength he has in his loins,
what power in the muscles of his belly!
[17] His tail sways like a cedar;
the sinews of his thighs are close-knit.
[18] His bones are tubes of bronze,
his limbs like rods of iron.

ANCENT MODELS OF MEANING AND BEING   **83**

[19] He ranks first among the works of God,
yet his Maker can approach him with his sword.
[20] The hills bring him their produce,
and all the wild animals play nearby.
[21] Under the lotus plants he lies,
hidden among the reeds in the marsh.
[22] The lotuses conceal him in their shadow;
the poplars by the stream surround him.
[23] When the river rages, he is not alarmed;
he is secure, though the Jordan should surge against his mouth.
[24] Can anyone capture him by the eyes,
or trap him and pierce his nose?

Job 41

[1] "Can you pull in the leviathan with a fishhook
or tie down his tongue with a rope?
[2] Can you put a cord through his nose
or pierce his jaw with a hook?
[3] Will he keep begging you for mercy?
Will he speak to you with gentle words?
[4] Will he make an agreement with you
for you to take him as your slave for life?
[5] Can you make a pet of him like a bird
or put him on a leash for your girls?
[6] Will traders barter for him?
Will they divide him up among the merchants?
[7] Can you fill his hide with harpoons
or his head with fishing spears?
[8] If you lay a hand on him,
you will remember the struggle and never do it again!
[9] Any hope of subduing him is false;
the mere sight of him is overpowering.
[10] No one is fierce enough to rouse him.
Who then is able to stand against me?
[11] Who has a claim against me that I must pay?
Everything under heaven belongs to me.

[12] "I will not fail to speak of his limbs,
his strength and his graceful form.

84   THE MEANING OF LIFE

[13] Who can strip off his outer coat?
Who would approach him with a bridle?
[14] Who dares open the doors of his mouth,
ringed about with his fearsome teeth?
[15] His back has rows of shields
tightly sealed together;
[16] each is so close to the next
that no air can pass between.
[17] They are joined fast to one another;
they cling together and cannot be parted.
[18] His snorting throws out flashes of light;
his eyes are like the rays of dawn.
[19] Firebrands stream from his mouth;
sparks of fire shoot out.
[20] Smoke pours from his nostrils
as from a boiling pot over a fire of reeds.
[21] His breath sets coals ablaze,
and flames dart from his mouth.
[22] Strength resides in his neck;
dismay goes before him.
[23] The folds of his flesh are tightly joined;
they are firm and immovable.
[24] His chest is hard as rock,
hard as a lower millstone.
[25] When he rises up, the mighty are terrified;
they retreat before his thrashing.
[26] The sword that reaches him has no effect,
nor does the spear or the dart or the javelin.
[27] Iron he treats like straw
and bronze like rotten wood.
[28] Arrows do not make him flee;
slingstones are like chaff to him.
[29] A club seems to him but a piece of straw;
he laughs at the rattling of the lance.
[30] His undersides are jagged potsherds,
leaving a trail in the mud like a threshing sledge.
[31] He makes the depths churn like a boiling caldron
and stirs up the sea like a pot of ointment.
[32] Behind him he leaves a glistening wake;
one would think the deep had white hair.

ANCIENT MODELS OF MEANING AND BEING **85**

[33] Nothing on earth is his equal-
a creature without fear.
[34] He looks down on all that are haughty;
he is king over all that are proud."

Job 42

Job

[1] Then Job replied to the LORD :

[2] "I know that you can do all things;
no plan of yours can be thwarted.
[3] You asked, 'Who is this that obscures my counsel without knowledge?'
Surely I spoke of things I did not understand,
things too wonderful for me to know.

[4] "You said, 'Listen now, and I will speak;
I will question you,
and you shall answer me.'
[5] My ears had heard of you
but now my eyes have seen you.
[6] Therefore I despise myself
and repent in dust and ashes."

Epilogue

[7] After the LORD had said these things to Job, he said to Eliphaz the Temanite, "I am angry with you and your two friends, because you have not spoken of me what is right, as my servant Job has. [8] So now take seven bulls and seven rams and go to my servant Job and sacrifice a burnt offering for yourselves. My servant Job will pray for you, and I will accept his prayer and not deal with you according to your folly. You have not spoken of me what is right, as my servant Job has." [9] So Eliphaz the Temanite, Bildad the Shuhite and Zophar the Naamathite did what the LORD told them; and the LORD accepted Job's prayer.
[10] After Job had prayed for his friends, the LORD made him prosperous again and gave him twice as much as he had before. [11] All his brothers and sisters and everyone who had known him before came and ate with him in his house. They comforted and consoled him over all the trouble the LORD had brought upon him, and each one gave him a piece of silver and a gold ring.
[12] The LORD blessed the latter part of Job's life more than the first. He had fourteen thousand sheep, six thousand camels, a thousand yoke of oxen and a thousand donkeys. [13] And he also had

86 THE MEANING OF LIFE

seven sons and three daughters. [14] The first daughter he named Jemimah, the second Keziah and the third Keren-Happuch. [15] Nowhere in all the land were there found women as beautiful as Job's daughters, and their father granted them an inheritance along with their brothers.
[16] After this, Job lived a hundred and forty years; he saw his children and their children to the fourth generation. [17] And so he died, old and full of years.

REVIEW / DISCUSSION QUESTIONS

1. How does the Adam & Eve story inform you about life and death in the world today?

2. How does Emily Dickenson (page 3) define Eden? How does this vary from how you define Eden?
   a. What emotions and attitudes does she associate with it?

   b. What is the basic way that people "make sense" out of life?

3. Define *mythopoeic* and describe why it is important.

4. What do the ancient sacred stories tell us about our "ROLE" in existence? Why are we here?

5. Creation Stories (pages 8, 10): What do the creation stories suggest about the nature and role of the sexes?

88 THE MEANING OF LIFE

6. What does this Eden story suggest about our "structure of responsibility"?

7. Write out (as clearly as you can) what you believe about where we come from.

8. Reflect upon your "mythic structure of origins" and write one sentence about how this basic "story" influences the following issues:
   a. Why am I here?

   b. What does the future hold?

   c. What does this say about how I relate with others?

   d. What does this say about how I relate with nature?

   e. What does this say about my desires and longings?

   f. Am I "good" or "bad"?

ANCIENT MODELS OF MEANING AND BEING   **89**

9. Define Torah and its contribution to human functioning.

10. Describe as best you can why mythopoeics is such a natural human phenomenon.

11. Read Leviticus 1-16. What are some basic guidelines, principles or structures within these chapters that are essential for human life?

12. .What is the most basic principle for life according to the Torah? How can we express this basic principle in our own lives?

13. Read Leviticus 18. What are three essential commitments that are required for the proper use of sex?

90   THE MEANING OF LIFE

14. If you had to give "instructions" to someone on how to live life, what would you say? Make up 5 commandments to guide life and nurture wellness.

15. A typical wellness model includes aspects of the following: Nutrition; Physical Activity; Spirituality; Family; Social; Occupational. Rate yourself between 1 and 10 on each of these scales (10 being the highest). What do you see in your own life that needs changing?

16. Review the poem by A.H. Clough (page 13)
    a.   What is the tone of the poem? How does the poet feel about society's response to the Ten Commandments?

    b.   What are your feelings about the Ten Commandments?

17. Read the summary of Quoheleth/ Ecclesiastes (page 55). What do you find in life that makes it meaningful?

18. What do you believe about life and the afterlife? Is there a "meaning OF life" or is "meaning to be found IN life"? What is the difference between these two statements?

19. How do we manage in the face of issues of pain, suffering and death?

20. How has reflecting on these issues changed you?

SECTION TWO

EASTERN & WESTERN FOUNDATIONS

CHAPTER 4:

An Oriental Model

"I hear, and I forget,

I see, and I remember,

I do, and I understand."

■ Confucius, 500 B.C.E.

The five hundred years before Christ was an astounding time of reflection upon life and its meaning, and even of psychology and neurobiology. Of the many fascinating discoveries and philosophies that formed during this era were the teachings of the classical Greek philosophers and of great oriental thinkers like the first Buddha and Confucius. Before engaging the very powerful influence of Greek thought and its impact upon the western world we will take some time and review the basics of oriental thought because it forms the basis of the Oriental attitudes toward psychology.

In the year 563 B.C.E. an Indian prince named Siddartha was born in what is now Nepal. Growing up in a very Hindu culture and being influenced by the mythic structures of that culture, Siddartha also sought to understand the meaning of his existence. While Siddartha Buddha lived a life of luxury, his occasional journeys away from his mansion caused him to reflect upon life. *What is the meaning of an Old Man, bent from life's work? What is the meaning of a man afflicted with serious illness? What is the meaning of a dead man in a funeral possession?* From these reflections upon life Siddartha realized that sickness, old age, and death are unavoidable. He became obsessed with the idea of inescapable human suffering.

Overwhelmed by this new revelation of life Siddartha left his family and wealth to seek the answer through mental and physical discipline, practicing Hindu Yoga techniques with several *Gurus* (literally: 'A teacher'). In the midst of this studying Siddartha was continually frustrated with his lack of progress. After a long period of fasting, Siddartha realized that continual deprivation would not bring about enlightenment, so he ate some food to gather his strength and began meditating under a Bohdi tree until the answer came to him.

Siddartha finally developed a philosophy for living a meaningful life and developed *The Middle Way* principle that forms the basis for a Buddhist lifestyle. In essence this approach is a simplistic model of holistic wellness by avoiding extremes and the strong desires of life. In engaging in this process Siddartha Buddha taught his way of engaging life to others.

96 THE MEANING OF LIFE

The more modern understanding of Siddhartha's teachings has sought to express his teachings in the language of psychology:

Divisions of Self within Buddhism

The Lesser Self : The ego, the consciousness of one's mind and body. The lesser self remains focused on individual limitations and the separation between the body and the world. The lesser self is created out of our own sense of inadequacy. As we move toward enlightenment, the lesser self diminishes.

The Greater Self: The greater self embraces the entire universe (very much a relic of Siddartha's Hindu upbringing) and everything found therein. The greater Self understands how interdependence ties everything together in a unified, non-separate whole.

Within Siddartha Buddha's teachings/legacy are the very basic notions of understanding life that follow a pattern of unavoidable realities. These realities, according to Siddartha, frame how we are to live and move and create meaning in life.

Siddartha Buddha also held to a principle of being conscious of our true state of being. Current terminology calls this *Right mindfulness*, that reminds us to become as aware as we can of what we actually are doing, experiencing, feeling, and what actually is motivating us at this moment, rather than getting stuck in some view of how we think we are "supposed to be."

While many in the west wrongly consider Buddha to be somehow anti-Christian, the fact is that Siddartha Buddha predated Jesus of Nazareth by over 500 years. Siddartha was in actual fact not interested in starting a religion (though he was strongly influenced by his own Hindu beliefs), nor was he particularly concerned about the existence or nature of God or what occurs after death. He was concerned about the existence of suffering and its influence upon people's lives, how to decrease it in this life, and how to make this life a good and satisfying one that is beneficial to ourselves and others. In many ways we can call the essential Buddhist teachings a combination of mythic structure and existential reflection forming an ethical or psychological structure for living life. Eventually however, the natural mythopoeic nature of people and society transformed this personal existential journey into a religion used to transmit his teachings.

Predominantly in oriental culture individuals consider themselves not just Buddhist or Confucianist or some other specific membership, but instead incorporate the teachings of these traditions as they apply to life. Therefore Buddhism has a clear and specific role in developing a meta-cognition structure for connecting the individual to the eternal and the universe and equips the individual to deal with basic issues of suffering, life and death. However, the societal structure and social relationships and norms are formed in a manner that generally follows the teachings of Confucius, with the self being defined in life by his/her relationships. Therefore, without relationships it can be argued that one does not exist, since one is defined by relationship to family, elders, community and state. Therefore the ultimate punishment in this model is disownment or family shame, for in such a structure the burden of this effectively creates a sense of non-being within the individual.

THE FOUR NOBLE TRUTHS

I. Suffering exists. It is part of the very structure of existence.

II. Suffering has a cause. Its cause is self-centered craving, and desire for that which will not be obtained. Out of this comes grabbing, clinging, or rejecting. Much of this is bound to fail because we fail to deeply realize the truth of impermanence, so that we grasp at the constant, changing flux of life as if it were something stable and fixed. These causes are part of a series of interconnected links of cause and effect that create a vicious circle from which there appears to be no escape. We meet new situations still encumbered with the viewed and attitudes of the past, which create still more ties that bind us to the wheel of suffering.

III. There is a way to end (or at least greatly reduce) suffering. Through letting go of conditioned states and views, and desires that will not be fulfilled, the cause of suffering falls away.

IV. A way to end (reduce) suffering is by following the eightfold path.

THE EIGHTFOLD PATH

1. Right Understanding, Especially Knowledge of the Four Noble Truths. The term "understanding" is often translated as "knowledge" or "views." "Understanding" seems to leave more latitude for thinking in terms of the broader conception of wisdom rather than the narrower one of intellectual knowledge alone.

2. Right Motivation (resolve). The determination to remove animosity, malice, and hatred from our consciousness, and also the determination to renounce worldly pleasures.

3. Right Speech. Telling the truth and avoiding lies, harsh language, frivolous gossip, and any remarks which may cause others unnecessary hardship or pain.

4. Right Action. Acting in ways that honor rather than destroy life, and refraining from stealing or immorality.

5. Right Livelihood. Finding an occupation that suits your own nature, which contributes to the world in some positive way, and which does not cause damage, difficulty, or hardship to others.

6. Right Effort. Directing the strength of your mind and body toward faithfully following the Eightfold Path.

7. Right Mindfulness. (Sometimes translated 'awareness') Letting go of thoughts of "I must have this," or "I must have that." Developing moment-by-moment awareness of what we are in fact doing in our lives and the world, and sensitivity to the effects of this. Learning to perceive the world and others clearly, without judgment or envy.

8. Right Concentration. Practicing meditative states which lead us in the direction of self-mastery and evenmindedness.

READ AND DECIDE FOR YOURSELF

Excerpts from:

TEACHINGS OF BUDDHA

SAYINGS OF CONFUCIUS

TEACHINGS OF BUDDHA

1. The Noble Truth of Suffering:

Birth is suffering.

Decay is suffering.

Death is suffering.

Sorrow, Lamentation, Pain, Grief, and Despair, are suffering.

Not to get what one desires, is suffering.

In short: the Five Groups of Existence are suffering these are Corporeality, Feeling, Perception, Mental Formations, and Consciousness)

2. The Noble Truth of the Origin of Suffering:

Suffering is due to the craving that results in fresh rebirth. The craving finds fresh delight by joining with pleasures here and there.

The craving arises and takes root wherever there are delightful and pleasurable things. It arises and takes root in the eye, ear, nose, tongue, body, and mind; in things like visual objects, sounds, smells, tastes, bodily impressions, and mind-objects; and in the consciousness, sense impression, feeling born of sense impression, perception, will, craving, thinking, and reflecting.

When an object is perceived and found pleasant one is attracted to the object, but if found unpleasant one is repelled. Attraction for and repulsion towards the objects arises thus. If one clings to ones experience. Out of the feelings of pleasant or unpleasant or indifference, one starts approving and clinging to such feelings. In this process lust springs up. This feeling of lust which is but clinging leads to the process of becoming (the effects of karma) and out of the process of becoming is shaped the future birth of a person. The birth causes decay, death, sorrow, lamentation, pain, grief and despair. Thus comes into existence the whole mass of suffering.

The sensuous craving causes accumulation of both the present suffering and the future suffering. Present suffering accumulates when out of sensuous craving people indulge in various forms of conflicts and quarrels or in wicked acts like stealing, robbery or seducing the wives of others which results either in deadly pain or in death.

The accumulation of future suffering arises when, after falling into various evil ways due to sensuous craving, beings die and at the dissolution of the body, descend downward into the abyss of hell or into an intense state of suffering and perdition.

Closely associated with the Noble Truth of Suffering is the law of karma. According to this law, all beings are owners (cause) as well as heirs (effect) of their deeds. Whether good or bad, they

100 THE MEANING OF LIFE

are the originators of all their actions. When these deeds ripen they will earn the fruit of their actions either in this life or in the next life or in any other future life. Thus beings who give birth to their actions, also eventually are born out of their own actions later on. As long as the beings are subjected to sensuous craving, this cycle of birth and rebirth and suffering from birth to birth goes on till the end of the world.

This is called the Noble Truth of the Origin of Suffering.

3. The Noble Truth of the Extinction of Suffering

Suffering ends only when the entire craving fades always and becomes extinct in the being. It ends only when the beings forsakes all craving and achieves complete liberation and detachment from it. Whether it is in the past, the present or the future, this cessation of all craving is possible only when a monk or a priest regards the pleasures and delightful objects of the world as impermanent, distasteful. And thus released from all forms of sensuous craving he does not return nor re-enter into the wheel of existence. This happens through the five fold process of extinction of craving, extinction of clinging, extinction of the effects of karma, extinction of rebirth and through the extinction of rebirth cessation of decay, death, sorrow, lamentation, suffering, grief and despair.

The Ego is but an illusion produced by the five fold process and maintained by the sensuous craving and life-sustaining energies. When the craving ceases the ego is no more nourished. But it continues its existence for some time till all its life-energies are exhausted. Then at the time of death it becomes completely dissolved resulting in the end of the five fold process itself.

Thus the process of Nirvana can be considered in two stages. The first stage of Nirvana happens during the life time of a person, when all his impurities are removed and he becomes an aha or a holy person. The second stage is set in motion after the death of the arhat when the fivefold process comes to an end. When the Arahat or the holy one passes away he attain the realm where there is nothing:" neither solid nor fluid, neither heat nor motion, neither this world nor any other world, neither the sun nor the moon." This is called "neither arising, nor passing away, neither standing still nor being born, nor dying. It is unborn, without source, uncreated and unformed real into which escape is possible for the beings through cessation of craving.

4. The Noble truth of the Path That Leads to the Extinction of Suffering

It is neither by indulging in sensuous cravings and pleasures, nor by subjecting oneself to painful, unholy and un-profitable self-torture, one can achieve freedom from suffering and rebirth. It is the middle path which the Perfect One found to be the most suitable for attaining peace and Nirvana. The middle path is also the Eightfold path which leads to suffering and rebirth.

BUDDHA'S TEACHINGS ON RIGHT-MINDEDNESS:

Right mindedness means to have thoughts that are free from the following:

1. lust,

2. ill-will and

3. cruelty.

Right Mindedness, is of two types: 1. The mundane right mindedness and the ultra mundane right mindedness. The first one means to have thoughts that are devoid of lust, ill-will and cruelty. This approach leads to worldly gains and good results. The second one involves thinking, considering, reasoning, ratiocination, application, keeping the mind holy, to be other worldly and pursuing the holy path. This path leads to gains that are other worldly.

Right Understanding leads to

1. Right understanding,

2. Right effort and

3. Right attentiveness.

Sayings of Confucius

Famous Sayings

Virtue is not left to stand alone. He who practices it will have.

They must often change, who would be constant in happiness or wisdom.

It is not possible for one to teach others who cannot teach his own family.

The superior man is modest in his speech but exceeds in his actions.

He who merely knows right principles is not equal to him who loves them

*To be able under all circumstances to practice five things constitutes perfect virtue;
Tthese five things are gravity, generosity of soul, sincerity, earnestness and kindness.*

We don't know yet about life, how can we know about death?

Mankind differs from the animals only by a little, and most people throw that away.

If you enjoy what you do, you'll never work another day in your life.

*The Master said, (the good man) does not grieve that other people do not recognize his merits.
His only anxiety is lest he should fail to recognize theirs.*

CHAPTER 5

THE GREEK TRADITION

Within the Greek tradition through Pythagoras we see ideas being formed by the mythic structure of a living universe that was eternal and divine. Such an idea is almost reminiscent of the Indo-Aryan teaching from the *Vayupurana* or the self-manifestation of the undifferentiated Brahman (Jacob, 1999). In the Greek structure the human psyche was a spark of the divine mind imprisoned in a mortal body. The ultimate aim of life was to rejoin the divine universal spirit. Philosophy then was simply a way of life for achieving this aim of reunion that results in the purification of the soul and the eventual escape from the wheel of birth. Interestingly enough, in this time period Indo-Aryan Hinduism was giving birth to Buddhism, which also reflected this cyclical image (Michalon, 2001)[45]. However, countering this were those more ancient cultures that blended the experiential and the mythical, like the Ugaritic and Semitic cultures of the millennia previous.

In contrast to Pythagoras, Socrates took a more independent approach while still including the two essential components for meaning making. Socrates focused his efforts on making a meaningful life by creating a mythic structure through an organized and structured form of understanding (Dillon, 2000). To this end Socrates again enacted the ancient process of developing a meaningful existence by incorporating a mythic structure to manage anxiety (and fill in the gaps in knowledge) and then find meaning in the everyday experiences of life. Through his mythic structure Socrates understood that the different forms of goodness (like honesty, courage, and soberness) were part of the same thing. While Socrates did not use these terms, essentially he affirmed that a mythic construct of reality must be formed within the individual.[46] Socrates argued for the unity of things, since, if goodness itself is identified with knowledge, it is not possible to maintain any essential distinctions between different forms of goodness— hence all virtues are really one. Actually Socrates went even beyond this to the position that all the other forms must be looked at in the light of the FORM OF THE GOOD (in essence, in light of a mythical structure).

---

45 Michalon, M (2001) argues that the key contribution of the Buddhist view to psychology is the concept of "self" and "selflessness". That is, that the self must recognize its interdependence with the cosmos and that without that context the "self" does essentially not exist. This notion then provides the sense of "good" and "bad" and "meaning" in the functioning of the ego and definition and strength of the ego.

46 Dillon (2000) notes that the role of function of "Dialogue" in the formation of the mythic structure and the grasping of the meaning of life is central to many great thinkers throughout history. Not only does Socrates support his model but it is also something that can be central to the Buddhist doctrine for understanding and expressing the great truths of life. In essence meaning can only come through the dynamic interaction with other minds, in order to form a large scheme of mythic meaning within which one can exist and derive meaning.

104 THE MEANING OF LIFE

It was in terms of the basic insight that "virtue is knowledge" that Socrates defined his philosophic mission; the identity was established in a simple but ingenious way (Dillon 2000). The ordinary Greek word for goodness, *arête,* means, not virtue in the popular sense, but rather, efficiency or excellence at a particular task (Samons, 2000). The efficiency in the making and the excellence of the product depend on having such knowledge of ends or purposes. In the same way, one can speak of the *arête* of the philosopher or the cobbler. Interestingly enough, the more ancient Semitic notion of *HOKMA* also incorporates this integrated issue of wisdom as being both encyclopaedic knowledge and practical skill (Bonvecchi, 1999)[47]. Further, the concepts of *Shal'm* and *Maat* as well as the Indo-Aryan concepts of *Kharma* and *Dharma* all express that general mythic sense of *rightness* and "everything in its right place ... existence organized in a way that it works".

In the ancient Greek context, while the sophists had been teaching efficiency *arête* in living without defining the universal end or aim of human life, Socrates realized that unless one first defines the purpose of human life through a mythic construct, one couldn't achieve *arête* or goodness in living (Adkins, 1985). Such knowledge was therefore of critical importance for good conduct, which alone follows excellence in living. However, in order to acquire such knowledge (of what Socrates viewed as a true construct, but was actually the natural mythopoeic function within us all), one must begin from scratch—with a deep conviction of one's ignorance (Pekarsky, 1994). This is the essential first step that serves to rid the mind of all prejudicial notions and delusions of wisdom. In a larger perspective we can see that Socrates was really speaking of the need to construct a mythic narrative of how the world works in order to fill in the gaps of human knowledge.

In the essential Socratic psychology the Socratic dialectic approach was therefore aimed first at getting people into such a confused state that they would be forced to admit their illogical and ignorant level of functioning (reject their current mythic structure or lack thereof). The second step was then to engage in a simpler dialogue that aimed at getting to the fullest comprehensive question of what constitutes wisdom, courage, goodness, justice and honesty (Pekarsky 1994). This was done through the examination of concrete circumstances. It was Socrates' contention that through the examination of reality there emerges an apprehension of the "being" for which we give an account in our questions and answers. In a sense Socrates was therefore simply advocating a *client directed* form of existential analysis, for the dialogical process was really nothing more than forming a community myth (albeit between only two people) and then developing a personal mythic structure within this wider and broader structure (Languilla, 1993)

---

47 Bonvencchi (1999) notes how "wisdom" can be used as an integrating factor to form the personal identity of an individual. The analysis process can then be used to evaluate the functioning of the "whole person" beyond the intra-psychic methodology of Freudian psychology.

(Jeffs, 2003).[48] Therefore, while the content may have been different from other cultures, Socrates' structure for meaning making was actually as common and human as any of the Socratic predecessors.

In the Socratic approach, the philosopher served as the midwife to the souls of people who struggled to give birth to the meaning of their own existence through a new mythopoeic structure. It was a practical understanding that was crucial where words like wisdom, justice, goodness and honesty were meaningful only in a mythic narrative that was a context of providing order to society and to the internal psyche of the individual (Languilla, 1993). The health and harmony of the psyche was, therefore, a matter of a proper or just balance among the parts of the psyche (namely the contextual myth and the ability of an individual to find a place within that mythic structure). Therefore, by equating goodness with a practical and encyclopaedic knowledge and not with pleasure as the Sophists did, Socrates had provided a meaning of what is "moral".

In a sense, the life and death of Socrates was of one cloth. For Socrates, true philosophers were to be engaged in studying death. This is not because death is "fashionable" but because death provides insight and structure to life. Such a thought was extremely common among the ancient Near-Eastern wisdom teachers, and always affirmed the need for a mythic structure for approaching life. As a true lover of wisdom, Socrates had been occupied in dying daily and not only knew the taste of immortality better than anyone, but reflected in his own personality the eternal truths of the ideal world. He had found the meaning of that simple ancient truth "like is known by like" (Hill, 1975) for his own soul had reflected the vision of the Good itself (Zuroff, 1982).[49]

The profound significance of Socrates' legacy for psychology lies in the fact that he connected the ancient existential structures for meaning with the vocabulary of the psyche. The *psyche* had a shadowy existence in Greek thought, where the *soma* was more or less identified with the body. Socrates clarifies this somewhat, claiming that it is the psyche that is the seat of the true self and self-motivation (in this Socrates was largely speaking of the mythopoeic narrative of the self). In this Socratic model of life it becomes imperative to care for the psyche since it is the true self and intra-psychic knowledge is important (Cooper, 2001)[50]. Indeed, after

---

48 Jeffs (2003) hints at the deep power of the Socratic method and one can logically relate this to psychology. For as Jeffs notes, the method used by Socrates was one of free expression and association (very Freudian) in the pursuit of understanding and the formation of a logical basis for understanding reality.

49 Zuroff (1982) in a social experiment takes this simple truth and displays how it applies to the construction of a person's social environment and social recollection. Interestingly the social constructs where shown to be stored with larger situational constructs which provides a good application of the meaning behind the importance of creating a large mythic construct within which to live, for without such a schema memory cannot be organized and retrieved effectively.

50 Cooper (2001) notes how Socrates subdivides the psychic structure and notes the role of the various intra-psychic functions of eros (desire), thymos (spiritedness), and how the external limitations of human experience interact with these basic instinctual drives, therefore knowledge of these intra-psychic parts is essential for self care and control.

106   THE MEANING OF LIFE

the Socratic conception of the psyche as personality "soul care" became recognized as an important issue. This mythical structure of internal care of the self then incorporated into the later mythology of Christian legends along the same theme.

The obvious connection with modern psychology is that Freud clearly carried the mythical structure of Socratic thought into the psychoanalytic prescriptions with the phrase, "know thyself" for cure and care of the psyche (Cooper, 2001). It is clear that Freud also found Oedipus as a paradigm, for self-knowledge is always painful. It is painful because in psychoanalysis one has to learn about the evil in oneself rather than the good in an ideal world; it also means freeing oneself from the morality of social constraint represented by an irrational superego. Parenthetically, we may also note the parallel between the Socratic and Freudian methods; the educator of the intellect and the therapist of the emotions both serve as aids in the individual's quest of self-knowledge.

As a premier apostle of the intellectual freedom it was Socrates who first focused on the prime value of the human psyche that he called humanity to know. In the Socratic world, it was reason that enabled humanity to attain the highest good and efficiency and organization. In the context of this study it can be said that Socrates showed the power of the mind to create one's mythic context, affirming that one is not a slave to society or religion for such a mythopoeic structure of beliefs.

Whereas Socrates was concerned with individual conduct, the good life, and happiness as an end, his pupil Plato developed a system of the world in which individual, society and the universe were all unified (Cropsey, 1995)[51]. Plato's grand synthesis of metaphysics, epistemology, knowledge, ethics and existence extends the Socratic morality internal organization to the external world. Plato's theory of reality and knowledge is therefore all of one piece, and is the foundation of the rest of his philosophy of human nature and society by going from the Socratic theme of the best state of the soul to the Platonic theme of the best state of society.

To derive the three parts of the soul from the three classes of society, and then to justify the classes on the basis of their correspondence to the natural state of affairs in the soul is indeed circular (Cooper, 2001). Therefore, in contrast to the Socratic notion of rebuilding your contextual mythic structure from the ground up, Plato was ready to draw from his context to form this mythic context.

Aristotle, the pupil of Plato, does seem to continue this idea of drawing from one's context to construct the mythic structure in which to understand life. However it is not the cultural

---

51 Plato's vision of the world recognizes the sheer power of mythopoeics in forming the psychological structure of people and society. Therefore, in the very early stages of his *Republic* he introduces artisans and the role of artisans to harness the mythopoeic forces of the psyche and constructing them in line with the goals and directions of the state. Therefore society has a role to play in creating the world which defines the individual interpretive structures and therefore the society of the future. Allen, J. (2002) "Plato: Morality and Immortality in Art" *Education Policy Review*. 104: 19-25.

context that Plato demands, nor the utter rejection of preconceptions that Socrates calls for. Rather, Aristotle took a more naturalistic bent by constructing models following logic and proven scientific knowledge, and in so doing created a new mythic structure (van Neikerk, 1999). This structure is one where the cosmos begins to take upon a living quality as "god".

In the end, however, Aristotle returns to the old refrain for meaning in life, where actions create meaning in a mythic worldview that he calls, "Virtue" (Lillegard, 2000). Indeed the Egyptian notion of *Maat*, and the West Semitic idea of *Shal'm* are also suggested. For Aristotle the good life is one of happiness: "Happiness is the activity of the soul in conformity with virtue" (Aristotle, 1969).

READ AND DECIDE FOR YOURSELF

Excerpts from:

MYTH OF THE CAVE (PLATO)

ON THE SACRED DISEASE (HIPPOCRATES)

ON DREAMS (ARISTOTLE)

PLATO'S MYTH OF THE CAVE

From THE REPUBLIC:

(An allegory for how our mind understands reality)

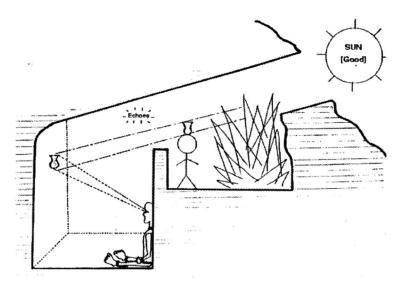

Now, I said, let me show in a figure how far our nature is enlightened or unenlightened: -- Behold! Human beings living in a underground den, which has a mouth open towards the light and reaching all along the den; here they have been from their childhood, and have their legs and necks chained so that they cannot move, and can only see before them, being prevented by the chains from turning round their heads. Above and behind them a fire is blazing at a distance, and between the fire and the prisoners there is a raised way; and you will see, if you look, a low wall built along the way, like the screen which marionette players have in front of them, over which they show the puppets. I see. And do you see, I said, men passing along the wall carrying all sorts of vessels, and statues and figures of animals made of wood and stone and various materials, which appear over the wall? Some of them are talking, others silent. You have shown me a strange image, and they are strange prisoners. Like ourselves, I replied; and they see only their own shadows, or the shadows of one another, which the fire throws on the opposite wall of the cave? True, he said; how could they see anything but the shadows if they were never allowed to move their heads? And of the objects that are being carried in like manner they would only see

110   THE MEANING OF LIFE

the shadows? Yes, he said. And if they were able to converse with one another, would they not suppose that they were naming what was actually before them? Very true. And suppose further that the prison had an echo which came from the other side, would they not be sure to fancy when one of the passers-by spoke that the voice which they heard came from the passing shadow? No question, he replied. To them, I said, the truth would be literally nothing but the shadows of the images. That is certain.

And now look again, and see what will naturally follow if the prisoners are released and disabused of their error. At first, when any of them is liberated and compelled suddenly to stand up and turn his neck round and walk and look towards the light, he will suffer sharp pains; the glare will distress him, and he will be unable to see the realities of which in his former state he had seen the shadows; and then conceive some one saying to him, that what he saw before was an illusion, but that now, when he is approaching nearer to being and his eye is turned towards more real existence, he has a clearer vision, -what will be his reply? And you may further imagine that his instructor is pointing to the objects as they pass and requiring him to name them, -will he not be perplexed? Will he not fancy that the shadows that he formerly saw are truer than the objects that are now shown to him? Far truer. And if he is compelled to look straight at the light, will he not have a pain in his eyes which will make him turn away to take and take in the objects of vision which he can see, and which he will conceive to be in reality clearer than the things which are now being shown to him? True, he now And suppose once more, that he is reluctantly dragged up a steep and rugged ascent, and held fast until he 's forced into the presence of the sun himself, is he not likely to be pained and irritated? When he approaches the light his eyes will be dazzled, and he will not be able to see anything at all of what are now called realities. Not all in a moment, he said. He will require to grow accustomed to the sight of the upper world. And first he will see the shadows best, next the reflections of men and other objects in the water, and then the objects themselves; then he will gaze upon the light of the moon and the stars and the spangled heaven; and he will see the sky and the stars by night better than the sun or the light of the sun by day? Certainly. Last of he will be able to see the sun, and not mere reflections of him in the water, but he will see him in his own proper place, and not in another; and he will contemplate him as he is. Certainly. He will then proceed to argue that this is he who gives the season and the years, and is the guardian of all that is in the visible world, and in a certain way the cause of all things that he and his fellows have been accustomed to behold? Clearly, he said, he would first see the sun and then reason about him. And when he remembered his old habitation, and the wisdom of the den and his fellow-prisoners, do you not suppose that he would felicitate himself on the change, and pity them? Certainly, he would. And if they were in the habit of conferring honors among themselves on those who were quickest to observe the passing shadows and to remark which of them went before, and which followed after, and which were together; and who were therefore best able to draw conclusions as to the future, do you think that he would care for such honors and glories, or envy the possessors of them? Would he not say with Homer, - Better to be the poor servant of a poor master, - and to endure anything, rather than think as they do and live after their manner? Yes, he said, I think that he would rather suffer anything than entertain these false

THE GREEK TRADITION 111

notions and live in this miserable manner. Imagine once more, I said, such an one coming suddenly out of the sun to be replaced in his old situation; would he not be certain to have his eyes full of darkness? To be sure, he said. And if there were a contest, and he had to compete in measuring the shadows with the prisoners who had never moved out of the den, while his sight was still weak, and before his eyes had become steady (and the time which would be needed to acquire this new habit of sight might be very considerable) would he not be ridiculous? Men would say of him that up he went and down he came without his eyes; and that it was better not even to think of ascending; and if any one tried to loose another and lead him up to the light, let them only catch the offender, and they would put him to death. No question, he said. This entire allegory, I said, you may now append, dear Glaucon, to the previous argument; the prison-house is the world of sight, the light of the fire is the sun, and you will not misapprehend me if you interpret the journey upwards to be the ascent of the soul into the intellectual world according to my poor belief, which, at your desire, I have expressed whether rightly or wrongly God knows. But, whether true or false, my opinion is that in the world of knowledge the idea of good appears last of all, and is seen only with an effort; and, when seen, is also inferred to be the universal author of all things beautiful and right, parent of light and of the lord of light in this visible world, and the immediate source of reason and truth in the intellectual; and that this is the power upon which he who would act rationally, either in public or private life must have his eye fixed. I agree, he said, as far as I am able to understand you. Moreover, I said, you must not wonder that those who attain to this beatific vision are unwilling to descend to human affairs; for their souls are ever hastening into the upper world where they desire to dwell; which desire of theirs is very natural, if our allegory may be trusted. Yes, very natural. And is there anything surprising in one who passes from divine contemplations to the evil state of man, misbehaving himself in a ridiculous manner; if, while his eyes are blinking and before he has become accustomed to the surrounding darkness, he is compelled to fight in courts of law, or in other places, about the images or the shadows of images of justice, and is endeavoring to meet the conceptions of those who have never yet seen absolute justice? Anything but surprising, he replied. Any one who has common sense will remember that the bewilderments of the eyes are of two kinds, and arise from two causes, either from coming out of the light or from going into the light, which is true of the mind's eye, quite as much as of the bodily eye; and he who remembers this when he sees any one whose vision is perplexed and weak, will not be too ready to laugh; he will first ask whether that soul of man has come out of the brighter light, and is unable to see because unaccustomed to the dark, or having turned from darkness to the day is dazzled by excess of light. And he will count the one happy in his condition and state of being, and he will pity the other; or, if he have a mind to laugh at the soul which comes from below into the light, there will be more reason in this than in the laugh which greets him who returns from above out of the light into the den. That, he said, is a very just distinction. But then, if I am right, certain professors of education must be wrong when they say that they can put a knowledge into the soul that was not there before, like sight into blind eyes. They undoubtedly say this, he replied. Whereas, our argument shows that the power and capacity of learning exists in the soul already; and that just as the eye was unable to turn from

112 THE MEANING OF LIFE

darkness to light without the whole body, so too the instrument of knowledge can only by the movement of the whole soul be turned from the world of becoming into that of being, and learn by degrees to endure the sight of being, and of the brightest and best of being, or in other words, of the good. Very true.

ON THE SACRED DISEASE

By Hippocrates

Written 400 B.C.E

Translated by Francis Adams[52]

(Teachings about how the "mind" is a physical thing.)

It is thus with regard to the disease called Sacred: it appears to me to be nowise more divine nor more sacred than other diseases, but has a natural cause from the originates like other affections. Men regard its nature and cause as divine from ignorance and wonder, because it is not at all like to other diseases. And this notion of its divinity is kept up by their inability to comprehend it, and the simplicity of the mode by which it is cured, for men are freed from it by purifications and incantations. But if it is reckoned divine because it is wonderful, instead of one there are many diseases which would be sacred; for, as I will show, there are others no less wonderful and prodigious, which nobody imagines to be sacred. The quotidian, tertian, and quartan fevers, seem to me no less sacred and divine in their origin than this disease, although they are not reckoned so wonderful. And I see men become mad and demented from no manifest cause, and at the same time doing many things out of place; and I have known many persons in sleep groaning and crying out, some in a state of suffocation, some jumping up and fleeing out of doors, and deprived of their reason until they awaken, and afterward becoming well and rational as before, although they be pale and weak; and this will happen not once but frequently. And there are many and various things of the like kind, which it would be tedious to state particularly.

They who first referred this malady to the gods appear to me to have been just such persons as the conjurors, purificators, mountebanks, and charlatans now are, who give themselves out for being excessively religious, and as knowing more than other people. Such persons, then, using the divinity as a pretext and screen of their own inability to of their own inability to afford any assistance, have given out that the disease is sacred, adding suitable reasons for this opinion, they have instituted a mode of treatment which is safe for themselves, namely, by applying purifications and incantations, and enforcing abstinence from baths and many articles of food which are unwholesome to men in diseases. Of sea substances, the surmullet, the blacktail, the mullet, and the eel; for these are the fishes most to be guarded against. And of fleshes, those of the goat, the stag, the sow, and the dog: for these are the kinds of flesh which are aptest to

---

[52] Accessed: http://classics.mit.edu/Hippocrates/sacred.html

114 THE MEANING OF LIFE

disorder the bowels. Of fowls, the cock, the turtle, and the bustard, and such others as are reckoned to be particularly strong. And of potherbs, mint, garlic, and onions; for what is acrid does not agree with a weak person. And they forbid to have a black robe, because black is expressive of death; and to sleep on a goat's skin, or to wear it, and to put one foot upon another, or one hand upon another; for all these things are held to be hindrances to the cure. All these they enjoin with reference to its divinity, as if possessed of more knowledge, and announcing beforehand other causes so that if the person should recover, theirs would be the honor and credit; and if he should die, they would have a certain defense, as if the gods, and not they, were to blame, seeing they had administered nothing either to eat or drink as medicines, nor had overheated him with baths, so as to prove the cause of what had happened. But I am of opinion that (if this were true) none of the Libyans, who live in the interior, would be free from this disease, since they all sleep on goats' skins, and live upon goats' flesh; neither have they couch, robe, nor shoe that is not made of goat's skin, for they have no other herds but goats and oxen. But if these things, when administered in food, aggravate the disease, and if it be cured by abstinence from them, godhead is not the cause at all; nor will purifications be of any avail, but it is the food which is beneficial and prejudicial, and the influence of the divinity vanishes.

Thus, they who try to cure these maladies in this way, appear to me neither to reckon them sacred nor divine. For when they are removed by such purifications, and this method of cure, what is to prevent them from being brought upon men and induced by other devices similar to these? So that the cause is no longer divine, but human. For whoever is able, by purifications conjurations, to drive away such an affection, will be able, by other practices, to excite it; and, according to this view, its divine nature is entirely done away with. By such sayings and doings, they profess to be possessed of superior knowledge, and deceive mankind by enjoining lustrations and purifications upon them, while their discourse turns upon the divinity and the godhead. And yet it would appear to me that their discourse savors not of piety, as they suppose, but rather of impiety, and as if there were no gods, and that what they hold to be holy and divine, were impious and unholy. This I will now explain.

For, if they profess to know how to bring down the moon, darken the sun, induce storms and fine weather, and rains and droughts, and make the sea and land unproductive, and so forth, whether they arrogate this power as being derived from mysteries or any other knowledge or consideration, they appear to me to practice impiety, and either to fancy that there are no gods, or, if there are, that they have no ability to ward off any of the greatest evils. How, then, are they not enemies to the gods? For if a man by magical arts and sacrifices will bring down the moon, and darken the sun, and induce storms, or fine weather, I should not believe that there was anything divine, but human, in these things, provided the power of the divine were overpowered by human knowledge and subjected to it. But perhaps it will be said, these things are not so, but, not withstanding, men being in want of the means of life, invent many and various things, and devise many contrivances for all other things, and for this disease, in every phase of the disease, assigning the cause to a god. Nor do they remember the same things once, but frequently. For, if they imitate a goat, or grind their teeth, or if their right side be convulsed, they say that the mother of the gods is the cause. But if they speak in a sharper and more intense tone, they resemble this state to a horse, and say that Poseidon is the cause. Or if any excrement be passed, which is often the case, owing to the violence of the disease, the appellation of Enodia is adhibited; or, if it be passed in smaller and denser masses, like bird's, it is said to be from Apollo Nomius. But if foam be emitted by the mouth, and the patient kick with his feet, Ares then gets the blame. But terrors which happen during the night, and fevers, and delirium, and jumpings out of bed, and frightful apparitions, and fleeing away,-all these they hold to be the plots of Hecate, and the invasions the and use purifications and incantations, and, as appears to me, make the divinity to be most wicked and most impious. For they purify those laboring under this disease, with the same sorts of blood and the other means that are used in the case of those who are stained with crimes, and of malefactors, or who have been enchanted by men, or who have done any wicked act; who ought to do the very reverse, namely, sacrifice and pray, and, bringing gifts to the temples, supplicate the gods. But now they do none of these things, but purify; and some of the purifications they conceal in the earth, and some they throw into the sea, and some they carry to the mountains where no one can touch or tread upon them. But these they ought to take to the temples and present to the god, if a god be the cause of the disease. Neither truly do I count it a worthy opinion to hold that the body of man is polluted by god, the most impure by the most holy; for were it defiled, or did it suffer from any other thing, it would be like to be purified and sanctified rather than polluted by god. For it is the divinity which purifies and sanctifies the greatest of offenses and the most wicked, and which proves our protection from them. And we mark out the boundaries of the temples and the groves of the gods, so that no one may pass them unless he be pure, and when we enter them we are sprinkled with holy water, not as being polluted, but as laying aside any other pollution which we formerly had. And thus it appears to me to hold, with regard to purifications.

But this disease seems to me to be no more divine than others; but it has its nature such as other diseases have, and a cause whence it originates, and its nature and cause are divine only just as much as all others are, and it is curable no less than the others, unless when, the from of time, it is confirmed, and has became stronger than the remedies applied. Its origin is hereditary, like that of other diseases. For if a phlegmatic person be born of a phlegmatic, and a bilious of a bilious, and a phthisical of a phthisical, and one having spleen disease, of another having disease of the spleen, what is to hinder it from happening that where the father and mother were subject to this disease, certain of their offspring should be so affected also? As the semen comes from all parts of the body, healthy particles will come from healthy parts, and unhealthy from unhealthy parts. And another great proof that it is in nothing more divine than other diseases is, that it occurs in those who are of a phlegmatic constitution, but does not attack the bilious. Yet, if it were more divine than the others, this disease ought to befall all alike, and make no distinction between the bilious and phlegmatic.

But the brain is the cause of this affection, as it is of other very great diseases, and in what manner and from what cause it is formed, I will now plainly declare. The brain of man, as in all other animals, is double, and a thin membrane divides it through the middle, and therefore the pain is not always in the same part of the head; for sometimes it is situated on either side, and sometimes the whole is affected; and veins run toward it from all parts of the body, many of which are small, but two are thick, the one from the liver, and the other from the spleen. And it is thus with regard to the one from the liver: a portion of it runs downward through the parts on the side, near the kidneys and the psoas muscles, to the inner part of the thigh, and extends to the foot. It is called vena cava. The other runs upward by the right veins and the lungs, and divides into branches for the heart and the right arm. The remaining part of it rises upward across the clavicle to the right side of the neck, and is superficial so as to be seen; near the ear it is concealed, and there it divides; its thickest, largest, and most hollow part ends in the brain; another small vein goes to the right ear, another to the right eye, and another to the nostril. Such are the distributions of the hepatic vein. And a vein from the spleen is distributed on the left side, upward and downward, like that from the liver, but more slender and feeble.

By these veins we draw in much breath, since they are the spiracles of our bodies inhaling air to themselves and distributing it to the rest of the body, and to the smaller veins, and they and afterwards exhale it. For the breath cannot be stationary, but it passes upward and downward, for if stopped and intercepted, the part where it is stopped becomes powerless. In proof of this, when, in sitting or lying, the small veins are compressed, so that the breath from the larger vein does not pass into them, the part is immediately seized with numbness; and it is so likewise with regard to the other veins.

This malady, then, affects phlegmatic people, but not bilious. It begins to be formed while the foetus is still in utero. For the brain, like the other organs, is depurated and grows before birth. If, then, in this purgation it be properly and moderately depurated, and neither more nor less than what is proper be secreted from it, the head is thus in the most healthy condition. If the secretion (melting) the from the brain be greater than natural, the person, when he grows up, will have his head diseased, and full of noises, and will neither be able to endure the sun nor cold. Or, if the melting take place from any one part, either from the eye or ear, or if a vein has become slender, that part will be deranged in proportion to the melting. Or, should depuration not take place, but congestion accumulate in the brain, it necessarily becomes phlegmatic. And such children as have an eruption of ulcers on the head, on the ears, and along the rest of the body, with copious discharges of saliva and mucus,-these, in after life, enjoy best health; for in this way the phlegm which ought to have been purged off in the womb, is discharged and cleared away, and persons so purged, for the most part, are not subject to attacks of this disease. But such as have had their skin free from eruptions, and have had no discharge of saliva or mucus, nor have undergone the proper purgation in the womb, these persons run the risk of being seized with this disease.

But should the defluxion make its way to the heart, the person is seized with palpitation and asthma, the chest becomes diseased, and some also have curvature of the spine. For when a defluxion of cold phlegm takes place on the lungs and heart, the blood is chilled, and the veins, being violently chilled, palpitate in the lungs and heart, and the heart palpitates, so that from this necessity asthma and orthopnoea supervene. For it does not receive the spirits as much breath as he needs until the defluxion of phlegm be mastered, and being heated is distributed to the veins, then it ceases from its palpitation and difficulty of breathing, and this takes place as soon as it obtains an abundant supply; and this will be more slowly, provided the defluxion be more abundant, or if it be less, more quickly. And if the defluxions be more condensed, the epileptic attacks will be more frequent, but otherwise if it be rarer. Such are the symptoms when the defluxion is upon the lungs and heart; but if it be upon the bowels, the person is attacked with diarrhoea.

And if, being shut out from all these outlets, its defluxion be determined to the veins I have formerly mentioned, the patient loses his speech, and chokes, and foam issues by the mouth, the teeth are fixed, the hands are contracted, the eyes distorted, he becomes insensible, and in some cases the bowels are evacuated. And these symptoms occur sometimes on the left side, sometimes on the right, and sometimes in both. The cause of everyone of these symptoms I will now explain. The man becomes speechless when the phlegm, suddenly descending into the veins, shuts out the air, and does not admit it either to the brain or to the vena cava, or to the ventricles, but interrupts the inspiration. For when a person draws in air by the mouth and nostrils, the breath goes first to the brain, then the greater part of it to the internal cavity, and part to the lungs, and part to the veins, and from them it is distributed to the other parts of the body along the veins; and whatever passes to the stomach cools, and does nothing more; and so also with regard to the lungs. But the air which enters the veins is of use (to the body) by entering the brain and its ventricles, and thus it imparts sensibility and motion to all the members, so that when the veins are excluded from the air by the phlegm and do not receive it, the man loses his speech and intellect, and the hands become powerless, and are contracted, the blood stopping and not being diffused, as it was wont; and the eyes are distorted owing to the veins being excluded from the air; and they palpitate; and froth from the lungs issues by the mouth. For when the breath does not find entrance to him, he foams and sputters like a dying person. And the bowels are evacuated in consequence of the violent suffocation; and the suffocation is produced when the liver and stomach ascend to the diaphragm, and the mouth of the stomach is shut up; this takes place when the breath does not enter by the mouth, as it is wont. The patient kicks with his feet when the air is shut up in the lungs and cannot find an outlet, owing to the phlegm; and rushing by the blood upward and downward, it occasions convulsions and pain, and therefore he kicks with his feet. All these symptoms he endures when the cold phlegm passes into the warm blood, for it congeals and stops the blood. And if the deflexion be copious and thick, it immediately proves fatal to him, for by its cold it prevails over the blood and congeals it; or, if it be less, it in the first place obtains the mastery, and stops the respiration; and then in the course of time, when it is diffused along the veins and mixed with much warm blood, it is thus overpowered, the veins receive the air, and the patient recovers his senses.

Of little children who are seized with this disease, the greater part die, provided the defluxion be copious and humid, for the veins being slender cannot admit the phlegm, owing to its thickness and abundance; but the blood is cooled and congealed, and the child immediately dies. But if the phlegm be in small quantity, and make a defluxion into both the veins, or to those on either side, the children survive, but exhibit notable marks of the disorder; for either the mouth

118   THE MEANING OF LIFE

is drawn aside, or an eye, the neck, or a hand, wherever a vein being filled with phlegm loses its tone, and is attenuated, and the part of the body connected with this vein is necessarily rendered weaker and defective. But for the most it affords relief for a longer interval; for the child is no longer seized with these attacks, if once it has contracted this impress of the disease, in consequence of which the other veins are necessarily affected, and to a certain degree attenuated, so as just to admit the air, but no longer to permit the influx of phlegm. However, the parts are proportionally enfeebled whenever the veins are in an unhealthy state. When in striplings the defluxion is small and to the right side, they recover without leaving any marks of the disease, but there is danger of its becoming habitual, and even increasing if not treated by suitable remedies. Thus, or very nearly so, is the case when it attacks children.

To persons of a more advanced age, it neither proves fatal, nor produces distortions. For their veins are capacious and are filled with hot blood; and therefore the phlegm can neither prevail nor cool the blood, so as to coagulate it, but it is quickly overpowered and mixed with the blood, and thus the veins receive the air, and sensibility remains; and, owing to their strength, the aforesaid symptoms are less likely to seize them. But when this disease attacks very old people, it therefore proves fatal, or induces paraplegia, because the veins are empty, and the blood scanty, thin, and watery. When, therefore, the defluxion is copious, and the season winter, it proves fatal; for it chokes up the exhalents, and coagulates the blood if the defluxion be to both sides; but if to either, it merely induces paraplegia. For the blood being thin, cold, and scanty, cannot prevail over the but being itself overpowered, it is coagulated, so that those parts in which the blood is corrupted, lose their strength.

The flux is to the right rather than to the left because the veins there are more capacious and numerous than on the left side, for on the one side they spring from the liver, and on the other from the spleen. The defluxion and melting down take place most especially in the case of children in whom the head is heated either by the sun or by fire, or if the brain suddenly contract a rigor, and then the phlegm is excreted. For it is melted down by the heat and diffusion of the but it is excreted by the congealing and contracting of it, and thus a defluxion takes place. And in some this is the cause of the disease, and in others, when the south wind quickly succeeds to northern breezes, it suddenly unbinds and relaxes the brain, which is contracted and weak, so that there is an inundation of phlegm, and thus the defluxion takes place. The defluxion also takes place in consequence of fear, from any hidden cause, if we are the at any person's calling aloud, or while crying, when one cannot quickly recover one's breath, such as often happens to children. When any of these things occur, the body immediately shivers, the person becoming speechless cannot draw his breath, but the breath (pneuma) stops, the brain is contracted, the blood stands still, and thus the excretion and defluxion of the phlegm take place. In children, these are the causes of the attack at first. But to old persons winter is most inimical. For when the head and brain have been heated at a great fire, and then the person is brought into cold and has a rigor, or when from cold he comes into warmth, and sits at the fire, he is apt to suffer in the same way, and thus he is seized in the manner described above. And there is much danger of the same thing occurring, if his head be exposed to the sun, but less so in summer, as the changes are not sudden.

THE GREEK TRADITION **119**

When a person has passed the twentieth year of his life, this disease is not apt to seize him, unless it has become habitual from childhood, or at least this is rarely or never the case. For the veins are filled with blood, and the brain consistent and firm, so that it does not run down into the veins, or if it do, it does not master the blood, which is copious and hot.

But when it has gained strength from one's childhood, and become habitual, such a person usually suffers attacks, and is seized with them in changes of the winds, especially in south winds, and it is difficult of removal. For the brain becomes more humid than natural, and is inundated with phlegm, so that the defluxions become more frequent, and the phlegm can no longer be the nor the brain be dried up, but it becomes wet and humid. This you may ascertain in particular, from beasts of the flock which are seized with this disease, and more especially goats, for they are most frequently attacked with it. If you will cut open the head, you will find the brain humid, full of sweat, and having a bad smell. And in this way truly you may see that it is not a god that injures the body, but disease. And so it is with man. For when the disease has prevailed for a length of time, it is no longer curable, as the brain is corroded by the phlegm, and melted, and what is melted down becomes water, and surrounds the brain externally, and overflows it; wherefore they are more frequently and readily seized with the disease. And therefore the disease is protracted, because the influx is thin, owing to its quantity, and is immediately overpowered by the blood and heated all through.

But such persons as are habituated to the disease know beforehand when they are about to be seized and flee from men; if their own house be at hand, they run home, but if not, to a deserted place, where as few persons as possible will see them falling, and they immediately cover themselves up. This they do from shame of the affection, and not from fear of the divinity, as many suppose. And little children at first fall down wherever they may happen to be, from inexperience. But when they have been often seized, and feel its approach beforehand, they flee to their mothers, or to any other person they are acquainted with, from terror and dread of the affection, for being still infants they do not know yet what it is to be ashamed.

Therefore, they are attacked during changes of the winds, and especially south winds, then also with north winds, and afterwards also with the others. These are the strongest winds, and the most opposed to one another, both as to direction and power. For, the north wind condenses the air, and separates from it whatever is muddy and nebulous, and renders it clearer and brighter, and so in like manner also, all the winds which arise from the sea and other waters; for they extract the humidity and nebulosity from all objects, and from men themselves, and therefore it (the north wind) is the most wholesome of the winds. But the effects of the south are the very reverse. For in the first place it begins by melting and diffusing the condensed air, and therefore it does not blow strong at first, but is gentle at the commencement, because it is not able at once to overcome the and compacted air, which yet in a while it dissolves. It produces the same effects upon the land, the sea, the fountains, the wells, and on every production which contains humidity, and this, there is in all things, some more, some less. For all these feel the effects of this wind, and from clear they become cloudy, from cold, hot; from dry, moist; and whatever ear then vessels are placed upon the ground, filled with wine or any other fluid, are affected with the south

120 THE MEANING OF LIFE

wind, and undergo a change. And the a change. And the sun, and the moon, it renders blunter appearance than they naturally are. When, then, it possesses such powers over things so great and strong, and the body is made to feel and undergo changes in the changes of the winds, it necessarily follows that the brain should be disolved and overpowered with moisture, and that the veins should become more relaxed by the south winds, and that by the north the healthiest portion of the brain should become contracted, while the most morbid and humid is secreted, and overflows externally, and that catarrhs should thus take place in the changes of these winds. Thus is this disease formed and prevails from those things which enter into and go out of the body, and it is not more difficult to understand or to cure than the others, neither is it more divine than other diseases.

Men ought to know that from nothing else but the brain come joys, delights, laughter and sports, and sorrows, griefs, despondency, and lamentations. And by this, in an especial manner, we acquire wisdom and knowledge, and see and hear, and know what are foul and what are fair, what are bad and what are good, what are sweet, and what unsavory; some we discriminate by habit, and some we perceive by their utility. By this we distinguish objects of relish and disrelish, according to the seasons; and the same things do not always please us. And by the same organ we become mad and delirious, and fears and terrors assail us, some by night, and some by day, and dreams and untimely wanderings, and cares that are not suitable, and ignorance of present circumstances, desuetude, and unskilfulness. All these things we endure from the brain, when it is not healthy, but is more hot, more cold, more moist, or more dry than natural, or when it suffers any other preternatural and unusual affection. And we become mad from its humidity. For when it is more moist than natural, it is necessarily put into motion, and the affection being moved, neither the sight nor hearing can be at rest, and the tongue speaks in accordance with the sight and hearing.

As long as the brain is at rest, the man enjoys his reason, but the depravement of the brain arises from phlegm and bile, either of which you may recognize in this manner: Those who are mad from phlegm are quiet, and do not cry out nor make a noise; but those from bile are vociferous, malignant, and will not be quiet, but are always doing something improper. If the madness be constant, these are the causes thereof. But if terrors and fears assail, they are connected with derangement of the brain, and derangement is owing to its being heated. And it is heated by bile when it is determined to the brain along the blood vessels running from the trunk; and fear is present until it returns again to the veins and trunk, when it ceases. He is grieved and troubled when the brain is unseasonably cooled and contracted beyond its wont. This it suffers from phlegm, and from the same affection the patient becomes oblivious. He calls out and screams at night when the brain is suddenly heated. The bilious endure this. But the phlegmatic are not heated, except when much blood goes to the brain, and creates an ebullition. Much blood passes along the aforesaid veins. But when the man happens to see a frightful dream and is in fear as if awake, then his face is in a greater glow, and the eyes are red when the patient is in fear. And the understanding meditates doing some mischief, and thus it is affected in sleep. But if, when awakened, he returns to himself, and the blood is again distributed along the veins, it ceases.

THE GREEK TRADITION 121

In these ways I am of the opinion that the brain exercises the greatest power in the man. This is the interpreter to us of those things which emanate from the air, when the brain happens to be in a sound state. But the air supplies sense to it. And the eyes, the ears, the tongue and the feet, administer such things as the brain cogitates. For in as much as it is supplied with air, does it impart sense to the body. It is the brain which is the messenger to the understanding. For when the man draws the breath into himself, it passes first to the brain, and thus the air is distributed to the rest of the body, leaving in the brain its acme, and whatever has sense and understanding. For if it passed first to the body and last to the brain, then having left in the flesh and veins the judgment, when it reached the brain it would be hot, and not at all pure, but mixed with the humidity from flesh and blood, so as to be no longer pure.

Wherefore, I say, that it is the brain which interprets the understanding. But the diaphragm has obtained its name (frenes) from accident and usage, and not from reality or nature, for I know no power which it possesses, either as to sense or understanding, except that when the man is affected with unexpected joy or sorrow, it throbs and produces palpitations, owing to its thinness, and as having no belly to receive anything good or bad that may present themselves to it, but it is thrown into commotion by both these, from its natural weakness. It then perceives beforehand none of those things which occur in the body, but has received its name vaguely and without any proper reason, like the parts about the heart, which are called auricles, but which contribute nothing towards hearing. Some say that we think with the heart, and that this is the part which is grieved, and experiences care. But it is not so; only it contracts like the diaphragm, and still more so for the same causes. For veins from all parts of the body run to it, and it has valves, so as to as to perceive if any pain or pleasurable emotion befall the man. For when grieved the body necessarily shudders, and is contracted, and from excessive joy it is affected in like manner. Wherefore the heart and the diaphragm are particularly sensitive, they have nothing to do, however, with the operations of the understanding, but of all but of all these the brain is the cause. Since, then, the brain, as being the primary seat of sense and of the spirits, perceives whatever occurs in the body, if any change more powerful than usual take place in the air, owing to the seasons, the brain becomes changed by the state of the air. For, on this account, the brain first perceives, because, I say, all the most acute, most powerful, and most deadly diseases, and those which are most difficult to be understood by the inexperienced, fall upon the brain.

And the disease called the Sacred arises from causes as the others, namely, those things which enter and quit the body, such as cold, the sun, and the winds, which are ever changing and are never at rest. And these things are divine, so that there is no necessity for making a distinction, and holding this disease to be more divine than the others, but all are divine, and all human. And each has its own peculiar nature and power, and none is of an ambiguous nature, or irremediable. And the most of them are curable by the same means as those by which any other thing is food to one, and injurious to another. Thus, then, the physician should understand and distinguish the season of each, so that at one time he may attend to the nourishment and increase, and at another to abstraction and diminution. And in this disease as in all others, he must strive not to feed the disease, but endeavor to wear it out by administering whatever is most opposed to

122 THE MEANING OF LIFE

each disease, and not that which favors and is allied to it. For by that which is allied to it, it gains vigor and increase, but it wears out and disappears under the use of that which is opposed to it. But whoever is acquainted with such a change in men, and can render a man humid and dry, hot and cold by regimen, could also cure this disease, if he recognizes the proper season for administering his remedies, without minding purifications, spells, and all other illiberal practices of a like kind.

ON DREAMS

Aristotle

Written 350 B.C.E

Translated by J. I. Beare[53]

Part 1

We must, in the next place, investigate the subject of the dream, and first inquire to which of the faculties of the soul it presents itself, i.e. whether the affection is one which pertains to the faculty of intelligence or to that of sense-perception; for these are the only faculties within us by which we acquire knowledge.

If, then, the exercise of the faculty of sight is actual seeing, that of the auditory faculty, hearing, and, in general that of the faculty of sense-perception, perceiving; and if there are some perceptions common to the senses, such as figure, magnitude, motion, &c., while there are others, as color, sound, taste, peculiar [each to its own sense]; and further, if all creatures, when the eyes are closed in sleep, are unable to see, and the analogous statement is true of the other senses, so that manifestly we perceive nothing when asleep; we may conclude that it is not by sense-perception we perceive a dream.

But neither is it by opinion that we do so. For [in dreams] we not only assert, e.g. that some object approaching is a man or a horse which would be an exercise of opinion , but that the object is white or beautiful, points on which opinion without sense-perception asserts nothing either truly or falsely. It is, however, a fact that the soul makes such assertions in sleep. We seem to see equally well that the approaching figure is a man, and that it is white. [In dreams], too, we think something else, over and above the dream presentation, just as we do in waking moments when we perceive something; for we often also reason about that which we perceive. So, too, in sleep we sometimes have thoughts other than the mere phantasms immediately before our minds. This would be manifest to any one who should attend and try, immediately on arising from sleep, to remember [his dreaming experience]. There are cases of persons who have seen such dreams, those, for example, who believe themselves to be mentally arranging a given list of subjects

---

53 Accessed: http://classics.mit.edu/Aristotle/dreams.html

124   THE MEANING OF LIFE

according to the mnemonic rule. They frequently find themselves engaged in something else besides the dream, viz. in setting a phantasm which they envisage into its mnemonic position. Hence it is plain that not every 'phantasm' in sleep is a mere dream-image, and that the further thinking which we perform then is due to an exercise of the faculty of opinion.

So much at least is plain on all these points, viz. that the faculty by which, in waking hours, we are subject to illusion when affected by disease, is identical with that which produces illusory effects in sleep. So, even when persons are in excellent health, and know the facts of the case perfectly well, the sun, nevertheless, appears to them to be only a foot wide. Now, whether the presentative faculty of the soul be identical with, or different from, the faculty of sense-perception, in either case the illusion does not occur without our actually seeing or [otherwise] perceiving something. Even to see wrongly or to hear wrongly can happen only to one who sees or hears something real, though not exactly what he supposes. But we have assumed that in sleep one neither sees, nor hears, nor exercises any sense whatever. Perhaps we may regard it as true that the dreamer sees nothing, yet as false that his faculty of sense-perception is unaffected, the fact being that the sense of seeing and the other senses may possibly be then in a certain way affected, while each of these affections, as duly as when he is awake, gives its impulse in a certain manner to his [primary] faculty of sense, though not in precisely the same manner as when he is awake. Sometimes, too, opinion says [to dreamers] just as to those who are awake, that the object seen is an illusion; at other times it is inhibited, and becomes a mere follower of the phantasm.

It is plain therefore that this affection, which we name 'dreaming', is no mere exercise of opinion or intelligence, but yet is not an affection of the faculty of perception in the simple sense. If it were the latter it would be possible [when asleep] to hear and see in the simple sense.

How then, and in what manner, it takes place, is what we have to examine. Let us assume, what is indeed clear enough, that the affection [of dreaming] pertains to sense-perception as surely as sleep itself does. For sleep does not pertain to one organ in animals and dreaming to another; both pertain to the same organ.

But since we have, in our work On the Soul, treated of presentation, and the faculty of presentation is identical with that of sense-perception, though the essential notion of a faculty of presentation is different from that of a faculty of sense-perception; and since presentation is the movement set up by a sensory faculty when actually discharging its function, while a dream appears to be a presentation (for a presentation which occurs in sleep-whether simply or in some particular way-is what we call a dream): it manifestly follows that dreaming is an activity of the faculty of sense-perception, but belongs to this faculty qua presentative.

Part 2

THE GREEK TRADITION   125

We can best obtain a scientific view of the nature of the dream and the manner in which it originates by regarding it in the light of the circumstances attending sleep. The objects of sense-perception corresponding to each sensory organ produce sense-perception in us, and the affection due to their operation is present in the organs of sense not only when the perceptions are actualized, but even when they have departed.

What happens in these cases may be compared with what happens in the case of projectiles moving in space. For in the case of these the movement continues even when that which set up the movement is no longer in contact [with the things that are moved]. For that which set them in motion moves a certain portion of air, and this, in turn, being moved excites motion in another portion; and so, accordingly, it is in this way that [the bodies], whether in air or in liquids, continue moving, until they come to a standstill.

This we must likewise assume to happen in the case of qualitative change; for that part which [for example] has been heated by something hot, heats [in turn] the part next to it, and this propagates the affection continuously onwards until the process has come round to its point of origination. This must also happen in the organ wherein the exercise of sense-perception takes place, since sense-perception, as realized in actual perceiving, is a mode of qualitative change. This explains why the affection continues in the sensory organs, both in their deeper and in their more superficial parts, not merely while they are actually engaged in perceiving, but even after they have ceased to do so. That they do this, indeed, is obvious in cases where we continue for some time engaged in a particular form of perception, for then, when we shift the scene of our perceptive activity, the previous affection remains; for instance, when we have turned our gaze from sunlight into darkness. For the result of this is that one sees nothing, owing to the excited by the light still subsisting in our eyes. Also, when we have looked steadily for a long while at one colour, e.g. at white or green, that to which we next transfer our gaze appears to be of the same colour. Again if, after having looked at the sun or some other brilliant object, we close the eyes, then, if we watch carefully, it appears in a right line with the direction of vision (whatever this may be), at first in its own colour; then it changes to crimson, next to purple, until it becomes black and disappears. And also when persons turn away from looking at objects in motion, e.g. rivers, and especially those which flow very rapidly, they find that the visual stimulations still present themselves, for the things really at rest are then seen moving: persons become very deaf after hearing loud noises, and after smelling very strong odours their power of smelling is impaired; and similarly in other cases. These phenomena manifestly take place in the way above described.

That the sensory organs are acutely sensitive to even a slight qualitative difference [in their objects] is shown by what happens in the case of mirrors; a subject to which, even taking it independently, one might devote close consideration and inquiry. At the same time it becomes plain from them that as the eye [in seeing] is affected [by the object seen], so also it produces a certain effect upon it. If a woman chances during her menstrual period to look into a highly polished mirror, the surface of it will grow cloudy with a blood-coloured haze. It is very hard to remove this stain from a new mirror, but easier to remove from an older mirror. As we have said before, the cause of this lies in the fact that in the act of sight there occurs not only a passion in the sense organ acted on by the polished surface, but the organ, as an agent, also produces an action, as is proper to a brilliant object. For sight is the property of an organ possessing brilliance and colour. The eyes, therefore, have their proper action as have other parts of the body. Because it is natural to the eye to be filled with blood vessels, a woman's eyes, during the period of menstrual flux and inflammation, will undergo a change, although her husband will not note this since his seed is of the same nature as that of his wife. The surrounding atmosphere, through which operates the action of sight, and which surrounds the mirror also, will undergo a change of the same sort that occurred shortly before in the woman's eyes, and hence the surface of the mirror is likewise affected. And as in the case of a garment, the cleaner it is the more quickly it is soiled, so the same holds true in the case of the mirror. For anything that is clean will show quite clearly a stain that it chances to receive, and the cleanest object shows up even the slightest stain. A bronze mirror, because of its shininess, is especially sensitive to any sort of contact (the movement of the surrounding air acts upon it like a rubbing or pressing or wiping); on that account, therefore, what is clean will show up clearly the slightest touch on its surface. It is hard to cleanse smudges off new mirrors because the stain penetrates deeply and is suffused to all parts; it penetrates deeply because the mirror is not a dense medium, and is suffused widely because of the smoothness of the object. On the other hand, in the case of old mirrors, stains do not remain because they do not penetrate deeply, but only smudge the surface.

From this therefore it is plain that stimulatory motion is set up even by slight differences, and that sense-perception is quick to respond to it; and further that the organ which perceives colour is not only affected by its object, but also reacts upon it. Further evidence to the same point is afforded by what takes place in wines, and in the manufacture of unguents. For both oil, when prepared, and wine become rapidly infected by the odours of the things near them; they not only acquire the odours of the things thrown into or mixed with them, but also those of the things which are placed, or which grow, near the vessels containing them.

In order to answer our original question, let us now, therefore, assume one proposition, which is clear from what precedes, viz. that even when the external object of perception has departed, the impressions it has made persist, and are themselves objects of perception: and [let us assume], besides, that we are easily deceived respecting the operations of sense-perception when we are excited by emotions, and different persons according to their different emotions; for example, the coward when excited by fear, the amorous person by amorous desire; so that, with but little resemblance to go upon, the former thinks he sees his foes approaching, the latter, that he sees the object of his desire; and the more deeply one is under the influence of the emotion, the less

THE GREEK TRADITION   127

similarity is required to give rise to these illusory impressions. Thus too, both in fits of anger, and also in all states of appetite, all men become easily deceived, and more so the more their emotions are excited. This is the reason too why persons in the delirium of fever sometimes think they see animals on their chamber walls, an illusion arising from the faint resemblance to animals of the markings thereon when put together in patterns; and this sometimes corresponds with the emotional states of the sufferers, in such a way that, if the latter be not very ill, they know well enough that it is an illusion; but if the illness is more severe they actually move according to the appearances. The cause of these occurrences is that the faculty in virtue of which the controlling sense judges is not identical with that in virtue of which presentations come before the mind. A proof of this is, that the sun presents itself as only a foot in diameter, though often something else gainsays the presentation. Again, when the fingers are crossed, the one object placed between them is felt [by the touch] as two; but yet we deny that it is two; for sight is more authoritative than touch. Yet, if touch stood alone, we should actually have pronounced the one object to be two. The ground of such false judgements is that any appearances whatever present themselves, not only when its object stimulates a sense, but also when the sense by itself alone is stimulated, provided only it be stimulated in the same manner as it is by the object. For example, to persons sailing past the land seems to move, when it is really the eye that is being moved by something else [the moving ship.]

Part 3

From this it is manifest that the stimulatory movements based upon sensory impressions, whether the latter are derived from external objects or from causes within the body, present themselves not only when persons are awake, but also then, when this affection which is called sleep has come upon them, with even greater impressiveness. For by day, while the senses and the intellect are working together, they (i.e. such movements) are extruded from consciousness or obscured, just as a smaller is beside a larger fire, or as small beside great pains or pleasures, though, as soon as the latter have ceased, even those that are trifling emerge into notice. But by night i.e. in sleep owing to the inaction of the particular senses, and their powerlessness to realize themselves, which arises from the reflux of the hot from the exterior parts to the interior, they i.e. the above 'movements' are borne in to the head quarters of sense-perception, and there display themselves as the disturbance (of waking life) subsides. We must suppose that, like the little eddies which are being ever formed in rivers, so the sensory movements are each a continuous process, often remaining like what they were when first started, but often, too, broken into other forms by collisions with obstacles. This [last mentioned point], moreover, gives the reason why no dreams occur in sleep immediately after meals, or to sleepers who are extremely young, e.g. to infants. The internal movement in such cases is excessive, owing to the heat generated from the food. Hence, just as in a liquid, if one vehemently disturbs it, sometimes no reflected image appears, while at other times one appears, indeed, but utterly distorted, so as to seem quite unlike its original; while, when once the motion has ceased, the reflected images are clear and plain; in the

128 THE MEANING OF LIFE

same manner during sleep the phantasms, or residuary movements, which are based upon the sensory impressions, become sometimes quite obliterated by the above described motion when too violent; while at other times the sights are indeed seen, but confused and weird, and the dreams which then appear are unhealthy, like those of persons who are atrabilious, or feverish, or intoxicated with wine. For all such affections, being spirituous, cause much commotion and disturbance. In sanguineous animals, in proportion as the blood becomes calm, and as its purer are separated from its less pure elements, the fact that the movement, based on impressions derived from each of the organs of sense, is preserved in its integrity, renders the dreams healthy, causes a [clear] image to present itself, and makes the dreamer think, owing to the effects borne in from the organ of sight, that he actually sees, and owing to those which come from the organ of hearing, that he really hears; and so on with those also which proceed from the other sensory organs. For it is owing to the fact that the movement which reaches the primary organ of sense comes from them, that one even when awake believes himself to see, or hear, or otherwise perceive; just as it is from a belief that the organ of sight is being stimulated, though in reality not so stimulated, that we sometimes erroneously declare ourselves to see, or that, from the fact that touch announces two movements, we think that the one object is two. For, as a rule, the governing sense affirms the report of each particular sense, unless another particular sense, more authoritative, makes a contradictory report. In every case an appearance presents itself, but what appears does not in every case seem real, unless when the deciding faculty is inhibited, or does not move with its proper motion. Moreover, as we said that different men are subject to illusions, each according to the different emotion present in him, so it is that the sleeper, owing to sleep, and to the movements then going on in his sensory organs, as well as to the other facts of the sensory process, [is liable to illusion], so that the dream presentation, though but little like it, appears as some actual given thing. For when one is asleep, in proportion as most of the blood sinks inwards to its fountain [the heart], the internal sensory movements, some potential, others actual accompany it inwards. They are so related [in general] that, if anything move the blood, some one sensory movement will emerge from it, while if this perishes another will take its place; while to one another also they are related in the same way as the artificial frogs in water which severally rise [in fixed succession] to the surface in the order in which the salt [which keeps them down] becomes dissolved. The residuary movements are like these: they are within the soul potentially, but actualize themselves only when the impediment to their doing so has been relaxed; and according as they are thus set free, they begin to move in the blood which remains in the sensory organs, and which is now but scanty, while they possess verisimilitude after the manner of cloud-shapes, which in their rapid metamorphoses one compares now to human beings and a moment afterwards to centaurs. Each of them is however, as has been said, the remnant of a sensory impression taken when sense was actualizing itself; and when this, the true impression, has departed, its remnant is still immanent, and it is correct to say of it, that though not actually Koriskos, it is like Koriskos. For when the person was actually perceiving, his controlling and judging sensory faculty did not call it Koriskos, but, prompted by this [impression], called the genuine person yonder Koriskos. Accordingly, this sensory impulse, which, when actually perceiving, it [the controlling faculty] describes (unless completely inhibited by the blood), it now [in dreams] when quasi-perceiving, receives from the movements persisting in the sense-organs, and mistakes it-an impulse that is merely like the true [objective] impression-for the true impression itself, while the effect of sleep is so great that it causes this mistake to pass unnoticed. Accordingly, just as if a finger be inserted beneath the eyeball without being observed, one object will not only present two visual images, but will create an opinion of its being two objects; while if it [the finger] be observed, the presentation will be the same, but the same opinion will not be formed of it; exactly so it is in states of sleep: if the sleeper perceives that he is asleep, and is conscious of the sleeping state during which the perception comes before his mind, it presents itself still, but something within him speaks to this effect: 'the image of Koriskos presents itself, but the real Koriskos is not present'; for often, when one is asleep, there is something in consciousness which declares that what then presents itself is but a dream. If, however, he is not aware of being asleep, there is nothing that will contradict the testimony of the bare presentation.

That what we here urge is true, i.e. that there are such presentative movements in the sensory organs, any one may convince himself, if he attends to and tries to remember the affections we experience when sinking into slumber or when being awakened. He will sometimes, in the moment of awakening, surprise the images that present themselves to him in sleep, and find that they are really but movements lurking in the organs of sense. And indeed some very young persons, if it is dark, though looking with wide-open eyes, see multitudes of phantom figures moving before them, so that they often cover up their heads in terror.

From all this, then, the conclusion to be drawn is, that the dream is a sort of presentation, and, more particularly, one which occurs in sleep; since the phantoms just mentioned are not dreams, nor is any other a dream which presents itself when the sense-perceptions are in a state of freedom. Nor is every presentation that occurs in sleep necessarily a dream. For in the first place, some persons [when asleep] actually, in a certain way, perceive sounds, light, savour, and contact; feebly, however, and, as it were, remotely. For there have been cases in which persons while asleep, but with the eyes partly open, saw faintly in their sleep (as they supposed) the light of a lamp, and afterwards, on being awakened, straightway recognized it as the actual light of a real lamp; while, in other cases, persons who faintly heard the crowing of cocks or the barking of dogs identified these clearly with the real sounds as soon as they awoke. Some persons, too, return answers to questions put to them in sleep. For it is quite possible that, of waking or sleeping, while the one is present in the ordinary sense, the other also should be present in a certain way. But none of these occurrences should be called a dream. Nor should the true thoughts, as distinct from the mere presentations, which occur in sleep [be called dreams]. The dream proper is a presentation based on the movement of sense impressions, when such presentation occurs during sleep, taking sleep in the strict sense of the term.

There are cases of persons who in their whole lives have never had a dream, while others dream

130 THE MEANING OF LIFE

when considerably advanced in years, having never dreamed before. The cause of their not having dreams appears somewhat like that which operates in the case of infants, and
that which operates immediately after meals. It is intelligible enough that no dream-presentation should occur to persons whose natural constitution is such that in them copious evaporation is borne upwards, which, when borne back downwards, causes a large quantity of motion. But it is not surprising that, as age advances, a dream should at length appear to them. Indeed, it is inevitable that, as a change is wrought in them in proportion to age or emotional experience, this reversal [from non-dreaming to dreaming] should occur also.

CHAPTER 6

CHRISTIAN AND ISLAMIC MODELS

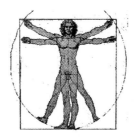

> *"Everyone who hears my words and lives them out is like a wise man who built his house upon the rock; and the rain fell, and the floods came, but it did not fall ..." And when Jesus finished these sayings, the crowds were astonished at his teaching, for he taught them as one who had authority.*
>
> *The Gospel according to Matthew*

In the Christian gospels, the messianic figure is a narrative of the supreme healer of the soul's imperfections, as well as the supreme creator of its perfection[54] with the goal of the divine kingdom being first the inevitable recognition of human imperfection and later the reorganized perfection of reality, being expressed by means of a pure love (Wood, 2003).

The Christ message of universal love[55], combined with the Socratic message of goodness via reason and knowledge, was in time turned into a comprehensive foundation for society; for what

---

54 According to an anonymous *Christian Science Monitor* article (1996 – Vol. 88) entitled "Thirsty", the Christ message based upon the Sermon on the Mount was one of healing through understanding. That is, happiness and inner peace was only to be achieved through a mythic construct of God (an understanding of God) that is relevant to everyday living. Through this understanding everyday living is infused with power and meaning.

55 It is important to note that "Christ" is a Greek term that is roughly equivalent to the Aramaic term "Messiah" which was so powerful for stirring national pride within Jews during the century following the reign of Julius Caesar. During this time period many revolutionaries claimed to be the anointed by the Jewish god to be the messiah in order to overthrow the foreign oppressors (first the helenizing Ptolemaic and Seleucid empires and then the Roman empire). Of course the most famous of these charismatic figures was the one known as *Joshua ben Joseph* in Aramaic, but most commonly called by the Greek translation, *Jesus the Christ*.

132   THE MEANING OF LIFE

both Socrates and the Christ legends affirm is that both the individual and society need the essentials of love and reason (Gill, 1991).

No one is righteous – All need love

According to St. John 7:53-8:11

But Jesus went to the Mount of Olives. And early in the morning he came again into the temple, and all the people were coming to Him; and He sat down and began to teach them. And the scribes and the Pharisees brought a woman caught in adultery, and having set her in the midst, they said to him, "Teacher, this woman has been caught in adultery, in the very act. Now in the Law of Moses its commands to stone such a woman; what then do you say?"

And they were saying this, testing him, in order that they might have grounds for accusing him. But Jesus stooped down, and with his fingers wrote on the ground. But when they persisted in asking him, he straightened up, and said to them, "He who is without sin among you, let him be the first to throw a stone at her."

And again he stooped down, and wrote on the ground. And when they heard it, they began to go out one by one, beginning with the older ones, and he was left alone, and the woman, where she had been in the midst. Jesus stood and looked a the woman, "Where are your accusers and those that condemned you?" She replied, "No one is left." Jesus replied, "Neither do I condemn you ... now go on your way and live rightly."

In many ways the Christian message was a great attempt at existential integration in understanding the psyche, as the doctrine of incarnation makes clear[56] (Gaultieri, 1968). In fact, this central tenet of incarnation may be regarded as the single-most important historical attempt at a radical integration of psyche and flesh and indeed the larger universe (Adams, 1999), a notion which Plato had torn asunder. Besides symbolizing an essential union of mind and body, the notion of Word becoming flesh (according to St. John 1) also underlines the individuation of the universal mind taking an individual form. (This is of course in contrast to the Gnostic Christians/Gnostic gospel accounts that emphasize a separation of flesh and spirit).

In many ways then, the Christian message is at its core along the same lines as the countless cultures before it. The idea of the salvation of all of creation, and the notion of resurrection was clearly in line with the integration of the psyche and soma (the physical and invisible). Indeed the notion of *Maat* or *Shal'm* is in many ways taken to its full and natural conclusion in the image of the Christian resurrection. However, the history of Christendom was such that Plato's separation

---

56 Adams (1999) notes that there is an essential phenomenon of human existence in the inter-permeating communion of self and world. The essence of life and meaning in the world "flows into" the self and becomes integrated as part of who one is. A self-awareness of this interconnection with the cosmos then results in a very different self concept.

CHRISTIAN AND ISLAMIC MODELS   **133**

of the visible and invisible began to infiltrate the Christian teachings of salvation until salvation was purely of the invisible.

The Sermon on the Mount

According to St. Mark (5: 3-12)

Blessed are the poor in spirit, for theirs is the kingdom of heaven. Blessed are those who mourn, for they shall be comforted. Blessed are the gentle, for they shall inherit the earth. Blessed are those who hunger and thirst for righteousness, for they shall be satisfied. Blessed are the merciful, for they shall receive mercy. Blessed are the pure in heart, for they shall see God. Blessed are the peacemakers, for they shall be called the children of God. Blessed are those who have been persecuted for the sake of righteousness, for theirs is the kingdom of heaven. Blessed are you when men cast insults at you, and persecute you falsely, on account of me. Rejoice and be glad, for your reward in heaven is great, for so they persecuted the prophets who were before you.

However, the depth of the actual Christ message in incarnation was deeper than most contemporaries could fathom (Gaultieri, 1968)[57]. It has therefore taken the great minds of thinkers like Augustine to plumb the depths of the epic journey of the human psyche in relation to this construct of resurrection. In Augustine's *Confessions* we see this most unsparing self-disclosure of human experience (McWilliam, 1995). For Augustine, there was a great existential component to the personal psyche, and intuitively he worked to know the universal mind of the creator and his own soul/psyche (McPherson, 2000). Indeed, this strong Augustinian notion went further as he was convinced that only through such knowledge would happiness in life be achieved. In Augustine's line of logic, since humanity was made in the image of the universal God, a searching self-examination was a way of knowing both one's own psyche and God. While one could know one's psyche through such intense introspection, one could only know God through the gift of God illuminating a receptive mind. It was not reason, but the mythical narrative that Augustine called "faith" which made this organization of the psyche possible; therefore one had to believe in the divine in order to understand, and understanding was the basis of happiness in

---

57 Of particular note is the non-synoptic thematic telling of the incarnation that was held within the main catholic tradition. In this literally there is the mythic formation of "the beginning" of all existence being a perfect idea and this perfect idea then became human (which was utterly against the typical Greek Gnostic idea of a separation of the "thought" and "physical"):

Εν αρκη ην ο λογος, και ο λογος ην προσ τον θεον και θεοσ ην ο λογος. Ουτοσ ην εν αρκη προς τον θεον. Πα ντα δι αυτου εγενετο, και κορι αυτου εγενετο υδε εν. ο γεγονεν. Και ο λογος σαρκ . – ΚΑΤΑ ΙΟΑΝΝΑΝ 1:1–2 & 14α̃ (John 1:1-2 & 14a) .

life. In many ways it was to date the clearest expression of an existential psychology; in other ways it was the same old construct, for in simplistic structural terms the mind must grasp a clear construct of the universe, and then find how he/she fits within this construct. This for Augustine was the essence of a meaningful life.[58]

---

[58] See Read For Yourself Section, this chapter– Samples of Augustine's Confessions to gain a clearer picture of what Augustine's construct of the universe was.

READ AND DECIDE FOR YOURSELF:

Excerpts from:

ROMANS / 1 CORINTHIANS

AUGUSTINE'S CONFESSIONS

136 THE MEANING OF LIFE

ROMANS / 1 CORINTHIANS

Romans 3

God's Faithfulness

[1]What advantage, then, is there in being a Jew, or what value is there in circumcision? [2]Much in every way! First of all, they have been entrusted with the very words of God.
[3]What if some did not have faith? Will their lack of faith nullify God's faithfulness? [4]Not at all! Let God be true, and every man a liar. As it is written:
    "So that you may be proved right when you speak
    and prevail when you judge."
[5]But if our unrighteousness brings out God's righteousness more clearly, what shall we say? That God is unjust in bringing his wrath on us? (I am using a human argument.) [6]Certainly not! If that were so, how could God judge the world? [7]Someone might argue, "If my falsehood enhances God's truthfulness and so increases his glory, why am I still condemned as a sinner?" [8]Why not say--as we are being slanderously reported as saying and as some claim that we say--"Let us do evil that good may result"? Their condemnation is deserved.

No One is Righteous

[9]What shall we conclude then? Are we any better? Not at all! We have already made the charge that Jews and Gentiles alike are all under sin. [10]As it is written:
    "There is no one righteous, not even one; [11]there is no one who understands, no one who seeks God.
[12]All have turned away, they have together become worthless; there is no one who does good, not even one." [13]"Their throats are open graves; their tongues practice deceit." "The poison of vipers is on their lips." [14]"Their mouths are full of cursing and bitterness." [15]"Their feet are swift to shed blood; [16]ruin and misery mark their ways, [17]and the way of peace they do not know." [18]"There is no fear of God before their eyes."
[19]Now we know that whatever the law says, it says to those who are under the law, so that every mouth may be silenced and the whole world held accountable to God. [20]Therefore no one will be declared righteous in his sight by observing the law; rather, through the law we become conscious of sin.

Righteousness Through Faith

CHRISTIAN AND ISLAMIC MODELS   137

[21]But now a righteousness from God, apart from law, has been made known, to which the Law and the Prophets testify. [22]This righteousness from God comes through faith in Jesus Christ to all who believe. There is no difference, [23]for all have sinned and fall short of the glory of God, [24]and are justified freely by his grace through the redemption that came by Christ Jesus. [25]God presented him as a sacrifice of atonement, through faith in his blood. He did this to demonstrate his justice, because in his forbearance he had left the sins committed beforehand unpunished-- [26]he did it to demonstrate his justice at the present time, so as to be just and the one who justifies those who have faith in Jesus.

[27]Where, then, is boasting? It is excluded. On what principle? On that of observing the law? No, but on that of faith. [28]For we maintain that a man is justified by faith apart from observing the law. [29]Is God the God of Jews only? Is he not the God of Gentiles too? Yes, of Gentiles too, [30]since there is only one God, who will justify the circumcised by faith and the uncircumcised through that same faith. [31]Do we, then, nullify the law by this faith? Not at all! Rather, we uphold the law.

Romans 4

Abraham Justified by Faith

[1]What then shall we say that Abraham, our forefather, discovered in this matter? [2]If, in fact, Abraham was justified by works, he had something to boast about--but not before God. [3]What does the Scripture say? "Abraham believed God, and it was credited to him as righteousness." [4]Now when a man works, his wages are not credited to him as a gift, but as an obligation. [5]However, to the man who does not work but trusts God who justifies the wicked, his faith is credited as righteousness. [6]David says the same thing when he speaks of the blessedness of the man to whom God credits righteousness apart from works:
[7]"Blessed are they whose transgressions are forgiven, whose sins are covered.
[8]Blessed is the man whose sin the Lord will never count against him."
[9]Is this blessedness only for the circumcised, or also for the uncircumcised? We have been saying that Abraham's faith was credited to him as righteousness. [10]Under what circumstances was it credited? Was it after he was circumcised, or before? It was not after, but before! [11]And he received the sign of circumcision, a seal of the righteousness that he had by faith while he was still uncircumcised. So then, he is the father of all who believe but have not been circumcised, in order that righteousness might be credited to them. [12]And he is also the father of the circumcised who not only are circumcised but who also walk in the footsteps of the faith that our father Abraham had before he was circumcised.

[13]It was not through law that Abraham and his offspring received the promise that he would be heir of the world, but through the righteousness that comes by faith. [14]For if those who live by law are heirs, faith has no value and the promise is worthless, [15]because law brings wrath. And where there is no law there is no transgression.

138 THE MEANING OF LIFE

[16]Therefore, the promise comes by faith, so that it may be by grace and may be guaranteed to all Abraham's offspring--not only to those who are of the law but also to those who are of the faith of Abraham. He is the father of us all. [17]As it is written: "I have made you a father of many nations." He is our father in the sight of God, in whom he believed--the God who gives life to the dead and calls things that are not as though they were.

[18]Against all hope, Abraham in hope believed and so became the father of many nations, just as it had been said to him, "So shall your offspring be." [19]Without weakening in his faith, he faced the fact that his body was as good as dead--since he was about a hundred years old--and that Sarah's womb was also dead. [20]Yet he did not waver through unbelief regarding the promise of God, but was strengthened in his faith and gave glory to God, [21]being fully persuaded that God had power to do what he had promised. [22]This is why "it was credited to him as righteousness." [23]The words "it was credited to him" were written not for him alone, [24]but also for us, to whom God will credit righteousness--for us who believe in him who raised Jesus our Lord from the dead. [25]He was delivered over to death for our sins and was raised to life for our justification.

Romans 5

Peace and Joy

[1]Therefore, since we have been justified through faith, we have peace with God through our Lord Jesus Christ, [2]through whom we have gained access by faith into this grace in which we now stand. And we rejoice in the hope of the glory of God. [3]Not only so, but we also rejoice in our sufferings, because we know that suffering produces perseverance; [4]perseverance, character; and character, hope. [5]And hope does not disappoint us, because God has poured out his love into our hearts by the Holy Spirit, whom he has given us.

[6]You see, at just the right time, when we were still powerless, Christ died for the ungodly. [7]Very rarely will anyone die for a righteous man, though for a good man someone might possibly dare to die. [8]But God demonstrates his own love for us in this: While we were still sinners, Christ died for us.

[9]Since we have now been justified by his blood, how much more shall we be saved from God's wrath through him! [10]For if, when we were God's enemies, we were reconciled to him through the death of his Son, how much more, having been reconciled, shall we be saved through his life! [11]Not only is this so, but we also rejoice in God through our Lord Jesus Christ, through whom we have now received reconciliation.

Death Through Adam, Life Through Christ

[12]Therefore, just as sin entered the world through one man, and death through sin, and in this way death came to all men, because all sinned-- [13]for before the law was given, sin was in the world. But sin is not taken into account when there is no law. [14]Nevertheless, death reigned from the

CHRISTIAN AND ISLAMIC MODELS **139**

time of Adam to the time of Moses, even over those who did not sin by breaking a command, as did Adam, who was a pattern of the one to come.
[15]But the gift is not like the trespass. For if the many died by the trespass of the one man, how much more did God's grace and the gift that came by the grace of the one man, Jesus Christ, overflow to the many! [16]Again, the gift of God is not like the result of the one man's sin: The judgment followed one sin and brought condemnation, but the gift followed many trespasses and brought justification. [17]For if, by the trespass of the one man, death reigned through that one man, how much more will those who receive God's abundant provision of grace and of the gift of righteousness reign in life through the one man, Jesus Christ.
[18]Consequently, just as the result of one trespass was condemnation for all men, so also the result of one act of righteousness was justification that brings life for all men. [19]For just as through the disobedience of the one man the many were made sinners, so also through the obedience of the one man the many will be made righteous.
[20]The law was added so that the trespass might increase. But where sin increased, grace increased all the more, [21]so that, just as sin reigned in death, so also grace might reign through righteousness to bring eternal life through Jesus Christ our Lord.

Romans 6

Dead to Sin, Alive in Christ

[1]What shall we say, then? Shall we go on sinning so that grace may increase? [2]By no means! We died to sin; how can we live in it any longer? [3]Or don't you know that all of us who were baptized into Christ Jesus were baptized into his death? [4]We were therefore buried with him through baptism into death in order that, just as Christ was raised from the dead through the glory of the Father, we too may live a new life.
[5]If we have been united with him like this in his death, we will certainly also be united with him in his resurrection. [6]For we know that our old self was crucified with him so that the body of sin might be done away with, that we should no longer be slaves to sin-- [7]because anyone who has died has been freed from sin.
[8]Now if we died with Christ, we believe that we will also live with him. [9]For we know that since Christ was raised from the dead, he cannot die again; death no longer has mastery over him. [10]The death he died, he died to sin once for all; but the life he lives, he lives to God.
[11]In the same way, count yourselves dead to sin but alive to God in Christ Jesus. [12]Therefore do not let sin reign in your mortal body so that you obey its evil desires. [13]Do not offer the parts of your body to sin, as instruments of wickedness, but rather offer yourselves to God, as those who have been brought from death to life; and offer the parts of your body to him as instruments of righteousness. [14]For sin shall not be your master, because you are not under law, but under grace.

Slaves to Righteousness

140   THE MEANING OF LIFE

[15]What then? Shall we sin because we are not under law but under grace? By no means! [16]Don't you know that when you offer yourselves to someone to obey him as slaves, you are slaves to the one whom you obey--whether you are slaves to sin, which leads to death, or to obedience, which leads to righteousness? [17]But thanks be to God that, though you used to be slaves to sin, you wholeheartedly obeyed the form of teaching to which you were entrusted. [18]You have been set free from sin and have become slaves to righteousness.

[19]I put this in human terms because you are weak in your natural selves. Just as you used to offer the parts of your body in slavery to impurity and to ever-increasing wickedness, so now offer them in slavery to righteousness leading to holiness. [20]When you were slaves to sin, you were free from the control of righteousness. [21]What benefit did you reap at that time from the things you are now ashamed of? Those things result in death! [22]But now that you have been set free from sin and have become slaves to God, the benefit you reap leads to holiness, and the result is eternal life. [23]For the wages of sin is death, but the gift of God is eternal life in Christ Jesus our Lord.

Romans 7

An Illustration From Marriage

[1]Do you not know, brothers--for I am speaking to men who know the law--that the law has authority over a man only as long as he lives? [2]For example, by law a married woman is bound to her husband as long as he is alive, but if her husband dies, she is released from the law of marriage. [3]So then, if she marries another man while her husband is still alive, she is called an adulteress. But if her husband dies, she is released from that law and is not an adulteress, even though she marries another man.

[4]So, my brothers, you also died to the law through the body of Christ, that you might belong to another, to him who was raised from the dead, in order that we might bear fruit to God. [5]For when we were controlled by the sinful nature, the sinful passions aroused by the law were at work in our bodies, so that we bore fruit for death. [6]But now, by dying to what once bound us, we have been released from the law so that we serve in the new way of the Spirit, and not in the old way of the written code.

Struggling With Sin

[7]What shall we say, then? Is the law sin? Certainly not! Indeed I would not have known what sin was except through the law. For I would not have known what coveting really was if the law had not said, "Do not covet." [8]But sin, seizing the opportunity afforded by the commandment, produced in me every kind of covetous desire. For apart from law, sin is dead. [9]Once I was alive apart from law; but when the commandment came, sin sprang to life and I died. [10]I found that the very commandment that was intended to bring life actually brought death.

CHRISTIAN AND ISLAMIC MODELS   141

[11]For sin, seizing the opportunity afforded by the commandment, deceived me, and through the commandment put me to death. [12]So then, the law is holy, and the commandment is holy, righteous and good. [13]Did that which is good, then, become death to me? By no means! But in order that sin might be recognized as sin, it produced death in me through what was good, so that through the commandment sin might become utterly sinful.

[14]We know that the law is spiritual; but I am unspiritual, sold as a slave to sin. [15]I do not understand what I do. For what I want to do I do not do, but what I hate I do. [16]And if I do what I do not want to do, I agree that the law is good. [17]As it is, it is no longer I myself who do it, but it is sin living in me. [18]I know that nothing good lives in me, that is, in my sinful nature. For I have the desire to do what is good, but I cannot carry it out. [19]For what I do is not the good I want to do; no, the evil I do not want to do--this I keep on doing. [20]Now if I do what I do not want to do, it is no longer I who do it, but it is sin living in me that does it.

[21]So I find this law at work: When I want to do good, evil is right there with me. [22]For in my inner being I delight in God's law; [23]but I see another law at work in the members of my body, waging war against the law of my mind and making me a prisoner of the law of sin at work within my members. [24]What a wretched man I am! Who will rescue me from this body of death? [25]Thanks be to God--through Jesus Christ our Lord!

So then, I myself in my mind am a slave to God's law, but in the sinful nature a slave to the law of sin.

Romans 8

Life Through the Spirit

[1]Therefore, there is now no condemnation for those who are in Christ Jesus, [2]because through Christ Jesus the law of the Spirit of life set me free from the law of sin and death. [3]For what the law was powerless to do in that it was weakened by the sinful nature, God did by sending his own Son in the likeness of sinful man to be a sin offering. And so he condemned sin in sinful man, [4]in order that the righteous requirements of the law might be fully met in us, who do not live according to the sinful nature but according to the Spirit.

[5]Those who live according to the sinful nature have their minds set on what that nature desires; but those who live in accordance with the Spirit have their minds set on what the Spirit desires. [6]The mind of sinful man is death, but the mind controlled by the Spirit is life and peace; [7]the sinful mind is hostile to God. It does not submit to God's law, nor can it do so. [8]Those controlled by the sinful nature cannot please God.

[9]You, however, are controlled not by the sinful nature but by the Spirit, if the Spirit of God lives in you. And if anyone does not have the Spirit of Christ, he does not belong to Christ. [10]But if Christ is in you, your body is dead because of sin, yet your spirit is alive because of righteousness. [11]And if the Spirit of him who raised Jesus from the dead is living in you, he who raised Christ from the dead will also give life to your mortal bodies through his Spirit, who lives

142　THE MEANING OF LIFE

in you.
[12]Therefore, brothers, we have an obligation--but it is not to the sinful nature, to live according to it. [13]For if you live according to the sinful nature, you will die; but if by the Spirit you put to death the misdeeds of the body, you will live, [14]because those who are led by the Spirit of God are sons of God. [15]For you did not receive a spirit that makes you a slave again to fear, but you received the Spirit of sonship. And by him we cry, "Abba, Father." [16]The Spirit himself testifies with our spirit that we are God's children. [17]Now if we are children, then we are heirs--heirs of God and co-heirs with Christ, if indeed we share in his sufferings in order that we may also share in his glory.

Future Glory

[18]I consider that our present sufferings are not worth comparing with the glory that will be revealed in us. [19]The creation waits in eager expectation for the sons of God to be revealed. [20]For the creation was subjected to frustration, not by its own choice, but by the will of the one who subjected it, in hope [21]that the creation itself will be liberated from its bondage to decay and brought into the glorious freedom of the children of God.
[22]We know that the whole creation has been groaning as in the pains of childbirth right up to the present time. [23]Not only so, but we ourselves, who have the firstfruits of the Spirit, groan inwardly as we wait eagerly for our adoption as sons, the redemption of our bodies. [24]For in this hope we were saved. But hope that is seen is no hope at all. Who hopes for what he already has? [25]But if we hope for what we do not yet have, we wait for it patiently.
[26]In the same way, the Spirit helps us in our weakness. We do not know what we ought to pray for, but the Spirit himself intercedes for us with groans that words cannot express. [27]And he who searches our hearts knows the mind of the Spirit, because the Spirit intercedes for the saints in accordance with God's will.

More Than Conquerors

[28]And we know that in all things God works for the good of those who love him, who have been called according to his purpose. [29]For those God foreknew he also predestined to be conformed to the likeness of his Son, that he might be the firstborn among many brothers. [30]And those he predestined, he also called; those he called, he also justified; those he justified, he also glorified.
[31]What, then, shall we say in response to this? If God is for us, who can be against us? [32]He who did not spare his own Son, but gave him up for us all--how will he not also, along with him, graciously give us all things? [33]Who will bring any charge against those whom God has chosen? It is God who justifies. [34]Who is he that condemns? Christ Jesus, who died – more than that, who was raised to life – is at the right hand of God and is also interceding for us. [35]Who shall separate us from the love of Christ? Shall trouble or hardship or persecution or famine or nakedness or danger or sword? [36]As it is written:

CHRISTIAN AND ISLAMIC MODELS   143

"For your sake we face death all day long;
     we are considered as sheep to be slaughtered." [37]No, in all these things we are more than conquerors through him who loved us. [38]For I am convinced that neither death nor life, neither angels nor demons, neither the present nor the future, nor any powers, [39]neither height nor depth, nor anything else in all creation, will be able to separate us from the love of God that is in Christ Jesus our Lord.

1 Corinthians 13

Love

[1]If I speak in the tongues of men and of angels, but have not love, I am only a resounding gong or a clanging cymbal. [2]If I have the gift of prophecy and can fathom all mysteries and all knowledge, and if I have a faith that can move mountains, but have not love, I am nothing. [3]If I give all I possess to the poor and surrender my body to the flames, but have not love, I gain nothing.
[4]Love is patient, love is kind. It does not envy, it does not boast, it is not proud. [5]It is not rude, it is not self-seeking, it is not easily angered, it keeps no record of wrongs. [6]Love does not delight in evil but rejoices with the truth. [7]It always protects, always trusts, always hopes, always perseveres.
[8]Love never fails. But where there are prophecies, they will cease; where there are tongues, they will be stilled; where there is knowledge, it will pass away. [9]For we know in part and we prophesy in part, [10]but when perfection comes, the imperfect disappears. [11]When I was a child, I talked like a child, I thought like a child, I reasoned like a child. When I became a man, I put childish ways behind me. [12]Now we see but a poor reflection as in a mirror; then we shall see face to face. Now I know in part; then I shall know fully, even as I am fully known.
[13]And now these three remain: faith, hope and love. But the greatest of these is love.

1 Corinthians 14

Gifts of Prophecy and Tongues

[1]Follow the way of love and eagerly desire spiritual gifts, especially the gift of prophecy. [2]For anyone who speaks in a tongue does not speak to men but to God. Indeed, no one understands him; he utters mysteries with his spirit. [3]But everyone who prophesies speaks to men for their strengthening, encouragement and comfort. [4]He who speaks in a tongue edifies himself, but he who prophesies edifies the church. [5]I would like every one of you to speak in tongues, but I would rather have you prophesy. He who prophesies is greater than one who speaks in tongues, unless he interprets, so that the church may be edified.
[6]Now, brothers, if I come to you and speak in tongues, what good will I be to you, unless I bring

144   THE MEANING OF LIFE

you some revelation or knowledge or prophecy or word of instruction? [7]Even in the case of lifeless things that make sounds, such as the flute or harp, how will anyone know what tune is being played unless there is a distinction in the notes? [8]Again, if the trumpet does not sound a clear call, who will get ready for battle? [9]So it is with you. Unless you speak intelligible words with your tongue, how will anyone know what you are saying? You will just be speaking into the air. [10]Undoubtedly there are all sorts of languages in the world, yet none of them is without meaning. [11]If then I do not grasp the meaning of what someone is saying, I am a foreigner to the speaker, and he is a foreigner to me. [12]So it is with you. Since you are eager to have spiritual gifts, try to excel in gifts that build up the church.

[13]For this reason anyone who speaks in a tongue should pray that he may interpret what he says. [14]For if I pray in a tongue, my spirit prays, but my mind is unfruitful. [15]So what shall I do? I will pray with my spirit, but I will also pray with my mind; I will sing with my spirit, but I will also sing with my mind. [16]If you are praising God with your spirit, how can one who finds himself among those who do not understand say "Amen" to your thanksgiving, since he does not know what you are saying? [17]You may be giving thanks well enough, but the other man is not edified.

[18]I thank God that I speak in tongues more than all of you. [19]But in the church I would rather speak five intelligible words to instruct others than ten thousand words in a tongue.

[20]Brothers, stop thinking like children. In regard to evil be infants, but in your thinking be adults. [21]In the Law it is written:

"Through men of strange tongues
    and through the lips of foreigners
 I will speak to this people,
    but even then they will not listen to me," says the Lord.

[22]Tongues, then, are a sign, not for believers but for unbelievers; prophecy, however, is for believers, not for unbelievers. [23]So if the whole church comes together and everyone speaks in tongues, and some who do not understand or some unbelievers come in, will they not say that you are out of your mind? [24]But if an unbeliever or someone who does not understand comes in while everybody is prophesying, he will be convinced by all that he is a sinner and will be judged by all, [25]and the secrets of his heart will be laid bare. So he will fall down and worship God, exclaiming, "God is really among you!"

Orderly Worship

[26]What then shall we say, brothers? When you come together, everyone has a hymn, or a word of instruction, a revelation, a tongue or an interpretation. All of these must be done for the strengthening of the church. [27]If anyone speaks in a tongue, two--or at the most three--should speak, one at a time, and someone must interpret. [28]If there is no interpreter, the speaker should keep quiet in the church and speak to himself and God.

[29]Two or three prophets should speak, and the others should weigh carefully what is said. [30]And if a revelation comes to someone who is sitting down, the first speaker should stop. [31]For you can

CHRISTIAN AND ISLAMIC MODELS   145

all prophesy in turn so that everyone may be instructed and encouraged. [32]The spirits of prophets are subject to the control of prophets. [33]For God is not a God of disorder but of peace.
[34]As in all the congregations of the saints, women should remain silent in the churches. They are not allowed to speak, but must be in submission, as the Law says. [35]If they want to inquire about something, they should ask their own husbands at home; for it is disgraceful for a woman to speak in the church.
[36]Did the word of God originate with you? Or are you the only people it has reached? [37]If anybody thinks he is a prophet or spiritually gifted, let him acknowledge that what I am writing to you is the Lord's command. [38]If he ignores this, he himself will be ignored.
[39]Therefore, my brothers, be eager to prophesy, and do not forbid speaking in tongues. [40]But everything should be done in a fitting and orderly way.

1 Corinthians 15

The Resurrection of Christ

[1]Now, brothers, I want to remind you of the gospel I preached to you, which you received and on which you have taken your stand. [2]By this gospel you are saved, if you hold firmly to the word I preached to you. Otherwise, you have believed in vain.
[3]For what I received I passed on to you as of first importance: that Christ died for our sins according to the Scriptures, [4]that he was buried, that he was raised on the third day according to the Scriptures, [5]and that he appeared to Peter, and then to the Twelve. [6]After that, he appeared to more than five hundred of the brothers at the same time, most of whom are still living, though some have fallen asleep. [7]Then he appeared to James, then to all the apostles, [8]and last of all he appeared to me also, as to one abnormally born.
[9]For I am the least of the apostles and do not even deserve to be called an apostle, because I persecuted the church of God. [10]But by the grace of God I am what I am, and his grace to me was not without effect. No, I worked harder than all of them--yet not I, but the grace of God that was with me. [11]Whether, then, it was I or they, this is what we preach, and this is what you believed.

The Resurrection of the Dead

[12]But if it is preached that Christ has been raised from the dead, how can some of you say that there is no resurrection of the dead? [13]If there is no resurrection of the dead, then not even Christ has been raised. [14]And if Christ has not been raised, our preaching is useless and so is your faith.
[15]More than that, we are then found to be false witnesses about God, for we have testified about God that he raised Christ from the dead. But he did not raise him if in fact the dead are not raised. [16]For if the dead are not raised, then Christ has not been raised either. [17]And if Christ has not been raised, your faith is futile; you are still in your sins. [18]Then those also who have fallen asleep in Christ are lost. [19]If only for this life we have hope in Christ, we are to be pitied more than all men.

146 THE MEANING OF LIFE

[20]But Christ has indeed been raised from the dead, the firstfruits of those who have fallen asleep. [21]For since death came through a man, the resurrection of the dead comes also through a man. [22]For as in Adam all die, so in Christ all will be made alive. [23]But each in his own turn: Christ, the firstfruits; then, when he comes, those who belong to him. [24]Then the end will come, when he hands over the kingdom to God the Father after he has destroyed all dominion, authority and power. [25]For he must reign until he has put all his enemies under his feet. [26]The last enemy to be destroyed is death. [27]For he "has put everything under his feet." Now when it says that "everything" has been put under him, it is clear that this does not include God himself, who put everything under Christ. [28]When he has done this, then the Son himself will be made subject to him who put everything under him, so that God may be all in all.

[29]Now if there is no resurrection, what will those do who are baptized for the dead? If the dead are not raised at all, why are people baptized for them? [30]And as for us, why do we endanger ourselves every hour? [31]I die every day--I mean that, brothers--just as surely as I glory over you in Christ Jesus our Lord. [32]If I fought wild beasts in Ephesus for merely human reasons, what have I gained? If the dead are not raised,

"Let us eat and drink,

for tomorrow we die." [33]Do not be misled: "Bad company corrupts good character." [34]Come back to your senses as you ought, and stop sinning; for there are some who are ignorant of God--I say this to your shame.

The Resurrection Body

[35]But someone may ask, "How are the dead raised? With what kind of body will they come?" [36]How foolish! What you sow does not come to life unless it dies. [37]When you sow, you do not plant the body that will be, but just a seed, perhaps of wheat or of something else. [38]But God gives it a body as he has determined, and to each kind of seed he gives its own body. [39]All flesh is not the same: Men have one kind of flesh, animals have another, birds another and fish another. [40]There are also heavenly bodies and there are earthly bodies; but the splendour of the heavenly bodies is one kind, and the splendour of the earthly bodies is another. [41]The sun has one kind of splendour, the moon another and the stars another; and star differs from star in splendour. [42]So will it be with the resurrection of the dead. The body that is sown is perishable, it is raised imperishable; [43]it is sown in dishonour, it is raised in glory; it is sown in weakness, it is raised in power; [44]it is sown a natural body, it is raised a spiritual body.

If there is a natural body, there is also a spiritual body. [45]So it is written: "The first man Adam became a living being"; the last Adam, a life-giving spirit. [46]The spiritual did not come first, but the natural, and after that the spiritual. [47]The first man was of the dust of the earth, the second man from heaven. [48]As was the earthly man, so are those who are of the earth; and as is the man from heaven, so also are those who are of heaven. [49]And just as we have borne the likeness of the earthly man, so shall we bear the likeness of the man from heaven.

[50]I declare to you, brothers, that flesh and blood cannot inherit the kingdom of God, nor does the

CHRISTIAN AND ISLAMIC MODELS   **147**

perishable inherit the imperishable. [51]Listen, I tell you a mystery: We will not all sleep, but we will all be changed-- [52]in a flash, in the twinkling of an eye, at the last trumpet. For the trumpet will sound, the dead will be raised imperishable, and we will be changed. [53]For the perishable must clothe itself with the imperishable, and the mortal with immortality. [54]When the perishable has been clothed with the imperishable, and the mortal with immortality, then the saying that is written will come true: "Death has been swallowed up in victory."

[55]"Where, O death, is your victory?

Where, O death, is your sting?" [56]The sting of death is sin, and the power of sin is the law. [57]But thanks be to God! He gives us the victory through our Lord Jesus Christ.

[58]Therefore, my dear brothers, stand firm. Let nothing move you. Always give yourselves fully to the work of the Lord, because you know that your labour in the Lord is not in vain.

148   THE MEANING OF LIFE

AUGUSTINE'S CONFESSIONS

Book Nine

Translated by E.B. Pusey[59]

9.1.1

O Lord, I am Thy servant; I am Thy servant, and the son of Thy Handmaid: Thou hast broken my bonds in sunder. I will offer to Thee The sacrifice of Let my heart and my tongue praise Thee; yea, let all my bones say, O Lord, who is like unto Thee? Let them say, and answer Thou me, and say unto my soul, I am thy salvation. Who am I, and what am I? What evil have not been either my deeds, or if not my deeds, my words, or if not my words, my will? But Thou, O Lord, are good and merciful, and Thy right hand had respect unto the depth of my death, and from the bottom of my heart emptied that abyss of corruption. And this Thy whole gift was, to nill what I willed, and to will what Thou willedst. But where through all those years, and out of what low and deep recess was my free-will called forth in a moment, whereby to submit my neck to Thy easy yoke, and my shoulders unto Thy light burden, O Christ Jesus, my Helper and my Redeemer? How sweet did it at once become to me, to want the sweetnesses of those toys! and what I feared to be parted from, was now a joy to part with. For Thou didst cast them forth from me, Thou true and highest sweetness. Thou castest them forth, and for them enteredst in Thyself, sweeter than all pleasure, though not to flesh and blood; brighter than all light, but more hidden than all depths, higher than all honour, but not to the high in their own conceits. Now was my soul free from the biting cares of canvassing and getting, and weltering in filth, and scratching off the itch of lust. And my infant tongue spake freely to Thee, my brightness, and my riches, and my health, the Lord my God.

9.2.2

And I resolved in Thy sight, not tumultuously to tear, but gently to withdraw, the service of my tongue from the marts of lip-labour: that the young, no students in Thy law, nor in Thy peace, but in lying dotages and law-skirmishes, should no longer buy at my mouth arms for their madness. And very seasonably, it now wanted but very few days unto the Vacation of the Vintage, and I resolved to endure them, then in a regular way to take my leave, and having been purchased by Thee, no more to return for sale. Our purpose then was known to Thee; but to men,

---

59 Accessed: http://ccat.sas.upenn.edu/jod/augustine/Pusey/book09

CHRISTIAN AND ISLAMIC MODELS 149

other than our own friends, was it not known. For we had agreed among ourselves not to let it out abroad to any: although to us, now ascending from the valley of tears, and singing that song of degrees, Thou hadst given sharp arrows, and destroying coals against the subtle tongue, which as though advising for us, would thwart, and would out of love devour us, as it doth its meat.

9.2.3

Thou hadst pierced our hearts with Thy charity, and we carried Thy words as it were fixed in our entrails: and the examples of Thy servants, whom for black Thou hadst made bright, and for dead, alive, being piled together in the receptacle of our thoughts, kindled and burned up that our heavy torpor, that we should not sink down to the abyss; and they fired us so vehemently, that all the blasts of subtle tongues from gainsayers might only inflame us the more fiercely, not extinguish us. Nevertheless, because for Thy Name's sake which Thou hast hallowed throughout the earth, this our vow and purpose might also find some to commend it, it seemed like ostentation not to wait for the vacation now so near, but to quit beforehand a public profession, which was before the eyes of all; so that all looking on this act of mine, and observing how near was the time of vintage which I wished to anticipate, would talk much of me, as if I had desired to appear some great one. And what end had it served me, that people should repute and dispute upon my purpose, and that our good should be evil spoken of.

9.2.4

Moreover, it had at first troubled me that in this very summer my lungs began to give way, amid too great literary labour, and to breathe deeply with difficulty, and by the pain in my chest to show that they were injured, and to refuse any full or lengthened speaking; this had troubled me, for it almost constrained me of necessity to lay down that burden of teaching, or, if I could be cured and recover, at least to intermit it. But when the full wish for leisure, that I might see how that Thou art the Lord, arose, and was fixed, in me; my God, Thou knowest, I began even to rejoice that I had this secondary, and that no feigned, excuse, which might something moderate the offence taken by those who, for their sons' sake, wished me never to have the freedom of Thy sons. Full then of such joy, I endured till that interval of time were run; it may have been some twenty days, yet they were endured manfully; endured, for the covetousness which aforetime bore a part of this heavy business, had left me, and I remained alone, and had been overwhelmed, had not patience taken its place. Perchance, some of Thy servants, my brethren, may say that I sinned in this, that with a heart fully set on Thy service, I suffered myself to sit even one hour in the chair of lies. Nor would I be contentious. But hast not Thou, O most merciful Lord, pardoned and remitted this sin also, with my other most horrible and deadly sins, in the holy water?

150 THE MEANING OF LIFE

9.3.5

Verecundus was worn down with care about this our blessedness, for that being held back by bonds, whereby he was most straitly bound, he saw that he should be severed from us. For himself was not yet a Christian, his wife one of the faithful; and yet hereby, more rigidly than by any other chain, was he let and hindered from the journey which we had now essayed. For he would not, he said, be a Christian on any other terms than on those he could not. However, he offered us courteously to remain at his country-house so long as we should stay there. Thou, O Lord, shalt reward him in the resurrection of the just, seeing Thou hast already given him the lot of the righteous. For although, in our absence, being now at Rome, he was seized with bodily sickness, and therein being made a Christian, and one of the faithful, he departed this life; yet hadst Thou mercy not on him only, but on us also: lest remembering the exceeding kindness of our friend towards us, yet unable to number him among Thy flock, we should be agonised with intolerable sorrow. Thanks unto Thee, our God, we are Thine: Thy suggestions and consolations tell us, Faithful in promises, Thou now requitest Verecundus for his country-house of Cassiacum, where from the fever of the world we reposed in Thee, with the eternal freshness of Thy Paradise: for that Thou hast forgiven him his sins upon earth, in that rich mountain, that mountain which yieldeth milk, Thine own mountain.

9.3.6

He then had at that time sorrow, but Nebridius joy. For although he also, not being yet a Christian, had fallen into the pit of that most pernicious error, believing the flesh of Thy Son to be a phantom: yet emerging thence, he believed as we did; not as yet endued with any Sacraments of Thy Church, but a most ardent searcher out of truth. Whom, not long after our conversion and regeneration by Thy Baptism, being also a faithful member of the Church Catholic, and serving Thee in perfect chastity and continence amongst his people in Africa, his whole house having through him first been made Christian, didst Thou release from the flesh; and now he lives in Abraham's bosom. Whatever that be, which is signified by that bosom, there lives my Nebridius, my sweet friend, and Thy child, O Lord, adopted of a freed man: there he liveth. For what other place is there for such a soul? There he liveth, whereof he asked much of me, a poor inexperienced man. Now lays he not his ear to my mouth, but his spiritual mouth unto Thy fountain, and drinketh as much as he can receive, wisdom in proportion to his thirst, endlessly happy. Nor do I think that he is so inebriated therewith, as to forget me; seeing Thou, Lord, Whom he drinketh, art mindful of us. So were we then, comforting Verecundus, who sorrowed, as far as friendship permitted, that our conversion was of such sort; and exhorting him to become faithful, according to his measure, namely, of a married estate; and awaiting Nebridius to follow us, which, being so near, he was all but doing: and so, lo! those days rolled by at length; for long and many they seemed, for the love I bare to the easeful liberty, that I might sing to Thee, from

CHRISTIAN AND ISLAMIC MODELS   151

my inmost marrow, My heart hath said unto Thee, I have sought Thy face: Thy face, Lord, will I seek.
9.4.7

Now was the day come wherein I was in deed to be freed of my Rhetoric Professorship, whereof in thought I was already freed. And it was done. Thou didst rescue my tongue, whence Thou hadst before rescued my heart. And I blessed Thee, rejoicing; retiring with all mine to the villa. What I there did in writing, which was now enlisted in Thy service, though still, in this breathing-time as it were, panting from the school of pride, my books may witness, as well what I debated with others, as what with myself alone, before Thee: what with Nebridius, who was absent, my Epistles bear witness. And when shall I have time to rehearse all Thy great benefits towards us at that time, especially when hasting on to yet greater mercies? For my remembrance recalls me, and pleasant is it to me, O Lord, to confess to Thee, by what inward goads Thou tamedst me; and how Thou hast evened me, lowering the mountains and hills of my high imaginations, straightening my crookedness, and smoothing my rough ways; and how Thou also subduedst the brother of my heart, Alypius, unto the name of Thy Only Begotten, our Lord and Saviour Jesus Christ, which he would not at first vouchsafe to have inserted in our writings. For rather would he have them savour of the lofty cedars of the Schools, which the Lord hath now broken down, than of the wholesome herbs of the Church, the antidote against serpents.

9.4.8

Oh, in what accents spake I unto Thee, my God, when I read the Psalms of David, those faithful songs, and sounds of devotion, which allow of no swelling spirit, as yet a Catechumen, and a novice in Thy real love, resting in that villa, with Alypius a Catechumen, my mother cleaving to us, in female garb with masculine faith, with the tranquillity of age, motherly love, Christian piety! Oh, what accents did I utter unto Thee in those Psalms, and how was I by them kindled towards Thee, and on fire to rehearse them, if possible, through the whole world, against the pride of mankind! And yet they are sung through the whole world, nor can any hide himself from Thy heat. With what vehement and bitter sorrow was I angered at the Manichees! and again I pitied them, for they knew not those Sacraments, those medicines, and were mad against the antidote which might have recovered them of their madness. How I would they had then been somewhere near me, and without my knowing that they were there, could have beheld my countenance, and heard my words, when I read the fourth Psalm in that time of my rest, and how that Psalm wrought upon me: When I called, the God of my righteousness heard me; in tribulation Thou enlarges me. Have mercy upon me, O Lord, and hear my prayer. Would that what I uttered on these words, they could hear, without my knowing whether they heard, lest they should think I spake it for their sakes! Because in truth neither should I speak the same things, nor in the same way, if I perceived that they heard and saw me; nor if I spake them would they so

152   THE MEANING OF LIFE

receive them, as when I spake by and for myself before Thee, out of the natural feelings of my soul.

9.4.9

I trembled for fear, and again kindled with hope, and with rejoicing in Thy mercy, O Father; and all issued forth both by mine eyes and voice, when Thy good Spirit turning unto us, said, O ye sons of men, how long slow of heart? why do ye love vanity, and seek after leasing? For I had loved vanity, and sought after leasing. And Thou, O Lord, hadst already magnified Thy Holy One, raising Him from the dead, and setting Him at Thy right hand, whence from on high He should send His promise, the Comforter, the Spirit of truth. And He had already sent Him, but I knew it not; He had sent Him, because He was now magnified, rising again from the dead, and ascending into heaven. For till then, the Spirit was not yet given, because Jesus was not yet glorified. And the prophet cries out, How long, slow of heart? why do ye love vanity, and seek after leasing? Know this, that the Lord hath magnified His Holy One. He cries out, How long? He cries out, Know this: and I so long, not knowing, loved vanity, and sought after leasing: and therefore I heard and trembled, because it was spoken unto such as I remembered myself to have been. For in those phantoms which I had held for truths, was there vanity and leasing; and I spake aloud many things earnestly and forcibly, in the bitterness of my remembrance. Which would they had heard, who yet love vanity and seek after leasing! They would perchance have been troubled, and have vomited it up; and Thou wouldest hear them when they cried unto Thee; for by a true death in the flesh did He die for us, who now interceded unto Thee for us.

9.4.10

I further read, Be angry, and sin not. And how was I moved, O my God, who had now learned to be angry at myself for things past, that I might not sin in time to come! Yea, to be justly angry; for that it was not another nature of a people of darkness which sinned for me, as they say who are not angry at themselves, and treasure up wrath against the day of wrath, and of the revelation of Thy just judgment. Nor were my good things now without, nor sought with the eyes of flesh in that earthly sun; for they that would have joy from without soon become vain, and waste themselves on the things seen and temporal, and in their famished thoughts do lick their very shadows. Oh that they were wearied out with their famine, and said, Who will show us good things? And we would say, and they hear, The light of Thy countenance is sealed upon us. For we are not that light which enlightened every man, but we are enlightened by Thee; that having been sometimes darkness, we may be light in Thee. Oh that they could see the eternal Internal, which having tasted, I was grieved that I could not show It them, so long as they brought me their heart in their eyes roving abroad from Thee, while they said, Who will show us good things? For there, where I was angry within myself in my chamber, where I was inwardly pricked, where I had sacrificed, slaying my old man and commencing the purpose of a new life, putting my trust in

CHRISTIAN AND ISLAMIC MODELS 153

Thee,- there hadst Thou begun to grow sweet unto me, and hadst put gladness in my heart. And I cried out, as I read this outwardly, finding it inwardly. Nor would I be multiplied with worldly goods; wasting away time, and wasted by time; whereas I had in Thy eternal Simple Essence other corn, and wine, and oil.

9.4.11

And with a loud cry of my heart I cried out in the next verse, O in peace, O for The Self-same! O what said he, I will lay me down and sleep, for who shall hinder us, when cometh to pass that saying which is written, Death is swallowed up in victory? And Thou surpassingly art the Self-same, Who art not changed; and in Thee is rest which forgetteth all toil, for there is none other with Thee, nor are we to seek those many other things, which are not what Thou art: but Thou, Lord, alone hast made me dwell in hope. I read, and kindled; nor found I what to do to those deaf and dead, of whom myself had been, a pestilent person, a bitter and a blind bawler against those writings, which are honied with the honey of heaven, and lightsome with Thine own light: and I was consumed with zeal at the enemies of this Scripture.

9.4.12

When shall I recall all which passed in those holy-days? Yet neither have I forgotten, nor will I pass over the severity of Thy scourge, and the wonderful swiftness of Thy mercy. Thou didst then torment me with pain in my teeth; which when it had come to such height that I could not speak, it came into my heart to desire all my friends present to pray for me to Thee, the God of all manner of health. And this I wrote on wax, and gave it them to read. Presently so soon as with humble devotion we had bowed our knees, that pain went away. But what pain? or how went it away? I was affrighted, O my Lord, my God; for from infancy I had never experienced the like. And the power of Thy Nod was deeply conveyed to me, and rejoicing in faith, I praised Thy Name. And that faith suffered me not to be at ease about my past sins, which were not yet forgiven me by Thy baptism.

9.5.13

The vintage-vacation ended, I gave notice to the Milanese to provide their scholars with another master to sell words to them; for that I had both made choice to serve Thee, and through my difficulty of breathing and pain in my chest was not equal to the Professorship. And by letters I signified to Thy Prelate, the holy man Ambrose, my former errors and present desires, begging his advice what of Thy Scriptures I had best read, to become readier and fitter for receiving so great grace. He recommended Isaiah the Prophet: I believe, because he above the rest is a more clear foreshower of the Gospel and of the calling of the Gentiles. But I, not understanding the first lesson in him, and imagining the whole to be like it, laid it by, to be resumed when better practised in our Lord's own words.

154 THE MEANING OF LIFE

9.6.14

Thence, when the time was come wherein I was to give in my name, we left the country and returned to Milan. It pleased Alypius also to be with me born again in Thee, being already clothed with the humility befitting Thy Sacraments; and a most valiant tamer of the body, so as, with unwonted venture, to wear the frozen ground of Italy with his bare feet. We joined with us the boy Adeodatus, born after the flesh, of my sin. Excellently hadst Thou made him. He was not quite fifteen, and in wit surpassed many grave and learned men. I confess unto Thee Thy gifts, O Lord my God, Creator of all, and abundantly able to reform our deformities: for I had no part in that boy, but the sin. For that we brought him up in Thy discipline, it was Thou, none else, had inspired us with it. I confess unto Thee Thy gifts. There is a book of ours entitled The Master; it is a dialogue between him and me. Thou knowest that all there ascribed to the person conversing with me were his ideas, in his sixteenth year. Much besides, and yet more admirable, I found in him. That talent struck awe into me. And who but Thou could be the workmaster of such wonders? Soon didst Thou take his life from the earth: and I now remember him without anxiety, fearing nothing for his childhood or youth, or his whole self. Him we joined with us, our contemporary in grace, to be brought up in Thy discipline.

And we were baptised, and anxiety for our past life vanished from us. Nor was I sated in those days with the wondrous sweetness of considering the depth of Thy counsels concerning the salvation of mankind. How did I weep, in Thy Hymns and Canticles, touched to the quick by the voices of Thy sweet-attuned Church! The voices flowed into mine ears, and the Truth distilled into my heart, whence the affections of my devotion overflowed, and tears ran down, and happy was I therein.

9.7.15

Not long had the Church of Milan begun to use this kind of consolation and exhortation, the brethren zealously joining with harmony of voice and hearts. For it was a year, or not much more, that Justina, mother to the Emperor Valentinian, a child, persecuted Thy servant Ambrose, in favour of her heresy, to which she was seduced by the Arians. The devout people kept watch in the Church, ready to die with their Bishop Thy servant. There my mother Thy handmaid, bearing a chief part of those anxieties and watchings, lived for prayer. We, yet unwarmed by the heat of Thy Spirit, still were stirred up by the sight of the amazed and disquieted city. Then it was first instituted that after the manner of the Eastern Churches, Hymns and Psalms should be sung, lest the people should wax faint through the tediousness of sorrow: and from that day to this the custom is retained, divers (yea, almost all) Thy congregations, throughout other parts of the world following herein.

CHRISTIAN AND ISLAMIC MODELS   155

9.7.16

Then didst Thou by a vision discover to Thy forenamed Bishop where the bodies of Gervasius and Protasius the martyrs lay hid (whom Thou hadst in Thy secret treasury stored uncorrupted so many years), whence Thou mightest seasonably produce them to repress the fury of a woman, but an Empress. For when they were discovered and dug up, and with due honour translated to the Ambrosian Basilica, not only they who were vexed with unclean spirits (the devils confessing themselves) were cured, but a certain man who had for many years been blind, a citizen, and well known to the city, asking and hearing the reason of the people's confused joy, sprang forth desiring his guide to lead him thither. Led thither, he begged to be allowed to touch with his handkerchief the bier of Thy saints, whose death is precious in Thy sight. Which when he had done, and put to his eyes, they were forthwith opened. Thence did the fame spread, thence Thy praises glowed, shone; thence the mind of that enemy, though not turned to the soundness of believing, was yet turned back from her fury of persecuting. Thanks to Thee, O my God. Whence and whither hast Thou thus led my remembrance, that I should confess these things also unto Thee? which great though they be, I had passed by in forgetfulness. And yet then, when the odour of Thy ointments was so fragrant, did we not run after Thee. Therefore did I more weep among the singing of Thy Hymns, formerly sighing after Thee, and at length breathing in Thee, as far as the breath may enter into this our house of grass.

9.8.17

Thou that makest men to dwell of one mind in one house, didst join with us Euodius also, a young man of our own city. Who being an officer of Court, was before us converted to Thee and baptised: and quitting his secular warfare, girded himself to Thine. We were together, about to dwell together in our devout purpose. We sought where we might serve Thee most usefully, and were together returning to Africa: whitherward being as far as Ostia, my mother departed this life. Much I omit, as hastening much. Receive my confessions and thanksgivings, O my God, for innumerable things whereof I am silent. But I will not omit whatsoever my soul would bring forth concerning that Thy handmaid, who brought me forth, both in the flesh, that I might be born to this temporal light, and in heart, that I might be born to Light eternal. Not her gifts, but Thine in her, would I speak of; for neither did she make nor educate herself. Thou createdst her; nor did her father and mother know what a one should come from them. And the sceptre of Thy Christ, the discipline of Thine only Son, in a Christian house, a good member of Thy Church, educated her in Thy fear. Yet for her good discipline was she wont to commend not so much her mother's diligence, as that of a certain decrepit maid-servant, who had carried her father when a child, as little ones used to be carried at the backs of elder girls. For which reason, and for her great age, and excellent conversation, was she, in that Christian family, well respected by its heads. Whence also the charge of her master's daughters was entrusted to her, to which she gave diligent heed, restraining them earnestly, when necessary, with a holy severity, and teaching them with a grave

156 THE MEANING OF LIFE

discretion. For, except at those hours wherein they were most temporately fed at their parents' table, she would not suffer them, though parched with thirst, to drink even water; preventing an evil custom, and adding this wholesome advice: "Ye drink water now, because you have not wine in your power; but when you come to be married, and be made mistresses of cellars and cupboards, you will scorn water, but the custom of drinking will abide." By this method of instruction, and the authority she had, she refrained the greediness of childhood, and moulded their very thirst to such an excellent moderation that what they should not, that they would not.

9.8.18

And yet (as Thy handmaid told me her son) there had crept upon her a love of wine. For when (as the manner was) she, as though a sober maiden, was bidden by her parents to draw wine out of the hogshead, holding the vessel under the opening, before she poured the wine into the flagon, she sipped a little with the tip of her lips; for more her instinctive feelings refused. For this she did, not out of any desire of drink, but out of the exuberance of youth, whereby it boils over in mirthful freaks, which in youthful spirits are wont to be kept under by the gravity of their elders. And thus by adding to that little, daily littles (for whoso despiseth little things shall fall by little and little), she had fallen into such a habit as greedily to drink off her little cup brim-full almost of wine. Where was then that discreet old woman, and that her earnest countermanding? Would aught avail against a secret disease, if Thy healing hand, O Lord, watched not over us? Father, mother, and governors absent, Thou present, who createdst, who callest, who also by those set over us, workest something towards the salvation of our souls, what didst Thou then, O my God? how didst Thou cure her? how heal her? didst Thou not out of another soul bring forth a hard and a sharp taunt, like a lancet out of Thy secret store, and with one touch remove all that foul stuff? For a maid-servant with whom she used to go to the cellar, falling to words (as it happens) with her little mistress, when alone with her, taunted her with this fault, with most bitter insult, calling her wine-bibber. With which taunt she, stung to the quick, saw the foulness of her fault, and instantly condemned and forsook it. As flattering friends pervert, so reproachful enemies mostly correct. Yet not what by them Thou doest, but what themselves purposed, dost Thou repay them. For she in her anger sought to vex her young mistress, not to amend her; and did it in private, either for that the time and place of the quarrel so found them; or lest herself also should have anger, for discovering it thus late. But Thou, Lord, Governor of all in heaven and earth, who turnest to Thy purposes the deepest currents, and the ruled turbulence of the tide of times, didst by the very unhealthiness of one soul heal another; lest any, when he observes this, should ascribe it to his own power, even when another, whom he wished to be reformed, is reformed through words of his.

9.9.19

CHRISTIAN AND ISLAMIC MODELS   157

Brought up thus modestly and soberly, and made subject rather by Thee to her parents, than by her parents to Thee, so soon as she was of marriageable age, being bestowed upon a husband, she served him as her lord; and did her diligence to win him unto Thee, preaching Thee unto him by her conversation; by which Thou ornamentedst her, making her reverently amiable, and admirable unto her husband. And she so endured the wronging of her bed as never to have any quarrel with her husband thereon. For she looked for Thy mercy upon him, that believing in Thee, he might be made chaste. But besides this, he was fervid, as in his affections, so in anger: but she had learnt not to resist an angry husband, not in deed only, but not even in word. Only when he was smoothed and tranquil, and in a temper to receive it, she would give an account of her actions, if haply he had overhastily taken offence. In a word, while many matrons, who had milder husbands, yet bore even in their faces marks of shame, would in familiar talk blame their husbands' lives, she would blame their tongues, giving them, as in jest, earnest advice: "That from the time they heard the marriage writings read to them, they should account them as indentures, whereby they were made servants; and so, remembering their condition, ought not to set themselves up against their lords." And when they, knowing what a choleric husband she endured, marvelled that it had never been heard, nor by any token perceived, that Patricius had beaten his wife, or that there had been any domestic difference between them, even for one day, and confidentially asking the reason, she taught them her practice above mentioned. Those wives who observed it found the good, and returned thanks; those who observed it not, found no relief, and suffered.

9.9.20

Her mother-in-law also, at first by whisperings of evil servants incensed against her, she so overcame by observance and persevering endurance and meekness, that she of her own accord discovered to her son the meddling tongues whereby the domestic peace betwixt her and her daughter-in-law had been disturbed, asking him to correct them. Then, when in compliance with his mother, and for the well-ordering of the family, he had with stripes corrected those discovered, at her will who had discovered them, she promised the like reward to any who, to please her, should speak ill of her daughter-in-law to her: and none now venturing, they lived together with a remarkable sweetness of mutual kindness.

9.9.21

This great gift also thou bestowedst, O my God, my mercy, upon that good handmaid of Thine, in whose womb Thou createdst me, that between any disagreeing and discordant parties where she was able, she showed herself such a peacemaker, that hearing on both sides most bitter things, such as swelling and indigested choler uses to break out into, when the crudities of enmities are breathed out in sour discourses to a present friend against an absent enemy, she never would disclose aught of the one unto the other, but what might tend to their reconcilement.

158 THE MEANING OF LIFE

A small good this might appear to me, did I not to my grief know numberless persons, who through some horrible and wide-spreading contagion of sin, not only disclose to persons mutually angered things said in anger, but add withal things never spoken, whereas to humane humanity, it ought to seem a light thing not to toment or increase ill will by ill words, unless one study withal by good words to quench it. Such was she, Thyself, her most inward Instructor, teaching her in the school of the heart.

9.9.22

Finally, her own husband, towards the very end of his earthly life, did she gain unto Thee; nor had she to complain of that in him as a believer, which before he was a believer she had borne from him. She was also the servant of Thy servants; whosoever of them knew her, did in her much praise and honour and love Thee; for that through the witness of the fruits of a holy conversation they perceived Thy presence in her heart. For she had been the wife of one man, had requited her parents, had governed her house piously, was well reported of for good works, had brought up children, so often travailing in birth of them, as she saw them swerving from Thee. Lastly, of all of us Thy servants, O Lord (whom on occasion of Thy own gift Thou sufferest to speak), us, who before her sleeping in Thee lived united together, having received the grace of Thy baptism, did she so take care of, as though she had been mother of us all; so served us, as though she had been child to us all.

9.10.23.

The day now approaching whereon she was to depart this life (which day Thou well knewest, we knew not), it came to pass, Thyself, as I believe, by Thy secret ways so ordering it, that she and I stood alone, leaning in a certain window, which looked into the garden of the house where we now lay, at Ostia; where removed from the din of men, we were recruiting from the fatigues of a long journey, for the voyage. We were discoursing then together, alone, very sweetly; and forgetting those things which are behind, and reaching forth unto those things which are before, we were enquiring between ourselves in the presence of the Truth, which Thou art, of what sort the eternal life of the saints was to be, which eye hath not seen, nor ear heard, nor hath it entered into the heart of man. But yet we gasped with the mouth of our heart, after those heavenly streams of Thy fountain, the fountain of life, which is with Thee; that being bedewed thence according to our capacity, we might in some sort meditate upon so high a mystery.

9.10.24

And when our discourse was brought to that point, that the very highest delight of the earthly senses, in the very purest material light, was, in respect of the sweetness of that life, not only not worthy of comparison, but not even of mention; we raising up ourselves with a more glowing

CHRISTIAN AND ISLAMIC MODELS 159

affection towards the "Self-same," did by degrees pass through all things bodily, even the very heaven whence sun and moon and stars shine upon the earth; yea, we were soaring higher yet, by inward musing, and discourse, and admiring of Thy works; and we came to our own minds, and went beyond them, that we might arrive at that region of never-failing plenty, where Thou feedest Israel for ever with the food of truth, and where life is the Wisdom by whom all these things are made, and what have been, and what shall be, and she is not made, but is, as she hath been, and so shall she be ever; yea rather, to "have been," and "hereafter to be," are not in her, but only "to be," seeing she is eternal. For to "have been," and to "be hereafter," are not eternal. And while we were discoursing and panting after her, we slightly touched on her with the whole effort of our heart; and we sighed, and there we leave bound the first fruits of the Spirit; and returned to vocal expressions of our mouth, where the word spoken has beginning and end. And what is like unto Thy Word, our Lord, who endureth in Himself without becoming old, and maketh all things new?

9.10.25

We were saying then: If to any the tumult of the flesh were hushed, hushed the images of earth, and waters, and air, hushed also the pole of heaven, yea the very soul be hushed to herself, and by not thinking on self surmount self, hushed all dreams and imaginary revelations, every tongue and every sign, and whatsoever exists only in transition, since if any could hear, all these say, We made not ourselves, but He made us that abideth for ever- If then having uttered this, they too should be hushed, having roused only our ears to Him who made them, and He alone speak, not by them but by Himself, that we may hear His Word, not through any tongue of flesh, nor Angel's voice, nor sound of thunder, nor in the dark riddle of a similitude, but might hear Whom in these things we love, might hear His Very Self without these (as we two now strained ourselves, and in swift thought touched on that Eternal Wisdom which abideth over all); -could this be continued on, and other visions of kind far unlike be withdrawn, and this one ravish, and absorb, and wrap up its beholder amid these inward joys, so that life might be for ever like that one moment of understanding which now we sighed after; were not this, Enter into thy Master's joy? And when shall that be? When we shall all rise again, though we shall not all be changed?

9.10.26

Such things was I speaking, and even if not in this very manner, and these same words, yet, Lord, Thou knowest that in that day when we were speaking of these things, and this world with all its delights became, as we spake, contemptible to us, my mother said, "Son, for mine own part I have no further delight in any thing in this life. What I do here any longer, and to what I am here, I know not, now that my hopes in this world are accomplished. One thing there was for which I desired to linger for a while in this life, that I might see thee a Catholic Christian before I died. My God hath done this for me more abundantly, that I should now see thee withal, despising earthly happiness, become His servant: what do I here?"

160 THE MEANING OF LIFE

9.11.27

What answer I made her unto these things, I remember not. For scarce five days after, or not much more, she fell sick of a fever; and in that sickness one day she fell into a swoon, and was for a while withdrawn from these visible things. We hastened round her; but she was soon brought back to her senses; and looking on me and my brother standing by her, said to us enquiringly, "Where was I?" And then looking fixedly on us, with grief amazed: "Here," saith she, "shall you bury your mother." I held my peace and refrained weeping; but my brother spake something, wishing for her, as the happier lot, that she might die, not in a strange place, but in her own land. Whereat, she with anxious look, checking him with her eyes, for that he still savoured such things, and then looking upon me: "Behold," saith she, "what he saith": and soon after to us both, "Lay," she saith, "this body any where; let not the care for that any way disquiet you: this only I request, that you would remember me at the Lord's altar, wherever you be." And having delivered this sentiment in what words she could, she held her peace, being exercised by her growing sickness.

9.11.28

But I, considering Thy gifts, Thou unseen God, which Thou instillest into the hearts of Thy faithful ones, whence wondrous fruits do spring, did rejoice and give thanks to Thee, recalling what I before knew, how careful and anxious she had ever been as to her place of burial, which she had provided and prepared for herself by the body of her husband. For because they had lived in great harmony together, she also wished (so little can the human mind embrace things divine) to have this addition to that happiness, and to have it remembered among men, that after her pilgrimage beyond the seas, what was earthly of this united pair had been permitted to be united beneath the same earth. But when this emptiness had through the fulness of Thy goodness begun to cease in her heart, I knew not, and rejoiced admiring what she had so disclosed to me; though indeed in that our discourse also in the window, when she said, "What do I here any longer?" there appeared no desire of dying in her own country. I heard afterwards also, that when we were now at Ostia, she with a mother's confidence, when I was absent, one day discoursed with certain of my friends about the contempt of this life, and the blessing of death: and when they were amazed at such courage which Thou hadst given to a woman, and asked, "Whether she were not afraid to leave her body so far from her own city?" she replied, "Nothing is far to God; nor was it to be feared lest at the end of the world, He should not recognise whence He were to raise me up." On the ninth day then of her sickness, and the fifty--sixth year of her age, and the three-and-thirtieth of mine, was that religious and holy soul freed from the body.

9.12.29

CHRISTIAN AND ISLAMIC MODELS 161

I closed her eyes; and there flowed withal a mighty sorrow into my heart, which was overflowing into tears; mine eyes at the same time, by the violent command of my mind, drank up their fountain wholly dry; and woe was me in such a strife! But when she breathed her last, the boy Adeodatus burst out into a loud lament; then, checked by us all, held his peace. In like manner also a childish feeling in me, which was, through my heart's youthful voice, finding its vent in weeping, was checked and silenced. For we thought it not fitting to solemnise that funeral with tearful lament, and groanings; for thereby do they for the most part express grief for the departed, as though unhappy, or altogether dead; whereas she was neither unhappy in her death, nor altogether dead. Of this we were assured on good grounds, the testimony of her good conversation and her faith unfeigned.

9.12.30

What then was it which did grievously pain me within, but a fresh wound wrought through the sudden wrench of that most sweet and dear custom of living together? I joyed indeed in her testimony, when, in that her last sickness, mingling her endearments with my acts of duty, she called me "dutiful," and mentioned, with great affection of love, that she never had heard any harsh or reproachful sound uttered by my mouth against her. But yet, O my God, Who madest us, what comparison is there betwixt that honour that I paid to her, and her slavery for me? Being then forsaken of so great comfort in her, my soul was wounded, and that life rent asunder as it were, which, of hers and mine together, had been made but one.

9.12.31

The boy then being stilled from weeping, Euodius took up the Psalter, and began to sing, our whole house answering him, the Psalm, I will sing of mercy and judgments to Thee, O Lord. But hearing what we were doing, many brethren and religious women came together; and whilst they (whose office it was) made ready for the burial, as the manner is, I (in a part of the house, where I might properly), together with those who thought not fit to leave me, discoursed upon something fitting the time; and by this balm of truth assuaged that torment, known to Thee, they unknowing and listening intently, and conceiving me to be without all sense of sorrow. But in Thy ears, where none of them heard, I blamed the weakness of my feelings, and refrained my flood of grief, which gave way a little unto me; but again came, as with a tide, yet not so as to burst out into tears, nor to change of countenance; still I knew what I was keeping down in my heart. And being very much displeased that these human things had such power over me, which in the due order and appointment of our natural condition must needs come to pass, with a new grief I grieved for my grief, and was thus worn by a double sorrow.

9.12.32

162 THE MEANING OF LIFE

And behold, the corpse was carried to the burial; we went and returned without tears. For neither in those prayers which we poured forth unto Thee, when the Sacrifice of our ransom was offered for her, when now the corpse was by the grave's side, as the manner there is, previous to its being laid therein, did I weep even during those prayers; yet was I the whole day in secret heavily sad, and with troubled mind prayed Thee, as I could, to heal my sorrow, yet Thou didst not; impressing, I believe, upon my memory by this one instance, how strong is the bond of all habit, even upon a soul, which now feeds upon no deceiving Word. It seemed also good to me to go and bathe, having heard that the bath had its name (balneum) from the Greek Balaneion for that it drives sadness from the mind. And this also I confess unto Thy mercy, Father of the fatherless, that I bathed, and was the same as before I bathed. For the bitterness of sorrow could not exude out of my heart. Then I slept, and woke up again, and found my grief not a little softened; and as I was alone in my bed, I remembered those true verses of Thy Ambrose. For Thou art the –

"Maker of all, the Lord,
And Ruler of the height,
Who, robing day in light, hast poured
Soft slumbers o'er the night,
That to our limbs the power
Of toil may be renew'd,
And hearts be rais'd that sink and cower,
And sorrows be subdu'd." -

9.12.33

And then by little and little I recovered my former thoughts of Thy handmaid, her holy conversation towards Thee, her holy tenderness and observance towards us, whereof I was suddenly deprived: and I was minded to weep in Thy sight, for her and for myself, in her behalf and in my own. And I gave way to the tears which I before restrained, to overflow as much as they desired; reposing my heart upon them; and it found rest in them, for it was in Thy ears, not in those of man, who would have scornfully interpreted my weeping. And now, Lord, in writing I confess it unto Thee. Read it, who will, and interpret it, how he will: and if he finds sin therein, that I wept my mother for a small portion of an hour (the mother who for the time was dead to mine eyes, who had for many years wept for me that I might live in Thine eyes), let him not deride me; but rather, if he be one of large charity, let him weep himself for my sins unto Thee, the Father of all the brethren of Thy Christ.

9.13.34

But now, with a heart cured of that wound, wherein it might seem blameworthy for an earthly feeling, I pour out unto Thee, our God, in behalf of that Thy handmaid, a far different kind of tears, flowing from a spirit shaken by the thoughts of the dangers of every soul that dieth in Adam. And although she having been quickened in Christ, even before her release from the flesh, had lived to the praise of Thy name for her faith and conversation; yet dare I not say that from what time Thou regeneratedst her by baptism, no word issued from her mouth against Thy Commandment. Thy Son, the Truth, hath said, Whosoever shall say unto his brother, Thou fool, shall be in danger of hell fire. And woe be even unto the commendable life of men, if, laying aside mercy, Thou shouldest examine it. But because Thou art not extreme in enquiring after sins, we confidently hope to find some place with Thee. But whosoever reckons up his real merits to Thee, what reckons he up to Thee but Thine own gifts? O that men would know themselves to be men; and that he that glorieth would glory in the Lord.

9.13.35

I therefore, O my Praise and my Life, God of my heart, laying aside for a while her good deeds, for which I give thanks to Thee with joy, do now beseech Thee for the sins of my mother. Hearken unto me, I entreat Thee, by the Medicine of our wounds, Who hung upon the tree, and now sitting at Thy right hand maketh intercession to Thee for us. I know that she dealt mercifully, and from her heart forgave her debtors their debts; do Thou also forgive her debts, whatever she may have contracted in so many years, since the water of salvation. Forgive her, Lord, forgive, I beseech Thee; enter not into judgment with her. Let Thy mercy be exalted above Thy justice, since Thy words are true, and Thou hast promised mercy unto the merciful; which Thou gavest them to be, who wilt have mercy on whom Thou wilt have mercy; and wilt have compassion on whom Thou hast had compassion.

9.13.36

And, I believe, Thou hast already done what I ask; but accept, O Lord, the free-will offerings of my mouth. For she, the day of her dissolution now at hand, took no thought to have her body sumptuously wound up, or embalmed with spices; nor desired she a choice monument, or to be buried in her own land. These things she enjoined us not; but desired only to have her name commemorated at Thy Altar, which she had served without intermission of one day: whence she knew the holy Sacrifice to be dispensed, by which the hand-writing that was against us is blotted out; through which the enemy was triumphed over, who summing up our offences, and seeking what to lay to our charge, found nothing in Him, in Whom we conquer. Who shall restore to Him the innocent blood? Who repay Him the price wherewith He bought us, and so take us from Him? Unto the Sacrament of which our ransom, Thy handmaid bound her soul by the bond of faith. Let none sever her from Thy protection: let neither the lion nor the dragon interpose himself by force or fraud. For she will not answer that she owes nothing, lest she be convicted and seized by the crafty accuser: but she will answer that her sins are forgiven her by Him, to Whom none can repay that price which He, Who owed nothing, paid for us.

9.13.37

May she rest then in peace with the husband before and after whom she had never any; whom she obeyed, with patience bringing forth fruit unto Thee, that she might win him also unto Thee. And inspire, O Lord my God, inspire Thy servants my brethren, Thy sons my masters, whom with voice, and heart, and pen I serve, that so many as shall read these Confessions, may at Thy Altar remember Monnica Thy handmaid, with Patricius, her sometimes husband, by whose bodies Thou broughtest me into this life, how I know not. May they with devout affection remember my parents in this transitory light, my brethren under Thee our Father in our Catholic Mother, and my fellow-citizens in that eternal Jerusalem which Thy pilgrim people sigheth after from their Exodus, even unto their return thither. That so my mother's last request of me, may through my confessions, more than through my prayers, be, through the prayers of many, more abundantly fulfilled to her.

CHAPTER 7

MIDDLE AGES AND RENAISSANCE

In the millennium to follow Augustine the Islamic world conquered and incorporated much of the Byzantine Empire. Through this time many monastic and mystic cultures flourished within both Islamic and Christian traditions throughout the region. One of the most significant was the Islamic sect of Sufi mystics (Levenson & Khilwati, 1999). This group of mystics incorporated ideas of the human soul and models of personality. A significant contribution was the idea of the Enneagram[60] where the nine key personality traits are balanced and provide the form of how a person will live within the Islamic mythic structure of existence (Hermanson, 2000). As such, the Islamic model for a meaningful life (in the Sufi tradition at least) was one of living within the mythic structure of "submitting to God" while finding one's niche through the balancing and counter-balancing of personality traits (Edwards, 1991). Within the 17th century of the Common Era we finally have the emergence of many strong thinkers for the nature of humanity and the way that meaning of, or in, life is formed. For Descartes, the mythic construct in which life was to be lived must be derived by reason. Though many may argue that Descartes was simply a product of his environment within Christendom, he did construct a very logical mythic schema within which to develop a model for meaning (Chung, 1999).

With the continued pressure of the Turkish Empire upon Western Europe in the 15th and 16th centuries there was a mass exodus of classically trained scholars from the east to the west. With this influx of excellent scholarship a renewed sense of vigour to seek understanding rather than relying upon doctrine crept into the Holy Roman Empire. One scholar was profoundly influenced by this new influx of thought and in turn profoundly changed the face of academia in the west— Erasmus of Rotterdam. A Dutch scholar, his attitudes seemed to echo those of William Ockham, who over a century earlier argued for breaking down complex constructs to get at the grain of truth. Erasmus himself called for an approach to education that could be summarized as *Ad Fontus* (Back to the Sources). This meant, simply, do not blindly trust what others say about an issue, go back to the basics and draw your own conclusions. (See a wonderful example of the depth and humour of Erasmus and his view on issues such as "folly" in this chapter's Read for Yourself Section).

Such a simple proposition had profound effects upon the entire history of Europe, for it was such education that inspired students like Martin Luther, and later John Calvin, to go back to the biblical sources and question the teachings of the Church. Such protestant movements also inspired universities to begin to break with doctrine (though it took over a century to do so) and

---

60 The term Ennea is Greek for "Nine" which indicates the number of personality traits that are to be balanced within an individual in order to provide the expression of the person's life.

166   THE MEANING OF LIFE

seek understanding. It was such a model of thinking that inspired Descartes to seek the essence of the mind/body/soul connection (which he concluded could be found in the Pineal gland of the brain).

Protestant Reformation/ The Refined Mythic Definition of the Mind

Following the teachings of Martin Luther and later John Calvin (and to a later and lesser extent, Ulrich Zwingli) the mythic structure for understanding human existence and the issue of mental health was refined to such a point within the 16th century that it set the stage for forming much of modern Europe. The Protestant declaration to Emperor Charles V and the presentation of the Augsburg Confession (and later its Confession/defence) did much to clarify the broken state of the human mind and its ultimate existential hope in God's loving attitude toward humanity:

"Our churches also teach that since the fall of Adam all men who are propagated according to nature are born in sin. That is to say, they are without fear of God, are without trust in god, and are concupiscent. And this disease or vice of origin is truly sin, which even now damns and brings eternal death on those who are not born again through baptism and the Holy Spirit."

- Apology of the Augsburg Confession – Article 2 – Original Sin.

Following the model of Socrates, Descartes began by doubting all present knowledge and models (Cottingham, 2002)[61]. The question as to whether he could be deceived was the basis of his "first philosophy" (Descartes, 1990) where he notes that doubting and even the awareness of being deceived secure the existence of a doubter and thereby affirms that at the very least, he exists. On the basis of his own existence he also affirms the existence of a perfect idea (namely God), for none other than God could be the source of the idea of God. Through his investigation

---

61 While Descartes goes through the Socratic process of acknowledging ignorance he does still believe in "belief". Descartes, throughout his writings, seems to acknowledge that "belief" is a central human function that we cannot avoid. His goal however is to identify and rid oneself of the "false beliefs" that skew our understanding of reality. Therefore Descartes seems to operate within a mythic structure that is constantly being reevaluated in the light of his studies. For according to Descartes basic mythic substructure, "sin" can infect knowledge and belief, skewing its focus away from the truth (Cottingham, 2002).

MIDDLE AGES AND RENAISSANCE   167

Descartes notes that people exist in the realms of the spirit and the mechanistic and therefore meaning must draw from the idea (the spirit) and be expressed in the mechanistic (the action).

Similar to Descartes, another 17th century thinker, Baruch Spinoza, expresses a view strikingly similar to the ancient west Semitic notions (Steinberg, 1998). This of course is not surprising considering Spinoza's Jewish ethnicity. However, his own community rejected him since he argued for the natural integration of the mythic structure in the material expression of the universe. Therefore, the idea of "god" was not separate from the material world as had become popular in religious thought[62]; rather, "god" was part of the physical and intimately linked with it. Therefore meaning only came from action that was in line with nature (Curley, 1985). Due to his views Spinoza was considered an atheist, though in truth his understanding of human psychology and human meaning was totally in line with the most ancient of religions (Segal, 2000).

Finally, in the late 1600's we see the emergence of the study of thought processes from a different perspective in the likes of John Locke (1632-1704). The unique approach of Locke was that he was not a great philosopher or theologian, like those who historically dealt with such issues of the mind. In stark contrast to René Descartes or Baruch Spinoza, Locke was in fact a physician by trade and occasionally a lab assistant to Sir Isaac Newton. In his straight-forward manner Locke pointed out that the mind functions by a mythic process of representations of objects. In essence, mental processes are *logo* representations of objects. Our minds fill in the gaps of our knowledge according to the mental picture we create and therefore no one really understands an object for human knowledge is really of two basic types: 1. Ideas/stories we form about objects 2. The processes we use to form stories and representations.

It was John Locke who coined the phrase *Tabula Rasa* (meaning: an empty slate) as a way of understanding the mind. The mind for Locke was an empty sheet upon which experience wrote its story and only after a significant amount of the basic story is written are we able to engage that story as our own personal mental thought processes. As a result, Locke believed that the philosophical ideas of free will were fundamentally wrong.

According to Locke, to ask whether or not we have free will is asking the wrong question. Locke pointed out that the proper question is "Are we free?" In essence, Locke argued that we believe ourselves to be free when we *can do what we want*, but we do not consciously will our own desires. Therefore Locke offered the simple statement, "We are slaves to our desires, but free to serve them" as his great philosophical statement on free will. Based upon this concept Locke therefore believed that the way to psychological wellness and satisfaction in life was the pursuit of happiness. As long as we are happy (getting what we want) we feel free and do not worry

---

62 Spinoza clearly sees humanity as an integration of the "idea" and "physical" and the intricate psychosomatic relationship between the mind and body. Indeed, relating to emotions and the existence of the person Spinoza argues that the mind and body are of the same substance. In his larger mythic structure Spinoza often refers to the organizing principles (ideas) and the physical as interchangeably "god" and "nature" not bothering to acknowledge any difference between the two. The essential integration of these aspects of nature and indeed of humanness is then simply a natural step along the line of Descartes (Curley, 1985).

about the slavery of our will. However even Locke could not be extricated from the mythic stories that defined his reality and concluded that in the end the self ought to seek to limit its desires for in the end we die and are judged by God ... and we will only be happy if we are in heaven.

READ AND DECIDE FOR YOURSELF:

Excerpts from:

IN PRAISE OF FOLLY
(ERASMUS OF ROTTERDAM)

DESCARTES' MEDITATIONS ON FIRST PHILOSOPHY
(BANACH'S OUTLINE)

BARUCH SPINOZA

JOHN LOCKE

THE CRITIQUE OF PRACTICAL REASON
(IMMANUEL KANT)

IN PRAISE OF FOLLY

Erasmus of Rotterdam

INTRODUCTION

To his friend THOMAS MORE, health:

As I was coming awhile since out of Italy for England, that I might not waste all that time I was to sit on horseback in foolish and illiterate fables, I chose rather one while to revolve with myself something of our common studies, and other while to enjoy the remembrance of my friends, of whom I left here some no less learned than pleasant. Among these you, my More, came first in my mind, whose memory, though absent yourself, gives me such delight in my absence, as when present with you I ever found in your company; than which, let me perish if in all my life I ever met with anything more delectable. And therefore, being satisfied that something was to be done, and that that time was no wise proper for any serious matter, I resolved to make some sport with the praise of folly. But who the devil put that in your head? you'll say. The first thing was your surname of More, which comes so near the word Moriae (folly) as you are far from the thing. And that you are so, all the world will cleat you. In the next place, I conceived this exercise of wit would not be least approved by you; inasmuch as you are wont to be delighted with such kind of mirth, that is to say, neither unlearned, if I am not mistaken, not altogether insipid, and in the whole course of your life have played the part of a Democtitus. And though such is the excellence of your judgment that it was even contrary to that of the people's, yet such is your incredible ability and sweetness of temper that you both can and delight to carry yourself to all men a man of all hours. Wherefore you will not only with good will accept this small declamation, but take upon you the defense of it, for as much as being dedicated to you, it is now no longer mine but yours. But perhaps there will not be wanting some wranglers that may cavil and charge me, partly that these toys are lighter than may become a divine, and partly more biting than may beseem the modesty of a Christian, and consequently exclaim that I resemble the ancient comedy, or another Lucian, and snarl at everything. But I would have them whom the lightness or foolery of the argument may offend to consider that mine is not the first of this kind, but the same thing that has been often practiced even by great authors: when Homer, so many ages since, did the like with the battle of frogs and mice; Virgil, with the gnat and puddings; Ovid, with the nut; when Polycrates and his corrector Isocrates extolled tyranny; Glauco, injustice; Favorinus, deformity and the quartan ague; Synescius, baldness; Lucian, the fly and flattery; when Seneca made such sport with Claudius' canonizations; Plutarch, with his dialogue between Ulysses and Gryllus; Lucian and Apuleius, with the ass; and some other, I know not who, with the hog that made his last will and testament, of which also even St. Jerome makes mention. And therefore if they please, let them suppose I played at tables for my diversion, or if they had rather have it so, that I rode on a hobbyhorse. For what injustice is it that when we allow every course of life its recreation, that study only should have none? Especially when such toys are not without their serious matter, and foolery is so handled that the reader that is not altogether thick-skulled may reap more benefit from it than from some men's crabbish and specious arguments. As when one, with long study and great pains, patches many pieces together on the praise of rhetoric or philosophy; another makes a panegyric to a prince; another encourages him to a war against the Turks; another tells you what will become of the world after himself is dead; and another finds out some new device for the better ordering of goat's wool: for as nothing is more trifling than to treat of serious matters triflingly, so nothing carries a better grace than so to discourse of trifles as a man may seem to have intended them least. For my own part, let other men judge of what I have written; though yet, unless an overweening opinion of myself may have made me blind in my own cause, I have praised folly, but not altogether foolishly. And now to say somewhat to that other cavil, of biting. This liberty was ever permitted to all men's wits, to make their smart, witty reflections on the common errors of mankind, and that too without offense, as long as this liberty does not run into licentiousness; which makes me the more admire the tender ears of the men of this age, that can away with solemn titles. No, you'll meet with some so preposterously religious that they will sooner endure the broadest scoffs even against Christ himself than hear the Pope or a prince be touched in the least, especially if it be anything that concerns their profit; whereas he that so taxes the lives of men, without naming anyone in particular, whither, I pray, may he be said to bite, or rather to teach and admonish? Or otherwise, I beseech you, under how many notions do I tax myself? Besides, he that spares no sort of men cannot be said to be angry with anyone in particular, but the vices of all. And therefore, if there shall happen to be anyone that shall say he is hit, he will but discover either his guilt or fear. Saint Jerome sported in this kind with more freedom and greater sharpness, not sparing sometimes men's very name. But I, besides that I have wholly avoided it, I have so moderated my style that the understanding reader will easily perceive my endeavors herein were rather to make mirth than bite. Nor have I, after the example of Juvenal, raked up that forgotten sink of filth and ribaldry, but laid before you things rather ridiculous than dishonest. And now, if there be anyone that is yet dissatisfied, let him at least remember that it is no dishonor to be discommended by Folly; and having brought her in speaking, it was but fit that I kept up the character of the person. But why do I run over these things to you, a person so excellent an advocate that no man better defends his client, though the cause many times be none of the best? Farewell, my best disputant More, and stoutly defend your Moriae.

THE PRAISE OF FOLLY

An oration, of feigned matter, spoken by Folly in her own person

At what rate so ever the world talks of me (for I am not ignorant what an ill report Folly has got, even among the most foolish), yet that I am that she, that only she, whose deity recreates both gods and men, even this is a sufficient argument, that I no sooner stepped up to speak to this full assembly than all your faces put on a kind of new and unwonted pleasantness. So suddenly have

172 THE MEANING OF LIFE

you cleared your brows, and with so frolic and hearty a laughter given me your applause, that in truth as many of you as I behold on every side of me seem to me no less than Homer's gods drunk with nectar and nepenthe; whereas before, you sat as lumpish and pensive as if you had come from consulting an oracle. And as it usually happens when the sun begins to show his beams, or when after a sharp winter the spring breathes afresh on the earth, all things immediately get a new face, new color, and recover as it were a certain kind of youth again: in like manner by but beholding me you have in an instant gotten another kind of countenance; and so what the otherwise great rhetoricians with their tedious and long-studied orations can hardly effect, to wit, to remove the trouble of the mind, I have done it at once with my single look.

But if you ask me why I appear before you in this strange dress, be pleased to lend me your ears, and I'll tell you; not those ears, I mean, you carry to church, but abroad with you, such as you are wont to prick up to jugglers, fools, and buffoons, and such as our friend Midas once gave to Pan. For I am disposed awhile to play the sophist with you; not of their sort who nowadays boozle young men's heads with certain empty notions and curious trifles, yet teach them nothing but a more than womanish obstinacy of scolding: but I'll imitate those ancients who, that they might the better avoid that infamous appellation of sophi or wise chose rather to be called sophists. Their business was to celebrate the praises of the gods and valiant men. And the like encomium shall you hear from me, but neither of Hercules nor Solon, but my own dear self, that is to say, Folly. Nor do I esteem a rush that call it a foolish and insolent thing to praise one's self. Be it as foolish as they would make it, so they confess it proper: and what can be more than that Folly be her own trumpet? For who can set me out better than myself, unless perhaps I could be better known to another than to myself ? Though yet I think it somewhat more modest than the general practice of our nobles and wise men who, throwing away all shame, hire some flattering orator or lying poet from whose mouth they may hear their praises, that is to say, mere lies; and yet, composing themselves with a seeming modesty, spread out their peacock's plumes and erect their crests, while this impudent flatterer equals a man of nothing to the gods and proposes him as an absolute pattern of all virtue that's wholly a stranger to it, sets out a pitiful jay in other's feathers, washes the blackamoor white, and lastly swells a gnat to an elephant. In short, I will follow that old proverb that says, "He may lawfully praise himself that lives far from neighbors." Though, by the way, I cannot but wonder at the ingratitude, shall I say, or negligence of men who, notwithstanding they honor me in the first place and are willing enough to confess my bounty, yet not one of them for these so many ages has there been who in some thankful oration has set out the praises of Folly; when yet there has not wanted them whose elaborate endeavors have extolled tyrants, agues, flies, baldness, and such other pests of nature, to their own loss of both time and sleep. And now you shall hear from me a plain extemporary speech, but so much the truer. Nor would I have you think it like the rest of orators, made for the ostentation of wit; for these, as you know, when they have been beating their heads some thirty years about an oration and at last perhaps produce somewhat that was never their own, shall yet swear they composed it in three days, and that too for diversion: whereas I ever liked it best to speak whatever came first out.

MIDDLE AGES AND RENAISSANCE   173

But let none of you expect from me that after the manner of rhetoricians I should go about to define what I am, much less use any division; for I hold it equally unlucky to circumscribe her whose deity is universal, or make the least division in that worship about which everything is so generally agreed. Or to what purpose, think you, should I describe myself when I am here present before you, and you behold me speaking? For I am, as you see, that true and only giver of wealth whom the Greeks call Moria, the Latins Stultitia, and our plain English Folly. Or what need was there to have said so much, as if my very looks were not sufficient to inform you who I am? Or as if any man, mistaking me for wisdom, could not at first sight convince himself by my face the true index of my mind? I am no counterfeit, nor do I carry one thing in my looks and an other in my breast. No, I am in every respect so like myself that neither can they dissemble me who arrogate to themselves the appearance and title of wise men and walk like asses in scarlet hoods, though after all their hypocrisy Midas' ears will discover their master. A most ungrateful generation of men that, when they are wholly given up to my party, are yet publicly ashamed of the name, as taking it for a reproach; for which cause, since in truth they are morotatoi, fools, and yet would appear to the world to be wise men and Thales, we'll even call them morosophous, wise fools.

Nor will it be amiss also to imitate the rhetoricians of our times, who think themselves in a manner gods if like horse leeches they can but appear to be double-tongued, and believe they have done a mighty act if in their Latin orations they can but shuffle in some ends of Greek like mosaic work, though altogether by head and shoulders and less to the purpose. And if they want hard words, they run over some worm-eaten manuscript and pick out half a dozen of the most old and obsolete to confound their reader, believing, no doubt, that they that understand their meaning will like it the better, out its particular grace; for if there happen to be any mote ambitious than others, they may give their applause with a smile, and, like the ass, shake their ears, that they may be thought to understand more than the rest of their neighbors.

But to come to the purpose: I have given you my name, but what epithet shall I add? What but that of the most foolish? For by what more proper name can so great a goddess as Folly be known to her disciples? And because it is not alike known to all from what stock I am sprung, with the Muses' good leave I'll do my endeavor to satisfy you. But yet neither the first Chaos, Orcus, Saturn, or Japhet, nor any of those threadbare, musty gods were my father, but Plutus, Riches; that only he, that is, in spite of Hesiod, Homer, nay and Jupiter himself, divum pater atque hominum rex, the father of gods and men, at whose single beck, as heretofore, so at present, all things sacred and profane are turned topsy-turvy. According to whose pleasure war, peace, empire, counsels, judgments, assemblies, wedlocks, bargains, leagues, laws, arts, all things light or serious--I want breath--in short, all the public and private business of mankind is governed; without whose help all that herd of gods of the poets' making, and those few of the better sort of the rest, either would not be at all, or if they were, they would be but such as live at home and keep a poor house to themselves. And to whomsoever he's an enemy, 'tis not Pallas herself that can befriend him; as on the contrary he whom he favors may lead Jupiter and his thunder in a string. This is my father and in him I glory. Nor did he produce me from his brain, as Jupiter that

174 THE MEANING OF LIFE

sour and ill-looked Pallas; but of that lovely nymph called Youth, the most beautiful and galliard of all the rest. Not was I, like that limping blacksmith, begot in the sad and irksome bonds of matrimony. Yet, mistake me not, 'twas not that blind and decrepit Plutus in Aristophanes that got me, but such as he was in his full strength and pride of youth; and not that only, but at such a time when he had been well heated with nectar, of which he had, at one of the banquets of the gods, taken a dose extraordinary.

And as to the place of my birth, forasmuch as nowadays that is looked upon as a main point of nobility, it was neither, like Apollo's, in the floating Delos, nor Venus-like on the rolling sea, nor in any of blind Homer's as blind caves: but in the Fortunate Islands, where all things grew without plowing or sowing; where neither labor, nor old age, nor disease was ever heard of; and in whose fields neither daffodil, mallows, onions, beans, and such contemptible things would ever grow, but, on the contrary, rue, angelica, bugloss, marjoram, trefoils, roses, violets, lilies, and all the gardens of Adonis invite both your sight and your smelling. And being thus born, I did not begin the world, as other children are wont, with crying; but straight perched up and smiled on my mother. Nor do I envy to the great Jupiter the goat, his nurse, forasmuch as I was suckled by two jolly nymphs, to wit, Drunkenness, the daughter of Bacchus, and Ignorance, of Pan. And as for such my companions and followers as you perceive about me, if you have a mind to know who they are, you are not like to be the wiser for me, unless it be in Greek: this here, which you observe with that proud cast of her eye, is Philautia, Self-love; she with the smiling countenance, that is ever and anon clapping her hands, is Kolakia, Flattery; she that looks as if she were half asleep is Lethe, Oblivion; she that sits leaning on both elbows with her hands clutched together is Misoponia, Laziness; she with the garland on her head, and that smells so strong of perfumes, is Hedone, Pleasure; she with those staring eyes, moving here and there, is Anoia, Madness; she with the smooth skin and full pampered body is Tryphe, Wantonness; and, as to the two gods that you see with them, the one is Komos, Intemperance, the other Ecgretos hypnos, Dead Sleep. These, I say, are my household servants, and by their faithful counsels I have subjected all things to my dominion and erected an empire over emperors themselves. Thus have you had my lineage, education, and companions .

And now, lest I may seem to have taken upon me the name of goddess without cause, you shall in the next place understand how far my deity extends, and what advantage by it I have brought both to gods and men. For, if it was not unwisely said by somebody, that this only is to be a god, to help men; and if they are deservedly enrolled among the gods that first brought in corn and wine and such other things as are for the common good of mankind, why am not I of right the alpha, or first, of all the gods? who being but one, yet bestow all things on all men. For first, what is more sweet or more precious than life? And yet from whom can it more properly be said to come than from me? For neither the crab-favoured Pallas' spear nor the cloudgathering Jupiter's shield either beget or propagate mankind; but even he himself, the father of gods and king of men at whose very beck the heavens shake, must lay by his forked thunder and those looks wherewith he conquered the giants and with which at pleasure he frightens the rest of the gods, and like a common stage player put on a disguise as often as he goes about that, which now

MIDDLE AGES AND RENAISSANCE **175**

and then he does, that is to say the getting of children: And the Stoics too, that conceive themselves next to the gods, yet show me one of them, nay the veriest bigot of the sect, and if he do not put off his beard, the badge of wisdom, though yet it be no more than what is common with him and goats; yet at least he must lay by his supercilious gravity, smooth his forehead, shake off his rigid principles, and for some time commit an act of folly and dotage. In fine, that wise man whoever he be, if he intends to have children, must have recourse to me. But tell me, I beseech you, what man is that would submit his neck to the noose of wedlock, if, as wise men should, he did but first truly weigh the inconvenience of the thing? Or what woman is there would ever go to it did she seriously consider either the peril of child-bearing or the trouble of bringing them up? So then, if you owe your beings to wedlock, you owe that wedlock to this my follower, Madness; and what you owe to me I have already told you. Again, she that has but once tried what it is, would she, do you think, make a second venture if it were not for my other companion, Oblivion? Nay, even Venus herself, notwithstanding whatever Lucretius has said, would not deny but that all her virtue were lame and fruitless without the help of my deity. For out of that little, odd, ridiculous May-game came the supercilious philosophers, in whose room have succeeded a kind of people the world calls monks, cardinals, priests, and the most holy popes. And lastly, all that rabble of the poets' gods, with which heaven is so thwacked and thronged, that though it be of so vast an extent, they are hardly able to crowd one by another.

But I think it is a small matter that you thus owe your beginning of life to me, unless I also show you that whatever benefit you receive in the progress of it is of my gift likewise. For what other is this? Can that be called life where you take away pleasure? Oh! Do you like what I say? I knew none of you could have so little wit, or so much folly, or wisdom rather, as to be of any other opinion. For even the Stoics themselves that so severely cried down pleasure did but handsomely dissemble, and railed against it to the common people to no other end but that having discouraged them from it, they might the more plentifully enjoy it themselves. But tell me, by Jupiter, what part of man's life is that that is not sad, crabbed, unpleasant, insipid, troublesome, unless it be seasoned with pleasure, that is to say, folly? For the proof of which the never sufficiently praised Sophocles in that his happy elegy of us, "To know nothing is the only happiness," might be authority enough, but that I intend to take every particular by itself.

And first, who knows not but a man's infancy is the merriest part of life to himself, and most acceptable to others? For what is that in them which we kiss, embrace, cherish, nay enemies succor, but this witchcraft of folly, which wise Nature did of purpose give them into the world with them that they might the more pleasantly pass over the toil of education, and as it were flatter the care and diligence of their nurses? And then for youth, which is in such reputation everywhere, how do all men favor it, study to advance it, and lend it their helping hand? And whence, I pray, all this grace? Whence but from me? by whose kindness, as it understands as little as may be, it is also for that reason the higher privileged from exceptions; and I am mistaken if, when it is grown up and by experience and discipline brought to savor something like man, if in the same instant that beauty does not fade, its liveliness decay, its pleasantness grow fat, and its briskness fail. And by how much the further it runs from me, by so much the less it lives, till it

176 THE MEANING OF LIFE

comes to the burden of old age, not only hateful to others, but to itself also. Which also were altogether insupportable did not I pity its condition, in being present with it, and, as the poets' gods were wont to assist such as were dying with some pleasant metamorphosis, . help their decrepitness as much as in me lies by bringing them back to a second childhood, from whence they are not improperly called twice children. Which, if you ask me how I do it, I shall not be shy in the point. I bring them to our River Lethe (for its springhead rises in the Fortunate Islands, and that other of hell is but a brook in comparison), from which, as soon as they have drunk down a long forgetfulness, they wash away by degrees the perplexity of their minds, and so wax young again.

But perhaps you'll say they are foolish and doting. Admit it; 'tis the very essence of childhood; as if to be such were not to be a fool, or that that condition had anything pleasant in it, but that it understood nothing. For who would not look upon that child as a prodigy that should have as much wisdom as a man?--according to that common proverb, "I do not like a child that is a man too soon." Or who would endure a converse or friendship with that old man who to so large an experience of things had joined an equal strength of mind and sharpness of judgment? And therefore for this reason it is that old age dotes; and that it does so, it is beholding to me. Yet, notwithstanding, is this dotard exempt from all those cares that distract a wise man; he is not the less pot companion, nor is he sensible of that burden of life which the more manly age finds enough to do to stand upright under it. And sometimes too, like Plautus' old man, he returns to his three letters, A.M.O., the most unhappy of all things living, if he rightly understood what he did in it. And yet, so much do I befriend him that I make him well received of his friends and no unpleasant companion; for as much as, according to Homer, Nestor's discourse was pleasanter than honey, whereas Achilles' was both bitter and malicious; and that of old men, as he has it in another place, florid. In which respect also they have this advantage of children, in that they want the only pleasure of the others' life, we'll suppose it prattling. Add to this that old men are more eagerly delighted with children, and they, again, with old men. "Like to like," quoted the Devil to the collier. For what difference between them, but that the one has more wrinkles and years upon his head than the other? Otherwise, the brightness of their hair, toothless mouth, weakness of body, love of mild, broken speech, chatting, toying, forgetfulness, inadvertency, and briefly, all other their actions agree in everything. And by how much the nearer they approach to this old age, by so much they grow backward into the likeness of children, until like them they pass from life to death, without any weariness of the one, or sense of the other.

And now, let him that will compare the benefits they receive by me, the metamorphoses of the gods, of whom I shall not mention what they have done in their pettish humors but where they have been most favorable: turning one into a tree, another into a bird, a third into a grasshopper, serpent, or the like. As if there were any difference between perishing and being another thing! But I restore the same man to the best and happiest part of his life. And if men would but refrain from all commerce with wisdom and give up themselves to be governed by me, they should never know what it were to be old, but solace themselves with a perpetual youth. Do but observe our grim philosophers that are perpetually beating their brains on knotty subjects, and for the most

MIDDLE AGES AND RENAISSANCE   177

part you'll find them grown old before they are scarcely young. And whence is it, but that their continual and restless thoughts insensibly prey upon their spirits and dry up their radical moisture? Whereas, on the contrary, my fat fools are as plump and round as a Westphalian hog, and never sensible of old age, unless perhaps, as sometimes it rarely happens, they come to be infected with wisdom, so hard a thing it is for a man to be happy in all things. And to this purpose is that no small testimony of the proverb, that says, "Folly is the only thing that keeps youth at a stay and old age afar off;" as it is verified in the Brabanders, of whom there goes this common saying, "That age, which is wont to render other men wiser, makes them the greater fools." And yet there is scarce any nation of a more jocund converse, or that is less sensible of the misery of old age, than they are. And to these, as in situation, so for manner of living, come nearest my friends the Hollanders. And why should I not call them mine, since they are so diligent observers of me that they are commonly called by my name?--of which they are so far from being ashamed, they rather pride themselves in it. Let the foolish world then be packing and seek out Medeas, Circes, Venuses, Auroras, and I know not what other fountains of restoring youth. I am sure I am the only person that both can, and have, made it good. 'Tis I alone that have that wonderful juice with which Memnon's daughter prolonged the youth of her grandfather Tithon. I am that Venus by whose favor Phaon became so young again that Sappho fell in love with him. Mine are those herbs, if yet there be any such, mine those charms, and mine that fountain that not only restores departed youth but, which is more desirable, preserves it perpetual. And if you all subscribe to this opinion, that nothing is better than youth or more execrable than age, I conceive you cannot but see how much you are indebted to me, that have retained so great a good and shut out so great an evil.

But why do I altogether spend my breath in speaking of mortals? …

But it is not my business to sift too narrowly the lives of prelates and priests for fear I seem to have intended rather a satire than an oration, and be thought to tax good princes while I praise the bad. And therefore, what I slightly taught before has been to no other end but that it might appear that there's no man can live pleasantly unless he be initiated to my rites and have me propitious to him. For how can it be otherwise when Fortune, the great directress of all human affairs, and myself are so all one that she was always an enemy to those wise men, and on the contrary so favorable to fools and careless fellows that all things hit luckily to them?

You have heard of that Timotheus, the most fortunate general of the Athenians, of whom came that proverb, "His net caught fish, though he were asleep;" and that "The owl flies;" whereas these others hit properly, wise men "born in the fourth month;" and again, "He rides Sejanus's his horse;" and "gold of Toulouse," signifying thereby the extremity of ill fortune. But I forbear the further threading of proverbs, lest I seem to have pilfered my friend Erasmus' adages. Fortune loves those that have least wit and most confidence and such as like that saying of Caesar, "The die is thrown." But wisdom makes men bashful, which is the reason that those wise men have so little to do, unless it be with poverty, hunger, and chimney corners; that they live

178 THE MEANING OF LIFE

such neglected, unknown, and hated lives: whereas fools abound in money, have the chief commands in the commonwealth, and in a word, flourish every way. For if it be happiness to please princes and to be conversant among those golden and diamond gods, what is more unprofitable than wisdom, or what is it these kind of men have, may more justly be censured? If wealth is to be got, how little good at it is that merchant like to do, if following the precepts of wisdom, he should boggle at perjury; or being taken in a lie, blush; or in the least regard the sad scruples of those wise men touching rapine and usury. Again, if a man sue for honors or church preferments, an ass or wild ox shall sooner get them than a wise man. If a man's in love with a young wench, none of the least humors in this comedy, they are wholly addicted to fools and are afraid of a wise man and flee him as they would a scorpion. Lastly, whoever intend to live merry and frolic, shut their doors against wise men and admit anything sooner. In brief, go whither you will, among prelates, princes, judges, magistrates, friends, enemies, from highest to lowest, and you'll find all things done by money; which, as a wise man condemns it, so it takes a special care not to come near him. What shall I say? There is no measure or end of my praises, and yet 'tis fit my oration have an end. And therefore I'll even break off; and yet, before I do it, 'twill not be amiss if I briefly show you that there has not been wanting even great authors that have made me famous, both by their writings and actions, lest perhaps otherwise I may seem to have foolishly pleased myself only, or that the lawyers charge me that I have proved nothing. After their example, therefore, will I allege my proofs, that is to say, nothing to the point.

And first, every man allows this proverb, "That where a man wants matter, he may best frame some." And to this purpose is that verse which we teach children, " 'Tis the greatest wisdom to know when and where to counterfeit the fool." And now judge yourselves what an excellent thing this folly is, whose very counterfeit and semblance only has got such praise from the learned. But more candidly does that fat plump "Epicurean bacon-hog," Horace, for so he calls himself, bid us "mingle our purposes with folly;" and whereas he adds the word bravem, short, perhaps to help out the verse, he might as well have let it alone; and again, " 'Tis a pleasant thing to play the fool in the right season;" and in another place, he had rather "be accounted a dotterel and sot than to be wise and made mouths at." And Telemachus in Homer, whom the poet praises so much, is now and then called nepios, fool: and by the same name, as if there were some good fortune in it, are the tragedians wont to call boys and striplings. And what does that sacred book of Iliads contain but a kind of counter-scuffle between foolish kings and foolish people? Besides, how absolute is that praise that Cicero gives of it! "All things are full of fools." For who does not know that every good, the more diffusive it is, by so much the better it is?

But perhaps their authority may be of small credit among Christians. We'll therefore, if you please, support our praises with some testimonies of Holy Writ also, in the first place, nevertheless, having forespoke our theologians that they'll give us leave to do it without offense. And in the next, forasmuch as we attempt a matter of some difficulty and it may be perhaps a little too saucy to call back again the Muses from Helicon to so great a journey, especially in a matter they are wholly strangers to, it will be more suitable, perhaps, while I play the divine and make my way through such prickly quiddities, that I entreat the soul of Scotus, a thing more

MIDDLE AGES AND RENAISSANCE **179**

bristly than either porcupine or hedgehog, to leave his scorebone awhile and come into my breast, and then let him go whither he pleases, or to the dogs. I could wish also that I might change my countenance, or that I had on the square cap and the cassock, for fear some or other should impeach me of theft as if I had privily rifled our masters' desks in that I have got so much divinity. But it ought not to seem so strange if after so long and intimate an acquaintance and converse with them I have picked up somewhat; when as that fig-tree-god Priapus hearing his owner read certain Greek words took so much notice of them that he got them by heart, and that cock in Lucian by having lived long among men became at last a master of their language.

But to the point under a fortunate direction. Ecclesiastes says in his first chapter, "The number of fools is infinite;" and when he calls it infinite, does he not seem to comprehend all men, unless it be some few whom yet 'tis a question whether any man ever saw? But more ingeniously does Jeremiah in his tenth chapter confess it, saying, "Every man is made a fool through his own wisdom;" attributing wisdom to God alone and leaving folly to all men else, and again, "Let not man glory in his wisdom." And why, good Jeremiah, would you not have a man glory in his wisdom? Because, he'll say, he has none at all. But to return to Ecclesiastes, who, when he cries out, "Vanity of vanities, all is vanity!" what other thoughts had he, do you believe, than that, as I said before, the life of man is nothing else but an interlude of folly? In which he has added one voice more to that justly received praise of Cicero's which I quoted before, viz., "All things are full of fools." Again, that wise preacher that said, "A fool changes as the moon, but a wise man is permanent as the sun," what else did he hint at in it but that all mankind are fools and the name of wise only proper to God? For by the moon interpreters understand human nature, and by the sun, God, the only fountain of light; with which agrees that which Christ himself in the Gospel denies, that anyone is to be called good but one, and that is God. And then if he is a fool that is not wise, and every good man according to the Stoics is a wise man, it is no wonder if all mankind be concluded under folly. Again Solomon, Chapter 15, "Foolishness," says he, "is joy to the fool," thereby plainly confessing that without folly there is no pleasure in life. To which is pertinent that other, "He that increases knowledge, increases grief; and in much understanding there is much indignation." And does he not plainly confess as much, Chapter 7, "The heart of the wise is where sadness is, but the heart of fools follows mirth"? by which you see, he thought it not enough to have learned wisdom without he had added the knowledge of me also. And if you will not believe me, take his own words, Chapter 1, "I gave my heart to know wisdom and knowledge, madness and folly." Where, by the way, 'tis worth your remark that he intended me somewhat extraordinary that he named me last. A preacher wrote it, and this you know is the order among churchmen, that he that is first in dignity comes last in place, as mindful, no doubt, whatever they do in other things, herein at least to observe the evangelical precept.

Besides, that folly is more excellent than wisdom the son of Sirach, whoever he was, clearly witnesses, Chapter 44, whose words, so help me, Hercules! I shall not once utter before you meet my induction with a suitable answer, according to the manner of those in Plato that dispute with Socrates. What things are more proper to be laid up with care, such as are rare and precious, or such as are common and of no account? Why do you give me no answer? Well, though you should dissemble, the Greek proverb will answer for you, "Foul water is thrown out of doors;" which, if any man shall be so ungracious as to condemn, let him know 'tis Aristotle's, the god of our masters. Is there any of you so very a fool as to leave jewels and gold in the street? In truth, I think not; in the most secret part of your house; nor is that enough; if there be any drawer in your iron chests more private than other, there you lay them; but dirt you throw out of doors. And therefore, if you so carefully lay up such things as you value and throw away what's vile and of no worth, is it not plain that wisdom, which he forbids a man to hide, is of less account than folly, which he commands him to cover? Take his own words, "Better is the man that hideth his folly than he that hideth his wisdom." Or what is that, when he attributes an upright mind without craft or malice to a fool, when a wise man the while thinks no man like himself? For so I understand that in his tenth chapter, "A fool walking by the way, being a fool himself, supposes all men to be fools like him." And is it not a sign of great integrity to esteem every man as good as himself, and when there is no one that leans not too much to other way, to be so frank yet as to divide his praises with another? Nor was this great king ashamed of the name when he says of himself that he is more foolish than any man. Nor did Paul, that great doctor of the Gentiles, writing to the Corinthians, unwillingly acknowledge it; "I speak," says he, "like a fool. I am more." As if it could be any dishonor to excel in folly.

But here I meet with a great noise of some that endeavor to peck out the crows' eyes; that is, to blind the doctors of our times and smoke out their eyes with new annotations; among whom my friend Erasmus, whom for honor's sake I often mention, deserves if not the first place yet certainly the second. O most foolish instance, they cry, and well becoming Folly herself! The apostle's meaning was wide enough from what you dream; for he spoke it not in this sense, that he would have them believe him a greater fool than the rest, but when he had said, "They are ministers of Christ, the same am I," and by way of boasting herein had equaled himself with to others, he added this by way of correction or checking himself, "I am more," as meaning that he was not only equal to the rest of the apostles in the work of the Gospel, but somewhat superior. And therefore, while he would have this received as a truth, lest nevertheless it might not relish their ears as being spoken with too much arrogance, he foreshortened his argument with the vizard of folly, "I speak like a fool," because he knew it was the prerogative of fools to speak what they like, and that too without offense. Whatever he thought when he wrote this, I leave it to them to discuss; for my own part, I follow those fat, fleshy, and vulgarly approved doctors, with whom, by Jupiter! a great part of the learned had rather err than follow them that understand the tongues, though they are never so much in the right. Not any of them make greater account of those smatterers at Greek than if they were daws. Especially when a no small professor, whose name I wittingly conceal lest those choughs should chatter at me that Greek proverb I have so often mentioned, "an ass at a harp," discoursing magisterially and theologically on this text, "I speak as a fool, I am more," drew a new thesis; and, which without the height of logic he could never have done, made this new subdivision--for I'll give you his own words, not only in form but matter also--"I speak like a fool," that is, if you look upon me as a fool for comparing myself with

MIDDLE AGES AND RENAISSANCE   181

those false apostles, I shall seem yet a greater fool by esteeming myself before them; though the same person a little after, as forgetting himself, runs off to another matter.

But why do I thus staggeringly defend myself with one single instance? As if it were not the common privilege of divines to stretch heaven, that is Holy Writ, like a cheverel; and when there are many things in St. Paul that thwart themselves, which yet in their proper place do well enough if there be any credit to be given to St. Jerome that was master of five tongues. Such was that of his at Athens when having casually espied the inscription of that altar, he wrested it into an argument to prove the Christian faith, and leaving out all the other words because they made against him, took notice only of the two last, viz., "To the unknown God;" and those too not without some alteration, for the whole inscription was thus: "To the Gods of Asia, Europe, and Africa; To the unknown and strange Gods." And according to his example do the sons of the prophets, who, forcing out here and there four or five expressions and if need be corrupting the sense, wrest it to their own purpose; though what goes before and follows after make nothing to the matter in hand, nay, be quite against it. Which yet they do with so happy an impudence that oftentimes the civilians envy them that faculty.

For what is it in a manner they may not hope for success in, when this great doctor (I had almost bolted out his name, but that I once again stand in fear of the Greek proverb) has made a construction on an expression of Luke, so agreeable to the mind of Christ as are fire and water to one another. For when the last point of danger was at hand, at which time retainers and dependents are wont in a more special manner to attend their protectors, to examine what strength they have, and prepare for the encounter, Christ, intending to take out of his disciples' minds all trust and confidence in such like defense, demands of them whether they wanted anything when he sent them forth so unprovided for a journey that they had neither shoes to defend their feet from the injuries of stones and briars nor the provision of a scrip to preserve them from hunger. And when they had denied that they wanted anything, he adds, "But now, he that hath a bag, let him take it, and likewise a scrip; and he that hath none, let him sell his coat and buy a sword." And now when the sum of all that Christ taught pressed only meekness, suffering, and contempt of life, who does not clearly perceive what he means in this place? to wit, that he might the more disarm his ministers, that neglecting not only shoes and scrip but throwing away their very coat, they might, being in a manner naked, the more readily and with less hindrance take in hand the work of the Gospel, and provide themselves of nothing but a sword, not such as thieves and murderers go up and down with, but the sword of the spirit that pierces the most inward parts, and so cuts off as it were at one blow all earthly affections, that they mind nothing but their duty to God. But see, I pray, whither this famous theologian wrests it. By the sword he interprets defense against persecution, and by the bag sufficient provision to carry it on. As if Christ having altered his mind, in that he sent out his disciples not so royally attended as he should have done, repented himself of his former instructions: or as forgetting that he had said, "Blessed are ye when ye are evil spoken of, despised, and persecuted, etc.," and forbade them to resist evil; for that the meek in spirit, not the proud, are blessed: or, lest remembering, I say, that he had compared them to sparrows and lilies, thereby minding them what small care they should take for the things of this

182   THE MEANING OF LIFE

life, was so far now from having them go forth without a sword that he commanded them to get one, though with the sale of their coat, and had rather they should go naked than want a brawling-iron by their sides. And to this, as under the word "sword" he conceives to be comprehended whatever appertains to the repelling of injuries, so under that of "scrip" he takes in whatever is necessary to the support of life. And so does this deep interpreter of the divine meaning bring forth the apostles to preach the doctrine of a crucified Christ, but furnished at all points with lances, slings, quarterstaffs, and bombards; lading them also with bag and baggage, lest perhaps it might not be lawful for them to leave their inn unless they were empty and fasting. Nor does he take the least notice of this, that he so willed the sword to be bought, reprehends it a little after and commands it to be sheathed; and that it was never heard that the apostles ever used or swords or bucklers against the Gentiles, though 'tis likely they had done it, if Christ had ever intended, as this doctor interprets.

There is another, too, whose name out of respect I pass by, a man of no small repute, who from those tents which Habakkuk mentions, "The tents of the land of Midian shall tremble," drew this exposition, that it was prophesied of the skin of Saint Bartholomew who was flayed alive. And why, forsooth, but because those tents were covered with skins? I was lately myself at a theological dispute, for I am often there, where when one was demanding what authority there was in Holy Writ that commands heretics to be convinced by fire rather than reclaimed by argument; a crabbed old fellow, and one whose supercilious gravity spoke him at least a doctor, answered in a great fume that Saint Paul had decreed it, who said, "Reject him that is a heretic, after once or twice admonition." And when he had sundry times, one after another, thundered out the same thing, and most men wondered what ailed the man, at last he explained it thus, making two words of one. "A heretic must be put to death." Some laughed, and yet there wanted not others to whom this exposition seemed plainly theological; which, when some, though those very few, opposed, they cut off the dispute, as we say, with a hatchet, and the credit of so uncontrollable an author. "Pray conceive me," said he, "it is written, 'Thou shalt not suffer a witch to live.' But every heretic bewitches the people; therefore, etc." And now, as many as were present admired the man's wit, and consequently submitted to his decision of the question. Nor came it into any of their heads that that law concerned only fortunetellers, enchanters, and magicians, whom the Hebrews call in their tongue "Mecaschephim," witches or sorcerers: for otherwise, perhaps, by the same reason it might as well have extended to fornication and drunkenness.

But I foolishly run on in these matters, though yet there are so many of them that neither Chrysippus, nor Didymus, volumes are large enough to contain them. I would only desire you to consider this, that if so great doctors may be allowed this liberty, you may the more reasonably pardon even me also, a raw, effeminate divine, if I quote not everything so exactly as I should. And so at last I return to Paul. "Ye willingly," says he, "suffer my foolishness," and again, "Take me as a fool," and further, "I speak it not after the Lord, but as it were foolishly," and in another place, "We are fools for Christ's sake." You have heard from how great an author how great praises of folly; and to what other end, but that without doubt he looked upon it as that one thing

MIDDLE AGES AND RENAISSANCE 183

both necessary and profitable. "If anyone among ye," says he, "seem to be wise, let him be a fool that he may be wise." And in Luke, Jesus called those two disciples with whom he joined himself upon the way, "fools." Nor can I give you any reason why it should seem so strange when Saint Paul imputes a kind of folly even to God himself. "The foolishness of God," says he, "is wiser than men." Though yet I must confess that Origen upon the place denies that this foolishness may be resembled to the uncertain judgment of men; of which kind is, that "the preaching of the cross is to them that perish foolishness."

But why am I so careful to no purpose that I thus run on to prove my matter by so many testimonies? when in those mystical Psalms Christ speaking to the Father says openly, "Thou knowest my foolishness." Nor is it without ground that fools are so acceptable to God. The reason perhaps may be this, that as princes carry a suspicious eye upon those that are over-wise, and consequently hate them--as Caesar did Brutus and Cassius, when he feared not in the least drunken Antony; so Nero, Seneca; and Dionysius, Plato--and on the contrary are delighted in those blunter and unlabored wits, in like manner Christ ever abhors and condemns those wise men and such as put confidence in their own wisdom. And this Paul makes clearly out when he said, "God hath chosen the foolish things of this world," as well knowing it had been impossible to have reformed it by wisdom. Which also he sufficiently declares himself, crying out by the mouth of his prophet, "I will destroy the wisdom of the wise, and cast away the understanding of the prudent."

And again, when Christ gives Him thanks that He had concealed the mystery of salvation from the wise, but revealed it to babes and sucklings, that is to say, fools. For the Greek word for babes is fools, which he opposes to the word wise men. To this appertains that throughout the Gospel you find him ever accusing the Scribes and Pharisees and doctors of the law, but diligently defending the ignorant multitude (for what other is that "Woe to ye Scribes and Pharisees" than woe to you, you wise men?), but seems chiefly delighted in little children, women, and fishers. Besides, among brute beasts he is best pleased with those that have least in them of the foxes' subtlety. And therefore he chose rather to ride upon an ass when, if he had pleased, he might have bestrode the lion without danger. And the Holy Ghost came down in the shape of a dove, not of an eagle or kite. Add to this that in Scripture there is frequent mention of harts, hinds, and lambs; and such as are destined to eternal life are called sheep, than which creature there is not anything more foolish, if we may believe that proverb of Aristotle "sheepish manners," which he tells us is taken from the foolishness of that creature and is used to be applied to dull-headed people and lack-wits. And yet Christ professes to be the shepherd of this flock and is himself delighted with the name of a lamb; according to Saint John, "Behold the Lamb of God!" Of which also there is much mention in the Revelation. And what does all this drive at, but that all mankind are fools--nay, even the very best?

And Christ himself, that he might the better relieve this folly, being the wisdom of the Father, yet in some manner became a fool when taking upon him the nature of man, he was found in shape as a man; as in like manner he was made sin that he might heal sinners. Nor did he work this cure any other way than by the foolishness of the cross and a company of fat apostles, not

184   THE MEANING OF LIFE

much better, to whom also he carefully recommended folly but gave them a caution against wisdom and drew them together by the example of little children, lilies, mustard-seed, and sparrows, things senseless and inconsiderable, living only by the dictates of nature and without either craft or care. Besides, when he forbade them to be troubled about what they should say before governors and straightly charged them not to inquire after times and seasons, to wit, that they might not trust to their own wisdom but wholly depend on him. And to the same purpose is it that that great Architect of the World, God, gave man an injunction against his eating of the Tree of Knowledge, as if knowledge were the bane of happiness; according to which also, St. Paul disallows it as puffing up and destructive; whence also St. Bernard seems in my opinion to follow when he interprets that mountain whereon Lucifer had fixed his habitation to be the mountain of knowledge.

Nor perhaps ought I to omit this other argument, that Folly is so gracious above that her errors are only pardoned, those of wise men never. Whence it is that they that ask forgiveness, though they offend never so wittingly, cloak it yet with the excuse of folly. So Aaron, in Numbers, if I mistake not the book, when he sues unto Moses concerning his sister's leprosy, "I beseech thee, my Lord, not to lay this sin upon us, which we have foolishly committed." So Saul makes his excuse of David, "For behold," says he, "I did it foolishly." And again, David himself thus sweetens God, "And therefore I beseech thee, O Lord, to take away the trespass of thy servant, for I have done foolishly," as if he knew there was no pardon to be obtained unless he had colored his offense with folly and ignorance. And stronger is that of Christ upon the cross when he prayed for his enemies, "Father, forgive them," nor does he cover their crime with any other excuse than that of unwittingness--because, says he, "they know not what they do." In like manner Paul, writing to Timothy, "But therefore I obtained mercy, for that I did it ignorantly through unbelief." And what is the meaning of "I did it ignorantly" but that I did it out of folly, not malice? And what of "Therefore I received mercy" but that I had not obtained it had I not been made more allowable through the covert of folly? For us also makes that mystical Psalmist, though I remembered it not in its right place, "Remember not the sins of my youth nor my ignorances." You see what two things he pretends, to wit, youth, whose companion I ever am, and ignorances, and that in the plural number, a number of multitude, whereby we are to understand that there was no small company of them.

But not to run too far in that which is infinite. To speak briefly, all Christian religion seems to have a kind of alliance with folly and in no respect to have any accord with wisdom. Of which if you expect proofs, consider first that boys, old men, women, and fools are more delighted with religious and sacred things than others, and to that purpose are ever next the altars; and this they do by mere impulse of nature. And in the next place, you see that those first founders of it were plain, simple persons and most bitter enemies of learning. Lastly there are no sort of fools seem more out of the way than are these whom the zeal of Christian religion has once swallowed up; so that they waste their estates, neglect injuries, suffer themselves to be cheated, put no difference between friends and enemies, abhor pleasure, are crammed with poverty, watchings, tears, labors, reproaches, loathe life, and wish death above all things; in short, they seem senseless to common understanding, as if their minds lived elsewhere and not in their own bodies; which, what else is it than to be mad? For which reason you must not think it so strange if the apostles seemed to be drunk with new wine, and if Paul appeared to Festus to be mad.

But now, having once gotten on the lion's skin, go to, and I'll show you that this happiness of Christians, which they pursue with so much toil, is nothing else but a kind of madness and folly; far be it that my words should give any offense, rather consider my matter. And first, the Christians and Platonists do as good as agree in this, that the soul is plunged and fettered in the prison of the body, by the grossness of which it is so tied up and hindered that it cannot take a view of or enjoy things as they truly are; and for that cause their master defines philosophy to be a contemplation of death, because it takes off the mind from visible and corporeal objects, than which death does no more. And therefore, as long as the soul uses the organs of the body in that right manner it ought, so long it is said to be in good state and condition; but when, having broken its fetters, it endeavors to get loose and assays, as it were, a flight out of that prison that holds it in, they call it madness; and if this happen through any distemper or indisposition of the organs, then, by the common consent of every man, 'tis downright madness. And yet we see such kind of men foretell things to come, understand tongues and letters they never learned before, and seem, as it were, big with a kind of divinity. Nor is it to be doubted but that it proceeds from hence, that the mind, being somewhat at liberty from the infection of the body, begins to put forth itself in its native vigor. And I conceive 'tis from the same cause that the like often happens to sick men a little before their death, that they discourse in strain above mortality as if they were inspired. Again, if this happens upon the score of religion, though perhaps it may not be the same kind of madness, yet 'tis so near it that a great many men would judge it no better, especially when a few inconsiderable people shall differ from the rest of the world in the whole course of their life. And therefore it fares with them as, according to the fiction of Plato, happens to those that being cooped up in a cave stand gaping with admiration at the shadows of things; and that fugitive who, having broke from them and returning to them again, told them he had seen things truly as they were, and that they were the most mistaken in believing there was nothing but pitiful shadows. For as this wise man pitied and bewailed their palpable madness that were possessed with so gross an error, so they in return laughed at him as a doting fool and cast him out of their company. In like manner the common sort of men chiefly admire those things that are most corporeal and almost believe there is nothing beyond them. Whereas on the contrary, these devout persons, by how much the nearer anything concerns the body, by so much more they neglect it and are wholly hurried away with the contemplation of things invisible. For the one give the first place to riches, the next to their corporeal pleasures, leaving the last place to their soul, which yet most of them do scarce believe, because they can't see it with their eyes. On the contrary, the others first rely wholly on God, the most unchangeable of all things; and next him, yet on this that comes nearest him, they bestow the second on their soul; and lastly, for their body, they neglect that care and condemn and flee money as superfluity that may be well spared; or if they are forced to meddle with any of these things, they do it carelessly and much against their wills, having as if they had it not, and possessing as if they possessed it not.

186 THE MEANING OF LIFE

There are also in each several things several degrees wherein they disagree among themselves. And first as to the senses, though all of them have more or less affinity with the body, yet of these some are more gross and blockish, as tasting, hearing, seeing, smelling, touching; some more removed from the body, as memory, intellect, and the will. And therefore to which of these the mind applies itself, in that lies its force. But holy men, because the whole bent of their minds is taken up with those things that are most repugnant to these grosser senses, they seem brutish and stupid in the common use of them. Whereas on the contrary, the ordinary sort of people are best at these, and can do least at the other; from whence it is, as we have heard, that some of these holy men have by mistake drunk oil for wine. Again, in the affections of the mind, some have a greater commerce with the body than others, as lust, desire of meat and sleep, anger, pride, envy; with which holy men are at irreconcilable enmity, and contrary, the common people think there's no living without them. And lastly there are certain middle kind of affections, and as it were natural to every man, as the love of one's country, children, parents, friends, and to which the common people attribute no small matter; whereas the other strive to pluck them out of their mind: unless insomuch as they arrive to that highest part of the soul, that they love their parents not as parents--for what did they get but the body? though yet we owe it to God, not them--but as good men or women and in whom shines the image of that highest wisdom which alone they call the chiefest good, and out of which, they say, there is nothing to be beloved or desired.

And by the same rule do they measure all things else, so that they make less account of whatever is visible, unless it be altogether contemptible, than of those things which they cannot see. But they say that in Sacraments and other religious duties there is both body and spirit. As in fasting they count it not enough for a man to abstain from eating, which the common people take for an absolute fast, unless there be also a lessening of his depraved affections: as that he be less angry, less proud, than he was wont, that the spirit, being less clogged with its bodily weight, may be the more intent upon heavenly things. In like manner, in the Eucharist, though, say they, it is not to be esteemed the less that 'tis administered with ceremonies, yet of itself 'tis of little effect, if not hurtful, unless that which is spiritual be added to it, to wit, that which is represented under those visible signs. Now the death of Christ is represented by it, which all men, vanquishing, abolishing, and, as it were, burying their carnal affections, ought to express in their lives and conversations that they may grow up to a newness of life and be one with him and the same one among another. This a holy man does, and in this is his only meditation. Whereas on the contrary, the common people think there's no more in that sacrifice than to be present at the altar and crowd next it, to have a noise of words and look upon the ceremonies. Nor in this alone, which we only proposed by way of example, but in all his life, and without hypocrisy, does a holy man fly those things that have any alliance with the body and is wholly ravished with things eternal, invisible, and spiritual. For which cause there's so great contrarity of opinion between them, and that too in everything, that each party thinks the other out of their wits; though that character, in my judgment, better agrees with those holy men than the common people: which yet will be more clear if, as I promised, I briefly show you that that great reward they so much fancy is nothing else but a kind of madness.

And therefore suppose that Plato dreamed of somewhat like it when he called the madness of lovers the most happy condition of all others. For he that's violently in love lives not in his own body but in the thing he loves; and by how much the farther he runs from himself into another, by so much the greater is his pleasure. And then, when the mind strives to rove from its body and does not rightly use its own organs, without doubt you may say 'tis downright madness and not be mistaken, or otherwise what's the meaning of those common sayings, "He does not dwell at home," "Come to yourself," "He's his own man again"? Besides, the more perfect and true his love is, the more pleasant is his madness. And therefore, what is that life hereafter, after which these holy minds so pantingly breathe, like to be? To wit, the spirit shall swallow up the body, as conqueror and more durable; and this it shall do with the greater ease because heretofore, in its lifetime, it had chanced and thinned it into such another nothing as itself. And then the spirit again shall be wonderfully swallowed up by the highest mind, as being more powerful than infinite parts; so that the whole man is to be out of himself nor to be otherwise happy in any respect, but that being stripped of himself, he shall participate of somewhat ineffable from that chiefest good that draws all things into itself. And this happiness though 'tis only then perfected when souls being joined to their former bodies shall be made immortal, yet forasmuch as the life of holy men is nothing but a continued meditation and, as it were, shadow of that life, it so happens that at length they have some taste or relish of it; which, though it be but as the smallest drop in comparison of that fountain of eternal happiness, yet it far surpasses all worldly delight, though all the pleasures of all mankind were all joined together. So much better are things spiritual than things corporeal, and things invisible than things visible; which doubtless is that which the prophet promises: "The eye hath not seen, nor the ear heard, nor has it entered into the heart of man to consider what God has provided for them that love Him." And this is that Mary's better part which is not taken away by change of life, but perfected.

And therefore they that are sensible of it, and few there are to whom this happens, suffer a kind of somewhat little differing from madness; for they utter many things that do not hang together, and that too not after the manner of men but make a kind of sound which they neither heed themselves, nor is it understood by others, and change the whole figure of their countenance, one while jocund, another while dejected, now weeping, then laughing, and again sighing. And when they come to themselves, tell you they know not where they have been, whether in the body or out of the body, or sleeping; nor do they remember what they have heard, seen, spoken, or done, and only know this, as it were in a mist or dream, that they were the most happy while they were so out of their wits. And therefore they are sorry they are come to themselves again and desire nothing more than this kind of madness, to be perpetually mad. And this is a small taste of that future happiness.

But I forget myself and run beyond my bounds. Though yet, if I shall seem to have spoken anything more boldly or impertinently than I ought, be pleased to consider that not only Folly but a woman said it; remembering in the meantime that Greek proverb, "Sometimes a fool may speak a word in season," unless perhaps you expect an epilogue, but give me leave to tell you you are

188 THE MEANING OF LIFE

mistaken if you think I remember anything of what I have said, having foolishly bolted out such a hodgepodge of words. 'Tis an old proverb, "I hate one that remembers what's done over the cup."

This is a new one of my own making: I hate a man that remembers what he hears. Wherefore farewell, clap your hands, live and drink lustily, my most excellent disciples of Folly.

The End

BANACH'S OUTLINE OF DESCARTES' MEDITATIONS ON FIRST PHILOSOPHY

An Outline of Descartes's Meditations on First Philosophy

Descartes's Arguments for Universal Doubt and the "Cogito" Argument

(An Outline of Meditations 1,2)[63]

<u>The argument for universal doubt:</u>

A. The dream argument:

1. I often have perceptions very much like the ones I usually have in sensation while I am dreaming.
2. There are no definite signs to distinguish dream experience from waking experience. therefore,
3. It is possible that I am dreaming right now and that all of my perceptions are false

B. Objection to the dream argument:

1. It could be argued that the images we form in dreams can only be composed of bits and pieces of real experience combined in novel ways. therefore,
2. Although we have reason to doubt the surface perceptual qualities of our perception, we have no reason to doubt the properties that we perceive the basic components of our experience to have. (In particular, there is no reason to doubt the mathematical properties that material bodies in general have.)

C. The deceiving God argument:

1. We believe that there is an all powerful God who has created us and who is all powerful.
2. He has in his power to make us be deceived even about matters of mathematical knowledge which we seem to see clearly. therefore,
3. It is possible that we are deceived even in our mathematical knowledge of the basic structure of the world.

D. Objections to the deceiving God argument:

1. We think that God is perfectly good and would not deceive us.
2. Some think that there does not exist such a powerful God.

---

[63] Accessed: ***http://www.anselm.edu/homepage/dbanach/medol.htm***

190   THE MEANING OF LIFE

E. Replies:

1. If it were repugnant to God's nature to deceive us, he would not allow us to be deceived at all.
2. If there is no God, we must assume the author of our being to be even less perfect, so that we have even more reason to doubt all our beliefs.

F. The demon argument:

1. Instead of assuming that God is the source of our deceptions, we will assume that there exists an evil demon, who is capable of deceiving us in the same way we supposed God to be able

Therefore, I have reason to doubt the totality of what my senses tell me as well as the mathematical knowledge that it seems I have.

The Argument for our Existence (the "Cogito"):

1. Even if we assume that there is a deceiver, from the very fact that I am deceived it follows that I exist.
2. In general it will follow from any state of thinking (e.g., imagining, sensing, feeling, reasoning) that I exist. While I can be deceived about the objective content of any thought, I cannot be deceived about the fact that I exist and that I seem to perceive objects with certain characteristics.
3. Since I only can be certain of the existence of myself insofar as I am thinking, I have knowledge of my existence only as a thinking thing (res cogitans).

The Argument that the Mind is More Certainly known than the Body:

1. It is possible that all knowledge of external objects, including my body, could be false as the result of the actions of an evil demon. It is not, however, possible that I could be deceived about my existence or my nature as a thinking thing.
2. a. Even Corporeal objects, such as my body, are known much more distinctly through the mind than through the body.
   b. The wax argument for (2a):

       i.   All the properties of the piece of wax that we perceive with the senses change as the wax melts.

       ii.   This is true as well of its primary properties, such as shape, extension, and size.

       iii.   Yet the wax remains the same piece of wax as it melts. therefore,

       iv.   Insofar as we know the wax, we know through our mind and faculty of judgment, not through our senses or imagination

MIDDLE AGES AND RENAISSANCE **191**

c. Therefore, every act of clear and distinct knowledge of corporeal matter also provides even more certain evidence for the existence and nature of ourselves as thinking things.

Therefore, our mind is much more clearly and distinctly known to us than our body.

General Outline of Meditations 3, 4, 5

Meditation Three:

Descartes proves God's existence and that He is not a deceiver, thereby allowing us to be sure that we are not deceived when we perceive things clearly and distinctly.

A. Summary of things of which I am certain and those which I still must doubt.

1. I am certain that I exist as a thinking thing.
2. I must still doubt both my senses and my intuitions concerning mathematical knowledge since God may have constituted me so as to be deceived even about those things I seem most certain.

Therefore, in order to become certain of anything else I must inquire into the existence of God and see whether He can be regarded as a deceiver.

B. Preliminary Discussion of Ideas

1. I have ideas that are like images of things. The most common cause of error is the judgment that these ideas are similar to things that exist outside of me.
2. There are three possible types of ideas: innate, those that originate in myself, and those that originate from something outside of me. We shall be most interested in the latter group.
3. Even though some ideas of apparent external objects come to me against my will, I cannot regard them as corresponding to external things. This is because:
    a. I may have some faculty which produces these ideas.
    b. Even if they come from outside me, I have no guarantee that they are similar to their causes.

Therefore, the principle upon which I have judged my ideas to be similar to external objects seems to be mistaken.

C. The argument for the existence of God from the fact that I have an idea of Him.

1. Besides its formal reality, which accounts for its mere existence as an idea, every idea also has objective reality according to the reality of the thing which it represents, or its object.

192   THE MEANING OF LIFE

2. There must be as much reality in the cause as there is in the effect. This applies to objective reality as well as formal reality.
3. I need not assume a cause greater than myself for any of my ideas of corporeal substance nor of other people or angels.
4. I have an idea of a perfect God, and this idea has more objective reality than any idea of a finite substance.
5. The idea of God could not have originated in me, since I am a finite substance.

Therefore, God must exist as the only possible cause of the objective reality found in my idea of Him.

D. Objections to the argument and replies.

1. Perhaps our idea of God is gotten from a negation of our limited properties.
   Reply - We must have an idea of perfection before we can have an idea of limitation.

2. Perhaps the idea of God is materially false.
   Reply - The idea of God is the most clear and distinct of our ideas.

3. Perhaps I am more perfect than I think and contain the perfections I attribute to my idea of God potentially.
   Reply - Potential reality is not enough to cause the objective reality of my idea, and I will never have the actual perfection needed since I am a finite being, always capable of improving

E. The argument from my existence:

It can also be argued that a cause more perfect than myself must be assumed to explain my coming into being and my continued existence. This cause must be God.

F. Objections to the argument from my existence.

1. Why must this more perfect being who is the cause of my idea of God and of my existence be taken to be God?
   Reply - Any finite cause must itself be caused by something else and the regress must end at some point with an infinite or perfect cause.

2. Why cannot there be several partial causes for my existence?
   Reply - Unity is one of the main perfections in my idea of God; this must have been caused by a unified being.

G. God cannot be seen as a deceiver, since He is perfect and deception depends upon some defect.

MIDDLE AGES AND RENAISSANCE   193

II. Meditation Four:

Descartes explains the possibility of error.

A. I know that God is not a deceiver and that God also created me along with all my capacities. I also know that I am often in error. This error cannot be due to the correct operation of any faculty which God has created in me, for this would make God a deceiver. I must inquire, therefore, into how it is possible that I can err even though I am the product of a benevolent God.

B. Error is due to the concurrent operation of the will and the intellect. No error is found in the intellect. Error consists in the will, in its judgments, going beyond what the intellect clearly and distinctly perceives to be the case.

C. God cannot be blamed for giving us a free or unlimited will which it is possible for us to abuse and thereby fall into error.

D. The way to avoid error is to refrain from judgment until our intellect sees the truth clearly and distinctly.

III. Meditation Five:

Descartes considers what properties we can know to belong to the essence of material things and also considers another way of proving God's existence by considering what properties we can know to belong to God's essence.

A. When I examine those ideas of corporeal objects that are distinct and not confused, I find that these are properties concerned with extension and duration: length, breadth, depth, size, shape, position, and movement.

1. When I discover particular things about these properties, it seems as if I am recalling something I already knew, something already within me.
2. Although they seem to be already in me, I am not the source of these ideas: they have their own immutable natures which would be the same whether or not I existed, or whether there exists any object that corresponds to these ideas.
3. Neither do these ideas come to me through the senses: I can form an idea that it is impossible to imagine or sense (such as the thousand sided figure mentioned in Meditation Six) and demonstrate many necessary truths concerning its nature.

B. The Ontological Argument for God's existence.

1. We have as a general principle that when I consider an idea, all that I perceive clearly and distinctly as pertaining to that thing really does pertain to it.
2. I understand clearly and distinctly that necessary existence belongs to the essence of God.
3. Therefore, existence really does belong to the essence of God and, hence, God exists.

194   THE MEANING OF LIFE

C. Objections to the argument.

    1.   In all other cases we separate existence from essence.
Reply - It is impossible to conceive a perfect being as lacking a perfection, existence.

    2.   Granted that we cannot think of God except as existing, still our thought does not make him exist.
Reply - It is the necessity of God's existence that imposes the necessity on our thought, not the other way around.

    3.   We need not assume that God has all perfections, including existence.
Reply - It is impossible in conceiving a supreme being to avoid attributing all perfections to Him.

D. The role of God in making knowledge possible.

    1.   Even though we naturally take those things we perceive clearly and distinctly to be true, if I were ignorant of God I could still find reason to doubt these things once my attention was not fixed firmly on their demonstration.

    2.   In particular I might think that I was constituted so as to be deceived about things that I believe I see quite evidently.

    3.   Once we are aware of God's existence and that he cannot have made us so as to be deceived about what we see clearly and distinctly, we cannot be deceived as long as we assent only to what we see clearly and distinctly. It does not matter if we are in fact dreaming; what our intellect tells us is wholly true.

    4.   Therefore, the truth and certainty of every science depends upon the knowledge of God.

Synoptic Outline of Meditation Six

On the Distinction of Mind and Body and the Existence of Material Objects

I. Introduction to the problem of the existence of material things.

A. I know that material objects exist insofar as they are objects of pure mathematics, since I clearly and distinctly perceive the mathematical primary properties of corporeal objects.

B. It also seems that my imagination gives me evidence of the existence of external objects. Therefore, we must investigate this faculty.

II. The distinction between Imagination and Intellect.

A. When I imagine something, I intuit that thing as present to my mind.

B. Imagination is thus distinct from thought since I can think of things without intuiting them as present. An example is a thousand sided figure, the chiligon. I can think of this even though I cannot form an image of it.

MIDDLE AGES AND RENAISSANCE   195

C. Effort is required for imagination, while it does not seem to be for Thought.

D. The faculty of Imagination is not essential to me. I can exist without this faculty.

E. In thought the mind turns on its own ideas. In imagination the mind turns toward the body.

Therefore,

F. The imagination seems to require the existence of the body, but this is only a probability. We cannot yet say certainly that a body exists.

III. The evidence for the existence of corporeal things from the senses.

A. Summary of old beliefs that I got from the senses: all of my impressions of the secondary properties of objects.

B. Reasons for thinking that these showed the existence of objects.

1. These ideas appeared against my will.
2. They are more vivid than those ideas I imagine.
3. All of the ideas that I form through imagination are composed out of components that come from the senses. Nothing is in the imagination that was not first in the senses.
4. I sense pain and pleasure in my body, but not in objects external to me.

C. Reasons for doubting that these things show that material objects exist,

1. The senses often show things to me about objects hat I know cannot be true. For example, a tower in the distance seems round when in fact it is square.
2. People sometimes fell pain in limbs that have been amputated, so the feeling of pain in our body gives no evidence for its existence.
3. It may be possible that I am dreaming.
4. I may be constituted by nature so as to be deceived about things I think I see clearly.
5. There may be some unknown faculty in me that produces these ideas in me even against my will.

IV. The argument for the distinction of mind and body and the existence of material objects.

A. The distinction of mind and body.

1. The argument from knowledge.
    a. If I clearly and distinctly understand one thing as distinct from another it is so.
    b. I am certain that I exist as a thinking thing, while I am not certain of the existence of my body. Therefore,
    c. I am a thinking thing and nothing else. My mind is distinct from my body.
2. The argument from extension.
    a. I am a thing that thinks and not an extended thing.

196   THE MEANING OF LIFE

      b. I have a distinct idea of body as an extended thing. Therefore,
      c. My mind is distinct from my body.

B. The argument that material objects exist.

1. I can understand myself without imagination and sense, but I cannot understand imagination and sense without attributing them to a thing that thinks.
2. Movement is a power of mine, but movement is a power only of extended things. Therefore,
3. It seems that although I am essentially a thinking thing, I am not only a thinking thing. It at least seems to me that I also have an extended body, but we must now see how we can be certain of this.
4. I not only have the power of passive sense, of examining the contents of my mind, but I also have active sense, the power of originating ideas within my mind. This faculty of active sense cannot be within me for two reasons:
      a. No intellection is required for this active sensing.
      b. These ideas come to me by active sense against my will. Therefore,
5. This faculty is in a substance other than myself.
6. This substance much have as much reality as the objective reality of the ideas it produces. Therefore,
7. This substance must be either God or an external extended body.
8. God is no deceiver.
9. He created me and gave me a great inclination to believe that these ideas come from corporeal things.
10. If they do not come from external objects, then God must be a deceiver. But this is an absurdity. Therefore,
11. Material objects exist.

C. These objects, however, may not be as they seem to us through the senses.

Having established the existence of external objects, Descartes goes on to consider whether our senses tell us the truth about them.

V. The relation of Mind and Body.

A. I am intimately joined with my body. Feelings of pain and pleasure are confused modes of perception arising out of my union with the body.

B. We have many ideas from sense, but our nature does not teach us to conclude anything from these unless there is an inquiry by the intellect. Mind, not the composite of mind and body is capable of knowing truth. Therefore,

C. The senses tell us only what is necessary for the welfare of the composite of mind and body.

MIDDLE AGES AND RENAISSANCE   197

D. With respect to the essences of things the senses are confused.

E. The poison objection: It would seem that it some cases our senses do not tell us what is best for the welfare of our body. For example, many poisons seem attractive to the senses, or an ill person may desire something injurious to her.

VI. Is God, therefore, to blame for giving us sensory faculties that sometimes lead us into harm?

A. The body is like a machine.

B. Mind and Body are distinct. This can be seen by noting that mind is indivisible, while body is divisible.

C. Mind is affected only by the brain, so all signals from the body must travel up into the brain.

D. Signals travel to the brain from the periphery of our body by means of animal spirits, so the system is like a cord running to the brain which can be pulled at any point along its length. Thus we can get signals in the brain that do not originate in our senses, but which we perceive as doing so. Therefore,

E. Even though this is the best possible arrangement to protect our body, it is possible to be deceived by a cause of a disturbance in our animal spirits within our body rather than outside it.

Thus God cannot be blamed for this arrangement.

VII. Being aware of this arrangement, I can use memory and intellect to avoid error by restricting my judgment to those things I perceive clearly and distinctly. We can return all those beliefs which we formerly took as doubtful, while disposing of those which led us astray.

BARUCH SPINOZA:

Summary and Biography[64]

Baruch Spinoza was born in 1632 in Amsterdam. He was the middle son in a prominent family of moderate means in Amsterdam's Portuguese-Jewish community. As a boy, he had undoubtedly been one of the star pupils in the congregation's Talmud Torah school. He was intellectually gifted, and this could not have gone unremarked by the congregation's rabbis. It is possible that Spinoza, as he made progress through his studies, was being groomed for a career as a rabbi. But he never made it into the upper levels of the curriculum, those which included advanced study of Talmud. At the age of seventeen, he was forced to cut short his formal studies to help run the family's importing business.

And then, on July 27, 1656, Spinoza was issued the harshest writ of cherem, or excommunication, ever pronounced by the Sephardic community of Amsterdam; it was never rescinded. We do not know for certain what Spinoza's "monstrous deeds" and "abominable heresies" were alleged to have been, but an educated guess comes quite easy. No doubt he was giving utterance to just those ideas that would soon appear in his philosophical treatises. In those works, Spinoza denies the immortality of the soul; strongly rejects the notion of a providential God -- the God of Abraham, Isaac and Jacob; and claims that the Law was neither literally given by God nor any longer binding on Jews. Can there be any mystery as to why one of history's boldest and most radical thinkers was sanctioned by an orthodox Jewish community?

To all appearances, Spinoza was content finally to have an excuse for departing from the community and leaving Judaism behind; his faith and religious commitment were, by this point, gone. Within a few years, he left Amsterdam altogether. By the time his extant correspondence begins, in 1661, he is living in Rijnsburg, not far from Leiden. While in Rijnsburg, he worked on the Treatise on the Emendation of the Intellect, an essay on philosophical method, and the Short Treatise on God, Man and His Well-Being, an initial but aborted effort to lay out his metaphysical, epistemological and moral views. His critical exposition of Descartes's Principles of Philosophy, the only work he published under his own name in his lifetime, was completed in 1663, after he had moved to Voorburg, outside The Hague. By this time, he was also working on what would eventually be called the Ethics, his philosophical masterpiece. However, when he saw the principles of toleration in Holland being threatened by reactionary forces, he put it aside to complete his "scandalous" Theological-Political Treatise, published anonymously and to great alarm in 1670. When Spinoza died in 1677, in The Hague, he was still at work on his Political

---

64 Accessed: http://plato.stanford.edu/entries/spinoza/

Treatise; this was soon published by his friends along with his other unpublished writings, including a Compendium to Hebrew Grammar.

Ethics

The Ethics is an ambitious and multifaceted work. It is also bold to the point of audacity, as one would expect of a systematic and unforgiving critique of the traditional philosophical conceptions of God, the human being and the universe, and, above all, of the religions and the theological and moral beliefs grounded thereupon. What Spinoza intends to demonstrate (in the strongest sense of that word) is the truth about God, nature and especially ourselves; and the highest principles of society, religion and the good life. Despite the great deal of metaphysics, physics, anthropology and psychology that take up Parts One through Three, Spinoza took the crucial message of the work to be ethical in nature. It consists in showing that our happiness and well-being lie not in a life enslaved to the passions and to the transitory goods we ordinarily pursue; nor in the related unreflective attachment to the superstitions that pass as religion, but rather in the life of reason. To clarify and support these broadly ethical conclusions, however, Spinoza must first demystify the universe and show it for what it really is. This requires laying out some metaphysical foundations, the project of Part One.

God or Nature

"On God" begins with some deceptively simple definitions of terms that would be familiar to any seventeenth century philosopher. "By substance I understand what is in itself and is conceived through itself"; "By attribute I understand what the intellect perceives of a substance, as constituting its essence"; "By God I understand a being absolutely infinite, i.e., a substance consisting of an infinity of attributes, of which each one expresses an eternal and infinite essence." The definitions of Part One are, in effect, simply clear concepts that ground the rest of his system. They are followed by a number of axioms that, he assumes, will be regarded as obvious and unproblematic by the philosophically informed ("Whatever is, is either in itself or in another"; "From a given determinate cause the effect follows necessarily"). From these, the first proposition necessarily follows, and every subsequent proposition can be demonstrated using only what precedes it. (References to the Ethics will be by part (I-V), proposition (p), definition (d), scholium (s) and corollary (c).)

In propositions one through fifteen of Part One, Spinoza presents the basic elements of his picture of God. God is the infinite, necessarily existing (that is, uncaused), unique substance of the universe. There is only one substance in the universe; it is God; and everything else that is, is in God.

Proposition 1: A substance is prior in nature to its affections.

Proposition 2: Two substances having different attributes have nothing in common with one another. (In other words, if two substances differ in nature, then they have nothing in common).

200 THE MEANING OF LIFE

Proposition 3: If things have nothing in common with one another, one of them cannot be the cause of the other.

Proposition 4: Two or more distinct things are distinguished from one another, either by a difference in the attributes [i.e., the natures or essences] of the substances or by a difference in their affections [i.e., their accidental properties].

Proposition 5: In nature, there cannot be two or more substances of the same nature or attribute.

Proposition 6: One substance cannot be produced by another substance.

Proposition 7: It pertains to the nature of a substance to exist.

Proposition 8: Every substance is necessarily infinite.

Proposition 9: The more reality or being each thing has, the more attributes belong to it.

Proposition 10: Each attribute of a substance must be conceived through itself.

Proposition 11: God, or a substance consisting of infinite attributes, each of which expresses eternal and infinite essence, necessarily exists. (The proof of this proposition consists simply in the classic "ontological proof for God's existence". Spinoza writes that "if you deny this, conceive, if you can, that God does not exist. Therefore, by axiom 7 ['If a thing can be conceived as not existing, its essence does not involve existence'], his essence does not involve existence. But this, by proposition 7, is absurd. Therefore, God necessarily exists, q.e.d.")

Proposition 12: No attribute of a substance can be truly conceived from which it follows that the substance can be divided.

Proposition 13: A substance which is absolutely infinite is indivisible.

Proposition 14: Except God, no substance can be or be conceived.

This proof that God -- an infinite, necessary and uncaused, indivisible being -- is the only substance of the universe proceeds in three simple steps. First, establish that no two substances can share an attribute or essence (Ip5). Then, prove that there is a substance with infinite attributes (i.e., God) (Ip11). It follows, in conclusion, that the existence of that infinite substance precludes the existence of any other substance. For if there were to be a second substance, it would have to have some attribute or essence. But since God has all possible attributes, then the attribute to be possessed by this second substance would be one of the attributes already possessed by God. But it has already been established that no two substances can have the same attribute. Therefore, there can be, besides God, no such second substance.

If God is the only substance, and (by axiom 1) whatever is, is either a substance or in a substance, then everything else must be in God. "Whatever is, is in God, and nothing can be or be conceived without God" (Ip15).

As soon as this preliminary conclusion has been established, Spinoza immediately reveals the objective of his attack. His definition of God -- condemned since his excommunication from the Jewish community as a "God existing in only a philosophical sense" -- is meant to preclude any anthropomorphizing of the divine being. In the scholium to proposition fifteen, he writes against "those who feign a God, like man, consisting of a body and a mind, and subject to passions. But how far they wander from the true knowledge of God, is sufficiently established by what has already been demonstrated." Besides being false, such an anthropomorphic conception of God can have only deleterious effects on human freedom and activity.

Much of the technical language of Part One is, to all appearances, right out of Descartes. But even the most devoted Cartesian would have had a hard time understanding the full import of propositions one through fifteen. What does it mean to say that God is substance and that everything else is "in" God? Is Spinoza saying that rocks, tables, chairs, birds, mountains, rivers and human beings are all properties of God, and hence can be predicated of God (just as one would say that the table "is red")? It seems very odd to think that objects and individuals -- what we ordinarily think of as independent "things" -- are, in fact, merely properties of a thing. Spinoza was sensitive to the strangeness of this kind of talk, not to mention the philosophical problems to which it gives rise. When a person feels pain, does it follow that the pain is ultimately just a property of God, and thus that God feels pain? Conundrums such as this may explain why, as of Proposition Sixteen, there is a subtle but important shift in Spinoza's language. God is now described not so much as the underlying substance of all things, but as the universal, immanent and sustaining cause of all that exists: "From the necessity of the divine nature there must follow infinitely many things in infinitely many modes, (i.e., everything that can fall under an infinite intellect)".

According to the traditional Judeo-Christian conception of divinity, God is a transcendent creator, a being who causes a world distinct from himself to come into being by creating it out of nothing. God produces that world by a spontaneous act of free will, and could just as easily have not created anything outside himself. By contrast, Spinoza's God is the cause of all things because all things follow causally and necessarily from the divine nature. Or, as he puts it, from God's infinite power or nature "all things have necessarily flowed, or always followed, by the same necessity and in the same way as from the nature of a triangle it follows, from eternity and to eternity, that its three angles are equal to two right angles" (Ip17s1). The existence of the world is, thus, mathematically necessary. It is impossible that God should exist but not the world. This does not mean that God does not cause the world to come into being freely, since nothing outside of God constrains him to bring it into existence. But Spinoza does deny that God creates the world by some arbitrary and undetermined act of free will. God could not have done otherwise. There are no possible alternatives to the actual world, and absolutely no contingency or spontaneity within that world. Everything is absolutely and necessarily determined.

202   THE MEANING OF LIFE

(Ip29): In nature there is nothing contingent, but all things have been determined from the necessity of the divine nature to exist and produce an effect in a certain way.

(Ip33): Things could have been produced by God in no other way, and in no other order than they have been produced.

There are, however, differences in the way things depend on God. Some features of the universe follow necessarily from God -- or, more precisely, from the absolute nature of one of God's attributes -- in a direct and unmediated manner. These are the universal and eternal aspects of the world, and they do not come into or go out of being. They include the most general laws of the universe, together governing all things in all ways. From the attribute of extension there follow the principles governing all extended objects (the truths of geometry) and laws governing the motion and rest of bodies (the laws of physics); from the attribute of thought, there follow laws of thought (understood by commentators to be either the laws of logic or the laws of psychology). Particular and individual things are causally more remote from God. They are nothing but "affections of God's attributes, or modes by which God's attributes are expressed in a certain and determinate way" (Ip25c).

There are two causal orders or dimensions governing the production and actions of particular things. On the one hand, they are determined by the general laws of the universe that follow immediately from God's natures. On the other hand, each particular thing is determined to act and to be acted upon by other particular things. Thus, the actual behavior of a body in motion is a function not just of the universal laws of motion, but also of the other bodies in motion and rest surrounding it and with which it comes into contact.

Spinoza's metaphysics of God is neatly summed up in a phrase that occurs in the Latin (but not the Dutch) edition of the Ethics: "God, or Nature", Deus, sive Natura: "That eternal and infinite being we call God, or Nature, acts from the same necessity from which he exists" (Part IV, Preface). It is an ambiguous phrase, since Spinoza could be read as trying either to divinize nature or to naturalize God. But for the careful reader there is no mistaking Spinoza's intention. The friends who, after his death, published his writings must have left out the "or Nature" clause from the more widely accessible Dutch version out of fear of the reaction that this identification would, predictably, arouse among a vernacular audience.

There are, Spinoza insists, two sides of Nature. First, there is the active, productive aspect of the universe -- God and his attributes, from which all else follows. This is what Spinoza, employing the same terms he used in the Short Treatise, calls Natura naturans, "naturing Nature". Strictly speaking, this is identical with God. The other aspect of the universe is that which is produced and sustained by the active aspect, Natura naturata, "natured Nature".

By Natura naturata I understand whatever follows from the necessity of God's nature, or from any of God's attributes, i.e., all the modes of God's attributes insofar as they are considered as things that are in God, and can neither be nor be conceived without God. (Ip29s).

Spinoza's fundamental insight in Book One is that Nature is an indivisible, uncaused, substantial whole -- in fact, it is the only substantial whole. Outside of Nature, there is nothing, and everything that exists is a part of Nature and is brought into being by Nature with a deterministic necessity. This unified, unique, productive, necessary being just is what is meant by 'God'. Because of the necessity inherent in Nature, there is no teleology in the universe. Nature does not act for any ends, and things do not exist for any set purposes. There are no "final causes" (to use the common Aristotelian phrase). God does not "do" things for the sake of anything else. The order of things just follows from God's essences with an inviolable determinism. All talk of God's purposes, intentions, goals, preferences or aims is just an anthropomorphizing fiction.

> *All the prejudices I here undertake to expose depend on this one: that men commonly suppose that all natural things act, as men do, on account of an end; indeed, they maintain as certain that God himself directs all things to some certain end, for they say that God has made all things for man, and man that he might worship God. (I, Appendix)*

God is not some goal-oriented planner who then judges things by how well they conform to his purposes. Things happen only because of Nature and its laws. "Nature has no end set before it . . . All things proceed by a certain eternal necessity of nature." To believe otherwise is to fall prey to the same superstitions that lie at the heart of the organized religions.

> *[People] find -- both in themselves and outside themselves -- many means that are very helpful in seeking their own advantage, e.g., eyes for seeing, teeth for chewing, plants and animals for food, the sun for light, the sea for supporting fish . . . Hence, they consider all natural things as means to their own advantage. And knowing that they had found these means, not provided them for themselves, they had reason to believe that there was someone else who had prepared those means for their use. For after they considered things as means, they could not believe that the things had made themselves; but from the means they were accustomed to prepare for themselves, they had to infer that there was a ruler, or a number of rulers of nature, endowed with human freedom, who had taken care of all things for them, and made all things for their use.*

> *And since they had never heard anything about the temperament of these rulers, they had to judge it from their own. Hence, they maintained that the Gods direct all things for the use of men in order to bind men to them and be held by men in the highest honor. So it has happened that each of them has thought up from his own temperament different ways of worshipping God, so that God might love them above all the rest, and direct the whole of Nature according to the needs of their blind desire and insatiable greed. Thus this prejudice was changed into superstition, and struck deep roots in their minds. (I, Appendix)*

A judging God who has plans and acts purposively is a God to be obeyed and placated. Opportunistic preachers are then able to play on our hopes and fears in the face of such a God. They prescribe ways of acting that are calculated to avoid being punished by that God and earn

THE MEANING OF LIFE

his rewards. But, Spinoza insists, to see God or Nature as acting for the sake of ends -- to find purpose in Nature -- is to misconstrue Nature and "turn it upside down" by putting the effect (the end result) before the true cause.

Nor does God perform miracles, since there are no departures whatsoever from the necessary course of nature. The belief in miracles is due only to ignorance of the true causes of phenomena.

> *If a stone has fallen from a room onto someone's head and killed him, they will show, in the following way, that the stone fell in order to kill the man. For if it did not fall to that end, God willing it, how could so many circumstances have concurred by chance (for often many circumstances do concur at once)? Perhaps you will answer that it happened because the wind was blowing hard and the man was walking that way. But they will persist: why was the wind blowing hard at that time? why was the man walking that way at that time? If you answer again that the wind arose then because on the preceding day, while the weather was still calm, the sea began to toss, and that the man had been invited by a friend, they will press on -- for there is no end to the questions which can be asked: but why was the sea tossing? why was the man invited at just that time? And so they will not stop asking for the causes of causes until you take refuge in the will of God, i.e., the sanctuary of ignorance. (I, Appendix)*

This is strong language, and Spinoza is clearly not unaware of the risks of his position. The same preachers who take advantage of our credulity will fulminate against anyone who tries to pull aside the curtain and reveal the truths of Nature. "One who seeks the true causes of miracles, and is eager, like an educated man, to understand natural things, not to wonder at them, like a fool, is generally considered and denounced as an impious heretic by whose whom the people honor as interpreters of nature and the Gods. For they know that if ignorance is taken away, then foolish wonder, the only means they have of arguing and defending their authority is also taken away."

The Human Being

In Part Two, Spinoza turns to the origin and nature of the human being. The two attributes of God of which we have cognizance are extension and thought. This, in itself, involves what would have been an astounding thesis in the eyes of his contemporaries, one that was usually misunderstood and always vilified. When Spinoza claims in Proposition Two that "Extension is an attribute of God, or God is an extended thing", he was almost universally -- but erroneously -- interpreted as saying that God is literally corporeal. For just this reason, "Spinozism" became, for his critics, synonymous with atheistic materialism.

According to one interpretation, God is indeed material, even matter itself, but this does not imply that God has a body. Another interpretation, however, one which will be adopted here, is that what is in God is not matter per se, but extension as an essence. And extension and thought are two distinct essences that have absolutely nothing in common. The modes or expressions of extension are physical bodies; the modes of thought are ideas. Because extension and thought have nothing in common, the two realms of matter and mind are causally closed systems.

MIDDLE AGES AND RENAISSANCE 205

Everything that is extended follows from the attribute of extension alone. Every bodily event is part of an infinite causal series of bodily events and is determined only by the nature of extension and its laws, in conjunction with its relations to other extended bodies. Similarly, every idea follows only from the attribute of thought. Any idea is an integral part of an infinite series of ideas and is determined by the nature of thought and its laws, along with its relations to other ideas. There is, in other words, no causal interaction between bodies and ideas, between the physical and the mental. There is, however, a thoroughgoing correlation and parallelism between the two series. For every mode in extension that is a relatively stable collection of matter, there is a corresponding mode in thought. In fact, he insists, "a mode of extension and the idea of that mode are one and the same thing, but expressed in two ways". Because of the fundamental and underlying unity of Nature, or of Substance, Thought and Extension are just two different ways of "comprehending" one and the same Nature. Every material thing thus has its own particular idea - - a kind of Platonic concept -- that expresses or represents it. Since that idea is just a mode of one of God's attributes -- Thought -- it is in God, and the infinite series of ideas constitutes God's mind. As he explains,

> A circle existing in nature and the idea of the existing circle, which is also in God, are one and the same thing, which is explained through different attributes. Therefore, whether we conceive nature under the attribute of Extension, or under the attribute of Thought, or under any other attribute, we shall find one and the same order, or one and the same connection of causes, i.e., that the same things follow one another.

It follows from this, he argues, that the causal relations between bodies is mirrored in the logical relations between God's ideas. Or, as Spinoza notes in Proposition Seven, "the order and connection of ideas is the same as the order and connection of things".

One kind of extended body, however, is significantly more complex than any others in its composition and in its dispositions to act and be acted upon. That complexity is reflected in its corresponding idea. The body in question is the human body; and its corresponding idea is the human mind or soul. The mind, then, like any other idea, is simply one particular mode of God's attribute, Thought. Whatever happens in the body is reflected or expressed in the mind. In this way, the mind perceives, more or less obscurely, what is taking place in its body. And through its body's interactions with other bodies, the mind is aware of what is happening in the physical world around it. But the human mind no more interacts with its body than any mode of Thought interacts with a mode of Extension.

One of the pressing questions in seventeenth century philosophy, and perhaps the most celebrated legacy of Descartes's dualism, is the problem of how two radically different substances such as mind and body enter into a union in a human being and cause effects in each other. How can the extended body causally engage the unextended mind, which is incapable of contact or motion, and "move" it, that is, cause mental effects such as pains, sensations and perceptions. Spinoza, in effect, denies that the human being is a union of two substances. The human mind and the human body are two different expressions -- under Thought and under Extension -- of one and

206 THE MEANING OF LIFE

the same thing: the person. And because there is no causal interaction between the mind and the body, the so-called mind-body problem does not, technically speaking, arise.

Knowledge

The human mind, like God, contains ideas. Some of these ideas -- sensory images, qualitative "feels" (like pains and pleasures), perceptual data -- are imprecise qualitative phenomena, being the expression in thought of states of the body as it is affected by the bodies surrounding it. Such ideas do not convey adequate and true knowledge of the world, but only a relative, partial and subjective picture of how things presently seem to be to the perceiver. There is no systematic order to these perceptions, nor any critical oversight by reason. "As long as the human Mind perceives things from the common order of nature, it does not have an adequate, but only a confused and mutilated knowledge of itself, of its own Body, and of external bodies" (IIp29c). Under such circumstances, we are simply determined in our ideas by our fortuitous and haphazard encounter with things in the external world. This superficial acquaintance will never provide us with knowledge of the essences of those things. In fact, it is an invariable source of falsehood and error. This "knowledge from random experience" is also the origin of great delusions, since we -- thinking ourselves free -- are, in our ignorance, unaware of just how we are determined by causes.

Adequate ideas, on the other hand, are formed in a rational and orderly manner, and are necessarily true and revelatory of the essences of things. "Reason", the second kind of knowledge (after "random experience"), is the apprehension of the essence of a thing through a discursive, inferential procedure. "A true idea means nothing other than knowing a thing perfectly, or in the best way." It involves grasping a thing's causal connections not just to other objects but, more importantly, to the attributes of God and the infinite modes (the laws of nature) that follow immediately from them. The adequate idea of a thing clearly and distinctly situates its object in all of its causal nexuses and shows not just that it is, but how and why it is. The person who truly knows a thing sees the reasons why the thing was determined to be and could not have been otherwise. "It is of the nature of Reason to regard things as necessary, not as contingent" (IIp44). The belief that some thing is accidental or spontaneous can be based only on an inadequate grasp of the thing's causal explanation, on a partial and "mutilated" familiarity with it. To perceive by way of adequate ideas is to perceive the necessity inherent in Nature.

Sense experience alone could never provide the information conveyed by an adequate idea. The senses present things only as they appear from a given perspective at a given moment in time. An adequate idea, on the other hand, by showing how a thing follows necessarily from one or another of God's attributes, presents it in its "eternal" aspects -- sub specie aeternitatis, as Spinoza puts it -- without any relation to time. "It is of the nature of Reason to regard things as necessary and not as contingent. And Reason perceives this necessity of things truly, i.e., as it is in itself. But this necessity of things is the very necessity of God's eternal nature. Therefore, it is of the nature of Reason to regard things under this species of eternity". The third kind of knowledge, intuition, takes what is known by Reason and grasps it in a single act of the mind.

MIDDLE AGES AND RENAISSANCE 207

Spinoza's conception of adequate knowledge reveals an unrivaled optimism in the cognitive powers of the human being. Not even Descartes believed that we could know all of Nature and its innermost secrets with the degree of depth and certainty that Spinoza thought possible. Most remarkably, because Spinoza thought that the adequate knowledge of any object, and of Nature as a whole, involves a thorough knowledge of God and of how things related to God and his attributes, he also had no scruples about claiming that we can, at least in principle, know God perfectly and adequately. "The knowledge of God's eternal and infinite essence that each idea involves is adequate and perfect" (IIp46). "The human Mind has an adequate knowledge of God's eternal and infinite essence" (Iip47). No other philosopher in history has been willing to make this claim. But, then again, no other philosopher identified God with Nature.

Passion and Action

Spinoza engages in such a detailed analysis of the composition of the human being because it is essential to his goal of showing how the human being is a part of Nature, existing within the same causal nexuses as other extended and mental beings. This has serious ethical implications. First, it implies that a human being is not endowed with freedom, at least in the ordinary sense of that term. Because our minds and the events in our minds are simply ideas that exist within the causal series of ideas that follows from God's attribute Thought, our actions and volitions are as necessarily determined as any other natural events. "In the Mind there is no absolute, or free, will, but the Mind is determined to will this or that by a cause that is also determined by another, and this again by another, and so to infinity."
What is true of the will (and, of course, of our bodies) is true of all the phenomena of our psychological lives. Spinoza believes that this is something that has not been sufficiently understood by previous thinkers, who seem to have wanted to place the human being on a pedestal outside of (or above) nature.

> *Most of those who have written about the Affects, and men's way of living, seem to treat, not of natural things, which follow the common laws of nature, but of things that are outside nature. Indeed they seem to conceive man in nature as a dominion within a dominion. For they believe that man disturbs, rather than follows, the order of nature, that he has absolute power over his actions, and that he is determined only by himself. (III, Preface)*

Descartes, for example, believed that if the freedom of the human being is to be preserved, the soul must be exempt from the kind of deterministic laws that rule over the material universe.
Spinoza's aim in Parts Three and Four is, as he says in his Preface to Part Three, to restore the human being and his volitional and emotional life into their proper place in nature. For nothing stands outside of nature, not even the human mind.

> *Nature is always the same, and its virtue and power of acting are everywhere one and the same, i.e., the laws and rules of nature, according to which all things happen, and change from one form to another, are always and everywhere the same. So the way of understanding the nature of*

208 THE MEANING OF LIFE

anything, of whatever kind, must also be the same, viz. through the universal laws and rules of nature.

Our affects -- our love, anger, hate, envy, pride, jealousy, etc. -- "follow from the same necessity and force of nature as the other singular things". Spinoza, therefore, explains these emotions -- as determined in their occurrence as are a body in motion and the properties of a mathematical figure -- just as he would explain any other things in nature. "I shall treat the nature and power of the Affects, and the power of the Mind over them, by the same Method by which, in the preceding parts, I treated God and the Mind, and I shall consider human actions and appetites just as if it were a Question of lines, planes, and bodies."

Our affects are divided into actions and passions. When the cause of an event lies in our own nature -- more particularly, our knowledge or adequate ideas -- then it is a case of the mind acting. On the other hand, when something happens in us the cause of which lies outside of our nature, then we are passive and being acted upon. Usually what takes place, both when we are acting and when we are being acted upon, is some change in our mental or physical capacities, what Spinoza calls "an increase or decrease in our power of acting" or in our "power to persevere in being". All beings are naturally endowed with such a power or striving. This conatus, a kind of existential inertia, constitutes the "essence" of any being. "Each thing, as far as it can by its own power, strives to persevere in its being." An affect just is any change in this power, for better or for worse. Affects that are actions are changes in this power that have their source (or "adequate cause") in our nature alone; affects that are passions are those changes in this power that originate outside of us.

What we should strive for is to be free from the passions -- or, since this is not absolutely possible, at least to learn how to moderate and restrain them -- and become active, autonomous beings. If we can acheive this, then we will be "free" to the extent that whatever happens to us will result not from our relations with things outside us, but from our own nature (as that follows from, and is ultimately and necessarily determined by the attributes of God of which our minds and bodies are modes). We will, consequently, be truly liberated from the troublesome emotional ups and downs of this life. The way to bring this about is to increase our knowledge, our store of adequate ideas, and eliminate as far as possible our inadequate ideas, which follow not from the nature of the mind alone but from its being an expresssion of how our body is affected by other bodies. In other words, we need to free ourselves from a reliance on the senses and the imagination, since a life of the senses and images is a life being affected and led by the objects around us, and rely as much as we can only on our rational faculties.

Because of our innate striving to persevere -- which, in the human being, is called "will" or "appetite" -- we naturally pursue those things that we believe will benefit us by increasing our power of acting and shun or flee those things that we believe will harm us by decreasing our power of acting. This provides Spinoza with a foundation for cataloguing the human passions. For the passions are all functions of the ways in which external things affect our powers or capacities. Joy [Laaetitiae, sometimes translated as "pleasure"], for example, is simply the movement or passage to a greater capacity for action. "By Joy . . . I shall understand that passion by which the Mind passes to a greater perfection" (IIIp11s). Being a passion, joy is always brought about by some external object. Sadness [Tristitiae, or "pain"], on the other hand, is the passage to a lesser state of perfection, also occasioned by a thing outside us. Love is simply Joy accompanied by an awareness of the external cause that brings about the passage to a greater perfection. We love that object that benefits us and causes us joy. Hate is nothing but "Sadness with the accompanying idea of an external cause". Hope is simply "an inconstant Joy which has arisen from the image of a future or past thing whose outcome we doubt". We hope for a thing whose presence, as yet uncertain, will bring about joy. We fear, however, a thing whose presence, equally uncertain, will bring about sadness. When that whose outcome was doubtful becomes certain, hope is changed into confidence, while fear is changed into despair.

All of the human emotions, in so far as they are passions, are constantly directed outward, towards things and their capacities to affect us one way or another. Aroused by our passions and desires, we seek or flee those things that we believe cause joy or sadness. "We strive to further the occurrence of whatever we imagine will lead to Joy, and to avert or destroy what we imagine is contrary to it, or will lead to Sadness." Our hopes and fears fluctuate depending on whether we regard the objects of our desires or aversions as remote, near, necessary, possible or unlikely. But the objects of our passions, being external to us, are completely beyond our control. Thus, the more we allow ourselves to be controlled by them, the more we are subject to passions and the less active and free we are. The upshot is a fairly pathetic picture of a life mired in the passions and pursuing and fleeing the changeable and fleeting objects that occasion them: "We are driven about in many ways by external causes, and . . . like waves on the sea, driven by contrary winds, we toss about, not knowing our outcome and fate" (IIIp59s). The title for Part Four of the Ethics reveals with perfect clarity Spinoza's evaluation of such a life for a human being: "On Human Bondage, or the Powers of the Affects". He explains that the human being's "lack of power to moderate and restrain the affects I call Bondage. For the man who is subject to affects is under the control, not of himself, but of fortune, in whose power he so greatly is that often, though he sees the better for himself, he is still forced to follow the worse". It is, he says, a kind of "sickness of the mind" to suffer too much love for a thing "that is liable to many variations and that we can never fully possess."

Virtue and Happiness

The solution to this predicament is an ancient one. Since we cannot control the objects that we tend to value and that we allow to influence our well-being, we ought instead to try to control our evaluations themselves and thereby minimize the sway that external objects and the passions have over us. We can never eliminate the passive affects entirely. We are essentially a part of nature, and can never fully remove outselves from the causal series that link us to external things. But we can, ultimately, counteract the passions, control them, and achieve a certain degree of relief from their turmoil.

The path to restraining and moderating the affects is through virtue. Spinoza is a psychological and ethical egoist. All beings naturally seek their own advantage -- to preserve

210   THE MEANING OF LIFE

their own being -- and it is right for them do so. This is what virtue consists in. Since we are thinking beings, endowed with intelligence and reason, what is to our greatest advantage is knowledge. Our virtue, therefore, consists in the pursuit of knowledge and understanding, of adequate ideas. The best kind of knowledge is a purely intellectual intuition of the essences of things. This "third kind of knowledge" -- beyond both random experience and ratiocination -- sees things not in their temporal dimension, not in their duration and in relation to other particular things, but under the aspect of eternity, that is, abstracted from all considerations of time and place and situated in their relationship to God and his attributes. They are apprehended, that is, in their conceptual and causal relationship to the universal essences (thought and extension) and the eternal laws of nature.

> *We conceive things as actual in two ways: either insofar as we conceive them to exist in relation to a certain time and place, or insofar as we conceive them to be contained in God and to follow from the necessity of the divine nature. But the things we conceive in this second way as true, or real, we conceive under a species of eternity, and to that extent they involve the eternal and infinite essence of God. (Vp39s)*

But this is just to say that, ultimately, we strive for a knowledge of God. The concept of any body involves the concept of extension; and the concept of any idea or mind involves the concept of thought. But thought and extension just are God's attributes. So the proper and adequate conception of any body or mind necessarily involves the concept or knowledge of God. "The third kind of knowledge proceeds from an adquate idea of certain attributes of God to an adequate knowledge of the essence of things, and the more we understand things in this way, the more we understand God." Knowledge of God is, thus, the Mind's greatest good and its greatest virtue.

What we see when we understand things through the third kind of knowledge, under the aspect of eternity and in relation to God, is the deterministic necessity of all things. We see that all bodies and their states follow necessarily from the essence of matter and the universal laws of physics; and we see that all ideas, including all the properties of minds, follow necessarily from the essence of thought and its universal laws. This insight can only weaken the power that the passions have over us. We are no longer hopeful or fearful of what shall come to pass, and no longer anxious or despondent over our possessions. We regard all things with equanimity, and we are not inordinately and irrationally affected in different ways by past, present or future events. The result is self-control and a calmness of mind.

> *The more this knowledge that things are necessary is concerned with singular things, which we imagine more distinctly and vividly, the greater is this power of the Mind over the affects, as experience itself also testifies. For we see that Sadness over some good which has perished is lessened as soon as the man who has lost it realizes that this good could not, in any way, have been kept. Similarly, we see that [because we regard infancy as a natural and necessary thing], no one pities infants because of their inability to speak, to walk, or to reason, or because they live so many years, as it were, unconscious of themselves. (Vp6s)*

MIDDLE AGES AND RENAISSANCE 211

Our affects themselves can be understood in this way, which further diminishes their power over us.

Spinoza's ethical theory is, to a certain degree, Stoic, and recalls the doctrines of thinkers such as Cicero and Seneca:

We do not have an absolute power to adapt things outside us to our use. Nevertheless, we shall bear calmly those things that happen to us contrary to what the principle of our advantage demands, if we are conscious that we have done our duty, that the power we have could not have extended itself to the point where we could have avoided those things, and that we are a part of the whole of nature, whose order we follow. If we understand this clearly and distinctly, that part of us which is defined by understanding, i.e., the better part of us, will be entirely satisfied with this, and will strive to persevere in that satisfaction. For insofar as we understand, we can want nothing except what is necessary, nor absolutely be satisfied with anything except what is true. (IV, Appendix)

What, in the end, replaces the passionate love for ephemeral "goods" is an intellectual love for an eternal, immutable good that we can fully and stably possess, God. The third kind of knowledge generates a love for its object, and in this love consists not joy, a passion, but blessedness itself. Taking his cue from Maimonides's view of human eudaimonia, Spinoza argues that the mind's intellectual love of God is our understanding of the universe, our virtue, our happiness, our well-being and our "salvation". It is also our freedom and autonomy, as we approach the condition wherein what happens to us follows from our nature (as a determinate and determined mode of one of God's attributes) alone and not as a result of the ways external things affect us. Spinoza's "free person" is one who bears the gifts and losses of fortune with equanimity, does only those things that he believes to be "the most important in life", takes care for the well-being of others (doing what he can to insure that they, too, achieve some relief from the disturbances of the passions through understanding), and is not anxious about death. The free person neither hopes for any eternal, otherworldly rewards nor fears any eternal punishments. He knows that the soul is not immortal in any personal sense, but is endowed only with a certain kind of eternity. The more the mind consists of true and adequate ideas (which are eternal), the more of it remains -- within God's attribute of Thought -- after the death of the body and the disappearance of that part of the mind that corresponds to the body's duration. This understanding of his place in the natural scheme of things brings to the free individual true peace of mind.

There are a number of social and political ramifications that follow from Spinoza's ethical doctrines of human action and well-being. Because disagreement and discord between human beings is always the result of our different and changeable passions, "free" individuals -- who all share the same nature and act on the same principles -- will naturally and effortlessly form a harmonious society. "Insofar as men are torn by affects that are passions, they can be contrary to one another . . .[But] insofar as men live according to the guidance of reason, they must do only those things that are good for human nature, and hence, for each man, i.e., those things that agree with the nature of each man. Hence, insofar as men live according to the guidance of reason, they must always agree among themselves" (IVp34-35). Free human beings will be mutually beneficial and useful, and will be tolerant of the opinions and even the errors of others. However, human beings do not generally live under the guidance of reason. The state or sovereign, therefore, is required in order to insure -- not by reason, but by the threat of force -- that individuals are protected from the unrestrained pursuit of self-interest on the part of other individuals. The transition from a state of nature, where each seeks his own advantage without limitation, to a civil state involves the universal renunciation of certain natural rights -- such as "the right everyone has of avenging himself, and of judging good and evil" -- and the investment of those prerogatives in a central authority. As long as human beings are guided by their passions, the state is necessary to bring it about that they "live harmoniously and be of assistance to one another".

John Locke (1689)

An Essay Concerning Human Understanding (1689). Excerpts from early in the work.[65]

CHAPTER II

NO INNATE PRINCIPLES IN THE MIND.

1. The way shown how we come by any knowledge, sufficient to prove it not innate. - It is an established opinion among some men, that there are in the understanding certain innate principles; some primarily notions, characters, as it were, stamped upon the mind of man, which the soul receives in its very first being and brings into the world with it. It would be sufficient to convince unprejudiced readers of the falseness of this supposition, if I should only show (as I hope I shall in the following parts of this discourse) how men, barely by the use of their natural faculties, may attain to all the knowledge they have, without the help of any innate impressions, and may arrive at certainty without any such original notions or principles. For I imagine, any one will easily grant, that it would be impertinent to suppose the ideas of colours innate in a creature to whom God hath given sight, and a power to receive them by the eyes from external objects: and no less unreasonable would it be to attribute several truths to the impressions of nature and innate characters, when we may observe in ourselves faculties fit to attain as easy and certain knowledge of them as if they were originally imprinted on the mind.

But because a man is not permitted without censure to follow his own thoughts in the search of truth, when they lead him ever so little out of the common road, I shall set down the reasons that made me doubt of the truth of that opinion as an excuse for my mistake, if I be in one; which I leave to be considered by those who, with me, dispose themselves to embrace truth wherever they find it.

2. General assent the great argument. - There is nothing more commonly taken for granted, than that there are certain principles, both speculative and practical (for they speak of both), universally agreed upon by all mankind; which therefore; they argue, must needs be constant impressions which the souls of men receive in their first beings, and which they bring into the world with them, as necessarily and really as they do any of their inherent faculties.

3. Universal consent proves nothing innate. - This argument, drawn from universal consent, has this misfortune in it, that if it were true in matter of fact that there were certain truths wherein all mankind agreed, it would not prove them innate, if there can be any other way shown, how men

---

[65] Accessed: http://www.marxists.org/reference/subject/philosophy/works/en/locke.htm

214 THE MEANING OF LIFE

may come to that universal agreement in the things they do consent in; which I presume may be done.

4. " What is, is; " and, " It is impossible for the same thing to be, and not to be," not universally assented to. - But, which is worse, this argument of universal consent, which is made use of to prove innate principles, seems to me a demonstration that there are none such; because there are none to which all mankind give an universal assent. I shall begin with the speculative, and instance in those magnified principles of demonstration: " Whatsoever is, is; " and "' It is impossible for the same thing to be, and not to be," which, of all others, I think, have the most allowed title to innate. These have so settled a reputation of maxims universally received that it will, no doubt, be thought strange if any one should seem to question it. But yet I take liberty to say, that these propositions are so far from having an universal assent, that there are a great part of mankind to whom they are not so much as known.

5. Not on the mind naturally, imprinted, because not known to children, idiots, etc. - For, first, it is evident, that all children and idiots have not the least apprehension or thought of them; and the want of that is enough to destroy that universal assent, which must needs be the necessary concomitant of all innate truths: it seeming to me near a contradiction to say, that there are truths imprinted on the soul which it perceives or understands not; imprinting, if it signify anything, being nothing else but the making certain truths to be perceived. For to imprint anything on the mind without the mind's perceiving it, seems to me hardly intelligible. If therefore children and idiots have souls, have minds, with those impressions upon them, they must unavoidably perceive them, and necessarily know and assent to these truths; Which, since they do not, it is evident that there are no such impressions. For if they are not notions naturally imprinted, how can they be innate? And if they are notions imprinted, how can they he unknown? To say, a notion is imprinted on the mind, and yet at the same time to say that the mind is ignorant of it, and never yet took notice of it, is to make this impression nothing. No proposition can he said to be in the mind which it never yet knew, which it was never yet conscious of. For if any one say, then, by the same reason, all propositions that are true, and the mind is capable ever of assenting to, may be said to be in the mind, and to the imprinted; since if any one can be said to be in the mind, which it never yet knew, it must be only because it is capable of knowing it; and so the mind is of all truths it ever shall know. Nay, thus truths may be imprinted on the mind which it never did, nor ever shall, know: for a man may live long and die at last in ignorance of many truths which his mind was capable of knowing, and that with certainty. So that if the capacity of knowing be the natural impression contended for, all the truths a man ever comes to know will, by this account, be every one of them innate: and this great point will amount to no more, but only to a very improper way of speaking; which, whilst it pretends to assert the contrary, says nothing different from those who deny innate principles. For nobody, I think, ever denied that the mind was capable of knowing several truths. The capacity, they say, is innate; the knowledge acquired. But then, to what end such contest for certain innate maxims? If truths can be imprinted on the understanding without being perceived I can see no difference there can be between any truths the

MIDDLE AGES AND RENAISSANCE   215

mind is capable of knowing in respect of their original: they must all be innate, or all adventitious; in vain shall a man go about to distinguish them. He therefore that talks of innate notions in the understanding, cannot (if he intend thereby any distinct sort of truths) mean such truths to be in the understanding as it never perceived, and is yet wholly ignorant of. For if these words ("to be in the understanding") have any propriety, they signify to be understood. So that, to be in the understanding and not to be understood; to be in the mind, and never to be perceived; is all one as to say, anything is, and is not, in the mind or understanding. If therefore these two propositions: "Whatsoever is ,is;" and, "It is impossible for the same thing to be, and not to be," are by nature imprinted, children cannot be ignorant of them; infants, and all that have souls, must necessarily have them in their understandings, know the truth of them, and assent to it.

6. That men know them when they come to the use of reason, answered. - To avoid this, it is usually answered, that all well know and assent to them, when they come to the use of reason; and this is enough to prove them innate. I answer,

7. Doubtful expressions, that have scarce any signification, go for clear results to those who, being prepossessed, take not the pains to examine even what they themselves say. For, to apply this answer with any tolerable sense to our present purpose, it must signify one of these two things; either, that, as soon as men come to the use of reason, these supposed native inscriptions come to be known and observed by them; or else, that the use and exercise of men's reasons assists them in the discovery of these principles, and certainly makes them known to them.

8. If reason discovered them, that would not prove them innate. - If they mean that by the use of reason men may discover these principles, and that this is sufficient to prove them innate, their way of arguing will stand thus: viz. That, whatever truths reason can certainly discover to us and make us firmly assent to, those are all naturally imprinted on the mind; since that universal assent which is made the mark of them, amounts to no more but this - that by the use of reason we are capable to come to a certain knowledge of, and assent to, them; and by this means there will be no difference between the maxims of the mathematicians and theorems they deduce from them: all must be equally allowed innate, they being all discoveries made by the use of reason and truths that a rational creature may certainly come to know, if he apply his thoughts rightly that way.

9. It is false that reason discovers them. - But how can these men think the use of reason necessary to discover principles that are supposed innate, when reason (if we may believe them) is nothing else but the faculty of deducing unknown truths from principles or propositions that are already known? That certainly can never be thought innate which we have need of reason to discover, unless, as I have said, we will have all the certain truths that reason ever teaches us to be innate. We may as well think the use of reason necessary to make our eyes discover visible objects as that there should be need of reason, or the exercise thereof to make the understanding see what is originally engraved in it, and cannot be in the understanding before it be perceived by it. So that to make reason discover these truths thus imprinted, is to say, that the use of reason discovers to a man what he knew before; and if men have those innate impressed truths

216   THE MEANING OF LIFE

originally, and before the use of reason and yet are always ignorant of them till they come to the use of reason, it is in effect to say that men know, and know them not, at the same time.

10. It will here perhaps be said, that mathematical demonstrations, and other truths that are not innate, are not assented to, as soon as proposed, wherein they are distinguished from these maxims and other innate truths. I shall have occasion to speak of assent upon the first proposing, more particularly by and by. I shall here only, and that very readily, allow, that these maxims and mathematical demonstrations are in this different - that the one has need of reason using of proofs to make them out and to gain our assent; but the other, as soon as understood, are, without any the least reasoning, embraced and assented to. But I withal beg leave to observe, that it lays open the weakness of this subterfuge which requires the use of reason for the discovery of these general truths, since it must be confessed, that in their discovery there is no use made of reasoning at all. And I think those who give this answer will not be forward to affirm, that the knowledge of this maxim, "That it is impossible for the same thing to be, and not to be," is a deduction of our reason. For this would be to destroy that bounty of nature they seem so fond of, whilst they make the knowledge of those principles to depend on the labour of our thoughts; for all reasoning is search and casting about, and requires pains and application. ...

BOOK II, CHAPTER I: OF IDEAS IN GENERAL, AND THEIR ORIGINAL.

1. Idea is the object of thinking. - Every man being conscious to himself, that he thinks, and that which his mind is applied about, whilst thinking, being the ideas that are there, it is past doubt that men have in their mind several ideas, such as are those expressed by the words, "whiteness, hardness, sweetness, thinking, motion, man, elephant, army, drunkenness," and others. It is in the first place then to be inquired, How he comes by them? I know it is a received doctrine, that men have native ideas and original characters stamped upon their minds in their very first being. This opinion I have at large examined already; and, I suppose, what I have said in the foregoing book will be much more easily admitted, when 1 have shown whence the understanding may get all the ideas it has, and by what ways and degrees they may come into the mind; for which I shall appeal to every one's own observation and experience.

2. All ideas come from sensation or reflection. - Let us then suppose the mind to be, as we say. white paper [tabula rasa], void of all characters without any ideas; how comes it to be furnished? Whence comes it by that vast store, which the busy and boundless fancy of man has painted on it with an almost endless variety? Whence has it all the materials of reason and knowledge? To this I answer, in one word, From experience: in that all our knowledge is founded, and from that it ultimately derives itself. Our observation, employed either about external sensible objects, or about the internal operations of our minds, perceived and reflected on by ourselves is that which supplies our understandings with all the materials of thinking. These two are the fountains of knowledge, from whence all the ideas we have, or can naturally have, do spring.

3. The object of sensation one source of ideas. - First. Our senses, conversant about particular sensible objects, do convey into the mind several distinct perceptions of things, according to those various ways wherein those objects do affect them; and thus we come by those ideas we have of yellow, white, heat, cold, soft, hard, bitter, sweet, and all those which we call sensible qualities; which when I say the senses convey into the mind, I mean, they from external objects convey into the mind what produces there those perceptions. This great source of most of the ideas we have., depending wholly upon our senses, and derived by them to the understanding, I call, "sensation."

4. The operations of our minds the other source of them. - Secondly. The other fountain, from which experience furnisheth the understanding with ideas, is the perception of the operations of our own minds within us, as it is employed about the ideas it has got; which operations, when the soul comes to reflect on and consider, do furnish the understanding with another set of ideas which could not be had from things without and such are perception, thinking, doubting, believing, reasoning, knowing, willing, and all the different actings of our own minds; which we, being conscious of, and observing in ourselves, do from these receive into our understandings as distinct ideas, as we do from bodies affecting our senses. This source of ideas every man has wholly in himself; and though it be not sense as having nothing to do with external objects, yet it is very like it, and might properly enough be called "internal sense." But as I call the other "sensation," so I call this " reflection," the ideas it affords being such only as the mind gets by reflecting on its own operations within itself. By reflection, then, in the following part of this discourse, I would be understood to mean that notice which the mind takes of its own operations, and the manner of them, by reason whereof there come to be ideas of these operations in the understanding. These two, I say, viz., external material things as the objects of sensation, and the operations of our own minds within as the objects of reflection, are to me, the only originals from whence all our ideas take their beginnings. The term "operations" here, I use in a large sense, as comprehending not barely the actions of the mind about its ideas, but some sort of passions arising sometimes from them, such as is the satisfaction or uneasiness arising from any thought.

5. All our ideas are of the one or the other of these. - The understanding seems to me not to have the least glimmering of any ideas which it doth not receive from one of these two. External objects furnish the mind with the ideas of sensible qualities, which are all those different perceptions they produce in us; and the mind furnishes the understanding with ideas of its own operations.

These, when we have taken a full survey of them, and their several modes, combinations, and relations, we shall find to contain all our whole stock of ideas, and that we have nothing in our mind which did not come in one of these two ways. Let anyone examine his own thoughts; and thoroughly search into his understanding, and then let him tell me, whether all the original ideas he has there, are any other than of the objects of his senses, or of the operations of his mind considered as objects of his reflection; and how great a mass of knowledge soever he imagines to be lodged there, he will, upon taking a strict view see that he has not any idea in his mind but

218 THE MEANING OF LIFE

what one of these two have imprinted, though perhaps with infinite variety compounded and enlarged by the understanding, as we shall see hereafter.

6. Observable in children. - He that attentively considers the state of a child at his first coming into the world, will have little reason to think him stored with plenty of ideas that are to de the matter of his future knowledge. It is by degrees he comes to be furnished with them; and though the ideas of obvious and familiar qualities imprint themselves before the memory begins to keep a register of time and order, yet it is often so late before some unusual qualities come in the way, that there are few men that cannot recollect the beginning of their acquaintance with them: and, if it were worth while, no doubt a child might be so ordered as to have but a very few even of the ordinary ideas till he were grown up to a man. But all that are born into the world being surrounded with bodies that perpetually and diversely affect them, variety of ideas whether care be taken about it, or no, are imprinted on the minds of children. Light and colours are busy at hand every where when the eye is but open; sounds and some tangible qualities fail not to solicit their proper senses and force an entrance to the mind; but yet I think it will be granted easily, that if a child were kept in a place where he never saw any other but black and white till he were a man, he would have no more ideas of scarlet or green, than he that from his childhood never tasted an oyster or a pine-apple has of those particular relishes.

7. Men are differently furnished with these according to the different objects they converse with. - Men then come to be furnished with fewer or more simple ideas from without, according as the objects they converse with afford greater or less variety; and from the operations of their minds within, according as they more or less reflect on them. For, though he that contemplates the operations of his mind cannot but have plain and clear ideas of them; yet, unless he turn his thoughts that way, and considers them attentively, he will no more have clear and distinct ideas of all the operations of his mind, and all that may be observed therein than he will have all the particular ideas of any landscape or of the parts and motions of a clock, who will not turn his eyes to it, and with attention heed all the parts of it. The picture or clock may be so placed, that they may come in his way every day; but yet he will have but a confused idea of all the parts they are made of, till he applies himself with attention to consider them each in particular. ...

CHAPTER III: OF IDEAS OF ONE SENSE

1. Division of simple ideas. - The better to conceive the ideas we receive from sensation, it may not be amiss for us to consider them in reference to the different ways whereby they make their approaches to our minds, and make themselves perceivable by us.

First, then, there are some which come into our minds by one sense only.

Secondly. There are others that convey themselves into the mind by more senses than one.

Thirdly. Others first are had from reflection only.

Fourthly. There are some that make themselves way, and are suggested to the mind, by all the ways of sensation and reflection.

We shall consider them apart under these several heads.

1. There are some ideas which have admittance only through one sense, which is peculiarly adapted to receive them. Thus light and colours, as white, red, yellow, blue, with their several degrees or shades and mixtures, as green, scarlet, purple, sea-green, and the rest, come in only by the eyes; all kinds of noises, sounds, and tones, only by the ears; the several tastes and smells, by the nose and palate. And if these organs, or the nerves which are the conduits to convey them from without to their audience in the brain, the mind's presence-room, (as I may so call it,) are, any of them, so disordered as not to perform their functions, they have no postern to be admitted by, no other way to bring themselves into view, and be received by the understanding.

The most considerable of those belonging to the touch are heat and cold, and solidity; all the rest - consisting almost wholly in the sensible configuration, as smooth and rough; or else more or less firm adhesion of the parts, as hard and soft, tough and brittle - are obvious enough.

2. I think it will be needless to enumerate all the particular simple ideas belonging to each sense. Nor indeed is it possible it we would, there being a great many more of them belonging to most of the senses than we have names for. The variety of smells, which are as many almost, if not more, than species of bodies in the world, do most of them want name. Sweet and stinking commonly serve our turn for these ideas, which in effect is little more than to call them pleasing or displeasing; though the smell of a rose and violet, both sweet, are certainly very distinct ideas. Nor are the different tastes that by, our palates we receive ideas of, much better provided with names. Sweet, bitter, sour, harsh, and salt, are almost all the epithets we have to denominate that numberless variety of relishes which are to be found distinct, not only in almost every sort of creatures but in the different parts of the same plant, fruit, or animal. The same may be said of colours and sounds. I shall therefore, in the account of simple ideas I am here giving, content myself to set down only such as are most material to our present purpose, or are in themselves less apt to be taken notice of, though they are very frequently the ingredients of our complex ideas; amongst which I think I may well account "solidity" which therefore I shall treat of in the next chapter.

THE CRITIQUE OF PRACTICAL REASON (1788)

Immanuel Kant

translated by Thomas Kingsmill Abbott

PREFACE – Excerpt from the first part of the work

PREFACE.

This work is called the Critique of Practical Reason, not of the pure practical reason, although its parallelism with the speculative critique would seem to require the latter term. The reason of this appears sufficiently from the treatise itself. Its business is to show that there is pure practical reason, and for this purpose it criticizes the entire practical faculty of reason. If it succeeds in this, it has no need to criticize the pure faculty itself in order to see whether reason in making such a claim does not presumptuously overstep itself (as is the case with the speculative reason). For if, as pure reason, it is actually practical, it proves its own reality and that of its concepts by fact, and all disputation against the possibility of its being real is futile.

With this faculty, transcendental freedom is also established; freedom, namely, in that absolute sense in which speculative reason required it in its use of the concept of causality in order to escape the antinomy into which it inevitably falls, when in the chain of cause and effect it tries to think the unconditioned. Speculative reason could only exhibit this concept (of freedom) problematically as not impossible to thought, without assuring it any objective reality, and merely lest the supposed impossibility of what it must at least allow to be thinkable should endanger its very being and plunge it into an abyss of scepticism.

Inasmuch as the reality of the concept of freedom is proved by an apodeictic law of practical reason, it is the keystone of the whole system of pure reason, even the speculative, and all other concepts (those of God and immortality) which, as being mere ideas, remain in it unsupported, now attach themselves to this concept, and by it obtain consistence and objective reality; that is to say, their possibility is proved by the fact that freedom actually exists, for this idea is revealed by the moral law.

Freedom, however, is the only one of all the ideas of the speculative reason of which we know the possibility a priori (without, however, understanding it), because it is the condition of the moral law which we know.* The ideas of God and immortality, however, are not conditions of the moral law, but only conditions of the necessary object of a will determined by this law; that is to say, conditions of the practical use of our pure reason. Hence, with respect to these ideas, we cannot affirm that we know and understand, I will not say the actuality, but even the possibility of them. However they are the conditions of the application of the morally determined will to its object, which is given to it a priori, viz., the summum bonum. Consequently in this practical point of view their possibility must be assumed, although we cannot theoretically know and understand it. To justify this assumption it is sufficient, in a practical point of view, that they contain no intrinsic impossibility (contradiction). Here we have what, as far as speculative reason is concerned, is a merely subjective principle of assent, which, however, is objectively valid for a reason equally pure but practical, and this principle, by means of the concept of freedom, assures objective reality and authority to the ideas of God and immortality. Nay, there is a subjective necessity (a need of pure reason) to assume them. Nevertheless the theoretical knowledge of reason is not hereby enlarged, but only the possibility is given, which heretofore was merely a problem and now becomes assertion, and thus the practical use of reason is connected with the elements of theoretical reason. And this need is not a merely hypothetical one for the arbitrary purposes of speculation, that we must assume something if we wish in speculation to carry reason to its utmost limits, but it is a need which has the force of law to assume something without which that cannot be which we must inevitably set before us as the aim of our action.

*Lest any one should imagine that he finds an inconsistency here when I call freedom the condition of the moral law, and hereafter maintain in the treatise itself that the moral law is the condition under which we can first become conscious of freedom, I will merely remark that freedom is the ratio essendi of the moral law, while the moral law is the ratio cognoscendi of freedom. For Pad not the moral law been previously distinctly thought in our reason, we should never consider ourselves justified in assuming such a thing as freedom, although it be not contradictory. But were there no freedom it would be impossible to trace the moral law in ourselves at all.

It would certainly be more satisfactory to our speculative reason if it could solve these problems for itself without this circuit and preserve the solution for practical use as a thing to be referred to, but in fact our faculty of speculation is not so well provided. Those who boast of such high knowledge ought not to keep it back, but to exhibit it publicly that it may be tested and appreciated. They want to prove: very good, let them prove; and the critical philosophy lays its arms at their feet as the victors. Quid statis? Nolint. Atqui licet esse beatis. As they then do not in fact choose to do so, probably because they cannot, we must take up these arms again in order to seek in the mortal use of reason, and to base on this, the notions of God, freedom, and immortality, the possibility of which speculation cannot adequately prove.

Here first is explained the enigma of the critical philosophy, viz.: how we deny objective reality to the supersensible use of the categories in speculation and yet admit this reality with respect to the objects of pure practical reason. This must at first seem inconsistent as long as this practical use is only nominally known. But when, by a thorough analysis of it, one becomes aware that the reality spoken of does not imply any theoretical determination of the categories and extension of our knowledge to the supersensible; but that what is meant is that in this respect an object belongs to them, because either they are contained in the necessary determination of the will a priori, or are inseparably connected with its object; then this inconsistency disappears,

222   THE MEANING OF LIFE

because the use we make of these concepts is different from what speculative reason requires. On the other hand, there now appears an unexpected and very satisfactory proof of the consistency of the speculative critical philosophy. For whereas it insisted that the objects of experience as such, including our own subject, have only the value of phenomena, while at the same time things in themselves must be supposed as their basis, so that not everything supersensible was to be regarded as a fiction and its concept as empty; so now practical reason itself, without any concert with the speculative, assures reality to a supersensible object of the category of causality, viz., freedom, although (as becomes a practical concept) only for practical use; and this establishes on the evidence of a fact that which in the former case could only be conceived. By this the strange but certain doctrine of the speculative critical philosophy, that the thinking subject is to itself in internal intuition only a phenomenon, obtains in the critical examination of the practical reason its full confirmation, and that so thoroughly that we should be compelled to adopt this doctrine, even if the former had never proved it at all.*

*The union of causality as freedom with causality as rational mechanism, the former established by the moral law, the latter by the law of nature in the same subject, namely, man, is impossible, unless we conceive him with reference to the former as a being in himself, and with reference to the latter as a phenomenon- the former in pure consciousness, the latter in empirical consciousness. Otherwise reason inevitably contradicts itself.

By this also I can understand why the most considerable objections which I have as yet met with against the Critique turn about these two points, namely, on the one side, the objective reality of the categories as applied to noumena, which is in the theoretical department of knowledge denied, in the practical affirmed; and on the other side, the paradoxical demand to regard oneself qua subject of freedom as a noumenon, and at the same time from the point of view of physical nature as a phenomenon in one's own empirical consciousness; for as long as one has formed no definite notions of morality and freedom, one could not conjecture on the one side what was intended to be the noumenon, the basis of the alleged phenomenon, and on the other side it seemed doubtful whether it was at all possible to form any notion of it, seeing that we had previously assigned all the notions of the pure understanding in its theoretical use exclusively to phenomena. Nothing but a detailed criticism of the practical reason can remove all this misapprehension and set in a clear light the consistency which constitutes its greatest merit.

So much by way of justification of the proceeding by which, in this work, the notions and principles of pure speculative reason which have already undergone their special critical examination are, now and then, again subjected to examination. This would not in other cases be in accordance with the systematic process by which a science is established, since matters which have been decided ought only to be cited and not again discussed. In this case, however, it was not only allowable but necessary, because reason is here considered in transition to a different use of these concepts from what it had made of them before. Such a transition necessitates a comparison of the old and the new usage, in order to distinguish well the new path from the old one and, at the same time, to allow their connection to be observed. Accordingly considerations of this kind, including those which are once more directed to the concept of freedom in the

MIDDLE AGES AND RENAISSANCE 223

practical use of the pure reason, must not be regarded as an interpolation serving only to fill up the gaps in the critical system of speculative reason (for this is for its own purpose complete), or like the props and buttresses which in a hastily constructed building are often added afterwards; but as true members which make the connexion of the system plain, and show us concepts, here presented as real, which there could only be presented problematically. This remark applies especially to the concept of freedom, respecting which one cannot but observe with surprise that so many boast of being able to understand it quite well and to explain its possibility, while they regard it only psychologically, whereas if they had studied it in a transcendental point of view, they must have recognized that it is not only indispensable as a problematical concept, in the complete use of speculative reason, but also quite incomprehensible; and if they afterwards came to consider its practical use, they must needs have come to the very mode of determining the principles of this, to which they are now so loth to assent. The concept of freedom is the stone of stumbling for all empiricists, but at the same time the key to the loftiest practical principles for critical moralists, who perceive by its means that they must necessarily proceed by a rational method. For this reason I beg the reader not to pass lightly over what is said of this concept at the end of the Analytic.

I must leave it to those who are acquainted with works of this kind to judge whether such a system as that of the practical reason, which is here developed from the critical examination of it, has cost much or little trouble, especially in seeking not to miss the true point of view from which the whole can be rightly sketched. It presupposes, indeed, the Fundamental Principles of the Metaphysic of Morals, but only in so far as this gives a preliminary acquaintance with the principle of duty, and assigns and justifies a definite formula thereof; in other respects it is independent.* It results from the nature of this practical faculty itself that the complete classification of all practical sciences cannot be added, as in the critique of the speculative reason. For it is not possible to define duties specially, as human duties, with a view to their classification, until the subject of this definition (viz., man) is known according to his actual nature, at least so far as is necessary with respect to duty; this, however, does not belong to a critical examination of the practical reason, the business of which is only to assign in a complete manner the principles of its possibility, extent, and limits, without special reference to human nature. The classification then belongs to the system of science, not to the system of criticism.

*A reviewer who wanted to find some fault with this work has hit the truth better, perhaps, than he thought, when he says that no new principle of morality is set forth in it, but only a new formula.

But who would think of introducing a new principle of all morality and making himself as it were the first discoverer of it, just as if all the world before him were ignorant what duty was or had been in thorough-going error? But whoever knows of what importance to a mathematician a formula is, which defines accurately what is to be done to work a problem, will not think that a formula is insignificant and useless which does the same for all duty in general.

In the second part of the Analytic I have given, as I trust, a sufficient answer to the objection of a truth-loving and acute critic* of the Fundamental Principles of the Metaphysic of Morals- a

224   THE MEANING OF LIFE

critic always worthy of respect the objection, namely, that the notion of good was not established before the moral principle, as be thinks it ought to have been.*[2] I have also had regard to many of the objections which have reached me from men who show that they have at heart the discovery of the truth, and I shall continue to do so (for those who have only their old system before their eyes, and who have already settled what is to be approved or disapproved, do not desire any explanation which might stand in the way of their own private opinion.)

*[See Kant's "Das mag in der Theoric ricktig seyn," etc. Werke, vol. vii, p. 182.]

*[2] It might also have been objected to me that I have not first defined the notion of the faculty of desire, or of the feeling of Pleasure, although this reproach would be unfair, because this definition might reasonably be presupposed as given in psychology. However, the definition there given might be such as to found the determination of the faculty of desire on the feeling of pleasure (as is commonly done), and thus the supreme principle of practical philosophy would be necessarily made empirical, which, however, remains to be proved and in this critique is altogether refuted. It will, therefore, give this definition here in such a manner as it ought to be given, in order to leave this contested point open at the beginning, as it should be. LIFE is the faculty a being has of acting according to laws of the faculty of desire. The faculty of DESIRE is the being's faculty of becoming by means of its ideas the cause of the actual existence of the objects of these ideas. PLEASURE is the idea of the agreement of the object, or the action with the subjective conditions of life, i.e., with the faculty of causality of an idea in respect of the actuality of its object (or with the determination of the forces of the subject to action which produces it). I have no further need for the purposes of this critique of notions borrowed from psychology; the critique itself supplies the rest. It is easily seen that the question whether the faculty of desire is always based on pleasure, or whether under certain conditions pleasure only follows the determination of desire, is by this definition left undecided, for it is composed only of terms belonging to the pure understanding, i.e., of categories which contain nothing empirical. Such precaution is very desirable in all philosophy and yet is often neglected; namely, not to prejudge questions by adventuring definitions before the notion has been completely analysed, which is often very late. It may be observed through the whole course of the critical philosophy (of the theoretical as well as the practical reason) that frequent opportunity offers of supplying defects in the old dogmatic method of philosophy, and of correcting errors which are not observed until we make such rational use of these notions viewing them as a whole.

When we have to study a particular faculty of the human mind in its sources, its content, and its limits; then from the nature of human knowledge we must begin with its parts, with an accurate and complete exposition of them; complete, namely, so far as is possible in the present state of our knowledge of its elements. But there is another thing to be attended to which is of a more philosophical and architectonic character, namely, to grasp correctly the idea of the whole, and from thence to get a view of all those parts as mutually related by the aid of pure reason, and by means of their derivation from the concept of the whole. This is only possible through the most intimate acquaintance with the system; and those who find the first inquiry too troublesome, and do not think it worth their while to attain such an acquaintance, cannot reach the second stage, namely, the general view, which is a synthetical return to that which had previously been given analytically. It is no wonder then if they find inconsistencies everywhere, although the gaps which these indicate are not in the system itself, but in their own incoherent train of thought.

I have no fear, as regards this treatise, of the reproach that I wish to introduce a new language, since the sort of knowledge here in question has itself somewhat of an everyday character. Nor even in the case of the former critique could this reproach occur to anyone who had thought it through and not merely turned over the leaves. To invent new words where the language has no lack of expressions for given notions is a childish effort to distinguish oneself from the crowd, if not by new and true thoughts, yet by new patches on the old garment. If, therefore, the readers of that work know any more familiar expressions which are as suitable to the thought as those seem to me to be, or if they think they can show the futility of these thoughts themselves and hence that of the expression, they would, in the first case, very much oblige me, for I only desire to be understood: and, in the second case, they would deserve well of philosophy. But, as long as these thoughts stand, I very much doubt that suitable and yet more common expressions for them can be found.*

*I am more afraid in the present treatise of occasional misconception in respect of some expressions which I have chosen with the greatest care in order that the notion to which they point may not be missed. Thus, in the table of categories of the Practical reason under the title of Modality, the Permitted, and forbidden (in a practical objective point of view, possible and impossible) have almost the same meaning in common language as the next category, duty and contrary to duty. Here, however, the former means what coincides with, or contradicts, a merely possible practical precept (for example, the solution of all problems of geometry and mechanics); the latter, what is similarly related to a law actually present in the reason; and this distinction is not quite foreign even to common language, although somewhat unusual. For example, it is forbidden to an orator, as such, to forge new words or constructions; in a certain degree this is permitted to a poet; in neither case is there any question of duty. For if anyone chooses to forfeit his reputation as an orator, no one can prevent him. We have here only to do with the distinction of imperatives into problematical, assertorial, and apodeictic. Similarly in the note in which I have pared the moral ideas of practical perfection in different philosophical schools, I have distinguished the idea of wisdom from that of holiness, although I have stated that essentially and objectively they are the same. But in that place I understand by the former only that wisdom to which man (the Stoic) lays claim; therefore I take it subjectively as an attribute alleged to belong to man. (Perhaps the expression virtue, with which also the made great show, would better mark the characteristic of his school.) The expression of a postulate of pure practical reason might give most occasion to misapprehension in case the reader confounded it with the signification of the postulates in pure mathematics, which carry apodeictic certainty with them. These, however, postulate the possibility of an action, the object of which has been previously recognized a priori in theory as possible, and that with perfect certainty. But the former postulates the possibility of an object itself (God and the immortality of the soul) from apodeictic practical laws, and therefore only for the purposes of a practical reason.

This certainty of the postulated possibility then is not at all theoretic, and consequently not apodeictic; that is to say, it is not a known necessity as regards the object, but a necessary supposition as regards the subject, necessary for the obedience to its objective but practical laws. It is, therefore, merely a necessary hypothesis. I could find no better expression for this rational necessity, which is subjective, but yet true and unconditional.

In this manner, then, the a priori principles of two faculties of the mind, the faculty of cognition and that of desire, would be found and determined as to the conditions, extent, and limits of their use, and thus a sure foundation be paid for a scientific system of philosophy, both theoretic and practical.

Nothing worse could happen to these labours than that anyone should make the unexpected discovery that there neither is, nor can be, any a priori knowledge at all. But there is no danger of

226 THE MEANING OF LIFE

this. This would be the same thing as if one sought to prove by reason that there is no reason. For we only say that we know something by reason, when we are conscious that we could have known it, even if it had not been given to us in experience; hence rational knowledge and knowledge a priori are one and the same. It is a clear contradiction to try to extract necessity from a principle of experience (ex pumice aquam), and to try by this to give a judgement true universality (without which there is no rational inference, not even inference from analogy, which is at least a presumed universality and objective necessity). To substitute subjective necessity, that is, custom, for objective, which exists only in a priori judgements, is to deny to reason the power of judging about the object, i.e., of knowing it, and what belongs to it. It implies, for example, that we must not say of something which often or always follows a certain antecedent state that we can conclude from this to that (for this would imply objective necessity and the notion of an a priori connexion), but only that we may expect similar cases (just as animals do), that is that we reject the notion of cause altogether as false and a mere delusion. As to attempting to remedy this want of objective and consequently universal validity by saying that we can see no ground for attributing any other sort of knowledge to other rational beings, if this reasoning were valid, our ignorance would do more for the enlargement of our knowledge than all our meditation. For, then, on this very ground that we have no knowledge of any other rational beings besides man, we should have a right to suppose them to be of the same nature as we know ourselves to be: that is, we should really know them. I omit to mention that universal assent does not prove the objective validity of a judgement (i.e., its validity as a cognition), and although this universal assent should accidentally happen, it could furnish no proof of agreement with the object; on the contrary, it is the objective validity which alone constitutes the basis of a necessary universal consent.

Hume would be quite satisfied with this system of universal empiricism, for, as is well known, he desired nothing more than that, instead of ascribing any objective meaning to the necessity in the concept of cause, a merely subjective one should be assumed, viz., custom, in order to deny that reason could judge about God, freedom, and immortality; and if once his principles were granted, he was certainly well able to deduce his conclusions therefrom, with all logical coherence. But even Hume did not make his empiricism so universal as to include mathematics. He holds the principles of mathematics to be analytical; and if his were correct, they would certainly be apodeictic also: but we could not infer from this that reason has the faculty of forming apodeictic judgements in philosophy also- that is to say, those which are synthetical judgements, like the judgement of causality. But if we adopt a universal empiricism, then mathematics will be included.

Now if this science is in contradiction with a reason that admits only empirical principles, as it inevitably is in the antinomy in which mathematics prove the infinite divisibility of space, which empiricism cannot admit; then the greatest possible evidence of demonstration is in manifest contradiction with the alleged conclusions from experience, and we are driven to ask, like Cheselden's blind patient, "Which deceives me, sight or touch?" (for empiricism is based on a necessity felt, rationalism on a necessity seen). And thus universal empiricism reveals itself as absolute scepticism. It is erroneous to attribute this in such an unqualified sense to Hume,* since he left at least one certain touchstone (which can only be found in a priori principles), although experience consists not only of feelings, but also of judgements.

*Names that designate the followers of a sect have always been accompanied with much injustice; just as if one said, "N is an Idealist." For although he not only admits, but even insists, that our ideas of external things have actual objects of external things corresponding to them, yet he holds that the form of the intuition does not depend on them but on the human mind.

However, as in this philosophical and critical age such empiricism can scarcely be serious, and it is probably put forward only as an intellectual exercise and for the purpose of putting in a clearer light, by contrast, the necessity of rational a priori principles, we can only be grateful to those who employ themselves in this otherwise uninstructive labour.

INTRODUCTION

Of the Idea of a Critique of Practical Reason.

The theoretical use of reason was concerned with objects of the cognitive faculty only, and a critical examination of it with reference to this use applied properly only to the pure faculty of cognition; because this raised the suspicion, which was afterwards confirmed, that it might easily pass beyond its limits, and be lost among unattainable objects, or even contradictory notions. It is quite different with the practical use of reason. In this, reason is concerned with the grounds of determination of the will, which is a faculty either to produce objects corresponding to ideas, or to determine ourselves to the effecting of such objects (whether the physical power is sufficient or not); that is, to determine our causality. For here, reason can at least attain so far as to determine the will, and has always objective reality in so far as it is the volition only that is in question. The first question here then is whether pure reason of itself alone suffices to determine the will, or whether it can be a ground of determination only as dependent on empirical conditions. Now, here there comes in a notion of causality justified by the critique of the pure reason, although not capable of being presented empirically, viz., that of freedom; and if we can now discover means of proving that this property does in fact belong to the human will (and so to the will of all rational beings), then it will not only be shown that pure reason can be practical, but that it alone, and not reason empirically limited, is indubitably practical; consequently, we shall have to make a critical examination, not of pure practical reason, but only of practical reason generally. For when once pure reason is shown to exist, it needs no critical examination. For reason itself contains the standard for the critical examination of every use of it. The critique, then, of practical reason generally is bound to prevent the empirically conditioned reason from claiming exclusively to furnish the ground of determination of the will. If it is proved that there is a [practical] reason, its employment is alone immanent; the empirically conditioned use, which claims supremacy, is on the contrary transcendent and expresses itself in demands and precepts which go quite beyond its

228 THE MEANING OF LIFE

sphere. This is just the opposite of what might be said of pure reason in its speculative employment. However, as it is still pure reason, the knowledge of which is here the foundation of its practical employment, the general outline of the classification of a critique of practical reason must be arranged in accordance with that of the speculative. We must, then, have the Elements and the Methodology of it; and in the former an Analytic as the rule of truth, and a Dialectic as the exposition and dissolution of the illusion in the judgements of practical reason. But the order in the subdivision of the Analytic will be the reverse of that in the critique of the pure speculative reason. For, in the present case, we shall commence with the principles and proceed to the concepts, and only then, if possible, to the senses; whereas in the case of the speculative reason we began with the senses and had to end with the principles. The reason of this lies again in this: that now we have to do with a will, and have to consider reason, not in its relation to objects, but to this will and its causality. We must, then, begin with the principles of a causality not empirically conditioned, after which the attempt can be made to establish our notions of the determining grounds of such a will, of their application to objects, and finally to the subject and its sense faculty. We necessarily begin with the law of causality from freedom, that is, with a pure practical principle, and this determines the objects to which alone it can be applied.

FIRST PART.

ELEMENTS OF PURE PRACTICAL REASON.

BOOK I. The Analytic of Pure Practical Reason.

CHAPTER I. Of the Principles of Pure Practical Reason.

I. DEFINITION.

Practical principles are propositions which contain a general determination of the will, having under it several practical rules. They are subjective, or maxims, when the condition is regarded by the subject as valid only for his own will, but are objective, or practical laws, when the condition is recognized as objective, that is, valid for the will of every rational being.

REMARK.

Supposing that pure reason contains in itself a practical motive, that is, one adequate to determine the will, then there are practical laws; otherwise all practical principles will be mere maxims. In case the will of a rational being is pathologically affected, there may occur a conflict of the maxims with the practical laws recognized by itself. For example, one may make it his maxim to let no injury pass unrevenged, and yet he may see that this is not a practical law, but only his own maxim; that, on the contrary, regarded as being in one and the same maxim a rule for the will of every rational being, it must contradict itself. In natural philosophy the principles of what happens, e.g., the principle of equality of action and reaction in the communication of motion) are at the same time laws of nature; for the use of reason there is theoretical and determined by the nature of the object. In practical philosophy, i.e., that which has to do only with the grounds of determination of the will, the principles which a man makes for himself are not laws by which one is inevitably bound; because reason in practical matters has to do with the subject, namely, with the faculty of desire, the special character of which may occasion variety in the rule. The practical rule is always a product of reason, because it prescribes action as a means to the effect. But in the case of a being with whom reason does not of itself determine the will, this rule is an imperative, i.e., a rule characterized by "shall," which expresses the objective necessitation of the action and signifies that, if reason completely determined the will, the action would inevitably take place according to this rule. Imperatives, therefore, are objectively valid, and are quite distinct from maxims, which are subjective principles. The former either determine the conditions of the causality of the rational being as an efficient cause, i.e., merely in reference to the effect and the means of attaining it; or they determine the will only, whether it is adequate to the effect or not. The former would be hypothetical imperatives, and contain mere precepts of skill; the latter, on the contrary, would be categorical, and would alone be practical laws. Thus maxims are principles, but not imperatives. Imperatives themselves, however, when they are conditional (i.e., do not determine the will simply as will, but only in respect to a desired effect, that is, when they are hypothetical imperatives), are practical precepts but not laws. Laws must be sufficient to determine the will as will, even before I ask whether I have power sufficient for a desired effect, or the means necessary to produce it; hence they are categorical: otherwise they are not laws at all, because the necessity is wanting, which, if it is to be practical, must be independent of conditions which are pathological and are therefore only contingently connected with the will. Tell a man, for example, that he must be industrious and thrifty in youth, in order that he may not want in old age; this is a correct and important practical precept of the will. But it is easy to see that in this case the will is directed to something else which it is presupposed that it desires; and as to this desire, we must leave it to the actor himself whether he looks forward to other resources than those of his own acquisition, or does not expect to be old, or thinks that in case of future necessity he will be able to make shift with little. Reason, from which alone can spring a rule involving necessity, does, indeed, give necessity to this precept (else it would not be an imperative), but this is a necessity dependent on subjective conditions, and cannot be supposed in the same degree in all subjects. But that reason may give laws it is necessary that it should only need to presuppose itself, because rules are objectively and universally valid only when they hold without any contingent subjective conditions, which distinguish one rational being from another. Now tell a man that he should never make a deceitful promise, this is a rule which only concerns his will, whether the purposes he may have can be attained thereby or not; it is the volition only which is to be determined a priori by that rule. If now it is found that this rule is practically right, then it is a law, because it is a categorical imperative. Thus, practical laws refer to the will only, without considering what is attained by its causality, and we may disregard this latter (as belonging to the world of sense) in order to have them quite pure.

230 THE MEANING OF LIFE

II. THEOREM I.

All practical principles which presuppose an object (matter) of the faculty of desire as the ground of determination of the will are empirical and can furnish no practical laws.

By the matter of the faculty of desire I mean an object the realization of which is desired. Now, if the desire for this object precedes the practical rule and is the condition of our making it a principle, then I say (in the first place) this principle is in that case wholly empirical, for then what determines the choice is the idea of an object and that relation of this idea to the subject by which its faculty of desire is determined to its realization. Such a relation to the subject is called the pleasure in the realization of an object. This, then, must be presupposed as a condition of the possibility of determination of the will. But it is impossible to know a priori of any idea of an object whether it will be connected with pleasure or pain, or be indifferent. In such cases, therefore, the determining principle of the choice must be empirical and, therefore, also the practical material principle which presupposes it as a condition.

In the second place, since susceptibility to a pleasure or pain can be known only empirically and cannot hold in the same degree for all rational beings, a principle which is based on this subjective condition may serve indeed as a maxim for the subject which possesses this susceptibility, but not as a law even to him (because it is wanting in objective necessity, which must be recognized a priori); it follows, therefore, that such a principle can never furnish a practical law.

III. THEOREM II.

All material practical principles as such are of one and the same kind and come under the general principle of self-love or private happiness.

Pleasure arising from the idea of the idea of the existence of a thing, in so far as it is to determine the desire of this thing, is founded on the susceptibility of the subject, since it depends on the presence of an object; hence it belongs to sense (feeling), and not to understanding, which expresses a relation of the idea to an object according to concepts, not to the subject according to feelings. It is, then, practical only in so far as the faculty of desire is determined by the sensation of agreeableness which the subject expects from the actual existence of the object. Now, a rational being's consciousness of the pleasantness of life uninterruptedly accompanying his whole existence is happiness; and the principle which makes this the supreme ground of determination of the will is the principle of self-love. All material principles, then, which place the determining ground of the will in the pleasure or pain to be received from the existence of any object are all of the same kind, inasmuch as they all belong to the principle of self-love or private happiness.

COROLLARY.

All material practical rules place the determining principle ofthe will in the lower desires; and if there were no purely formal laws of the will adequate to determine it, then we could not admit any higher desire at all.

REMARK I.

It is surprising that men, otherwise acute, can think it possible to distinguish between higher and lower desires, according as the ideas which are connected with the feeling of pleasure have their origin in the senses or in the understanding; for when we inquire what are the determining grounds of desire, and place them in some expected pleasantness, it is of no consequence whence the idea of this pleasing object is derived, but only how much it pleases. Whether an idea has its seat and source in the understanding or not, if it can only determine the choice by presupposing a feeling of pleasure in the subject, it follows that its capability of determining the choice depends altogether on the nature of the inner sense, namely, that this can be agreeably affected by it. However dissimilar ideas of objects may be, though they be ideas of the understanding, or even of the reason in contrast to ideas of sense, yet the feeling of pleasure, by means of which they constitute the determining principle of the will (the expected satisfaction which impels the activity to the production of the object), is of one and the same kind, not only inasmuch as it can only be known empirically, but also inasmuch as it affects one and the same vital force which manifests itself in the faculty of desire, and in this respect can only differ in degree from every other ground of determination. Otherwise, how could we compare in respect of magnitude two principles of determination, the ideas of which depend upon different faculties, so as to prefer that which affects the faculty of desire in the highest degree. The same man may return unread an instructive book which he cannot again obtain, in order not to miss a hunt; he may depart in the midst of a fine speech, in order not to be late for dinner; he may leave a rational conversation, such as he otherwise values highly, to take his place at the gaming-table; he may even repulse a poor man whom he at other times takes pleasure in benefiting, because he has only just enough money in his pocket to pay for his admission to the theatre. If the determination of his will rests on the feeling of the agreeableness or disagreeableness that he expects from any cause, it is all the same to him by what sort of ideas he will be affected.

The only thing that concerns him, in order to decide his choice, is, how great, how long continued, how easily obtained, and how often repeated, this agreeableness is. just as to the man who wants money to spend, it is all the same whether the gold was dug out of the mountain or washed out of the sand, provided it is everywhere accepted at the same value; so the man who cares only for the enjoyment of life does not ask whether the ideas are of the understanding or the senses, but only how much and how great pleasure they will give for the longest time. It is only those that would gladly deny to pure reason the power of determining the will, without the presupposition of any feeling, who could deviate so far from their own exposition as to describe as quite heterogeneous what they have themselves previously brought under one and the same principle. Thus, for example, it is observed that we can find pleasure in the mere exercise of power, in the consciousness of our strength of mind in overcoming obstacles which are opposed to our designs, in the culture of our mental talents, etc.; and we justly call these more refined pleasures and enjoyments, because they are more in our power than others; they do not wear out, but rather increase the capacity for further enjoyment of them, and while they delight they at the same time cultivate. But to say on this account that they determine the will in a different way and

232 THE MEANING OF LIFE

not through sense, whereas the possibility of the pleasure presupposes a feeling for it implanted in us, which is the first condition of this satisfaction; this is just as when ignorant persons that like to dabble in metaphysics imagine matter so subtle, so supersubtle that they almost make themselves giddy with it, and then think that in this way they have conceived it as a spiritual and yet extended being. If with Epicurus we make virtue determine the will only by means of the pleasure it promises, we cannot afterwards blame him for holding that this pleasure is of the same kind as those of the coarsest senses. For we have no reason whatever to charge him with holding that the ideas by which this feeling is excited in us belong merely to the bodily senses. As far as can be conjectured, he sought the source of many of them in the use of the higher cognitive faculty, but this did not prevent him, and could not prevent him, from holding on the principle above stated, that the pleasure itself which those intellectual ideas give us, and by which alone they can determine the will, is just of the same kind.

Consistency is the highest obligation of a philosopher, and yet the most rarely found. The ancient Greek schools give us more examples of it than we find in our syncretistic age, in which a certain shallow and dishonest system of compromise of contradictory principles is devised, because it commends itself better to a public which is content to know something of everything and nothing thoroughly, so as to please every party.

The principle of private happiness, however much understanding and reason may be used in it, cannot contain any other determining principles for the will than those which belong to the lower desires; and either there are no [higher] desires at all, or pure reason must of itself alone be practical; that is, it must be able to determine the will by the mere form of the practical rule without supposing any feeling, and consequently without any idea of the pleasant or unpleasant, which is the matter of the desire, and which is always an empirical condition of the principles. Then only, when reason of itself determines the will (not as the servant of the inclination), it is really a higher desire to which that which is pathologically determined is subordinate, and is really, and even specifically, distinct from the latter, so that even the slightest admixture of the motives of the latter impairs its strength and superiority; just as in a mathematical demonstration the least empirical condition would degrade and destroy its force and value. Reason, with its practical law, determines the will immediately, not by means of an intervening feeling of pleasure or pain, not even of pleasure in the law itself, and it is only because it can, as pure reason, be practical, that it is possible for it to be legislative.

REMARK II.

To be happy is necessarily the wish of every finite rational being, and this, therefore, is inevitably a determining principle of its faculty of desire. For we are not in possession originally of satisfaction with our whole existence- a bliss which would imply a consciousness of our own independent self-sufficiency this is a problem imposed upon us by our own finite nature, because we have wants and these wants regard the matter of our desires, that is, something that is relative to a subjective feeling of pleasure or pain, which determines what we need in order to be satisfied with our condition. But just because this material principle of determination can only be empirically known by the subject, it is impossible to regard this problem as a law; for a law being objective must contain the very same principle of determination of the will in all cases and for all rational beings. For, although the notion of happiness is in every case the foundation of practical relation of the objects to the desires, yet it is only a general name for the subjective determining principles, and determines nothing specifically; whereas this is what alone we are concerned with in this practical problem, which cannot be solved at all without such specific determination. For it is every man's own special feeling of pleasure and pain that decides in what he is to place his happiness, and even in the same subject this will vary with the difference of his wants according as this feeling changes, and thus a law which is subjectively necessary (as a law of nature) is objectively a very contingent practical principle, which can and must be very different in different subjects and therefore can never furnish a law; since, in the desire for happiness it is not the form (of conformity to law) that is decisive, but simply the matter, namely, whether I am to expect pleasure in following the law, and how much. Principles of self-love may, indeed, contain universal precepts of skill (how to find means to accomplish one's purpose), but in that case they are merely theoretical principles;* as, for example, how he who would like to eat bread should contrive a mill; but practical precepts founded on them can never be universal, for the determining principle of the desire is based on the feeling pleasure and pain, which can never be supposed to be universally directed to the same objects.

*Propositions which in mathematics or physics are called practical ought properly to be called technical. For they For they have nothing to do with the determination of the theoretical they only point out how the certain must is to be produced and are, therefore, just as theoretical as any propositions which express the connection of a cause with an effect. Now whoever chooses the effect must also choose the cause.

Even supposing, however, that all finite rational beings were thoroughly agreed as to what were the objects of their feelings of pleasure and pain, and also as to the means which they must employ to attain the one and avoid the other; still, they could by no means set up the principle of self-love as a practical law, for this unanimity itself would be only contingent. The principle of determination would still be only subjectively valid and merely empirical, and would not possess the necessity which is conceived in every law, namely, an objective necessity arising from a priori grounds; unless, indeed, we hold this necessity to be not at all practical, but merely physical, viz., that our action is as inevitably determined by our inclination, as yawning when we see others yawn. It would be better to maintain that there are no practical laws at all, but only counsels for the service of our desires, than to raise merely subjective principles to the rank of practical laws, which have objective necessity, and not merely subjective, and which must be known by reason a priori, not by experience (however empirically universal this may be). Even the rules of corresponding phenomena are only called laws of nature (e.g., the mechanical laws), when we either know them really a priori, or (as in the case of chemical laws) suppose that they would be known a priori from objective grounds if our insight reached further. But in the case of merely subjective practical principles, it is expressly made a condition that they rest, not on objective, but on subjective conditions of choice, and hence that they must always be represented

234   THE MEANING OF LIFE

as mere maxims, never as practical laws. This second remark seems at first sight to be mere verbal refinement, but it defines the terms of the most important distinction which can come into consideration in practical investigations.

IV. THEOREM II.

A rational being cannot regard his maxims as practical universal laws, unless he conceives them as principles which determine the will, not by their matter, but by their form only.

By the matter of a practical principle I mean the object of the will. This object is either the determining ground of the will or it is not. In the former case the rule of the will is subjected to an empirical condition (viz., the relation of the determining idea to the feeling of pleasure and pain), consequently it can not be a practical law. Now, when we abstract from a law all matter, i.e., every object of the will (as a determining principle), nothing is left but the mere form of a universal legislation. Therefore, either a rational being cannot conceive his subjective practical principles, that is, his maxims, as being at the same time universal laws, or he must suppose that their mere form, by which they are fitted for universal legislation, is alone what makes them practical laws.

REMARK.

The commonest understanding can distinguish without instruction what form of maxim is adapted for universal legislation, and what is not. Suppose, for example, that I have made it my maxim to increase my fortune by every safe means. Now, I have a deposit in my hands, the owner of which is dead and has left no writing about it. This is just the case for my maxim. I desire then to know whether that maxim can also bold good as a universal practical law. I apply it, therefore, to the present case, and ask whether it could take the form of a law, and consequently whether I can by my maxim at the same time give such a law as this, that everyone may deny a deposit of which no one can produce a proof. I at once become aware that such a principle, viewed as a law, would annihilate itself, because the result would be that there would be no deposits. A practical law which I recognise as such must be qualified for universal legislation; this is an identical proposition and, therefore, self-evident. Now, if I say that my will is subject to a practical law, I cannot adduce my inclination (e.g., in the present case my avarice) as a principle of determination fitted to be a universal practical law; for this is so far from being fitted for a universal legislation that, if put in the form of a universal law, it would destroy itself.

It is, therefore, surprising that intelligent men could have thought of calling the desire of happiness a universal practical law on the ground that the desire is universal, and, therefore, also the maxim by which everyone makes this desire determine his will. For whereas in other cases a universal law of nature makes everything harmonious; here, on the contrary, if we attribute to the maxim the universality of a law, the extreme opposite of harmony will follow, the greatest opposition and the complete destruction of the maxim itself and its purpose. For, in that case, the will of all has not one and the same object, but everyone has his own (his private welfare), which may accidentally accord with the purposes of others which are equally selfish, but it is far from suffing for a law; because the occasional exceptions which one is permitted to make are endless, and cannot be definitely embraced in one universal rule. In this manner, then, results a harmony like that which a certain satirical poem depicts as existing between a married couple bent on going to ruin, "O, marvellous harmony, what he wishes, she wishes also"; or like what is said of the pledge of Francis I to the Emperor Charles V, "What my brother Charles wishes that I wish also" (viz., Milan). Empirical principles of determination are not fit for any universal external legislation, but just as little for internal; for each man makes his own subject the foundation of his inclination, and in the same subject sometimes one inclination, sometimes another, has the preponderance. To discover a law which would govern them all under this condition, namely, bringing them all into harmony, is quite impossible.

V. PROBLEM I.

Supposing that the mere legislative form of maxims is alone the sufficient determining principle of a will, to find the nature of the will which can be determined by it alone.

Since the bare form of the law can only be conceived by reason, and is, therefore, not an object of the senses, and consequently does not belong to the class of phenomena, it follows that the idea of it, which determines the will, is distinct from all the principles that determine events in nature according to the law of causality, because in their case the determining principles must themselves be phenomena. Now, if no other determining principle can serve as a law for the will except that universal legislative form, such a will must be conceived as quite independent of the natural law of phenomena in their mutual relation, namely, the law of causality; such independence is called freedom in the strictest, that is, in the transcendental, sense; consequently, a will which can have its law in nothing but the mere legislative form of the maxim is a free will.

VI. PROBLEM II.

Supposing that a will is free, to find the law which alone is competent to determine it necessarily.

Since the matter of the practical law, i.e., an object of the maxim, can never be given otherwise than empirically, and the free will is independent on empirical conditions (that is, conditions belonging to the world of sense) and yet is determinable, consequently a free will must find its principle of determination in the law, and yet independently of the matter of the law. But, besides the matter of the law, nothing is contained in it except the legislative form. It is the legislative form, then, contained in the maxim, which can alone constitute a principle of determination of the [free] will.

REMARK.

Thus freedom and an unconditional practical law reciprocally imply each other. Now I do not ask here whether they are in fact distinct, or whether an unconditioned law is not rather merely the consciousness of a pure practical reason and the latter identical with the positive concept of freedom; I only ask, whence begins our knowledge of the unconditionally practical,

236 THE MEANING OF LIFE

whether it is from freedom or from the practical law? Now it cannot begin from freedom, for of this we cannot be immediately conscious, since the first concept of it is negative; nor can we infer it from experience, for experience gives us the knowledge only of the law of phenomena, and hence of the mechanism of nature, the direct opposite of freedom. It is therefore the moral law, of which we become directly conscious (as soon as we trace for ourselves maxims of the will), that first presents itself to us, and leads directly to the concept of freedom, inasmuch as reason presents it as a principle of determination not to be outweighed by any sensible conditions, nay, wholly independent of them. But how is the consciousness, of that moral law possible? We can become conscious of pure practical laws just as we are conscious of pure theoretical principles, by attending to the necessity with which reason prescribes them and to the elimination of all empirical conditions, which it directs. The concept of a pure will arises out of the former, as that of a pure understanding arises out of the latter. That this is the true subordination of our concepts, and that it is morality that first discovers to us the notion of freedom, hence that it is practical reason which, with this concept, first proposes to speculative reason the most insoluble problem, thereby placing it in the greatest perplexity, is evident from the following consideration: Since nothing in phenomena can be explained by the concept of freedom, but the mechanism of nature must constitute the only clue; moreover, when pure reason tries to ascend in the series of causes to the unconditioned, it falls into an antinomy which is entangled in incomprehensibilities on the one side as much as the other; whilst the latter (namely, mechanism) is at least useful in the explanation of phenomena, therefore no one would ever have been so rash as to introduce freedom into science, had not the moral law, and with it practical reason, come in and forced this notion upon us. Experience, however, confirms this order of notions. Suppose some one asserts of his lustful appetite that, when the desired object and the opportunity are present, it is quite irresistible. [Ask him]- if a gallows were erected before the house where he finds this opportunity, in order that he should be hanged thereon immediately after the gratification of his lust, whether he could not then control his passion; we need not be long in doubt what he would reply. Ask him, however- if his sovereign ordered him, on pain of the same immediate execution, to bear false witness against an honourable man, whom the prince might wish to destroy under a plausible pretext, would he consider it possible in that case to overcome his love of life, however great it may be. He would perhaps not venture to affirm whether he would do so or not, but he must unhesitatingly admit that it is possible to do so. He judges, therefore, that he can do a certain thing because he is conscious that he ought, and he recognizes that he is free- a fact which but for the moral law he would never have known.

REVIEW / DISCUSSION QUESTIONS

1. What do you believe about the nature of suffering? How do the teachings of Siddartha Buddha inform or influence your view on suffering in life?

2. What are the *Psyche* and *Soma* in Greek thought?

3. How do Socrates, Plato and Aristotle differ in their views of the Psyche?

4. Summarize what Hippocrates learned about brain function and its relationship to the body.

238 THE MEANING OF LIFE

5.   Summarize Aristotle's view of dreams.

6.   Briefly describe three main points of Jesus the Christ's teachings.

7.   What was most important according to Jesus' teachings:
      a.   Spirituality, Beliefs or Actions?

      b.   Why do you hold this opinion?

8.   What do the death/resurrection and teachings of Jesus tell us about our understanding of humanity and our source of hope? (Read 1 Corinthians 15)

9. According to St. Augustine's *Confessions* what was his mythic schema (framework for making life meaningful)?

10. According to Rene Descartes' *First Philosophy* what is the process of questioning and knowing that we must go through in order to understand reality? Compare this to your own process of "knowing" (if you have one).

11. Describe how you see the integration of reality (what is your schema of reality) and how it compares to Baruch Spinoza's view of the integration of all things.

SECTION THREE

THE FOUR-HEADED MONSTER

CHAPTER 8

COGNITIVE PSYCHOLOGY

> *Those of our fellowmen who are dissatisfied with this state of things and who desire something more for their momentary peace of mind may look for it where they can find it. We shall not blame them for doing so; but we cannot help them and cannot change our own way of thinking on their account.*
>
> ■ Sigmund Freud - 1932

The formal beginnings of psychology as a discipline seem to universally fall back to one man, Wilhelm Wundt (1832-1920), who formally began an experimental laboratory in psychology in 1879. This date is the time when psychology came into its own as a modern science of the mind. Many of the conceptual and methodological tools that were forming in German academia for a hundred years previous were finally used in an l institutional space for formal and recognized research. A medical doctor by trade, Wundt began teaching at the University of Leipzig in 1874, teaching courses in philosophy, physiology and eventually in the new discipline of *psychology.*

Shortly after establishing the world's first formal psychological laboratory Wundt recognized the need for a scholarly journal to publish the numerous research papers coming out of his new laboratory. In 1881 the journal *Psychological Studies* began publication and quickly spread the news of this new discipline and the research done within Wundt's laboratory.

The emergence of this new discipline within Europe did not, of course, go unnoticed in North America. A medical doctor by the name of William James (1842-1910) was clearly very interested in Wundt's work at Leipzig and can in some senses be considered the founder of the *functionalism* trend within American psychology. In contrast to the European emphasis of a *structuralism* approach (essentially asking *WHAT* questions) James turned the attention to *HOW* questions.

This functionalist spirit that was to define North American psychology is best illustrated by the work of Granville Stanley Hall (1844-1924). G. Stanley Hall began his graduate studies attending seminary at Union Theological Seminary in New York and later studied philosophy in Germany. Finally, at the age of thirty-two he enrolled at Harvard to study under William James in the area of Psychology while also spending time studying under Wundt in Germany. Hall became the first recipient of a Ph.D. in Psychology within North America and quickly became a defining force within this new discipline.

244   THE MEANING OF LIFE

While *structuralist* psychology was forming in German universities and *functionalist* psychology was forming in American universities, a movement of applied psychology was forming in England and France. This new emerging use of psychology brought with it the application of psychology for the service of public institutions. The first attempts of this practical emphasis can be seen in Francis Galton's work on individual differences and Cattell's unsuccessful attempt to measure intelligence.

At the beginning of the 20th century, success was just around the corner as we had the emergence of the Paris psychologist Alfred Binet (1857-1911) and his interest in measuring intelligence. After years of trail and error Binet discovered that it was easier to tell the individual differences in complex thinking tasks and therefore used this as a basis for measuring intelligence.

Binet, along with his colleague, Theodore Simon, successfully developed the first usable intelligence test, published in 1905. The Binet-Simon Scales' publishing rights were later purchased by Lewis Turman (for the cost of $1) and translated and adapted into the Stanford-Binet Intelligence Scale that is still the standard of intelligence testing.

While psychology has grown and changed shape over the past century, it is still a child with four heads. That is to say, there are four main schools that can incorporate most of what is termed Psychology: Behaviourism, Psychoanalysis, Cognitive Psychology and the Humanistic school of psychology.

READ AND DECIDE FOR YOURSELF:

Excerpts from:

EUGENICS: ITS DEFINITION, SCOPE AND AIMS
(FRANCIS GALTON)

HEREDITARY TALENT AND CHARACTER
(FRANCIS GALTON)

NEW METHODS FOR THE DIAGNOSIS OF THE INTELLECTUAL LEVEL OF SUBNORMALS
(ALFRED BINET)

EUGENICS: ITS DEFINITION, SCOPE, AND AIMS.

Francis Galton

THE AMERICAN JOURNAL OF SOCIOLOGY

Volume X; July, 1904; Number 1

Read before the Sociological Society at a meeting in the School of Economies
(London University), on May 16, 1904. Professor Karl Pearson, F.R.S., in the chair.

EUGENICS is the science which deals with all influences that improve the inborn qualities of a race; also with those that develop them to the utmost advantage. The improvement of the inborn qualities, or stock, of some one human population will alone be discussed here.

What is meant by improvement ? What by the syllable *eu* in "eugenics," whose English equivalent is "good"? There is considerable difference between goodness in the several qualities and in that of the character as a whole. The character depends largely on the *proportion* between qualities, whose balance may be much influenced by education. We must therefore leave morals as far as possible out of the discussion, not entangling ourselves with the almost hopeless difficulties they raise as to whether a character as a whole is good or bad. Moreover, the goodness or badness of character is not absolute, but relative to the current form of civilization. A fable will best explain what is meant. Let the scene be the zoological gardens in the quiet hours of the night, and suppose that, as in old fables, the animals are able to converse, and that some very wise creature who had easy access to all the cages, say a philosophic sparrow or rat, was engaged in collecting the opinions of all sorts of animals with a view of elaborating a system of absolute morality. It is needless to enlarge on the contrariety of ideals between the beasts that prey and those they prey upon, between those of the animals that have to work hard for their food and the sedentary parasites that cling to their bodies and suck their blood, and so forth. A large number of suffrages in favor of maternal affection would be obtained, but most species of fish would repudiate it, while among the voices of birds would be heard the musical protest of the cuckoo. Though no agreement could be reached as to absolute morality, the essentials of eugenics may be easily defined. All creatures would agree that it was better to be healthy than sick, vigorous than weak, well-fitted than ill-fitted for their part in life; in short, that it was better to be good rather than bad specimens of their kind, whatever that kind might be. So with men. There are a vast number of conflicting ideals, of alternative characters, of incompatible civilizations; but they are wanted to give fullness and interest to life. Society would be very dull if every man resembled the highly estimable Marcus Aurelius or Adam Bede. The aim of eugenics is to represent each class or sect by its best specimens; that done, to leave them to work out their common civilization in their own way.

A considerable list of qualities can easily be compiled that nearly everyone except *"cranks"* would take into account when picking out the best specimens of his class. It would include health, energy, ability, manliness, and courteous disposition. Recollect that the natural differences between dogs are highly marked in all these respects., and that men are quite as variable by nature as other animals of like species. Special aptitudes would be assessed highly by those who possessed them, as the artistic faculties by artists, fearlessness of inquiry and veracity by scientists, religious absorption by mystics, and so on. There would be self-sacrificers, self-tormentors, and other exceptional idealists; but the representatives of these would be better members of a community than the body of their electors. They would have more of those qualities that are needed in a state--more vigor, more ability, and more consistency of purpose. The community might be trusted to refuse representatives of criminals, and of others whom it rates as undesirable.

Let us for a moment suppose that the practice of eugenics should hereafter raise the average quality of our nation to that of its better moiety at the present day, and consider the gain. The general tone of domestic, social, and political life would be higher. The race as a whole would be less foolish, less frivolous, less excitable, and politically more provident than now. Its demagogues who *"played* to the gallery" would play to a more sensible gallery than at present. We should be better fitted to fulfil our vast imperial opportunities. Lastly, men of an order of ability which is now very rare would become more frequent, because, the level out of which they rose would itself have risen.

The aim of eugenics is to bring as many influences as can be reasonably employed, to cause the useful classes in the community to contribute *more* than their proportion to the next generation. The course of procedure that lies within the functions of a learned and active society, such as the sociological may become, would be somewhat as follows:

1. Dissemination of a knowledge of the laws of heredity, so far as they are surely known, and promotion of their further study. Few seem to be aware how greatly the knowledge of what may be termed the *actuarial* side of heredity has advanced in recent years. The *average* closeness of kinship in each degree now admits of exact definition and of being treated mathematically, like birth- and death-rates, and the other topics with which actuaries are concerned.

2. Historical inquiry into the rates with which the various classes of society (classified according to civic usefulness.) have contributed to the population at various times, in ancient and modern nations. There is strong reason for believing that national rise and decline is closely connected with this influence. It seems to be the tendency of high civilization to check fertility in the upper classes,- through numerous causes, some of which are well. known, others are inferred, and others again are wholly obscure. The latter class are apparently analogous to those which

bar the fertility of most species of wild animals in zoological gardens. Out of the hundreds and thousands of species that have been tamed, very few indeed are fertile when their liberty is restricted and their struggles for livelihood are abolished; those which are so, and are otherwise useful to man, becoming domesticated. There is perhaps some connection between this obscure action and the disappearance of most savage races when brought into contact with high civilization, though there are other and well-known concomitant causes. But while most barbarous races disappear, some, like the negro, do not. It may therefore be expected that types of our race will be found to exist which can be highly civilized without losing fertility; nay, they may become more fertile under artificial conditions, as is the case with many domestic animals.

3. Systematic collection of facts showing the circumstances under which large and thriving families have most frequently originated; in other words, the *conditions* of eugenics. The definition of a thriving family, that will pass muster for the moment at least, is one in which the children have gained distinctly superior positions to those who were their classmates in early life. Families may be considered *"large"* that contain not less than three adult male children. It would be no great burden to a society including many members who had eugenics at heart, to initiate and to preserve a large collection of such records for the use of statistical students. The committee charged with the task would have to consider very carefully the form of their circular and the persons intrusted to distribute it. They should ask only for as much useful information as could be easily, and would be readily, supplied by any member of the family appealed to. The point to be ascertained is the *status* of the two parents at the time of their marriage, whence its more or less eugenic character might have been predicted, if the larger knowledge that we now hope to obtain had then existed. Some account would be wanted of their race, profession, and residence; also of their own respective parentages, and of their brothers and sisters. Finally the reasons would be required, why the children deserved to be entitled a "thriving" family. This manuscript collection might hereafter develop into a *"golden* book" of thriving families. The Chinese, whose customs have often much sound sense, make their honors retrospective. We might learn from them to show that respect to the parents of noteworthy children which the contributors of such valuable assets to the national wealth richly deserve. The act of systematically collecting records of thriving families would have the further advantage of familiarizing the public with the fact that eugenics had at length become a subject of serious scientific study by an energetic society.

4. Influences affecting marriage. The remarks of Lord Bacon in his essay on *Death* may appropriately be quoted here. He says with the view of minimizing its terrors: "There is no passion in the mind of men so weak but it mates and masters the fear of

death ..... Revenge triumphs over death; love slights it; honour aspireth to it; grief flyeth to it; fear pre-occupateth it." Exactly the same kind of considerations apply to marriage. The passion of love seems so overpowering that it may be thought folly to try to direct its course. But plain facts do not confirm this view. Social influences of all kinds have immense power in the end, and they are very various. If unsuitable marriages from the eugenic point of view were banned socially, or even regarded with the unreasonable disfavor which some attach to cousin-marriages, very few would be made. The multitude of marriage restrictions that have proved prohibitive among uncivilized people would require a volume to describe.

5. Persistence in setting forth the national importance of eugenics. There are three stages to be passed through: (I) It must be made familiar as an academic question, until its exact importance has been understood and accepted as a fact. (2) It must be recognized as a subject whose practical development deserves serious consideration. (3) It must be introduced into the national conscience, like a new religion. It has, indeed, strong claims to become an orthodox religious, tenet of the future, for eugenics co-operate with the workings of nature by securing that humanity shall be represented by the fittest races. What nature does blindly, slowly, and ruthlessly, man may do providently, quickly, and kindly. As it lies within his power, so it becomes his duty to work in that direction. The improvement of our stock seems to me one of the highest objects that we can reasonably attempt. We are ignorant of the ultimate destinies of humanity, but feel perfectly sure that it is as noble a work to raise its level, in the sense already explained, as it would be disgraceful to abase it. I see no impossibility in eugenics becoming a religious dogma among mankind, but its details must first be worked out sedulously in the study. Overzeal leading to hasty action would do harm, by holding out expectations of a near golden age, which will certainly be falsified and cause the science to be discredited. The first and main point is to secure the general intellectual acceptance of eugenics as a hopeful and most important study. Then let its principles work into the heart of the nation, which will gradually give practical effect to them in ways that we may not wholly foresee.

HEREDITARY TALENT AND CHARACTER.

Francis Galton (1865)

Originally published in Macmillan's Magazine, 12, 157-166, 318-327.

PART I

The power of man over animal life, in producing whatever varieties of form he pleases, is enormously great. It would seem as though the physical structure of future generations was almost as plastic as clay, under the control of the breeder's will. It is my desire to show more pointedly than -- so far as I am aware -- has been attempted before, that mental qualities are equally under control.

A remarkable misapprehension appears to be current as to the fact of the transmission of talent by inheritance. It is commonly asserted that the children of eminent men are stupid; that, where great power of intellect seems to have been inherited, it has descended through the mother's side; and that one son commonly runs away with the talent of a whole family. My own inquiries have led me to a diametrically opposite conclusion. I find that talent is transmitted by inheritance in a very remarkable degree; that the mother has by no means the monopoly of its transmission; and that whole families of persons of talent are more common than those in which one member only is possessed of it. I justify my conclusions by the statistics I now proceed to adduce, which I believe are amply sufficient to command conviction. They are only a part of much material I have collected, for a future volume on this subject; all of which points in the same direction. I should be very grateful to any of my readers for information that may help me in my further inquiries.

In investigating the hereditary transmission of talent, we must ever bear in mind our ignorance of the laws which govern the inheritance even of physical features. We know to, a certainty that the latter exist, though we do not thoroughly understand their action. · The breeders of our domestic animals have discovered many rules by experience, and act upon them to a nicety. But we have not advanced, even to this limited extent, in respect to the human race. It has been nobody's business to study them; and the study is difficult for many reasons. Thus, only two generations are likely to be born during the life of any observer; clothing conceals shape; and each individual rarely marries more than once. Nevertheless, all analogy assures us that the physical features of man are equally transmissible with those of brutes. The resemblances between parent and offspring as they [p. 158] appear to a casual observer, are just as close in one case as in the other; and, therefore, as a nearer scrutiny has established strict laws of hereditary transmission in brutes, we have every reason for believing that the same could also be discovered in the case of man.

So far as I am aware, no animals have ever been bred for general intelligence. Special aptitudes are thoroughly controlled by the breeder. He breeds dogs that point, that retrieve, that fondle, or that bite; but, no one has ever yet attempted to breed for high general intellect, irrespective of all other qualities. It would be a most interesting subject for an attempt. We hear constantly of prodigies of dogs, whose very intelligence makes them of little value as slaves. When they are wanted, they are apt to be absent on their own errands. They are too critical of their master's conduct. For instance, an intelligent dog shows marked contempt for an unsuccessful sportsman. He will follow nobody along a road that leads on a well-known tedious errand. He does not readily forgive a man who wounds his self-esteem. He is often a dexterous thief and a sad hypocrite. For these reasons an over-intelligent dog is not an object of particular desire, and therefore, I suppose, no one has ever thought of encouraging a breed of wise dogs. But it mould be a most interesting occupation for a country philosopher to pick up, the cleverest dogs he could hear of, and mate them together, generation after generation -- breeding purely for intellectual power, and disregarding shape, size, and every other quality.

As no experiment of this description has ever been made, I cannot appeal to its success. I can only say that the general resemblances in mental qualities between parents and offspring, in man and brute, are every whit as near as the resemblance of their physical features; and I must leave the existence of actual laws in the former case to be a matter of inference from the analogy of the latter. Resemblance frequently fails where we might expect it to hold; but we may fairly ascribe the failure to the influence of conditions that we do not yet comprehend. So long as we have a plenitude of evidence in favour of the hypothesis of the hereditary descent of talent, we need not be disconcerted when negative evidence brought against us. We must reply that just the same argument might have been urged against the transmission of physical features of our domestic animals; yet our breeders have discovered certain rules, and make their living by acting upon them. They know, with accurate prevision, when particular types of animals are mated together, what will be the character of the offspring. They can say that such and such qualities will be reproduced to a certainty. That others are doubtful; for they may appear in some of the descendants and not in the rest. Lastly, that there are yet other qualities, excessive in one parent and defective in the other, that will be counterbalanced and be transmitted to the offspring in a moderate proportion.

I maintain by analogy that this prevision could be equally attained respect to the mental qualities, though I cannot prove it. All I can show is that talent and peculiarities of character are found in the children, when they have existed in either of the parents, to an extent beyond all question greater than in the children of ordinary persons. It is a fact, neither to be denied nor be considered of importance, that the children of men of genius are frequently of mediocre intellect. The qualities each individual are due to the combined influence of his two parents; and remarkable qualities of the one have been neutralized in the offspring by the opposite or defective qualities of the other. It is natural that contrast of qualities, in the parents' dispositions, should occur as frequently as harmony; for one of the many foundations of friendship and of the marriage union is a difference of character; each individual seeking thereby to supplement the

252 THE MEANING OF LIFE

qualities in which he feels his own nature to be deficient. We have also good reason to believe that every special talent or character depends [p. 159] on a variety of obscure conditions, the analysis of which has never yet been seriously attempted. It is easy to conceive that the entire character might be considerably altered, owing to the modification of any one of these conditions.

As a first step in my investigation, I sought a biographical work, of manageable size, that should contain the lives of the chief men of genius whom the world is known to have produced. I ultimately selected that of Sir Thomas Phillips, in his well-known work of reference, "The Million of Facts;" because it is compiled with evident discrimination, and without the slightest regard to the question on which I was engaged. It is, moreover, prefaced --- "It has been attempted to record, in brief, only the ORIGINAL MINDS, who founded or originated. Biography in general is filled with mere imitators, or with men noted only for chance of birth, or necessary position in society." I do not mean to say that Sir Thomas Phillips's selection is the best that could have been made, for he was a somewhat crochety [*sic*] writer. It did not, however, much matter whose biography I adopted, so long as it had been written in the above-mentioned spirit and so long as I determined to abide stedfastly [*sic*] within its limits, without yielding to the temptation of supplying obvious omissions, in a way favourable to any provisional theory.

According to this select biography, I find that 605 notabilities lived between the years 1453 and 1853. And among these are no less than 102 relationships, or 1 in 6, according to the following list:

(see diagram, right)

It will be observed that the number is swelled by four large families, such as those of Gronovius and Stephens, of six [p. 160] members each, and of the Medici and the House of Orange, of four members

Art.	Lit. & science.	More distant.	Brothers.	Father & son.	Number.	NOTABLE PERSONS.
-	-	1	-	2	3	J. Adams, Pres. U.S.A.; son Samuel also patriot; nephew, J. Quincey, president.
-	2	-	2	-	2	W. Belsham, historian; brother of T. Belsham, Unitarian minister.
-	3	-	-	2	3	J. Bernouilli, father of James and uncle of John, all mathematicians.
3	-	-	-	2	3	Breughel, father and two sons, painters.
-	2	-	-	2	2	Buxtorf, father and son, Hebraists.
3	-	1	2	-	3	Caracci. An. and Ag. brothers, Lud. cousin, painter.
-	1	-	2	-	2	Cartwright, reformer; brother, mechanist.
-	3	-	-	3	3	Casini, grandfather, father, and son, all mathematicians.
-	1	2	-	-	2	Cooper, Privy Councillor to Cromwell; grandson, literary.
-	-	-	2	-	2	De Witt, two brothers, patriots.
-	-	-	-	3	3	Elizabeth, queen, daughter of Henry VIII. and granddaughter of Sir T. Bullen.
-	2	-	2	-	2	Fontana, two brothers, natural philosophers.
-	2	-	-	2	2	Forster, father and son, naturalists (Cook's voyages).
-	6	-	-	6	6	Gronovius, sons and grandsons, six in all, learned critics.
-	1	-	-	2	3	Gustavus Adolphus, father of Christina and grandson of Gustavus Vasa.
-	2	-	-	2	2	Herschel, father and son, astronomers.
-	2	-	2	-	2	Hunter, two brothers, anatomists.
-	2	2	-	-	2	Jussieu, uncle and nephew, botanists.
-	-	-	-	4	4	Medici, grandfather, father, and son, and Catherine.
-	-	-	-	2	2	Orleans, Egalité, and son Louis Philippe.
-	-	-	2	-	2	Ostade, two brothers, painters.
-	4	-	4	-	4	Perrault, four brothers, all writers.
-	1	-	-	2	2	Penn, admiral; son, Quaker writer.
-	-	2	-	-	4	Phillibert, Prince of Orange; cousin William, whose son was Maurice. His grandson was our William III.
-	-	-	-	2	2	Pitt, father and son, statesmen.
-	2	-	-	2	2	Scaliger, classical critic; son also.
-	-	-	2	-	2	Sforzas, father and son.
-	1	2	-	-	2	Shaftesbury, statesman; grandson, author.
-	1	-	-	2	2	Sheridan, father and son.
-	1	-	-	2	2	Staël, Madam, daughter of Necker, financier.
-	6	-	-	6	6	Stephens, family of six, critics and editors.
2	-	-	-	2	2	Teniers, father and son, painters.
-	-	-	-	2	2	Tytler, historian and poet; son, Lord Woodhouselee.
2	-	-	-	2	2	Vanderwelde, father and son, painters.
-	2	-	2	-	2	Vanderwurf, two brothers, famous for small history.
-	-	1	2	-	3	Valnoo, two brothers, and nephew, painters.
-	1	-	-	2	2	Walpole, Sir Robert, statesman; Sir Horace, author.
-	-	-	-	2	2	Van Tromp, father and son, admirals.
-	1	2	-	-	2	Villiers, statesman; grandson, the reprobate poet.
-	2	-	-	2	2	Vossius, father, son, and other relatives, all writers.
-	2	-	-	2	2	Warton, editor of Pope; son, poet.
9	52	14	22	66	102	

each. The two first might be objected to, as hardly worthy of the distinguished place they occupy. But we must adhere to our biography; there are many more relationships that could very fairly have been added, as a set-off against these names. Such are two more Vanderweldes, and the family of Richelieu; besides others, like Hallam the historian, and Watt the mechanic, whose sons died early, full of the highest promise. Even if sixteen names were struck out of our list, the proportion of the relationship would remain as 86/605, or 1 in 7. And these are almost wholly referable to transmission of talent through the male line; for eminent mothers do not find a place in mere biographical lists. The overwhelming force of a statistical fact like this renders counter-arguments of no substantial effect.

Next, let us examine a biographical list of much greater extension. I have selected for this purpose an excellent brief dictionary by Mr. C. Hone.[*1*] It is not yet published, but part of its proof sheets have been obligingly lent to me. The entire work appears to contain some 19,000 names; it is, therefore, more than thirty times as extensive as the list we have hitherto been considering. I have selected one part only of this long series of names for examination, namely, those that begin with the letter M. There are 1141 names that remain under this letter, after eliminating those of sovereigns, and also of all persons who died before A.D. 1453. Out of these, 103 or 1 in 11 are either fathers and sons, or brothers; and I am by no means sure that I have succeeded in hunting out all the relationships that might be found to exist among them.

It will be remarked that the proportion of distinguished relationships becomes smaller, as we relax the restrictions of our selection; and it is reasonable that it should be so, for we then include in our lists the names of men who have been inducted into history through other conditions than the possession of eminent talent.

Again, if we examine into the relationships of the notabilities of the present day, we obtain even larger proportions. Walford's :Men of the Time" contains an account of the distinguished men of England, the Continent and America, who are now alive. Under the letter A there are 85 names of men, and no less than 25 of these, or 1 in 3-1/2, have relatives also in the list; 12 of them are brothers, and 11 fathers and sons.

Abbott, Rev. Jacob (U.S.A.), author on religions and moral subjects.

Abbott, Rev. John, younger brother of above, author on religious and moral subjects.

A'Beckett, Sir William, author, Solicitor-Gen. of New South Wales, and brother of late Gilbert Abbott A'Beckett.

Adam, Jean Victor, painter, son of an eminent engraver.

Adams, American minister, son of John Quincey Adams.

Ainsworth, William Francis, editor of "Journal of Natural and Geographical Science," "Explorations in Asia-Minor and Kurdistan."

Ainsworth, William Harrison, novelist, cousin of above.

Aïvazooski, Gabriel, Armenian, born in the Crimea, Professor of European and Oriental languages, and member of Historical Institute of France.

254 THE MEANING OF LIFE

Aïvazooski, Ivan, a marine painter, brother of above.

Albermarile, Earl of (brother of Keppel)

Albert, Prince (brother).

Aldis, Sir Charles, medical.

Aldis, Charles J.B. medical, son of above.

Alexander, James Waddell, American divine (son of a Professor).

Alexander, Joseph Addison, Professor of Ancient languages, and of Biblical and Ecclesiastical history, brother of the above.

Alison, Sir Archibald, historian, son of author of "Essays on Taste;" his mother belonged to "a family which has for two centuries been eminent in mathematics and the exact sciences."

Ampère, member of French Academy, and Professor in College of France (literary), son of the celebrated physicist of the same name

Arago, Etienne, journalist and theatrical writer, brother of the celebrated philosopher.

Argyropopulo, statesman, son of grand interpreter to the Porte.

Aristarchi, ecclesiastic and statesman, son of Grand interpreter to the Porte.

Arnold, Matthew, son of late Dr. Arnold.

Arwidson, Librarian R. Library, Stockholm. author, son of a person who held a, high position in the Church.

Ashburton, Lord, son of Rt. Hon. Alexander Baring. [p. 161]

Azeglio, Massimo, statesman and painter

Azeglio, Marquis, *nephew* of the above, diplomatist and painter.

So if we examine the biographies of artists. In Bryan's large "Dictionary of Painters," the letter a contains 391 names of men, of whom 65 are near relatives, or 1 in 6: 33 of them are fathers and sons, 30 are brothers. In Fétis "Biographie Universelle des Musiciens" the letter S contains 515 names, of which 50 are near relations, or 1 in 10. Two-third are fathers and sons, one-third are brothers.

It is justly to be urged, in limitation of the enormous effect of hereditary influence, implied by the above figures, that when a parent has achieved great eminence, his son will be placed in a more favourable position for advancement, than if he had been the son of an ordinary person. Social position is an especially important aid to success in statesmanship and generalship; for it is notorious that neither the Legislature nor the army afford, in their highest ranks, an open arena to the ablest intellects. The sons of the favoured classes are introduced early in life to both these fields of trial, with every encouragement to support them. Those of the lower classes are delayed and discouraged in their start; and when they are near the coveted goal, they find themselves aged. They are too late: they are not beaten by the superior merit of their contemporaries, but by time; as was once touchingly remarked by Sir De Lacy Evans.

COGNITIVE PSYCHOLOGY   255

In order to test the value of hereditary influence with greater precision, we should therefore extract from our biographical list the names (they are 330) of those that have achieved distinction in the more open fields of science and literature. There is no favour here beyond the advantage of a good education. Whatever spur may be given by the desire to maintain the family fame and whatever opportunities are afforded by abundant leisure, are more than neutralised by those influences which commonly lead the heirs of fortune to idleness and dilettantism.

Recurring to our list, we find fifty-one men who have distinguished relations. Therefore, no less than 51/605, or one distinguished man in every twelve has a father, son, or brother, distinguished in literature. To take a round number at a venture, we may be sure that there have been far more than a million students educated in Europe during the last four centuries, being an average of only 2,500 in each a [*sic*] year. According to our list, about 330 of these, or only 1 in 3,000, achieved eminent distinction: yet of those who did so, 1 in 12 was related to a distinguished man. Keeping to literature alone, it is 51 to 330 = 1 to 6-1/2, that a very distinguished literary man has a very distinguished literary relative, and it is (leaving out the Gronovius and Stephenses) 20 to 330 = 1 to 16, and 12 to 330·=1 to 28, that the relationship is father and son, or brother and brother, respectively.

The Law is, by far, the most open to fair competition of all the professions; and of all offices in the law there is none that is more surely the reward of the most distinguished intellectual capacity than that of the Lord Chancellor. It therefore becomes an exceedingly interesting question to learn what have been the relationships of our Lord Chancellors. Are they to any notable degree the children, or the parents, or the brothers of very eminent men? Lord Campbell's "Lives of the Chancellors" forms a valuable biographical dictionary for the purpose of this investigation. I have taken it just as it stands; including; as Lord Campbell does, certain Lord Keepers and Commissioners of the Great Seal, as of equal rank with the Chancellors. I may further mention, that many expressions in Lord Campbell's works show that he was a disbeliever in hereditary influence.

Now what are the facts? Since Henry VIII.'s time, when Chancellors ceased to be ecclesiastics, and were capable of marrying, we have had thirty-nine Chancellors, &c. whose lives have been written by Lord Campbell, of whom the following had eminent relationships :-- [p. 162]

> Sir Nicholas Bacon, Lord Keeper: son, Lord Chancellor Bacon.
>
> Coventry: son of a very learned judge of the Common Pleas.
>
> Bacon : father as above.
>
> Littleton: son of a judge.
>
> Whitelock: son of a judge, father of two sons, one of great eminence as a lawyer, the other as a soldier.
>
> Herbert : three son. One had high command in army ; the second, the great naval officer, created Lord Torrington; the third, Chief Justice of Queen's Bench.

256   THE MEANING OF LIFE

Finch, son of Speaker of House of Commons, and first cousin to the Lord Chancellor Finch of previous years, had a son who "almost rivalled his father" and who was made Solicitor-General and Earl of Aylesford.

Macclesfield: son, President of Royal Society.

Talbot: father was bishop, consecutively, of Oxford, Salisbury and Durham; had sons, of one of whom there were great hopes, but he died young; the other "succeeded to his father's virtues."

Hardwick had five sons, all very distinguished. One, a man of letters ; second, Lord Chancellor Yorke; third, an ambassador; fourth, "talented as the others;" fifth, Bishop of Ely.

Northington: father was "one of the most accomplished men of his day. "

Pratt: father was Chief Justice of King's Bench; his son was distinguished for public service.

Yorke: father was Lord Chancellor Hadwicke. (See above.)

Bathurst: father was the Lord Bathurst of Queen Anne's time; his son was the Lord Bathurst who filled high office under George III. and IV.

Erskine: his brothers were nearly as eminent. The whole family was most talented.

Eldon: brother was the famous Lord Stowell, Judge of Admiralty.

Thus out of the 39 Chancellors 16 had kinsmen of eminence. 13 of them -- viz. Sir Nicholas Bacon, Lord Bacon, Coventry, Littleton, Whitelock, Herbert, Finch, Hardwick, Pratt, Yorke, Bathurst, Erskine, and Eldon -- had kinsmen of great eminence. In other words, 13 out of 39 -- that is, 1 in every 3 -- are remarkable instances of hereditary influence.

It is astonishing to remark the number of the Chancellors, who rose from mediocre social positions, showing how talent makes its way at the Bar, and how utterly insufficient are favouritism and special opportunities to win the great legal prize of the Chancellorship. It is not possible accurately, and it is hardly worth while roughly, to calculate the numerical value of hereditary influence in obtaining the Chancellorship. It is sufficient to say that it is enormous. We must not only reckon the number of students actually at the Chancery bar, and that the Lord Chancellor was the foremost man among them, but we must reckon the immense number of schools in England, in any one of which, if a boy shows real marks of eminence is pretty sure to be patronised and passed on to a better place of education; whence by exhibitions, and subsequently by University scholarships and fellowships, he may become educated as a lawyer. I believe, from these reasons, that the chances of the son of a Lord Chancellor to be himself also a Chancellor, supposing he enters the law, to be more than a thousandfold greater than if he were the son of equally rich but otherwise undistinguished parents. It does not appear an accident that, out of 54 Lord Chancellors or Lord Keepers, two -- viz. Sir Nicholas Bacon and Lord Hardwick -

COGNITIVE PSYCHOLOGY 257

- should have had sons who were also Chancellors, when we bear in mind the very eminent legal relationships of Herbert, Finch, Eldon, and the rest.

The intellectual force of English boys has, up to almost the present date, been steadily directed to classical education. Classics form the basis of instruction at our grammar schools, so that every boy who possesses signal classical aptitudes has a chance of showing them. Those who are successful obtain exhibitions and other help, and ultimately find their way to the great arena of competition of University life.

The senior classic at Cambridge is not only the foremost of the 300 youths who take their degrees in the same year, but he is the foremost of perhaps a tenth part of the classical intellect of his generation, throughout all England. No industry, without eminent natural talent to back it, could possibly raise a youth into that position.

The institution of the class list at Cambridge dates from. 1824; so there, [p. 163] have been 41 senior classics up to the present year, Wherever two names had been bracketed together, I selected the one that stood best in other examinations and then extracted the following names from the list of them, as instances of hereditary influence:--

> 1827. Kennedy: father was a classics of eminence; two brothers, see below; another brother, almost equally distinguished in classics.
>
> 1828. Selwyn: brother M.P. for Cambridge, an eminent lawyer.
>
> 1830. Wordsworth: nephew to the poet, brother of an almost equally distinguished classic, son of the Master of Trinity.
>
> 1831. Kennedy (see above.)
>
> 1832. Lushington: brother (see below); nephew to the Right Hon. Sir Stephen Lushington. The family has numerous other members of eminent talent.
>
> 1834. Kennedy (see above).
>
> 1835. Goulbourn: father, Chancellor of the Exchequer, nephew of Sergeant Goulbourn, cousin to Dr. Goulbourn, Head Master of Rugby the well-known preacher.
>
> 1835. Vaughan : many relations like those of Goulbourn, including the Judge, the Professor at Oxford, and Mr. Hawkins. (See below)
>
> 1842. Denman : father was the eminent Chief Justice Lord Denman.
>
> 1846. Lushington: brother (see above).
>
> 1854. Hawkins: see Vaughan.
>
> 1855. Butler: son of Senior Wrangler of 1794; three brothers, of whom two held University Scholarships in Oxford, and the other was a double first-class man at Cambridge.

258 THE MEANING OF LIFE

12 of the 41, or about 1 in 3-1/2, show these influences in a more or less marked degree; 7 of them, or 1 in 6, viz. 3 Kennedy, 1 Wordsworth, 2 Lushington, and 1 Butler, very much so.

The data we have been considering are summed up in the following table:--

Number of cases.		Occurrence of near male relationship.	Percentages.	
			Distinguished father has a distinguished son.	Distinguished man has a distinguished brother.
605	All the men of "original minds" (Sir T. Phillips) and of every profession between 1453 and 1853	1 in 6 cases.	6 times in 100 cases.	2 times in 100 cases.
85	Living notabilities (Walford's "Men of the Times," letter A)	1 in 3½ cases.	7 ,, ,,	7 ,, ,,
391	Painters of all dates (Bryan's Dicty. A)	1 in 6 cases.	5 ,, ,,	4 ,, ,,
515	Musicians (Fétis Dicty. A)	1 in 10 cases.	6 ,, ,,	3 ,, ,,
54	Lord Chancellors (Lord Campbell) .	1 in 3 cases.	16 ,, ,,	4 ,, ,,
41	Senior Classics of Cambridge . . .	1 in 4 cases.	Too recent	10 ,, ,,
	Averages	1 in 6 cases.	8 in 100 cases.	5 in 100 cases.

Everywhere is the enormous power or hereditary influence forced on our attention. If we take a list of the most brilliant standard writers of the last few years, we shall find a large share of the number have distinguished relationships. It would be difficult to set off, against the following instances, the same number of names of men of equal eminence, whose immediate relatives were undistinguished. Bronté (Jane Eyre and her two sisters); Bulwer (and his brother the ambassador); Disraeli (father, author of "Curiosities of Literature"); Hallam (son, the subject of "In Memoriam"); Kingsley(two brothers eminent novelists, two others no less talented); Lord Macaulay (son of Zachary Macaulay); Miss Martineau (and her brother); Merivale, Herman and Charles (brothers); Dean Stanley (father the bishop, and popular writer on birds); Thackeray (daughter, authoress of "Elizabeth"); Tennyson (brother also a poet); Mrs. Trollope (son, Anthony).

As we cannot doubt that the transmission of talent is as much through the side of the mother as through that of the father, how vastly would the offspring be improved, supposing distinguished women to be commonly married to distinguished men, generation after [p. 164] generation, their qualities being in harmony and not in contrast, according to rules of which we are now ignorant, but which a study of the subject would be sure to evolve!

It has been said by Bacon that "great men have no continuance." I, however, find that very great men are certainly not averse to the other sex, for some such have been noted for their illicit intercourses, and, I believe, for a corresponding amount of illegitimate issue. Great lawyers are especially to be blamed in this, even more than poets, artists, or great commanders. It seems natural to believe that a person who is not married, or who, if married, does not happen to have children, should feel himself more vacant to the attractions of a public or a literary career than if he had the domestic cares and interests of a family to attend to. Thus, if we take a list of the leaders in science of the present day, the small number of them who have families is very remarkable. Perhaps the best selection of names we can make, is from those who have filled the annual scientific office of President of the British Association. We will take the list of the commoners simply, lest it should be objected, though unjustly, that some of the noblemen who have occupied the chair were not wholly indebted to their scientific attainments for that high position. Out of twenty-two individuals, about one-third have children; one-third are or have been married and have no children; and one-third have never been married. Among the children of those who have had families, the names of Frank Buckland and Alexander Herschel are already well-known to the public.

There has been a popular belief that men of great intellectual eminence, are usually of feeble constitution, and of a dry and cold disposition. There may be such instances, but I believe the general rule to be exactly the opposite. Such men, so far as my observation and reading extend, are usually more manly and genial than the average, and by the aid of these very qualities, they obtain a recognised ascendancy. It is a great and common mistake to suppose that high intellectual powers are commonly associated with puny frames and small physical strength. Men of remarkable eminence are almost always men of vast powers of work. Those among them that have fallen into sedentary ways will frequently astonish their friends by their physical feats, when they happen to be in the mood of a vacation ramble. The Alpine Club contains a remarkable number of men of fair literary and scientific distinction; and these are among the strongest and most daring of the climbers. I believe, from my own recollections of the thews and energies of my contemporaries and friends of many years at Cambridge, that the first half-dozen class-men in classics or mathematics would have beaten, out of all proportion, the last half-dozen class-men in any trial of physical strength or endurance. Most notabilities have been great eaters and excellent digesters, on literally the same principle that the furnace which can raise more steam than is usual for one of its size burn more freely and well than is common. Most great men are vigorous animals, with exuberant powers, and an extreme devotion to a cause. There is no reason to suppose that, in breeding for the highest order of intellect, we should produce a sterile or a feeble race.

Many forms of civilization have been peculiarly unfavourable to the hereditary transmission of rare talent. None of them mere more prejudicial to it than that of the Middle Ages, where almost every youth of genius was attracted into the Church, and enrolled in the ranks of a celibate clergy.

Another great hindrance to it is a costly tone of society, like that of our own, where it becomes a folly for a rising man to encumber himself with domestic expenses, which custom exacts, and which are larger than his resources are able to meet. Here also genius is celibate, at least during the best period of manhood.

260   THE MEANING OF LIFE

A spirit of caste is also bad, which [p. 165] compels a man of genius to select his wife from a narrow neighborhood or from the members of a few families.

But a spirit of clique is not bad. I understand that in Germany it is very much the custom for professors to marry the daughters of other professors, and I have some reason to believe, but am anxious for further information before I can feel sure of it, that the enormous intellectual digestion of German literary men, which far exceeds that of the corresponding class of our own country-men, may, in some considerable degree, be traceable to this practice.

So far as beauty is concerned, the custom of many countries, of the nobility purchasing the handsomest girls they could find for their wives, has laid the foundation of a higher type of features among the ruling classes. It is not so very long ago in England that it was thought quite natural that the strongest lance at the tournament should win the fairest or the noblest lady. The lady was the prize to be tilted for. She rarely objected to the arrangement, because her vanity was gratified by the *éclat* of the proceeding. Now history is justly charged with a tendency to repeat itself. We may, therefore, reasonably look forward to the possibility, I do not venture to say the probability, of a recurrence of some such practice of competition. What an extraordinary effect might be produced on our race, if its object was to unite in marriage those who possessed the finest and most suitable natures, mental moral, and physical!

Let us, then, give reins to our fancy, and imagine a Utopia -- or a Laputa, if you will -- in which a system of competitive examination for girls, as well as for youths, had been so developed as to embrace every important quality of mind and body, and where a considerable sum was yearly allotted to the endowment of such marriages as promised to yield children who would grow into eminent servants of the State. We may picture to ourselves an annual ceremony in that Utopia or Laputa, in which the Senior Trustee of the Endowment Fund would address ten deeply-blushing young men, all of twenty-five years old, in the following terms :

> *"Gentlemen, I have to announce the results of a public examination, conducted on established principles; which show that you occupy the foremost places in your year, in respect to those qualities of talent, character, and bodily vigour which are proved, on the whole, to do most honour and best service to our race. An examination has also been conducted on established principles among all the young ladies of this country who are now of the age of twenty-one, and I need hardly remind you, that this examination takes note of grace, beauty, health, good temper, accomplished housewifery, and disengaged affections, in addition to noble qualities of heart and brain. By a careful investigation of the marks you have severally obtained, and a comparison of them, always on established principles, with those obtained by the most distinguished among the young ladies, we have been enabled to select ten of their names with especial reference to your individual qualities. It appears that marriages between you and these ten ladies, according to the list I hold in my hand, would offer the probability of unusual happiness to yourselves, and, what is of paramount interest to the State, would probably result in an extraordinarily talented issue. Under these*

circumstances, if any or all of these marriages should be agreed upon, the sovereign herself will give away the brides, at a high and solemn festival, six months hence, in Westminster abbey. We, on our part, are prepared, in each case, to assign 5,000l. as a wedding-present, and to defray the cost of maintaining and educating your children, out of the ample funds entrusted to our disposal by the State."

If a twentieth part of the cost and pains were spent in measures for the improvement of the human race that is spent on the improvement of the breed of horses and cattle, what a galaxy of genius might we not create! We [p. 166] might introduce prophets and high priests of our civilization into a world as surely as we can propagate idiots by mating *crétins*. Men and women of the present day are, to those we might hope to bring into existence, what the pariah dogs of the streets of an Eastern town are to our own highly bred varieties.

The feeble nations of the world are necessarily giving way before the nobler varieties of mankind; and even the best of these, so far as we know them, seem unequal to their work. The average culture of mankind is become so much high, than it was, and the branches of knowledge and history so various and extended, that few are capable even of comprehending the exigencies of our modern civilization; much less fulfilling them. We are living in a sort of intellectual anarchy, for want of master minds. The general intellectual capacity of our leaders requires to be raised, and also to be differentiated. We want abler commanders, statesmen, thinkers, inventors, and artists. The natural qualifications of our race are no greater than they used to be in semi-barbarous times, though the conditions amid which we are born are vastly more complex than of old. The foremost minds of the present day seem to stagger and halt under an intellectual load too heavy for their powers.

To be continued.

SECOND PAPER[2]

I have shown, in my previous paper, that intellectual capacity is so largely transmitted by descent that, out of every hundred sons of men distinguished in the open professions, no less than eight are found to have rivalled their fathers in eminence. It must be recollected that success of this kind implies the simultaneous inheritance of many points of character, in addition to mere intellectual capacity. A man must inherit good health, a love of mental work, a strong purpose, and considerable ambition, in order to achieve successes of the high order of which we are speaking. The deficiency of any one of these qualities would certainly be injurious, and probably be fatal to his chance of obtaining great distinction. But more than this: the proportion we have arrived at takes [p. 319] no account whatever of one-half of the hereditary influences that form the nature of the child My particular method of inquiry did not admit of regard being paid to the influences transmitted by the mother, whether they had strengthened or weakened those transmitted by the father. Lastly, though the talent and character of both of the parents might, in any particular case, be of a remarkably noble order, and thoroughly congenial, yet they would

262 THE MEANING OF LIFE

necessarily have such mongrel antecedents that it would be absurd to expect their children to invariably equal them in their natural endowments. The law of atavism prevents it. When we estimate at its true importance this accumulation of impediments in the way of the son of a distinguished father rivalling his parent -- the mother being selected, as it were, at haphazard -- we cannot but feel amazed at the number of instances in which a successful rivalship has occurred. Eight per cent. is as large a proportion as could have been expected on the most stringent hypothesis of hereditary transmission. No one, I think, can doubt, from the facts and analogies I have brought forward, that, if talented men were mated with talented women, of the same mental and physical characters as themselves, generation after generation, we might produce a highly-bred human race, with no more tendency to revert to meaner ancestral types than is shown by our long-established breeds of race-horses and fox-hounds.

It may be said that, even granting the validity of my arguments, it would be impossible to carry their indications into practical effect. For instance, if we divided the rising generation into two castes, A and B, Of which a was selected for natural gifts, and B was the refuse, then, supposing marriage was confined within the pale of the caste to which each individual belonged, it might be objected that we should simply differentiate our race -- that we should create a good and a bad caste, but we should not improve the race as a whole. I reply that this is by no means the necessary result. There remains another very important law to be brought into play. Any agency, however indirect, that would somewhat hasten the marriages in caste A, and retard those in caste B, would result in a larger proportion of children being born to A than to B, and would end by wholly eliminating B, and replacing it by A.

Let us take a definite case, in order to give precision to our ideas We will suppose the population to be, in the first instance, stationary; A and B to be equal in numbers; and the children of each married pair who survive to maturity to be rather more than 2-1/2 in the case of A, and rather less than 1-1/2 in the case of B. This no extravagant hypothesis. Half the population of the British Isles are born of mothers under the age of thirty years.

The result in the first generation would be that the total population would be unchanged, but that only one-third part of it would consist of the children of B In the second generation, the descendants of B would be reduced to two-ninths of their original numbers, but the total population would begin to increase, owing to the greater preponderance of the prolific caste A. At this point the law of natural selection mould powerfully assist in the substitution of caste A for caste B, by pressing heavily on the minority of weakly and incapable men.

The customs that affect the direction and date of marriages are already numerous. In many families, marriages between cousins are discouraged and checked. Marriages, in other respects appropriate, are very commonly deferred, through prudential considerations, If it was generally felt that intermarriages between A and B were as unadvisable as they are supposed to be between cousins, and that marriages in A ought to be hastened, on the ground of prudential considerations, while those in B ought to be discouraged and retarded, then, I believe, we should have agencies amply sufficient to eliminate B in a few generations.

I hence conclude that the improvement of the breed of mankind is no [p. 320] insuperable difficulty. If everybody were to agree on the improvement of the race of man being a matter of the very utmost importance, and if the theory of the hereditary transmission of qualities in men was as thoroughly understood as it is in the case of our domestic animals, I see no absurdity in supposing that, in some way or other, the improvement would be carried into effect.

It remains for me in the present article to show that hereditary influence is as clearly marked in mental aptitudes as in general intellectual power. I will then enter into some of the considerations which my views on hereditary talent and character naturally suggest.

I will first quote a few of those cases in which characteristics have been inherited that clearly depend on peculiarities of organization. Prosper Lucas was among our earliest encyclopædists on this subject. It is distinctly shown by him, and agreed to by others, such as Mr. G. Lewes, that predisposition to any form of disease, or any malformation, may become an inheritance. Thus disease of the heart is hereditary; so are tubercles in the lungs ; so also are diseases of the brain, of the liver, and of the kidney; so are diseases of the eye and of the ear. General maladies are equally inheritable, as gout and madness. Longevity on the one hand, and premature deaths on the other, go by descent. If we consider a class of peculiarities, more recondite in their origin than these, we shall still find the law of inheritance to hold good. A morbid susceptibility to contagious disease, or to the poisonous effects of opium, or of calomel, and an aversion to the taste of meat, are all found to be inherited. So is a craving for drink, or for gambling, strong sexual passion, a proclivity to pauperism, to crimes of violence, and to crimes of fraud.

There are certain marked types of character, justly associated with marked types of feature and of temperament. We hold, axiomatically, that the latter are inherited (the case being too notorious, and too consistent with the analog afforded by brute animals, to render argument necessary), and we therefore infer the same of the former For instance, the face of the combatant is square, coarse, and heavily jawed. It differs from that of the ascetic, the voluptuary, the dreamer, and the charlatan.

Still more strongly marked than these, are the typical features and characters of different races of men. The Mongolians, Jews, Negroes, Gipsies [*sic*], and American Indians; severally propagate their Binds; and each kind differs in character and intellect, as well as in colour and shape, from the other four. They, and a vast number of other races, form a class of instances worthy of close investigation, in which peculiarities of character are invariably transmitted from the parents to the offspring.

In founding argument on the innate character of different races, it is necessary to bear in mind the exceeding docility of man. His mental habits in mature life are the creatures of social discipline, as well as of inborn aptitudes, and it is impossible to ascertain what is due to the latter alone, except by observing several individuals of the same race, reared under various influences, and noting the peculiarities of character that invariably assert themselves. But, even when we have imposed these restrictions to check a hasty and imaginative conclusion, we find there remain abundant data to prove an astonishing diversity in the natural characteristics of different races. It

264   THE MEANING OF LIFE

will be sufficient for our purpose if we fix our attention upon the peculiarities of one or two of them.

The race of the American Indians is spread over an enormous area, and through every climate; for it reaches from the frozen regions of the North, through the equator, down to the inclement regions of the South. It exists in thousands of disconnected communities, speaking nearly as many different languages. It has been subjected to a strange variety of political influences, such as its own despotisms in Peru, Mexico, Natchez, and Bogota, and its [p. 321 numerous republics, large and small. Members of the race have been conquered and ruled by military adventures from Spain and Portugal; others have been subjugated to Jesuitical rule; numerous settlements have been made by strangers on its soil; and, finally, the north of the continent has been colonized by European races. Excellent observers have watched the American Indians under all these influences, and their almost unanimous conclusion is as follows :--

The race is divided into many varieties, but it has fundamentally the same character throughout the whole of America. The men, and in a less degree the women, are naturally cold, melancholic, patient, and taciturn. A father, mother, and their children, are said to live together in a hut, like persons assembled by accident, not tied by affection. The youths treat their parents with neglect, and often with such harshness and insolence as to horrify Europeans who have witnessed their conduct. The mothers have been seen to commit infanticide without the slightest discomposure, and numerous savage tribes have died out in consequence of this practice. The American Indians are eminently non-gregarious. They nourish a sullen reserve, and show little sympathy with each other, even when in great distress. The Spaniards had to enforce the common duties of humanity by positive laws. They are strangely taciturn. When not engaged in action they will sit whole days in one posture without opening their lips, and wrapped up in their narrow thoughts. They usually march in Indian file, that is to say, in a long line, at some distance from each other, without exchanging a word. They keep the same profound silence in rowing a canoe, unless they happen to be excited by some extraneous cause. On the other hand, their patriotism and local attachments are strong, and they have an astonishing sense of personal dignity. The nature of the American Indians appears to contain the minimum of affectionate and social qualities compatible with the continuance of their race.

Here, then, is a well-marked type of character, that formerly prevailed over a large part of the globe, with which other equally marked types of character in other regions are strongly contrasted. Take, for instance, the typical West African Negro. He is more unlike the Red man in his mind than in his body. Their characters are almost opposite, one to the other. The Red man has great patience great reticence, great; dignity, and no passion; the Negro has strong impulsive passions, and neither patience, reticence, nor dignity, He is warm-hearted, loving towards his master's children, and idolised by the children in return. He is eminently gregarious for he is always jabbering, quarrelling, tom-tom-ing, or dancing. He is remarkably domestic, and he is endowed with such constitutional vigour, and is so prolific, that his race is irrepressible.

The Hindu, the Arab, the Mongol, the Teuton, and very many more, have each of them their peculiar characters. We have not space to analyse them on this occasion; but, whatever they are, they are transmitted, generation after generation, as truly as their physical forms.

What is true for the entire race is equally true for its varieties. If we were to select persons mho mere born with a type of character that we desired to intensify, -- suppose it was one that approached to some ideal standard of perfection -- and if we compelled marriage within the limits of the society so selected, generation after generation; there can be no doubt that the offspring would ultimately be born with the qualities we sought, as surely as if we had been breeding for physical features, and not for intellect or disposition.

Our natural constitution seems to bear as direct and stringent a relation to that of our forefathers as any other physical effect does to its cause. Our bodies, minds, and capabilities of development have been derived from them. Everything we possess at our birth is a heritage from our ancestors.

Can we hand anything down to our children, that we have fairly won by [p. 322] our own independent exertions? Will our children be born with more virtuous dispositions, if we ourselves have acquired virtuous habits? Or are we no more than passive transmitters of a nature we have received, and which we have no power to modify? There are but a few instances in which habit even seems to be inherited. The chief among them are such as those of dogs being born excellent pointers; of the attachment to man shown by dogs; and of the fear of man, rapidly learnt and established among the birds of newly-discovered islands. But all of these admit of being accounted for on other grounds than the hereditary transmission of habits. Pointing is, in some faint degree, a natural disposition of all dogs. Breeders have gradually improved upon it, and created the race we now possess. There is nothing to show that the reason why dogs are born staunch pointers is that their parents bad been broken into acquiring an artificial habit. So as regards the fondness of dogs for man. It is inherent to a great extent in the genus. The dingo, or wild dog of Australia, is attached to the man mho has caught him when a puppy, and clings to him even although he is turned adrift to hunt for his own living. This quality in dogs is made more intense by the custom of selection. The savage dogs are lost or killed; the tame ones are kept and bred from. Lastly, as regards the birds. As soon as any of their flock has learned to fear, I presume that its frightened movements on the approach of man form a language that is rapidly and unerringly understood by the rest, old or young; and that, after a few repetitions, of the signal, man becomes an object of well-remembered mistrust. Moreover, just as natural selection has been shown to encourage love of man in domestic dogs, so it tends to encourage fear of man in all wild animals -- the tamer varieties perishing owing to their misplaced confidence, and the wilder ones continuing their breed.

If we examine the question from the opposite side, a List of life-long habits in the parents might be adduced which leave no perceptible trace on their descendants. I cannot ascertain that, the son of an old soldier learns his drill more quickly than the son of an artizan, I am assured that the sons of fishermen, whose ancestors have pursued the same calling time out of mind, are just as sea-sick as the sons of landsmen when they first go to sea. I cannot discover that the castes of

266   THE MEANING OF LIFE

India show signs of being naturally endowed with special aptitudes. If the habits of an individual are transmitted to his descendants, it is as Darwin says, in a very small degree, and is hardly, if at all, traceable.

We shall therefore take an approximately correct view of the origin of our life, if we consider our own embryos to have sprung immediately from the embryos whence our parents were developed, and these from the embryos of *their* parents, and so on for ever. We should in this way look on the nature of mankind, and perhaps on that of the whole animated creation, as one continuous system, ever pushing out new branches in all directions, that variously interlace, and that bud into separate lives at every point of interlacement.

This simile does not at all express the popular notion of life. Most persons seem to have a vague idea that a new element, specially fashioned in heaven, and not transmitted by simple descent, is introduced into the body of every newly-born infant. Such a notion is unfitted to stand upon any scientific basis with which we are acquainted. It is impossible it should be true, unless there exists some property or quality in man that is not transmissible by descent. But the terms *talent* and *character* are exhaustive: they include the whole of man's spiritual nature so far as we are able to understand it. No other class of qualities is known to exist, that we might suppose to have been interpolated from on high. Moreover, the idea is improbable from *à priori* [*sic*] considerations, because there is no other instance in which creative power operates under our own observation at the [p. 323] present day, except it may be in the freedom in action of our own wills. Whenever else we turn off our eyes, we see nothing but law and order, and effect following cause.

But though, when me look back to our ancestors, the embryos of our progenitors may be conceived to have been developed, in each generation, immediately from the one that preceded it, yet we cannot take so restricted a view when we look forward. The interval that separates the full-grown animal from its embryo is too important to be disregarded. It is in this interval that Darwin's law of natural selection comes into play; and those conditions are entered into, which affect, we know not how, the "individual variation" of the offspring. I mean those that cause dissimilarity among brothers and sisters who are born successively, while twins, produced simultaneously, are often almost identical. If it were possible that embryos should descend directly from embryos, there might be developments in every direction, and the world would be filled with monstrosities. But this is not the order of nature. It is her fiat that the natural tendencies of animals should never disaccord long and widely with the conditions under which they are placed. Every animal before it is of an age to bear offspring, has to undergo frequent stern examinations before the board of nature, under the law of natural selection; where to be "plucked" is not necessarily disgrace, but is certainly death. Never let it be forgotten that man, as a reasonable being, has the privilege of not being helpless under the tyranny of uncongenial requirements, but that he can, and that he does, modify the subjects in which nature examines him, and that he has considerable power in settling beforehand the relative importance in the examination that shall be assigned to each separate subject.

COGNITIVE PSYCHOLOGY   267

It becomes a question of great interest how far moral monstrosities admit of being bred. Is there any obvious law that assigns a limit to the propagation of supremely vicious or supremely virtuous natures? In strength, agility, and other physical qualities Darwin's law of natural selection acts with unimpassioned, merciless severity. The weakly die in the battle for life; the stronger and more capable individuals are alone permitted to survive, and to bequeath their constitutional vigour to future generations. Is there any corresponding rule in respect to moral character? I believe there is, and I have already hinted at it when speaking of the American Indians. I am prepared to maintain that its action, by insuring a certain fundamental unity m the quality of the affections, enables men and the higher order of animals to sympathise in some degree with each other, and also, that this law forms the broad basis of our religious sentiments.

Animal life, in all but the very lowest classes, depends on at least one, and, more commonly, on all of the four following principles:-- There must be affection, and it must be of four kinds : sexual, parental, filial and social. The absolute deficiency of any one of these would be a serious hindrance, if not a bar to the continuance of any race. Those who possessed all of them, in the strongest measure, would, speaking generally, have an advantage in the struggle for existence. Without sexual affection, there would be no marriages, and no children; without parental affection, the children would be abandoned; without filial affection, they would stray and perish; and, without the social, each individual would be single-handed against rivals who were capable of banding themselves into tribes. Affection for others as well as for self, is therefore a necessary part of animal character. Disinterestedness is as essential to a brute's well-being as selfishness. No animal lives for itself alone, but also, at least occasionally, for its parent, its mate, its offspring, or its fellow. Companionship is frequently more grateful to an animal than abundant food. The safety of her young is considered by many a mother as a paramount object to her own. The passion for a mate is equally strong. The gregarious bird posts itself during its turn of duty as watchman on a tree, [p. 324] by the side of the feeding flock. Its zeal to serve the common cause exceeds its care to attend to its own interests. Extreme selfishness is not a common vice. Narrow thoughts of self by no means absorb the minds of ordinary men; they occupy a secondary position in the thoughts of the more noble and generous of our race. A large part of an Englishman's life is devoted to others or to the furtherance of general ideas, and not to directly personal ends. The Jesuit toils for his order, not for himself. Many plan for that which they can never live to see. At the hour of death they are still planning. An incompleted will, which might work unfairness among those who would succeed to the property of a dying man, harasses his mind. Personal obligations of all sorts press as heavily as in the fulness of health, although the touch of death is known to be on the point of cancelling them. It is so with animals. A dog's thoughts are towards his master, even when he suffers the extremest pain. His mind is largely filled at all times with sentiments of affection. But disinterested feelings are more necessary to man than to any other animal, because of the long period of his dependent childhood, and also because of his great social needs, due to his physical helplessness. Darwin's law of natural selection mould therefore be expected to develop these sentiments among men, even among the lowest barbarians, to a greater degree than among animals.

268   THE MEANING OF LIFE

I believe that our religious sentiments spring primarily from these four sources. The institution of celibacy is an open acknowledgment that the theistic and human affections are more or less convertible; I mean that by starving the one class the other becomes more intense and absorbing. In savages, the theistic sentiment is chiefly, if not wholly, absent. I would refer my readers, who may hesitate in accepting this assertion, to the recently published work of my friend Sir John Lubbock, "Prehistoric Times," p. 467-472, where the reports of travellers on the religion of savages are very ably and fairly collated. The theistic sentiment is secondary, not primary. It becomes developed within us under the influence of reflection and reason. All evidence tends to show that main is directed to the contemplation and love of God by instincts that he shares with the whole animal world, and that primarily appeal to the love of his neighbour.

Moral monsters are born among Englishmen, even at the present day; and, when they are betrayed by their acts, the law puts them out of the way, by the prison or the gallows, and so prevents them from continuing their breed. Townley, the murderer, is an instance in point. He behaved with decorum and propriety; he was perfectly well-conducted to the gaol officials, and he corresponded with his mother in a style that was certainly flippant, but was not generally considered to be insane. However, with all this reasonableness of disposition, he could not be brought to see that he had done anything particularly wrong in murdering the girl that was disinclined to marry him. He was thoroughly consistent in his disregard for life, because, when his own existence became wearisome, he ended it with perfect coolness, by jumping from an upper staircase. It is a notable fact that a man without a conscience, like Townley, should be able to mix in English society for years, just like other people.

How enormous is the compass of the scale of human character, which reaches from dispositions like those we have just described, to that of a Socrates! How various are the intermediate types of character that commonly fall under everybody's notice, and how differently are the principles of virtue measured out to different natures! We can clearly observe the extreme diversity of character in children. Some are naturally generous and open, others mean and tricky; some are warm and loving, others cold and heartless; some are meek and patient, others obstinate and self-asserting; some few have the tempers of angels, and at least as many have the tempers of devils. In the [p. 325] same way, as I showed in my previous paper, that by selecting men and women of rare and similar talent, and mating them together, generation after generation, an extraordinarily gifted race might be developed, so a yet more rigid selection, having regard to their moral nature, would, I believe, result in a no less marked improvement of their natural disposition.

Let us consider an instance in which different social influences have modified the inborn dispositions of a nation. The North American people has been bred from the most restless and combative class of Europe. Whenever, during the last ten or twelve generations, a political or religious party has suffered defeat, its prominent members, whether they were the best, or only the noisiest, have been apt to emigrate to America, as a refuge from persecution. Men fled to America for conscience' [sic] sake, and for that of unappreciated patriotism. Every scheming knave, and every brutal ruffian, who feared the arm of the law, also turned his eyes in the same direction. Peasants and artisans, whose spirit rebelled against the tyranny of society and the monotony of their daily life, and men of a higher position, who chafed under conventional restraints, all yearned towards America. Thus the dispositions of the parents of the American people have been exceedingly varied, and usually extreme, either for good or for evil. But in one respect they almost universally agreed. Every head of an emigrant family brought with him a restless character, and a spirit apt to rebel. If we estimate the moral nature of Americans from their present social state, we shall find it to be just what me might have expected from such a parentage. They are enterprising, defiant, and touchy; impatient of authority; furious politicians; very tolerant of fraud and violence; possessing much high and generous spirit, and some true religious feeling, but strongly addicted to cant.

We have seen that the law of natural selection develops disinterested affection of a varied character even in animals and barbarian man. Is the same law different in its requirements when acting on civilized man? It is no doubt more favourable on the whole to civilized progress, but we must not expect to find as yet many marked signs of its action. As a matter of history, our Anglo-Saxon civilization is only skin-deep. It is but eight hundred years, or twenty-six generations, since the Conquest, and the ancestors of the large majority of Englishmen were the merest boors at a much later date than that. It is said that among the heads of the noble houses of England there can barely be found one that has a right to claim the sixteen quarterings -- that is to say, whose great-great-grandparents were, all of them (sixteen in number), entitled to carry arms. Generally the nobility of a family is represented by only a few slender rills among a multiplicity of non-noble sources.

The most notable quality that the requirements of civilization have hitherto bred in us, living as me do in a rigorous climate and on a naturally barren soil, is the instinct of continuous steady labour. This is alone possessed by civilized races, and it is possessed in a far greater degree by the feeblest individuals among them than by the most able-bodied savages. Unless a man can work hard and regularly in England, he becomes an outcast. If he only works by fits and starts he has not a chance of competition with steady workmen. An artizan who has variable impulses, and wayward moods, is almost sure to end in intemperance and ruin. In short, men who are born with wild and irregular dispositions, even though they contain much that is truly noble, are alien to the spirit of a civilized country, and they and their breed are eliminated from it by the law of selection. On the other hand, a wild, untameable restlessness is innate with savages. I have collected numerous instances where children of a low race have been separated at an early age from their parents, and reared as part of a settler's family, quite apart from their own people. Yet, after years of civilized ways, in some fit of passion, or under [p. 326] some craving, like that of a bird about to emigrate, they have abandoned their home, flung away their dress, and sought their countrymen in the bush, among whom they have subsequently been found living in contented barbarism, without a vestige of their gentle nurture. This is eminently the case with the Australians, and I have heard of many others in South Africa. There are also numerous instances in England where the restless nature of gipsy [sic] half-blood asserts itself with irresistible force.

270   THE MEANING OF LIFE

Another difference, which may either be due to natural selection or to original difference of race, is the fact that savages seem incapable of progress after the first few years of their life. The average children of all races are much on a par. Occasionally, those of the lower races are more precocious than the Anglo-Saxons; as a brute beast of a few weeks old is certainly more apt and forward than a child of the same age. But, as the years go by, the higher races continue to progress, while the lower ones gradually stop. They remain children in mind, with the passions of grown men. Eminent genius commonly asserts itself in tender years, but it continues long to develop. The highest minds in the highest race seem to have been those who had the longest boyhood. It is not those who were little men in early youth who have succeeded. Here I may remark that, in the great mortality that besets the children of our poor, those who are members of precocious families, and who are therefore able to help in earning wages at a very early age, have a marked advantage over their competitors. They, on the whole, live, and breed their like, while the others die. But, if this sort of precocity be unfavourable to a race -- if it be generally followed by an early arrest of development, and by a premature old age -- then modern industrial civilization, in encouraging precocious varieties of men, deteriorates the breed.

Besides these three points of difference -- endurance of steady labour, tameness of disposition, and prolonged development -- I know of none that very markedly distinguishes the nature of the lower classes of civilized man from that of barbarians. In the excitement of a pillaged town the English soldier is just as brutal as the savage. Gentle manners seem, under those circumstances, to have been a mere gloss thrown by education over a barbarous nature. One of the effects of civilization is to diminish the rigour of the application of the law of natural selection, It preserves weakly lives, that would have perished in barbarous lands. The sickly children of a wealthy family have a better chance of living and rearing offspring than the stalwart children of a poor one. As with the body, so with the mind. Poverty is more adverse to early marriages than is natural bad temper, or inferiority of intellect. In civilized society, money interposes her ægis between the law of natural selection and very many of its rightful victims. Scrofula and madness are naturalised among us by wealth; short-sightedness is becoming so. There seems no limit to the morbific [*sic*] tendencies of body or mind that might accumulate in a land where the law of primogeniture was general, and where riches were more esteemed than personal qualities. Neither is there any known limit to the intellectual and moral grandeur of nature that might be introduced into aristocratical families, if their representatives, who have such rare privilege in winning wives that please them best, should invariably, generation after generation, marry with a view of transmitting those noble qualities to their descendants. Inferior blood in the representative of a family might be eliminated from it in a few generations. The share that a man retains in the constitution of his remote descendants is inconceivably small. The father transmits, on an average, one-half of his nature, the grandfather one-fourth, the great-grandfather one-eighth; the share decreasing step by step, in a geometrical ration with great rapidity. Thus the man who claims descent from a Norman baron, who accompanied William the Conqueror twenty-six generations ago, has so minute a share of that baron's influence in his [p. 327] constitution, that, if he weighs fourteen stone, the part of him which may be ascribed to the baron (supposing, of course, there have been no additional lines of relationship) is only one-fiftieth of a grain in weight -- an amount ludicrously disproportioned to the value popularly ascribed to ancient descent. As a stroke of policy, I question if the head of a great family, or a prince, would not give more strength to his position, by marrying a wife who would bear him talented sons, than one who would merely bring him the support of high family connexions.

With the few but not insignificant exceptions we have specified above, still barbarians in our nature, and we show it in a thousand ways. The children who dabble and dig in the dirt have inherited the instincts of untold generations of barbarian forefathers, who dug with their nails for a large fraction of their lives. Our ancestors were grubbing by the hour, each day, to get at the roots they chiefly lived upon. They had to grub out pitfalls for their game, holes for their palisades and hut-poles, hiding-places, and ovens. Man became a digging animal by nature; and so we see the delicately-reared children of our era very ready to revert to primeval habits. Instinct breaks out in them, just as it does in the silk-haired, boudoir-nurtured spaniel, with a ribbon round its neck, that runs away from the endearments of its mistress, to sniff and revel in some road-side mess of carrion.

It is a common theme of moralists of many creeds, that man is born with an imperfect nature. He has lofty aspirations, but there is a weakness in his disposition that incapacitates him from carrying his nobler purposes into effect. He sees that some particular course of action is his duty, and should be his delight; but his inclinations are fickle and base, and do not conform to his better judgment. The whole moral nature of man is tainted with sin, which prevents him from doing the things he knows to be right.

I venture to offer an explanation of this apparent anomaly, which seems perfectly satisfactory from a scientific point of view. It is neither more nor less than that the development of our nature, under Darwin's law of natural selection, has not yet overtaken the development of our religious civilization. Man was barbarous but yesterday, and therefore it is not to be expected that the natural aptitudes of his race should already have become moulded into accordance with his very recent advance. We men of the present centuries are like animals suddenly transplanted among new conditions of climate and of food: our instincts fail us under the altered circumstances.

My theory is confirmed by the fact that the members of old civilizations are far less sensible than those newly converted from barbarism of their nature being inadequate to their moral needs. The conscience of a negro is aghast at his own wild, impulsive nature, and is easily stirred by a preacher, but it is scarcely possible to ruffle the self-complacency of a steady-going Chinaman.

The sense of original sin would show, according to my theory, not that man was fallen from a high estate, but that he was rapidly rising from a low one. It would therefore confirm the conclusion that has been arrived at by every independent line of ethnological research -- that our forefathers were utter savages from the beginning; and, that, after myriads of years of barbarism, our race has but very recently grown to be civilized and religious.

272 THE MEANING OF LIFE

NEW METHODS FOR THE DIAGNOSIS OF THE INTELLECTUAL LEVEL OF SUBNORMALS

Alfred Binet (1905)

First published in *L'Année Psychologique*, *12*, 191-244.

This translation by Elizabeth S. Kite first appeared in 1916 in *The development of intelligence in children*. Vineland, NJ: Publications of the Training School at Vineland.

Before explaining these methods let us recall exactly the conditions of the problem which we are attempting to solve. Our purpose is to be able to measure the intellectual capacity of a child who is brought to us in order to know whether he is normal or retarded. We should therefore, study his condition at the time and that only. We have nothing to do either with his past history or with his future; consequently we shall neglect his etiology, and we shall make no attempt to distinguish between acquired and congenital idiocy; for a stronger reason we shall set aside all consideration of pathological anatomy which might explain his intellectual deficiency. So much for his past. As to that which concerns his future, we shall exercise the same abstinence; we do not attempt to establish or prepare a prognosis and we leave unanswered the question of whether this retardation is curable, or even improvable. We shall limit ourselves to ascertaining the truth in regard to his present mental state.

Furthermore, in the definition of this state, we should make some restrictions. Most subnormal children, especially those in the schools, are habitually grouped in two categories, those of backward intelligence, and those who are unstable. This latter class, which certain *alienists* call moral imbeciles, do not necessarily manifest inferiority of intelligence; they are turbulent, vicious, rebellious to all discipline; they lack sequence of ideas, and probably power of attention. It is a matter of great delicacy to make the distinction between children who are unstable, and those who have rebellious dispositions. Elsewhere we have insisted upon the necessity of instructors not treating as unstable, that is as pathological cases, those children whose character is not sympathetic with their own. It would necessitate a long study, and probably a very difficult one, to establish the distinctive signs which separate the unstable from the undisciplined. For the present we shall not take up this study. We shall set the unstable aside, and shall consider only that which bears upon those who are backward in intelligence.

This is not, however, to be the only limitation of our subject because backward states of intelligence present several different types. There is the insane type -- or the type of intellectual decay -- which consists in a progressive loss of former acquired intelligence. Many epileptics, who suffer from frequent attacks, progress toward insanity. It would be possible and probably very important, to be able to make the distinction between those with decaying intelligence on the one hand, and those of inferior intelligence on the other. But as we have determined to limit on this side also, the domain of our study, we shall rigorously exclude all forms of insanity and decay. Moreover we believe that these are rarely present in the schools, and need not be taken into consideration in the operation of new classes for subnormals.

Another distinction is made between those of inferior intelligence and degenerates. The latter are subjects in whom occur clearly defined, episodical phenomena, such as impulsions, obsessions, deliriums. We shall eliminate the degenerates as well as the insane.

Lastly, we should say a word upon our manner of studying those whom most alienists call idiots but whom we here call of inferior intelligence. The exact nature of this inferiority is not known; and today without other proof, one very prudently refuses to liken this state to that of an arrest of normal development. It certainly seems that the intelligence of these beings has undergone a certain arrest; but it does not follow that the disproportion between the degree of intelligence and the age is the only characteristic of their condition. There is also in many cases, most probably a deviation in the development, a perversion. The idiot of fifteen years, who, like a baby of three, is making his first verbal attempts, can not be completely likened to a three-year old child, because the latter is normal, but the idiot is not. There exists therefore between them, necessarily, differences either apparent or hidden. The careful study of idiots shows, among some of them at least, that whereas certain faculties are almost wanting, others are better developed. They have therefore certain aptitudes. Some have a good auditory or musical memory, and a whole repertoire of songs; others have mechanical ability. If all were carefully examined, many examples of these partial aptitudes would probably be found.

Our purpose is in no wise to study, analyze, or set forth the aptitudes of those of inferior intelligence. That will be the object of a later work. Here we shall limit ourselves to the measuring of their general intelligence. We shall determine their intellectual level, and, in order the better to appreciate this level, we shall compare it with that of normal children of the same age or of an analogous level. The reservations previously made as to the true conception of arrested development, will not prevent our finding great advantage in a methodical comparison between those of inferior and those of normal intelligence.

To what method should we have recourse in making our diagnosis of the intellectual level? No one method exists, but there are a number of different ones which should be used cumulatively, because the question is a very difficult one to solve, and demands rather a collaboration of methods. It is important that the practitioner be equipped in such a manner that he shall use, only as accessory, the information given by the parents of the child, so that he may always be able to verify this information, or, when necessary, dispense with it. In actual practice quite the opposite occurs. When the child is taken to the clinic the physician listens a great deal to the parents and questions the child very little, in fact scarcely looks at him, allowing himself to be influenced by a very strong presumption that the child is intellectually inferior. If, by a chance not likely to occur, but which would be most interesting some time to bring about, the physician were submitted to the test of selecting the subnormals from a mixed group of children, he would

274   THE MEANING OF LIFE

certainly find himself in the midst of grave difficulties, and would commit many errors especially in cases of slight defect.

The organization of methods is especially important because, as soon as the schools for subnormals are in operation, one must be on his guard against the attitude of the parents. Their sincerity will be worth very little when it is in conflict with their interests. If the parents wish the child to remain in the regular school, they will not be silent concerning his intelligence. "My child understands everything," they will say, and they will be very careful not to give any significant information in regard to him. If, on the contrary, they wish him to be admitted into an institution where gratuitous board and lodging are furnished, they will change completely. They will be capable even of teaching him how to simulate mental debility. One should, therefore, be on his guard against all possible frauds.

In order to recognize the inferior states of intelligence we believe that three different methods should be employed. We have arrived at this synthetic view only after many years of research, but we are now certain that each of these methods renders some service. These methods are:

1. *The medical method*, which aims to appreciate the anatomical, physiological, and pathological signs of inferior intelligence.

2. *The pedagogical method*, which aims to judge of the intelligence according to the sum of acquired knowledge.

3. *The psychological method*, which makes direct observations and measurements of the degree of intelligence.

From what has gone before it is easy to see the value of each of these methods. The medical method is indirect because it conjectures the mental from the physical. The pedagogical method is more direct; but the psychological is the most direct of all because it aims to measure the state of the intelligence as it is at the present moment. It does this by experiments which oblige the subject to make an effort which shows his capability in the way of comprehension, judgment, reasoning, and invention.

I. THE PSYCHOLOGICAL METHOD

The fundamental idea of this method is the establishment of what we shall call a measuring scale of intelligence. This scale is composed of a series of tests of increasing difficulty, starting from the, lowest intellectual level that can be observed, and ending with that of average normal intelligence. Each group in the series corresponds to a different mental level.

This scale properly speaking does not permit the measure of the intelligence,[*1*] because intellectual qualities are not superposable, and therefore cannot be measured as linear surfaces are measured, but are on the contrary, a classification, a hierarchy among diverse intelligences; and for the necessities of practice this classification is equivalent to a measure. We shall therefore be able to know, after studying two individuals, if one rises above the other and to how many degrees, if one rises above the average level of other individuals considered as normal, or if he remains below. Understanding the normal progress of intellectual development among normals, we shall be able to determine how many years such an individual is advanced or retarded. In a word we shall be able to determine to what degrees of the scale idiocy, imbecility, and moronity [2] correspond.

The scale that we shall describe is not a theoretical work; it is the result of long investigations, first at the Salpêtrière, and afterwards in the primary schools of Paris, with both normal and subnormal children. These short psychological questions have been given the name of tests. The use of tests is today very common, and there are even contemporary authors who have made a specialty of organizing new tests according to theoretical views, but who have made no effort to patiently try them out in the schools. Theirs is an amusing occupation, comparable to a person's making a colonizing expedition into Algeria, advancing always only upon the map, without taking off his dressing gown. We place but slight confidence in the tests invented by these authors and we have borrowed nothing from them. All the tests which we propose have been repeatedly tried, and have been retained from among many, which after trial have been discarded. We can certify that those which are here presented have proved themselves valuable.

We have aimed to make all our tests simple, rapid, convenient, precise, heterogeneous, holding the subject in continued contact with the experimenter, and bearing principally upon the faculty of judgment. Rapidity is necessary for this sort of examination. It is impossible to prolong it beyond twenty minutes without fatiguing the subject. During this maximum of twenty minutes, it must be turned and turned about in every sense, and at least ten tests must be executed, so that not more than about two minutes can be given to each. In spite of their interest, we were obliged to proscribe long exercises. For example, it would be very instructive to know how a subject learns by heart a series of sentences. We have often tested the advantage of leaving a person by himself with a lesson of prose or verse after having said to him, "Try to learn as much as you can of this in five minutes." Five minutes is too long for our test, because during that time the subject escapes us; it may be that he becomes distracted or thinks of other things; the test loses its clinical character and becomes too scholastic. We have therefore reluctantly been obliged to renounce testing the rapidity and extent of the memory by this method. Several other equivalent examples of elimination could be cited. In order to cover rapidly a wide field of observation, it goes without saying that the tests should be heterogeneous.

Another consideration. Our purpose is to evaluate a level of intelligence. It is understood that we here separate natural intelligence and instruction. It is the intelligence alone that we seek to measure, by disregarding in so far as possible, the degree of instruction which the subject possesses. He should, indeed, be considered by the examiner as a complete ignoramus knowing neither how to read nor write. This necessity forces us to forego a great many exercises having a verbal, literary or scholastic character. These belong to a pedagogical examination. We believe that we have succeeded in completely disregarding the acquired information of the subject. We give him nothing to read, nothing to write, and submit him to no test in which he might succeed

THE MEANING OF LIFE

by means of rote learning. In fact we do not even notice his inability to read if a case occurs. It is simply the level of his natural intelligence that is taken into account.

But here we must come to an understanding of what meaning to give to that word so vague and so comprehensive, "the intelligence." Nearly all the phenomena with which psychology concerns itself are phenomena of intelligence; sensation, perception, are intellectual manifestations as much as reasoning. Should we therefore bring into our examination the measure of sensation after the manner of the psycho-physicists? Should we put to the test all of his psychological processes? A slight reflection has shown us that this would indeed be wasted time.

It seems to us that in intelligence there is a fundamental faculty, the alteration or the lack of which, is of the utmost importance for practical life. This faculty is judgment, otherwise called good sense, practical sense, initiative, the faculty of adapting one's self to circumstances. To judge well, to comprehend well, to reason well, these are the essential activities of intelligence. A person may be a moron or an imbecile if he is lacking in judgment; but with good judgment he can never be either. Indeed the rest of the intellectual faculties seem of little importance in comparison with judgment. What does it matter, for example, whether the organs of sense function normally? Of what import that certain ones are hyperesthetic, or that others are anesthetic or are weakened? *Laura Bridgman, Helen Keller* and their fellow-unfortunates were blind as well as deaf, but this did not prevent them from being very intelligent. Certainly this is demonstrative proof that the total or even partial integrity of the senses does not form a mental factor equal to judgment. We may measure the acuteness of the sensibility of subjects; nothing could be easier. But we should do this, not so much to find out the state of their sensibility as to learn the exactitude of their judgment.

The same remark holds good for the study of the memory. At first glance, memory being a psychological phenomenon of capital importance, one would be tempted to give it a very conspicuous part in an examination of intelligence. But memory is distinct from and independent of judgment. One may have good sense and lack memory. The reverse is also common. Just at the present time we are observing a backward girl who is developing before our astonished eyes a memory very much greater than our own. We have measured that memory and we are not deceived regarding it. Nevertheless that girl presents a most beautifully classic type of imbecility.

As a result of all this investigation, in the scale which we present we accord the first place to judgment; that which is of importance to us is not certain errors which the subject commits, but absurd errors, which prove that he lacks judgment. We have even made special provision to encourage people to make absurd replies. In spite of the accuracy of this directing idea, it will be easily understood that it has been impossible to permit of its regulating exclusively our examinations. For example, one can not make tests of judgment on children of less than two years when one begins to watch their first gleams of intelligence. Much is gained when one can discern in them traces of coördination, the first delineation of attention and memory. We shall therefore bring out in our lists some tests of memory; but so far as we are able, we shall give these tests such a turn as to invite the subject to make absurd replies, and thus under cover of a test of memory, we shall have an appreciation of their judgment.

MEASURING SCALE OF INTELLIGENCE

General recommendations. The examination should take place in a quiet room, quite isolated, and the child should be called in alone without other children. It is important that when a child sees the experimenter for the first time, he should be reassured by the presence of someone he knows, a relative, an attendant, or a school superintendent. The witness should be instructed to remain passive and mute, and not to intervene in the examination either by word or gesture.

The experimenter should receive each child with a friendly familiarity to dispel the timidity of early years. Greet him the moment he enters, shake hands with him and seat him comfortably. If he is intelligent enough to understand certain words, awaken his curiosity, his pride. If he refuses to reply to a test, pass to the next one, or perhaps offer him a piece of candy; if his silence continues, send him away until another time. These are little incidents that frequently occur in an examination of the mental state, because in its last analysis, an examination of this kind is based upon the good will of the subject.

We here give the technique of each question. It will not suffice simply to read what we have written in order to be able to conduct examinations. A good experimenter can be produced only by example and imitation, and nothing equals the lesson gained from the thing itself. Every person who wishes to familiarize himself with our method of examination should come to our school. Theoretical instruction is valuable only when it merges into practical experience. Having made these reservations, let us point out the principal errors likely to be committed by inexperienced persons. There are two: the first consists in recording the gross results without making psychological observations, without noticing such little facts as permit one to give to the gross results their true value. The second error, equally frequent, is that of making suggestions. An inexperienced examiner has no idea of the influence of words; he talks too much, he aids his subject, he puts him on the track, unconscious of the help he is thus giving. He plays the part of pedagogue, when he should remain psychologist. Thus his examination is vitiated. It is a difficult art to be able to encourage a subject, to hold his attention, to make him do his best without giving aid in any form by an unskillful suggestion.[*3*]

THE SERIES OF TESTS

1. "Le Regard" [4]

In this test the examiner seeks to discover if there exists that coordination in the movement of the head and the eyes which is associated with the act of vision. If such coordination does exist it proves that the subject not only sees but more than that he "regards" (that is he is able to follow with his eyes a moving object).

Procedure. A lighted match is slowly moved before the eyes of the subject in such a way as to provoke a movement of the head or of the eyes to follow the flame. If a first attempt does not

278   THE MEANING OF LIFE

succeed the experiment should be tried again after a little while. It is preferable to operate in a quiet place where no kind of distraction is likely to occur. It is not important that the subject follow the movements of the match constantly for any length of time or persistently. The least sign of coördination of the movements of vision is sufficient, if it leaves no doubt in the mind of the examiner.

Additional remarks. The observation of a few spontaneous phenomena may well be noted. Thus it is possible sometimes for the examiner, by fixing his gaze steadily upon the child, to satisfy himself that the child really coordinates for a moment. If the subject is afflicted with or suspected of blindness, the visual stimulus may be replaced by an auditory stimulus. For example, call him loudly, or better, ring a little bell behind his head and notice if he turns his head toward the sound, or if he has any peculiar facial expression which would indicate that he hears. The reaction of attention to sound seems to develop later than the reaction to light. We have observed children who, when a bell was rung behind the head, would not make a single movement in order to hear better, and yet would follow with their eyes the lighted match. It is scarcely necessary to add that the child who hides his face behind his hand when questioned, or who replies to your smile by a smile, or who walks about the room without knocking against obstacles, stove, chairs, wall, table, proves by his behavior that he coordinates the movements of vision, arid thus he has passed the first test.

2. Prehension Provoked by a Tactile Stimulus

Here the purpose is to discover whether the coordination exists between a tactile stimulus of the hand, and the movement of seizing and carrying to the mouth.

Procedure. A small object, easily handled, for example a piece of wood, is placed in contact with the hand of the child in order to determine if he succeeds in seizing the object, holding it in his hand without letting it fall, and carrying it to his mouth. It is well to stimulate the contact either on the back of the hand or on the palm, and note the results. It is possible that the subject, after having taken the little object, loosens his fingers and lets it fall. It is necessary in that case to try again with a little patience, in order to learn if the letting go came of a chance distraction, or if the subject is not capable of performing the muscular act which would consist in carrying it to his mouth.

3. Prehension Provoked by a Visual Perception

Here the purpose is to find whether coordination exists between the sight of an object and its prehension, when the object is not placed in contact with the hand of the subject.

Procedure. The object is presented to his view and within reach of his hand, in a manner to provoke an intentional movement of his hand to take it. This third test is passed when the subject, following a visual perception of the object, makes a movement of the hand towards the object, reaches, seizes and carries it to his mouth. A small cube of white wood, easy to handle is used. In these presentations it is not forbidden to speak and hence the object is offered to the child as follows: "Here is a little object, take it, it is for you -- Come now, pay attention, etc." If the subject understands, so much the better for him; if he does not understand the sound of these words has the advantage of attracting. his attention. Moreover the examiner makes gestures and makes them more naturally if he talks at the same time.

4. Recognition of Food

Here the purpose is to discover whether the subject can make the distinction by sight between familiar food and what can not be eaten.

Procedure. A piece of chocolate (half a bar) and a little cube of white wood of similar dimensions are successively presented. The test is to see if the subject, by sight alone, makes the distinction between the two objects before carrying them to his mouth. Does he carry only the chocolate to his mouth and begin to eat it? Does he refuse to take the piece of wood, or having taken it does he push it away, or again does he hold it in his hand without putting it to his mouth?

Tests 3 and 4 can be made rapidly as a single experiment. A piece of chocolate is first shown to the child and his attention is drawn to it. Note whether he tries to take it or not. If he makes no effort to attain it, and is not distracted by anything, place the chocolate in the palm of his hand, and note what happens. If on the contrary he takes the chocolate which is shown him and carries it to his mouth, the chocolate is taken from him, and the piece of wood put in its place, to see if he carries this new object also to his mouth.

Although these tests succeed with very many children by appealing to their greediness, it often happens that a willful child, or one frightened by the sight of the examiner whom he does not know, turns away from him and refuses to look at what is shown him. These movements of defense indicate already a mentality that corresponds most likely to the fourth degree. The experimenter must be armed with patience and gentleness. He may have a relative, an attendant, or any other person who knows the child, present the chocolate, but he must carefully note the behavior of the child throughout the operation. If the attack of anger, or tears, or fear lasts too long, the examination is necessarily suspended to be taken up at a more favorable time. These are the disappointments to which *alienists* are accustomed.

5. Quest of Food Complicated by a Slight Mechanical Difficulty

This test is designed to bring into play a rudiment of memory, an effort of will, and a coordination of movements.

Procedure. First be sure that the child recognizes the candy or bonbon to be used in this experiment. Then while he is watching you, wrap the bonbon in a piece of paper. Present it to him and carefully note his movements. Does he remember that the paper contains a bonbon? Does he reject it as a useless object, or does he try to pull it apart? Does he carry the covered morsel to his

280 THE MEANING OF LIFE

mouth? Does he eat the paper or does he make some effort to unfold it? Does he completely succeed in unfolding it, or does he seem satisfied with one attempt? Does he present the covered morsel to some one else as if to ask his aid?

6. Execution of Simple Commands and Imitation of Simple Gestures

This test involves various motor coördinations, and associations between certain movements, and the understanding of the significance of certain gestures. In these tests the subject enters for the first time into social relations with the experimenter and it is therefore necessary that he understand the will and desires of the latter. It is the beginning of inter-psychology.

Procedure. As soon as the subject enters the room say good morning to him with expression, give him your hand with accentuated gesture to see if he understands the salutation and if he knows how to shake hands. In cases where the subject walks in, ask him to be seated; this permits one to see whether he understands the meaning of the invitation and if he knows the use of a chair. Throw some object on the. floor and request him by gestures as well as by speech to pick it up and give it back. Make him get up, shut the door, send him away, call him back. So much for commands. Imitation of simple gestures is accomplished by fixing his attention by repeating several times, "Look at me carefully," and when his attention is gained, by saying "Do as I do." The examiner then claps his hands together, puts them in the air, on the shoulders, behind the back; he turns the thumbs one about the other, raises the foot, etc. All this mimicry must be conducted gaily with the air of play. It is sufficient if a single well marked imitation is provoked; the rest is unnecessary. Do not confound the inaptitude for imitation, with bad humor, ill-will, or timidity.

7. Verbal Knowledge of Objects

The object of this test is to discover if associations exist between things and their names. Comprehension and the first possibilities of language are here studied. This test is a continuation of the previous one and represents the second degree of communication between individuals; the first degree is made through imitation, the second through words.

Procedure. This test is composed of two parts. In the first place the examiner names a part of the body and asks the child to point to it. The. questions may relate to the head, the hair, the eyes, the feet, the hands, the nose, the ears, the mouth. Ask the child with a smile "Where is your head?" If he seems embarrassed or timid, encourage him by aiding him a little. "There is your head," pointing it out and touching it if the child does not seem to understand what is wanted of him. On the other hand if he replies by a correct designation to the first question go no further, because if he knows where his head is he should know equally well where are his ears and his mouth. Give him therefore some more difficult questions, for example, his cheek, his eyebrow, his heart.

The second part of the experiment consists in making him designate familiar objects, a string, a cup, a key. Bring the child to the table and by means of gestures indicate the objects and turn his attention to them. When his attention is fixed upon the objects tell him to give you the one you name. "Give me the cup. Give me the key, etc." The cup, the key, the string are the three objects asked for. It is of little importance that he shows awkwardness in taking and presenting them. The essential is that by the play of the countenance and gestures, he indicates clearly that he distinguishes these objects by their names. It is preferable to keep these three objects, others less familiar should be rejected, as for instance a box of matches, a cork, etc. The test is made with three objects in order to avoid the right designation by simple chance. With backward children the following facts may present themselves. They do not know the name of the object presented to them, but having understood that they are to designate an object, they point to anything that is on the table. This is a manner of reacting very common among idiots and imbeciles. They make mistakes but they do not realize it, being in fact very well satisfied with their achievements. Here is another source of error to be avoided. In consequence of their extreme docility, many backward children may be bewildered by the least contradiction. When they have handed you a cup, if you ask them "Isn't this a key?" some might make a sign of acquiescence. This is a test of suggestibility of which more will be said further on. To a blind child, give objects to be recognized by the sense of touch.

8. Verbal Knowledge of Pictures

This exercise is the same as the preceding one with this difference only, that the objects are replaced by pictures which, in consequence of the diminished size and the reduction to a plane surface, are a little more difficult to recognize than in nature, and more than this in a picture the objects must be sought for.

Procedure. We make use of a print borrowed from the picture-book of Inspector Lacabe and Mlle. Goergin. This print in colors represents a complex family scene. We show the print to the child and ask him to designate successively the following objects: the window, mamma, big sister, little sister, little girl, cat, broom, basket, bouquet, duster, coffee-mill. The questions are asked in this way: "Where is the window?" or "Tell me where the window is," or "Show me the window," or "Put your finger on the window."

The last suggestion is generally unnecessary because the child has a tendency to place his forefinger, generally a dirty one, upon the detail which is named for him. If he makes an error in designation be careful not to correct it, but make a note of it. In a psychological examination of this kind, one must never point out to a child the errors which he makes. The examiner is not a pedagogue. It is rare that those who take an interest in the picture can not designate the principal details named to them. The incapable ones give no attention to the picture and do not seem to comprehend what is wanted of them. It is interesting to study the attitude of a child during this test. There are two acts to be accomplished, one a search for the object, the other the recognition of the object. At once in the search the aptitudes or inaptitudes betray themselves. Many defective persons show an excess of eagerness to designate the object, which in itself is a sign of faulty attention. They point out at once without waiting to comprehend. They sometimes point out

282   THE MEANING OF LIFE

before one has finished the sentence. "Where is the -----," said with a suspension in the voice, and already their finger is placed haphazard upon the picture. Such as these do not hunt with care and are incapable of suspending their judgment. This is, it seems to us, a striking characteristic of a weak mind. The child must be closely studied in order to find if, in spite of this special manner, he really knows the names of the objects. A reprimand gently given will sometimes put him on his guard, "No, no, pay attention, you go too fast," and if the question is repeated he will often give a correct answer.

In other cases, errors are sometimes made through suggestibility. The subject seems to imagine that he will commit a fault if he does not designate some object when the question is asked, and out of compliance or of timidity, he makes an erroneous designation for an object whose name he does not know, or which he does not succeed in finding. Notice again, the more reasonable attitude of those who, not knowing the name of the object, refrain from pointing it out but continue the search or reply distinctly, "I do not know." It is rare that an imbecile uses that little phrase. The avowal of ignorance is a proof of judgment and is always a good indication.

9. Naming of Designated Objects

This test is the opposite of the preceding one. It shows the passing from the thing to the word. It also is executed by the use of pictures.

Procedure. Here we make use of another colored print borrowed from the same collection as the preceding. We place it before the eyes of the child and designate with a pencil different objects while asking each time, "What is this?" The objects upon which we place the pencil are the little girl, the dog, the boy, the father, the lamp-lighter, the sky, the advertisement. For the lamp-lighter we ask what he does. Here as elsewhere it is unnecessary to exhaust the complete series of questions unless the subject fails. One or two positive replies are sufficient to satisfy the requirements of the test. This test permits us to know the vocabulary and the pronunciation of the child. Defects of pronunciation, so frequent in the young, are a serious source of embarrassment. It often requires a very indulgent ear to recognize the right word in an indistinct and very brief murmur, and in a case of this sort the examiner will do well to use an interrogation point. Added to the difficulties which proceed from faulty pronunciation, are those brought about by a special vocabulary. Many little children though normal use a vocabulary invented or deformed by them, which is understood only by themselves and their parents.

Additional remarks. Tests 7, 8, and 9 do not constitute differing degrees in the rigorous sense of the word, that is to say they are not tests corresponding to different levels of intelligence. We have ascertained that generally with subnormals those who can pass test 7, pass 8 and also 9. These would therefore be tests of equal rank. We have kept them, however, because these tests occupy an important place in our measuring scale of intelligence, as they constitute a borderline test between imbecility and idiocy. It is useful to have this borderline solidly placed and all these tests will serve as buttresses.

Observations, such as one may make every day on those afflicted with general paralysis, aphasia, or simply people very much fatigued, show that it is much more difficult to pass from the object to the word than it is to pass from the word to the object, or we may say, that one recognizes a word more easily than one finds it. It does not seem clear up to the present that this observation is also applicable to inferior states of intelligence.

10. Immediate Comparison of Two Lines of Unequal Lengths [5]

As we enter the field of what may properly be called psychological experimentation, we shall find it difficult to define which mental functions are being exercised because they are very numerous. Here the child must understand that it is a question of comparison, that the comparison is between two lines that are shown to him; he must understand the meaning of the words, "Show me the longer." He must be capable of comparing, that is of bringing together a conception and an image, and of turning his mind in the direction of searching for a difference. We often have illusions as to the simplicity of psychical processes, because we judge them in relation to others, still more complex. In fact here is a test which will seem to show but little mentality in those who are able to execute it; nevertheless when analyzed it reveals a great complexity.

Procedure. The subject is presented successively with three pieces of paper upon each of which two lines, drawn in ink, are to be compared. Each piece of paper measures 15 by 20 cm.; the lines are drawn lengthwise of the paper, on the same level, and separated by a space of 5 mm. The lines are respectively 4 and 3 cm. in length and one-half of a millimeter in width. On the first sheet the longer line is at the right and on the other two at the left. Each sheet is shown to the subject while saying to him, "Which is the longer line?" Note if his reply is correct but do not tell him. In order to eliminate haphazard replies, it is well to repeat the whole series at least twice. The end is not to discover just how far the accuracy of the child's glance may go, but simply to find if he is capable of making a correct comparison between two lines. Many subnormals are incapable of this; but they act as though they were capable; they seem to understand what is said to them and each time put the finger upon one of the lines saying, "This one." It is necessary to recognize those subjects whose errors are not, strictly speaking, faults of comparison but absence of comparison. It often happens that the subject constantly chooses the line on the same side for the longer, for example always the one on the right side. This manner of reacting would be a sign of defect were it not that one encounters the same thing with some normals.

11. Repetition of Three Figures [6]

This is a test of immediate memory and voluntary attention.

Procedure. Looking the subject squarely in the eye to be sure his attention is fixed, one pronounces three figures, after having told him to repeat them. Choose figures that do not follow each other, as for instance 3, 0, 8, or 5, 9, 7, Pronounce the three figures in the same voice without accentuating one more than the others and without rhythm, but with a certain energy. The

284 THE MEANING OF LIFE

rapidity to be observed is two figures per second. Listen carefully and record the repetition which is made. Often the first attempt is unsuccessful because the subject has not clearly understood and commences to repeat the first figure the moment he hears it; he must be made to be quiet, renew the explanation and commence the pronunciation of another series of figures. There are certain subjects who can not repeat a single figure; in general these are the ones whose mental condition is such that they have not understood anything at all of what is asked of them. Others repeat only a single figure, the first or the last; others pronounce more than three. Special attention must be given to those whose error consists in pronouncing a greater number of figures than that which is said, or in pronouncing a series of figures in their natural order. An individual who, when asked to repeat 3, 0, 8, replies 2, 3, 4, 5, commits a serious error, which would cause one to suspect mental debility. But on the other hand it is true that all feeble-minded and all imbeciles do not commit this error, and that many young normals may commit it. Be careful to notice also if the subject seems satisfied with his reply when this is obviously and grossly false; this indicates an absence of judgment which constitutes an aggravated condition.

Let us say, apropos of this test, that it is important to make a distinction between errors of attention and of adaptation on the one hand, and errors of judgment on the other. When a failure is produced by distraction it is not very important. Thus it may happen that a subject does not repeat the three figures the first time. Begin again and if he succeeds the second time in retaining them he should be considered as having passed the test. A little farther on we shall have to deal with tests of judgment properly so-called, and three or four difficulties will be presented for solution. In this last case, failure will be much more serious, because it can not be due to inattention and the test cannot be considered as passed unless the solutions are given complete.

12. Comparison of Two Weights [7]

This is a test of attention, of comparison and of the muscular sense.

Procedure. Place side by side on the table before the subject two small cubical boxes having the same dimensions, (23 mm. on a side) and the same color, but of different weights. The boxes, weighted by grains of lead rolled in cotton and not perceptible by shaking, weigh 3 grams and 12 grams respectively. The subject is asked to find out which is the heavier. The operation terminated, two other cubes of 6 and 15 grams respectively are given him to compare, and again 3 grams and 15 grams. If the subject hesitates or seems to be going haphazard, start over again mixing the cubes in order to be sure that he really compares the weights.

At the injunction, "See the two boxes, now tell me which is the heavier," many young subjects designate haphazard one of the two boxes without testing the weights. This error, all the more naive since the two are exactly alike in appearance, does not prove that the subject is incapable of weighing them in his hand and of judging of the weights while exercising muscular sense. One must then order him to take the boxes in his hand and weigh them. Some are very awkward, and

COGNITIVE PSYCHOLOGY   285

put the two boxes into one hand at the same time to weigh them. One must again interfere and teach him how to put a box in each hand and weigh the two simultaneously.

Additional remarks. Following this weighing of two boxes of different weight and equal volume, one can propose to weigh two boxes of equal weight but different volume. The illusion which is produced under these circumstances is well known. With the weights equal, the larger box will appear lighter; and the apparent difference of weight increases with the difference of volume. Investigations have been made to determine whether this illusion takes place with backward children, and it has been observed by Demoor that there are certain ones who are not affected by it, something which we ourselves have recently verified. We put before the defective children long boxes of white wood, of the same weight, the largest one 24 x 4 x 4 cm., the smallest 12 x 2 x 2 cm., the medium one 18 x 3 x 3 cm. Like many normal children our subnormals, when given two for comparison and asked "Which is the heavier," pointed out the larger. The first naive response has but little significance. If one insists, if one tells the subject to weigh them in his hand, it sometimes happens that subnormals either cling to their first designation, or abandon it altogether and find the smaller one the heavier; in the latter case they are sensitive to the illusion. It seems to us that before declaring that a subnormal is not sensitive, one must first find if he can compare two weights, and whether he is able to judge which is the heavier of two weights having the same volume. Having made this preliminary test, one will perceive that very many subnormals are insensible to the illusion because they are incapable of comparing weights. What they lack therefore is a more elementary aptitude.

13. Suggestibility

Suggestibility is by no means a test of intelligence, because very many persons of superior intelligence are susceptible to suggestion, through distraction, timidity, fear of doing wrong, or some preconceived idea. Suggestion produces effects which from certain points of view closely resemble the natural manifestations of feeble-mindedness; in fact suggestion disturbs the judgment, paralyzes the critical sense, and forces us to attempt unreasonable or unfitting acts worthy of a defective. It is therefore necessary, when examining a child suspected of retardation, not to give a suggestion unconsciously, for thus artificial debility is produced which might make the diagnosis deceptive. If a person is forced to give an absurd reply by making use of an alternative pronounced in an authoritative voice, it does not in the least prove that he is lacking in judgment. But this source of error being once recognized and set aside, it is none the less interesting to bring into the examination a precise attempt at suggestion, and note what happens. It is a means of testing the force of judgment of a subject and his power of resistance. [*8*]

Procedure. The proof of suggestibility which we have devised does not give rise to a special experiment: it complicates by a slight addition other exercises which we have already described.

(a) *Designation of* objects *named by the experimenter.* When we :ask the child (test 7) to show us the thread, the cup, the thimble, we add, "Show me the button." On the empty table there is no

286 THE MEANING OF LIFE

button, there are only the three preceding objects and yet by gesture and look we invite the subject to search for the button on the table. It is a suggestion by personal action, developing obedience. Certain ones obey quickly and easily, presenting to us again the cup or no matter what other objects. Their suggestibility is complete. Others resist a little, pout, while feigning to hunt for it on the table, or in the cup; they do not reply, but cover their embarrassment by a search which they continue indefinitely if not interrupted. One should consider this attitude as a sufficient expression of resistance, and go no further. It would be unnecessary as we are not seeking a victory over them. Lastly, those least affected by suggestion, reply clearly, "I do not know," or "There is no button." Some laugh.

(b) *Designation of parts of a picture named by the experimenter.* When the child has looked at the picture and we have asked him to point out the window, etc., at the very last say, "Where is the patapoum?" and then "Where is the nitchevo?" words that have no sense for him. These demands are made in the same manner as the preceding ones. Here again we find the three types, children who docilely designate any object whatever, others who search indefinitely without finding anything, and again others who declare, "There is none."

(c) *Snare of lines.* Following the three pairs of unequal lines, which serve to show the correctness of comparison, we place before the subject three other similar sheets each containing two equal lines. We present them saying, "And here?" Led on by the former replies he has a tendency, an acquired force, for again finding one line longer than the other. Some succumb to the snare completely. Others stop at the first pair and declare, "They are equal," but at the second and third they say one of the lines is longer than the other. Others find them all equal but hesitate. Others again fall into the snare without a shadow of hesitation.

14. Verbal Definition of Known Objects

Vocabulary, some general notions, ability to put a simple idea into words, are all brought to light by means of this test.

Procedure. Ask the child what is a house, a horse, a fork, a mamma. This is the conversation that takes place: "Do you know what a ------ is?" If the child answers yes then ask him: "Very well, then tell me what it is." Try to overcome his silence a little and his timidity. Aid him, only when necessary, by giving him an example: "A dog, it barks," and then see if the child understands and approves that definition.

Very young normal *children* of two or three years, reply to questions of this kind with enthusiasm. They ordinarily reply in terms of use, "A fork is to eat with." This is typical. Record the answer verbatim. Some will keep silent, some give absurd, incomprehensible replies, or again will repeat the word, " A house, it is a house."

15. Repetition of Sentences of Fifteen Words [9]

This is a test of immediate memory, so far as it concerns the recollection of words; a proof of voluntary attention, naturally because voluntary attention must accompany all psychological experiments; lastly it is a test of language.

Procedure. First be sure that the child is listening carefully, then, after having warned him that he will have to repeat what is said to him, pronounce slowly, intelligibly, the following sentence: *I get up in the morning, I dine at noon, I go to bed at night.* Then make a sign for him to repeat. Often the child, still not very well adapted, has not fully understood. Never repeat a sentence but go on to another. When the subject repeats it write down verbatim what he says. Many even among normals make absurd repetitions, for example: "I go to bed at noon." Often the child replaces the cultured expression "I dine" for a more familiar form, "I eat." The fact of being able to repeat the sentence correctly after the first hearing is a good sign. The second sentence is easier than the first, *In the summer the weather is beautiful; in winter snow falls.* Here is the third, *Germaine has been bad, she has not worked, she will be scolded.* Now we give five sentences quite difficult to understand:

The horse-chestnut tree in the garden throws upon the ground the faint shade of its new young leaves

The horse draws the carriage, the road is steep and the carriage is heavy.

It is one o'clock in the afternoon, the house is silent, the cat sleeps in *the shade.*

One should not say all that he thinks, but he must think all that he says.

The spirit of criticism must not be confounded with the spirit of contradiction.

16. Comparison of Known Objects from Memory

288 THE MEANING OF LIFE

This is an exercise in ideation, in the notion of differences, and somewhat in powers of observation.

Procedure. One asks what difference there is between paper and cardboard, between a fly and a butterfly, between a piece of wood and a piece of glass. First be sure that the subject knows these objects. Ask him, "Have you seen paper?" "Do you know what cardboard is?" Thus ask him about all the objects before drawing his attention to the difference between them. It may happen that little Parisians, even though normal, and eight or nine years old, have never seen a butterfly. These are examples of astounding ignorance, but we have found, what is still more extraordinary, Parisians of ten years who have never seen the Seine.

After being assured that the two objects to be compared are known, demand their difference. If the word is not understood, take notice and afterward choose more familiar language. "In what are they not alike? How are they not alike?" Three classes of replies may be expected. First, that of the children who have no comprehension of what is desired of them. When asked the difference between cardboard and paper, they reply, "The cardboard." When one has provoked replies of this kind, the explanation must be renewed with patience to see if there is not some means of making oneself understood. Second, the absurd replies, such as, "The fly is larger than the butterfly," "The wood is thicker than the glass," or "The butterfly flies and so does the fly." Third, the correct reply.

17. Exercise of Memory on Pictures

This is a test of attention and visual memory.

Procedure. The subject is told that several pictures will be shown to him, which he will be allowed to look at for thirty seconds, and that he must then repeat the names of the objects seen, from memory. There are thirteen pictures, each 6 by 6 centimeters, representing the following objects: clock, key, nail, omnibus, barrel, bed, cherry, rose, mouth of a beast, nose, head of a child, eggs, landscape. These pictures are pasted on two cardboards and are shown simultaneously. Measure the time of exposure with the second hand of the watch. In order that the subject shall not become absorbed in one picture, say to him, "Make haste. Look at all." The thirty seconds passed, the examiner writes from dictation the names of the pictures the subject recalls.

This test does indeed give an idea of the memory of a person, but two subjects may have very unequal memories of the same picture; one of them may recall only one detail while another recalls the whole. Moreover there is a weak point in this test in that it may be affected by failure of attention. It is sufficient that a fly should alight, a door should open, a cock should crow, or for the subject to have a desire to use his handkerchief during the thirty seconds, to disturb the work of memorizing. If the result is altogether lacking, the test should be repeated with another collection of pictures to find whether the first error was the result of distraction.

18. Drawing a Design from Memory

This is a test of attention, visual memory, and a little analysis.

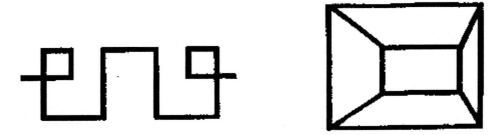

DESIGN TO BE DRAWN FROM MEMORY AFTER BEING STUDIED 10 SECONDS

Procedure. The subject is told that two designs will be shown to him, which he will be allowed to look at for ten seconds, and which he must then draw from memory. Excite his emulation. The two designs which we reproduce here, are shown to him and left exposed for ten seconds. (Regulate the time by the second hand of a watch; the time must be exact within one or two seconds.) Then see that the subject commences the reproduction of the design without loss of time.

Marking the results of this test, that is the errors committed, is a delicate operation. Simply note if the reproduction is absolutely correct; or if without being correct it resembles the model; or if, on the contrary, it bears no resemblance whatever to it.

19. Immediate Repetition of Figures

This is a test of immediate memory and immediate attention.

Procedure. This is the same as for the three figures, see above Here the errors noted for the three figures take on greater proportions. One must be on the watch for errors of judgment. A normal may fail but the manner is different.

20. Resemblances of Several Known Objects Given from Memory

This is a test of memory, conscious recognition of resemblances, power of observation.

290   THE MEANING OF LIFE

Procedure. This test closely resembles test 16, except that here resemblances are to be indicated instead of differences. It may be surprising to learn that children have a good deal of trouble noting resemblances; they much more willingly find differences in the objects given them to compare. One must insist a good deal and show them that although unlike two objects may be somewhat similar. Here are the questions to be asked:

In what are a poppy and blood alike?

How are a fly, an ant, a butterfly, a flea alike?

In what way are a newspaper, a label, a picture alike?

Under test 16 we have indicated the precautions that must be taken, notably that of assuring oneself that the child knows the objects to be compared. There are little Parisians who have never seen poppies or ants.

21. Comparison of Lengths

This is a test in exactness of glance in rapid comparison.

Procedure. In this test one presents a series of pairs of lines. One line of each pair is 30 mm. long and the other varies from 31 to 35 mm. These lines are drawn on the pages of a blank book, 15 by 30 cm.; there are only two lines on a page. They extend in the same direction, end to end, separated by 5 mm. The longer occupies first the right then the left of the page. There are fifteen pairs. After placing them in order one begins by showing the pair where the difference is greatest. The subject is asked to point out the longer of the two lines.

We then present, in another blank book, a series of pairs of lines very much more difficult to estimate. The pages of this book are 20 by 30 cm.; the constant line is 100 mm. long, the variable ranging from 101 to 103 mm. The exact comparison of such long lines is beyond the ability of many adults. The number of pairs is twelve.

22. Five Weights to be Placed in Order [10]

This test requires a direct concentration of attention, an appreciation of weight, and the memory of judgment.

Procedure. Five little boxes of the same color and volume are placed in a group on the table. They weigh respectively 3, 6, 9, 12, and 15 grams. They are shown to the subject while saying to him: "Look at these little boxes, they have not the same weight; you are going to arrange them here in their right order. Here to the left first the heaviest weight; next, the one a little less heavy; here one a little less heavy; here one a little less heavy, and here the lightest one." This explanation is difficult to give in childish terms. It must be attempted, however, and repeated if one perceives that it is not understood.

The explanation terminated, one must observe with attention the attitude of the child. One child does not understand, *puts* nothing in order; another arranges the weights very well but does not compare them; he takes one at random and puts it at the left as the heaviest, without comparing it with the others, and places those remaining without weighing them. A third tries them a little, but noticeably goes at it blindly. The reading of the weights which is inscribed on each, shows us the errors.

There are three classes to distinguish. First, the subject who goes at random without comparing, often committing a serious error, four degrees for example. Second, the subject who compares, but makes a slight error of one or two degrees. Third, the one who has the order exact. We propose to estimate the errors in this test by taking account of the displacement that must be made to re-establish the correct order. Thus in the following example: 12, 9, 6, 3, 15, -- 15 is not in its place, and the error is of four degrees because it must make four moves to find the place where it belongs. All the others must be changed one degree. The sum of the changes indicates the total error which is of eight degrees. It is necessary to make a distinction between those who commit slight errors of inattention, and those who by the enormity of an error of 6 or 8 prove that they act at random.

23. Gap in Weights

As soon as the subject has correctly arranged the weights and only then, tell him that one of the weights is to be taken away while he closes his eyes, and that he is to discover which has been taken away by weighing them in his hand. The operation demanded of him is delicate. One must note that he does not cheat by reading the marking on the box. If there is any fear of this, wrap the boxes in paper.

24. Exercise upon Rhymes [11]

This exercise requires an ample vocabulary, suppleness of mind, spontaneity, intellectual activity.

Procedure. Begin by asking the subject if he knows what a rhyme is. Then explain by means of examples: "Rhymes are words that end in the same way. Thus 'grenouille' [frog]rhymes with 'citrouille,' [pumpkin] because it is the same sound 'ouille.' 'Compote' [compote] rhymes with 'carotte,' [carrot] they both end with 'ote.' 'Baton' [stick] rhymes with 'macaron,' [macaroon, or a round badge or medal] and with 'citron' [lemon]. Here the rhyme is on 'on.' [*12*] Do you now understand what a rhyme is? Very well, you must find all the rhymes you can. The word with which you must find rhymes is 'obéissance' [obedience]. [*13*] Come, begin, find some." In order to accomplish this test, the subject must not only find rhymes, which is partly a matter of imagination, but he must understand the preceding explanation, which is a matter of judgment. There are subjects who remain silent who either have not understood or are unable to find

292   THE MEANING OF LIFE

rhymes. Others are more loquacious but the false rhymes they cite prove that they have not comprehended. The minute having elapsed, renew the explanation and try the test again.

25. Verbal Gaps to be Filled

This test thought out and proposed by Professor Ebbinghaus of Berlin, varies in significance according to its mode of use. It consists essentially in this: a word of a text is omitted and the subject is asked to replace it. The nature of the intellectual work by which the gap is filled, varies according to the case. This may be a test of memory, a test of style, or a test of judgment. In the sentence: "Louis IX was born in ------" the gap is filled by memory. "The crow ----- his feathers with his beak;" in this the idea of the suppressed word is not at all obscure, and the task consists in finding the proper word. We may say in passing, that according to the opinion of several teachers before whom we have tried it, this kind of exercise furnishes excellent scholastic training. Lastly, in sentences of the nature of those we have chosen, the filling of the gaps requires an attentive examination and an appreciation of the facts set forth by the sentence. It is therefore an exercise of judgment.

Procedure. We have simplified it by suppressing all explanations. The words forming the gap are intentionally placed at the end of the sentence. It is sufficient to read the text with expression, then suspend the voice with the tone of interrogation when one arrives at the gap. The subject naturally fills in the gap. If he does not do so spontaneously, urge him a little by saying, "Finish. What must one say?" Once the operation is set going it continues easily.

The operator knows the true words of the text which have been suppressed. He should not yield to the temptation of considering those the only correct ones. He must examine and weigh with care all the words that are given him. Some are good, others altogether bad, nonsensical or absurd. There will be all degrees.

Here is the text with the gaps. The words to be suppressed are in italics.

> The weather is clear, the sky is (1) *blue*. The sun has quickly dried the linen which the women have spread on the line. The cloth, white as snow, dazzles the (2) eyes.[*] The women gather up the large sheets which are as stiff as though they had been (3) *starched*. They shake them and hold them by the four (4) *corners*. Then they snap the sheets with a (5) *noise*. Meanwhile the housewife irons the fine linen. She takes the irons one after the other and places them on the (6) *stove*. Little Mary who is dressing her doll would like to do some (7) *ironing*, but she has not had permission to touch the (8) *irons*.

26. Synthesis of Three Words in One Sentence [14]

This exercise is a test in spontaneity, facility of invention and combination, aptitude to construct sentences.

Procedure. Three words are proposed: Paris, river, fortune. Ask that a sentence be made using those three words. It is necessary to be very clear, and to explain to those who may not chance to know what a sentence is. Many subjects remain powerless before this difficulty, which is beyond their capacity. Others can make a sentence with a given word but they cannot attain to the putting of three words in a single sentence.

27. Reply to an Abstract Question [15]

This test is one of the most important of all, for the diagnosis of mental debility. It is rapid, easily given, sufficiently precise. It consists in placing the subject in a situation presenting a difficulty of an abstract nature. Any mind which is not apt in abstraction succumbs here.

Procedure. This consists in reading the beginning of a sentence and suspending the voice when one arrives at the point, and repeating, "What ought one to do?" The sentences are constructed in such a manner that the slight difficulty of comprehension which they present, comes from the ideas rather than from the words. The child who does not understand, is hindered less by his ignorance of the language than by his lack of ability to seize an abstract idea. There are twenty-five questions. The first are very easy and tend to put the subject at his ease. We do not reproduce them here as they will be found farther on with the results.

Here are only four of the sentences. They are among those of medium difficulty.

1. When one has need of good advice -- what must one do?
2. Before making a decision about a very important affair -- what must one do?
3. When anyone has offended you and asks you to excuse him -- what ought you to do?
4. When one asks your opinion of someone whom you know only a little -- what ought you to say?

It is often a delicate matter to estimate the value of a reply. Sometimes the subject does not gather all the shades of the question and the reply is too simple, not absolutely adequate to the demand. Nevertheless one must be satisfied if it expresses sense, if it proves that the general bearing of the question has been grasped.

In other cases the reply is equivocal; it would be excellent if it came from a dilletante [sic], or a decadent, because of the double meaning which is ironically evoked. It is of no value in the mouth of a school child. Thus to the first question, "When one has need of good advice --" a child replied, "one says nothing." We suppose he has not understood but if this had been an ironical reply, one might have found in it a curious meaning. As a matter of fact, these uncertainties, which are truly matters of conscience with the examiner, present themselves but rarely. Ordinarily the interpretation is easy because one knows already about what to expect from his subject.

294   THE MEANING OF LIFE

28. Reversal of the Hands of a Clock

This is a test of reasoning, attention, visual imagery.

Procedure. First ask the subject if he knows how to tell time. In case his answer is in the affirmative, put him to the test because it is not best to trust his word. There are imbeciles who say they know how to tell time and give extravagant answers when a watch is given them to read. It is important to note this error in judgment. Having found that the subject knows how to tell time, remind him that the long hand indicates the minutes and the short hand the hours. Then say to him, " Suppose that it is a quarter of three, do you clearly see where the long hand is, and the short hand? Very well, now suppose the long hand is changed to the place where the short hand is, and the short hand to the place of the long, what time is it?" Reverse the hands for the following hours: twenty minutes past six; four minutes of three. The correct solutions are, half past four, and a quarter past eleven.

The subject must not see the face of a watch nor make the design upon paper, or his cuff or his nail to aid his imagination. As the experiment is made individually, supervision is easy.

When the subject gives the two solutions correctly, one can push him a little further, imposing a question much more difficult. Say to him, "For each of the hours that you have indicated, the reversal of the hands brings about the result that you have found; nevertheless this result is not altogether correct. The transposition indicated is not altogether possible. By analyzing the case with care, tell me why."

This test permits of varying degrees of accuracy in the replies. First, certain ones are not able to make any transposition; they give no solution, or else it is absolutely incorrect. Others who come nearer the truth give a solution which is partially correct; for example, only one of the hands is rightly placed, or perhaps an error of symmetry has been committed, one has put to the right what ought to have been at the left or inversely. The third category is that of subjects who give correct solutions. Finally the fourth is composed of those who give a correct solution and are capable of criticizing the slight inaccuracies.

29. Paper Cutting [16]

This exercise calls for voluntary attention, reasoning, visual imagery, but not for vocabulary.

Procedure. Take two sheets of white paper of the same dimensions. Call the attention of the subject to their equality. "You see they are alike." Lay the first one on the table, fold the other into two equal parts slowly before the subject, then fold again into two equal parts at right angles to the first fold. The sheet is now folded in four equal divisions. On the edge that presents a single fold, cut out with the scissors, a triangle. Take away the triangular piece of paper without allowing the subject to study it, but show him the folded paper, and say to him: "The sheet of paper is now cut. If I were to open it, it would no longer resemble the first sheet of paper here on the table; there will be a hole in it. Draw on this first sheet of paper what I shall see when I unfold

COGNITIVE PSYCHOLOGY   295

this one." It is important that the experimenter say neither more nor less than our text, and that he compel himself to employ the words chosen by us although scarcely exact and accurate. The subject now draws upon the first sheet the result of the cutting which he has just witnessed. He should not be allowed to handle the perforated sheet. Some subjects look a little at the perforation, others rely upon their imagination and begin at once to draw. The less intelligent simply draw an angle placed no matter where on the white page, or perhaps a triangle whose form and dimensions are not those of the cut. A little closer observation causes some to consider the form and dimensions. Somewhat better is the triangle replaced by a diamond drawn in the center of the page. Although better, it is still not the correct result, for to be correct two diamonds must be drawn, one in the center of each half of the paper. This test interests everybody. It requires no development of style. It has nothing literary, and rests upon entirely different faculties than those required by preceding tests. Moreover the correctness of the result is easy to grade.

CHAPTER 9

BEHAVIOURISM

While behaviourism is viewed globally as primarily an American school, historically the major influences of behaviourism were from Europe. While some argue that the philosophical antecedents of behaviourism can be found in the Greek reductionist philosophies of Leucippus and Democritus (whereby only the atoms and the void are real), the fact is that modern Russian studies actually form its basis.

In the late 19th century a popular Russian philosopher and physiologist by the name of Ivan Sechenov (1829-1905) argued that a key to understanding people was in their physiological reactions to stress. In essence, Sechenov advocated an emphasis upon the environmental reactive/ interpretive nature of people, arguing that it accounts for over 99% of our formation as individuals. However, Sechenov's views were so radical that they were only truly accepted after the work of a later Russian researcher popularised the notion of behaviourism.

Ivan Petrovich Pavlov (1849-1936) began his academic career studying physics but soon became absorbed in physiology and studied primarily the nervous system and nerves related to the heart and digestion. It was an experiment about the physiology of digestion that led him logically to create a science of conditioned reflexes. In his study of the reflex regulation of the activity of the digestive glands, Pavlov paid special attention to the phenomenon of what was termed "psychic secretion" which is caused by food stimuli at a distance from an animal. A series of experiments causes Pavlov to reject the subjective interpretation of "psychic salivary secretion" and, on the basis of Sechenov's hypothesis that psychic activity was of a reflexive nature, he concluded that this was a reflex, though temporary and conditioned.

This radical discovery earned Pavlov a number of global honours beginning with his induction into the Russian Academy of Science in 1901 and a Nobel Prize in 1904. Then, in 1907, he was elected Academician of the Russian Academy of Science and in 1912 Pavolov received an honorary doctorate from Cambridge University. Finally, after the October Revolution in Russia, a special governmental decree signed by Lenin on January 24, 1921, notes "...*the outstanding scientific services of Academician I.P. Pavlov, which are of enormous significance to the working class of the whole world.*" (See Read For Yourself Section, this chapter, for a sample of Pavlov's work).

While all will acknowledge the contributions of Sechenov and Pavlov to the school of Behaviourism, it was John B. Watson (1878-1958) who planted the school in American psychology. Today behaviourism stands as a powerful force within American psychology and in many ways forms the basis of the multi-national corporate strategies that have come to typify the American style of marketing and economics as well. It is a powerful legacy for a man born into a humble Baptist family from South Carolina.

Receiving his Ph.D. from the University of Chicago (in Philosophy and Psychology) in 1903, he went on to study biology and physiology. After studying the behaviour of children he fell in line with Pavlov's notions and concluded that humans were simply complicated animals that functioned on the basis of conditioned responses to the environment. Such views clearly led him away from the views of people like Sigmund Freud, and in the 1920's Watson predicted that Freudian psychoanalysis would be rejected as utterly false within his lifetime.

As a professor at John's Hopkins University, J.B. Watson was quickly making a name for himself as a powerful force for Behavioural Psychology when an affair with an assistant ended both his academic career and his marriage. However, John Watson's understanding of human psychology (and particularly his brand of behaviourism) was quickly recognized by the corporate world. In 1924 he became vice president of the largest advertising agency in the United States, thereby demonstrating the economic benefits of understanding human behaviour and psychology.

Due to the clear economic power that could be exploited through basic conditioning the school of Behavioural Psychology became firmly rooted within the world of American academia. While Pavlov was Russian, and Watson never returned to teaching after his forced resignation at John's Hopkins, these two figures remain the core pillars of this movement.

Following in the footsteps of Pavlov and Watson were other innovators in behaviourism theory and the emergence of a new and more technical approach to behaviourism led by the likes of Clark L. Hull (1884-1952) who popularized behaviourism in the American academic community. Hull's work at various universities across the United States (including Yale) quickly confirmed that Hull was a powerful theorist and leader in academic psychological research. Among Hull's accomplishments was his central role in the development of quantitative approaches to behaviour.

Hull's vastly complex theories reduced human experience into a mathematically guided theory for learning and principles of behaviour. These theories were anchored by the basic principles of stimuli and responses that were mediated by personal variables of drive, fatigue, conditioned habit strength and perceived incentive, resulting in what has been referred to as the *stimulus intensity dynamism*. Through this complex system a behaviourism perspective of learning was developed that was seen by the rest of the world to be an uniquely North American approach to psychology.

Following in the same vein as Hull was Edward C. Tolman (1886-1959), an even more extreme behaviourist than Hull, as Tolman noted, who was purely concerned with behaviour rather than cognition. As such, many have argued about Tolman being much of a psychological theorist, however his theory of molar (larger units) behaviourism was of a sufficient contribution (to what had largely been molecular [smaller units] of Watson style behaviourism) that it is noteworthy. Of course, Hull and Tolman are most important to American behaviourism because they influenced a new generation of theorists, including a boy named Burrhus Frederic Skinner of Susquehanna, Pennsylvania (1904-1990).

Without a doubt B.F. Skinner became the modern icon for the standard characteristics of behaviourism. A graduate of Harvard (the most behaviourism driven psychology program in America at its time) B.F. Skinner did not consider himself to be a behaviourist. However, after joining the faculty at the University of Minnesota his attitudes began to change and he eventually returned to his roots, teaching at Harvard. Through a long progression of his theories Skinner finally put forward his prime principle of *Operant Conditioning.* Skinner differentiated this from Pavlovian conditioning by stressing the relation of the response and reinforcement. For Skinner, Pavlov's conditioning was a *Type II* conditioning where reinforcement correlated with a stimulus. In contrast, his Operant Conditioning was *Type I* that was correlated with a response. Therefore Skinner pointed out that his principles *dealt with the conditioning of voluntary behaviour* (in contrast to Pavlov's principle of the conditioning of autonomic behaviour).

READ AND DECIDE FOR YOURSELF:

Excerpts from:

LECTURE ON THE WORK OF THE CEREBRAL HEMISPHERE
(IVAN PETROVICH PAVLOV)

THE CONFLICTING PSYCHOLOGIES OF LEARNING—A WAY OUT
(CLARK L. HULL)

PSYCHOLOGY AS THE BEHAVIOURIST VIEWS IT
(JOHN B. WATSON)

TWO TYPES OF CONDITIONED REFLEX AND A PSEUDO TYPE
(B. F. SKINNER)

LECTURE ON THE WORK OF THE CEREBRAL HEMISPHERE, LECTURE ONE

Ivan Petrovich Pavlov (1924)

Source: from Experimental Psychology and other essays, 1957, published by Philosophical Library, NY. One lecture reproduced in full. [66]

Gentlemen,

One cannot but be struck by a comparison of the following facts. First, the cerebral hemispheres, the higher part of the central nervous system, is a rather impressive organ. In structure it is exceedingly complex, comprising millions and millions (in man - even billions) of cells, i.e., centres or foci of nervous activity. These cells vary in size, shape and arrangement and are connected with each other by countless branches. Such structural complexity naturally suggests a very high degree of functional complexity. Consequently, it would seem that a boundless field of investigation is offered here for the physiologist. Secondly, take the dog, man's companion and friend since prehistoric times, in its various roles as hunter, sentinel, etc. We know that this complex behaviour of the dog, its higher nervous activity (since no one will dispute that this is higher nervous activity), is chiefly associated with the cerebral hemispheres. If we remove the cerebral hemispheres in the dog (Goltz and others), it becomes incapable of performing not only the roles mentioned above, but even of looking after itself. It becomes profoundly disabled and will die unless well cared for. This implies that both in respect of structure and function, the cerebral hemispheres perform considerable physiological work.

Let us turn now to man. His entire higher nervous activity is also dependent on the normal structure and functioning of the cerebral hemispheres. The moment the complex structure of his hemispheres is damaged or disturbed in one way or another, he also becomes an invalid; he can no longer freely associate with his fellows as an equal and must be isolated.

In amazing contrast to this boundless activity of the cerebral hemispheres is the scant content of the present-day physiology of these hemispheres. Up to 1870 there was no physiology of the cerebral hemispheres at all; they seemed inaccessible to the physiologist. It was in that year that Fritsch and Hitzig first successfully applied the ordinary physiological methods of stimulation and destruction to their study. Stimulation of certain parts of the cerebral cortex regularly evoked contractions in definite groups of the skeletal muscles (the cortical motor region). Extirpation of

---

66 Accessed: *http://www.marxists.org/reference/subject/philosophy/works/ru/pavlov.htm*

302   THE MEANING OF LIFE

these parts led to certain disturbances in the normal activity of the corresponding groups of muscles.

Shortly afterwards H. Munk, Ferrier and others demonstrated that other regions of the cortex, seemingly not susceptible to artificial stimulation, are also functionally differentiated. Removal of these parts leads to defects in the activity of certain receptor organs - the eye, the ear and the skin.

Many researchers have been thoroughly investigating these phenomena. More precision and more details have been obtained, especially as regards the motor region, and this knowledge has even found practical application in medicine; however, investigation as vet has not gone far beyond the initial point. The essential fact is that the entire higher and complex behaviour of the animal, which is dependent on the cerebral hemispheres, as shown by the previously mentioned experiment by Goltz with the extirpation of the hemispheres in a dog, has hardly been touched upon in these investigations and is not included even in the programme of current physiological research, what do the facts relating to the cerebral hemispheres, which are now at the disposal of the physiologist, explain with regard to the behaviour of the higher animals? Is there a general scheme of the higher nervous activity? What kind of general rules govern this activity? The contemporary physiologist finds himself truly empty-handed when he has to answer these lawful questions. While the object of investigation is highly complex in relation to structure, and extremely rich in function, research in this sphere remains, as it were, in a blind alley, unable to open up before the physiologist the boundless vistas which might have been expected.

Why is this so? The reason is clear, the work of the cerebral hemispheres has never been regarded from the same point of view as that of other organs of the body, or even other parts of the central nervous system. It has been described as special psychical activity - which we feel and apprehend in ourselves and which we suppose exists in animals by analogy with human beings. Hence the highly peculiar and difficult position of the physiologist. On the one hand, the study of the cerebral hemispheres, as of all other parts of the organism, seems to come within the scope of physiology, but on the other hand, it is an object of study by a special branch of science - psychology. What, then, should be the attitude of the physiologist? Should he first acquire psychological methods and knowledge and only then begin to study the activity of the cerebral hemispheres? But there is a real complication here. It is quite natural that physiology, in analysing living matter, should always base itself on the more exact and advanced sciences - mechanics, physics and chemistry. But here we are dealing with an altogether different matter, since in this particular case we should have to rely on a science which has no claim to exactness as compared with physiology. Until recently discussion revolved even around the question whether psychology should be considered a natural science or a science at all. Without going deeply into this question, I should like to cite some facts which, although crude and superficial, seem to me very convincing. Even the psychologists themselves do not regard their science as being exact. Not so long ago James, an outstanding American psychologist, called psychology not a science, but a "hope for science." Another striking illustration has been provided by Wundt, formerly a physiologist, who became a celebrated psychologist and philosopher and even the founder of the so-called experimental psychology. Prior to the war, in 1913, a discussion took place in Germany as to the advisability of separating the psychological branch of science from the philosophical in the universities, i.e., of having two separate chairs instead of one. Wundt opposed separation, one of his arguments being the impossibility of establishing a common and obligatory examination programme' in psychology, since each professor had his own ideas of the essence of psychology. Is it not clear, then, that psychology has not yet reached the stage of an exact science?

This being the case, there is no need for the physiologist to have recourse to psychology. In view of the steadily developing natural science it would be more logical to expect that not psychology should render assistance to the physiology of the cerebral hemispheres, but, on the contrary, physiological investigation of the activity of this organ in animals should lay the foundation for the exact scientific analysis of the human subjective world. Consequently, physiology must follow its own path - the path blazed for it long ago. Taking as his starting-point the assumption that the functioning of the animal's organism, unlike that of the human being, is similar to the work of a machine, Descartes' three hundred years ago evolved the idea of the reflex as the basic activity of the nervous system. Descartes regarded every activity of the organism as a natural response to certain external agents and believed that the connection between the active organ and the given agent, that is, between cause and effect, is achieved through a definite nervous path. In this way the study of the activity of the animal nervous system was placed on the firm basis of natural science. In the eighteenth, nineteenth and twentieth centuries the idea of the reflex had been extensively used by physiologists, but only in their work on the lower parts of the central nervous system; gradually, however, they began to study its higher parts, until finally, after Sherrington's classical works on spinal reflexes, Magnus, his successor, established the reflex nature of all the basic locomotor activities of the organism. And so experiment fully justified the idea of the reflex which , thereafter, was used in the study of the central nervous system almost up to the cerebral hemispheres. It is to be hoped that the more complex activities of the organism, including the basic locomotor reflexes - states so far referred to in psychology as anger, fear, playfulness, etc. - will soon be related to the simple reflex activity of the subcortical parts of the brain.

A bold attempt to apply the idea of the reflex to the cerebral hemispheres not only of animals but also of man, was made by I. M. Sechenov, the Russian physiologist, on the basis of the contemporary physiology of the nervous system. In a paper published in Russian in 1863 and entitled Reflexes of the Brain Sechenov characterised the activity of the cerebral hemispheres as reflex, i.e., determined activity. He regarded thoughts as reflexes in which the effector end is inhibited, and affects as exaggerated reflexes with a wide irradiation of excitation. A like attempt has been made in our time by Ch. Richet who introduced the concept of the psychical reflex in which the reaction to a given stimulus is determined by its union with the traces left in the cerebral hemispheres by previous stimuli. Generally, the recent physiology of the higher nervous activity related to the cerebral hemispheres tends to associate acting stimulation with traces left by previous ones (associative memory - according to J. Loeb; training, education by experience -

according to other physiologists). But this was mere theorising. The time had come for a transition to the experimental analysis of the subject, and from the objective external aspect, as is the case with any other branch of natural science. This transition was determined by comparative physiology which had just made its appearance as a result of the influence of the theory of evolution. Now that it had turned its attention to the entire animal kingdom, physiology, in dealing with its lower representatives, was forced, of necessity, to abandon the anthropomorphic concept and concentrate on the scientific elucidation of the relations between the external agents influencing the animal and the responsive external activity, the locomotor reaction of the latter. This gave birth to J. Loeb's doctrine of animal tropisms; to the suggestion by Beer, Bethe and Uexküll of an objective terminology for designating the animal reactions; and finally, to the investigation by zoologists of the behaviour of the lower representatives of the animal world, by means of purely objective methods, by comparing the effect of external influences on the animal with its responsive external activity - as for example in the classical work of Jennings, etc.

Influenced by this new tendency in biology and having a practical cast of mind, American psychologists who also became interested in comparative psychology displayed a tendency to subject the external activity of animals to experimental analysis under deliberately induced conditions. Thorndike's Animal Intelligence (1898) must be regarded as the starting-point for investigations of this kind. In these investigations the animal was kept in a box and food placed outside, within sight. The animal, naturally, tried to reach the food, but to do so it had to open the door which in the different experiments was fastened in a different way. Tables and charts registered the speed and the manner in which the animal solved this problem. The entire process was interpreted as the formation of an association, connection between the visual and the tactile stimulation and the locomotor activity. Afterwards by means of this method, and by modifications of it, researchers studied numerous questions relating to the associative ability of various animals. Almost simultaneously with the above-mentioned work by Thorndike, of which I was not then aware, I too had arrived at the idea of the need for a similar attitude to the subject. The following episode, which occurred in my laboratory, gave birth to the idea.

While making a detailed investigation of the digestive glands I had to busy myself also with the so-called psychical stimulation of the glands. When, together with one of my collaborators, I attempted a deeper analysis of this fact, at first in the generally accepted way, i.e., psychologically, visualising the probable thoughts and feelings of the animal, I stumbled on a fact unusual in laboratory practice. I found myself unable to agree with my colleague; each of us stuck to his point of view, and we were unable to convince each other by certain experiments. This made me definitely reject any further psychological discussion of the subject, and I decided to investigate it in a purely objective way, externally, i.e., strictly recording all stimuli reaching the animal at the given moment and observing its corresponding responses either in the form of movements or in the form of salivation (as occurred in this particular case).

This was the beginning of the investigations that I have carried on now for the past twenty-five years with the participation of numerous colleagues who joined hand and brain with me in this work and to whom I am deeply grateful. We have, of course, passed through different stages, and the subject has been advanced only gradually. At first we had but a few separate facts at our disposal, but today so much material has been accumulated by us that we can make an attempt to present it in a more or less systematised form. I am now in a position to place before you a physiological theory of the activity of the cerebral hemispheres which at any rate conforms much more to the structural and functional complexity of this organ than the theory which until now has been based on a few fragmentary, though very important, facts of modern physiology.

Thus, research along these new lines of strictly objective investigation of the higher nervous activity has been carried out mainly in my laboratories (with the participation of a hundred colleagues); work along the same lines has been carried out also by American psychologists. As for other physiological laboratories, so far only a few have begun, starting somewhat later, to investigate this subject, but in most cases their work is still in the initial stage. So far there has been one essential point of difference in the research of the Americans and in ours. Since in the case of the Americans the objective investigation is being conducted by psychologists, this means that, although psychologists study the facts from the purely external - aspect, nevertheless, in posing the problems, in analysing and formulating the results, they tend to think more in terms of psychology. The result is that with the exception of the group of "behaviourists" their work does not bear a purely physiological character. Whereas, we, having started from physiology, invariably and strictly adhere to the physiological point of view, and we are investigating and systematising the whole subject solely in a physiological way.

I shall now pass to an exposition of our material, but before doing so I should like to touch on the concept of the reflex in general, on reflexes in physiology and the so-called instincts.

In the main we base ourselves on Descartes' concept of the reflex. Of course, this is a genuinely scientific concept, since the phenomenon implied by it can be strictly determined. It means that a certain agent of the external world, or of the organism's internal medium produces a certain effect in one or other nervous receptor, which is transformed into a nervous process, into nervous excitation. The excitation is transmitted along certain nerve fibres, as if along an electric cable, to the central nervous system; thence, thanks to the established nervous connections, it passes along other nerve fibres to the working organ, where it in its turn is transformed into a special activity of the cells of this organ. Thus, the stimulating agent proves to be indispensably connected with the definite activity of the organism, as cause and effect.

It is quite obvious that the entire activity of the organism is governed by definite laws. If the animal were not (in the biological sense) strictly adapted to the surrounding world, it would, sooner or later, cease to exist. If instead of being attracted by food, the animal turned away from it, or instead of avoiding fire threw itself into it, and so on, it would perish. The animal must so react to the environment that all its responsive activity ensures its existence. The same is true if we think of life in terms of mechanics, physics and chemistry. Every material system can exist as an entity only so long as its internal forces of attraction, cohesion, etc., are equilibrated with the external forces influencing it. This applies in equal measure to such a simple object as a stone and to the most complex chemical substance, and it also holds good for the organism. As a definite material system complete in itself, the organism can exist only so long as it is in equilibrium with

306   THE MEANING OF LIFE

the environment; the moment this equilibrium is seriously disturbed, the organism ceases to exist as a particular system. Reflexes are the elements of this constant adaptation or equilibration. Physiologists have studied and are studying numerous reflexes, these indispensable, machine-like reactions of the organism, which at the same time are inborn, i.e., determined by the peculiar organisation of the given nervous system. Reflexes, like the belts of machines made by human hands, are of two kinds: the positive and the negative inhibitory, in other words, those which excite certain activities and those which inhibit them. Although investigation of these reflexes by physiologists has been under way for a long time, it is, of course, a long way from being finished. More and more new reflexes are being discovered; the properties of the receptor organs, on the surface on which it is walking. In what way does it differ, say, from inclining the head and closing the lids when something flashes near the eye? We should call the latter a defensive reflex, and the first an alimentary instinct, although in the case of the pecking, if it is caused by the sight of a stain, nothing but inclining the head and a movement of the beak occurs.

Further, it has been noted that instincts are more complex than reflexes. But there are exceedingly complex reflexes which no one designates as instincts. Take, for example, vomiting. This is a highly complex action and one that involves extraordinary co-ordination of a large number of muscles, both striated and smooth, usually employed in other functions of the organism and spread over a large area. It also involves the secretion of various glands which normally. participate in quite different activities of the organism.

The fact that instincts involve a long chain of successive actions, while reflexes are, so to speak, one-storeyed, has also been regarded as a point of distinction between them. By way of example let us take the building of a nest, or of animal dwellings in general. Here, of course, we have a long chain of actions: the animal must search for the material', bring it to the site and put it together and secure it. If we regard this as a reflex, we must assume that the ending of one reflex excites a new one, or, in other words, that these are chain-reflexes. But such chain activities are by no means peculiar to instincts alone. We are familiar with many reflexes which are also interlocked. Here is an instance. When we stimulate an afferent nerve, for example, the n. ischiadicus, there takes place a reflex rise of blood pressure. This is the first reflex. The high pressure in the left ventricle of the heart and in the first part of the aorta acts as a stimulus to another reflex: it stimulates the endings of the n. depressoris cordis which evokes a depressor reflex moderating the effect of the first reflex. Let us take the chain-reflex recently established by Magnus. A cat, even deprived of the cerebral hemispheres will in most cases fall on its feet when thrown from a height. How does this occur? The change in the spatial position of the otolithic organ of the ear causes a certain reflex contraction of the muscles in the neck, which restores the animal's head to a normal position in relation to the horizon. This is the first reflex. The end of this reflex - the contraction of the muscles in the neck and the righting of the head in general - stimulates a fresh reflex on certain muscles of the trunk and limbs which come into action and, in the end, restore the animal's proper standing posture.

Yet another difference between reflexes and instincts has been assumed, namely, that instincts often depend on the internal state or condition of the organism. For instance, a bird builds its nest only in the mating season. Or, to take a simpler example, when the animal is sated, it is no longer attracted by food and stops eating. The same applies to the sexual instinct, which is connected with the age of the organism, as well as with the state of the reproductive glands. In general the hormones, products of the glands of internal secretion, are of considerable importance in this respect. But this, too, is not a peculiar property of the instincts alone. The intensity of any reflex, as well as its presence or absence, directly depends on the state of excitability of the reflex centres which in turn always depends on the chemical and physical properties of the blood (automatic stimulation of the centres) and on the interaction of different reflexes.

Finally, importance is sometimes attached to the fact that reflexes are related to the activity of separate organs, whereas instincts involve the activity of the organism as a whole, i.e., actually the whole skeleto-muscular system. However, we know from the works of Magnus and de Kleyn that standing, walking, and bodily balance in general, are reflexes.

Thus, reflexes and instincts alike are natural reactions of the organism to certain stimulating agents, and consequently there is no need to designate them by different terms. The term "reflex" is preferable, since a strictly scientific sense has been imparted to it from the very outset.

The aggregate of these reflexes constitutes the foundation of the nervous activity both in men and animals. Consequently, thorough study of all these fundamental nervous reactions of the organism is, of course, a matter of great importance. Unfortunately, as already mentioned, this is a long way from having been accomplished, especially in the case of those reflexes which are called instincts. Our knowledge of these instincts is very limited and fragmentary. We have but a rough classification of them - alimentary, self-defensive, sexual, parental and social. But almost each of these groups often includes numerous separate reflexes, some of which have not been even identified by us, while some are confused with others or, at least, they are not fully appreciated by us as to their vital importance. To what extent this subject remains unelucidated and how full it is still of gaps can be demonstrated by this example from my own experience.

Once, in the course of our experimental work which I shall describe presently, we were puzzled by the peculiar behaviour of our animal. This was a tractable dog with which we were on very friendly terms. The dog was given a rather easy assignment. It was placed in the stand and had its movements restricted only by soft loops fastened round its leys (to which at first it did not react at all). Nothing else was done except to feed it repeatedly at intervals of several minutes. At first the dog was quiet and ate willingly, but as time went on it became more and more excited: it began to struggle against the surrounding objects, tried to break loose, pawing at the floor, gnawing the supports of the stand, etc. This ceaseless muscular exertion brought on dyspnoea and a continuous secretion of saliva; this persisted for weeks, becoming worse and worse, with the result that the dog was no longer fit for our experimental work. This phenomenon puzzled us for a long time. We advanced many hypotheses as to the possible reason for this unusual behaviour, and although we had by then acquired sufficient knowledge of the behaviour of dogs, our efforts were in vain until it occurred to us that it might be interpreted quite simply - as the manifestation of a freedom reflex, and that the dog would not remain quiet so long as its movements were constrained. We overcame this reflex by means of another - a food reflex, We began to feed the

308 THE MEANING OF LIFE

dog only in the stand. At first it ate sparingly and steadily lost weight, but gradually it began to eat more - until it consumed the whole of its daily ration. At the same time it became quiet during the experiments; the freedom reflex was thus inhibited. It is obvious that the freedom reflex is one of the most important reflexes, or, to use a more general term, reactions of any living being. But this reflex is seldom referred to, as if it were not finally recognised. James does not enumerate it even among the special human reflexes (instincts). Without a reflex protest against restriction of an animal's movements any insignificant obstacle in its way would interfere with the performance of certain of its important functions. As we know, in some animals the freedom reflex is so strong that when placed in captivity they reject food, pine away and die.

Let us turn to another example. There is a reflex which is still insufficiently appreciated and which can be termed the investigatory reflex. I sometimes call it the "What-is-it?" reflex. It also belongs to the fundamental reflexes and is responsible for the fact that given the slightest change in the surrounding world both man and animals immediately orientate their respective receptor organs towards the agent evoking the change. The biological significance of this reflex is enormous. If the animal were not provided with this reaction, its life, one may say, would always hang by a thread. In man this reflex is highly developed, manifesting itself in the form of an inquisitiveness which gives birth to scientific thought, ensuring for us a most reliable and unrestricted orientation in the surrounding world. Still less elucidated and differentiated is the category of negative, inhibitory reflexes (instincts) induced by any strong stimuli, or even by weak but unusual stimuli. So-called animal hypnotism belongs, of course, to this category.

Thus, the fundamental nervous reactions both of man and animals are inborn in the form of reflexes. And I repeat once more that it is highly important to have a complete list of these reflexes and properly to classify them, since, as we shall see later, all the remaining nervous activity of the organism is based on these reflexes.

However, although the reflexes just described constitute the fundamental condition for the safety of the organism in the surrounding nature, they in themselves are not sufficient to ensure a lasting, stable and normal existence for the organism. This is proved by the following experiment, carried out on a dog in which the cerebral hemispheres have been extirpated. Besides the internal reflexes, such a dog retains the fundamental external reflexes. It is attracted by food; it keeps away from destructive stimuli; it displays the investigatory reflex pricking up its ears and lifting its head to sound. It possesses the freedom reflex as well, and strongly resists any attempt at capture. Nevertheless, it is an invalid and would not survive without care. Evidently something vital is missing in its nervous activity. But what? It is impossible not to see that the number of stimulating agents evoking reflex reactions in this dog has decreased considerably, that the stimuli act at a very short distance and are of a very elementary and very general character, being undifferentiated. Hence, the equilibrium of this higher organism with the environment in a wide sphere of its life has also become very elementary, limited and obviously inadequate.

Let us now revert to the simple example with which we began our investigations. When food or some unpalatable substance gets into the mouth of the animal, it evokes a secretion of saliva which moistens, dissolves and chemically alters the food, or in the case of disagreeable substances removes them and cleanses the mouth. This reflex is caused by the physical and chemical properties of the above-mentioned substances when they come in contact with the mucous membrane of the oral cavity. However, a ' similar secretary reaction is produced by the same substances when placed at a distance from the dog and act on it only by appearance and smell. Moreover, even the sight of the vessel from which the dog is fed suffices to evoke salivation, and what is more, this reaction can be produced by the sight of the person who usually brings the food, even by the sound of his footsteps in the next room. All these numerous, distant, complex and delicately differentiated stimuli lose their effect irretrievably when the dog is deprived of the cerebral hemispheres; only the physical and chemical properties of substances, when they come in contact with the mucous membrane of the mouth, retain their effect. Meanwhile, the processing significance of the lost stimuli is, in normal conditions, very great. Dry food immediately encounters plenty of the required liquid; unpalatable substances, which often destroy the mucous membrane of the mouth, are removed from it by a layer of saliva rapidly diluted and so on. But their significance is still greater when they bring into action the motor component of the alimentary reflex, i.e., when the seeking of food is effected.

Here is another important example of the defensive reflex. The strong animals prey on those smaller and weaker, and the latter must inevitably perish if they begin to defend themselves only when the fangs and claws of the enemy are already in their flesh. But the situation is quite different when the defensive reaction arises at the sight and sound of the approaching foe. The weak animal has a chance of escaping by seeking cover or in flight.

What, then, would be our general summing up of this difference in attitude of the normal and of the decorticated animal to the external world? What is the general mechanism of this distinction and what is its basic principle?

It is not difficult to see that in normal conditions the reactions of the organism are evoked not only by those agents of the external world that are essential for the organism, i.e., the agents that bring direct benefit or harm to the organism, but by other countless agents which are merely signals of the first agents, as demonstrated above. It is not the sight and sound of the strong animal which destroy the smaller and weaker animal, but its fangs and its claws. However. the signalling, or to use Sherrington's term, the distant stimuli, although comparatively limited in number, play a part in the afore-mentioned reflexes. The essential feature of the higher nervous activity, with which we shall be concerned and which in the higher animal is probably inherent in the cerebral hemispheres alone, is not only the action of countless signalling stimuli, rather it is the important fact that in certain conditions their physiological action changes.

In the above-mentioned salivary reaction now one particular vessel acted as a signal, now another, now one man, now another - strictly depending on the vessel that contained the food or the unpalatable substances before they were introduced in the dog's mouth, and which person brought and gave them to the dog. This, clearly, makes the machine-like activity of the organism still more precise and perfect. The environment of the animal is so infinitely complex and is so continuously in a state of flux, that the intricate and complete system of the organism has the

310   THE MEANING OF LIFE

chance of becoming equilibrated with the environment only if it is also in a corresponding state of constant flux.

Hence, the fundamental and most general activity of the cerebral hemispheres is signalling, the number of signals being infinite and the signalisation variable.

THE CONFLICTING PSYCHOLOGIES OF LEARNING — A WAY OUT

Clark L. Hull (1935)

First published in *Psychological Review*, *42*, 491-516.

INTRODUCTION

One of the most striking things about the present state of the theory of learning and of psychological theory in general is the wide disagreement among individual psychologists. Perhaps the most impressive single manifestation of the extent of this disagreement is contained in 'Psychologies of 1925' [2] and 'Psychologies of 1930' [3]. In these works we find earnestly defending themselves against a world of enemies, a hormic psychology, an act psychology, a functional psychology, a structural psychology, a Gestalt psychology, a reflexology psychology, a behavioristic psychology, a response psychology, a dynamic psychology, a factor psychology, a psychoanalytical psychology, and a psychology of dialectical materialism -- at least a dozen.

No one need be unduly disturbed by the mere fact of conflict as such; that in itself contains an element of optimism, since it indicates an immense amount of interest and genuine activity which are entirely favorable for the advancement of any science. What disturbs many psychologists who are solicitous for the advancement of the science of psychology is [p. 492] that of which these disagreements are symptomatic. To put the matter in an extreme form: if all of these twelve psychologies should be in specific disagreement on a given point, then at least eleven of them must be wrong, and in such welter of error the twelfth may very well be wrong also; at all events, it is difficult under such circumstances to see how all can be right about everything.

The obvious implication of this general situation has recently called out a timely little book by Grace Adams [4] entitled, 'Psychology: science or superstition?' In this work she points out what we all know only too well -- that among psychologists there is not only a bewilderingly large diversity of opinion, but that we are divided into sects, too many of which show emotional and other signs of religious fervor. This emotionalism and this inability to progress materially toward agreement obviously do not square with the ideals of objectivity and certainty which we associate with scientific investigation; they are, on the other hand, more than a little characteristic of metaphysical and theological controversy. Such a situation leads to the suspicion that we have not yet cast off the unfortunate influences of our early associations with metaphysicians. Somehow we have permitted ourselves to fall into essentially unscientific practices. Surely all

312   THE MEANING OF LIFE

psychologists truly interested in the welfare of psychology as a science, whatever their theoretical bias may be, should cooperate actively to correct this.

But before we can mend a condition we must discover the basis of the difficulty. A clue to this is furnished by the reassuring fact that persisting disagreements among us do not concern to any considerable extent the results of experiment, but are confined almost entirely to matters of theory. It is the thesis of this paper that such a paradoxical disparity between scientific experiment and scientific theory not only ought not to exist but that it need not and actually will not exist if the theory is truly scientific. It will be convenient in approaching this problem first to secure a little perspective by recalling the essential characteristics of some typical scientific procedures. [p. 493]

FOUR TYPICAL SCIENTIFIC PROCEDURES

There are many approaches to the discovery of truth; for our present purposes these may be grouped roughly under four heads. The simplest method of discovery is random observation -- the trusting to chance that some valuable datum may turnup in the course of miscellaneous search and experiment. It is hardly conceivable that there ever will come a time in science when an experimenter will not need to be on the alert for the appearance of significant but unexpected phenomena. A classical example of the occasionally immense significance of such accidentally encountered observations is the discovery of the X-ray.

A second method of very wide and successful application in the search for truth is that sometimes known as systematic exploration. This seems to be the method advocated by Francis Bacon in his 'Novum Organum'. [5] In modern times the discovery of salversan, by Ehrlich, illustrates in a general way this indispensable type of research procedure.

A third method widely employed in scientific investigations is that of the experimental testing of isolated hypotheses. Such isolated hypotheses often come as intuitions or hunches from we know not where; they occasionally appear in the form of prevailing traditions which are as yet inadequately tested by experiment. An example of the latter is the wide-spread belief that tobacco smoking interferes with the learning and thought processes. [6]

A fourth procedure in the discovery of truth, and the one which particularly concerns us here, is found in experiments which are directed by systematic and integrated theory rather than by isolated and vagrant hypotheses. Such systematic theoretical developments are exemplified by relativity theory, chiefly in the hands of Einstein ([7], 299), and by quantum theory [8], in the hands of a large number of individuals including Bohr, Rutherford, Heisenberg, Schrodinger, Dirac, and others. Perhaps the best-known investigation motivated by relativity theory is the astronomical observation whereby [p. 494] it was demonstrated that the image of a star whose light rays had passed close to the sun showed a certain amount of displacement from its true position, conforming both as to direction and amount with deductions made from the theory ([7],370). Possibly one of the most striking recent experiments based on quantum theory is the well-known discovery and isolation of 'heavy' water, at Columbia University a few months ago, by Professor Urev.

Our special concern here is to point out that this fourth type of investigation, in addition to yielding facts of intrinsic importance, has the great virtue of indicating the truth or falsity of the theoretical system from which the phenomena were originally deduced. If the theories of a science really agree with the experimental evidence, and if there is general agreement as to this evidence, there should be a corresponding agreement regarding theory. An examination of the nature of scientific theoretical systems and their relationship to the fourth type of scientific procedure just considered should aid us in coping with the paradox presented by the present unfortunate state of psychological theory. [9]

FOUR ESSENTIALS OF SOUND SCIENTIFIC THEORY

It is agreed on all hands that Isaac Newton's 'Principia' is a classic among systematic theories in science. It starts with eight explicitly stated definitions and three postulates (laws of motion) ([10], pp. 1-13), and from these deduces by a rigorous process of reasoning the complex structure of the system. Many persons who may not be overly familiar with the technical details of classical mathematical physics will be able to understand the essentials of such a system from our knowledge of ordinary Euclidian geometry, which as a systematic structure is substantially similar. In the geometries we have our definitions, our postulates (axioms), and, following these, the remarkable sequence of interrelated and inter- [p. 495] locking theorems which flow so beautifully by deduction from the basic assumptions. In a truly scientific system, however, a considerable number of the theorems must constitute specific hypotheses capable of concrete confirmation or refutation. This was eminently true of Newton's system. For a very longtime the Newtonian physics stood this test, though finally certain important deductions from his postulates failed of confirmation, and it fell. Had Newton's system not been firmly anchored to observable fact, its overthrow would not have been possible and we would presumably be having at the present time emotionally warring camps of Newtonians and Einsteinians. Fortunately, we are spared this spectacle.

To summarize in a formal and systematic manner, it maybe said that for a candidate to be considered as a sound scientific theory it must satisfy four basic criteria. [11]

I. The definitions and postulates of a scientific system should be stated in a clear and unambiguous manner, they should be consistent with one another, and they should be of such a nature that they permit rigorous deductions.

II. The labor of deducing the potential implications of the postulates of the system should be performed with meticulous care and exhibited, preferably step by step and in full detail. It is these deductions which constitute the substance of a system.

III. The significant theorems of a truly scientific system must take the form of specific statements of the outcome of concrete experiments or observations. The

314 THE MEANING OF LIFE

experiments in question may be those which have already been performed, but of particular significance are those which have not previously been carried out or even planned. It is among these latter, especially, that crucial tests of a theoretical system will be found. [*12*] [p. 496]

IV. The theorems so deduced which concern phenomena not already known must be submitted to carefully controlled experiments. The outcome of these critical experiments, as well as of all previous ones, must agree with the corresponding theorems making up the system.

Let us consider briefly some of the more important reasons why a sound scientific system should possess these four characteristics. Consider the first: If the postulates of an alleged system are not stated clearly they can hardly be known to the scientific public which may wish to evaluate the system. Moreover, if the postulates have never been explicitly written out by the sponsor of the system, the chances are high that they are not clear even to him. And, obviously, if the definitions and postulates of a system are not clear to the sponsor of the system, neither he nor anyone else can make specific and definite deductions from them.

Second, deductions must be performed with rigor because only in this way can their implications become known. Obviously, until the implications of the postulates are known they cannot possibly be submitted to experimental test; and unless the deductions are rigorous the experimental test will be futile because it will have no real bearing on the soundness of the postulates. Indeed, without rigorous deductions a would-be system is nothing more than a vague and nebulous point of view.

Third, the deductions must be related specifically to the concrete data of the science in question, since otherwise they cannot be submitted to the absolutely indispensable experimental test. It is here that scientific theory differs (or *should* differ) sharply from metaphysical speculations such as concern ethics and theology. Metaphysics does not permit this continuous check on the validity of the deductions, which largely accounts for the interminable wrangles characteristic of that literature. This criterion accordingly becomes in- [p. 497] valuable in distinguishing psychological metaphysics from scientific psychological theory. By this criterion much of what at present passes as theory in our literature must be regarded as metaphysical, *i.e.*, as essentially unscientific.

Fourth, the labor of setting up the critical experiments designed to verify or refute the theorems thus rigorously deduced from the postulates must be performed thoroughly and impartially because, once more, we shall otherwise lack the indispensable objective test of the truth of the system.

It scarcely needs to be added that there is nothing either radical or new in the above criteria of sound scientific theory; on the contrary, the program is conservative and respectable to an eminent degree. Indeed, it has been accepted in science for at least two hundred years. Our purpose is mainly to urge that we really put into practice what we, with the other sciences, have known for a very long time. This we evidently have not done; otherwise we would not be confronted with the glaring paradox of the wildest confusion in the matter of theory coupled with substantial agreement in the field of experiment.

Is Rigorous Theory In Psychology Possible?

No doubt many will feel that such standards of scientific theory may be suitable for theoretical physics, but that they are quite impossible in psychology, at least for the present. To take such a view is equivalent to holding that we can have no genuinely scientific theory in psychology. This is indeed conceivable, but if so we ought not to pretend to have theories at all. If scientific theories are really impossible in psychology, the quicker we recognize it, the better. There are signs, however, that the beginnings of a genuinely scientific theory of mammalian behavior are already on their way. Extremely promising examples of such achievements in intimately related fields have been published by Crozier [*13*] and by Hecht [*14*]. The recent work of Gulliksen [*15*], in which he presents a genuinely rational equation for the learning curve, as distinguished from an empirically fitted formula, offers promise of a larger development in the field of mammalian learning. [p. 498]

It is probably not accidental that all three of the above studies are essentially mathematical. At present, on the other hand, the superficial appearance of the concepts regarding learning which are current among our theorists does not suggest ready mathematical treatment. And while this condition is probably more apparent than real, it serves to raise the important question as to whether rigorous logical deductions can be made on the basis of such quasi-mathematical concepts as have so far emerged from behavior experiments.

There is reason to believe that a genuinely scientific system may be constructed from such materials, and that the difficulty of making such theoretical constructs is not nearly so great as their rarity might lead one to expect. Obviously, the best evidence for such a belief is actual performance. Accordingly, the following section (pp. 501 *ff*) of this paper is given over to the presentation of a suggested miniature scientific system based on typical quasi-mathematical concepts. This has been developed by means of a form of reasoning analogous to that employed in ordinary geometrical proofs. In it an effort has been made to conform to the criteria laid down above as necessary for a sound theoretical development. It is hoped that it will aid in making clear in some concrete detail the theoretical methodology here being advocated. Let us, accordingly, proceed to the critical examination of this miniature theoretical system in the light of our four formal criteria of what scientific theory should be.

At the beginning (pp. 501 *ff*.) there will be found a series of eleven definitions: of rote series, of the learning of rote series, of excitatory tendency, of inhibitory tendency, of spanning, of actual and of effective strength of excitatory tendencies, of remote excitatory tendency, of trace conditioned reaction, and so on.

Next there appears (p. 503) a Series of explicitly stated postulates: that the remote excitatory tendencies of Ebbinghaus exist; that remote excitatory tendencies of Ebbinghaus possess the same behavior characteristics as do the trace conditioned reflexes of Pavlov (Lepley's hypothesis); that the period of delay of trace conditioned reflexes possesses an [p. 499] inhibition of delay; that

316   THE MEANING OF LIFE

inhibitions are additive; that caffeine retards the accumulation of inhibition; that inhibitions diminish more rapidly with the lapse of time than do related excitatory tendencies, and so on. So much for the first criterion.

There follows (pp. 504 *ff*) a series of eleven theorems derived by a formal process of reasoning from the preceding postulates and definitions. For the most part each step of the reasoning is explicitly stated and the logical source of each is conscientiously given. In this connection it is to be observed that the deduction or proof of each theorem is a complex multiple-link logical construct involving the joint action of numerous principles or postulates, as contrasted with simple syllogistic reasoning where but two premises are employed. Moreover, it is to be noted that the system is an integrated one not only in that all the theorems are derived from the same postulates, but also in that the later theorems are dependent on the earlier ones in the form of a logical hierarchy, very much as in systems of geometry. In the derivation of these eleven theorems an attempt has thus been made to conform to the second criterion of a satisfactory scientific system.

Let us now proceed to the examination of this theorem hierarchy from the point of view of the third and fourth criteria.

The first four theorems, while logically necessary for the derivation of the later ones, do not themselves permit any direct experimental test. It is believed, however, that all of the others are sufficiently concrete and specific to permit definite experimental confirmation or refutation. Consider, for example, Theorem V. In plain language, this states that *the central portion of a rote series is more difficult to memorize than are the two ends*. This is, of course, a fact long known to experimentalists." [16][17] Theorem VI, which states that [p. 500] *the difficulty of learning syllables increases most rapidly at the ends of the series but the rate of increase is less and less as the point of maximum difficulty is approached*, has also long been a laboratory commonplace. [16] Theorem VII states that the reaction times of the syllables of a rote series will be shortest at the ends and progressively longer as the middle is approached; this is a case of a deduction actually made in advance of experiment. Recently, however, the deduction has had experimental confirmation. [18]

Now, let us look at Theorem VIII. This theorem means that syllables in the middles of partially learned series are known better a short time after the termination of practice than they are immediately at the conclusion of practice. It is particularly to be noted that this theorem flies directly in the face of the old and time-honored principle of forgetting; i.e., it demands that performance shall improve instead of deteriorate with the passage of time. When this deduction was first performed our logic seemed to be carrying us into a topsy-turvy world, but our postulates presented us with no alternative; scientific theory is concerned with inflexible logic rather than with predictions based on intuitions or wishes. A year or two after the deduction was made, Ward submitted it to critical experimental test and found the theoretical expectation fully and completely substantiated. [18]

BEHAVIOURISM 317

And so we could go on through Theorems IX and X. It will suffice to say that Theorem IX has recently been experimentally verified by Ward [*18*] after the deduction was made, and that Theorem X states a striking law of economy of learning long known to the literature (18, 375 *ff.*).

Finally we come to Theorem XI. Stripped of technical verbiage, this theorem means that the peak of difficulty in the middle of a rote series when learned by massed practice under the influence of caffeine will be lower than when learned by massed practice in the normal condition. Two or three years after this deduction had been made, the author set up an experiment [p. 501] especially to test it. When the experiment was completed and the data tabulated, it was found that the deduction was not verified -- the peak of difficulty in the middle of the series was a little higher under caffeine than in the control series, where the subjects learned the material in a normal condition [*19*]. Here, then, is a case where a definite deduction has been flatly controverted by fact.

Clearly, where a theory is opposed by a fact, the fact has the right of way. In a situation of this kind something is obviously wrong, presumably with one or more of the postulates involved in the deduction. In this particular case suspicion naturally rests most heavily on Postulate VI. At all events, Theorem XI serves to round out and give a further note of realism to this miniature scientific theoretical system. It is a noteworthy event, in the present status of psychological theory, to have a deduction sufficiently anchored by logic to the postulates of the system that a collision with a stubborn experimental fact shall be able to force a revision of the system. It is reasonably safe to assume that the rarity of such collisions at present is not due to the infallibility of current theoretical constructs. Until our systems become sufficiently clear and definite for this kind of event to be of fairly frequent occurrence, we may well suspect that what passes as theory among us is not really making contact with our experimental facts.

A MINIATURE SCIENTIFIC THEORETICAL SYSTEM BY WAY OF ILLUSTRATION

Definitions

I. A rote series is a number of nonsense syllables presented visually one at a time for constant periods (*e.g.*, three seconds) with only a fraction of a second between exposures. The subject learns to speak each syllable while its predecessor is still in view, the overt immediate stimulus for each overt reaction being the visual stimulus arising from the preceding syllable.

II. A rote series is said to be learned when the subject can correctly anticipate each successive syllable throughout a single repetition.

III. An 'excitatory tendency,' as emanating from a stimulus, is a tendency for a reaction to take place more certainly and, in case it does occur, to do so more vigorously other things equal, soon after the organism has received said stimulus than at other times.

IV. An 'inhibitory tendency' is one which has the capacity to weaken the action potentiality of a concurrent excitatory tendency.

V. A syllable reaction tendency is said to be spanned by a remote excitatory [p. 502] tendency and by the parallel inhibition of delay (Postulate III) when said syllable reaction tendency falls between the stimulus syllable and the response syllable associated with the remote excitatory tendency and the parallel inhibition of delay in question.

VI. The 'actual' strength of In excitatory tendency is that strength it would display for action if uncomplicated by concurrent inhibitory tendencies.

VII. The 'effective' strength of an excitatory tendency is that strength it displays in action under whatever conditions of inhibition may exist at the time.

VIII. A remote excitatory tendency is an excitatory influence, initiated by a syllable as a stimulus, exerted upon any other syllable as a reaction with, the exception of the syllable immediately following the stimulus syllable.

IX. A trace conditioned reaction is an S - R relationship (acquired in isolation by a special conditioning technique) which has the characteristic that an appreciable interval (e.g., sixteen seconds) may elapse between the presentation of the overt stimulus and the taking place of the overt response [20]

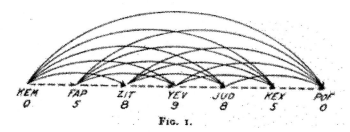

Fig. 1.

Diagrammatic representation of both the immediate and the remote forward excitatory tendencies assumed to be operative in rote series. The straight broken arrows represent immediate excitatory tendencies and the curved solid arrows represent remote excitatory tendencies. The number of remote excitatory tendencies spanning a given syllable, such as ZIT, is given by the formula $(n - 1)(N - n)$ where N is the total number of syllables in the series and n is the ordinal number of the syllable whose span value is under consideration. Thus, in the above example, $N = 7$ and the n for ZIT $=3$. Accordingly, $n - 1 = 2$ and $N - n = 4$. Consequently, ZIT should have a 2 X 4 or 8 remote excitatory tendencies spanning it. The truth of this computation may be verified by counting the number of curved lines immediately above the syllable in question. The number of remote excitatory tendencies spanning the several syllables is given beneath each. [p. 503]

X. 'Massed practice' is a method of learning in which the series is run through from beginning to end almost continuously, i.e., with a pause only of from ten to twenty seconds between successive repetitions.

XI. 'Distributed practice' is a method of learning in which an appreciable interval of time (e.g., one hour or more) is interposed between ,successive repetitions; otherwise it is the some as 'massed practice.'

Postulates

I. Rote series possess functionally potent remote excitatory tendencies extending forward from each syllable of the series as an overt stimulus to every syllable placed later in the series as an overt response except the response syllable immediately following the stimulus syllable. (Ebbinghaus, [21], 106.)

II. The remote excitatory tendencies of Ebbinghaus possess the same characteristics as the trace conditioned reflexes of Pavlov. (Lepley's hypothesis, [22]; [23].)

III. The period of delay of trace conditioned reflexes possesses a power to inhibit(temporarily) to a certain extent the functional strength of excitatory tendencies, the reactions of which would otherwise tend to take place during such period. (Pavlov, [24], 173.)

IV. The inhibition of delay of each succeeding degree of remoteness (distance between overt stimulus and overt response) decreases progressively, each additional increment in remoteness diminishing the inhibition, on the average, by a constant amount. (Assumed by rough analogy to corresponding excitatory tendencies, [21], 106.)

V. Inhibitions of delay operative at the same time summate arithmetically. (Assumed from analogy to excitatory tendencies, [25], 36)

VI. Inhibitions of delay accumulate to a lesser degree when the subject is under the influence of caffeine than do associated excitatory tendencies. (Evans, [26], 365.)VII. When learning is performed by massed practice, the ratio of the actual strength of excitatory tendency to the inhibition of delay is, on the average, constant throughout the learning process, and such as usually to leave a positive effective strength of excitatory tendency. (Assumed as a first approximation.)

VIII. Inhibitory tendencies in the early stages of weakening through the lapse of time diminish more rapidly than do associated excitatory tendencies. (Pavlov, [24],99 and 58 ff.)

320 THE MEANING OF LIFE

IX. A constant minimal strength of excitatory tendency is necessary to make re-call possible even when no concurrent inhibition is present. (Assumed.)X. The total aggregate actual excitatory tendency exerted on a syllable as a reaction tendency is, on the average, a constant for all syllables in a given list at a given time. (Assumed.)

XI. A constant minimal 'effective' strength is required of any given excitatory tendency for it to pass the threshold of overt reaction. (Assumed.)

XII. Under the conditions of rote learning, each repetition of a rote series adds, on the average, a constant positive increment to the actual strength of each excitatory tendency of the series. (Pillsbury, [27], 370)

XIII. The greater the functional or 'effective' strength of the excitatory tendency evoking a reaction, the less, on the average, will be the time elapsing between the stimulus and the reaction. (Simley, [28])

XIV. The 'actual' strength of excitatory tendencies accumulated through repetitions is not influenced by the previous presence of superposed inhibitions of delay. (Assumed.) [p. 504]

Theorems

I

If the number of syllabics in a rote series is N, and the ordinal number of a particular syllables counting from the beginning is n, the syllabic as a reaction tendency will be spanned by $(n-1)$ $(N-n)$ remote excitatory tendencies.

1. It is evident (Postulate I and Fig. I) that a given syllable in a rote series (Definition I) is spanned (Definition V) by remote excitatory tendencies definition VIII) all of which originate in the syllables anterior to itself and which terminate in syllables posterior to itself; *i.e.*, each syllable anterior to a given syllable has a remote excitatory tendency extending to each syllable posterior to said syllable n.

2. Since there are $(n-1)$ syllables anterior to a given syllable and $(N-n)$ syllables posterior to it, it follows from (1) and Postulate 1 that there must be $(n-1)$ $(N-n)$ remote excitatory tendencies spanning any given syllable as a reaction.

II

Within any rote series, the mean degree of remoteness of remote excitatory tendencies spanning a given syllabic is the same for all syllables, viz,

$$\frac{N+1}{2}$$

1. In continuous series the terms of which increase by constant steps, the mean of the series as a whole will be given by the mean of the values appearing at the respective ends of the series.

2. By Postulate 1 (and Fig. 1), the remote excitatory tendencies spanning a given syllable and originating in a particular syllable, satisfy the conditions of (1).

3. Take any syllable, n, of a rote series. It is evident (Fig. 1 and Postulate 1) that those remote excitatory tendencies originating in syllable 1 and which span syllables must have as their greatest length the distance in intervals from the last syllable of the series to the first syllable of the series, *i.e.*, N - *1* intervals, and for their shortest value the distance in intervals from syllable 1 to syllable $n+1$, *i.e.*, $n+$ 1 - 1, or simply n intervals.

4. From (1), (2), and (3) it follows that the remote excitatory tendencies of the set emanating from syllable 1 have as their mean that of N - 1 and n, or

$$\frac{N+n-1}{2} \, .$$

5. It is evident also (Postulate 1 and Fig. 1), that the excitatory tendencies of the set emanating from the second syllable must all be one step less in distance than those emanating from syllable 1, *i.e.*, that their mean value must be

$$\frac{N+n-1}{2} - 1 \; ;$$

    that the mean of those emanating from syllable 3 must be

$$\frac{N+n-1}{2} - 2 \, ,$$

    and so on, the amount subtracted from the fraction in the case of the mean of the last set being one less than the total number of sets.

6. But by (2) of Theorem 1, the number of such sets is n - 1. It follows from (5) that the value subtracted from the fraction which appears in the formula representing the mean of the last set must be $(n$ - 1$)$ - 1, or n - 2.

7. From (4), (5) and (6), the final mean of the series must be

322   THE MEANING OF LIFE

$$\frac{N + n - 1}{2} - (n - 2).$$

But by (5) and (6) the means of the several series constitute a continuous series exhibiting constant step intervals. Therefore, by (1), the mean of these means must be given by the mean of the first and last means of the series. [p. 505]

8. By (5), (6), and (7), the mean extent of the series of means must be

$$\frac{\dfrac{N + n - 1}{2} + \dfrac{N + n - 1}{2} - (n - 2)}{2}$$

which becomes

$$\frac{N + n - 1 + N + n - 1 - 2n + 4}{4}$$

The n's disappear, leaving

$$\frac{2N + 2}{4} \quad \text{or} \quad \frac{N + 1}{2}.$$

9. But since by assumption n was any syllable, it follows from (7) that the mean length of remote excitatory tendencies spanning any syllable is like that of all the others, viz.,

$$\frac{N + 1}{2}$$

III

The total inhibition of delay operative at any given syllable position is measured by the number of remote excitatory tendencies spanning that syllable position.

1. By Postulates II and III and Definition IX, the intervals of delay of remote excitatory tendencies are the loci of inhibitions of delay.

2. By Postulate IV, the magnitude of these inhibitions of delay is a decreasing linear function of the degree of remoteness of the excitatory tendency in question.

BEHAVIOURISM 323

3. It follows from (1) and (2) and Theorem II that the mean magnitude of inhibition (Definition IV) effective at any given syllable position in the series must be like that of all other syllable positions.

4. But if the mean inhibition of delay at all syllable positions is the same, it follows that the total inhibition at any given syllable position must be strictly proportional to the number of remote excitatory tendencies spanning that syllable position.

5. From (4) and Postulate V the theorem follows.

IV

The number of repetitions required for mastery of any particular syllabic of a rote series is $T + Ri$, (where T is a constant representing the number of repetitions required to produce learning when no inhibition is present, and Ri is a linear function of the number of spannings, *i.e.* of $(n - 1) (N - n)$.

1. By Postulates IX and XII and Definition II, a finite basic number of repetitions, T, will be required to produce the strength of excitatory tendency (Definition III) necessary to evoke reaction when there is no inhibition present.

2. By Postulate X and Definition VI, T must be a constant throughout any given rote series.

3. By Postulates XI and XII and Definitions IV and VII, there must be added to the threshold constant, T, certain repetitions to overcome any inhibitions present.

4. By Postulates V and XII, the number of repetitions at a given syllable will be a direct linear function of the aggregate inhibition at that syllable.

5. By (4) and Theorem III, the number of repetitions required to override the inhibition at any point within a given series must be a linear function of the value $(n - 1) (N - n)$.

6. From (2) and (5) it follows that the number of repetitions required for mastery of a rote series at any given point must be the sum of those required to pass the thres- [p. 506] hold of recall, T, plus those required to overcome the adverse influence of inhibition,$(n - 1) (N - n)$, *i.e.*, it must be $T + Ri$ where the latter is a linear function of $(n - 1) (N - n)$.

V

The number of repetitions required for mastery of the individual syllables of a role series is greater in the central region of the series than at either end, the position of maximum difficulty falling at point

324 THE MEANING OF LIFE

$$\frac{N+1}{2}.$$

1. Since, by Theorem IV, T in the expression $T + $ Ri is a constant, it follows that the variability in the number of repetitions required for the mastery of the several portions of a rote series will be a direct linear function of $(n - 1) (N - n)$ only, since Ri is a linear function of $(n - 1) (N - n)$.

2. If, now, we substitute in this formula the successive ordinal values at the beginning of any tote series, taking the length of the series at any convenient value such as N =9, we have,

> Syllable number (n), 1 2 3 4 5 6 7 8 9
> Unite of repetition to learn, o 7 12 15 16 15 12 7 o

It may be seen by on inspection of the series of values in (2) that the number of repetitions required for mastery increases continuously from the ends toward the middle of the easier, the maximum falling at point 5, which may be expressed by

$$\frac{N+1}{2}.$$

Thus we have a concrete demonstration of the truth of the theorem for a particular series. [_29_]

VI

The rate of increase in the number of repetitions required for mastery in a rote series progressively diminishes as the point of maximum difficulty is approached from either end,

1. Taking any convenient length of series such as one of eight syllables (N = 8), [p. 507] we have by Theorem IV the formula $T + $ Ri, remembering that T is constant and Ri is a linear function of $(n - 1) (N - n)$.

> Syllable number (n), 1 2 3 4 5 6 7 8
> Units of repetition to learn, 0 6 10 12 12 10 6 0

2. Here it may be seen that the units of repetition required for mastery increase by 6 points from syllable 1 to syllable 2, by 4 points from syllable 2 to syllable 3, and by 2 points from syllable 3 to syllable q; *i.e.*, the rate of increase in difficulty progressively diminishes as the middle is approached.

3. A corresponding inspection reveals the same type of progression from the posterior end of the series as point

$$\frac{N+1}{2}$$

is approached.

4. (1), (2), and (3) constitute a concrete demonstration of the truth of the theorem for a particular series. [30]

VII

The reaction times of the syllables of a rote series learned by massed practice will be shortest at the end positions and progressively longer the farther the syllable from the end of the series.

1. By Theorem V, syllables require an increasing number of repetitions to learn as the point of maximal difficulty of the series is approached from either end.

2. From (I) and Postulates XI and XII and Definition VII, it follows that the syllables near the ends of the series will rise above the threshold of recall progressively earlier than the syllables farther from the ends. [p. 508]

3. From (2), Definition I, and Postulate XII, it follows that the syllables near the ends of the series will be over learned more than those at the middle, *i.e.*, they will have progressively stronger effective excitatory tendencies (Definition VII) as their distance from the middle of the series increases.

4. By (3) and Postulate XIII the theorem follows.

VIII

In rote series learned to a variable but incomplete degree by massed practice, the number of successful reactions in the middle portion of the series will be greater after a certain period of no practice than at once after the conclusion of learning.

1. By Theorems I and III and Postulate VII, it follows that throughout the learning of rote series where the learning is performed by massed practice there will be variable but finite amounts of inhibition operative on the excitatory tendencies of syllables in the interior of series, *i.e.*, upon all but the two end syllables.

2. By Definition IV, this will depress the effective reactive capacity of such excitatory tendencies (Definition VII) below their actual values.

326 THE MEANING OF LIFE

3. But, by Postulate VIII, inhibitions at first diminish more rapidly during the passage of time than do the associated excitatory tendencies.

4. By (3), during a given interval of no practice the inhibitory tendency will decrease by a finite amount.

5. It follows from (2) and (3) and Postulate XIV that in the early stages of a period of no practice following the learning of a rote series, the effective excitatory strengths of the interior syllables as reaction tendencies will be greater by finite amounts than at the conclusion of learning.

6. From (5) it follows that all syllables as reaction tendencies whose excitatory strengths are above the reaction threshold at the conclusion of incomplete learning will remain above after the period of no practice.

7. Since the degree of learning before interruption varies from one series to another (as here assumed), it follows that of those reaction tendencies which are below the threshold of recall some will differ from the threshold by an amount less than the finite amount indicated in (4).

8. From (3) and (7) it follows that certain syllables which are below the threshold of recall at the conclusion of incomplete learning will be above it at the conclusion of an optimal interval early in the period of no practice.

9. The group of effective reaction tendencies above the threshold at the conclusion of learning (6) added to the group which pass the threshold after an optimal interval of no practice (8) will make a sum larger than the former alone, from which the theorem follows.

IX

In just barely learned role series the reaction time of syllables in the interior of the series will be shorter after an optimal period of no practice than for the corresponding individual syllables at the conclusion of learning by massed practice.

1. By reasoning analogous to that of (1), (2), (3), and (4) Of the proof for TheoremVIII, it follows that the effective excitatory strength of just-learned syllables in the middle of rote series will be greater at some point early in the period of no practice than at the conclusion of learning by massed practice (Definition X).

2. By (1) and Postulate XIII, this increased excitatory strength will be accompanied by shortened reaction time, from which the theorem follows. [p. 509]

X

Rote series will be learned with fewer repetitions by distributed practice than by massed practice.

1. By Theorems II, III, and IV, the most difficult syllables to memorize of a rote series are loaded with inhibitions of delay.

2. By Definition XI, the method of distributed practice involves appreciable periods of time between repetitions. By Postulate VIII these time intervals, if not too long, will dissipate the inhibition more rapidly than the associated excitatory tendency. It follows that for a given amount of training the method of distributed practice will yield relatively less accumulated inhibition than by massed practice.

3. From (2) it follows (Postulates XI and XII) that the method of distributed repetitions will bring the most difficult syllable above the threshold of recall with fewer repetitions than will be the case by the method of massed repetitions.

4. But, by Definitions I and III, the number of repetitions required to learn rote series is that required to learn the most difficult single syllable.

5. By (3) and (4)1 the theorem follows.

XI

The value obtained by dividing the number of repetitions required to bring syllables above the threshold at the ends of role series, by the number required in the middle of the same series, will be larger when the learning is done under the influence of caffeine than when done in the normal condition, the learning in both cases to be performed by massed practice.

1. By Theorem V, the middles of rote series learned by massed practice require more repetitions for learning than do the ends.

2. From (1) it follows that the number of repetitions per syllable for learning at the ends divided by the number at the middle Re/Rm will yield a value less than 1.

3. Now, by Postulate VI, inhibitions accumulate to a lesser degree, other things equal, when the learning is performed under the influence of caffeine. It follows from this and Theorems II and III that less inhibition will accumulate in the middle of the series in question when learning is performed under the influence of caffeine.

4. By (3), Definition IV, and Postulate XII, it follows that the middle syllables will be learned with less repetitions under caffeine than in the normal condition, i.e., that Rm will be smaller than normal. Since caffeine has no such influence on syllables not inhibited, Re will remain the same.

5. But to reduce Rm in the division Re/Rm will increase the resulting values.

328 THE MEANING OF LIFE

6. From (5) the theorem follows.

SOME PROBLEMS CONNECTED WITH
THE EVALUATION OF PSYCHOLOGICAL THEORY

The recognized principles of science, then, provide us with a method which seems capable of bringing some kind of order out of the present chaos in theoretical psychology. Moreover, the program appears to be one to which all theorists, however diverse their postulates provided they are not essentially metaphysical or mystical, may subscribe. Indeed, it seems to be so firmly rooted in the traditions and essential logic [p. 510] of science that all would-be theoretical work will ultimately come to be judged by the scientific public according to this standard, regardless of the views of the theorists themselves. This brings us to the consideration of certain concrete problems which arise when an attempt is made to evaluate the claims of competing theoretical systems.

In the first place, it should be obvious that all mere systems of classification must be rejected. A dictionary may be systematic, but it can hardly be rated as a theoretical system even when the terms are largely of new coinage. Merely to call a bit of learning behavior a case of 'closure' or 'insight' on the one hand, or a case of 'conditioning' or 'trial-and-error' on the other, will not serve. Such systems cannot pass even the first criterion. [*31*]

Next we must consider the nature of the concepts and postulates which are admissible as the basis for psychological theory. Some psychologists appear to have assumed that only principles incapable of direct observational verification [*32*] should be admitted as postulates, whereas others may conceivably have assumed that only principles capable of direct observational verification should be admitted. In a similar manner, one group of theorists may insist that the postulates from which psychological systems evolve must be concerned with *parts*, while another group may insist that they must concern *wholes*. One group of theorists may insist that the postulates must come solely from conditioned reflex experiments, whereas to another group such postulates might not be at all acceptable. [p. 511]

From the present point of view this argument is quite footless. Actually, all such groups beg the main question. The question at issue is: Can more theorems which will be confirmed in the laboratory be deduced from postulates which are principles of dynamics, or more from postulates which are principles of mechanics, or more from a combination of both types of postulates; can more sound theorems be deduced from postulated parts, or more from postulated wholes, or more from a combination of the two? These are matters which should properly await the outcome of trial; it is conceivable that numerous distinct sets of postulates may prove more or less successful.

The history of scientific practice so far shows that, in the main, the credentials of scientific postulates have consisted in what the postulates can do, rather than in some metaphysical quibble about where they came from. If a set of postulates is really bad it will sooner or later get its user into trouble with experimental results. On the other hand, no matter how bad it looks at first, if a set of postulates consistently yields valid deductions of laboratory results, it *must* be good. [*33*] In a word, a complete *laissez-faire* policy should obtain in regard to postulates. Let the psychological theorist begin with neurological postulates, or stimulus-response postulates, or structural postulates, or functional postulates, or factor postulates, or organismic postulates, or Gestalt postulates, or sign-Gestalt postulates, or hormonic postulates, or mechanistic postulates, or dynamic postulates, or postulates concerned with the nature of consciousness, or the postulates of dialectical materialism, and no questions should be asked about his beginning save those of consistency and the principle of parsimony.

Third, we must be extremely careful to insure the rigor of our deductions. Perhaps the most common fallacy in current would-be theories is the *non sequitur* -- the supposed conclusion simply does not follow from the postulates. [p. 512]

In particular we must be on our guard against might be called the 'anthropomorphic fallacy. By this is meant deduction the critical point of which turns out to be an implicit statement which, if made explicit, would be something like, "If I were a rat and were in that situation I would do so and so." Such elements in a deduction make it a travesty because the very problem at issue is whether a system is able to deduce from its postulates alone what a normal man (or rat) would do under particular conditions. It is this fallacy which justifies the inveterate aversion of scientists for anthropomorphism. It is true that as a practical guide to the expectation of what a rat, or an ape, or a child, or another man will actually do in an as yet untried situation such an approach is, of course, of value and should be used. But predictions arrived at in such a way are of no value as scientific theory because a truly scientific theory seeks to deduce what anthropomorphism reaches by intuition or by naive assumption. Prophecies as to the outcome of untried experiments based merely on such anthropomorphic intuitions should be credited to the institutional genius of the prophet rather than to the theoretical system to which the prophet may adhere. Predictions, however successful, can have no evidential value as to the credibility of the prophet's system until he is willing and able to exhibit the logic by which his predictions flow from the postulates of that system, and until this logic is really rigorous, until it consists of something more than the feeble *non-sequiturs* too often presented in our literature as scientific explanations.

SUMMARY AND CONCLUSIONS

Scientific theory in its best sense consists of the strict logical deduction from definite postulates of what should be observed under specified conditions. [*35*] If the deductions are lacking or are logically invalid, there is no theory; if the deductions involve conditions of observation which are impossible of attainment, the theory is metaphysical rather than scientific; and if the deduced phenomenon is not observed [p. 513] when the conditions are fulfilled, the theory is false. Classifications of the phenomena of a science may have distinct expository and pedagogical convenience, but convenience cannot be said to be true or false. Points of view in science may possess the virtue of fertility by suggesting new directions of investigations, but neither can fertility be said to be true or false. On the other hand, truly scientific theory, from its very nature, must permit the observational determination of its truth or falsity.

It is believed that upon the above conceptions of scientific theory may be based a robust hope of bringing order out of our present theoretical chaos. It is conceivable, of course, that more

330   THE MEANING OF LIFE

than one scientific system may be able to deduce the major phenomena of learning. However, the history of scientific theory has shown that successful duplicate explanations of the same natural phenomena have usually turned out to be at bottom the same. Accordingly, we may expect that when we have put our scientific house in order there will be little more disagreement in the field of theory than in the field of experiment, and presumably such disagreements as appear will prove to be but temporary.

Assuming both the possibility and the desirability of such an outcome, the question arises as to how it can most promptly be achieved. First, it is believed that the thing most urgently needed at the present moment is a clear statement of postulates with accompanying definitions of terms. Second, these postulates should be followed by the step-by-step deduction of the theorems making up the body of the system. No doubt the meticulous presentation of the logic behind the theorems of a system may at first strike certain readers as pedantic. Moreover, it is an unfortunate fact that for per-sons untrained in a particular system, the more rigorous the logic the more difficult it becomes to comprehend. It is encouraging, however, to note that difficulty of comprehension by the tyro has not prevented the development of mathematical theory in the older sciences, and with them rigor of deduction has not usually been regarded as pedantry. A number of indications point to a considerable development [p. 514] of this kind of theoretical work in psychology within the immediate future.

As this development proceeds, we may anticipate that those systems or points of view which are unable to satisfy the postulational requirements of truly scientific theory will come to be known for what they are, and will lose adherents. The proponents of other points of view may be expected gradually to clarify their basic postulates and from these to evolve systems of rigorously proved theorems. Of this latter group of systems, presumably, it will be found impossible to apply the experimental check to the theorems of some because the systems in question either do not specify clearly the conditions under which phenomena should occur or else they are not clear as to exactly what phenomena are to be expected. Some systems, on the other hand, will doubtless succeed in making genuine contact with experimental facts. Of these, some will probably present such a high proportion of experimental non-confirmations that the confirmations actually observed maybe attributable to mere chance.

Finally, let us hope, there will survive a limited number of systems which show a degree of successes appreciably in excess of what chance would produce. Occasionally, in such cases, a failure of a theorem to agree with experimental observation may be accounted for plausibly on the basis of a known and recognized factor operating in such a way as to over-ride the action represented by the theorem. Unless this can be done, however, the postulates of the system must be revised until they yield theorems agreeing with both the new and the old facts, after which there will be made new deductions which will be checked against new experiments, and so on in recurring cycles. Thus theoretical truth is not absolute, but relative.

It seems likely that as the process of theoretical development goes on the surviving systems will show two fairly distinct types of relationship. First, there will be systems which attempt explanations on different levels such as the perceptual level, the stimulus-response level, the neuro-anatomical level, and the neuro-physiological level. It is conceivable that each [p. 515] might develop a perfect system on its own level. In that case each lower level should be able to deduce the relevant basic postulates of the system above it in the hierarchy of systems. Here, of course, would be supplementation rather than conflict.

Second, there may be some systems which attempt explanation at the same level. However diverse such systems may appear at the beginning, they may be expected gradually to display an essential identity as they go through successive revisions, the differences at length consisting in nothing but the terms employed. Those systems which concern different but related aspects of learning, by the process of expansion, will finally come to overlap. This overlapping will convert them into approximately the same status as the groups just mentioned, and a gradually approached outcome of substantial agreement may similarly be anticipated. Thus systems may expand by a process of integration.

Finally, sound scientific theory has usually led not only to prediction but to control; abstract principles in the long run have led to concrete application. With powerful deductive instruments at our disposal we should be able to predict the outcome of learning not only under untried laboratory conditions, but under as yet untried conditions of practical education. We should be able not only to predict what rats will do in a maze under as yet untried circumstances, but what a man will do under the complex conditions of everyday life. In short, the attainment of a genuinely scientific theory of mammalian behavior offers the promise of development in the understanding and control of human conduct in its immensely varied aspects which will be comparable to the control already achieved over inanimate nature, and of which the modern world is in such dire need.

Footnotes

[1] The substance of this paper was read as a portion of the symposium on 'Psychological theories of learning,' at the Pittsburgh meeting of the A. A. A. S., December 28, 1934.
The writer is indebted to Dr. Robert T. Ross for the material appearing in notes 7 and 8. Dr. Ross has also read and criticized the entire manuscript. Professor Max Wertheimer and Dr. George Katona also read and criticized an early form of the manuscript.

[2] Murchison, C., (Editor), Psychologies of 1925, Worcester: Clark University Press, 1925.

[3] [Murchison, C.,] Psychologies of 1934 Worcester: Clark University Press, 1925.

[4] Adams, G., Psychology: science or superstition?, New York; Covici Friede, 1931.

[5] Bacon, F., Advancement of learning and novurn organum, Revised edition, Colonial Press, 1900.

[6] Hull, C. L., The influence of tobacco smoking on mental and motor efficiency, Psychol. Monog., 1924, 33, No. 150.

[7] Haas, A., Introduction to theoretical physics, Vol. II (trans. from the 3rd and 4th editions by T. Verschoyle), London: Constable and Co., 1925.

[8] Reiche, F., The quantum theory (trans. by H. S. Hatfield and H. L. Prose), N. Y.: E. P. Dutton and Co., 1930.

[9] This emphasis on the fourth type of experimental approach is not to be understood as an advocacy of it as an exclusive method in psychology; neither is it being urged that theoretical considerations are paramount. Many approaches are necessary to produce a well-rounded science. Some temperaments will prefer one approach, some another, thus leading to a useful division of labor.

332 THE MEANING OF LIFE

[10] Newton, Issac, Mathematical principles (Trans. by F. Cajori), Univ. of California Press, 1934.

[11] As the reader examines these items it might be illuminating for him to consider the particular theoretical system which is his special aversion, and judge whether or not it passes each successive criterion. After having thus fortified himself, he might proceed cautiously to a similar examination of the system which he favors.

[12] For this reason it is especially desirable for the advancement of science that the proponents of theoretical systems publish the deductions of the outcome of as yet untried experiments. The failure of subsequent experimental verification of such deductions should not be regarded as in any way discrediting the author. Instead, it should be considered merely a normal incident in the evolution of science. Fortunately, in such situations it is the hypothesis which is on trial, not the proponent's reputation as a seer.

[13] Crozier, W. J., Chemoreception, from A handbook of general experimental psychology, edited by Carl Murchison, Worcester: Clark University Press, 1934.

[14] Hecht, S., Vision: II. The nature of the photoreceptor process, from A handbook of general experimental psychology, edited by Carl Murchison, Worcester: Clark University Press, 1934.

[15] Gulliksen, H. A., A rational equation of the learning curve based on Thorndike's law, J. *General Psychol.*, 1934, 395-434.

[16] Robinson, E. S., and Brown, M. A., Effect of serial position on memorization, *Amer. J. Psychol.*, 37, 538-552.

[17] It is to be noted, however, that while the general picture of series difficulty as shown by experiment agrees with the theorem, there is disagreement in detail. The theorem demands that the maximum difficulty appear in the exact center of the series, whereas it actually appears a little posterior to the center. This, of course, reflects an inadequacy in the theory and calls for a revision of postulates. This systematic reconstruction has already gone far enough to correct the difficulty here considered. This may serve as an example of the successive-approximation procedure characteristic of theoretical development in science. The revised construct will be given in connection with a full statement of the system to be contained in a contemplated publication.

[18] Ward, L. B., Retention over short intervals of time, Thesis presented for the degree of Doctor of Philosophy, Yale University, 1934 (On file in the Yale University Library).

[19] [Hull, C. L.] The influence of caffeine and other factors on the phenomena of rote learning. *General Psychol.*, 1935, 13, 249-274.

[20] What is spoken of as the 'overt' stimulus of a trace conditioned reaction is not regarded as the 'actual' stimulus. The 'overt' stimulus is supposed to set in motion some kind of slowly changing internal sequence more or less characteristic of each such stimulus. It is the stimulus value of the phase of this sequence immediately preceding the reinforcing stimulus which is regarded as the 'actual' stimulus of the trace conditioned reaction. It thus comes about that the stimulus of POF (Fig. I) is compounded of 6 elements from as many different sources, whereas that of FAP arises from a single source. But, so far as is now known, the ease of conditioning is not influenced by the complexity of the stimulus, so that the 'actual' strength of the excitatory tendencies to the arousal of POF and FAP should be alike so far as this factor is concerned. This means, necessarily, that the *immediate* excitatory tendency from KEX to POF must be appreciably weaker than that from KEM to FAP or even from ZIT to YEV. This last deduction is obviously capable of experimental test.

[21] Ebbinghaus, H. Memory (trans. by H. A. Ruger and C. E. Bussenius), N. Y.: Teachers College, Columbia University, 1913.

[22] Lepley, W. M., A theory of serial learning and forgetting based upon conditioned reflex principles, *Psychol. REV.*, 1932, so, 279-288.

[23] [Lepley, W. M.] Serial reactions considered as conditioned reactions, *Psychol. Monog.*, 1934. No. 205.

[24] Pavlov, I. P., Conditioned reflexes (trans. by G. V. Anrep), Oxford University Press, 1927.

[25] Sherrington, C. S., The integrative action of the nervous system, New Haven: Yale University Press, 1906.

[26] Evans, C. LA, Recent advances in physiology, Phila.: P. Blakiston's Son and Co., 1926.

[27] Pillsbury, WA BA, The fundamentals of psychology, N. Y.: Macmillan, 1927.

[28] Simley, O. H., The relation of subliminal to supraliminal learning, *Arch. Psychol.*, 1933, No. 146.

[29] A deduction of the essential portion of this theorem is yielded by the calculus

$$R_1 = a + m(n-1)(N-n)$$

Expanding we have,

$$R_I = a - m[+n^2 + n(N+1) - N]$$

Differentiating with respect to

$$\frac{dR_I}{dn} = m[-2n + (N+1)]$$

at the maximum,

$$\frac{dR_I}{dn} = 0$$

whence

$$-2n + (N+1) = 0$$

and solving for n we have,

$$n = \frac{N+1}{2}$$

therefore, the position of maximum difficulty falls at the point

$$\frac{N+1}{2}$$

[30] A deduction of the essential portion of this theorem is yielded by the calculus (see note to Theorem V):
It follows from

$$\frac{dR_I}{dn} = m[-2n + (N+1)]$$

(where m is positive)

that

$$\frac{d^2 R_I}{dn^2} = -2m$$

whence if

$$n < \frac{N+1}{2}$$

$$\frac{dR_I}{dn} \text{ is positive}$$

$$\frac{d^2 R_I}{dn^2} \text{ is negative}$$

whence, the curve increases toward the right with decreasing slope

334 THE MEANING OF LIFE

$$\frac{dR_1}{dn} \text{ is negative}$$

$$\frac{d^2 R_1}{dn^2} \text{ is positive}$$

whence, the curve decreases toward the right with increasing (negative) slope.

[31] It appears to be at this point that most current attempts in the field of psychological theory break down. Their concepts appear not to be of such a nature that significant theorems may be drawn from them by a rigorous logic. A theoretical system without proven theorems is a paradox, to say the least.

[32] The postulates of a system may be susceptible of two types of verification -- one indirect and the other direct. Indirect verification occurs when a deduction from a combination of postulates is observationally confirmed. The failure of such a verification throws doubt on the soundness of all of the postulates involved. This particular doubt is removed when appropriate change is made in one or more of these postulates so that deductions from them conform not only to the new observations but to all those phenomena previously deduced and verified. All postulates are susceptible of indirect verification, but some postulates permit direct verification and some do not. Postulates regarding the positions and movements of electrons, for example, permit indirect verification but not direct observation.

[33] Consider the Riemannian geometry, which insists that the sum of the angles of a triangle is greater than two right angles ([*34*], 58). This is repugnant to common sense, yet Einstein used the Riemannian geometry as the basis for making the greatest single advance in scientific theory since the time of Newton.

[34] Poincaré, The foundations of science (trans. by G. B. Halsted), The Science Press, 1929.

[35] Truth, for the purposes of the present paper, is to be understood as a theoretical deduction which has been verified by observation

[36] *Classics* editor=s note: The following reference was included in Hull=s Reference list but was not referred to in the text:

Kreuger, W. C. F., Effect of overlearning on retention, *J. Exper. Psychol.*, 1929, 12, 71-78.

[MS. received April 12, 1935]

Psychology as the Behaviorist Views It.

John B. Watson (1913).

First published in *Psychological Review, 20*, 158-177

Psychology as the behaviorist views it is a purely objective experimental branch of natural science. Its theoretical goal is the prediction and control of behavior. *Introspection* forms no essential part of its methods, nor is the scientific value of its data dependent upon the readiness with which they lend themselves to interpretation in terms of consciousness. The behaviorist, in his efforts to get a unitary scheme of animal response, recognizes *no dividing line between man and brute*. The behavior of man, with all of its refinement and complexity, forms only a part of the behaviorist's total scheme of investigation.

It has been maintained by its followers generally that psychology is a study of the science of the phenomena of *consciousness*. It has taken as its problem, on the one hand, the analysis of complex mental states (or processes) into *simple elementary constituents*, and on the other the construction of complex states when the elementary constituents are given. The world of physical objects (stimuli, including here anything which may excite activity in a receptor), which forms the total phenomena of the natural scientist, is looked upon merely as means to an end. That end is the production of mental states that may be 'inspected' or 'observed'. The psychological object of observation in the case of an emotion, for example, is the mental state itself. The problem in emotion is the determination of the number and kind of elementary constituents present, their loci, intensity, order of appearance, etc. It is agreed that introspection is the method *par excellence* by means of which mental states may be manipulated for purposes of psychology. On this assumption, behavior data (including under this term everything which goes under the name of *comparative psychology*) have no value *per se*. They possess significance only in so far as they may throw light upon conscious states.*1* Such data must have at least an analogical or indirect reference to belong to the realm of psychology.

Indeed, at times, one finds psychologists who are sceptical of even this analogical reference. Such scepticism is often shown by the question which is put to the student of behavior, 'what is the bearing of animal work upon human psychology?' I used to have to study over this question. Indeed it always embarrassed me somewhat. I was interested in my own work and felt that it was important, and yet I could not trace any close connection between it and psychology as my questioner understood psychology. I hope that such a confession will clear the atmosphere to such an extent that we will no longer have to work under false pretences. We must frankly admit that the facts so important to us which we have been able to glean from extended work upon the senses of animals by the behavior method have contributed only in a fragmentary way to the general theory of human sense organ processes, nor have they suggested new points of

336 THE MEANING OF LIFE

experimental attack. The enormous number of experiments which we have carried out upon learning have likewise contributed little to human psychology. It seems reasonably clear that some kind of compromise must be affected: either psychology must change its viewpoint so as to take in *facts of behavior*, whether or not they have bearings upon the problems of 'consciousness'; or else behavior must stand alone as a wholly separate and independent science. Should human psychologists fail to look with favor upon our overtures and refuse to modify their position, the behaviorists will be driven to using human beings as subjects and to employ methods of investigation which are exactly comparable to those now employed in the animal work.

Any other hypothesis than that which admits the independent value of behavior material, regardless of any bearing such material may have upon consciousness, will inevitably force us to the *absurd position* of attempting to *construct* the conscious content of the animal whose behavior we have been studying. On this view, after having determined our animal's ability to learn, the simplicity or complexity of its methods of learning, the effect of past habit upon present response, the range of stimuli to which it ordinarily responds, the widened range to which it can respond under experimental conditions -- in more general terms, its various problems and its various ways of solving them -- we should still feel that the task is unfinished and that the results are worthless, until we can interpret them by analogy in the light of consciousness. Although we have solved our problem we feel uneasy and unrestful because of our definition of psychology: we feel forced to say something about the possible mental processes of our animal. We say that, having no eyes, its stream of consciousness cannot contain brightness and color sensations as we know them -- having no taste buds this stream can contain no sensations of sweet, sour, salt and bitter. But on the other hand, since it does respond to thermal, tactual and organic stimuli, its conscious content must be made up largely of these sensations; and we usually add, to protect ourselves against the reproach of being *anthropomorphic*, 'if it has any consciousness'. Surely this doctrine which calls for an anological interpretation of all behavior data may be shown to be false: the position that the standing of an observation upon behavior is determined by its fruitfulness in yielding results which are interpretable only in the narrow realm of (really human) consciousness.

This emphasis upon analogy in psychology has led the behaviorist somewhat afield. Not being willing to throw off the yoke of consciousness he feels impelled to make a place in the scheme of behavior where the rise of consciousness can be determined. This point has been a shifting one. A few years ago certain animals were supposed to possess 'associative memory', while certain others were supposed to lack it. One meets this search for the origin of consciousness under a good many disguises. Some of our texts state that consciousness arises at the moment when reflex and instinctive activities fail properly to conserve the organism. A perfectly adjusted organism would be lacking in consciousness. On the other hand whenever we find the presence of diffuse activity which results in habit formation, we are justified in assuming consciousness. I must confess that these arguments had weight with me when I began the study of behavior. I fear that a good many of us are still viewing behavior problems with something like this in mind. More than one student in behavior has attempted to frame criteria of the *psychic* -- to devise a set of objective, structural and functional criteria which, when applied in the particular instance, will enable us to decide whether such and such responses are positively conscious, merely indicative of consciousness, or whether they are purely 'physiological'. Such problems as these can no longer satisfy behavior men. It would be better to give up the province altogether and admit frankly that the study of the behavior of animals has no justification, than to admit that our search is of such a 'will o' the wisp' character. One can assume either the presence or the absence of consciousness anywhere in the *phylogenetic scale* without affecting the problems of behavior by one jot or one tittle; and without influencing in any way the mode of experimental attack upon them. On the other hand, I cannot for one moment assume that the paramecium responds to light; that the rat learns a problem more quickly by working at the task five times a day than once a day, or that the human child exhibits plateaux in his learning curves. These are questions which vitally concern behavior and which must be decided by direct observation under experimental conditions.

This attempt to reason by analogy from human conscious processes to the conscious processes in animals, and *vice versa*: to make consciousness, as the human being knows it, the center of reference of all behavior, forces us into a situation similar to that which existed in biology in Darwin's time. The whole Darwinian movement was judged by the bearing it had upon the origin and development of the human race. Expeditions were undertaken to collect material which would establish the position that the rise of the human race was a perfectly natural phenomenon and not an act of special creation. Variations were carefully sought along with the evidence for the heaping up effect and the weeding out effect of selection; for in these and the other Darwinian mechanisms were to be found factors sufficiently complex to account for the origin and race differentiation of man. The wealth of material collected at this time was considered valuable largely in so far as it tended to develop the concept of evolution in man. It is strange that this situation should have remained the dominant one in biology for so many years. The moment zoology undertook the experimental study of evolution and descent, the situation immediately changed. Man ceased to be the center of reference. I doubt if any experimental biologist today, unless actually engaged in the problem of race differentiation in man, tries to interpret his findings in terms of human evolution, or ever refers to it in his thinking. He gathers his data from the study of many species of plants and animals and tries to work out the laws of inheritance in the particular type upon which he is conducting experiments. Naturally, he follows the progress of the work upon race differentiation in man and in the descent of man, but he looks upon these as special topics, equal in importance with his own yet ones in which his interests will never be vitally engaged. It is not fair to say that all of his work is directed toward human evolution or that it must be interpreted in terms of human evolution. He does not have to dismiss certain of his facts on the inheritance of coat color in mice because, forsooth, they have little bearing upon the differentiation of the *genus homo* into separate races, or upon the descent of the *genus homo* from some more primitive stock.

In psychology we are still in that stage of development where we feel that we must select our material. We have a general place of discard for processes, which we anathematize so far as their value for psychology is concerned by saying, 'this is a reflex'; 'that is a purely physiological fact

338 THE MEANING OF LIFE

which has nothing to do with psychology'. We are not interested (as psychologists) in getting all of the processes of adjustment which the animal as a whole employs, and in finding how these various responses are associated, and how they fall apart, thus working out a systematic scheme for the prediction and control of response in general. Unless our observed facts are indicative of consciousness, we have no use for them, and unless our apparatus and method are designed to throw such facts into relief, they are thought of in just as disparaging a way. I shall always remember the remark one distinguished psychologist made as he looked over the color apparatus designed for testing the responses of animals to monochromatic light in the attic at Johns Hopkins. It was this: 'And they call this psychology!'

I do not wish unduly to criticize psychology. It has failed signally, I believe, during the fifty-odd years of its existence as an experimental discipline to make its place in the world as an undisputed natural science. Psychology, as it is generally thought of, has something esoteric in its methods. If you fail to reproduce my findings, it is not due to some fault in your apparatus or in the control of your stimulus, but it is due to the fact that your *introspection is untrained.*[2] The attack is made upon the observer and not upon the experimental setting. In physics and in chemistry the attack is made upon the experimental conditions. The apparatus was not sensitive enough, impure chemicals were used, etc. In these sciences a better technique will give reproducible results. Psychology is otherwise. if you can't observe 3-9 states of clearness in attention, your introspection is poor. if, on the other hand, a feeling seems reasonably clear to you, your introspection is again faulty. You are seeing too much. Feelings are never clear.

The time seems to have come when psychology must discard all reference to consciousness; when it need no longer delude itself into thinking that it is making mental states the object of observation. We have become so enmeshed in speculative questions concerning the elements of mind, the nature of conscious content (for example, *imageless thought*, attitudes, and *Bewusstseinslage*, etc.) that I, as an experimental student, feel that something is wrong with our premises and the types of problems which develop from them. There is no longer any guarantee that we all mean the same thing when we use the terms now current in psychology. Take the case of sensation. A sensation is defined in terms of its attributes. One psychologist will state with readiness that the attributes of a visual sensation are *quality, extension, duration, and intensity.* Another will add *clearness.* Still another that of *order.* I doubt if any one psychologist can draw up a set of statements describing what he means by sensation which will be agreed to by three other psychologists of *different training.* Turn for a moment to the question of the number of isolable sensations. Is there an extremely large number of color sensations -- or only four, red, green, yellow and blue? Again, yellow, while psychologically simple, can be obtained by superimposing red and green spectral rays upon the same diffusing surface! If, on the other hand, we say that every just noticeable difference in the spectrum is a simple sensation, and that every just noticeable increase in the white value of a given colour gives simple sensations, we are forced to admit that the number is so large and the conditions for obtaining them so complex that the concept of sensation is unusable, either for the purpose of analysis or that of synthesis. *Titchener*, who has fought the most valiant fight in this country for a psychology based upon

BEHAVIOURISM 339

introspection, feels that these differences of opinion as to the number of sensations and their attributes; as to whether there are relations (in the sense of elements) and on the many others which seem to be fundamental in every attempt at analysis, are perfectly natural in the present undeveloped state of psychology. While it is admitted that every growing science is full of unanswered questions, surely only those who are wedded to the system as we now have it, who have fought and suffered for it, can confidently believe that there will ever be any greater uniformity than there is now in the answers we have to such questions. I firmly believe that two hundred years from now, unless the introspective method is discarded, psychology will still be divided on the question as to whether auditory sensations have the quality of 'extension', whether intensity is an attribute which can be applied to color, whether there is a difference in 'texture' between image and sensation and upon many hundreds of others of like character.

The condition in regard to other mental processes is just as chaotic. Can image type be experimentally tested and verified? Are recondite thought processes dependent mechanically upon imagery at all? Are psychologists agreed upon what feeling is? One states that feelings are attitudes. Another finds them to be groups of organic sensations possessing a certain solidarity. Still another and larger group finds them to be new elements correlative with and ranking equally with sensations.

My psychological quarrel is not with the systematic and structural psychologist alone. The last fifteen years have seen the growth of what is called *functional psychology*. This type of psychology decries the use of elements in the static sense of the structuralists. It throws emphasis upon the biological significance of conscious processes instead of upon the analysis of conscious states into introspectively isolable elements. I have done my best to understand the difference between functional psychology and structural psychology. Instead of clarity, confusion grows upon me. The terms sensation, perception, affection, emotion, volition are used as much by the functionalist as by the structuralist. The addition of the word 'process' ('mental act as a whole', and like terms are frequently met) after each serves in some way to remove the corpse of ccontent' and to leave 'function' in its stead. Surely if these concepts are elusive when looked at from a content standpoint, they are still more deceptive when viewed from the angle of function, and especially so when function is obtained by the introspection method. It is rather interesting that no functional psychologist has carefully distinguished between 'perception' (and this is true of the other psychological terms as well) as employed by the systematist, and cperceptual process' as used in functional psychology. It seems illogical and hardly fair to criticize the psychology which the systematist gives us, and then to utilize his terms without carefully showing the changes in meaning which are to be attached to them. I was greatly surprised some time ago when I opened Pillsbury's book and saw psychology defined as the 'science of behavior'. A still more recent text states that psychology is the 'science of mental behavior'. When I saw these promising statements I thought, now surely we will have texts based upon different lines. After a few pages the science of behavior is dropped and one finds the conventional treatment of sensation, perception, imagery, etc., along with certain shifts in emphasis and additional facts which serve to give the author's personal imprint.

340 THE MEANING OF LIFE

One of the difficulties in the way of a consistent functional psychology is the *parallelistic hypothesis*. If the functionalist attempts to express his formulations in terms which make mental states really appear to function, to play some active role in the world of adjustment, he almost inevitably lapses into terms which are connotative of *interaction*. When taxed with this he replies that it is more convenient to do so and that he does it to avoid the circumlocution and clumsiness which are inherent in any thoroughgoing parallelism.*3* As a matter of fact I believe the functionalist actually thinks in terms of interaction and resorts to parallelism only when forced to give expression to his views. I feel that *behaviorism* is the only consistent and logical functionalism. In it one avoids both the Scylla of parallelism and the Charybdis of interaction. Those time-honored relics of philosophical speculation need trouble the student of behavior as little as they trouble the student of physics. The consideration of the mind-body problem affects neither the type of problem selected nor the formulation of the solution of that problem. I can state my position here no better than by saying that I should like to bring my students up in the same ignorance of such hypotheses as one finds among the students of other branches of science.

This leads me to the point where I should like to make the argument constructive. I believe we can write a psychology, define it as Pillsbury, and never go back upon our definition: never use the terms consciousness, mental states, mind, content, introspectively verifiable, imagery, and the like. I believe that we can do it in a few years without running into the absurd terminology of Beer, Bethe, Von Uexküll, Nuel, and that of the so-called objective schools generally. It can be done in terms of stimulus and response, in terms of habit formation, habit integrations and the like. Furthermore, I believe that it is really worth while to make this attempt now.

The psychology which I should attempt to build up would take as a starting point, first, the observable fact that organisms, man and animal alike, do adjust themselves to their environment by means of hereditary and habit equipments. These adjustments may be very adequate or they may be so inadequate that the organism barely maintains its existence; secondly, that certain stimuli lead the organisms to make the responses. In a system of psychology completely worked out, given the response the stimuli can be predicted; given the stimuli the response can be predicted. Such a set of statements is crass and raw in the extreme, as all such generalizations must be. Yet they are hardly more raw and less realizable than the ones which appear in the psychology texts of the day. I possibly might illustrate my point better by choosing an everyday problem which anyone is likely to meet in the course of his work. Some time ago I was called upon to make a study of certain species of birds. Until I went to Tortugas I had never seen these birds alive. When I reached there I found the animals doing certain things: some of the acts seemed to work peculiarly well in such an environment, while others seemed to be unsuited to their type of life. I first studied the responses of the group as a whole and later those of individuals. In order to understand more thoroughly the relation between what was habit and what was hereditary in these responses, I took the young birds and reared them. In this way I was able to study the order of appearance of hereditary adjustments and their complexity, and later the beginnings of habit formation. My efforts in determining the stimuli which called forth such adjustments were crude indeed. Consequently my attempts to control behavior and to produce responses at will did not meet with much success. Their food and water, sex and other social relations, light and temperature conditions were all beyond control in a field study. I did find it possible to control their reactions in a measure by using the nest and egg (or young) as stimuli. It is not necessary in this paper to develop further how such a study should be carried out and how work of this kind must be supplemented by carefully controlled laboratory experiments. Had I been called upon to examine the natives of some of the Australian tribes, I should have gone about my task in the same way. I should have found the problem more difficult: the types of responses called forth by physical stimuli would have been more varied, and the number of effective stimuli larger. I should have had to determine the social setting of their lives in a far more careful way. These savages would be more influenced by the responses of each other than was the case with the birds. Furthermore, habits would have been more complex and the influences of past habits upon the present responses would have appeared more clearly. Finally, if I had been called upon to work out the psychology of the educated European, my problem would have required several lifetimes. But in the one I have at my disposal I should have followed the same general line of attack. In the main, my desire in all such work is to gain an accurate knowledge of adjustments and the stimuli calling them forth. My final reason for this is to learn general and particular methods by which I may control behavior. My goal is not 'the description and explanation of states of consciousness as such', nor that of obtaining such proficiency in mental gymnastics that I can immediately lay hold of a state of consciousness and say, 'this, as a whole, consists of gray sensation number 350, Of such and such extent, occurring in conjunction with the sensation of cold of a certain intensity; one of pressure of a certain intensity and extent,' and so on *ad infinitum*. If psychology would follow the plan I suggest, the educator, the physician, the jurist and the business man could utilize our data in a practical way, as soon as we are able, experimentally, to obtain them. Those who have occasion to apply psychological principles practically would find no need to complain as they do at the present time. Ask any physician or jurist today whether scientific psychology plays a practical part in his daily routine and you will hear him deny that the psychology of the laboratories finds a place in his scheme of work. I think the criticism is extremely just. One of the earliest conditions which made me dissatisfied with psychology was the feeling that there was no realm of application for the principles which were being worked out in content terms.

What gives me hope that the behaviorist's position is a defensible one is the fact that those branches of psychology which have already partially withdrawn from the parent, experimental psychology, and which are consequently less dependent upon introspection are today in a most flourishing condition. Experimental pedagogy, the psychology of drugs, the psychology of advertising, legal psychology, the psychology of tests, and psychopathology are all vigorous growths. These are sometimes wrongly called 'practical' or 'applied' psychology. Surely there was never a worse misnomer. In the future there may grow up vocational bureaus which really apply psychology. At present these fields are truly scientific and are in search of broad generalizations which will lead to the control of human behavior. For example, we find out by experimentation whether a series of stanzas may be acquired more readily if the whole is learned at once, or

342 THE MEANING OF LIFE

whether it is more advantageous to learn each stanza separately and then pass to the succeeding. We do not attempt to apply our findings. The application of this principle is purely voluntary on the part of the teacher. In the psychology of drugs we may show the effect upon behavior of certain doses of caffeine. We may reach the conclusion that caffeine has a good effect upon the speed and accuracy of work. But these are general principles. We leave it to the individual as to whether the results of our tests shall be applied or not. Again, in legal testimony, we test the effects of recency upon the reliability of a witness's report. We test the accuracy of the report with respect to moving objects, stationary objects, color, etc. It depends upon the judicial machinery of the country to decide whether these facts are ever to be applied. For a 'pure' psychologist to say that he is not interested in the questions raised in these divisions of the science because they relate indirectly to the application of psychology shows, in the first place, that he fails to understand the *scientific aim* in such problems, and secondly, that he is not interested in a psychology which concerns itself with human life. The only fault I have to find with these disciplines is that much of their material is stated in terms of introspection, whereas a statement in terms of objective results would be far more valuable. There is no reason why appeal should ever be made to consciousness in any of them. Or why introspective data should ever be sought during the experimentation, or published in the results. In experimental pedagogy especially one can see the desirability of keeping all of the results on a purely objective plane. If this is done, work there on the human being will be comparable directly with the work upon animals. For example, at Hopkins, Mr. Ulrich has obtained certain results upon the distribution of effort in learning -- using rats as subjects. He is prepared to give comparative results upon the effect of having an animal work at the problem once per day, three times per day, and five times per day. Whether it is advisable to have the animal learn only one problem at a time or to learn three abreast. We need to have similar experiments made upon man, but we care as little about his 'conscious processes' during the conduct of the experiment as we care about such processes in the rats.

I am more interested at the present moment in trying to show the necessity for maintaining uniformity in experimental procedure and in the method of stating results in both human and animal work, than in developing any ideas I may have upon the changes which are certain to come in the scope of human psychology. Let us consider for a moment the subject of the range of stimuli to which animals respond. I shall speak first of the work upon vision in animals. We put our animal in a situation where he will respond (or learn to respond) to one of two monochromatic lights. We feed him at the one (positive) and punish him at the other (negative). In a short time the animal learns to go to the light at which he is fed. At this point questions arise which I may phrase in two ways: I may choose the psychological way and say 'does the animal see these two lights as I do, *i.e.,* as two distinct colors, or does he see them as two grays differing in brightness, as does the totally color blind?' Phrased by the behaviorist, it would read as follows: 'Is my animal responding upon the basis of the difference in intensity between the two stimuli, or upon the difference in wavelengths?' He nowhere thinks of the animal's response in terms of his own experiences of colors and grays. He wishes to establish the fact whether wavelength is a factor in that animal's adjustment.*4* If so, what wave-lengths are effective and what differences in wave-length must be maintained in the different regions to afford bases for differential responses? If wave-length is not a factor in adjustment he wishes to know what difference in intensity will serve as a basis for response, and whether that same difference will suffice throughout the spectrum. Furthermore, he wishes to test whether the animal can respond to wavelengths which do not affect the human eye. He is as much interested in comparing the rat's spectrum with that of the chick as in comparing it with man's. The point of view when the various sets of comparisons are made does not change in the slightest.

However we phrase the question to ourselves, we take our animal after the association has been formed and then introduce certain control experiments which enable us to return answers to the questions just raised. But there is just as keen a desire on our part to test man under the same conditions, and to state the results in both cases in common terms.

The man and the animal should be placed as nearly as possible under the same experimental conditions. Instead of feeding or punishing the human subject, we should ask him to respond by setting a second apparatus until standard and control offered no basis for a differential response. Do I lay myself open to the charge here that I am using introspection? My reply is not at all; that while I might very well feed my human subject for a right choice and punish him for a wrong one and thus produce the response if the subject could give it, there is no need of going to extremes even on the platform I suggest. But be it understood that I am merely using this second method as an abridged behavior method.*5* We can go just as far and reach just as dependable results by the longer method as by the abridged. In many cases the direct and typically human method cannot be safely used. Suppose, for example, that I doubt the accuracy of the setting of the control instrument, in the above experiment, as I am very likely to do if I suspect a defect in vision? It is hopeless for me to get his introspective report. He will say: 'There is no difference in sensation, both are reds, identical in quality.' But suppose I confront him with the standard and the control and so arrange conditions that he is punished if he responds to the 'control' but not with the standard. I interchange the positions of the standard and the control at will and force him to attempt to differentiate the one from the other. If he can learn to make the adjustment even after a large number of trials it is evident that the two stimuli do afford the basis for a differential response. Such a method may sound nonsensical, but I firmly believe we will have to resort increasingly to just such method where we have reason to distrust the language method.

There is hardly a problem in human vision which is not also a problem in animal vision: I mention the limits of the spectrum, threshold values, *absolute and relative*, flicker, *Talbot's law*, *Weber's law*, field of vision, the *Purkinje phenomenon*, etc. Every one is capable of being worked out by behavior methods. Many of them are being worked out at the present time.

I feel that all the work upon the senses can be consistently carried forward along the lines I have suggested here for vision. Our results will, in the end, give an excellent picture of what each organ stands for in the way of function. The anatomist and the physiologist may take our data and show, on the one hand, the structures which are responsible for these responses, and, on the other, the physics-chemical relations which are necessarily involved (physiological chemistry of nerve and muscle) in these and other reactions.

344 THE MEANING OF LIFE

The situation in regard to the study of memory is hardly different. Nearly all of the memory methods in actual use in the laboratory today yield the type of results I am arguing for. A certain series of *nonsense syllables* or other material is presented to the human subject. What should receive the emphasis are the rapidity of the habit formation, the errors, peculiarities in the form of the curve, the persistence of the habit so formed, the relation of such habits to those formed when more complex material is used, etc. Now such results are taken down with the subject's introspection. The experiments are made for the purpose of discussing the mental machinery[6] involved in learning, in recall, recollection and forgetting, and not for the purpose of seeking the human being's way of shaping his responses to meet the problems in the terribly complex environment into which he is thrown, nor for that of showing the similarities and differences between man's methods and those of other animals.

The situation is somewhat different when we come to a study of the more complex forms of behavior, such as imagination, judgment, reasoning, and conception. At present the only statements we have of them are in content terms.[7] Our minds have been so warped by the fifty-odd years which have been devoted to the study of states of consciousness that we can envisage these problems only in one way. We should meet the situation squarely and say that we are not able to carry forward investigations along all of these lines by the behavior methods which are in use at the present time. In extenuation I should like to call attention to the paragraph above where I made the point that the introspective method itself has reached a *cul-de-sac* with respect to them. The topics have become so threadbare from much handling that they may well be put away for a time. As our methods become better developed it will be possible to undertake investigations of more and more complex forms of behavior. Problems which are now laid aside will again become imperative, but they can be viewed as they arise from a new angle and in more concrete settings.

Will there be left over in psychology a world of pure psychics, to use Yerkes' term? I confess I do not know. The plans which I most favor for psychology lead practically to the ignoring of consciousness in the sense that that term is used by psychologists today. I have virtually denied that this realm of psychics is open to experimental investigation. I don't wish to go further into the problem at present because it leads inevitably over into metaphysics. If you will grant the behaviorist the right to use consciousness in the same way that other natural scientists employ it - that is, without making consciousness a special object of observation - you have granted all that my thesis requires.

In concluding, I suppose I must confess to a deep bias on these questions. I have devoted nearly twelve years to experimentation on animals. It is natural that such a one should drift into a theoretical position which is in harmony with his experimental work. Possibly I have put up a straw man and have been fighting that. There may be no absolute lack of harmony between the position outlined here and that of functional psychology. I am inclined to think, however, that the two positions cannot be easily harmonized. Certainly the position I advocate is weak enough at present and can be attacked from many standpoints. Yet when all this is admitted I still feel that the considerations which I have urged should have a wide influence upon the type of psychology which is to be developed in the future. What we need to do is to start work upon psychology, making *behavior, not consciousness,* the objective point of our attack. Certainly there are enough problems in the control of behavior to keep us all working many lifetimes without ever allowing us time to think of *consciousness an sich.* Once launched in the undertaking, we will find ourselves in a short time as far divorced from an introspective psychology as the psychology of the present time is divorced from faculty psychology.

Summary

1. Human psychology has failed to make good its claim as a natural science. Due to a mistaken notion that its fields of facts are conscious phenomena and that introspection is the only direct method of ascertaining these facts, it has enmeshed itself in a series of speculative questions which, while fundamental to its present tenets, are not open to experimental treatment. In the pursuit of answers to these questions, it has become further and further divorced from contact with problems which vitally concern human interest.

2. Psychology, as the behaviorist views it, is a purely objective, experimental branch of natural science which needs introspection as little as do the sciences of chemistry and physics. It is granted that the behavior of animals can be investigated without appeal to consciousness. Heretofore the viewpoint has been that such data have value only in so far as they can be interpreted by analogy in terms of consciousness. The position is taken here that the behavior of man and the behavior of animals must be considered on the same plane; as being equally essential to a general understanding of behavior. It can dispense with consciousness in a psychological sense. The separate observation of 'states of consciousness', is, on this assumption, no more a part of the task of the psychologist than of the physicist. We might call this the return to a non-reflective and nave use of consciousness. In this sense consciousness may be said to be the instrument or tool with which all scientists work. Whether or not the tool is properly used at present by scientists is a problem for philosophy and not for psychology.

3. From the viewpoint here suggested the facts on the behavior of amoebæ have value in and for themselves without reference to the behavior of man. In biology studies on race differentiation and inheritance in amœbæ form a separate division of study which must be evaluated in terms of the laws found there. The conclusions so reached may not hold in any other form. Regardless of the possible lack of generality, such studies must be made if evolution as a whole is ever to be regulated and controlled. Similarly the laws of behavior in amœbæ, the range of responses, and the determination of effective stimuli, of habit formation, persistency of habits, interference and reinforcement of habits, must be determined and evaluated in and for themselves, regardless of their generality, or of their bearing upon such laws in other forms, if the phenomena of behavior are ever to be brought within the sphere of scientific control.

4. This suggested elimination of states of consciousness as proper objects of investigation in themselves will remove the barrier from psychology which exists between it and the other

346 THE MEANING OF LIFE

sciences. The findings of psychology become the functional correlates of structure and lend themselves to explanation in physico-chemical terms.

5. Psychology as behavior will, after all, have to neglect but few of the really essential problems with which psychology as an introspective science now concerns itself. In all probability even this residue of problems may be phrased in such a way that refined methods in behavior (which certainly must come) will lead to their solution.

References

1 That is, either directly upon the conscious state of the observer or indirectly upon the conscious state of the experimenter.

2 In this connection I call attention to the controversy now on between the adherents and the opposers of imageless thought. The 'types of reactors' (sensory and motor) were also matters of bitter dispute. The complication experiment was the source of another war of words concerning the accuracy of the opponents' introspection.

3 My colleague, Professor H. C. Warren, by whose advice this article was offered to the Review, believes that the parallelist can avoid the interaction terminology completely by exercising a little care.

4 He would have exactly the same attitude as if he were conducting an experiment to show whether an ant would crawl over a pencil laid across the trail or go round it.

5 I should prefer to look upon this abbreviated method, where the human subject is told in words, for example, to equate two stimuli; or to state in words whether a given stimulus is present or absent, etc., as the language method in behavior. It in no way changes the status of experimentation. The method becomes possible merely by virtue of the fact that in the particular case the experimenter and his animal have systems of abbreviations or shorthand behavior signs (language), any one of which may stand for a habit belonging to the repertoire both of the experimenter and his subject. To make the data obtained by the language method virtually the whole of behavior -- or to attempt to mould all of the data obtained by other methods in terms of the one which has by all odds the most limited range -- is putting the cart before the horse with a vengeance.

6 They are often undertaken apparently for the purpose of making crude pictures of what must or must not go on in the nervous system.

7 There is need of questioning more and more the existence of what psychology calls imagery. Until a few years ago I thought that centrally aroused visual sensations were as clear as those peripherally aroused. I had never accredited myself with any other kind. However, closer examination leads me to deny in my own case the presence of imagery in the Galtonian sense. The whole doctrine of the centrally aroused image is, I believe, at present, on a very insecure foundation. Angell as well as Fernald reach the conclusion that an objective determination of image type is impossible. It would be an interesting confirmation of their experimental work if we should find by degrees that we have been mistaken in building up this enormous structure of the centrally aroused sensation (or image).

The hypothesis that all of the so-called 'higher thought' processes go on in terms of faint reinstatements of the original muscular act (including speech here) and that these are integrated into systems which respond in serial order (associative mechanisms) is, I believe, a tenable one. It makes reflective processes as mechanical as habit. The scheme of habit which James long ago described - where each return or afferent current releases the next appropriate motor discharge - is as true for ,thought processes' as for overt muscular acts. Paucity of 'imagery' would be the rule. In other words, wherever there are thought processes there are faint contractions of the systems of musculature involved in the overt exercise of the customary act, and especially in the still finer systems of musculature involved in speech. If this is true, and I do not see how it can be gainsaid, imagery becomes a mental luxury (even if it really exists) without any functional significance whatever. If experimental procedure justifies this hypothesis, we shall have at hand tangible phenomena which may be studied as behavior material. I should say that the day when we can study reflective processes by such methods is about as far off as the day when we can tell by physicochemical methods the difference in the structure and arrangement of molecules between living protoplasm and inorganic substances. The solutions of both problems await the advent of methods and apparatus.

[After writing this paper I heard the addresses of Professors Thorndike and Angell, at the Cleveland meeting of the American Psychological Association. I hope to have the opportunity to discuss them at another time. I must even here attempt to answer one question raised by Thorndike.
Thorndike [...] casts suspicions upon ideo-motor action. If by ideo-motor action he means just that and would not include sensori-motor action in his general denunciation, I heartily agree with him. I should throw out imagery altogether and attempt to show that practically all natural thought goes on in terms of sensori-motor processes in the larynx (but not in terms of 'imageless thought') which rarely come to consciousness in any person who has not groped for imagery in the psychological laboratory. This easily explains why so many of the welleducated laity know nothing of imagery. I doubt if Thorndike conceives of the matter in this way. He and Woodworth seem to have neglected the speech mechanisms.

It has been shown that improvement in habit comes unconsciously. The first we know of it is when it is achieved -- when it becomes an object. I believe that 'consciousness' has just as little to do with improvement in thought processes. Since, according to my view, thought processes are really motor habits in the larynx, improvements, short cuts, changes, etc., in these habits are brought about in the same way that such changes are produced in other motor habits. This view carries with it the implication that there are no reflective processes (centrally initiated processes): The individual is always examining objects, in the one case objects in the now accepted sense, in the other their substitutes, viz., the movements in the speech musculature. From this it follows that there is no theoretical limitation of the behavior method. There remains, to be sure, the practical difficulty, which may never be overcome, of examining speech movements in the way that general bodily behavior may be examined.]

TWO TYPES OF CONDITIONED REFLEX AND A PSEUDO TYPE[*]

B.F. Skinner (1935)[1]

From the Biological Laboratories of Harvard University

First published in Journal of General Psychology, 12, 66-77.

A conditioned reflex is said to be conditioned in the sense of being dependent for its existence or state upon the occurrence of a certain kind of event, having to do with the presentation of a reinforcing stimulus. A definition that includes much more than this simple notion will probably not be applicable to all cases. At almost any significant level of analysis a distinction must be made between at least two major types of conditioned reflex. These may be represented, with examples, in the following way (where S = stimulus, R = response, $(S - R)$ = reflex, -> = "is followed by," and [ ] = "the strength of" the inclosed reflex):

TYPE I

$S_0 \longrightarrow R_0 \longrightarrow S_1 \longrightarrow R_1$

(A) LEVER — PRESSING   FOOD — SALIVATION, EATING
(B)   "   "   SHOCK — WITHDRAWAL, EMOTIONAL CHANGE

Given such a sequence, where $[S_1\text{-}R_1] \sim = 0$,[2] conditioning occurs as a change in $[S_0\text{-}R_0]$ - an increase in strength (positive conditioning) in (*a*) and a decrease (negative conditioning) in (*b*).[p.67]

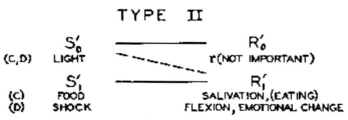

TYPE II

$S'_0 \longrightarrow R'_0$
(C,D) LIGHT   r (NOT IMPORTANT)

$S'_1 \longrightarrow R'_1$
(C) FOOD   SALIVATION, (EATING)
(D) SHOCK   FLEXION, EMOTIONAL CHANGE

Given the simultaneous or successive presentation of S'_0 and S'_1, where $[S'_1 - R'_1] \sim = 0$,[2] conditioning occurs as an increase in $[S'_0 - R'_1]$.
Differences between the types are as follows:

1. In Type I, $S_o \rightarrow R_o \rightarrow S_1$, where R_o necessarily intervenes between the stimuli; in Type II, $S'_o \rightarrow S'_1$, where R'_1 is ignored.[3] In I, R_o is important; it becomes the conditioned response. In II, R'_o is irrelevant (except when it is relevant in another sense by conflicting with R'_1) and may actually disappear.

Since conditioning of the second type may take place even when S'_1 occurs after R'_o, Paradigm II, Example (*c*), may be written for this case as follows:

light --------------- *r* ----------------> food ---------------salivation,

when it is identical with I. But the result is not to reduce the two types to a single form. Both kinds of conditioning proceed simultaneously but separately. If *r* is "turning toward the light," for example, and if the food is withheld until turning takes place, [light - turning] will increase according to I while [light-salivation] will increase according to II. The same result is obtained with negative conditioning. Example (*d*) gives, upon delaying S'_1.

light -------------- *r* ---------------> shock --------------- flexion, etc.,

where [light--*r*] will decrease according to I, while [light-flexion] increases according to II.

In the special case in which R_o and R'_1 are of the same form, the two kinds can apparently not be separated. If, for example, some unconditioned salivation is supposed to be elicitable by a light,[4] we may substitute "salivation" for *r*, to obtain

light - salivation I ---------------> food - salivation II.

Both [light - salivation I] and [light - salivation II] will increase, with apparently no possible distinction. This is a very special case and is also in no sense a reduction to a single type.

2. In I, $(S_o - R_o)$ occurs normally in the absence of $(S_1 - R_1)$, [p.68] and its strength may be measured without interfering with the reinforcing action of S_1. In II S'_1 must be withheld whenever a measurement of $[S'_o - R'_1]$, the conditioned reflex, is taken, because S'_1 also evokes R'_1. Some amount of extinction necessarily ensues in the second case.

3. Since S'_1 must be withheld in measuring $[S'_o - R'_1]$, R'_1 must be independent of any property of S'_1 not possessed by S'_o. In Example (*c*) salivation may become attached to the light as a conditioned response of Type II; but seizing, chewing, and swallowing, which are also responses

350 THE MEANING OF LIFE

to S'_1, must not be included in the paradigm since they require the presence of parts of S'_1 which cannot be supplied by S'_0.

A special restriction on Paradigm II is therefore necessary. Where S'_0 is of a very simple sort (a tone, for example), the properties possessed in addition to S'_0 by S'_1 are practically equal to S'_1, and we may express the restriction in terms of a general distinction between two kinds of response. The first kind require no external point of reference in their elicitation or description. Typical examples are: glandular activities (salivation), local muscular responses (flexion, wink, breathing movements, production of sounds), and facilitation and inhibition.[5]

The second kind require points of reference for their elicitation or description which are not supplied by the organism itself, but by the stimulus. Examples are: orientation toward the source of a sound, approaching a light, and touching, seizing and manipulating objects (such as a lever or food). Our present rule is that responses of the second kind cannot be substituted for R'_1 in Paradigm II, unless S' also supplies the required points of reference.

4. In Type I, $[S_0 - R_0] \sim = 0$ before conditioning takes place. The reflex-to-be-conditioned must be elicited at least once as an unconditioned "investigatory" reflex. In Type II, $[S'_0 - R'_1]$ may begin at zero and usually does. In Type I the *state* of the reflex is "conditioned" by the occurrence of the reinforcing sequence, but its *existence* is not. A distinction between a conditioned and an unconditioned relfex is here less significant, because all examples of the [p.69] former have necessarily been examples of the latter. There are no exclusively conditioned reflexes in this type. Since $[S'_0 - R'_1]$ may begin at zero, a new reflex may be created in conditioning of the second type. And since practically any stimulus may be attached to R'_1 in Paradigm II, a very large number of new reflexes can thus be derived. Conditioning of Type I, on the other hand, is not a device for increasing the repertory of reflexes; R_0 continues to be elicited by the one stimulus with which it began.

There are three reflexes in Paradigm II, but only two in I.

5. The significant change in Type I may be either an increase or a decrease in strength; in Type II it is an increase only, even when $[S'_0 - R'_1]$ does not begin at zero.

In Type I stimuli may be divided into two classes, positively and negatively conditioning, according to whether they produce an increase or decrease when used as reinforcement. The distinction cannot be made in Type II, where a reflex may be negative in another sense (a reflex of "avoidance," for example), but where its strength only increases during conditioning.

6. In Type I the conditioned reflex $(S_0 - R_0)$ may be associated with any drive; in Type II the reflex $(S'_0 - R'_1)$ is necessarily attached to the drive specified by R'_1.

BEHAVIOURISM   351

This point may require some comment. In the present use of the term a drive is an inferred variable of which the strength of a group of reflexes is a function (2). Hunger, for example, is a variable (H) a change in which is responsible for concurrent changes in the strength (a) of all unconditioned reflexes concerned with the ingestion of food, (b) of all conditioned reflexes (of either type) in which the reinforcing stimulus is concerned with the ingestion of food, and (c) to a much lesser extent of all "investigatory" reflexes. In Paradigm I, Example a (lever - pressing) is originally a function of H to some slight extent under (c) above. After conditioning it varies with H according to (b), over a wide range probably equal to that of any unconditioned reflex under (a). Conditioning of Type I is really the becoming attached to a group of reflexes varying as a function of some drive. This is a much more comprehensive description of the process than to define it as an increase in strength, where the drive is assumed to remain constant at a significant value. But the identity of H in the present case is [p.70] determined only by our choice of a reinforcing reflex. Given (S_1 - R_1) of another drive, say thirst, then (S_o - R_o) will become conditioned by attaching itself to the group varying with thirst, and will not vary with H except to some slight extent under (c).

This is a characteristic wholly lacking in Type II. Here R' is originally part of the unconditioned reflex and the drive to which it belongs is definitely fixed.

7. A minor difference is in the way in which the stimulus-to-be-conditioned usually acts. In Type I, S_o is usually part of a larger field, and R_o occurs as the result of the eventual prepotency of S_o over other stimuli. In Type II, S'_o is usually suddenly presented to the organism. The significance of this difference, which is not absolute, will appear later.

We shall now consider a third type of relation which involves a discrimination. It may be based upon a conditioned reflex of either type, but we shall begin with I. To establish a discrimination subdivide S_o into two classes on the basis of a selected property or component member (3, 4). For example, let the lever stimulate either in the presence of a light (L), when the stimulus may be written as $S_{A.B..L..}$ (subcripts indicate properties or components), or in the dark, when the stimulus is $S_{A.B...}$. Continue to reinforce the re-response to one of them, say $S_{A.B..L..}$, and extinguish or negatively condition the response to the other by breaking the sequence at S_1 or by introducing as S_1 of the negatively conditioning kind (Difference 5). When this has been done, $[S_{A.B..L..}\text{---}R_o] >$ $[S_{A.B..}\text{---}R_o]$. And at any value of the underlying drive such that ($S_{A.B..L}\text{---}R_o$) is usually elicited but ($S_{AB..}\text{---}R_o$) is not, there exists the following condition. Given an organism in the presence of $S_{AB..}$ ordinarily unresponsive, the presentation of L will be followed by a response. For the sake of comparison we may set up a paradigm in imitation of II as follows:

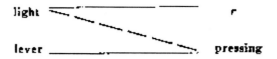

The relation between the light and the response to the lever might be called pseudo-conditioned reflex. It has some of the characteristics of Type II: the original response to the light is irrelevant [p.71] (Difference 1); the relation may be wholly absent prior to the "conditioning" (Difference 4); it changes in a positive direction only (Difference 5); and the "stimulus" is usually of the presented kind (Difference 7). In all these respects it differs from Type I, although the example is based upon a reflex of that type. I many other respects it differs from both types. A reinforcing reflex is not included in the paradigm, but must be added as a third or fourth reflex. The response is not principally to the light, but to the lever; the light is only a component member of the whole stimulus, and "light-pressing" is not legitimately the expression of a reflex. The lever cannot be removed to show the conditioned effectiveness of the light as in Type II; instead, the response to the lever alone must be extinguished - a characteristic that we have not met before.

In spite of these differences it is often said (in similar cases) that the light becomes the "conditioned stimulus for the response to the lever" just as it becomes the stimulus for salivation. This is a confusion with Type II which obviously arises from a neglect of the extinguished reflex. The relation of pressing the lever to the lever itself is ignored and only the relation to the light taken into account. The lever comes to be treated, not as a source of stimulation, but as part of the apparatus, relevant to the response only for mechanical reasons. When the discrimination is based upon a response not requiring an external point of reference (Difference 3), the chance of this neglect increases enormously. If we substitute "flexion of a leg" for "pressing a lever" (and continue for the moment with Type I), S_o in Paradigm I is not directly observable; we simply wait until a flexion appears, then reinforce. Having established (S_o - R_o) as a conditioned reflex of some strength, we subdivide our inferred S_o as before, extinguish ($S_{AB..}$ - R_o), and reinforce ($S_{AB..L..}$ - R_o). When the discrimination has been set up, we have a condition in which the organism is ordinarily unresponsive but immediately responds with flexion upon presentation of the light.

Our inability to demonstrate S_o makes it difficult to show the discriminative nature of this relation; but it is by no means impossible to find other grounds, as we may see by comparing it with a true reflex of Type II. Let the presentation of the light be followed by a shock to the foot until the light alone elicits flexion. The resulting reflex is superficially similar to the relation of light and [p.72] flexion that we have just examined, but fundamentally the two cases are unlike. Assuming that no immediate difference can in fact be detected,[6] we may still show differences by referring forward or backward to the history of the organism. The two relations have been established in different ways and their continued existence depends upon reinforcement from different stimuli. The discriminative drive relation also varies with an arbitrarily chosen drive, while the conditioned reflex is necessarily attached to the drive to which shock-flexion belongs.

These differences are chiefly due, however, to the use of a conditioned reflex of Type I in setting up the discrimination. In a pseudo-conditioned reflex based upon Type II the distinction is much less sure. Here we are invariably able to neglect the extinguished member because R'_1 is of the kind not requiring an external point of reference (Difference 3), and we can minimize its importance in other ways. Given a conditioned reflex of this kind:

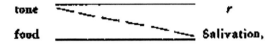

if we establish a discrimination between the tone and the tone-plus-a light (reinforcing the resonse to the latter), we obtain the following condition: an organism in the presence of the tone, ordinarily unresponsive, will respond upon presentation of the light. The only difference between this relation and a true reflex of Type II is the extinction of the response to the tone, which is evidence that a discrimination has taken place. The reinforcement of tone and light should condition responses to both of these stimuli; but we observe that the organism is unresponsive in the presence of the tone alone.

Now, this surviving difference may be reduced at will by reducing the significance of S'_o in the basic reflex of the pseudo-type. If we lower the intensity of the tone or choose another stimulus of a less important kind, we may approach as closely as we please to a conditioned reflex of Type II. We cannot actually reach Type II in [p.73] this way, but we can easily reach a point at which our pseudo-reflex is identical with any actual experimental example of that type. This is true because some amount of discrimination is practically always involved in cases of Type II. When we put a dog into a stand, present a light and then food, the food reinforces not only the light but the stimulation from the stand. Merely putting the dog into the stand again should elicit salivation according to Paradigm II. In practice this is a disturbing effect, which must be eliminated through extinction. So long as it occurs, any actual case of Type II must be formulated as a pseudo-conditioned reflex. If S_G is the stimulation affecting the organism in addition to S_o, then S_o Paradigm II should read $S_G + S_o$. The effect upon S_G is extinguished through lack of reinforcement in the absence of S_o, and the result is a discrimination: an organism is the presence of S_G, ordinarily unresponsive, responds when S_o is added. The importance of this criticism will depend upon the relative magnitudes of S_G and S_o. In the optimal experiment S_G may be reduced to a value that is insignificant in comparison with ordinary values of S_o.

The partially discriminative nature of Type II is invetable. It is not important in Type I because of Difference 1. Paradigm I contains an implicit specification that S_o is active or has just acted at the moment of reinforcement, since it specifies that S_1 is to be withheld until R_o has occurred. The reinforced stimulus is really S_o and not $S_G + S_o$ (it is the lever, in our example, not the whole

354   THE MEANING OF LIFE

stimulating field presented by the apparatus). Paradigm II contains no specification of the activity of S_o ; and the reinforcing action of S'_1 must be supposed to extend to S_G as well as to S_o. In practice an active state at the moment of reinforcement is usually insured by presenting S_o suddenly.[7] This might be included as an additional provision in Paradigm II, but the provision really required is that S_o, and no part of S_G, be active at the moment of reinforcement. This is not easily arranged. We cannot wholly avoid the generalized action of the reinforcement in Type II because of the lack of dependence of S'_1 upon R'_o.

One characteristic of the pseudo-conditioned reflex is the variety [p.74] of the forms of its "stimulus". We have assumed that in our two fundamental paradigms any stimulus had ultimately the dimensions of energy (although we have often used the shorthand device of speaking of the source of the energy - as, for example, "lever"). In the pseudo type, however, the "stimulus" can be a single property. It can be the intensity of the stimulus, or some such qualitative aspect as pitch or hue. It can be a change from one value of a property to another, or the absence of a property, or a duration. The reason why this is possible is that the other properties of the stimulus can be relegated to S_G for extinction. If the *pitch* of a tone is to be a conditioned "stimulus," the tone itself must first become one also, and the response to its other properties must be extinguished by extinguishing the responses to tones of other pitches. In a true conditioned reflex this cannot be done. Although it is common to speak of properties as stimuli (1), the presence of a property in the position of a stimulus is a certain indication that a pseudo-conditioned reflex is really in quesiton. A property alone cannot be used in either true type because it implies extinction; most of the real stimulus must be relegated to S_G, and the requirement that the value of S_G be negligible cannot therefore be satisfied.

The position of a pseudo-conditioned reflex may be summarized as follows. When the pseudo-reflex is based upon a reflex of Type I and when R_o requires external points of reference, there are important practical and theoretical reasons why a separate formulation is demanded. When R_o does not require external points of reference, there are fewer differences, but a separate formulation is still necessary. When the pseudo type is based upon a reflex of Type II, the distinction is weakened but should still be made, except when S_G can be reduced to a very low value relative to S'_o. In the last case a practical distinction is impossible, not because of an identity of types, but because of the failure of Type II to appear experimentally in a pure form.

It is a tempting hypothesis that II is not an authentic type but may be reduced to a discrimination based on Type I. But this has not been shown; we have not reduced the pseudo type to Type II or *vice versa*. Nor have we come very near it. The present pseudo-reflex which resembles II most closely requires of that type for its establishment. It is probably more than a coincidence that [p.75] a discrimination based upon Type I has so many of the properties of II, but the reduction to a single type appears from our present evidence to be highly improbable, desirable though it would be as an immense simplification. The differences that we have noted are not easily

BEHAVIOURISM **355**

disposed of. Still more improbable is a reduction of I to II, since the first step supplied by the pseudo type is then lacking.

To the differences we have listed might be added differences in the parts played by the two types in the economy of the organism. The essence of Type II is the substitution of one stimulus for another, or, as Pavlov has put it, signalization (1). It *prepares* the organism by obtaining the elicitation of a response before the original stimulus has begun to act, and it does this by letting any stimulus that has *incidently* accompanied or anticipated the original stimulus act in its stead. In Type I there is no substitution of stimuli and consequently no signalization. Type I acts in another way: the organism selects from a large repertory of unconditioned reflexes those of which the repetition is important with respect to certain elementary functions and discards those of which it is unimportant. The conditioned response of Type I does not prepare for the reinforcing stimulus, it *produces* it. The stimulus-to-be-conditioned is never in any sense incidental.

Type I plays the more important rôle. When an organism comes accidentally[*8*] upon a new kind of food, which it seizes and eats, both kinds of conditioning presumably occur. When the visible radiation from the food next stimulates the organism, salivation is evoked according to Paradigm II. This secretion remains useless until the food is actually seized and eaten. But seizing and eating will depend upon the same accidental factors as before unless conditioning of Type I has also occurred - that is, unless the strength of the reflex (food-seizing) has increased. Thus while a reflex of Type II prepares the organism, a reflex of Type I obtains the food for which the preparation is made. And this is in general a fair characterization of the relative importance of the two types. As Pavlov has said, conditioned stimuli are important in providing saliva before food is received, but "even greater is their importance when they evoke the motor component of the complex reflex of nutrition, i.e., [p.7 6] when they act as stimuli to the reflex of seeking food." (1, p.13).[9] Although "the reflex of seeking food" is an unfortunate expression, it refers clearly enough to behavior characteristic of Type I.

Footnotes

[*] Accepted for publication by Carl Murchison of the Editorial Board and received in the Editorial Office, June 4, 1934.

[1] Society of Fellows, Harvard University.

[2] This expression specifies the presence of some amount of drive (2).

[3] For convenience we shall omit the case of simultaneous stimuli in Type II.

[4] See Difference 4 below for this general requirement in Type I.

[5] Where conditioned facilitation and inhibition are defined by substituting for R'_1 in Paradigm II the expressions "Incr. [S" - R"]" and "Decr. [S" - R"]" respectively. (Incr. = "increase in"; Decr. = "decrease in").

[6] This is a generous assumption since some evidence for the presence of S_o can usually be found. A difference in the character of the response might also be shown (in the case of the true reflex it may be accompanied by changes in breathing rate, for example, which would be lacking in the pseudo reflex).

356 THE MEANING OF LIFE

[7] This is our explanation of Difference 7. Another explanation might be added. If S'_0 is active for any length of time prior to S_1 it will have an extinguishing effect. This cannot be said of Type I.

[8] That is to say, as the result of weak investigatory reflexes.

[9] This is a doubly interesting statement because Pavlov has confined his own investigations practically exclusively to conditioned reflexes of the second type. It ought to be said that he usually regards this type as adequate for the whole field. Thus he says that the "function of the hemispheres" is signalization (1, p.17), although signalization is, as we have seen, a characteristic of Type II only.

CHAPTER 10

PSYCHOANALYSIS

Like the movement of Behaviourism, Psychoanalysis is more than a theory—it is an intellectual movement that continues to have a deep and pervasive influence on many fields of study. The sheer popularity and pervasiveness of this school is clear through the association of its founder with psychology in general, Sigmund Freud.

Sigmund Freud (1856-1939) was born in Moravia to a Jewish family and grew up under the growing wave of anti-Semitism in Europe. As a talented young student Freud was no different than his contemporaries that formed the field of psychology. Having a strong education in physiology like Wundt and Pavlov, he might have followed the same bio-psychological route had he not entered into realm of psychological therapy.

At the beginning of Freud's career he entered the realm of clinical practice largely as a clinical neurologist who was seeking to deal with the neural disorders of his patients. Freud was drawn mostly to the disorder of *Hysteria* that was a neuroses that was all too common. It must be noted that today the term used for *Hysteria* is *Dissociative Disorder* and the term *neuroses* is currently unfashionable, but at Freud's time was used to describe what was thought to be a disorder of nerve structures.

As early as 1895, Freud was torn by what he saw as two divergent needs within clinical practice. The first need was Freud's desire to conduct scientific, quantitative study of mental functioning in order to develop a theory of mental functioning and from this fulfil the second need of finding what causes psychopathology from what is originally normal psychology. This obsession to find the aetiology of psychopathology led Freud to study childhood development and models of thinking, eventually forming a general guiding thesis that adult neurotic symptoms find their ultimate cause in a childhood trauma or disgusting thought. At the time, this event or thought has no pathological effect, but it lies dormant and is unconsciously reawakened and expressed as a symptom years later.

While this is the basic guiding tenet that Freud formed early in his life, his overall views on psychoanalytic theory and practice evolved throughout his life. Indeed, oftentimes the theories attributed to Sigmund Freud were truly clarified by Freud's daughter, Anna (who herself was a powerful force in psychoanalytic theory, particularly in the realm of Child Psychology). Despite the great diversity of principles set forward by Freud throughout his career, some basic tenets of his understanding of the human psychic structure have become permanent fixtures of the psychological vocabulary.

According to the psychoanalytic view, the personality consists of three systems: the *id*, the *ego*, and the *superego*. The *id* is the biological component that functions as a basic instinctual drive that is needed for human survival. The id is ruled by the pleasure principle of avoiding pain and gaining pleasure. The id is an unchanging biologically controlled mechanism that never matures and is outside the realm of our conscious control. The *ego* is the psychological component that interacts with the external world and governs and controls the drives of the id and the social expectations of the superego. The *ego* is ruled by the *reality principle* that mediates what is within oneself and what is not. Finally, the *superego* is the social/ judicial branch of the personality that incorporates the mythic stories of the community and uses the power of guilt and shame to influence the ego.

The force of the control of the ego and the superego over the id can at times cause *Anxiety*. In psychoanalytic theory there are three types of anxiety: Moral, Neurotic and Reality Based. Reality anxiety is the fear of danger from the external world and is recognized as essential for survival. In contrast to this, the other types of anxiety are concerned with the balance of power within the individual and "who will rule the house". Neurotic anxiety, for example, is the fear that the instincts will get out of hand, and moral anxiety is fear of one's own conscience (like feeling guilty for breaking a rule of the social group). In order to deal with these types of anxiety a person then develops Ego-defence mechanisms that begin to deny or distort reality in order to manage the anxiety. These mechanisms include the typical Freudian defences of Repression, Denial, Reaction Formation, Projection, Displacement, Rationalization, Sublimation, Regression, Compensation, Identification and Introjection.

Through Freud's clinical experience he also developed the theory that how we use these defence mechanisms and how we manage our psychic balance of power is all formed in the first six years of our life. This basic pattern of human functioning was, according to Freud, found in the stages of psycho-sexual development that form around issues of trust, emotion and acceptance of sexual feelings. A child starts at the *oral stage* where basic nurturing is needed or else feelings of greediness will develop. As the child enters the *anal stage* between 1-3 years he/she learns to master him/herself and the joy of relative independence. Ages 3-6 include the *phallic stage* of emerging sexual identity and the desire to form relationships with the parent of the opposite sex. The *Latency stage* from 6-12 involves the interest of forming peer friendships and discovery of the outer world. Then, at age 12, the *genital stage* emerges with the old themes of the phallic stage coupled with a burst of sexual energy. According to Freud, how an individual develops through these stages dictates how an individual will function throughout life and is the root source of the development of psychological dysfunction.

Despite Freud's legacy of psychoanalysis and the psychic structure, he was in fact more concerned with the role of meaning in life and was extremely well read in the mythic literature of many cultures. Freud's writings often took great pains to either revise ancient perspectives or to criticize them openly (but never ignore them), for Freud recognized, as did the ancients, that the mythopoeic force of the human psyche is central to understanding both the individual, and society, and ultimately the meaning of life.

Of course Freud did not single-handedly build the entire theoretical foundations of the psychoanalytic school. Another theorist by the name of Alfred Adler (1870-1937), who worked as a physician in Vienna was also president of the Vienna Psychoanalytic Society until he resigned in 1911. While Adler was a colleague of Freud until 1911, it was after this time that

Adler broke away from Freud in favour of a neo-Freudian perspective that was more individualistic. In so doing, Adler rejected Freud's foundational principle of a psychic structure and argued that people can only be understood as a whole, stressing the unity of the personality and the complete integration of the parts while emphasizing the purposeful nature of behaviour.

In essence, Adler rejected Freud's biological/instinctual/structural model of the psyche and instead focused on the formation of subjective feelings of inferiority. Adler argued that such feelings cause us to strive for creativity, mastery and success. Therefore what is central in life is not our instinctual drive, but rather what we do with the abilities we possess and how this fits into a mythic structure of our ideal (which is typically formed by age 6). In many ways Adler pulled the basic Freudian ideas that had been skewed into a structural model back into an existential frame. In so doing Adler viewed as central to his therapy the client's subjective frame of reference.

In many ways Adler was Freudian, but this was overshadowed by his recognition of the importance of the mythopoeic subjective reality of the individual as a whole. With such an emphasis it could be argued that Adler was of a phenomenological orientation (though not to the degree of those to be discussed in a later chapter). However, Adler did admit that life in its reality is far less important than how the individual believes life to be. Therefore Adler's approach to counselling rests on the collaborative effort between therapist and client in the process of identifying and exploring *mistaken goals* and *faulty assumptions* about life. In Freudian terms it amounts to rebuilding and re-educating the superego and the ego to function in a way that is well thought out and conscious. Of course, Alfred Adler would prefer to say that it was helping a person gain conscious control and awareness of their values, beliefs and expectations for life in order to become a more complete person. (See Read For Yourself Section, this chapter, for further information on Adler's perspective on life).

Such a sentiment acknowledging the value of the mythopoeic is not limited to Alfred Adler. Indeed, another of Freud's colleagues is among the most recognized proponents of mythic thought as the basis of being human. This proponent was Carl Gustav Jung. Though Jung (1875-1961) was associated with Freud's psychoanalytic movement from 1907-1913, Jung was a thinker who was largely independent of Freud. While on the surface Jung holds some similarities to Freud, the underlying philosophies about people and the role of the unconscious is very different.

The largest difference between Freud and Jung was in their outlook of religion, for while Freud railed against religion at times, Jung (the son of a minister and a student of all the world's religions) viewed religion as the basic expression of the human psyche (in a positive way, which is in contrast to Freud's view). In so doing, Jung believed that the total person is a collection and interaction of the *personal unconscious* (the storehouse of personal experience and organizing stories) and the *collective unconscious* (the cultural and historical experiences and stories that form our context).

In mythopoeic terms, a person's personality (*Psyche*) is formed through a mixture of personal stories of the personal unconscious that borrows heavily from the collective unconscious

360 THE MEANING OF LIFE

and forms into mythic *archetypes* or patterns of understanding existence. These *archetypes* are frames for stories of meaning, life, death, struggle and ways of making meaning out of human existence (religion etc). As the person lives within the community one then places upon oneself a mythic image or *persona* (after the play actor's mask). This public image of the person is a guiding form, but not the substance of a person. For example, a *persona* of a person may be as a mother and this is formed within the *collective archetype* of what a mother is to be, but neither the *archetype* nor the *persona* is the sum of the individual.

However, while Jung was a prolific writer on the role of myth in the psychodynamic function of human life he is likely best known for his work on attitudes. Jung viewed all people to engage in an attitude of inwardness and solitude (introversion) or outgoing social activity (extroversion). Jung believed in four basic psychological functions: thinking, feeling, sensation, and intuition. All functions are prevalent in all people, but there are nevertheless strong preferences so that a given function may be clearly dominant in a given personality. Such personality typing has been transformed over the past 50 years into many of the psychological tests known today. The most popular test based upon Jung's personality typing is the Myers-Briggs Personality Test.

When it came to psychotherapy Jung still relied upon Freud's basic psychoanalytic method with his own unique twist. This twist was in the analysis and discovery of the collective unconscious influences and archetypes within a person's mythic story. This was done through the analysis of daydreams, word association tests and even a client's art.

Even within his personal life Jung was caught up in discovering his own persona (masks) and the influences upon his own personal unconscious, not to mention the collective unconscious of human society. This personal quest lead Jung to delve deep into his own creative works reflected in a personal diary (which came to be known as the "Red Book"). Following Jung's death, his Red Book reflections only served to bolster his popularity as the authority on the mythopoeic process of human experience.

READ AND DECIDE FOR YOURSELF:

Excerpts from:

WHAT LIFE SHOULD MEAN TO YOU
(ALFRED ADLER)

A PHILOSOPHY OF LIFE
(SIGMUND FREUD)

ESSAY ON PSYCHOLOGICAL TYPES
(C.G. JUNG)

---

67 Reproduced on: http://www.marxists.org/reference/subject/philosophy/works/at/adler.htm

362   THE MEANING OF LIFE

WHAT LIFE SHOULD MEAN TO YOU (1933) CHAPTER 2[68]

Alfred Adler (1931)

Chapter 2. Mind and Body

MEN have always debated whether the mind governs the body or the body governs the mind. Philosophers have joined in the controversy and taken one position or the other; they have called themselves idealists or materialists; they have brought up arguments by the thousand; and the question still seems as vexed and unsettled as ever. Perhaps Individual Psychology may give some help towards a solution; for in Individual Psychology we are really confronted with the living interactions of mind and body. Someone's mind and body is here to be treated; and if our treatment is wrongly based we shall fail to help him. Our theory must definitely grow from experience; it must definitely stand the test of application. We are living amongst these interactions, and we have the strongest challenge to find the right point of view.

The findings of Individual Psychology remove much of the tension from this problem. It no longer remains a plain 'either ... or'. We see that both mind and body are expressions of life: they are parts of the whole of life. And we begin to understand their reciprocal relations in that whole. The life of man is the life of a moving being, and it would not be sufficient for him to develop body alone. A plant is rooted: it stays in one place and cannot move. It would be very surprising, therefore, to discover that a plant had a mind; or at least a mind in any sense which we could comprehend. If a plant could foresee or project consequences, the faculty would be useless to it. What advantage would it be for the plant to think: 'Here is someone coming. In a minute he will tread on me, and I shall be dead underfoot'? The plant would still be unable to move out of the way.

All moving beings, however, can foresee and reckon up the direction in which to move; and this fact makes it necessary to postulate that they have minds or souls.

Sense, sure, you have,
Else you could not have motion.
[Hamlet, Act III, Scene 4]

This foreseeing the direction of movement is the central principle of the mind. As soon as we have recognised it we are in a position to understand how the mind governs the body it sets the goal for movements. Merely to initiate a random movement from moment to moment would never be enough: there must be a goal for the strivings. Since it is the mind's function to decide a point towards which movement is to be made, it occupies the governing position in life. At the

---

68 Reproduced on: http://www.marxists.org/reference/subject/philosophy/works/at/adler.htm

same time, the body influences the mind; it is the body which must be moved. The mind can move the body only in accordance with the possibilities which the body possesses and those which it can be trained to develop. If, for example, the mind proposes to move the body to the moon, it will fail unless it discovers a technique suited to the body's limitations.

Men are more engaged in movement than any other beings. They do not only move in more ways - as we can see in the complicated movements of their hands - but they are also more capable, by means of their movements, of moving the environment around them. We should expect, therefore, that the ability to foresee would be most highly developed in the human mind, and that men would give the clearest evidence of a purposive striving to improve their whole position with respect to their whole situation.

In every human being, moreover, we can discover behind all partial movements towards partial goals one single inclusive movement. All our strivings are directed towards a position in which a feeling of security has been achieved, a feeling that all the difficulties of life have been overcome and that we have emerged finally, in relation to the whole situation around us, safe and victorious. With this purpose in view, all movements and expressions must be coordinated and brought into a unity: the mind is compelled to develop as if to achieve a final ideal goal. It is no different with the body; the body also strives to be a unity. It, too, develops towards an ideal goal pre-existent in the germ. If, for example, the skin is broken all the body is busy in making itself whole again. The body, however, is not merely left alone to unfold its potentialities: the mind can help it in its development. The value of exercise and training, and of hygiene in general, have all been proved; and these are all aids for the body supplied by the mind in its striving towards the final goal.

From the first days of life, uninterruptedly till the end, this partnership of growth and development continues. Body and mind are co-operating as indivisible parts of one whole. The mind is like a motor, dragging with it all the potentialities which it can discover in the body, helping to bring the body into a position of safety and superiority to all difficulties. In every movement of the body, in every expression and symptom, we can see the impress of the mind's purpose. A man moves. There is meaning in his movement. He moves his eyes, his tongue, the muscles of his face. His face has an expression, a meaning. It is mind that puts meaning there. Now we can begin to see what psychology, or the science of mind, really deals with. The province of psychology is to explore the meaning involved in all the expressions of an individual, to find the key to his goal, and ta compare it with the goals of others.

In striving for the final goal of security, the mind is always faced with the necessity of making the goal concrete; of calculating 'security lies in this particular point; it is reached by going in this particular direction'. Here, of course, the chance of a mistake occurs; but without a quite definite goal and direction-setting there could be no movement at all. If I lift my hand, there must be a goal for the movement already in my mind. The direction which the mind chooses may be, in reality, disastrous; but it is chosen because the mind conceives it mistakenly as the most advantageous. All psychological mistakes are thus mistakes in choosing the direction of

364 THE MEANING OF LIFE

movement. The goal of security is common to all human beings; but some of them mistake the direction in which security lies and their concrete movements lead them astray.

If we see an expression or symptom and fail to recognise the meaning behind it, the best way to understand it is, first of all, to reduce it in outline to a bare movement. Let us take, for example, the expression of stealing. To steal is to remove property from another person to oneself. Let us now examine the goal of the movement: the goal is to enrich oneself, and to feel more secure by possessing more. The point at which the movement sets out is therefore a feeling of being poor and deprived. The next step is to find out in what circumstances the individual is placed and in what conditions he feels deprived. Finally we can see whether he is taking the right way to change these circumstances and overcome his feeling of being deprived; whether the movement is in the right direction, or whether he has mistaken the method of securing what he desires. We need not criticise his final goal; but we may be able to point out that he has chosen a mistaken way in making it concrete.

The changes which the human race has made in its environment we call our culture; and our culture is the result of all the movements which the minds of men have initiated for their bodies. Our work is inspired by our minds. The development of our bodies is directed and aided by our minds. In the end we shall not be able to find a single human expression which is not filled with the purposiveness of the mind. It is by no means desirable, however, that the mind should overstress its own part. If we are to overcome difficulties, bodily fitness is necessary. The mind is engaged, therefore, in governing the environment in such a way that the body can be defended - so that it can be protected from sickness, disease and death, from damage, accidents and failures of function. This is the purpose served by our ability to feel pleasure and pain, to create phantasies and to identify ourselves with good and bad situations. The feelings put the body in shape to meet a situation with a definite type of response. Phantasies and identifications are methods of foreseeing; but they are also more: they stir up the feelings in accordance with which the body will act. In this way the feelings of an individual bear the impress of the meaning he gives to life and of the goal he has set for his strivings. To a great extent, though they rule his body, they do not depend on his body: they will always depend primarily on his goal and his consequent style of life.

Clearly enough, it is not the style of life alone that governs an individual. His attitudes do not create his symptoms without further help. For action they must be reinforced by feelings. What is new in the outlook of Individual Psychology is our observation that the feelings are never in contradiction to the style of life. Where there is a goal, the feelings always adapt themselves to its attainment. We are no longer, therefore, in the realm of physiology or biology; the rise of feelings cannot be explained by chemical theory and cannot be predicted by chemical examination. In Individual Psychology we must presuppose the physiological processes, but we are more interested in the psychological goal. It is not so much our concern that anxiety influences the sympathetic and parasympathetic nerves. We look, rather, for the purpose and end of anxiety.

With this approach anxiety cannot be taken as rising from the suppression of sexuality, or as being left behind as the result of disastrous birth-experiences. Such explanations are beside the mark. We know that a child who is accustomed to be accompanied, helped and supported by its mother may find anxiety whatever its source - a very efficient weapon for controlling its mother. We are not satisfied with a physical description of anger; our experience has shown us that anger is a device to dominate a person or a situation. We can take it for granted that every bodily and mental expression must be based on inherited material; but our attention is directed to the use which is made of this material in striving to achieve a definite goal. This, it seems, is the only real psychological approach.

In every individual we see that feelings have grown and developed in the direction and to the degree which were essential to the attainment of his goal. His anxiety or courage, cheerfulness or sadness, have always agreed with his style of life: their proportionate strength and dominance has been exactly what we could expect. A man who accomplishes his goal of superiority by sadness cannot be gay and satisfied with his accomplishments. He can only be happy when he is miserable. We can notice also that feelings appear and disappear at need. A patient suffering from agoraphobia loses the feeling of anxiety when he is at home or when he is dominating another person. All neurotic patients exclude every part of life in which they do not feel strong enough to be the conqueror.

The emotional tone is as fixed as the style of life. The coward, for example, is always a coward, even though he is arrogant with weaker people or seems courageous when he is shielded by others. He may fix three locks on his door, protect himself with police dogs and mantraps and insist that he is full of courage. Nobody will be able to prove his feeling of anxiety; but the cowardice of his character is shown sufficiently by the trouble he has taken to protect himself.

The realm of sexuality and love gives a similar testimony. The feelings belonging to sex always appear when an individual desires to approach his sexual goal. By concentration, he tends to exclude conflicting tasks and incompatible interests; and thus he evokes the appropriate feelings and functions. The lack of these feelings and functions - as in impotence, premature ejaculation, perversion and frigidity - is established by refusing to exclude inappropriate tasks and interests. Such abnormalities are always induced by a mistaken goal of superiority and a mistaken style of life. We always find in such cases a tendency to expect consideration rather than to give it, a lack of social feeling, and a failure in courage and optimistic activity.

A patient of mine, a second child, suffered very profoundly from inescapable feelings of guilt. Both his father and his elder brother laid great emphasis on honesty. When the boy was seven years old he told his teacher in school that he had done a piece of homework by himself, although, as a matter of fact, his brother had done it for him. The boy concealed his guilty feelings for three years. At last he went to see the teacher and confessed his awful lie. The teacher merely laughed at him. Next he went to his father in tears and confessed a second time. This time he was more successful. The father was proud of his boy's love of truth; he praised and consoled him. In spite of the fact that his father had absolved him, the boy continued to be depressed. We can hardly avoid the conclusion that this boy was occupied in proving his great integrity and scrupulousness by accusing himself so bitterly for such a trifle. The high moral atmosphere of his

366 THE MEANING OF LIFE

home gave him the impulse to excel in integrity. He felt inferior to his elder brother in school work and social attractiveness; and he tried to achieve superiority by a sideline of his own.

Later in life he suffered from other self-reproaches. He masturbated and was never completely free from cheating in his studies. His feelings of guilt always increased before he took an examination. As he went on he collected difficulties of this sort. By means of his sensitive conscience he was much more burdened than his brother; and thus he had an excuse prepared for all failures to equal him. When he left the university, he planned to do technical work; but his compulsory feelings of guilt grew so poignant that he prayed through the whole day that God would forgive him. He was thus left without time for working.

By now his condition was so bad that he was sent to an asylum, and there he was considered as incurable. After a time, however, he improved and left the asylum, but asked permission to be readmitted if he should suffer a relapse. He changed his occupation and studied the history of art. The time came around for his examinations. He went to church on a public holiday. He threw himself down before the great crowd and cried out, 'I am the greatest sinner of all men.' In this way again he succeeded in drawing attention to his sensitive conscience.

After another period in the asylum he returned home. One day he came down to lunch naked. He was a well-built man and on this point he could compete well with his brother and with other people.

His feelings of guilt were means to make him appear more honest than others and in this way he was struggling to achieve superiority. His struggles, however, were directed towards the useless side of life. His escape from examinations and occupational work gives a sign of cowardice and a heightened feeling of inadequacy; and his whole neurosis was a purposive exclusion of every activity in which he feared a defeat. The same striving for superiority by shabby means is evident in his prostration in church and his sensational entrance into the dining-room. His style of life demanded them and the feelings he induced were entirely appropriate.

It is, as we have already seen, in the first four or five years of life that the individual is establishing the unity of his mind and constructing the relations between mind and body. He is taking his hereditary material and the impressions he receives from the environment and is adapting them to his pursuit of superiority. By the end of the fifth year his personality has crystallised. The meaning he gives to life, the goal he pursues, his style of approach, and his emotional disposition are all fixed. They can be changed later; but they can be changed only if he becomes free from the mistake involved in his childhood crystallisation. just as all his previous expressions were coherent with his interpretation of life, so now, if he is able to correct the mistake, his new expressions will be coherent with his new interpretation.

It is by means of his organs that an individual comes into touch with his environment and receives impressions from it. We can see, therefore, from the way he is training his body, the kind of impression he is prepared to receive from his environment and the use he is trying to make of his experience. If we notice the way he looks and listens and what it is that attracts his attention, we have learned much about him. This is the reason why postures have such an importance; they show us the training of the organs and the use which is being made of them to select impressions. Postures are always conditioned by meanings.

Now we can add to our definition of psychology. Psychology is the understanding of an individual's attitude towards the impressions of his body. We can also begin to see how the great differences between human minds come to arise. A body which is ill-suited to the environment and has difficulty in fulfilling the demands of the environment will usually be felt by the mind as a burden. For this reason children who have suffered from imperfect organs meet with greater hindrances than usual for their mental development. It is harder for their minds to influence, move and govern their bodies towards a position of superiority. A greater effort of mind is needed, and mental concentration must be higher than with others if they are to secure the same object. So the mind becomes overburdened and they become self-centred and egoistic. When a child is always occupied with the imperfection of its organs and the difficulties of movement, it has no attention to spare for what is outside itself. It finds neither the time nor the freedom to interest itself in others, and in consequence grows up with a lesser degree of social feeling and ability to co-operate.

Imperfect organs offer many handicaps but these handicaps are by no means an inescapable fate. If the mind is active on its own part and trains hard to overcome the difficulties, the individual may very well succeed in being as successful as those who were originally less burdened. Indeed, children with imperfect organs very often accomplish, in spite of their obstacles, more than children who start with more normal instruments. The handicap was a stimulus to go further ahead. A boy, for example, may suffer unusual stress through the imperfection of his eyes. He is more occupied in trying to see; he gives more attention to the visible world; he is more interested in distinguishing colours and forms. In the end, he comes to have a much greater experience of the visible world than children who never needed to struggle or to pay attention to small distinctions. Thus an imperfect organ can turn out to be the source of great advantages; but only if the mind has found the right technique for overcoming difficulties. Among painters and poets a great proportion are known to have suffered from imperfections of sight. These imperfections have been governed by well-trained minds; and finally their possessors could use their eyes to more purpose than others who were more nearly normal. The same kind of compensation can be seen, perhaps more easily, among left-handed children who have not been recognised as left-handed. At home, or in the beginning of their school-days, they were trained to use their imperfect right hands. Thus they were really not so well equipped for writing, drawing or handicraft. We might expect, if the mind can be used to overcome such difficulties, that often this imperfect right hand would develop a high degree of artistry. This is precisely what happens. In many instances left-handed children learn to have better handwriting than others, more talent for drawing and painting, or more skin in craftsmanship. By finding the right technique, by interest, training and exercise, they have turned disadvantage into advantage.

Only a child who desires to contribute to the whole, whose interest is not centred in himself, can train successfully to compensate for defects. If children desire only to rid themselves of difficulties, they will continue backward. They can keep up their courage only ff they have a

368 THE MEANING OF LIFE

purpose in view for their efforts and ff the achievement of this purpose is more important to them than the obstacles which stand in the way. It is a question of where their interest and attention is directed. If they are striving towards an object external to themselves, they will quite naturally train and equip themselves to achieve it. Difficulties win represent no more than positions which are to be conquered on their way to success. If, on the other hand, their interest hes in stressing their own drawbacks or in fighting these drawbacks with no purpose except to be free from them, they will be able to make no real progress. A clumsy right hand cannot be trained into a skilful right hand by taking thought, by wishing that it were less clumsy, or even by avoiding clumsiness. It can become so only by exercise in practical achievements; and the incentive to the achievement must be more deeply felt than the discouragement at the hitherto existent clumsiness. If a child is to draw together his powers and overcome his difficulties, there must be a goal for his movements outside of himself; a goal based on interest in reality, interest in others, and interest in co-operation.

A good example of hereditary capital and the use to which it may be turned was given me by my investigations into families which suffered from inferiority of the kidney tract. Very often children in these families suffered from enuresis. The organ inferiority is real; it can be shown in the kidney or the bladder or in the existence of a spina bifida; and often a corresponding imperfection of the lumbar segment can be suspected from a naevus or birth-mole on the skin in that area. The organ inferiority, however, by no means accounts sufficiently for the enuresis. The child is not under the compulsion of his organs; and he uses them in his own way. Some children, for example, will wet the bed at night and never wet themselves during the day. Sometimes the habit will disappear suddenly, upon a change in the environment or in the attitude of the parents. Enuresis can be overcome, except among feeble-minded children, ff the child ceases to use the imperfection of his organs for a mistaken purpose.

Mainly, however, children who suffer from enuresis are being stimulated not to overcome it but to continue it. A skilful mother can give the right training; but if the mother is not skilful an unnecessary weakness persists. Often in families which suffer from kidney troubles or bladder troubles everything to do with urinating is over-stressed. Mothers will then mistakenly try very hard to stop the enuresis. If the child notices how much value is placed on this point, he will very probably resist. It will give him a very good opportunity to assert his opposition to this kind of education. If a child resists the treatment which his parents give him, he will always find his way to attack them at their point of greatest weakness. A very well-known sociologist in Germany has discovered that a surprising proportion of criminals spring from families which are occupied in the suppression of crime; from the families of judges, policemen, or prison warders. Often the children of teachers are obstinately backward. In my own experience I have often found this true; and I have found also a surprising number of neurotic children among the children of doctors and of delinquent children among the children of ministers of religion. In a similar way, the children whose parents over-stress urination have a very clear way open for them to show that they have wills of their own.

Enuresis can also provide us with a good example of how dreams are used to stir up emotions appropriate to the actions we intend. Often children who wet the bed dream that they have got out of bed and gone to the toilet. In this way they have excused themselves; now they are perfectly right to wet the bed. The purpose which enuresis serves is generally to attract notice, to subordinate others, to occupy their attention in the night-time as well as the day. Sometimes it is to antagonise them; the habit is a declaration of enmity. From every angle, we can see that enuresis is really a creative expression; the child is speaking with his bladder instead of his mouth. The organic imperfection does no more than offer him the means for the expression of his opinion.

Children who express themselves in this way are always suffering from a tension. Generally they belong to the class of spoiled children who have lost their position of being the unique centre of attention. Another child has been born, perhaps, and they find it more difficult to secure the undivided attention of their mothers. Enuresis thus represents a movement to come in closer contact with the mother, even by unpleasant means. It says, in effect, 'I am not so far advanced as you think: I must still be watched'. In different circumstances, or with a different organ imperfection, they would have chosen other means. They might have used sound, for example, to establish the connection, in which case they would have been restless and cried during the night. Some children walk in their sleep, have nightmares, fall out of bed, or become thirsty and call for water. The psychological background for these expressions is similar. The choice of symptom depends in part on the organic situation and in part on the attitude of the environment.

Such cases show very well the influence which the mind exerts over the body. In all probability the mind does not only affect the choice of a particular bodily symptom; it is governing and influencing the whole building-up of the body. We have no direct proof of this hypothesis; and it is difficult to see how a proof could ever be established. The evidence, however, seems clear enough. If a boy is timid, his timidity is reflected in his whole development. He will not care for physical achievements; or, rather, he will not think of them as possible for himself. In consequence, it will not occur to him to train his muscles in an efficient way, and he will exclude all the impressions from outside that would ordinarily be a stimulus to muscular development. Other children, who allow themselves to be influenced and interested in the training of their muscles, will go farther ahead in physical fitness; he, because his interest is blocked, will remain behind.

From such consideration we can fairly conclude that the whole form and development of the body is affected by the mind and reflects the errors or deficiencies of the mind. We can often observe bodily expressions which are plainly the end results of mental failings, where the right way to compensate for a difficulty has not been discovered. We may be sure, for example, that the endocrine glands themselves can be influenced in the first four or five years of life. Imperfect glands never have a compulsive influence on conduct; on the other hand, they are being continuously affected by the whole environment, by the direction in which the child seeks to receive impressions, and by the creative activity of its mind in this interesting situation.

370 THE MEANING OF LIFE

Another piece of evidence would perhaps be more readily understood and accepted, since it is more familiar and leads towards a temporary expression, not towards a fixed disposition of the body. To a certain degree every emotion finds some bodily expression. The individual will show his emotion in some visible form; perhaps in his posture and attitude, perhaps in his face, perhaps in the trembling of his legs and knees. Similar changes could be found in the organs themselves. If he flushes or turns pale, for example, the circulation of the blood is affected. In anger, anxiety, sorrow or any other emotion, the body always speaks; and each individual's body speaks in a language of its own. When one man is in a situation in which he is afraid, he trembles; the hair of another will stand on end; a third will have palpitations of the heart. Still others will sweat or choke, speak in a hoarse voice, or shrink physically and cower away. Sometimes the tonus of the body is affected, the appetite lost, or vomiting induced. With some it is the bladder which is mainly irritated by such emotions, with others the sexual organs. Many children feel stimulated in the sexual organs when taking examinations; and it is well known that criminals will frequently go to a house of prostitution, or to their sweethearts, after they have committed a crime. In the realm of science we find psychologists who claim that sex and anxiety go together and psychologists who claim that they have not the remotest connection. Their point of view depends on their personal experience; with some there is a connection, with others not.

All of these responses belong to different types of individuals. They could probably be discovered to be to some extent hereditary, and physical expressions of this kind will often give us hints of the weaknesses and peculiarities of the family tree. Other members of the family may make a very similar bodily response. What is most interesting here, however, is to see how, by means of the emotions, the mind is able to activate the physical conditions. The emotions and their physical expressions tell us how the mind is acting and reacting in a situation which it interprets as favourable or unfavourable. In an outburst of temper, for example, the individual has wished to overcome his imperfections as quickly as possible. The best way has seemed to be to hit, accuse or attack another individual. The anger, in its turn, influences the organs: mobilises them for action or lays an additional stress on them. Some people when they are angry have stomach trouble at the same time, or grow red in the face. Their circulation is altered to such a degree that a headache ensues. We shall generally find unadmitted rage or humiliation behind attacks of migraine, or habitual headaches; and with some people anger results in trigeminal neuralgia or fits of an epileptic nature.

The means by which the body is influenced have never been completely explored, and we shall probably never have a full account of them. A mental tension affects both the voluntary system and the vegetative nerve system. Where there is tension, there is action in the voluntary system. The individual drums on the table, plucks at his lips or tears up pieces of paper. If he is tense, he has to move in some way. Chewing a pencil or a cigar gives him an outlet for his tension. These movements show us that he feels himself too much confronted by some situation. It is the same whether he blushes when he is among strangers, begins to tremble or exhibits a tic; they are all results of tension. By means of the vegetative system, the tension is communicated to the whole body; and so, with every emotion, the whole body is itself in a tension. The manifestations of this tension, however, are not as clear at every point; and we speak of symptoms only in those points where the results are discoverable., If we examine more closely we shall find that every part of the body is involved in an emotional expression; and that these physical expressions are the consequences of the action of the mind and the body. It is always necessary to look for these reciprocal actions of the mind on the body, and of the body on the mind, since both of them are parts of the whole with which we are concerned.

We may reasonably conclude from such evidence that a style of life and a corresponding emotional disposition exert a continuous influence on the development of the body. If it is true that a child crystallises its style of life very early, we should be able to discover., if we are experienced enough, the resulting physical expressions in later life. A courageous individual will show the effects of his attitude in his physique. His body will be differently built up; the tonus of his muscles will be stronger, the carriage of his body will be firmer. Posture probably influences very considerably the development of the body and perhaps accounts in part for the better tonus of the muscles. The expression of the face is different in the courageous individual, and, in the end, the whole cast of features. Even the conformation of the skull may be affected.

Today it would be difficult to deny that the mind can influence the brain. Pathology has shown cases where an individual has lost the ability to read or write through a lesion in the left hemisphere, but has been able to recover this ability by training other parts of the brain. It often happens that an individual has an apoplectic stroke and there is no possibility of repairing the damaged part of the brain; and yet other parts of the brain compensate, restore the functions of the organs and so complete once more the brain's faculties. This fact is especially important in helping us to show the possibilities of the educational application of Individual Psychology. If the mind can exercise such an influence over the brain; if the brain is no more than the tool of the mind - its most important tool, but still only its tool - then we can find ways to develop and improve this tool. No one born with a certain standard of brain need remain inescapably bound by it all his life: methods may be found to make the brain better fitted for life.

A mind which has fixed its goal in a mistaken direction - which ' for example, is not developing the ability to co-operate - will fail to exercise a helpful influence on the growth of the brain. For this reason we find that many children who lack the ability to co-operate show, in later life, that they have not developed their intelligence, their ability to understand. Since the whole bearing of an adult reveals the influence of the style of life which he built up in the first four or five years, since we can see visibly before us the results of his scheme of apperception and the meaning which he has given to life, we can discover the blocks in co-operation from which he is suffering, and help to correct his failures. Already in Individual Psychology we have the first steps towards this science.

Many authors have pointed out a constant relationship between the expressions of the mind and those of the body. None of them, it seems, has attempted to discover the bridge between the two. Kretschmer, for example, has described how, in the build of the body, we can discover a correspondence with a certain type of mind. He is thus able to distinguish types into which he fits

372   THE MEANING OF LIFE

a great proportion of mankind. There are, for instance, the pyknoids, round-faced individuals with short noses and a tendency to corpulence; the men of whom Julius Caesar speaks:

> *'Let me have men about me that are fat;*
> *Sleek-headed men and such as sleep o' nights."*

With such a physique Kretschmer correlates specific mental characteristics; but his work does not make clear the reasons for this correlation. In our own conditions, individuals of this physique do not appear as suffering from organ imperfection; their bodies are well suited to our culture. Physically they feel equal to others. They have confidence in their own strength. They are not tense and, if they wished to fight, they would feel capable of fighting. They have no need, however, to look on others as their enemies or to struggle with life as if it were hostile. One school of psychology would call them extroverts, but would offer no explanation. We should expect them to be extroverts, because they suffer no trouble from their bodies.

A contrasting type which Kretschmer distinguishes is the schizoid, either infantile or unusually tall, long-nosed, with an egg-shaped head. These he believes to be reserved and introspective; and if they suffer from mental disturbances, they become schizophrenic. They are of the other type of which Caesar speaks:

> *"'Yond Cassius has a lean and hungry look;*
> *He thinks too much; such men are dangerous."*

Perhaps these individuals suffered from imperfect organs and grew up more self-interested, more pessimistic and more 'introverted'. Perhaps they made more claims for help, and when they found that they were not sufficiently considered, became bitter and suspicious. We can find, however, as Kretschmer admits, many mixed types, and even pyknoid types who have developed with the mental characteristics attributed to schizoids. We could understand this if their circumstances had burdened them in another way, and they had become timid and discouraged. We could probably, by systematic discouragement, make any child into a person who behaved like a schizoid.

If we had much experience behind us, we could recognise from all the partial expressions of an individual the degree of his ability to co-operate. Without knowing it, people have always been looking for such signs. The necessity for co-operation is always pressing us; and hints have already been discovered, not scientifically but intuitively, to show us how to orient ourselves better in this chaotic life. In the same way we can see that before all the great adjustments of history the mind of the people had already recognised the necessity for adjustment and was striving to achieve it. So long as the striving is only instinctive, mistakes can easily be made. People have always disliked individuals who had very noticeable physical peculiarities, disfigured persons or hunchbacks. Without knowing it, they were judging them as less fitted for co-operation. This was a great mistake, but their judgment was probably founded on experience.

The way had not yet been found to increase the degree of co-operation in individuals who suffered from these peculiarities; their drawbacks were therefore over-emphasised, and they became the victims of popular superstition.

Let us now summarise our position. In the first four or five years of life the child unifies its mental strivings and establishes the root relationships between its mind and its body. A fixed style of life is adopted, with a corresponding emotional and physical habitus. Its development includes a larger or smaller degree of co-operation; and it is from this degree of co-operation that we learn to judge and understand the individual. In all failures the highest common measure is a small degree of ability to cooperate. We can now give a still further definition of psychology: it is the understanding of deficiencies in co-operation. Since the mind is a unity and the same style of life runs through all its expressions, all of an individual's emotions and thoughts must be consonant with his style of life. If we see emotions that apparently cause difficulties and run counter to the individual's own welfare, it is completely useless to begin by trying to change these emotions. They are the right expression of the individual's style of life, and they can be uprooted only if he changes his style of life.

Here Individual Psychology gives us a special hint for our educational and therapeutic outlook. We must never treat a symptom or a single expression: we must discover the mistake made in the whole style of life, in the way the mind has interpreted its experiences, in the meaning it has given to life, and in the actions with which it has answered the impressions received from the body and from the environment. This is the real task of psychology. It is not properly to be called psychology if we stick pins into a child and see how far it jumps, or tickle it and see how loud it laughs. These enterprises, so common among modem psychologists, may in fact tell us something of an individual's psychology; but only in so far as they give evidence of a fixed and particular style of life. Styles of life are the proper subject-matter of psychology and the material for investigation; and schools which take any other subject-matter are occupied, in the main part, with physiology or biology. This holds true of those who investigate stimuli and reactions; those who attempt to trace the effect of a trauma or shocking experience; and those who examine inherited abilities and look to see how they unfold themselves. In Individual Psychology, however, we are considering the psyche itself, the unified mind; we are examining the meaning which individuals give to the world and to themselves, their goals, the direction of their strivings, and the approaches they make to the problems of life. The best key which we so far possess for understanding psychological differences is given by examining the degree of ability to co-operate.

374 THE MEANING OF LIFE

Summary of Alfred Adler's Development Model:[69]

(This table is a broad simplification of Adler's theory.)

POSITION	FAMILY SITUATION	CHILD'S CHARACTERISTICS
ONLY	Birth is a miracle. Parents have no previous experience. Retains 200% attention from both parents. May become rival of one parent. Can be over-protected and spoiled.	Likes being the center of adult attention. Often has difficulty sharing with siblings and peers. Prefers adult company and uses adult language.
OLDEST	Dethroned by next child. Has to learn to share. Parent expectations are usually very high. Often given resposnsibility and expected to set an example.	May become authoritarian or strict. Feels power is his right. Can become helpful if encouraged. May turn to father after birth of next child.
SECOND	He has a pacemaker. There is always someone ahead.	Is more competitive, wants to overtake older child. May become a rebel or try to outdo everyone. Competition can deteriorate into rivalry.
MIDDLE	Is "sandwiched" in. May feel squeezed out of a position of privilege and significance.	May be even-tempered, "take it or leave it" attitude. May have trouble finding a place or become a fighter of injustice.
YOUNGEST	Has many mothers and fathers. Older children try to educate him. Never dethroned.	Wants to be bigger than the others. May have huge plans that never work out. Can stay the "baby." Frequently spoiled.
TWIN	One is usually stronger or more active.	Can have identity problems.

---

[69] http://ourworld.compuserve.com/homepages/hstein/birthord.htm

		Parents may see one as the older.	Stronger one may become the leader.
"GHOST CHILD"		Child born after the death of the first child may have a "ghost" in front of him. Mother may become over-protective.	Child may exploit mother's over-concern for his well-being, or he may rebel, and protest the feeling of being compared to an idealized memory.
ADOPTED CHILD		Parents may be so thankful to have a child that they spoil him. They may try to compensate for the loss of his biological parents.	Child may become very spoiled and demanding. Eventually, he may resent or idealize the biological parents.
ONLY BOY AMONG GIRLS		Usually with women all the time, if father is away.	May try to prove he is the man in the family, or become effeminate.
ONLY GIRL AMONG BOYS		Older brothers may act as her protectors.	Can become very feminine, or a tomboy and outdo the brothers. May try to please the father.
ALL BOYS		If mother wanted a girl, can be dressed as a girl.	Child may capitalize on assigned role or protest it vigorously.
ALL GIRLS		May be dressed as a boy.	Child may capitalize on assigned role or protest it vigorously.

GENERAL NOTES

1. The psychological situation of each child in the family is different.

2. The child's opinion of himself and his situation determines his choice of attitude.

3. If more than 3 years separate children, sub-groups of birth order may form.

4. A child's birth order position may be seized by another child if circumstances permit.

5. Competition may be expressed in choice of interests or development of characteristics.

6. Birth order is sometimes not a major influences on personality development. The other potentially significant influences are: organ inferiority, parental attitudes, social & economic position, and gender roles.

7. For more comprehensive information about birth order, read: *What Life Could Mean to You*, by Alfred Adler; *The Individual Psychology of Alfred Adler*, edited by Heinz and Rowena Ansbacher; and *Lydia Sicher: An Adlerian Perspective*, edited by Adele Davidson.

8. Adler speculated that birth order differences would begin to disappear when families became less competitive and autocratic, and more cooperative and democratic.

LECTURE XXXV (1932) A PHILOSOPHY OF LIFE

Sigmund Freud (1932)

Source: New Introductory Lectures on Psycho-analysis (1933). [70]

LADIES AND GENTLEMEN - In the last lecture we were occupied with trivial everyday affairs, with putting, as it were, our modest house in order. We will now take a bold step, and risk an answer to a question which has repeatedly been raised in non-analytic quarters, namely, the question whether psychoanalysis leads to any particular Weltanschauung, and if so, to what.'Weltanschauung' is, I am afraid, a specifically German notion, which it would be difficult to translate into a foreign language. If I attempt to give you a definition of the word, it can hardly fail to strike you as inept. By Weltanschauung, then, I mean an intellectual construction that gives a unified solution of all the problems of our existence in virtue of a comprehensive hypothesis, a construction, therefore, in which no question is left open and in which everything in which we are interested finds a place. It is easy to see that the possession of such a Weltanschauung is one of the ideal wishes of mankind. When one believes in such a thing, one feels secure in life, one knows what one ought to strive after, and how one ought to organise one's emotions and interests to the best purpose.

If that is what is meant by a Weltanschauung, then the question is an easy one for psychoanalysis to answer. As a specialised science, a branch of psychology - 'depth-psychology' or psychology of the unconscious - it is quite unsuited to form a Weltanschauung of its own; it must accept that of science in general. The scientific Weltanschauung is, however, markedly at variance with our definition. The unified nature of the explanation of the universe is, it is true, accepted by science, but only as a programme whose fulfilment is postponed to the future. Otherwise it is distinguished by negative characteristics, by a limitation to what is, at any given time, knowable, and a categorical rejection of certain elements which are alien to it. It asserts that there is no other source of knowledge of the universe but the intellectual manipulation of carefully verified observations, in fact, what is called research, and that no knowledge can be obtained from revelation, intuition or inspiration. It appears that this way of looking at things came very near to receiving general acceptance during the last century or two. It has been reserved for the present century to raise the objection that such a Weltanschauung is both empty and unsatisfying, that it overlooks all the spiritual demands of man, and all the needs of the human mind.

---

70 Accessed: http://www.marxists.org/reference/subject/philosophy/works/at/freud.htm

This objection cannot be too strongly repudiated. It cannot be supported for a moment, for the spirit and the mind are the subject of scientific investigation in exactly the same way as any non-human entities. Psycho-analysis has a peculiar right to speak on behalf of the scientific Weltanschauung in this connection, because it cannot be accused of neglecting the part occupied by the mind in the universe. The contribution of psychoanalysis to science consists precisely in having extended research to the region of the mind. Certainly without such a psychology science would be very incomplete. But if we add to science the investigation of the intellectual and emotional functions of men (and animals), we find that nothing has been altered as regards the general position of science, that there are no new sources of knowledge or methods of research. Intuition and inspiration would be such, if they existed; but they can safely be counted as illusions, as fulfilments of wishes. It is easy to see, moreover, that the qualities which, as - we have shown, are expected of a Weltanschauung have a purely emotional basis. Science takes account of the fact that the mind of man creates such demands and is ready to trace their source, but it has not the slightest ground for thinking them justified. On the contrary, it does well to distinguish carefully between illusion (the results of emotional demands of that kind) and knowledge.

This does not at all imply that we need push these wishes contemptuously aside, or under-estimate their value in the lives of human beings. We are prepared to take notice of the fulfilments they have achieved for themselves in the creations of art and in the systems of religion and philosophy; but we cannot overlook the fact that it would be wrong and highly inexpedient to allow such things to be carried over into the domain of knowledge. For in that way one would open the door which gives access to the region of the psychoses, whether individual or group psychoses, and one would drain off from these tendencies valuable energy which is directed towards reality and which seeks by means of reality to satisfy wishes and needs as far as this is possible.

From the point of view of science we must necessarily make use of our critical powers in this direction, and not be afraid to reject and deny. It is inadmissible to declare that science is one field of human intellectual activity, and that religion and philosophy are others, at least as valuable, and that science has no business to interfere with the other two, that they all have an equal claim to truth, and that everyone is free to choose whence he shall draw his convictions and in what he shall place his belief. Such an attitude is considered particularly respectable, tolerant, broad-minded and free from narrow prejudices. Unfortunately it is not tenable; it shares all the pernicious qualities of an entirely unscientific Weltanschauung and in practice comes to much the same thing. The bare fact is that truth cannot be tolerant and cannot admit compromise or limitations, that scientific research looks on the whole field of human activity as its own, and must adopt an uncompromisingly critical attitude towards any other power that seeks to usurp any part of its province.

Of the three forces which can dispute the position of science, religion alone is a really serious enemy. Art is almost always harmless and beneficent, it does not seek to be anything else but an illusion. Save in the case of a few people who are, one might say, obsessed by art, it never

THE MEANING OF LIFE

dares to make any attacks on the realm of reality. Philosophy is not opposed to science, it behaves itself as if it were a science, and to a certain extent it makes use of the same methods; but it parts company with science, in that it clings to the illusion that it can produce a complete and coherent picture of the universe, though in fact that picture must needs fall to pieces with every new advance in our knowledge. Its methodological error lies in the fact that it over-estimates the epistemological value of our logical operations, and to a certain extent admits the validity of other sources of knowledge, such as intuition. And often enough one feels that the poet Heine is not unjustified when he says of the philosopher:

> *'With his night-cap and his night-shirt tatters,*
> *He botches up the loop-holes in the structure of the world.'*

But philosophy has no immediate influence on the great majority of mankind; it interests only a small number even of the thin upper stratum of intellectuals, while all the rest find it beyond them. In contradistinction to philosophy, religion is a tremendous force, which exerts its power over the strongest emotions of human beings. As we know, at one time it included everything that played any part in the mental life of mankind, that it took the place of science, when as yet science hardly existed, and that it built up a Weltanschauung of incomparable consistency and coherence which, although it has been severely shaken, has lasted to this day.

If one wishes to form a true estimate of the full grandeur of religion, one must keep in mind what it undertakes to do for men. It gives them information about the source and origin of the universe it assures them of protection and final happiness amid the changing vicissitudes of life, and it guides their thoughts and actions by means of precepts which are backed by the whole force of its authority. It fulfils, therefore, three functions. In the first place, it satisfies man's desire for knowledge; it is here doing the same thing that science attempts to accomplish by its own methods, and here, therefore, enters into rivalry with it. It is to the second function that it performs that religion no doubt owes the greater part of its influence. In so far as religion brushes away men's fear of the dangers and vicissitudes of life, in so far as it assures them of a happy ending, and comforts them in their misfortunes, science cannot compete with it. Science, it is true, teaches how one can avoid certain dangers and how one can combat many sufferings with success; it would be quite untrue to deny that science is a powerful aid to human beings, but in many cases it has to leave them to their suffering, and can only advise them to submit to the inevitable. In the performance of its third function, the provision of precepts, prohibitions and restrictions, religion is furthest removed from science. For science is content with discovering and stating the facts. It is true that from the applications of science rules and recommendations for behaviour may be deduced. In certain circumstances they may be the same as those which are laid down by religion, but even so the reasons for them will be different.

It is not quite clear why religion should combine these three functions. What has the explanation of the origin of the universe to do with the inculcation of certain ethical precepts? Its assurances of protection and happiness are more closely connected with these precepts. They are the reward for the fulfilment of the commands; only he who obeys them can count on receiving these benefits, while punishment awaits the disobedient. For the matter of that something of the same kind applies to science; for it declares that anyone who disregards its inferences is liable to suffer for it.

One can only understand this remarkable combination of teaching, consolation and precept in religion if one subjects it to genetic analysis. We may begin with the most remarkable item of the three, the teaching about the origin of the universe for why should a cosmogony be a regular element of religious systems? The doctrine is that the universe was created by a being similar to man, but greater in every respect, in power, wisdom and strength of passion, in fact by an idealised superman. Where you have animals as creators of the universe, you have indications of the influence of totemism, which I shall touch on later, at any rate with a brief remark. It is interesting to notice that this creator of the universe is always a single god, even when many gods are believed in. Equally interesting is the fact that the creator is nearly always a male, although there is no lack of indication of the existence of female deities, and many mythologies make the creation of the world begin precisely with a male god triumphing over a female goddess, who is degraded into a monster. This raises the most fascinating minor problems, but we must hurry on. The rest of our enquiry is made easy because this God-Creator is openly called Father. Psycho-analysis concludes that he really is the father, clothed in the grandeur in which he once appeared to the small child. The religious man's picture of the creation of the universe is the same as his picture of his own creation.

If this is so, then it is easy to understand how it is that the comforting promises of protection and the severe ethical commands are found together with the cosmogony. For the same individual to whom the child owes its own existence, the father (or, more correctly, the parental function which is composed of the father and the mother), has protected and watched over the weak and helpless child, exposed as it is to all the dangers which threaten in the external world; in its father's care it has felt itself safe. Even the grown man, though he may know that he possesses greater strength, and though he has greater insight into the dangers of life, rightly feels that fundamentally he is just as helpless and unprotected as he was in childhood and that in relation to the external world he is still a child. Even now, therefore, he cannot give up the protection which he has enjoyed as a child. But he has long ago realised that his father is a being with strictly limited powers and by no means endowed with every desirable attribute. He therefore looks back to the memory-image of the overrated father of his childhood, exalts it into a Deity, and brings it into the present and into reality. The emotional strength of this memory-image and the lasting nature of his need for protection are the two supports of his belief in God.

The third main point of the religious programme, its ethical precepts, can also be related without any difficulty to the situation of childhood. In a famous passage, which I have already quoted in an earlier lecture, the philosopher Kant speaks of the starry heaven above us and the moral law within us as the strongest evidence for the greatness of God. However odd it may sound to put these two side by side - for what can the heavenly bodies have to do with the question whether one man loves another or kills him? - nevertheless it touches on a great

380 THE MEANING OF LIFE

psychological truth. The same father (the parental function) who gave the child his life, and preserved it from the dangers which that life involves, also taught it what it may or may not do, made it accept certain limitations of its instinctual wishes, and told it what consideration it would be expected to show towards its parents and brothers and sisters, if it wanted to be tolerated and liked as a member of the family circle, and later on of more extensive groups. The child is brought up to know its social duties by means of a system of love-rewards and punishments, and in this way it is taught that its security in life depends on its parents (and, subsequently, other people) loving it and being able to believe in its love for them. This whole state of affairs is carried over by the grown man unaltered into his religion. The prohibitions and commands of his parents live on in his breast as his moral conscience; God rules the world of men with the help of the same system of rewards and punishments, and the degree of protection and happiness which each individual enjoys depends on his fulfilment of the demands of morality; the feeling of security, with which he fortifies himself against the dangers both of the external world and of his human environment, is founded on his love of God and the consciousness of God's love for him. Finally, he has in prayer a direct influence on the divine will, and in - that way insures for himself a share in the divine omnipotence.

I am sure that while you have been listening to me a whole host of questions must have come into your minds which you would like to have answered. I cannot undertake to do so here and now, but I am perfectly certain that none of these questions of detail would shake our thesis that the religious Weltanschauung is determined by the situation that subsisted in our childhood. It is therefore all the more remarkable that, in spite of its infantile character, it nevertheless has a forerunner. There was, without doubt, a time when there was no religion and no gods. It is known as the age of animism. Even at that time the world was full of spirits in the semblance of men (demons, as we call them), and all the objects in the external world were their dwelling-place or perhaps identical with them; but there was no supreme power which had created them all which controlled them, and to which it was possible to turn for protection and aid. The demons of animism were usually hostile to man, but it seems as though man had more confidence in himself in those days than later on. He was no doubt in constant terror of these evil spirits, but he defended himself against them by means of certain actions to which he ascribed the power to drive them away. Nor did he think himself entirely powerless in other ways. If he wanted something from nature - rain, for instance-he did not direct a prayer to the Weather-god, but used a spell, by means of which he expected to exert a direct influence over nature; he himself made something which resembled rain. In his fight against the powers of the surrounding world his first weapon was magic, the first forerunner of our modern technology. We suppose that this confidence in magic is derived from the over-estimation of the individual's own intellectual operations, from the belief in the 'omnipotence of thoughts', which, incidentally, we come across again in our obsessional neurotics. We may imagine that the men of that time were particularly proud of their acquisition of speech, which must have been accompanied by a great facilitation of thought. They attributed magic power to the spoken word. This feature was later on taken over by religion. 'And God said: Let there be light, and there was light.' But the fact of magic actions shows that animistic man did not rely entirely on the force of his own wishes. On the contrary, he depended for success upon the performance of an action which would cause Nature to imitate it. If he wanted it to rain, he himself poured out water; if he wanted to stimulate the soil to fertility, he offered it a performance of sexual intercourse in the fields.

You know how tenaciously anything that has once found psychological expression persists. You will therefore not be surprised to hear that a great many manifestations of animism have lasted up to the present day, mostly as what are called superstitions, side by side with and behind religion. But more than that, you can hardly avoid coming to the conclusion that our philosophy has preserved essential traits of animistic modes of thought such as the over-estimation of the magic of words and the belief that real processes in the external world follow the lines laid down by our thoughts. It is, to be sure, an animism without magical practices. On the other hand, we should expect to find that in the age of animism there must already have been some kind of morality, some rules governing the intercourse of men with one another. But there is no evidence that they were closely bound up with animistic beliefs. Probably they were the immediate expression of the distribution of power and of practical necessities.

It would be very interesting to know what determined the transition from animism to religion; but you may imagine in what darkness this earliest epoch in the evolution of the human mind is still shrouded. It seems to be a fact that the earliest form in which religion appeared was the remarkable one of totemism, the worship of animals, in the train of which followed the first ethical commands, the taboos. In a book called Totem and Taboo, I once worked out a suggestion in accordance with which this change is to be traced back to an upheaval in the relationships in the human family. The main achievement of religion, as compared with animism, lies in the psychic binding of - the fear of demons. Nevertheless, the evil spirit still has a place in the religious system as a relic of the previous age.

So much for the pre-history of the religious Weltanschauung. Let us now turn to consider what has happened since, and what is still going on under our own eyes. The scientific spirit, strengthened by the observation of natural processes, began in the course of time to treat religion as a human matter, and to subject it to a critical examination. This test it failed to pass. In the first place, the accounts of miracles roused a feeling of surprise and disbelief, since they contradicted everything that sober observation had taught, and betrayed all too clearly the influence of human imagination. In the next place, its account of the nature of the universe had to be rejected, because it showed evidence of a lack of knowledge which bore the stamp of earlier days, and because, owing to increasing familiarity with the laws of nature, it had lost its authority. The idea that the universe came into being through an act of generation or creation, analogous to that which produces an individual human being, no longer seemed to be the most obvious and self-evident hypothesis; for the distinction between living and sentient beings and inanimate nature had become apparent to the human mind, and had made it impossible to retain the original animistic theory. Besides this, one must not overlook the influence of the comparative study of different religious systems, and the impression they give of mutual exclusiveness and intolerance.

382   THE MEANING OF LIFE

Fortified by these preliminary efforts, the scientific spirit at last summoned up courage to put to the test the most important and the most emotionally significant elements of the religious Weltanschauung. The truth could have been seen at any time, but it was long before anyone dared to say it aloud: the assertions made by religion that it could give protection and happiness to men, if they would only fulfil certain ethical obligations, were unworthy of belief. It seems not to be true that there is a power in the universe which watches over the well-being of every individual with parental care and brings all his concerns to a happy ending. On the contrary, the destinies of man are incompatible with a universal principle of benevolence or with - what is to some degree contradictory - a universal principle of justice. Earthquakes, floods and fires do not differentiate between the good and devout man and the sinner and unbeliever. And, even if we leave inanimate nature out of account and consider the destinies of individual men in so far as they depend on their relations with others of their own kind, it is by no means the rule that virtue is rewarded and wickedness punished, but it happens often enough that the violent, the crafty and the unprincipled seize the desirable goods of the earth for themselves, while the pious go empty away. Dark, unfeeling and unloving powers determine human destiny; the system of rewards and punishments, which, according to religion, governs the world, seems to have no existence. This is another occasion for abandoning a portion of the animism which has found refuge in religion.

The last contribution to the criticism of the religious Weltanschauung has been made by psychoanalysis, which has traced the origin of religion to the helplessness of childhood, and its content to the persistence of the wishes and needs of childhood into maturity. This does not precisely imply a refutation of religion, but it is a necessary rounding off of our knowledge about it, and, at least on one point, it actually contradicts it, for religion lays claim to a divine origin. This claim, to be sure, is not false, if our interpretation of God is accepted.

The final judgment of science on the religious Weltanschauung, then, runs as follows. While the different religions wrangle with one another as to which of them is in possession of the truth, in our view the truth of religion may be altogether disregarded. Religion is an attempt to get control over the sensory world, in which we are placed, by means of the wish-world, which we have developed inside us as a result of biological and psychological necessities. But it cannot achieve its end. Its doctrines carry with them the stamp of the times in which they originated, the ignorant childhood days of the human race. Its consolations deserve no trust. Experience teaches us that the world is not a nursery. The ethical commands, to which religion seeks to lend its weight, require some other foundation instead, for human society cannot do without them, and it is dangerous to link up obedience to them with religious belief. If one attempts to assign to religion its place in man's evolution, it seems not so much to be a lasting acquisition as a parallel to the neurosis which the civilised individual must pass through on his way from childhood to maturity.

You are, of course, perfectly free to criticise this account of mine, and I am prepared to meet you half-way. What I have said about the gradual crumbling of the religious Weltanschauung was no doubt an incomplete abridgment of the whole story; the order of the separate events was not quite correctly given, and the co-operation of various forces towards the awakening of the scientific spirit was not traced. I have also left out of account the alterations which occurred in the religious Weltanschauung itself, both during the period of its unchallenged authority and afterwards under the influence of awakening criticism. Finally I have, strictly speaking, limited my remarks to one single form of religion, that of the Western peoples. I have, as it were, constructed a lay-figure for the purposes of a demonstration which I desired to be as rapid and as impressive as possible. Let us leave on one side the question of whether my knowledge would in any case have been sufficient to enable me to do it better or more completely. I am aware that you can find all that I have said elsewhere, and find it better said; none of it is new. But I am firmly convinced that the most careful elaboration of the material upon which the problems of religion are based would not shake these conclusions.

As you know, the struggle between the scientific spirit and the religious Weltanschauung is not yet at an end; it is still going on under our very eyes to-day. However little psychoanalysis may make use as a rule of polemical weapons, we will not deny ourselves the pleasure of looking into this conflict. Incidentally, we may perhaps arrive at a clearer understanding of our attitude towards the Weltanschauung. You will see how easily some of the arguments which are brought forward by the supporters of religion can be disproved; though others may succeed in escaping refutation.

The first objection that one hears is to the effect that it is an impertinence on the part of science to take religion as a subject for its investigations, since religion is something supreme, something superior to the capacities of the human understanding, something which must not be approached with the sophistries of criticism. In other words, science is not competent to sit in judgment on religion. No doubt it is quite useful and valuable, so long as it is restricted to its own province; but religion does not lie in that province, and with religion it can have nothing to do. If we are not deterred by this brusque dismissal, but enquire on what grounds religion bases its claim to an exceptional position among human concerns, the answer we receive, if indeed we are honoured with an answer at all, is that religion cannot be measured by human standards, since it is of divine origin, and has been revealed to us by a spirit which the human mind cannot grasp. It might surely be thought that nothing could be more easily refuted than this argument; it is an obvious petitio principii, a 'begging of the question'. The point which is being called in question is whether there is a divine spirit and a revelation; and it surely cannot be a conclusive reply to say that the question be asked, because the Deity cannot be called in question. What is happening here is the same kind of thing as we meet with occasionally in our analytic work. If an otherwise intelligent patient denies a suggestion on particularly stupid grounds, his imperfect logic is evidence for the existence of a particularly strong motive for his making the denial, a motive which can only be of an affective nature and serve to bind an emotion.

Another sort of answer may be given, in which a motive of this kind is openly admitted. Religion must not be critically examined, because it is the highest, most precious and noblest thing that the mind of man has brought forth, because it gives expression to the deepest feelings, and is the only thing that makes the world bearable and life worthy of humanity. To this we need not reply by disputing this estimate of religion, but rather by drawing attention to another aspect

384 THE MEANING OF LIFE

of the matter. We should point out that it is not a question of the scientific spirit encroaching upon the sphere of religion, but of religion encroaching upon the sphere of scientific thought. Whatever value and importance religion may have, it has no right to set any limits to thought, and therefore has no right to except itself from the application of thought.

Scientific thought is, in its essence, no different from the normal process of thinking, which we all, believers and unbelievers alike, make use of when we are going about our business in everyday life. It has merely taken a special form in certain respects: it extends its interest to things which have no immediately obvious utility, it endeavours to eliminate personal factors and emotional influences, it carefully examines the trustworthiness of the sense perceptions on which it bases its conclusions, it provides itself with new perceptions which are not obtainable by everyday means, and isolates the determinants of these new experiences by purposely varied experimentation. Its aim is to arrive at correspondence with reality, that is to say with what exists outside us and independently of us, and, as experience has taught us, is decisive for the fulfilment or frustration of our desires. This correspondence with the real external world we call truth. It is the aim of scientific work, even when the practical value of that work does not interest us. When, therefore, religion claims that it can take the place of science and that, because it is beneficent and ennobling, it must therefore be true, that claim is, in fact, an encroachment, which, in the interests of everyone, should be resisted. It is asking a great deal of a man, who has learnt to regulate his everyday affairs in accordance with the rules of experience and with due regard to reality, that he should entrust precisely what affects him most nearly to the care of an authority which claims as its prerogative freedom from all the rules of rational thought. And as for the protection that religion promises its believers, I hardly think that any of us would be willing even to enter a motorcar if the driver informed us that he drove without allowing himself to be distracted by traffic regulations, but in accordance with the impulses of an exalted imagination.

And indeed the ban which religion has imposed upon thought in the interests of its own preservation is by no means without danger both for the individual and for society. Analytic experience has taught us that such prohibitions, even though they were originally confined to some particular field, have a tendency to spread, and then become the cause of severe inhibitions in people's lives. In women a process of this sort can be observed to follow from the prohibition against their occupying themselves, even in thought, with the sexual side of their nature. The biographies of almost all the eminent people of past times show the disastrous results of the inhibition of thought by religion. Intellect, on the other hand, - or rather, to call it by a more familiar name, reason - is among the forces which may be expected to exert a unifying influence upon men - creatures who can be held together only with the greatest difficulty, and whom it is therefore scarcely possible to control. Think how impossible human society would be if everyone had his own particular multiplication table and his own private units of weight and length. Our best hope for the future is that the intellect - the scientific spirit, - reason - should in time establish a dictatorship over the human mind. The very nature of reason is a guarantee that it would not fail to concede to human emotions and to all that is determined by them the position to which they are entitled. But the common pressure exercised by such a domination of reason would prove to be the strongest unifying force among men, and would prepare the way for further unifications. Whatever, like the ban laid upon thought by religion, opposes such a development is a danger for the future of mankind.

The question may now be asked why religion does not put an end to this losing fight by openly declaring: 'It is a fact that I cannot give you what men commonly call truth; to obtain that, you must go to science. But what I have to give you is incomparably more beautiful, more comforting and more ennobling than anything that you could ever get from science. And I therefore say to you that it is true in a different and higher sense.' The answer is easy to find. Religion cannot make this admission, because if it did it would lose all influence over the mass of mankind. The ordinary man knows only one 'truth' - truth in the ordinary sense of the word. What may be meant by a higher, or a highest, truth, he cannot imagine. Truth seems to him as little capable of having degrees as death, and the necessary leap from the beautiful to the true is one that he cannot make. Perhaps you will agree with me in thinking that he is right in this.

The struggle, therefore, is not yet at an end. The followers of the religious Weltanschauung act in accordance with the old maxim: the best defence is attack. 'What', they ask, 'is this science that presumes to depreciate our religion, which has brought salvation and comfort to millions of men for many thousands of years? What has science for its part so far accomplished? What more can be expected of it? On its own admission, it is incapable of comforting or ennobling us. We will leave that on one side, therefore, though it is by no means easy to give up such benefits. But what of its teaching? Can it tell us how the world began, and what fate is in store for it? Can it even paint for us a coherent picture of the universe, and show us where the unexplained phenomena of life fit in, and how spiritual forces are able to operate on inert matter? If it could do that we should not refuse it our respect. But it has done nothing of the sort, not one single problem of this kind has it solved. It gives us fragments of alleged knowledge, which it cannot harmonise with one another, it collects observations of uniformities from the totality of events, and dignifies them with the name of laws and subjects them to its hazardous interpretations. And with what a small degree of certitude does it establish its conclusions! All that it teaches is only provisionally true; what is prized to-day as the highest wisdom is overthrown tomorrow and experimentally replaced by something else. The latest error is then given the name of truth. And to this truth we are asked to sacrifice our highest good!'

Ladies and Gentlemen - In so far as you yourselves are supporters of the scientific Weltanschauung I do not think you will be very profoundly shaken by this critic's attack. In Imperial Austria an anecdote was once current which I should like to call to mind in this connection. On one occasion the old Emperor was receiving a deputation from a political party which he disliked: 'This is no longer ordinary opposition', he burst out, 'this is factious opposition.' In just the same way you will find that the reproaches made against science for not having solved the riddle of the universe are unfairly and spitefully exaggerated. Science has had too little time for such a tremendous achievement. It is still very young, a recently developed human activity. Let us bear in mind, to mention only a few dates, that only about three hundred years have passed since Kepler discovered the laws of planetary movement; the life of Newton,

386 THE MEANING OF LIFE

who split up light into the colours of the spectrum, and put forward the theory of gravitation, came to an end in 1727, that is to say a little more than two hundred years ago; and Lavoisier discovered oxygen shortly before the French Revolution. I may be a very old man to-day, but the life of an individual man is very short in comparison with the duration of human development, and it is a fact that I was alive when Charles Darwin published his work on the origin of species. In the same year, 1859, Pierre Curie, the discoverer of radium, was born. And if you go back to the beginnings of exact natural science among the Greeks, to Archimedes, or to Aristarchus of Samos (circa 250 B.C.), the forerunner of Copernicus, or even to the tentative origins of astronomy among the Babylonians, you will only be covering a very small portion of the period which anthropology requires for the evolution of man from his original ape-like form, a period which certainly embraces more than a hundred thousand years. And it must not be forgotten that the last century has brought with it such a quantity of new discoveries and such a great acceleration of scientific progress that we have every reason to look forward with confidence to the future of science.

It has to be admitted that the other objections are valid within certain limits. Thus it is true that the path of science is slow, tentative and laborious. That cannot be denied or altered. No wonder that the gentlemen of the opposition are dissatisfied; they are spoilt, they have had an easier time of it with their revelation. Progress in scientific work is made in just the same way as in an analysis. The analyst brings expectations with him to his work, but he must keep them in the background. He discovers something new by observation, now here and now there, and at first the bits do not fit together. He puts forward suppositions, he brings up provisional constructions, and abandons them if they are not confirmed; he must have a great deal of patience, must be prepared for all possibilities, and must not jump at conclusions for fear of their leading him to overlook new and unexpected factors. And in the end the whole expenditure of effort is rewarded, the scattered discoveries fall into place and he obtains an understanding of a whole chain of mental events; he has finished one piece of work and is ready for the next. But the analyst is unlike other scientific workers in this one respect, that he has to do without the help which experiment can bring to research.

But the criticism of science which I have quoted also contains a great deal of exaggeration. It is not true to say that it swings blindly from one attempt to another, and exchanges one error for the next. As a rule the man of science works like a sculptor with a clay model, who persistently alters the first rough sketch, adds to it and takes away from it, until he has obtained a satisfactory degree of similarity to some object, whether seen or imagined. And, moreover, at least in the older and more mature sciences, there is already a solid foundation of knowledge, which is now only modified and elaborated and no longer demolished. The outlook, in fact, is not so bad in the world of science.

And finally, what is the purpose of all these passionate disparagements of science? In spite of its present incompleteness and its inherent difficulties, we could not do without it and could not put anything else in its place. There is no limit to the improvement of which it is capable, and this can certainly not be said of the religious Weltanschauung. The latter is complete in its essentials; if it is an error, it must remain one for ever. No attempt to minimise the importance of science can alter the fact that it attempts to take into account our dependence on the real external world, while religion is illusion and derives its strength from the fact that it falls in with our instinctual desires.

I must now go on to mention some other types of Weltanschauung that are in opposition to the scientific one; I do so, however, unwillingly, because I know that I am not competent to form a judgment upon them. I hope, therefore, that you will bear this confession in mind in listening to what I have to say, and that if your interest is aroused you will go elsewhere for more trustworthy information.

In the first place I ought at this point to name the various philosophical systems which have ventured to draw a picture of the world, as it is reflected in the minds of thinkers whose eyes are as a rule turned away from it. But I have already attempted to give a general characterisation of philosophy and its methods, and I believe I am more unfitted than almost anyone to pass the individual systems under review. I shall ask you, therefore, instead to turn your attention to two other phenomena which, particularly in these days, cannot be ignored.

The Weltanschauung to which I shall first refer is, as it were, a counterpart of political anarchism, and may perhaps have emanated from it. No doubt there have been intellectual nihilists of this kind before, but at the present day the theory of relativity of modern physics seems to have gone to their heads. It is true that they start out from science, but they succeed in forcing it to cut the ground from under its own feet, to commit suicide, as it were; they make it dispose of itself by getting it to refute its own premises. One often has an impression that this nihilism is only a temporary attitude, which will only be kept up until this task has been completed. When once science has been got rid of, some kind of mysticism, or, indeed, the old religious Weltanschauung, can spring up in the space that has been left vacant. According to this anarchistic doctrine, there is no such thing as truth, no assured knowledge of the external world. What we give out as scientific truth is only the product of our own needs and desires, as they are formulated under varying external conditions; that is to say, it is illusion once more. Ultimately we find only what we need to find, and see only what we desire to see. We can do nothing else. And since the criterion of truth, correspondence with an external world, disappears, it is absolutely immaterial what views we accept. All of them are equally true and false. And no one has a right to accuse anyone else of error.

For a mind which is interested in epistemology, it would be tempting to enquire into the contrivances and sophistries by means of which the anarchists manage to elicit a final product of this kind from science. One would no doubt be brought up against situations like the one involved in the familiar example of the Cretan who says that all Cretans are liars. But I am not desirous, nor am I capable, of going deeper into this. I will merely remark that the anarchistic theory only retains its remarkable air of superiority so long as it is concerned with opinions about abstract things; it breaks down the moment it comes in contact with practical life. Now the behaviour of men is guided by their opinions and knowledge, and the same scientific spirit which speculates

388 THE MEANING OF LIFE

about the structure of the atom or the origin of man is concerned in the building of a bridge that will bear its load. If it were really a matter of indifference what we believed, if there were no knowledge which was distinguished from among our opinions by the fact that it corresponds with reality, then we might just as well build our bridges of cardboard as of stone, or inject a tenth of a gram of morphia into a patient instead of a hundredth, or take tear-gas as a narcotic instead of ether. But the intellectual anarchists themselves would strongly repudiate such practical applications of their theory.

The other opposing Weltanschauung is to be taken far more seriously, and in this case I very deeply regret the insufficiency of my knowledge. I dare say that you know more about this subject than I do and that you have long ago taken up your position for or against Marxism. The investigations of Karl Marx into the economic structure of society and into the influence of various forms of economic organisation upon all departments of human life have in our day acquired an authority that cannot be denied. How far they are right or wrong in detail, I naturally do not know. I gather that it is not easy even for better informed people to decide. Some of the propositions in Marx's theory seem strange to me, such as that the evolution of forms of society is a process of natural history, or that the changes in social stratification proceed from one another in the manner of a dialectical process. I am by no means certain that I understand these statements rightly; moreover, they do not sound 'materialistic' but like traces of the obscure Hegelian philosophy under the influence of which Marx at one time passed. I do not know how I can throw off the view which I share with other laymen, who are inclined to trace back the formation of classes in society to the struggles which went on from the beginning of history between various human hordes. These hordes differed to a slight degree from one another; and it is my view that social differences go back to these original differences of tribe or race. Psychological factors, such as the amount of constitutional aggressiveness and also the degree of cohesion within the horde, and material factors, such as the possession of better weapons, decided the victory. When they came to live together in the same territory, the victors became the masters and the conquered the slaves. There is no sign in all this of natural laws or conceptual modifications; on the other hand, we cannot fail to recognise the influence which the progressive control over natural forces exerts on the social relationships between men, since men always place their newly won powers at the service of their aggressiveness, and use them against one another. The introduction of metals, of bronze and iron, put an end to whole cultural epochs and their social institutions. I really believe that gunpowder and fire-arms overthrew chivalry and the domination of the aristocracy, and that the Russian despotism was already doomed before the war was lost, since no amount of in-breeding among the ruling families of Europe could have produced a race of Tsars capable of withstanding the explosive force of dynamite.

It may be, indeed, that with the present economic crisis which followed upon the Great War we are merely paying the price of our latest triumph over Nature, the conquest of the air. This does not sound very convincing, but at least the first links in the chain of argument are clearly recognisable. The policy of England was based on the security guaranteed by the seas which encircle her coasts. The moment Blériot flew over the Channel in his aeroplane this protective isolation was broken through; and on the night on which, in a time of peace, a German Zeppelin made an experimental cruise over London, war against Germany became a certainty. Nor must the threat of submarines be forgotten in this connection.

I am almost ashamed of treating a theme of such importance and complexity in such a slight and inadequate manner, and I am also aware that I have not said anything that is new to you. I only wanted to call your attention to the fact that the factor of man's control over Nature, from which he obtains his weapons for his struggle with his fellow-men, must of necessity also affect his economic arrangements. We seem to have travelled a long way from the problems of a Weltanschauung, but we shall soon come back to the point. The strength of Marxism obviously does not lie in its view of history or in the prophecies about the future which it bases upon that view, but in its clear insight into the determining influence which is exerted by the economic conditions of man upon his intellectual, ethical and artistic reactions. A whole collection of correlations and causal sequences were thus discovered, which had hitherto been almost completely disregarded. But it cannot be assumed that economic motives are the only ones which determine the behaviour of men in society. The unquestionable fact that different individuals, races and nations behave differently under the same economic conditions in itself proves that the economic factor cannot be the sole determinant. It is quite impossible to understand how psychological factors can be overlooked where the reactions of living human beings are involved; for not only were such factors already concerned in the establishment of these economic conditions but even in obeying these conditions, men can do no more than set their original instinctual impulses in motion - their self-preservative instinct, their love of aggression, their need for love and their impulse to attain pleasure and avoid pain. In an earlier lecture we have emphasised the importance of the part played by the super-ego, which represents tradition and the ideals of the past, and which will resist for some time the pressure exerted by new economic situations. And, finally, we must not forget that the mass of mankind, subjected though they are to economic necessities, are borne on by a process of cultural development - some call it civilisation - which is no doubt influenced by all the other factors, but is equally certainly independent of them in its origin; it is comparable to an organic process, and is quite capable of itself having an effect upon the other factors. It displaces the aims of the instincts, and causes men to rebel against what has hitherto been tolerable; and, moreover, the progressive strengthening of the scientific spirit seems to be an essential part of it. If anyone were in a position to show in detail how these different factors - the general human instinctual disposition, its racial variations and its cultural modifications - behave under the influence of varying social organisation, professional activities and methods of subsistence, how these factors inhibit or aid one another - if, I say, anyone could show this, then he would not only have improved Marxism but would have made it into a true social science. For sociology, which deals with the behaviour of man in society, can be nothing other than applied psychology. Strictly speaking, indeed, there are only two sciences - psychology, pure and applied, and natural science.

390 THE MEANING OF LIFE

When at last the far-reaching importance of economic conditions began to be realised, the temptation arose to bring about an alteration in them by means of revolutionary interference, instead of leaving the change to the course of historical development. Theoretical Marxism, as put into effect in Russian Bolshevism, has acquired the energy, the comprehensiveness and the exclusiveness of a Weltanschauung, but at the same time it has acquired an almost uncanny resemblance to what it is opposing. Originally it was itself a part of science, and, in its realisation, was built up on science and technology, but it has nevertheless established a ban upon thought which is as inexorable as was formerly that of religion. All critical examination of the Marxist theory is forbidden, doubts of its validity are as vindictively punished as heresy once was by the Catholic Church. The works of Marx, as the source of revelation, have taken the place of the Bible and the Koran, although they are no freer from contradictions and obscurities than those earlier holy books.

And although practical Marxism has remorselessly swept away all idealistic systems and illusions, it has nevertheless developed illusions itself, which are no less dubious and unverifiable than their predecessors. It hopes, in the course of a few generations, so to alter men that they will be able to live together in the new order of society almost without friction, and that they will do their work voluntarily. In the meantime it moves elsewhere the instinctual barriers which are essential in any society, it directs outwards the aggressive tendencies which threaten every human community, and finds its support in the hostility of the poor against the rich, and of the hitherto powerless against the former holders of power. But such an alteration in human nature is very improbable. The enthusiasm with which the mob follow the Bolshevist lead at present, so long as the new order is incomplete and threatened from outside, gives no guarantee for the future, when it will be fully established and no longer in danger. In exactly the same way as religion, Bolshevism is obliged to compensate its believers for the sufferings and deprivations of the present life by promising them a better life hereafter, in which there will be no unsatisfied needs. It is true that this paradise is to be in this world; it will be established on earth, and will be inaugurated within a measurable time. But let us remember that the Jews, whose religion knows nothing of a life beyond the grave, also expected the coming of the Messiah here on earth, and that the Christian Middle Ages constantly believed that the Kingdom of God was at hand.

There is no doubt what the answer of Bolshevism to these criticisms will be. 'Until men have changed their nature', it will say, 'one must employ the methods which are effective with them today. One cannot do without compulsion in their education or a ban upon thinking or the application of force, even the spilling of blood; and if one did not awake in them the illusions you speak of, one would not be able to bring them to submit to this compulsion.' And it might politely ask us to say how else it could be done. At this point we should be defeated. I should know of no advice to give. I should admit that the conditions of this experiment would have restrained me, and people like me, from undertaking it; but we are not the only ones concerned. There are also men of action, unshakeable in their convictions, impervious to doubt, and insensitive to the sufferings of anyone who stands between them and their goal. It is owing to such men that the tremendous attempt to institute a new order of society of this kind is actually being carried out in

Russia now. At a time when great nations are declaring that they expect to find their salvation solely from a steadfast adherence to Christian piety, the upheaval in Russia - in spite of all its distressing features - seems to bring a promise of a better future. Unfortunately, neither our own misgivings nor the fanatical belief of the other side give us any hint of how the experiment will turn out. The future will teach us. Perhaps it will show that the attempt has been made prematurely and that a fundamental alteration of the social order will have little hope of success until new discoveries are made that will increase our control over the forces of Nature, and so make easier the satisfaction of our needs. It may be that only then will it be possible for a new order of society to emerge which will not only banish the material want of the masses, but at the same time meet the cultural requirements of individual men. But even so we shall still have to struggle for an indefinite length of time with the difficulties which the intractable nature of man puts in the way of every kind of social community.

Ladies and Gentlemen - Let me in conclusion sum up what I had to say about the relation of psychoanalysis to the question of a Weltanschauung. Psychoanalysis is not, in my opinion, in a position to create a Weltanschauung of its own. It has no need to do so, for it is a branch of science, and can subscribe to the scientific Weltanschauung. The latter, however, hardly merits such a high-sounding name, for it does not take everything into its scope, it is incomplete and it makes no claim to being comprehensive or to constituting a system. Scientific thought is still in its infancy; there are very many of the great problems with which it has as yet been unable to cope. A Weltanschauung based upon science has, apart from the emphasis it lays upon the real world, essentially negative characteristics, such as that it limits itself to truth and rejects illusions. Those of our fellowmen who are dissatisfied with this state of things and who desire something more for their momentary peace of mind may look for it where they can find it. We shall not blame them for doing so; but we cannot help them and cannot change our own way of thinking on their account.

ESSAY ON PSYCHOLOGICAL TYPES

C. G. Jung (1921)

Translation by H. Godwyn Baynes (1923)[71]

CHAPTER X
GENERAL DESCRIPTION OF THE TYPES
A. INTRODUCTION

In the following pages I shall attempt a general description of the types, and my first concern must be with the two general types I have termed introverted and extraverted. But, in addition, I shall also try to give a certain characterization of those special types whose particularity is due to the fact that his most differentiated function plays the principal role in an individual's adaptation or orientation to life. The former I would term *general attitude types,* since they are distinguished by the direction of general interest or libido movement, while the latter I would call *function-types.*

The general-attitude types, as I have pointed out more than once, are differentiated by their particular attitude to the object. The introvert's attitude to the object is an abstracting one; at bottom, he is always facing the problem of how libido can be withdrawn from the object, as though an attempted ascendancy on. the part of the object had to be continually frustrated. The extravert, on the contrary, maintains a positive relation to the object. To such an extent does he affirm its importance that his subjective attitude is continually being orientated by, and related to the object. An fond, the object can never have sufficient value; for him, therefore, its importance must always be paramount.

The two types are so essentially different, presenting so striking a contrast, that their existence, even to the [p. 413] uninitiated in psychological matters becomes an obvious fact, when once attention has been drawn to it. Who does not know those taciturn, impenetrable, often shy natures, who form such a vivid contrast to these other open, sociable, serene maybe, or at least friendly and accessible characters, who are on good terms with all the world, or, even when disagreeing with it, still hold a relation to it by which they and it are mutually affected.

Naturally, at first, one is inclined to regard such differences as mere individual idiosyncrasies. But anyone with the opportunity of gaining a fundamental knowledge of many men will soon discover that such a far-reaching contrast does not merely concern the individual

---

71 http://psychclassics.yorku.ca/Jung/types.htm

case, but is a question of typical attitudes, with a universality far greater than a limited psychological experience would at first assume. In reality, as the preceding chapters will have shown, it is a question of a fundamental opposition; at times clear and at times obscure, but always emerging whenever we are dealing with individuals whose personality is in any way pronounced. Such men are found not only among the educated classes, but in every rank of society; with equal distinctness, therefore, our types can be demonstrated among labourers and peasants as among the most differentiated members of a nation. Furthermore, these types override the distinctions of sex, since one finds the same contrasts amongst women of all classes. Such a universal distribution could hardly arise at the instigation of consciousness, ie. as the result of a conscious and deliberate choice of attitude. If this were the case, a definite level of society, linked together by a similar education and environment and, therefore, correspondingly localized, would surely have a majority representation of such an attitude. But the actual facts are just the reverse, for the types have, apparently, quite a random distribution. [p. 414] In the same family one child is introverted, and another extraverted.

Since, in the light of these facts, the attitude-type regarded as a general phenomenon having an apparent random distribution, can be no affair of conscious judgment or intention, its existence must be due to some unconscious instinctive cause. The contrast of types, therefore, as a, universal psychological. phenomenon, must in some way or other have its biological precursor.

The relation between subject and object, considered biologically, is always a relation of adaptation, since every relation between subject and object presupposes mutually modifying effects from either side. These modifications constitute the adaptation. The typical attitudes to the object, therefore, are adaptation processes. Nature knows two fundamentally different ways of adaptation, which determine the further existence of the living organism the one is by increased fertility, accompanied by a relatively small degree of defensive power and individual conservation; the other is by individual equipment of manifold means of self-protection, coupled with a relatively insignificant fertility. This biological contrast seems not merely to be the analogue, but also the general foundation of our two psychological modes of adaptation, At this point a mere general indication must suffice; on the one hand, I need only point to the peculiarity of the extravert, which constantly urges him to spend and propagate himself in every way, and, on the other, to the tendency of the introvert to defend himself against external claims, to conserve himself from any expenditure of energy directly related to the object, thus consolidating for himself the most secure and impregnable position.

Blake's intuition did not err when he described the two forms as the "prolific" and the "devouring" [1] As is [p. 415] shown by the general biological example, both forms are current and successful after their kind ; this is equally true of the typical attitudes. What the one brings about by a multiplicity of relations, the other gains by monopoly.

The fact that often in their earliest years children display an unmistakable typical attitude forces us to assume that it cannot possibly be the struggle for existence, as it is generally understood, which constitutes the compelling factor in favour of a definite attitude. We might, however, demur, and indeed with cogency, that even the tiny infant, the very babe at the breast,

394 THE MEANING OF LIFE

has already an unconscious psychological adaptation to perform, inasmuch as the special character of the maternal influence leads to specific reactions in the child. This argument, though appealing to incontestable facts, has none the less to yield before the equally unarguable fact that two children of the same mother may at a very early age exhibit opposite types, without the smallest accompanying change in the attitude of the mother. Although nothing would induce me to underestimate the well-nigh incalculable importance of parental influence, this experience compels me to conclude that the decisive factor must be looked for in the disposition of the child. The fact that, in spite of the greatest possible similarity of external conditions, one child will assume this type while another that, must, of course, in the last resort he ascribed to individual disposition. Naturally in saying this I only refer to those cases which occur under normal conditions. Under abnormal conditions, i.e. when there is an extreme and, therefore, abnormal attitude in the mother, the children can also be coerced into a relatively similar attitude; but this entails a violation of their individual disposition, which quite possibly would have assumed another type if no abnormal and disturbing external influence had intervened. As a rule, whenever such a falsification of type takes place as a result of external [p. 416] influence, the individual becomes neurotic later, and a cur can successfully be sought only in a development of that attitude which corresponds with the individual's natural way.

As regards the particular disposition, I know not what to say, except that there are clearly individuals who have either a greater readiness and capacity for one way, or for whom it is more congenial to adapt to that way rather than the other. In the last analysis it may well be that physiological causes, inaccessible to our knowledge, play a part in this. That this may be the case seems to me not improbable, in view of one's experience that a reversal of type often proves exceedingly harmful to the physiological well-being of the organism, often provoking an acute state of exhaustion.

B. THE EXTRAVERTED TYPE

In our descriptions of this and the following type it will be necessary, in the interest of lucid and comprehensive presentation, to discriminate between the conscious and unconscious psychology. Let us first lend our minds to a description of the phenomena of consciousness.

(1)THE GENERAL ATTITUDE OF CONSCIOUSNESS

Everyone is, admittedly, orientated by the data with which the outer world provides him ; yet we see that this may be the case in a way that is only relatively decisive. Because it is cold out of doors, one man is persuaded to wear his overcoat, another from a desire to become hardened finds this unnecessary; one man admires the new tenor because all the world admires him, another withholds his approbation not because he dislikes him but because in his view the subject of general admiration is not thereby proved to be admirable; one submits to [p. 417] a given state of affairs because his experience argues nothing else to be possible, another is convinced that, although it has repeated itself a thousand times in the same way, the thousand and first will be different. The former is orientated by the objective data; the latter reserves a view, which is, as it were, interposed between himself and the objective fact. Now, when the orientation to the object and to objective facts is so predominant that the most frequent and essential decisions and actions are determined, not by subjective values but by objective relations, one speaks of an extraverted attitude. When this is habitual, one speaks of an extraverted type. If a man so thinks, feels, and acts, in a word so *lives,* as to correspond *directly* with objective conditions and their claims, whether in a good sense or ill, he is extraverted. His life makes it perfectly clear that it is the objective rather than the subjective value which plays the greater role as the determining factor of his consciousness. He naturally has subjective values, but their determining power has less importance than the external objective conditions. Never, therefore, does he expect to find any absolute factors in his own inner life, since the only ones he knows are outside himself. Epimetheus-like, his inner life succumbs to the external necessity, not of course without a struggle; which, however, always ends in favour of the objective determinant. His entire consciousness looks outwards to the world, because the important and decisive determination always comes to him from without. But it comes to him from without, only because that is where he expects it. All the distinguishing characteristics of his psychology, in so far as they do not arise from the priority of one definite psychological function or from individual peculiarities, have their origin in this basic attitude. *Interest* and *attention* follow objective happenings and, primarily, those of the immediate environment. Not [p. 418] only persons, but things, seize and rivet his interest. His *actions,* therefore, are also governed by the influence of persons and things. They are directly related to objective data and determinations, and are, as it were, exhaustively explainable on these grounds. Extraverted action is recognizably related to objective conditions. In so far it is not purely reactive to environmental stimuli, it character is constantly applicable to the actual circumstances, and it finds adequate and appropriate play within the limits of the objective situation. It has no serious tendency to transcend these bounds. The same holdsgood for interest: objective occurrences have a well-nigh inexhaustible charm, so that in the normal course the extravert's interest makes no other claims.

The moral laws which govern his action coincide with the corresponding claims of society, *i.e.* with the generally valid moral view-point. If the generally valid view were different, the subjective moral guiding line would also be different, without the general psychological habitus being in any way changed. It might almost seem, although it, is by no means the case, that this rigid determination by objective factors would involve an altogether ideal and complete adaptation to general conditions of life. An *accommodation* to objective data, such as we have described, must, of course, seem a complete adaptation to the extraverted view, since from this standpoint no other criterion exists. But from a higher point of view, it is by no means granted that the standpoint of objectively given, facts is the normal one under all circumstances. Objective conditions may be either temporarily or locally abnormal. An individual who is accommodated to such con certainly conforms to the abnormal style of his surroundings, but, in relation to the universally valid laws of life. He is, in common with his milieu, in an abnormal position. The individual may, however, thrive in such surroundings [p. 419] but only to the point when he, together with his whole milieu, is destroyed for transgressing the universal laws of life. He must

396   THE MEANING OF LIFE

inevitably participate in this downfall with the same completeness as he was previously adjusted to the objectively valid situation. He is adjusted, but not adapted, since adaptation demands more than a mere frictionless participation in the momentary conditions of the immediate environment. (Once more I would point to Spitteler's Epimetheus). Adaptation demands an observance of laws far more universal in their application than purely local and temporary conditions. Mere adjustment is the limitation of the normal extraverted type. On the one hand, the extravert owes his normality to his ability to fit into existing conditions with relative ease. He naturally pretends to nothing more than the satisfaction of existing objective possibilities, applying himself, for instance, to the calling which offers sound prospective possibilities in the actual situation in time and place. He tries to do or to make just what his milieu momentarily needs and expects from him, and abstains from every innovation that is not entirely obvious, or that in any way exceeds the expectation of those around him. But on the other hand, his normality must also depend essentially upon whether the extravert takes into account the actuality of his subjective needs and requirements; and this is just his weak point, for the tendency of his type has such a strong outward direction that even the most obvious of all subjective facts, namely the condition of his own body, may quite easily receive inadequate consideration. The body is not sufficiently objective or 'external,' so that the satisfaction of simple elementary requirements which are indispensable to physical well-being are no longer given their place. The body accordingly suffers, to say nothing of the soul. Although, as a rule, the extravert takes small note of [p. 420] this latter circumstance, his intimate domestic circle perceives it all the more keenly. His loss of equilibrium is perceived by himself only when abnormal bodily sensations make themselves felt.

These tangible facts he cannot ignore. It is natural he should regard them as concrete and 'objective', since for his mentality there exists only this and nothing more -- in himself. In others he at once sees "imagination" at work. A too extraverted attitude may actually become so regardless of the subject that the latter is entirely sacrificed to so-called objective claims; to the demands, for instance, of a continually extending business, because orders lie claiming one's attention or because profitable possibilities are constantly being opened up which must instantly be seized.

This is the extravert's danger; he becomes caught up in objects, wholly losing himself in their toils. The functional (nervous) or actual physical disorders which result from this state have a compensatory significance, forcing the subject to an involuntary self-restriction. Should the symptoms be functional, their peculiar formation may symbolically express the psychological situation; a singer, for instance, whose fame quickly reaches a dangerous pitch tempting him to a disproportionate outlay of energy, is suddenly robbed of his high tones by a nervous inhibition. A man of very modest beginnings rapidly reaches a social position of great influence and wide prospects, when suddenly he is overtaken by a psychogenic state, with all the symptoms of mountain-sickness. Again, a man on the point of marrying an idolized woman of doubtful character, whose value he extravagantly over-estimates, is seized with a spasm of the oesophagus, which forces him to a regimen of two cups of milk in the day, demanding his three-hourly attention. All visits to his fianceé are thus effectually stopped, and no choice is left to him [p.

421] but to busy himself with his bodily nourishment. A man who through his own energy and enterprise has built up a vast business, entailing an intolerable burden of work, is afflicted by nervous attacks of thirst, as a result of which he speedily falls a victim to hysterical alcoholism.

Hysteria is, in my view, by far the most frequent neurosis with the extraverted type. The classical example of hysteria is always characterized by an exaggerated rapport with the members of his circle, and a frankly imitatory accommodation to surrounding conditions. A constant tendency to appeal for interest and to produce impressions upon his milieu is a basic trait of the hysterical nature. A correlate to this is his proverbial suggestibility, his pliability to another person's influence. Unmistakable extraversion comes out in the communicativeness of the hysteric, which occasionally leads to the divulging of purely phantastic contents; whence arises the reproach of the hysterical lie.

To begin with, the 'hysterical' character is an exaggeration of the normal attitude; it is then complicated by compensatory reactions from the side of the unconscious, which manifests its opposition to the extravagant extraversion in the form of physical disorders, whereupon an introversion of psychic energy becomes unavoidable. Through this reaction of the unconscious, another category of symptoms arises which have a more introverted character. A morbid intensification of phantasy activity belongs primarily to this category. From this general characterization of the extraverted attitude, let us now turn to a description of the modifications, which the basic psychological functions undergo as a result of this attitude. [p. 422]

(II) THE ATTITUDE OF THE UNCONSCIOUS

It may perhaps seem odd that I should speak of attitude of the 'unconscious'. As I have already sufficiently indicated, I regard the relation of the unconscious to the conscious as compensatory. The unconscious, according to this view, has as good a claim to an I attitude' as the conscious.

In the foregoing section I emphasized the tendency to a certain one-sidedness in the extraverted attitude, due to the controlling power of the objective factor in the course, of psychic events. The extraverted type is constantly tempted to give himself away (apparently) in favour of the object, and to assimilate his subject to the object. I have referred in detail to the ultimate consequences of this exaggeration of the extraverted attitude, viz. to the injurious suppression of the subjective factor. It is only, to be expected, therefore, that a psychic compensation of the conscious extraverted attitude will lay especial weight upon the subjective factor, i.e. we shall have to prove a strong egocentric tendency in the unconscious. Practical experience actually furnishes this proof. I do not wish to enter into a casuistical survey at this point, so must refer my readers to the ensuing sections, where I shall attempt to present the characteristic attitude of the unconscious from the angle of each function-type, In this section we are merely concerned with the compensation of a general extraverted attitude; I shall, therefore, confine myself to an equally general characterization of the compensating attitude of the unconscious.

The attitude of the unconscious as an effective complement to the conscious extraverted attitude has a definitely introverting character. It focusses libido upon the subjective factor, *i.e.* all

398   THE MEANING OF LIFE

those needs and claims which are stifled or repressed by a too extraverted conscious [p. 423] attitude. It may be readily gathered from what has been said in the previous section that a purely objective orientation does violence to a multitude of subjective emotions, intentions, needs, and desires, since it robs them of the energy which is their natural right. Man is not a machine that one can reconstruct, as occasion demands, upon other lines and for quite other ends, in the hope that it will then proceed to function, in a totally different way, just as normally as before. Man bears his age-long history with him in his very structure is written the history of mankind.

The historical factor represents a vital need, to which a wise economy must respond. Somehow the past must become vocal, and participate in the present. Complete assimilation to the object, therefore, encounters the protest of the suppressed minority, elements belonging to the past and existing from the beginning. From this quite general consideration it may be understood why it is that the unconscious claims of the extraverted type have an essentially primitive, infantile, and egoistical character. When Freud says that the unconscious is "only able to wish", this observation contains a large measure of truth for the unconscious of the extraverted type. Adjustment and assimilation to objective data prevent inadequate subjective impulses from reaching consciousness. These tendencies (thoughts, wishes, affects, needs, feelings, etc.) take on a regressive character corresponding with the degree of their repression, ie. the less they are recognized, the more infantile and archaic they become. The conscious attitude robs them of their relatively disposable energycharge, only leaving them the energy of which it cannot deprive them. This remainder, which still possesses a potency not to be under-estimated, can be described only as primeval instinct. Instinct can never be rooted out from an individual by any arbitrary measures; it requires [p. 424] the slow, organic transformation of many generations to effect a radical change, for instinct is the energic [sic] expression of a definite organic foundation.

Thus with every repressed tendency a considerable sum of energy ultimately remains. This sum corresponds with the potency of the instinct and guards its effectiveness, notwithstanding the deprivation of energy which made it unconscious. The measure of extraversion in the conscious attitude entails a like degree of infantilism and archaism in the attitude of the unconscious. The egoism which so often characterizes the extravert's unconscious attitude goes far beyond mere childish selfishness; it even verges upon the wicked and brutal. It is here we find in fullest bloom that incest-wish described by Freud. It is self-evident that these things are entirely unconscious, remaining altogether hidden from the eyes of the uninitiated observer so long as the extraversion of the conscious attitude does not reach an extreme stage. But wherever an exaggeration of the conscious standpoint takes place, the unconscious also comes to light in a symptomatic form, i.e. the unconscious egoism, infantilism, and archaism lose their original compensatory characters, and appear in more or less open opposition to the conscious attitude. This process begins in the form of an absurd exaggeration of the conscious standpoint, which is aimed at a further repression of the unconscious, but usually ends in a reductio ad absurdum of the conscious attitude, i.e. a collapse. The catastrophe may be an objective one, since the objective aims gradually become falsified by the subjective. I remember the case of a printer who, starting as a mere employé, worked his way up through two decades of hard struggle, till at last he was the independent possessor of a very extensive business. The more the business extended, the more it increased its hold upon him, until gradually every other interest [p. 425] was allowed to become merged in it. At length he was completely enmeshed in its toils, and, as we shall soon see, this surrender eventually proved his ruin. As a sort of compensation to his exclusive interest in the business, certain memories of his childhood came to life. As a child he had taken great delight in painting and drawing. But, instead of renewing this capacity for its own sake as a balancing side-interest, he canalized it into his business and began to conceive 'artistic' elaborations of his products. His phantasies unfortunately materialized: he actually began to produce after his own primitive and infantile taste, with the result that after a very few years his business went to pieces. He acted in obedience to one of our 'civilized ideals', which enjoins the energetic man to concentrate everything upon the one end in view. But he went too far, and merely fell a victim to the power of his subjective infantile claims.

But the catastrophic solution may also be subjective, i.e. in the form of a nervous collapse. Such a solution always comes about as a result of the unconscious counterinfluence, which can ultimately paralyse conscious action. In which case the claims of the unconscious force themselves categorically upon consciousness, thus creating a calamitous cleavage which generally reveals itself in two ways: either the subject no longer knows what he really wants and nothing any longer interests him, or he wants too much at once and has too keen an interest-but in impossible things. The suppression of infantile and primitive claims, which is often necessary on "civilized" grounds, easily leads to neurosis, or to the misuse of narcotics such as alcohol, morphine, cocaine, etc. In more extreme cases the cleavage ends in suicide.

It is a salient peculiarity of unconscious tendencies that, just in so far as they are deprived of their energy by a lack of conscious recognition, they assume a correspond- [p. 426] ingly destructive character, and as soon as this happen their compensatory function ceases. They cease to have a compensatory effect as soon as they reach a depth or stratum that corresponds with a level of culture absolutely incompatible with our own. From this moment the unconscious tendencies form a block, which is opposed to the conscious attitude in every respect ; such a bloc inevitably leads to open conflict.

In a general way, the compensating attitude of the unconscious finds expression in the process of psychic equilibrium. A normal extraverted attitude does not, of course, mean that the individual behaves invariably in accordance with the extraverted schema. Even in the same individual many psychological happenings may be observed, in which the mechanism of introversion is concerned. A habitus can be called extraverted only when the mechanism of extraversion predominates. In such a case the most highly differentiated function has a constantly extraverted application, while the inferior functions are found in the service of introversion, i.e. the more valued function, because the more conscious, is more completely subordinated to conscious control and purpose, whilst the less conscious, in other words, the partly unconscious inferior functions are subjected to conscious free choice in a much smaller degree.

The superior function is always the expression of the conscious personality, its aim, its will, and its achievement, whilst the inferior functions belong to the things that happen to one. Not that

400 THE MEANING OF LIFE

they merely beget blunders, e.g. lapsus linguae or lapsus calami, but they may also breed half or three-quarter resolves, since the inferior functions also possess a slight degree of consciousness. The extraverted feeling type is a classical example of this, for he enjoys an excellent feeling rapport with his entourage, yet occasionally opinions of an incomparable tactlessness [p. 427] will just happen to him. These opinions have their source in his inferior and subconscious thinking, which is only partly subject to control and is insufficiently related to the object ; to a large extent, therefore, it can operate without consideration or responsibility.

In the extraverted attitude the inferior functions always reveal a highly subjective determination with pronounced egocentricity and personal bias, thus demonstrating their close connection with the unconscious. Through their agency the unconscious is continually coming to light. On no account should we imagine that the unconscious lies permanently buried under so many overlying strata that it can only be uncovered, so to speak, by a laborious process of excavation. On the contrary, there is a constant influx of the unconscious into the conscious psychological process; at times this reaches such a pitch that the observer can decide only with difficulty which character-traits are to be ascribed to the conscious, and which to the unconscious personality. This difficulty occurs mainly with persons whose habit of expression errs rather on the side of profuseness. Naturally it depends very largely also upon the attitude of the observer, whether he lays hold of the conscious or the unconscious character of a personality. Speaking generally a judging observer will tend to seize the conscious character, while a perceptive observer will be influenced more by the unconscious character, since judgement is chiefly interested in the conscious motivation of the psychic process, while perception tends to register the mere happening. But in so far as we apply perception and judgment in equal measure, it may easily happen that a personality appears to us as both introverted and extraverted, so that we cannot at once decide to which attitude the superior function belongs. In such cases only a thorough analysis of the function qualities can help us to a sound opinion. During the analysis we must observe which [p. 428] function is placed under the control and motivation of consciousness, and which functions have an accidental and spontaneous character. The former is always more highly differentiated than the latter, which also possess many infantile and primitive qualities. Occasionally the former function gives the impression of normality, while the latter have something abnormal or pathological about them.

(III) THE PECULIARITIES OF THE BASIC PSYCHOLOGICAL FUNCTIONS IN THE EXTRAVERTED ATTITUDE

1. Thinking

As a result of the general attitude of extraversion, thinking is orientated by the object and objective data. This orientation of thinking produces a noticeable peculiarity.

Thinking in general is fed from two sources, firstly from subjective and in the last resort unconscious roots, and secondly from objective data transmitted through sense perceptions.

PSYCHOANALYSIS   401

Extraverted thinking is conditioned in a larger measure by these latter factors than by the former. judgment always presupposes a criterion ; for the extraverted judgment, the valid and determining criterion is the standard taken from objective conditions, no matter whether this be directly represented by an objectively perceptible fact, or expressed in an objective idea ; for an objective idea, even when subjectively sanctioned, is equally external and objective in origin. Extraverted thinking, therefore, need not necessarily be a merely concretistic thinking it may equally well be a purely ideal thinking, if, for instance, it can be shown that the ideas with which it is engaged are to a great extent borrowed from without, i.e. are transmitted by tradition and education. The criterion of judgment, therefore, as to whether or no a thinking is extraverted, hangs directly upon the question: by [p. 429] which standard is its judgment governed -- is it furnished from without, or is its origin subjective? A further criterion is afforded by the direction of the thinker's conclusion, namely, whether or no the thinking has a preferential direction outwards. It is no proof of its extraverted nature that it is preoccupied with concrete objects, since I may be engaging my thoughts with a concrete object, either because I am abstracting my thought from it or because I am concretizing my thought with it. Even if I engage my thinking with concrete things, and to that extent could be described as extraverted, it yet remains both questionable and characteristic as regards the direction my thinking will take; namely, whether in its further course it leads back again to objective data, external facts, and generally accepted ideas, or not. So far as the practical thinking of the merchant, the engineer, or the natural science pioneer is concerned, the objective direction is at once manifest. But in the case of a philosopher it is open to doubt, whenever the course of his thinking is directed towards ideas. In such a case, before deciding, we must further enquire whether these ideas are mere abstractions from objective experience, in which case they would merely represent higher collective concepts, comprising a sum of objective facts ; or whether (if they are clearly not abstractions from immediate experience) they may not be derived from tradition or borrowed from the intellectual atmosphere of the time. In the latter event, such ideas must also belong to the category of objective data, in which case this thinking should also be called extraverted.

Although I do not propose to present the nature of introverted thinking at this point, reserving it for a later section, it is, however, essential that I should make a few statements about it before going further. For if one considers strictly what I have just said concerning [p. 430] extraverted thinking, one might easily conclude that such a statement includes everything that is generally understood as thinking. It might indeed be argued that a thinking whose aim is concerned neither with objective facts nor with general ideas scarcely merits the name 'thinking'. I am fully aware of the fact that the thought of our age, in common with its most eminent representatives, knows and acknowledges only the extraverted type of thinking. This is partly due to the fact that all thinking which attains visible form upon the world's surface, whether as science, philosophy, or even art, either proceeds direct from objects or flows into general ideas. On either ground, although not always completely evident it at least appears essentially intelligible, and therefore relatively valid. In this sense it might be said that the extraverted intellect, i.e. the mind that is orientated by objective data, is actually the only one recognized.

402 THE MEANING OF LIFE

There is also, however -- and now I come to the question of the introverted intellect -- an entirely different kind of thinking, to which the term I "thinking" can hardly be denied: it is a kind that is neither orientated by the immediate objective experience nor is it concerned with general and objectively derived ideas. I reach this other kind of thinking in the following way. When my thoughts are engaged with a concrete object or general idea in such a way that the course of my thinking eventually leads me back again to my object, this intellectual process is not the only psychic proceeding taking place in me at the moment. I will disregard all those possible sensations and feelings which become noticeable as a more or less disturbing accompaniment to my train of thought, merely emphasizing the fact that this very thinking process which proceeds from objective data and strives again towards the object stands also in a constant relation to the subject. This relation is a condition sine qua non, without which no think- [p. 431] ing process whatsoever could take place. Even though my thinking process is directed, as far as possible, towards objective data, nevertheless it is *my* subjective process, and it can neither escape the subjective admixture nor yet dispense with it. Although I try my utmost to give a completely objective direction to my train of thought, even then I cannot exclude the parallel subjective process with its all-embracing participation, without extinguishing the very spark of life from my thought. This parallel subjective process has a natural tendency, only relatively avoidable, to subjectify objective facts, *i.e.* to assimilate them to the subject.

Whenever the chief value is given to the subjective process, that other kind of thinking arises which stands opposed to extraverted thinking, namely, that purely subjective orientation of thought which I have termed introverted. A thinking arises from this other orientation that is neither determined by objective facts nor directed towards objective data -- a thinking, therefore, that proceeds from subjective data and is directed towards subjective ideas or facts of a subjective character. I do not wish to enter more fully into this kind of thinking here; I have merely established its existence for the purpose of giving a necessary complement to the extraverted thinking process, whose nature is thus brought to a clearer focus.

When the objective orientation receives a certain predominance, the thinking is extraverted. This circumstance changes nothing as regards the logic of thought -- it merely determines that difference between thinkers which James regards as a matter of temperament. The orientation towards the object, as already explained, makes no essential change in the thinking function; only its appearance is altered. Since it is governed by objective data, it has the appearance of being captivated by the object, as though without the external orientation it simply could not [p. 432] exist. Almost it seems as though it were a sequence of external facts, or as though it could reach its highest point only when chiming in with some generally valid idea. It seems constantly to be affected by objective data, drawing only those conclusions which substantially agree with these. Thus it gives one the impression of a certain lack of freedom, of occasional short-sightedness, in spite of every kind of adroitness within the objectively circumscribed area. What I am now describing is merely the impression this sort of thinking makes upon the observer, who must himself already have a different standpoint, or it would be quite impossible for him to observe the phenomenon of extraverted thinking. As a result of his different standpoint he merely sees its aspect, not its nature; whereas the man who himself possesses this type of thinking is able to seize its nature, while its aspect escapes him. judgment made upon appearance only cannot be fair to the essence of the thing-hence the result is depreciatory. But essentially this thinking is no less fruitful and creative than introverted thinking, only its powers are in the service of other ends. This difference is perceived most clearly when extraverted thinking is engaged upon material, which is specifically an object of the subjectively orientated thinking. This happens, for instance, when a subjective conviction is interpreted analytically from objective facts or is regarded as a product or derivative of objective ideas. But, for our 'scientifically' orientated consciousness, the difference between the two modes of thinking becomes still more obvious when the subjectively orientated thinking makes an attempt to bring objective data into connections not objectively given, i.e. to subordinate them to a subjective idea. Either senses the other as an encroachment, and hence a sort of shadow effect is produced, wherein either type reveals to the other its least favourable aspect, The subjectively orientated thinking then appears [p. 433] quite arbitrary, while the extraverted thinking seems to have an incommensurability that is altogether dull and banal. Thus the two standpoints are incessantly at war.

Such a conflict, we might think, could be easily adjusted if only we clearly discriminated objects of a subjective from those of an objective nature. Unfortunately, however, such a discrimination is a matter of impossibility, although not a few have attempted it. Even if such a separation were possible, it would be a very disastrous proceeding, since in themselves both orientations are one-sided, with a definitely restricted validity; hence they both require this mutual correction. Thought is at once sterilized, whenever thinking is brought, to any great extent, under the influence of objective data, since it becomes degraded into a mere appendage of objective facts; in which case, it is no longer able to free itself from objective data for the purpose of establishing an abstract idea. The process of thought is reduced to mere 'reflection', not in the sense of 'meditation', but in the sense of a mere imitation that makes no essential affirmation beyond what was already visibly and immediately present in the objective data. Such a thinking-process leads naturally and directly back to the objective fact, but never beyond it ; not once, therefore, can it lead to the coupling of experience with an objective idea. And, vice versa, when this thinking has an objective idea for its object, it is quite unable to grasp the practical individual experience, but persists in a more or less tautological position. The materialistic mentality presents a magnificent example of this.

When, as the result of a reinforced objective determination, extraverted thinking is subordinated to objective data, it entirely loses itself, on the one hand, in the individual experience, and proceeds to amass an accumulation of undigested empirical material. The oppressive mass of more or less disconnected individual experiences [p. 434] produces a state of intellectual dissociation, which, on the other hand, usually demands a psychological compensation. This must consist in an idea, just as simple as it is universal, which shall give coherence to the heaped-up but intrinsically disconnected whole, or at least it should provide an inkling of such a connection. Such ideas as "matter" or "energy" are suitable for this purpose. But, whenever thinking primarily depends not so much upon external facts as upon an accepted or

404   THE MEANING OF LIFE

second-hand idea, the very poverty of the idea provokes a compensation in the form of a still more impressive accumulation of facts, which assume a one-sided grouping in keeping with the relatively restricted and sterile point of view; whereupon many valuable and sensible aspects of things automatically go by the board. The vertiginous abundance of the socalled scientific literature of to-day owes a deplorably high percentage of its existence to this misorientation.

2. The Extraverted Thinking Type

It is a fact of experience that all the basic psychological functions seldom or never have the same strength or grade of development in one and the same individual. As a rule, one or other function predominates, in both strength and development. When supremacy among the psychological functions is given to thinking, i.e. when the life of an individual is mainly ruled by reflective thinking so that every important action proceeds from intellectually considered motives, or when there is at least a tendency to conform to such motives, we may fairly call this a *thinking type*. Such a type can be either introverted or extraverted. We will first discuss the *extraverted thinking type*.

In accordance with his definition, we must picture a, man whose constant aim -- in so far, of course, as he is a [p. 435] pure type -- is to bring his total life-activities into relation with intellectual conclusions, which in the last resort are always orientated by objective data, whether objective facts or generally valid ideas. This type of man gives the deciding voice-not merely for himself alone but also on behalf of his entourage-either to the actual objective reality or to its objectively orientated, intellectual formula. By this formula are good and evil measured, and beauty and ugliness determined. All is right that corresponds with this formula; all is wrong that contradicts it; and everything that is neutral to it is purely accidental. Because this formula seems to correspond with the meaning of the world, it also becomes a world-law whose realization must be achieved at all times and seasons, both individually and collectively. Just as the extraverted thinking type subordinates himself to his formula, so, for its own good, must his entourage also obey it, since the man who refuses to obey is wrong -- he is resisting the world-law, and is, therefore, unreasonable, immoral, and without a conscience. His moral code forbids him to tolerate exceptions; his ideal must, under all circumstances, be realized; for in his eyes it is the purest conceivable formulation of objective reality, and, therefore, must also be generally valid truth, quite indispensable for the salvation of man. This is not from any great love for his neighbour, but from a higher standpoint of justice and truth. Everything in his own nature that appears to invalidate this formula is mere imperfection, an accidental miss-fire, something to be eliminated on the next occasion, or, in the event of further failure, then clearly a sickness.

If tolerance for the sick, the suffering, or the deranged should chance to be an ingredient in the formula, special provisions will be devised for humane societies, hospitals, prisons, colonies, etc., or at least extensive plans for such projects. For the actual execution of these schemes the [p. 436] motives of justice and truth do not, as a rule, suffice; still devolve upon real Christian charity, which I to do with feeling than with any intellectual 'One really should' or I one must' figure largely in this programme. If the formula is wide enough, it may play a very useful rôle in social life, with a reformer or a ventilator of public wrongs or a purifier of the public conscience, or as the propagator of important innovations. But the more rigid the formula, the more, does he develop into a grumbler, a crafty reasoner, and a self-righteous critic, who would like to impress both himself and others into one schema.

We have now outlined two extreme figures, between which terminals the majority of these types may be graduated.

In accordance with the nature of the extraverted attitude, the influence and activities of such personalities are all the more favourable and beneficent, the further one goes from the centre. Their best aspect is to be found at the periphery of their sphere of influence. The further we penetrate into their own province, the more do the unfavourable results of their tyranny impress us. Another life still pulses at the periphery, where the truth of the formula can be sensed as an estimable adjunct to the rest. But the further we probe into the special sphere where the formula operates, the more do we find life ebbing away from all that fails to coincide with its dictates. Usually it is the nearest relatives who have to taste the most disagreeable results of an extraverted formula, since they are the first to be unmercifully blessed with it. But above all the subject himself is the one who suffers most -- which brings us to the other side of the psychology of this type.

The fact that an intellectual formula never has been and never will be discovered which could embrace the [p. 437] abundant possibilities of life in a fitting expression must lead -- where such a formula is accepted -- to an inhibition, or total exclusion, of other highly important forms and activities of life. In the first place, all those vital forms dependent upon feeling will become repressed in such a type, as, for instance, aesthetic activities, taste, artistic sense, the art of friendship, etc. Irrational forms, such as religious experiences, passions and the like, are often obliterated even to the point of complete unconsciousness. These, conditionally quite important, forms of life have to support an existence that is largely unconscious. Doubtless there are exceptional men who are able to sacrifice their entire life to one definite formula; but for most of us a permanent life of such exclusiveness is impossible. Sooner or later -- in accordance with outer circumstances and inner gifts -- the forms of life repressed by the intellectual attitude become indirectly perceptible, through a gradual disturbance of the conscious conduct of life. Whenever disturbances of this kind reach a definite intensity, one speaks of a neurosis. In most cases, however, it does not go so far, because the individual instinctively allows himself some preventive extenuations of his formula, worded, of course, in a suitable and reasonable way. In this way a safety-valve is created.

The relative or total unconsciousness of such tendencies or functions as are excluded from any participation in the conscious attitude keeps them in a relatively undeveloped state. As compared with the conscious function they are inferior. To the extent that they are unconscious, they become merged with the remaining contents of the unconscious, from which they acquire a bizarre character. To the extent that they are conscious, they only play a secondary rôle, although one of considerable importance for the whole psychological picture.

406   THE MEANING OF LIFE

Since feelings are the first to oppose and contradict [p. 438] the rigid intellectual formula, they are affected first this conscious inhibition, and upon them the most intense repression falls. No function can be entirely eliminated -- it can only be greatly distorted. In so far as feelings allow themselves to be arbitrarily shaped and subordinated, they have to support the intellectual conscious attitude and adapt themselves to its aims. Only to a certain degree, however, is this possible; a part of the feeling remains insubordinate, and therefore must be repressed. Should the repression succeed, it disappears from consciousness and proceeds to unfold a subconscious activity, which runs counter to conscious aims, even producing effects whose causation is a complete enigma to the individual. For example, conscious altruism, often of an extremely high order, may be crossed by a secret self-seeking, of which the individual is wholly unaware, and which impresses intrinsically unselfish actions with the stamp of selfishness. Purely ethical aims may lead the individual into critical situations, which sometimes have more than a semblance of being decided by quite other than ethical motives. There are guardians of public morals or voluntary rescue-workers who suddenly find themselves in deplorably compromising situations, or in dire need of rescue. Their resolve to save often leads them to employ means which only tend to precipitate what they most desire to avoid. There are extraverted idealists, whose desire to advance the salvation of man is so consuming that they will not shrink from any lying and dishonest means in the pursuit of their ideal. There are a few painful examples in science where investigators of the highest esteem, from a profound conviction of the truth and general validity of their formula, have not scrupled to falsify evidence in favour of their ideal. This is sanctioned by the formula; the end justifieth the means. Only an inferior feeling-function, operating seductively [p. 439] and unconsciously, could bring about such aberrations in otherwise reputable men.

The inferiority of feeling in this type manifests itself also in other ways. In so far as it corresponds with the dominating positive formula, the conscious attitude becomes more or less impersonal, often, indeed, to such a degree that a very considerable wrong is done to personal interests. When the conscious attitude is extreme, all personal considerations recede from view, even those which concern the individual's own person. His health is neglected, his social position deteriorates, often the most vital interests of his family are violated -- they are wronged morally and financially, even their bodily health is made to suffer -- all in the service of the ideal. At all events personal sympathy with others must be impaired, unless they too chance to be in the service of the same formula. Hence it not infrequently happens that his immediate family circle, his own children for instance, only know such a father as a cruel tyrant, whilst the outer world resounds with the fame of his humanity. Not so much in spite of as because of the highly impersonal character of the conscious attitude, the unconscious feelings are highly personal and oversensitive, giving rise to certain secret prejudices, as, for instance, a decided readiness to misconstrue any objective opposition to his formula as personal ill-will, or a constant tendency to make negative suppositions regarding the qualities of others in order to invalidate their arguments beforehand-in defence, naturally, of his own susceptibility. As a result of this unconscious sensitiveness, his expression and tone frequently becomes sharp, pointed, aggressive, and insinuations multiply. The feelings have an untimely and halting character, which is always a mark of the inferior function. Hence arises a pronounced tendency to resentment. However generous the individual sacrifice [p. 440] to the intellectual goal may be, the feelings are correspondingly petty, suspicious, crossgrained, and conservative. Everything new that is not already contained formula is viewed through a veil of unconscious and is judged accordingly. It happened only in middle of last century that a certain physician, famed his humanitarianism, threatened to dismiss an assistant for daring to use a thermometer, because the formula decreed that fever shall be recognized by the pulse. There are, of course, a host of similar examples.

Thinking which in other respects may be altogether blameless becomes all the more subtly and prejudicially, affected, the more feelings are repressed. An intellectual standpoint, which, perhaps on account of its actual intrinsic value, might justifiably claim general recognition, undergoes a characteristic alteration through the influence of this unconscious personal sensitiveness; it becomes rigidly dogmatic. The personal self-assertion is transferred to the intellectual standpoint. Truth is no longer left to work her natural effect, but through an identification with the subject she is treated like a sensitive darling whom an evil-minded critic has wronged. The critic is demolished, if possible with personal invective, and no argument is too gross to be used against him. Truth must be trotted out, until finally it begins to dawn upon the public that it is not so much really a question of truth as of her personal procreator.

The dogmatism of the intellectual standpoint, however, occasionally undergoes still further peculiar modifications from the unconscious admixture of unconscious personal feelings; these changes are less a question of feeling, in the stricter sense, than of contamination from other unconscious factors which become blended with the repressed feeling in the unconscious. Although reason itself offers proof, that every intellectual formula can be no more than [p. 441] a partial truth, and can never lay claim, therefore, to autocratic authority; in practice, the formula obtains so great an ascendancy that, beside it, every other standpoint and possibility recedes into the background. It replaces all the more general, less defined, hence the more modest and truthful, views of life. It even takes the place of that general view of life which we call religion. Thus the formula becomes a religion, although in essentials it has not the smallest connection with anything religious. Therewith it also gains the essentially religious character of absoluteness. It becomes, as it were, an intellectual superstition. But now all those psychological tendencies that suffer under its repression become grouped together in the unconscious, and form a counter-position, giving rise to paroxysms of doubt. As a defence against doubt, the conscious attitude grows fanatical. For fanaticism, after all, is merely overcompensated doubt. Ultimately this development leads to an exaggerated defence of the conscious position, and to the gradual formation of an absolutely antithetic unconscious position; for example, an extreme irrationality develops, in opposition to the conscious rationalism, or it becomes highly archaic and superstitious, in opposition to a conscious standpoint imbued with modern science. This fatal opposition is the source of those narrow-minded and ridiculous views, familiar to the historians of science, into which many praiseworthy pioneers have ultimately blundered. It not infrequently happens in a man of this type that the side of the unconscious becomes embodied in a woman.

408 THE MEANING OF LIFE

In my experience, this type, which is doubtless familiar to my readers, is chiefly found among men, since thinking tends to be a much more dominant function in men than in women. As a rule, when thinking achieves the mastery in women, it is, in my experience, a kind of thinking which results from a prevailingly intuitive activity of mind. [p. 442]

The thought of the extraverted thinking type is, positive, i.e. it produces. It either leads to new facts or to general conceptions of disparate experimental material. Its judgment is generally synthetic. Even when it analyses, it constructs, because it is always advancing beyond the, analysis to a new combination, a further conception which reunites the analysed material in a new way or adds some., thing further to the given material. In general, therefore, we may describe this kind of judgment as predicative. In any case, characteristic that it is never absolutely depreciatory or destructive, but always substitutes a fresh value for one that is demolished. This quality is due to the fact that thought is the main channel into which a thinking-type's energy flows. Life steadily advancing shows itself in the man's thinking, so that his ideas maintain a progressive, creative character. His thinking neither stagnates, nor is it in the least regressive. Such qualities cling only to a thinking that is not given priority in consciousness. In this event it is relatively unimportant, and also lacks the character of a positive vital activity. It follows in the wake of other functions, it becomes Epimethean, it has an 'esprit de l'escalier' quality, contenting itself with constant ponderings and broodings upon things past and gone, in an effort to analyse and digest them. Where the creative element, as in this case, inhabits another function, thinking no longer progresses it stagnates. Its judgment takes on a decided inherency-character, i.e. it entirely confines itself to the range of the given material, nowhere overstepping it. It is contented with a more or less abstract statement, and fails to impart any value to the experimental material that was not already there.

The inherency-judgment of such extraverted thinking is objectively orientated, i.e. its conclusion always expresses the objective importance of experience. Hence, not only does it remain under the orientating influence of objective [p. 443] data, but it actually rests within the charmed circle of the individual experience, about which it affirms nothing that was not already given by it. We may easily observe this thinking in those people who cannot refrain from tacking on to an impression or experience some rational and doubtless very valid remark, which, however, in no way adventures beyond the given orbit of the experience. At bottom, such a remark merely says 'I have understood it -- I can reconstruct it.' But there the matter also ends. At its very highest, such a judgment signifies merely the placing of an experience in an objective setting, whereby the experience is at once recognized as belonging to the frame.

But whenever a function other than thinking possesses priority in consciousness to any marked degree, in so far as thinking is conscious at all and not directly dependent upon the dominant function, it assumes a negative character. In so far as it is subordinated to the dominant function, it may actually wear a positive aspect, but a narrower scrutiny will easily prove that it simply mimics the dominant function, supporting it with arguments that unmistakably contradict the laws of logic proper to thinking. Such a thinking, therefore, ceases to have any interest for our present discussion. Our concern is rather with the constitution of that thinking which cannot be subordinated to the dominance of another function, but remains true to its own principle. To observe and investigate this thinking in itself is not easy, since, in the concrete case, it is more or less constantly repressed by the conscious attitude. Hence, in the majority of cases, it first must be retrieved from the background of consciousness, unless in some unguarded moment it should chance to come accidentally to the surface. As a rule, it must be enticed with some such questions as 'Now what do you really think?' or, again, 'What is your private view [p. 444] about the matter?' Or perhaps one may even use a little cunning, framing the question something this: 'What do you imagine, then, that I really think about the matter?' This latter form should be chosen when the real thinking is unconscious and, therefore projected. The thinking that is enticed to the surface this way has characteristic qualities; it was these I had in mind just now when I described it as negative. It habitual mode is best characterized by the two words 'nothing but'. Goethe personified this thinking in the figure of Mephistopheles. It shows a most distinctive tendency to trace back the object of its judgment to some banality or other, thus stripping it of its own independent significance. This happens simply because it is represented as being dependent upon some other commonplace thing. Wherever a conflict, apparently essential in nature, arises between two men, negative thinking mutters 'Cherchez la femme'. When a man champions or advocates a cause, negative thinking makes no inquiry as to the importance of the thing, but merely asks 'How much does he make by it?' The dictum ascribed to Moleschott: "Der Mensch ist, was er isst" (" Man is what he eats ") also belongs to this collection, as do many more aphorisms and opinions which I need not enumerate.

The destructive quality of this thinking as well as its occasional and limited usefulness, hardly need further elucidation. But there still exists another form of negative thinking, which at first glance perhaps would scarcely be recognized as such I refer to the theosophical thinking which is to-day rapidly spreading in every quarter of the globe, presumably as a reaction phenomenon to the materialism of the epoch now receding. Theosophical thinking has an air that is not in the least reductive, since it exalts everything to transcendental and world-embracing ideas. A dream, for instance, is no [p. 445] longer a modest dream, but an experience upon 'another plane'. The hitherto inexplicable fact of telepathy is ,very simply explained by 'vibrations' which pass from one man to another. An ordinary nervous trouble is quite simply accounted for by the fact that something has collided with the astral body. Certain anthropological peculiarities of the dwellers on the Atlantic seaboard are easily explained by the submerging of Atlantis, and so on. We have merely to open a theosophical book to be overwhelmed by the realization that everything is already explained, and that 'spiritual science' has left no enigmas of life unsolved. But, fundamentally, this sort of thinking is just as negative as materialistic thinking. When the latter conceives psychology as chemical changes taking place in the cell-ganglia, or as the extrusion and withdrawal of cell-processes, or as an internal secretion, in essence this is just as superstitious as theosophy. The only difference lies in the fact that materialism reduces all phenomena to our current physiological notions, while theosophy brings everything into the concepts of Indian metaphysics. When we trace the dream to an overloaded stomach, the dream is not thereby explained, and when we explain telepathy as 'vibrations', we have said just as little.

410   THE MEANING OF LIFE

Since, what are 'vibrations'? Not only are both methods of explanation quite impotent -- they are actually destructive, because by interposing their seeming explanations they withdraw interest from the problem, diverting it in the former case to the stomach, and in the latter to imaginary vibrations, thus preventing any serious investigation of the problem. Either kind of thinking is both sterile and sterilizing. Their negative quality consists in this it is a method of thought that is indescribably cheap there is a real poverty of productive and creative energy. It is a thinking taken in tow by other functions. [p. 446]

3. Feeling

Feeling in the extraverted attitude is orientated by objective data, i.e. the object is the indispensable determinant of the kind of feeling. It agrees with objective values. If one has always known feeling as a subjective fact, the nature of extraverted feeling will not immediately be understood, since it has freed itself as fully as possible from the subjective factor, and has, instead, become wholly subordinated to the influence of the object. Even where it seems to show a certain independence of the quality of the concrete object, it is none the less under the spell of. traditional or generally valid standards of some sort. I may feel constrained, for instance, to use the predicate 'beautiful' or 'good', not because I find the object 'beautiful' or 'good' from my own subjective feeling, but because it is fitting and politic so to do; and fitting it certainly is, inasmuch as a contrary opinion would disturb the general feeling situation. A feeling-judgment such as this is in no way a simulation or a lie -- it is merely an act of accommodation. A picture, for instance, may be termed beautiful, because a picture that is hung in a drawing-room and bearing a well-known signature is generally assumed to be beautiful, or because the predicate 'ugly' might offend the family of the fortunate possessor, or because there is a benevolent intention on the part of the visitor to create a pleasant feeling-atmosphere, to which end everything must be felt as agreeable. Such feelings are governed by the standard of the objective determinants. As such they are genuine, and represent the total visible feeling-function.

In precisely the same way as extraverted thinking strives to rid itself of subjective influences, extraverted feeling has also to undergo a certain process of differentiation, before it is finally denuded of every subjective [p. 447] trimming. The valuations resulting from the act of feeling either correspond directly with objective values or at least chime in with certain traditional and generally known standards of value. This kind of feeling is very largely responsible for the fact that so many people flock to the theatre, to concerts, or to Church, and what is more, with correctly adjusted positive feelings. Fashions, too, owe their existence to it, and, what is far more valuable, the whole positive and wide-spread support of social, philanthropic, and such like cultural enterprises. In such matters, extraverted feeling proves itself a creative factor. Without this feeling, for instance, a beautiful and harmonious sociability would be unthinkable. So far extraverted feeling is just as beneficent and rationally effective as extraverted thinking. But this salutary effect is lost as soon as the object gains an exaggerated influence. For, when this happens, extraverted feeling draws the personality too much into the object, i.e. the object assimilates the person, whereupon the personal character of the feeling, which constitutes its principal charm, is lost. Feeling then becomes cold, material, untrustworthy. It betrays a secret aim, or at least arouses the suspicion of it in an impartial observer. No longer does it make that welcome and refreshing impression the invariable accompaniment of genuine feeling; instead, one scents a pose or affectation, although the egocentric motive may be entirely unconscious.

Such overstressed, extraverted feeling certainly fulfils æsthetic expectations, but no longer does it speak to the heart; it merely appeals to the senses, or -- worse still -- to the reason. Doubtless it can provide æsthetic padding for a situation, but there it stops, and beyond that its effect is nil. It has become sterile. Should this process go further, a strangely contradictory dissociation of feeling develops; every object is seized upon with feeling- [p. 448] valuations, and numerous relationships are made which are inherently and mutually incompatible. Since such aberrations would be quite impossible if a sufficiently emphasized subject were present, the last vestige of a real personal standpoint also becomes suppressed. The subject becomes so swallowed up in individual feeling processes that to the observer it seems as though there were no longer a subject of feeling but merely a feeling process. In such a condition feeling has entirely forfeited its original human warmth, it gives an impression of pose, inconstancy, unreliability, and in the worst cases appears definitely hysterical.

4. The Extraverted Feeling-Type

In so far as feeling is, incontestably, a more obvious peculiarity of feminine psychology than thinking, the most pronounced feeling-types are also to be found among women. When extraverted feeling possesses the priority we speak of an extraverted feeling-type. Examples of this type that I can call to mind are, almost without exception, women. She is a woman who follows the guiding-line of her feeling. As the result of education her feeling has become developed into an adjusted function, subject to conscious control. Except in extreme cases, feeling has a personal character, in spite of the fact that the subjective factor may be already, to a large extent, repressed. The personality appears to be adjusted in relation to objective conditions. Her feelings correspond with objective situations and general values. Nowhere is this more clearly revealed than in the so-called 'love-choice'; the 'suitable' man is loved, not another one; he is suitable not so much because he fully accords with the fundamental character of the woman -- as a rule she is quite uninformed about this -- but because [p. 449] he meticulously corresponds in standing, age, capacity, height, and family respectability with every reasonable requirement. Such a formulation might, of course, be easily rejected as ironical or depreciatory, were I not fully convinced that the love-feeling of this type of woman completely corresponds with her choice. It is genuine, and not merely intelligently manufactured. Such 'reasonable' marriages exist without number, and they are by no means the worst. Such women are good comrades to their husbands and excellent mothers, so long as husbands or children possess the conventional psychic constitution. One can feel 'correctly', however, only when feeling is disturbed by nothing else. But nothing disturbs feeling so much as thinking. It is at once intelligible, therefore, that this type should repress thinking as much as possible. This does not mean to say that such a woman does not think at all; on the contrary, she may even think a great deal and very ably, but her thinking is

412   THE MEANING OF LIFE

never sui generis; it is, in fact, an Epimethean appendage to her feeling. What she cannot feel, she cannot consciously think. 'But I can't think what I don't feel', such a type said to me once in indignant tones. As far as feeling permits, she can think very well, but every conclusion, however logical, that might lead to a disturbance of feeling is rejected from the outset. It is simply not thought. And thus everything that corresponds with objective valuations is good: these things are loved or treasured; the rest seems merely to exist in a world apart.

But a change comes over the picture when the importance of the object reaches a still higher level. As already explained above, such an assimilation of subject to object then occurs as almost completely to engulf the subject of feeling. Feeling loses its personal character -- it becomes feeling per se; it almost seems as though the [p. 450] personality were wholly dissolved in the feeling of the moment. Now, since in actual life situations constantly and successively alternate, in which the feeling-tones released are not only different but are actually mutually contrasting, the personality inevitably becomes dissipated in just so many different feelings. Apparently, he is this one moment, and something completely different the next -- apparently, I repeat, for in reality such a manifold personality is altogether impossible. The basis of the ego always remains identical with itself, and, therefore, appears definitely opposed to the changing states of feeling. Accordingly the observer senses the display of feeling not so much as a personal expression of the feeling-subject as an alteration of his ego, a mood, in other words. Corresponding with the degree of dissociation between the ego and the momentary state of feeling, signs of disunion with the self will become more or less evident, i.e. the original compensatory attitude of the unconscious becomes a manifest opposition. This reveals itself, in the first instance, in extravagant demonstrations of feeling, in loud and obtrusive feeling predicates, which leave one, however, somewhat incredulous. They ring hollow; they are not convincing. On the contrary, they at once give one an inkling of a resistance that is being overcompensated, and one begins to wonder whether such a feeling-judgment might not just as well be entirely different. In fact, in a very short time it actually is different. Only a very slight alteration in the situation is needed to provoke forthwith an entirely contrary estimation of the selfsame object. The result of such an experience is that the observer is unable to take either judgment at all seriously. He begins to reserve his own opinion. But since, with this type, it is a matter of the greatest moment to establish an intensive feeling rapport with his environment, redoubled efforts are now required [p. 451] to overcome this reserve. Thus, in the manner of the circulus vitiosus, the situation goes from bad to worse. The more the feeling relation with the object becomes overstressed, the nearer the unconscious opposition approaches the surface.

We have already seen that the extraverted feeling type, as a rule, represses his thinking, just because thinking is the function most liable to disturb feeling. Similarly, when thinking seeks to arrive at pure results of any kind, its first act is to exclude feeling, since nothing is calculated to harass and falsify thinking so much as feeling-values. Thinking, therefore, in so far as it is an independent function, is repressed in the extraverted feeling type. Its repression, as I observed before, is complete only in so far as its inexorable logic forces it to conclusions that are incompatible with feeling. It is suffered to exist as the servant of feeling, or more accurately its slave. Its backbone is broken; it may not operate on its own account, in accordance with its own laws, Now, since a logic exists producing inexorably right conclusions, this must happen somewhere, although beyond the bounds of consciousness, i.e. in the unconscious. Pre-eminently, therefore, the unconscious content of this type is a particular kind of thinking. It is an infantile, archaic, and negative thinking.

So long as conscious feeling preserves the personal character, or, in other words, so long as the personality does not become swallowed up by successive states of feeling, this unconscious thinking remains compensatory. But as soon as the personality is dissociated, becoming dispersed in mutually contradictory states of feeling, the identity of the ego is lost, and the subject becomes unconscious. But, because of the subject's lapse into the unconscious, it becomes associated with the unconscious thinking -- function, therewith assisting the unconscious [p. 452] thought to occasional consciousness. The stronger the conscious feeling relation, and therefore, the more 'depersonalized,' it becomes, the stronger grows the unconscious opposition. This reveals itself in the fact that unconscious ideas centre round just the most valued objects, which are thus pitilessly stripped of their value. That thinking which always thinks in the 'nothing but' style is in its right place here, since it destroys the ascendancy of the feeling that is chained to the object.

Unconscious thought reaches the surface in the form of irruptions, often of an obsessing nature, the general character of which is always negative and depreciatory. Women of this type have moments when the most hideous thoughts fasten upon the very objects most valued by their feelings. This negative thinking avails itself of every infantile prejudice or parallel that is calculated to breed doubt in the feeling-value, and it tows every primitive instinct along with it, in the effort to make 'a nothing but' interpretation of the feeling. At this point, it is perhaps in the nature of a side-remark to observe that the collective unconscious, i.e. the totality of the primordial images, also becomes enlisted in the same manner, and from the elaboration and development of these images there dawns the possibility of a regeneration of the attitude upon another basis.

Hysteria, with the characteristic infantile sexuality of its unconscious world of ideas, is the principal form of neurosis with this type.

5. Recapitulation of Extraverted Rational Types

I term the two preceding types rational or judging types because they are characterized by the supremacy of the reasoning and the judging functions. It is a general distinguishing mark of both types that their life is, to a [p. 453] large extent, subordinated to reasoning judgment. But we must not overlook the point, whether by 'reasoning' we are referring to the standpoint of the individual's subjective psychology, or to the standpoint of the observer, who perceives and judges from without. For such an observer could easily arrive at an opposite judgment, especially if he has a merely intuitive apprehension of the behaviour of the observed, and judges accordingly. In its totality, the life of this type is never dependent upon reasoning judgment alone; it is influenced in almost equal degree by unconscious irrationality. If observation is restricted to behaviour, without any concern for the domestic interior of the individual's consciousness, one may get an

414   THE MEANING OF LIFE

even stronger impression of the irrational and accidental character of certain unconscious manifestations in the individual's behaviour than of the reasonableness of his conscious purposes and motivations. I, therefore, base my judgment upon what the individual feels to be his conscious psychology. But I am prepared to grant that we may equally well entertain a precisely opposite conception of such a psychology, and present it accordingly. I am also convinced that, had I myself chanced to possess a different individual psychology, I should have described the rational types in the reversed way, from the standpoint of the unconscious-as irrational, therefore. This circumstance aggravates the difficulty of a lucid presentation of psychological matters to a degree not to be underestimated, and immeasurably increases the possibility of misunderstandings. The discussions which develop from these misunderstandings are, as a rule, quite hopeless, since the real issue is never joined, each side speaking, as it were, in a different tongue. Such experience is merely one reason the more for basing my presentation upon the subjective conscious psychology of the individual, since there, at least, one has a definite objective footing, which completely [p. 454] drops away the moment we try to ground psychological principles upon the unconscious. For the observed, in this case, could undertake no kind of co-operation, because there is nothing of which he is not more informed than his own unconscious. The judgment would entirely devolve upon the observer -- a certain guarantee that its basis would be his own individual psychology, which would infallibly be imposed upon the observed. To my mind, this is the case in the psychologies both of Freud and of Adler. The individual is completely at the mercy of the arbitrary discretion of his observing critic -- which can never be the case when the conscious psychology of the observed is accepted as the basis. After all, he is the only competent judge, since he alone knows his own motives.

The reasonableness that characterizes the conscious management of life in both these types, involves a conscious exclusion of the accidental and non-rational. Reasoning judgment, in such a psychology, represents a power that coerces the untidy and accidental things of life into definite forms; such at least is its aim. Thus, on the one hand, a definite choice is made among the possibilities of life, since only the rational choice is consciously accepted; but, on the other hand, the independence and influence of those psychic functions which perceive life's happenings are essentially restricted. This limitation of sensation and intuition is, of course, not absolute. These functions exist, for they are universal; but their products are subject to the choice of the reasoning judgment. It is not the absolute strength of sensation, for instance, which turns the scales in the motivation of action, but judgment, Thus, in a certain sense, the perceiving-functions share the same fate as feeling in the case of the first type, or thinking in that of the second. They are relatively repressed, and therefore in an inferior state of differentiation. This circumstance gives a particular stamp to the unconscious [p. 455] of both our types; what such men do consciously and intentionally accords with reason (their reason of course), but what happens to them corresponds either with infantile, primitive sensations, or with similarly archaic intuitions. I will try to make clear what I mean by these latter concepts in the sections that follow. At all events, that which happens to this type is irrational (from their own standpoint of course). Now, since there are vast numbers of men whose lives consist in what happens to them more than in actions resulting from reasoned intention, it might conceivably happen, that such a man, after careful analysis, would describe both our types as irrational. We must grant him, however, that only too often a man's unconscious makes a far stronger impression upon one than his conscious, and that his actions often have considerably more weight and meaning than his reasoned motivations.

The rationality of both types is orientated objectively, and depends upon objective data. Their reasonableness corresponds with what passes as reasonable from the collective standpoint. Subjectively they consider nothing rational save what is generally considered as such. But reason is also very largely subjective and individual. In our case this share is repressed -- increasingly so, in fact, the more the significance of the object is exalted, Both the subject and subjective reason, therefore, are always threatened with repression and, when it descends, they fall under the tyranny of the unconscious, which in this case possesses most unpleasant qualities. We have already spoken of its thinking. But, in addition, there are primitive sensations, which reveal themselves in compulsive forms, as, for instance, an abnormal compulsive pleasure seeking in every conceivable direction ; there are also primitive intuitions, which can become a positive torture to the individuals concerned, not to mention their entourage. Everything disagreeable and painful, everything disgusting, [p. 456] ugly, and evil is scented out or suspected, and these as a rule only correspond with half-truths, than which nothing is more calculated to create misunderstandings of the most poisonous kind. The powerful influence of the opposing unconscious contents necessarily brings about a frequent interruption of the rational conscious government, namely, a striking subservience to the element of chance, so that, either by virtue of their sensational value or unconscious significance, accidental happenings acquire a compelling influence.

6. Sensation

Sensation, in the extraverted attitude, is most definitely conditioned by the object. As sense-perception, sensation is naturally dependent upon the object. But, just as naturally, it is also dependent upon the subject; hence, there is also a subjective sensation, which after its kind is entirely different from the objective. In the extraverted attitude this subjective share of sensation, in so far as its conscious application is concerned, is either inhibited or repressed. As an irrational function, sensation is equally repressed, whenever a rational function, thinking or feeling, possesses the priority, ie. it can be said to have a conscious function, only in so far as the rational attitude of consciousness permits accidental perceptions to become conscious contents; in short, realizes them. The function of sense is, of course, absolute in the stricter sense; for example, everything is seen or heard to the farthest physiological possibility, but not everything attains that threshold value which a perception must possess in order to be also apperceived. It is a different matter when sensation itself possesses priority, instead of merely seconding another function. In this case, no element of objective sensation is excluded and nothing repressed (with the exception of the subjective share [p. 457] already mentioned). Sensation has a preferential objective determination, and those objects which release the strongest sensation are decisive for the individual's psychology. The result of this is a pronounced sensuous hold to the object. Sensation,

416   THE MEANING OF LIFE

therefore, is a vital function, equipped with the potentest [sic] vital instinct. In so far as objects release sensations, they matter; and, in so far as it lies within the power of sensation, they are also fully accepted into consciousness, whether compatible with reasoned judgment or not. As a function its sole criterion of value is the strength of the sensation as conditioned by its objective qualities. Accordingly, all objective processes, in so far as they release sensations at all, make their appearance in consciousness. It is, however, only concrete, sensuously perceived objects or processes which excite sensations in the extraverted attitude; exclusively those, in fact, which everyone in all times and places would sense as concrete. Hence, the orientation of such an individual corresponds with purely concrete reality. The judging, rational functions are subordinated to the concrete facts of sensation, and, accordingly, possess the qualities of inferior differentiation, i.e. they are marked by a certain negativity, with infantile and archaic tendencies. The function most affected by the repression, is, naturally, the one standing opposite to sensation, viz. intuition, the function of unconscious perception.

7. The Extraverted Sensation Type

No other human type can equal the extraverted sensation-type in realism. His sense for objective facts is extraordinarily developed. His life is an accumulation of actual experience with concrete objects, and the more pronounced he is, the less use does he make of his experience. In certain cases the events of his life hardly deserve [p. 458] the name 'experience'. He knows no better use for this sensed 'experience' than to make it serve as a guide to fresh sensations; anything in the least 'new' that comes within his circle of interest is forthwith turned to a sensational account and is made to serve this end. In so far as one is disposed to regard a highly developed sense for sheer actuality as very reasonable, will such men be esteemed rational. In reality, however, this is by no means the case, since they are equally subject to the sensation of irrational, chance happenings, as they are to rational behaviour.

Such a type -- the majority arc men apparently -- does not, of course, believe himself to be 'subject' to sensation. He would be much more inclined to ridicule this view as altogether inconclusive, since, from his standpoint, sensation is the concrete manifestation of life -- it is simply the fulness [sic] of actual living. His aim is concrete enjoyment, and his morality is similarly orientated. For true enjoyment has its own special morality, its own moderation and lawfulness, its own unselfishness and devotedness. It by no means follows that he is just sensual or gross, for he may differentiate his sensation to the finest pitch of æsthetic purity without being the least unfaithful, even in his most abstract sensations, to his principle of objective sensation. Wulfen's Cicerone des r¨cksichtlosen Lebensgenusses is the unvarnished confession of a type of this sort. From this point of view the book seems to me worth reading.

Upon the lower levels this is the man of tangible reality, with little tendency either for reflection or commanding purpose. To sense the object, to have and if possible to enjoy sensations, is his constant motive. He is by no means unlovable; on the contrary, he frequently has a charming and lively capacity for enjoyment; he is sometimes a jolly fellow, and often a refined æsthete. [p. 459]

In the former case, the great problems of life hinge upon a good or indifferent dinner; in the latter, they are questions of good taste. When he 'senses', everything essential has been said and done. Nothing can be more than concrete and actual; conjectures that transcend or go beyond the concrete are only permitted on condition that they enhance sensation. This need not be in any way a pleasurable reinforcement, since this type is not a common voluptuary; he merely desires the strongest sensation, and this, by his very nature, he can receive only from without. What comes from within seems to him morbid and objectionable. In so far as lie thinks and feels, he always reduces down to objective foundations, i.e. to influences coming from the object, quite unperturbed by the most violent departures from logic. Tangible reality, under any conditions, makes him breathe again. In this respect he is unexpectedly credulous. He will, without hesitation, relate an obvious psychogenic symptom to the falling barometer, while the existence of a psychic conflict seems to him a fantastic abnormality. His love is incontestably rooted in the manifest attractions of the object. In so far as he is normal, he is conspicuously adjusted to positive reality -- conspicuously, because his adjustment is always visible. His ideal is the actual; in this respect he is considerate. He has no ideals related to ideas -- he has, therefore, no sort of ground for maintaining a hostile attitude towards the reality of things and facts. This expresses itself in all the externals of his life. He dresses well, according to his circumstances ; he keeps a good table for his friends, who are either made comfortable or at least given to understand that his fastidious taste is obliged to impose certain claims upon his entourage. He even convinces one that certain sacrifices are decidedly worth while for the sake of style.

But the more sensation predominates, so that the [p. 460] sensing subject disappears behind the sensation, the more unsatisfactory does this type become. Either he develops into a crude pleasure-seeker or he becomes an unscrupulous, designing sybarite. Although the object is entirely indispensable to him, yet, as something existing in and through itself, it is none the less depreciated. It is ruthlessly violated and essentially ignored, since now its sole use is to stimulate sensation. The hold upon the object is pushed to the utmost limit. The unconscious is, accordingly, forced out of its me[accent]tier as a compensatory function and driven into open opposition. But, above all, the repressed intuitions begin to assert themselves in the form of projections upon the object. The strangest conjectures arise; in the case of a sexual object, jealous phantasies and anxiety-states play a great role. More acute cases develop every sort of phobia, and especially compulsive symptoms. The pathological contents have a remarkable air of unreality, with a frequent moral or religious colouring. A pettifogging captiousness often develops, or an absurdly scrupulous morality coupled with a primitive, superstitious and 'magical' religiosity, harking back to abstruse rites. All these things have their source in the repressed inferior functions, which, in such cases, stand in harsh opposition to the conscious standpoint; they wear, in fact, an aspect that is all the more striking because they appear to rest upon the most absurd suppositions, in complete contrast to the conscious sense of reality. The whole culture of thought and feeling seems, in this second personality, to be twisted into a morbid primitiveness; reason is hair-splitting sophistry -- morality is dreary moralizing and palpable Pharisaism -- religion is absurd superstition -- intuition, the noblest of human gifts, is a mere personal subtlety,

418   THE MEANING OF LIFE

a sniffing into every corner; instead of searching the horizon, it recedes to the narrowest gauge of human meanness. [p. 461]

The specially compulsive character of the neurotic symptoms represent the unconscious counterweight to the laisser aller morality of a purely sensational attitude, which, from the standpoint of rational judgment, accepts without discrimination, everything that happens. Although this lack of basic principles in the sensation-type does not argue an absolute lawlessness and lack of restraint, it at least deprives him of the quite essential restraining power of judgment. Rational judgment represents a conscious coercion, which the rational type appears to impose upon himself of his own free will. This compulsion overtakes the sensation-type from the unconscious. Moreover, the rational type's link to the object, from the very existence of a judgment, never means such an unconditioned relation as that which the sensation-type has with the object. When his attitude reaches an abnormal one-sidedness, he is in danger of falling just as deeply into the arms of the unconscious as he consciously clings to the object. When he becomes neurotic, he is much harder to treat in the rational way, because the functions to which the physician must appeal are in a relatively undifferentiated state; hence little or no trust can be placed in them. Special means of bringing emotional pressure to bear are often needed to make him at all conscious.

8. Intuition

Intuition as the function of unconscious perception is wholly directed upon outer objects in the extraverted attitude. Because, in the main, intuition is an unconscious process, the conscious apprehension of its nature is a very difficult matter. In consciousness, the intuitive function is represented by a certain attitude of expectation, a perceptive and penetrating vision, wherein only the subsequent result can prove, in every case, how much was [p. 462] 'perceived-into', and how much actually lay in the object.

Just as sensation, when given the priority, is not a mere reactive process of no further importance for the object, but is almost an action which seizes and shapes the object, so it is with intuition, which is by no means a mere perception, or awareness, but an active, creative process that builds into the object just as much as it takes out. But, because this process extracts the perception unconsciously, it also produces an unconscious effect in the object. The primary function of intuition is to transmit mere images, or perceptions of relations and conditions, which could be gained by the other functions, either not at all, or only by very roundabout ways. Such images have the value of definite discernments, and have a decisive bearing upon action, whenever intuition is given the chief weight; in which case, psychic adaptation is based almost exclusively upon intuition. Thinking, feeling, and sensation are relatively repressed; of these, sensation is the one principally affected, because, as the conscious function of sense, it offers the greatest obstacle to intuition. Sensation disturbs intuition's clear, unbiassed, na[umlaut]ive awareness with its importunate sensuous stimuli; for these direct the glance upon the physical superficies, hence upon the very things round and beyond which intuition tries to peer. But since intuition, in the extraverted attitude, has a prevailingly objective orientation, it actually comes very near to sensation; indeed, the expectant attitude towards outer objects may, with almost equal probability, avail itself of sensation. Hence, for intuition really to become paramount, sensation must to a large extent be suppressed. I am now speaking of sensation as the simple and direct sense-reaction, an almost definite physiological and psychic datum. This must be expressly established beforehand, because, if I ask the intuitive how he is [p. 463] orientated, he will speak of things which are quite indistinguishable from sense-perceptions. Frequently he will even make use of the term 'sensation'. He actually has sensations, but he is not guided by them per se, merely using them as directing-points for his distant vision. They are selected by unconscious expectation. Not the strongest sensation, in the physiological sense, obtains the crucial value, but any sensation whatsoever whose value happens to become considerably enhanced by reason of the intuitive's unconscious attitude. In this way it may eventually attain the leading position, appearing to the intuitive's consciousness indistinguishable from a pure sensation. But actually it is not so.

Just as extraverted sensation strives to reach the highest pitch of actuality, because only thus can the appearance of a complete life be created, so intuition tries to encompass the greatest possibilities, since only through the awareness of possibilities is intuition fullysatisfied. Intuition seeks to discover possibilities in the objective situation; hence as a mere tributary function (viz. when not in the position of priority) it is also the instrument which, in the presence of a hopelessly blocked situation, works automatically towards the issue, which no other function could discover. Where intuition has the priority, every ordinary situation in life seems like a closed room, which intuition has to open. It is constantly seeking outlets and fresh possibilities in external life. In a very short time every actual situation becomes a prison to the intuitive; it burdens him like a chain, prompting a compelling need for solution. At times objects would seem to have an almost exaggerated value, should they chance to represent the idea of a severance or release that might lead to the discovery of a new possibility. Yet no sooner have they performed their office, serving intuition as a ladder or a bridge, than they [p. 464] appear to have no further value, and are discarded as mere burdensome appendages. A fact is acknowledged only in so far as it opens up fresh possibilities of advancing beyond it and of releasing the individual from its operation. Emerging possibilities are compelling motives from which intuition cannot escape and to which all else must be sacrificed.

9. The Extraverted Intuitive Type

Whenever intuition predominates, a particular and unmistakable psychology presents itself. Because intuition is orientated by the object, a decided dependence upon external situations is discernible, but it has an altogether different character from the dependence of the sensational type. The intuitive is never to be found among the generally recognized reality values, but he is always present where possibilities exist. He has a keen nose for things in the bud pregnant with future promise. He can never exist in stable, long-established conditions of generally acknowledged though limited value: because his eye is constantly ranging for new possibilities, stable conditions have an air of impending suffocation. He seizes hold of new objects and new

420   THE MEANING OF LIFE

ways with eager intensity, sometimes with extraordinary enthusiasm, only to abandon them cold-bloodedly, without regard and apparently without remembrance, as soon as their range becomes clearly defined and a promise of any considerable future development no longer clings to them. As long as a possibility exists, the intuitive is bound to it with thongs of fate. It is as though his whole life went out into the new situation. One gets the impression, which he himself shares, that he has just reached the definitive turning point in his life, and that from now on nothing else can seriously engage his thought and feeling. How- [p. 465] ever reasonable and opportune it may be, and although every conceivable argument speaks in favour of stability, a day will come when nothing will deter him from regarding as a prison, the self-same situation that seemed to promise him freedom and deliverance, and from acting accordingly. Neither reason nor feeling can restrain or discourage him from a new possibility, even though it may run counter to convictions hitherto unquestioned. Thinking and feeling, the indispensable components of conviction, are, with him, inferior functions, possessing no decisive weight; hence they lack the power to offer any lasting. resistance to the force of intuition. And yet these are the only functions that are capable of creating any effectual compensation to the supremacy of intuition, since they can provide the intuitive with that judgment in which his type is altogether lacking. The morality of the intuitive is governed neither by intellect nor by feeling; he has his own characteristic morality, which consists in a loyalty to his intuitive view of things and a voluntary submission to its authority, Consideration for the welfare of his neighbours is weak. No solid argument hinges upon their well-being any more than upon his own. Neither can we detect in him any great respect for his neighbour's convictions and customs; in fact, he is not infrequently put down as an immoral and ruthless adventurer. Since his intuition is largely concerned with outer objects, scenting out external possibilities, he readily applies himself to callings wherein he may expand his abilities in many directions. Merchants, contractors, speculators, agents, politicians, etc., commonly belong to this type.

Apparently this type is more prone to favour women than men; in which case, however, the intuitive activity reveals itself not so much in the professional as in the social sphere. Such women understand the art of utilizing every social opportunity; they establish right social con- [p. 466] nections; they seek out lovers with possibilities only to abandon everything again for the sake of a new possibility.

It is at once clear, both from the standpoint of political economy and on grounds of general culture, that such a type is uncommonly important. If well-intentioned, with an orientation to life not purely egoistical, he may render exceptional service as the promoter, if not the initiator of every kind of promising enterprise. He is the natural advocate of every minority that holds the seed of future promise. Because of his capacity, when orientated more towards men than things, to make an intuitive diagnosis of their abilities and range of usefulness, he can also 'make' men. His capacity to inspire his fellow-men with courage, or to kindle enthusiasm for something new, is unrivalled, although he may have forsworn it by the morrow. The more powerful and vivid his intuition, the more is his subject fused and blended with the divined possibility. He animates it; he

PSYCHOANALYSIS   421

presents it in plastic shape and with convincing fire; he almost embodies it. It is not a mere histrionic display, but a fate.

This attitude has immense dangers -- all too easily the intuitive may squander his life. He spends himself animating men and things, spreading around him an abundance of life -- a life, however, which others live, not he. Were he able to rest with the actual thing, he would gather the fruit of his labours; yet all too soon must he be running after some fresh possibility, quitting his newly planted field, while others reap the harvest. In the end he goes empty away. But when the intuitive lets things reach such a pitch, he also has the unconscious against him. The unconscious of the intuitive has a certain similarity with that of the sensation-type. Thinking and feeling, being relatively repressed, produce infantile and archaic thoughts and feelings in the unconscious, which may be compared [p. 467] with those of the countertype. They likewise come to the surface in the form of intensive projections, and are just as absurd as those of the sensation-type, only to my mind they lack the other's mystical character; they are chiefly concerned with quasi-actual things, in the nature of sexual, financial, and other hazards, as, for instance, suspicions of approaching illness. This difference appears to be due to a repression of the sensations of actual things. These latter usually command attention in the shape of a sudden entanglement with a most unsuitable woman, or, in the case of a woman, with a thoroughly unsuitable man; and this is simply the result of their unwitting contact with the sphere of archaic sensations. But its consequence is an unconsciously compelling tie to an object of incontestable futility. Such an event is already a compulsive symptom, which is also thoroughly characteristic of this type. In common with the sensation-type, he claims a similar freedom and exemption from all restraint, since he suffers no submission of his decisions to rational judgment, relying entirely upon the perception of chance, possibilities. He rids himself of the restrictions of reason, only to fall a victim to unconscious neurotic compulsions in the form of oversubtle, negative reasoning, hair-splitting dialectics, and a compulsive tie to the sensation of the object. His conscious attitude, both to the sensation and the sensed object, is one of sovereign superiority and disregard. Not that he means to be inconsiderate or superior -- he simply does not see the object that everyone else sees; his oblivion is similar to that of the sensation-type -- only, with the latter, the soul of the object is missed. For this oblivion the object sooner or later takes revenge in the form of hypochondriacal, compulsive ideas, phobias, and every imaginable kind of absurd bodily sensation. [p. 468]

10. Recapitulation of Extraverted Irrational Types

I call the two preceding types irrational for reasons already referred to; namely, because their commissions and omissions are based not upon reasoned judgment but upon the absolute intensity of perception. Their perception is concerned with simple happenings, where no selection has been exercised by the judgment. In this respect both the latter types have a considerable superiority over the two judging types. The objective occurrence is both law-determined and accidental. In so far as it is law-determined, it is accessible to reason; in so far as it is accidental, it is not. One might reverse it and say that we apply the term law-determined to the occurrence

422 THE MEANING OF LIFE

appearing so to our reason, and where its regularity escapes us we call it accidental. The postulate of a universal lawfulness remains a postulate of reason only; in no sense is it a postulate of our functions of perception. Since these are in no way grounded upon the principle of reason and its postulates, they are, of their very nature, irrational. Hence my term 'irrational' corresponds with the nature of the perception-types. But merely because they subordinate judgment to perception, it would be quite incorrect to regard these types as unreasonable. They are merely in a high degree empirical; they are grounded exclusively upon experience, so exclusively, in fact, that as a rule, their judgment cannot keep pace with their experience. But the functions of judgment are none the less present, although they eke out a largely unconscious existence. But, since the unconscious, in spite of its separation from the conscious subject, is always reappearing on the scene, the actual life of the irrational types exhibits striking judgments and acts of choice, which take the form of apparent sophistries, cold-hearted criticisms, and an apparently purposeful [p. 469] selection of persons and situations. These traits have a rather infantile, or even primitive, stamp; at times they are astonishingly naive, but at times also inconsiderate, crude, or outrageous. To the rationally orientated mind, the real character of such people might well appear rationalistic and purposeful in the bad sense. But this judgment would be valid only for their unconscious, and, therefore, quite incorrect for their conscious psychology, which is entirely orientated by perception, and because of its irrational nature is quite unintelligible to the rational judgment. Finally, it may even appear to a rationally orientated mind that such an assemblage of accidentals, hardly deserves the name 'psychology.' The irrational type balances this contemptuous judgment with an equally poor impression of the rational; for he sees him as something only half alive, whose only aim in life consists in fastening the fetters of reason upon everything living, and wringing his own neck with criticisms. Naturally, these are gross extremes; but they occur.

From the standpoint of the rational type, the irrational might easily be represented as a rational of inferior quality; namely, when he is apprehended in the light of what happens to him. For what happens to him is not the accidental-in that he is master-but, in its stead, he is overtaken by rational judgment and rational aims. This fact is hardly comprehensible to the rational mind, but its unthinkableness merely equals the astonishment of the irrational, when he discovers someone who can set the ideas of reason above the living and actual event. Such a thing seems scarcely credible to him. It is, as a rule, quite hopeless to look to him for any recognition of principles in this direction, since a rational understanding is just as unknown and, in fact, tiresome to him as the idea of making a contract, without mutual discussion and obligations, appears unthinkable to the rational type. [p. 470]

This point brings me to the problem of the psychic relation between the representatives of the different types. Following the terminology of the French school of hypnotists, the psychic relation among the more modern psychiatrists is termed I 'rapport'. Rapport chiefly consists in a feeling of actual accord, in spite of recognised differences. In fact, the recognition of existing differences, in so far as they are common to both, is already a rapport, a feeling of accord. If we make this feeling conscious to a rather high degree in an actual case, we discover that it has not merely the quality of a feeling that cannot be analysed further, but it also has the nature of an insight or cognitional content, representing the point of agreement in a conceptual form. This rational presentation is exclusively valid for the rational types; it by no means applies to the irrational, whose rapport is based not at all upon judgment but upon the parallelism of actual living events. His feeling of accord is the common perception of a sensation or intuition. The rational would say that rapport with the irrational depends purely upon chance. If, by some accident, the objective situations are exactly in tune, something like a human relationship takes place, but nobody can tell what will be either its validity or its duration. To the rational type it is often a very bitter thought that the relationship will last only just so long as external circumstances accidentally produce a mutual interest. This does not occur to him as being especially human, whereas it is precisely in this situation that the irrational sees a humanity of quite singular beauty. Accordingly each regards the other as a man destitute of relationships, upon whom no reliance can be placed, and with whom one can never get on decent terms. Such a result, however, is reached only when one consciously tries to make some estimate of the nature of one's relationships with one's fellow-men. Although a psychological conscientiousness of [p. 471] this kind is by no means usual, yet it frequently happens that, notwithstanding an absolute difference of standpoint, a kind of rapport does take place, and in the following way. The one assumes with unspoken projection that the other is, in all essential points, of the same opinion as himself, while the other divines or senses an objective community of interest, of which, however, the former has no conscious inkling and whose existence he would at once dispute, just as it would never occur to the latter that his relationship must rest upon a common point-of-view. A rapport of this kind is by far the most frequent; it rests upon projection, which is the source of many subsequent misunderstandings.

Psychic relationship, in the extraverted attitude, is always regulated by objective factors and outer determinants. What a man is within has never any decisive significance. For our present-day culture the extraverted attitude is the governing principle in the problem of human relationship; naturally, the introverted principle occurs, but it is still the exception, and has to appeal to the tolerance of the age.

C. THE INTROVERTED TYPE

(I) THE GENERAL ATTITUDE OF CONSCIOUSNESS

As I have already explained in section A (1) of the present chapter, the introverted is distinguished from the extraverted type by the fact that, unlike the latter, who is prevailingly orientated by the object and objective data, he is governed by subjective factors. In the section alluded to I mentioned, inter alia, that the introvert interposes a subjective view between the perception of the object and his own action, which prevents the action from assuming a character that corresponds with the objective situation. Naturally, this is a special case, mentioned by way of [p. 472] example, and merely intended to serve as a simple illustration. But now we must go in quest of more general formulations.

424   THE MEANING OF LIFE

Introverted consciousness doubtless views the external conditions, but it selects the subjective determinants as the decisive ones. The type is guided, therefore, by that factor of perception and cognition which represents the receiving subjective disposition to the sense stimulus. Two persons, for example, see the same object, but they never see it in such a way as to receive two identically similar images of it. Quite apart from the differences in the personal equation and mere organic acuteness, there often exists a radical difference, both in kind and degree, in the psychic assimilation of the perceived image. Whereas the extraverted type refers pre-eminently to that which reaches him from the object, the introvert principally relies upon that which the outer impression constellates [sic] in the subject. In an individual case of apperception, the difference may, of course, be very delicate, but in the total psychological economy it is extremely noticeable, especially in the form of a reservation of the ego. Although it is anticipating somewhat, I consider that point of view which inclines, with Weininger, to describe this attitude as philautic, or with other writers, as autoerotic, egocentric, subjective, or egoistic, to be both misleading in principle and definitely depreciatory. It corresponds with the normal bias of the extraverted attitude against the nature of the introvert. We must not forget-although extraverted opinion is only too prone to do so-that all perception and cognition is not purely objective: it is also subjectively conditioned. The world exists not merely in itself, but also as it appears to me. Indeed, at bottom, we have absolutely no criterion that could help us to form a judgment of a world whose nature was unassimilable by the subject. If we were to ignore the subjective factor, it [p. 473] would mean a complete denial of the great doubt as to the possibility of absolute cognition. And this would mean a rechute into that stale and hollow positivism which disfigured the beginning of our epoch -- an attitude of intellectual arrogance that is invariably accompanied by a crudeness of feeling, and an essential violation of life, as stupid as it is presumptuous. Through an overvaluation of the objective powers of cognition, we repress the importance of the subjective factor, which simply means the denial of the subject. But what is the subject? The subject is man -- we are the subject. Only a sick mind could forget that cognition must have a subject, for there exists no knowledge and, therefore, for us, no world where 'I know' has not been said, although with this statement one has already expressed the subjective limitation of all knowledge.

The same holds good for all the psychic functions: they have a subject which is just as indispensable as the object. It is characteristic of our present extraverted valuation that the word 'subjective' occasionally rings almost like a reproach or blemish; but in every case the epithet 'merely subjective' means a dangerous weapon of offence, destined for that daring head, that is not unceasingly convinced of the unconditioned superiority of the object. We must, therefore, be quite clear as to what meaning the term 'subjective' carries in this investigation. As the subjective factor, then, I understand that psychological action or reaction which, when merged with the effect of the object, makes a new psychic fact. Now, in so far as the subjective factor, since oldest times and among all peoples, remains in a very large measure identical with itself -- since elementary perceptions and cognitions are almost universally the same -- it is a reality that is just as firmly established as the outer object. If this were not so, any sort of permanent and essentially changeless reality [p. 474] would be altogether inconceivable, and any understanding with posterity would be a matter of impossibility. Thus far, therefore, the subjective factor is something that is just as much a fact as the extent of the sea and the radius of the earth. Thus far, also, the subjective factor claims the whole value of a world-determining power which can never, under any circumstances, be excluded from our calculations. It is the other world-law, and the man who is based upon it has a foundation just as secure, permanent, and valid, as the man who relies upon the object But, just as the object and objective data remain by no means always the same, inasmuch as they are both perishable and subject to chance, the subjective factor is similarly liable to variability and individual hazard. Hence its value is also merely relative. The excessive development of the introverted standpoint in consciousness, for instance, does not lead to a better or sounder application of the subjective factor, but to an artificial subjectification of consciousness, which can hardly escape the reproach 'merely subjective'. For, as a countertendency to this morbid subjectification, there ensues a desubjectification of consciousness in the form of an exaggerated extraverted attitude which richly deserves Weininger's description "misautic". Inasmuch as the introverted attitude is based upon a universally present, extremely real, and absolutely indispensable condition of psychological adaptation, such expressions as 'philautic', 'egocentric', and the like are both objectionable and out of place, since they foster the prejudice that it is invariably a question of the beloved ego. Nothing could be more absurd than such an assumption. Yet one is continually meeting it when examining the judgments of the extravert upon the introvert. Not, of course, that I wish to ascribe such an error to individual extraverts; it is rather the present generally accepted extraverted view which is by no means restricted to the extraverted [p. 475] type; for it finds just as many representatives in the ranks of the other type, albeit very much against its own interest. The reproach of being untrue to his own kind is justly levelled at the latter, whereas, this, at least, can never be charged against the former.

The introverted attitude is normally governed by the psychological structure, theoretically determined by heredity, but which to the subject is an ever present subjective factor. This must not be assumed, however, to be simply identical with the subject's ego, an assumption that is certainly implied in the above mentioned designations of Weininger; it is rather the psychological structure of the subject that precedes any development of the ego. The really fundamental subject, the Self, is far more comprehensive than the ego, because the former also embraces the unconscious, while the latter is essentially the focal point of consciousness. Were the ego identical with the Self, it would be unthinkable that we should be able to appear in dreams in entirely different forms and with entirely different meanings. But it is a characteristic peculiarity of the introvert, which, moreover, is as much in keeping with his own inclination as with the general bias, that he tends to confuse his ego with the Self, and to exalt his ego to the position of subject of the psychological process, thus effecting that morbid subjectification of consciousness, mentioned above, which so alienates him from the object.

The psychological structure is the same. Semon has termed it 'mneme',[2] whereas I call it the 'collective unconscious'. The individual Self is a portion, or excerpt, or representative, of

426   THE MEANING OF LIFE

something universally present in all living creatures, and, therefore, a correspondingly graduated kind of psychological process, which is born anew in every creature. Since earliest times, the inborn manner of acting [p. 476] has been called instinct, and for this manner of psychic apprehension of the object I have proposed the term archetype. I may assume that what is understood by instinct is familiar to everyone. It is another matter with the archetype. This term embraces the same idea as is contained in 'primordial image' (an expression borrowed from Jakob Burckhardt), and as such I have described it in Chapter xi of this book. I must here refer the reader to that chapter, in particular to the definition of 'image'.

The archetype is a symbolical formula, which always begins to function whenever there are no conscious ideas present, or when such as are present are impossible upon intrinsic or extrinsic grounds. The contents of the collective unconscious are represented in consciousness in the form of pronounced tendencies, or definite ways of looking at things. They are generally regarded by the individual as being determined by the object-incorrectly, at bottom-since they have their source in the unconscious structure of the psyche, and are only released by the operation of the object. These subjective tendencies and ideas are stronger than the objective influence; because their psychic value is higher, they are superimposed upon all impressions. Thus, just as it seems incomprehensible to the introvert that the object should always be decisive, it remains just as enigmatic to the extravert how a subjective standpoint can be superior to the objective situation. He reaches the unavoidable conclusion that the introvert is either a conceited egoist or a fantastic doctrinaire. Recently he seems to have reached the conclusion that the introvert is constantly influenced by an unconscious power-complex. The introvert unquestionably exposes himself to this prejudice; for it cannot be denied that his definite and highly generalized mode of expression, which apparently excludes every other view from the outset, lends a certain countenance to [p. 477] this extraverted opinion. Furthermore, the very decisiveness and inflexibility of the subjective judgment, which is superordinated to all objective data, is alone sufficient to create the impression of a strong egocentricity. The introvert usually lacks the right argument in presence of this prejudice; for he is just as unaware of the unconscious, though thoroughly sound presuppositions of his subjective judgment, as he is of his subjective perceptions. In harmony with the style of the times, he looks without, instead of behind his own consciousness for the answer. Should he become neurotic, it is the sign of a more or less complete unconscious identity of the ego with the Self, whereupon the importance of the Self is reduced to nil, while the ego becomes inflated beyond reason. The undeniable, world-determining power of the subjective factor then becomes concentrated in the ego, developing an immoderate power claim and a downright foolish egocentricity. Every psychology which reduces the nature of man to unconscious power instinct springs from this foundation. For example, Nietzsche's many faults in taste owe their existence to this subjectification of consciousness.

(II) THE UNCONSCIOUS ATTITUDE

The superior position of the subjective factor in consciousness involves an inferiority of the objective factor. The object is not given that importance which should really belong to it. Just as it plays too great a role in the extraverted attitude, it has too little to say in the introverted. To the extent that the introvert's consciousness is subjectified, thus bestowing undue importance upon the ego, the object is placed in a position which in time becomes quite untenable. The object is a factor of undeniable power, while the ego is something very restricted [p. 478] and transitory. It would be a very different matter if the Self opposed the object. Self and world are commensurable factors; hence a normal introverted attitude is just as valid, and has as good a right to existence, as a normal extraverted attitude. But, if the ego has usurped the claims of the subject, a compensation naturally develops under the guise of an unconscious reinforcement of the influence of the object. Such a change eventually commands attention, for often, in spite of a positively convulsive attempt to ensure the superiority of the ego, the object and objective data develop an overwhelming influence, which is all the more invincible because it seizes upon the individual unawares, thus effecting an irresistible invasion of consciousness. As a result of the ego's defective relation to the object -- for a will to command is not adaptation -- a compensatory relation to the object develops in the unconscious, which makes itself felt in consciousness as an unconditional and irrepressible tie to the object. The more the ego seeks to secure every possible liberty, independence, superiority, and freedom from obligations, the deeper does it fall into the slavery of objective facts. The subject's freedom of mind is chained to an ignominious financial dependence, his unconcernedness of action suffers now and again, a distressing collapse in the face of public opinion, his moral superiority gets swamped in inferior relationships, and his desire to dominate ends in a pitiful craving to be loved. The chief concern of the unconscious in such a case is the relation to the object, and it affects this in a way that is calculated to bring both the power illusion and the superiority phantasy to utter ruin. The object assumes terrifying dimensions, in spite of conscious depreciation. Detachment from, and command of, the object are, in consequence, pursued by the ego still more violently. Finally, the ego surrounds itself by a regular system of safeguards (Adler has ably [p. 479] depicted these) which shall at least preserve the illusion of superiority. But, therewith, the introvert severs himself completely from the object, and either squanders his energy in defensive measures or makes fruitless attempts to impose his power upon the object and successfully assert himself. But these efforts are constantly being frustrated by the overwhelming impressions he receives from the object. It continually imposes itself upon him against his will; it provokes in him the most disagreeable and obstinate affects, persecuting him at every step. An immense, inner struggle is constantly required of him, in order to 'keep going.' Hence Psychoasthenia is his typical form of neurosis, a malady which is characterized on the one hand by an extreme sensitiveness, and on the other by a great liability to exhaustion and chronic fatigue.

An analysis of the personal unconscious yields an abundance of power phantasies coupled with fear of the dangerously animated objects, to which, as a matter of fact, the introvert easily falls a victim. For a peculiar cowardliness develops from this fear of the object; he shrinks from making either himself or his opinion effective, always dreading an intensified influence on the part of the object. He is terrified of impressive affects in others, and is hardly ever free from the dread of falling under hostile influence. For objects possess terrifying and powerful qualities for

428   THE MEANING OF LIFE

him-qualities which he cannot consciously discern in them, but which, through his unconscious perception, he cannot choose but believe in. Since his conscious relation to the object is relatively repressed, its exit is by way of the unconscious, where it becomes loaded with the qualities of the unconscious. These qualities are primarily infantile and archaic. His relation to the object, therefore, becomes correspondingly primitive, taking on all those peculiarities which characterize the primitive objectrelationship. Now it seems as though objects possessed [p. 480] magical powers. Strange, new objects excite fear and distrust, as though concealing unknown dangers; objects long rooted and blessed by tradition are attached to his soul as by invisible threads; every change has a disturbing, if not actually dangerous aspect, since its apparent implication is a magical animation of the object. A lonely island where only what is permitted to move moves, becomes an ideal. Auch Einer, the novel by F. Th. Vischer, gives a rich insight into this side of the introvert's psychology, and at the same time shows the underlying symbolism of the collective unconscious, which in this description of types I am leaving on one side, since it is a universal phenomenon with no especial connection with types.

(III) PECULIARITIES OF THE BASIC PSYCHOLOGICAL FUNCTIONS IN THE INTROVERTED ATTITUDE

1. Thinking

When describing extraverted thinking, I gave a brief characterization of introverted thinking, to which at this stage I must make further reference. Introverted thinking is primarily orientated by the subjective factor. At the least, this subjective factor is represented by a subjective feeling of direction, which, in the last resort, determines judgment. Occasionally, it is a more or less finished image, which to some extent, serves as a standard. This thinking may be conceived either with concrete or with abstract factors, but always at the decisive points it is orientated by subjective data. Hence, it does not lead from concrete experience back again into objective things, but always to the subjective content, External facts are not the aim and origin of this thinking, although the introvert would often like to make it so appear. It begins in the subject, and returns to the subject, although it may [p. 481] undertake the widest flights into the territory of the real and the actual. Hence, in the statement of new facts, its chief value is indirect, because new views rather than the perception of new facts are its main concern. It formulates questions and creates theories; it opens up prospects and yields insight, but in the presence of facts it exhibits a reserved demeanour. As illustrative examples they have their value, but they must not prevail. Facts are collected as evidence or examples for a theory, but never for their own sake. Should this latter ever occur, it is done only as a compliment to the extraverted style. For this kind of thinking facts are of secondary importance; what, apparently, is of absolutely paramount importance is the development and presentation of the subjective idea, that primordial symbolical image standing more or less darkly before the inner vision. Its aim, therefore, is never concerned with an intellectual reconstruction of concrete actuality, but with the shaping of that dim image into a resplendent idea. Its desire is to reach reality; its goal is to see how external facts fit into, and fulfil, the framework of the idea; its actual creative power is proved by the fact that this thinking can also create that idea which, though not present in the external facts, is yet the most suitable, abstract expression of them. Its task is accomplished when the idea it has fashioned seems to emerge so inevitably from the external facts that they actually prove its validity.

But just as little as it is given to extraverted thinking to wrest a really sound inductive idea from concrete facts or ever to create new ones, does it lie in the power of introverted thinking to translate its original image into an idea adequately adapted to the facts. For, as in the former case the purely empirical heaping together of facts paralyses thought and smothers their meaning, so in the latter case introverted thinking shows a dangerous tendency [p. 482] to coerce facts into the shape of its image, or by ignoring them altogether, to unfold its phantasy image in freedom. In such a case, it will be impossible for the presented idea to deny its origin from the dim archaic image. There will cling to it a certain mythological character that we are prone to interpret as 'originality', or in more pronounced cases' as mere whimsicality; since its archaic character is not transparent as such to specialists unfamiliar with mythological motives. The subjective force of conviction inherent in such an idea is usually very great; its power too is the more convincing, the less it is influenced by contact with outer facts. Although to the man who advocates the idea, it may well seem that his scanty store of facts were the actual ground and source of the truth and validity of his idea, yet such is not the case, for the idea derives its convincing power from its unconscious archetype, which, as such, has universal validity and everlasting truth. Its truth, however, is so universal and symbolic, that it must first enter into the recognized and recognizable knowledge of the time, before it can become a practical truth of any real value to life. What sort of a causality would it be, for instance, that never became perceptible in practical causes and practical results?

This thinking easily loses itself in the immense truth of the subjective factor. It creates theories for the sake of theories, apparently with a view to real or at least possible facts, yet always with a distinct tendency to go over from the world of ideas into mere imagery. Accordingly many intuitions of possibilities appear on the scene, none of which however achieve any reality, until finally images are produced which no longer express anything externally real, being 'merely' symbols of the simply unknowable. It is now merely a mystical thinking and quite as unfruitful as that empirical thinking whose sole operation is within the framework of objective facts. [p. 483]

Whereas the latter sinks to the level of a mere presentation of facts, the former evaporates into a representation of the unknowable, which is even beyond everything that could be expressed in an image. The presentation of facts has a certain incontestable truth, because the subjective factor is excluded and the facts speak for themselves. Similarly, the representing of the unknowable has also an immediate, subjective, and convincing power, because it is demonstrable from its own existence. The former says 'Est, ergo est' ('It is ; therefore it is') ; while the latter says 'Cogito, ergo cogito' (' I think ; therefore I think'). In the last analysis, introverted thinking arrives at the evidence of its own subjective being, while extraverted thinking is driven to the evidence of its complete identity with the objective fact. For, while the extravert really denies himself in his

430   THE MEANING OF LIFE

complete dispersion among objects, the introvert, by ridding himself of each and every content, has to content himself with his mere existence. In both cases the further development of life is crowded out of the domain of thought into the region of other psychic functions which had hitherto existed in relative unconsciousness. The extraordinary impoverishment of introverted thinking in relation to objective facts finds compensation in an abundance of unconscious facts. Whenever consciousness, wedded to the function of thought, confines itself within the smallest and emptiest circle possible -- though seeming to contain the plenitude of divinity -- unconscious phantasy becomes proportionately enriched by a multitude of archaically formed facts, a veritable pandemonium of magical and irrational factors, wearing the particular aspect that accords with the nature of that function which shall next relieve the thought-function as the representative of life. If this should be the intuitive function, the 'other side' will be viewed with the eyes of a Kubin or a Meyrink. If it is the feeling-function, [p. 484] there arise quite unheard of and fantastic feeling-relations, coupled with feeling-judgments of a quite contradictory and unintelligible character. If the sensation-function, then the senses discover some new and never-before-experienced possibility, both within and without the body. A closer investigation of such changes can easily demonstrate the reappearance of primitive psychology with all its characteristic features. Naturally, the thing experienced is not merely primitive but also symbolic; in fact, the older and more primeval it appears, the more does it represent the future truth: since everything ancient in our unconscious means the coming possibility.

Under ordinary circumstances, not even the transition to the 'other side' succeeds -- still less the redeeming journey through the unconscious. The passage across is chiefly prevented by conscious resistance to any subjection of the ego to the unconscious reality and to the determining reality of the unconscious object. The condition is a dissociation-in other words, a neurosis having the character of an inner wastage with increasing brain-exhaustion -- a psychoasthenia, in fact.

2. The Introverted Thinking Type

Just as Darwin might possibly represent the normal extraverted thinking type, so we might point to Kant as a counter-example of the normal introverted thinking type. The former speaks with facts; the latter appeals to the subjective factor. Darwin ranges over the wide fields of objective facts, while Kant restricts himself to a critique of knowledge in general. But suppose a Cuvier be contrasted with a Nietzsche: the antithesis becomes even sharper.

The introverted thinking type is characterized by a priority of the thinking I have just described. Like his [p. 485] extraverted parallel, he is decisively influenced by ideas; these, however, have their origin, not in the objective data but in the subjective foundation. Like the extravert, he too will follow his ideas, but in the reverse direction: inwardly not outwardly. Intensity is his aim, not extensity. In these fundamental characters he differs markedly, indeed quite unmistakably from his extraverted parallel. Like every introverted type, he is almost completely lacking in that which distinguishes his counter type, namely, the intensive relatedness to the object. In the case of a human object, the man has a distinct feeling that he matters only in a negative way, i.e., in milder instances he is merely conscious of being superfluous, but with a more extreme type he feels himself warded off as something definitely disturbing. This negative relation to the object-indifference, and even aversion-characterizes every introvert; it also makes a description of the introverted type in general extremely difficult. With him, everything tends to disappear and get concealed. His judgment appears cold, obstinate, arbitrary, and inconsiderate, simply because he is related less to the object than the subject. One can feel nothing in it that might possibly confer a higher value upon the object; it always seems to go beyond the object, leaving behind it a flavour of a certain subjective superiority. Courtesy, amiability, and friendliness may be present, but often with a particular quality suggesting a certain uneasiness, which betrays an ulterior aim, namely, the disarming of an opponent, who must at all costs be pacified and set at ease lest he prove a disturbing- element. In no sense, of course, is he an opponent, but, if at all sensitive, he will feel somewhat repelled, perhaps even depreciated. Invariably the object has to submit to a certain neglect; in worse cases it is even surrounded with quite unnecessary measures of precaution. Thus it happens that this type tends to [p. 486] disappear behind a cloud of misunderstanding, which only thickens the more he attempts to assume, by way of compensation and with the help of his inferior functions, a certain mask of urbanity, which often presents a most vivid contrast to his real nature. Although in the extension of his world of ideas he shrinks from no risk, however daring, and never even considers the possibility that such a world might also be dangerous, revolutionary, heretical, and wounding to feeling, he is none the less a prey to the liveliest anxiety, should it ever chance to become objectively real. That goes against the grain. When the time comes for him to transplant his ideas into the world, his is by no means the air of an anxious mother solicitous for her children's welfare; he merely exposes them, and is often extremely annoyed when they fail to thrive on their own account. The decided lack he usually displays in practical ability, and his aversion from any sort of re[accent]clame assist in this attitude. If to his eyes his product appears subjectively correct and true, it must also be so in practice, and others have simply got to bow to its truth. Hardly ever will he go out of his way to win anyone's appreciation of it, especially if it be anyone of influence. And, when he brings himself to do so, he is usually so extremely maladroit that he merely achieves the opposite of his purpose. In his own special province, there are usually awkward experiences with his colleagues, since he never knows how to win their favour; as a rule he only succeeds in showing them how entirely superfluous they are to him. In the pursuit of his ideas he is generally stubborn, head-strong, and quite unamenable to influence. His suggestibility to personal influences is in strange contrast to this. An object has only to be recognized as apparently innocuous for such a type to become extremely accessible to really inferior elements. They lay hold of him from the [p. 487] unconscious. He lets himself be brutalized and exploited in the most ignominious way, if only he can be left undisturbed in the pursuit of his ideas. He simply does not see when he is being plundered behind his back and wronged in practical ways: this is because his relation to the object is such a secondary matter that lie is left without a guide in the purely objective valuation of his product. In thinking out his problems to the utmost of his ability, he also complicates them, and constantly becomes entangled in every possible scruple.

432   THE MEANING OF LIFE

However clear to himself the inner structure of his thoughts may be, he is not in the least clear where and how they link up with the world of reality. Only with difficulty can he persuade himself to admit that what is clear to him may not be equally clear to everyone. His style is usually loaded and complicated by all sorts of accessories, qualifications, saving clauses, doubts, etc., which spring from his exacting scrupulousness. His work goes slowly and with difficulty. Either he is taciturn or he falls among people who cannot understand him; whereupon he proceeds to gather further proof of the unfathomable stupidity of man. If he should ever chance to be understood, he is credulously liable to overestimate. Ambitious women have only to understand how advantage may be taken of his uncritical attitude towards the object to make an easy prey of him; or he may develop into a misanthropic bachelor with a childlike heart. Then, too, his outward appearance is often gauche, as if he were painfully anxious to escape observation; or he may show a remarkable unconcern, an almost childlike naivete. In his own particular field of work he provokes violent contradiction, with which he has no notion how to deal, unless by chance he is seduced by his primitive affects into biting and fruitless polemics. By his wider circle he is counted inconsiderate and domineering. But the [p. 488] better one knows him, the more favourable one's judgment becomes, and his nearest friends are well aware how to value his intimacy. To people who judge him from afar he appears prickly, inaccessible, haughty; frequently he may even seem soured as a result of his anti-social prejudices. He has little influence as a personal teacher, since the mentality of his pupils is strange to him. Besides, teaching has, at bottom, little interest for him, except when it accidentally provides him with a theoretical problem. He is a poor teacher, because while teaching his thought is engaged with the actual material, and will not be satisfied with its mere presentation.

With the intensification of his type, his convictions become all the more rigid and unbending. Foreign influences are eliminated; he becomes more unsympathetic to his peripheral world, and therefore more dependent upon his intimates. His expression becomes more personal and inconsiderate and his ideas more profound, but they can no longer be adequately expressed in the material at hand. This lack is replaced by emotivity and susceptibility. The foreign influence, brusquely declined from without, reaches him from within, from the side of the unconscious, and he is obliged to collect evidence against it and against things in general which to outsiders seems quite superfluous. Through the subjectification of consciousness occasioned by his defective relationship to the object, what secretly concerns his own person now seems to him of chief importance. And he begins to confound his subjective truth with his own person. Not that he will attempt to press anyone personally with his convictions, but he will break out with venomous and personal retorts against every criticism, however just. Thus in every respect his isolation gradually increases. His originally fertilizing ideas become destructive, because poisoned by a kind of sediment of bitterness. His struggle against the influences emanating [p. 489] from the unconscious increases with his external isolation, until gradually this begins to cripple him. A still greater isolation must surely protect him from the unconscious influences, but as a rule this only takes him deeper into the conflict which is destroying him within.

PSYCHOANALYSIS 433

The thinking of the introverted type is positive and synthetic in the development of those ideas which in ever increasing measure approach the eternal validity of the primordial images. But, when their connection with objective experience begins to fade, they become mythological and untrue for the present situation. Hence this thinking holds value only for its contemporaries, just so long as it also stands in visible and understandable connection with the known facts of the time. But, when thinking becomes mythological, its irrelevancy grows until finally it gets lost in itself. The relatively unconscious functions of feeling, intuition, and sensation, which counterbalance introverted thinking, are inferior in quality and have a primitive, extraverted character, to which all the troublesome objective influences this type is subject to must be ascribed. The various measures of self-defence, the curious protective obstacles with which such people are wont to surround themselves, are sufficiently familiar, and I may, therefore, spare myself a description of them. They all serve as a defence against 'magical' influences; a vague dread of the other sex also belongs to this category.

3. Feeling

Introverted feeling is determined principally by the subjective factor. This means that the feeling-judgment differs quite as essentially from extraverted feeling as does the introversion of thinking from extraversion. It is unquestionably difficult to give an intellectual presentation of the introverted feeling process, or even an approximate [p. 490] description of it, although the peculiar character of this kind of feeling simply stands out as soon as one becomes aware of it at all. Since it is primarily controlled by subjective preconditions, and is only secondarily concerned with the object, this feeling appears much less upon the surface and is, as a rule, misunderstood. It is a feeling which apparently depreciates the object; hence it usually becomes noticeable in its negative manifestations. The existence of a positive feeling can be inferred only indirectly, as it were. Its aim is not so much to accommodate to the objective fact as to stand above it, since its whole unconscious effort is to give reality to the underlying images. It is, as it were, continually seeking an image which has no existence in reality, but of which it has had a sort of previous vision. From objects that can never fit in with its aim it seems to glide unheedingly away. It strives after an inner intensity, to which at the most, objects contribute only an accessory stimulus. The depths of this feeling can only be divined -- they can never be clearly comprehended. It makes men silent and difficult of access; with the sensitiveness of the mimosa, it shrinks from the brutality of the object, in order to expand into the depths of the subject. It puts forward negative feeling-judgments or assumes an air of profound indifference, as a measure of self-defence.

Primordial images are, of course, just as much idea as feeling. Thus, basic ideas such as God, freedom, immortality are just as much feeling-values as they are significant as ideas. Everything, therefore, that has been said of the introverted thinking refers equally to introverted feeling, only here everything is felt while there it was thought. But the fact that thoughts can generally be expressed more intelligibly than feelings demands a more than ordinary descriptive or artistic capacity before the real wealth of this feeling can be even approximately [p. 491] presented or

434   THE MEANING OF LIFE

communicated to the outer world. Whereas subjective thinking, on account of its unrelatedness, finds great difficulty in arousing an adequate understanding, the same, though in perhaps even higher degree, holds good for subjective feeling. In order to communicate with others it has to find an external form which is not only fitted to absorb the subjective feeling in a satisfying expression, but which must also convey it to one's fellowman in such a way that a parallel process takes place in him. Thanks to the relatively great internal (as well as external) similarity of the human being, this effect can actually be achieved, although a form acceptable to feeling is extremely difficult to find, so long as it is still mainly orientated by the fathomless store of primordial images. But, when it becomes falsified by an egocentric attitude, it at once grows unsympathetic, since then its major concern is still with the ego. Such a case never fails to create an impression of sentimental self-love, with its constant effort to arouse interest and even morbid self-admiration just as the subjectified consciousness of the introverted thinker, striving after an abstraction of abstractions, only attains a supreme intensity of a thought-process in itself quite empty, so the intensification of egocentric feeling only leads to a contentless passionateness, which merely feels itself. This is the mystical, ecstatic stage, which prepares the way over into the extraverted functions repressed by feeling, just as introverted thinking is pitted against a primitive feeling, to which objects attach themselves with magical force, so introverted feeling is counterbalanced by a primitive thinking, whose concretism and slavery to facts passes all bounds. Continually emancipating itself from the relation to the object, this feeling creates a freedom, both of action and of conscience, that is only answerable to the subject, and that may even renounce all traditional values. But so much the more [p. 492] does unconscious thinking fall a victim to the power of objective facts.

4. The Introverted Feeling Type

It is principally among women that I have found the priority of introverted feeling. The proverb 'Still waters run deep' is very true of such women. They are mostly silent, inaccessible, and hard to understand; often they hide behind a childish or banal mask, and not infrequently their temperament is melancholic. They neither shine nor reveal themselves. Since they submit the control of their lives to their subjectively orientated feeling, their true motives generally remain concealed. Their outward demeanour is harmonious and inconspicuous; they reveal a delightful repose, a sympathetic parallelism, which has no desire to affect others, either to impress, influence, or change them in any way. Should this outer side be somewhat emphasized, a suspicion of neglectfulness and coldness may easily obtrude itself, which not seldom increases to a real indifference for the comfort and well-being of others. One distinctly feels the movement of feeling away from the object. With the normal type, however, such an event only occurs when the object has in some way too strong an effect. The harmonious feeling atmosphere rules only so long as the object moves upon its own way with a moderate feeling intensity, and makes no attempt to cross the other's path. There is little effort to accompany the real emotions of the object, which tend to be damped and rebuffed, or to put it more aptly, are 'cooled off' by a negative feeling-judgment. Although one may find a constant readiness for a peaceful and harmonious companionship, the unfamiliar object is shown no touch of amiability, no gleam of responding warmth, but is met by a manner of apparent indifference or repelling coldness. [p. 493]

One may even be made to feel the superfluousness of one's own existence. In the presence of something that might carry one away or arouse enthusiasm, this type observes a benevolent neutrality, tempered with an occasional trace of superiority and criticism that soon takes the wind out of the sails of a sensitive object. But a stormy emotion will be brusquely rejected with murderous coldness, unless it happens to catch the subject from the side of the unconscious, i.e. unless, through the animation of some primordial image, feeling is, as it were, taken captive. In which event such a woman simply feels a momentary laming, invariably producing, in due course, a still more violent resistance, which reaches the object in his most vulnerable spot. The relation to the object is, as far as possible, kept in a secure and tranquil middle state of feeling, where passion and its intemperateness are resolutely proscribed. Expression of feeling, therefore, remains niggardly and, when once aware of it at all, the object has a permanent sense of his undervaluation. Such, however, is not always the case, since very often the deficit remains unconscious; whereupon the unconscious feeling-claims gradually produce symptoms which compel a more serious attention.

A superficial judgment might well be betrayed, by a rather cold and reserved demeanour, into denying all feeling to this type. Such a view, however, would be quite false; the truth is, her feelings are intensive rather than extensive. They develop into the depth. Whereas, for instance, an extensive feeling of sympathy can express itself in both word and deed at the right place, thus quickly ridding itself of its impression, an intensive sympathy, because shut off from every means of expression, gains a passionate depth that embraces the misery of a world and is simply benumbed. It may possibly make an extravagant irruption, leading to some staggering act of an almost heroic character, to which, however, neither the object nor [p. 494] the subject can find a right relation. To the outer world, or to the blind eyes of the extravert, this sympathy looks like coldness, for it does nothing visibly, and an extraverted consciousness is unable to believe in invisible forces.

Such misunderstanding is a characteristic occurrence in the life of this type, and is commonly registered as a most weighty argument against any deeper feeling relation with the object. But the underlying, real object of this feeling is only dimly divined by the normal type. It may possibly express its aim and content in a concealed religiosity anxiously shielded, from profane eyes, or in intimate poetic forms equally safeguarded from surprise; not without a secret ambition to bring about some superiority over the object by such means. Women often express much of it in their children, letting their passionateness flow secretly into them.

Although in the normal type, the tendency, above alluded to, to overpower or coerce the object once openly and visibly with the thing secretly felt, rarely plays a disturbing role, and never leads to a serious attempt in this direction, some trace of it, none the less, leaks through into the personal effect upon the object, in the form of a domineering influence often difficult to define. It is sensed as a sort of stifling or oppressive feeling which holds the immediate circle

436 THE MEANING OF LIFE

under a spell. It gives a woman of this type a certain mysterious power that may prove terribly fascinating to the extraverted man, for it touches his unconscious. This power is derived from the deeply felt, unconscious images; consciousness, however, readily refers it to the ego, whereupon the influence becomes debased into personal tyranny. But, wherever the unconscious subject is identified with the ego, the mysterious power of the intensive feeling is also transformed into banal and arrogant ambition, vanity, and [p. 495] petty tyranny. This produces a type of woman most regrettably distinguished by her unscrupulous ambition and mischievous cruelty. But this change in the picture leads also to neurosis.

So long as the ego feels itself housed, as it were, beneath the heights of the unconscious subject, and feeling reveals something higher and mightier than the ego, the type is normal. The unconscious thinking is certainly archaic, yet its reductions may prove extremely helpful in compensating the occasional inclinations to exalt the ego into the subject. But, whenever this does take place by dint of complete suppression of the unconscious reductive thinking-products, the unconscious thinking goes over into opposition and becomes projected into objects. Whereupon the now egocentric subject comes to feel the power and importance of the depreciated object. Consciousness begins to feel 'what others think'. Naturally, others are thinking, all sorts of baseness, scheming evil, and contriving all sorts of plots, secret intrigues, etc. To prevent this, the subject must also begin to carry out preventive intrigues, to suspect and sound others, to make subtle combinations. Assailed by rumours, he must make convulsive efforts to convert, if possible, a threatened inferiority into a superiority. Innumerable secret rivalries develop, and in these embittered struggles not only will no base or evil means be disdained, but even virtues will be misused and tampered with in order to play the trump card. Such a development must lead to exhaustion. The form of neurosis is neurasthenic rather than hysterical; in the case of women we often find severe collateral physical states, as for instance anæmia and its sequelæ.

5. Recapitulation of Introverted Rational Types

Both the foregoing types are rational, since they are founded upon reasoning, judging functions. Reasoning [p. 496] judgment is based not merely upon objective, but also upon subjective, data. But the predominance of one or other factor, conditioned by a psychic disposition often existing from early youth, deflects the reasoning function. For a judgment to be really reasonable it should have equal reference to both the objective and the subjective factors, and be able to do justice to both. This, however, would be an ideal case, and would presuppose a uniform development of both extraversion and introversion. But either movement excludes the other, and, so long as this dilemma persists, they cannot possibly exist side by, side, but at the most successively. Under ordinary circumstances, therefore, an ideal reason is impossible. A rational type has always a typical reasonal variation. Thus, the introverted rational types unquestionably have a reasoning judgment, only it is a judgment whose leading note is subjective. The laws of logic are not necessarily deflected, since its onesidedness lies in the premise. The premise is the predominance of the subjective factor existing beneath every conclusion and colouring every judgment. Its superior value as compared with the objective factor is self-evident from the beginning. As already stated, it is not just a question of value bestowed, but of a natural disposition existing before all rational valuation. Hence, to the introvert rational judgment necessarily appears to have many nuances which differentiate it from that of the extravert. Thus, to the introvert, to mention the most general instance, that chain of reasoning which leads to the subjective factor appears rather more reasonable than that which leads to the object. This difference, which in the individual case is practically insignificant, indeed almost unnoticeable, effects unbridgeable oppositions in the gross; these are the more irritating, the less we are aware of the minimal standpoint displacement produced by the psychological premise in the individual case. A [p. 497] capital error regularly creeps in here, for one labours to prove a fallacy in the conclusion, instead of realizing the difference of the psychological premise. Such a realization is a difficult matter for every rational type, since it undermines the apparent, absolute validity of his own principle, and delivers him over to its antithesis, which certainly amounts to a catastrophe.

Almost more even than the extraverted is the introverted type subject to misunderstanding: not so much because the extravert is a more merciless or critical adversary, than he himself can easily be, but because the style of the epoch in which he himself participates is against him. Not in relation to the extraverted type, but as against our general accidental world-philosophy, he finds himself in the minority, not of course numerically, but from the evidence of his own feeling. In so far as he is a convinced participator in the general style, he undermines his own foundations, since the present style, with its almost exclusive acknowledgment of the visible and the tangible, is opposed to his principle. Because of its invisibility, he is obliged to depreciate the subjective factor, and to force himself to join in the extraverted overvaluation of the object. He himself sets the subjective factor at too low a value, and his feelings of inferiority are his chastisement for this sin. Little wonder, therefore, that it is precisely our epoch, and particularly those movements which are somewhat ahead of the time, that reveal the subjective factor in every kind of exaggerated, crude and grotesque form of expression. I refer to the art of the present day.

The undervaluation of his own principle makes the introvert egotistical, and forces upon him the psychology of the oppressed. The more egotistical he becomes, the stronger his impression grows that these others, who are apparently able, without qualms, to conform with the present style, are the oppressors against whom he must guard and [p. 498] protect himself. He does not usually perceive that he commits his capital mistake in not depending upon the subjective factor with that same loyalty and devotion with which the extravert follows the object By the undervaluation of his own principle, his penchant towards egoism becomes unavoidable, which, of course, richly deserves the prejudice of the extravert. Were he only to remain true to his own principle, the judment of 'egoist' would be radically false; for the justification of his attitude would be established by its general efficacy, and all misunderstandings dissipated.

6. Sensation

Sensation, which in obedience to its whole nature is concerned with the object and the objective stimulus, also undergoes a considerable modification in the introverted attitude. It, too, has a subjective factor, for beside the object sensed there stands a sensing subject, who

438   THE MEANING OF LIFE

contributes his subjective disposition to the objective stimulus. In the introverted attitude sensation is definitely based upon the subjective portion of perception. What is meant by this finds its best illustration in the reproduction of objects in art. When, for instance, several painters undertake to paint one and the same landscape, with a sincere attempt to reproduce it faithfully, each painting will none the less differ from the rest, not merely by virtue of a more or less developed ability, but chiefly because of a different vision; there will even appear in some of the paintings a decided psychic variation, both in general mood and in treatment of colour and form. Such qualities betray a more or less influential co-operation of the subjective factor. The subjective factor of sensation is essentially the same as in the other functions already spoken of. It is an unconscious disposition, which alters [p. 499] the sense-perception at its very source, thus depriving it of the character of a purely objective influence. In this case, sensation is related primarily to the subject, and only secondarily to the object. How extraordinarily strong the subjective factor can be is shown most clearly in art. The ascendancy of the subjective factor occasionally achieves a complete suppression of the mere influence of the object; but none the less sensation remains sensation, although it has come to be a perception of the subjective factor, and the effect of the object has sunk to the level of a mere stimulant. Introverted sensation develops in accordance with this subjective direction. A true sense-perception certainly exists, but it always looks as though objects were not so much forcing their way into the subject in their own right as that the subject were seeing things quite differently, or saw quite other things than the rest of mankind. As a matter of fact, the subject perceives the same things as everybody else, only, he never stops at the purely objective effect, but concerns himself with the subjective perception released by the objective stimulus. Subjective perception differs remarkably from the objective. It is either not found at all in the object, or, at most, merely suggested by it; it can, however, be similar to the sensation of other men, although not immediately derived from the objective behaviour of things. It does not impress one as a mere product of consciousness -- it is too genuine for that. But it makes a definite psychic impression, since elements of a higher psychic order are perceptible to it. This order, however, does not coincide with the contents of consciousness. It is concerned with presuppositions, or dispositions of the collective unconscious, with mythological images, with primal possibilities of ideas. The character of significance and meaning clings to subjective perception. It says more than the mere image of the object, though naturally only to him for whom the [p. 500] subjective factor has some meaning. To another, a reproduced subjective impression seems to suffer from the defect of possessing insufficient similarity with the object; it seems, therefore, to have failed in its purpose. Subjective sensation apprehends the background of the physical world rather than its surface. The decisive thing is not the reality of the object, but the reality of the subjective factor, i.e. the primordial images, which in their totality represent a psychic mirror-world. It is a mirror, however, with the peculiar capacity of representing the present contents of consciousness not in their known and customary form but in a certain sense sub specie aeternitatis, somewhat as a million-year old consciousness might see them. Such a consciousness would see the becoming and the passing of things beside their present and momentary existence, and not only that, but at the same time it would also see that Other, which was before their becoming and will be after their passing hence. To this consciousness the present moment is improbable. This is, of course, only a simile, of which, however, I had need to give some sort of illustration of the peculiar nature of introverted sensation. Introverted sensation conveys an image whose effect is not so much to reproduce the object as to throw over it a wrapping whose lustre is derived from age-old subjective experience and the still unborn future event. Thus, mere sense impression develops into the depth of the meaningful, while extraverted sensation seizes only the momentary and manifest existence of things.

7. The Introverted Sensation Type

The priority of introverted sensation produces a definite type, which is characterized by certain peculiarities. It is an irrational type, inasmuch as its selection among occurrences is not primarily rational, but is guided rather [p. 501] by what just happens. Whereas, the extraverted sensation-type is determined by the intensity of the objective influence, the introverted type is orientated by the intensity of the subjective sensation-constituent released by the objective stimulus. Obviously, therefore, no sort of proportional relation exists between object and sensation, but something that is apparently quite irregular and arbitrary judging from without, therefore, it is practically impossible to foretell what will make an impression and what will not. If there were present a capacity and readiness for expression in any way commensurate with the strength of sensation, the irrationality of this type would be extremely evident. This is the case, for instance, when the individual is a creative artist. But, since this is the exception, it usually happens that the characteristic introverted difficulty of expression also conceals his irrationality. On the contrary, he may actually stand out by the very calmness and passivity of his demeanour, or by his rational self-control. This peculiarity, which often leads the superficial judgment astray, is really due to his unrelatedness to objects. Normally the object is not consciously depreciated in the least, but its stimulus is removed from it, because it is immediately replaced by a subjective reaction, which is no longer related to the reality of the object. This, of course, has the same effect as a depreciation of the object. Such a type can easily make one question why one should exist at all; or why objects in general should have any right to existence, since everything essential happens without the object. This doubt may be justified in extreme cases, though not in the normal, since the objective stimulus is indispensable to his sensation, only it produces something different from what was to be surmised from the external state of affairs. Considered from without, it looks as though the effect of the object [p. 502] did not obtrude itself upon the subject. This impression is so far correct inasmuch as a subjective content does, in fact, intervene from the unconscious, thus snatching away the effect of the object. This intervention may be so abrupt that the individual appears to shield himself directly from any possible influence of the object. In any aggravated or well-marked case, such a protective guard is also actually present. Even with only a slight reinforcement of the unconscious, the subjective constituent of sensation becomes so alive that it almost completely obscures the objective influence. The results of this are, on the one hand, a feeling of complete depreciation on the part of the object, and, on the other, an illusory

440 THE MEANING OF LIFE

conception of reality on the part of the subject, which in morbid cases may even reach the point of a complete inability to discriminate between the real object and the subjective perception. Although so vital a distinction vanishes completely only in a practically psychotic state, yet long before that point is reached subjective perception may influence thought, feeling, and action to an extreme degree, in spite of the fact that the object is clearly seen in its fullest reality. Whenever the objective influence does succeed in forcing its way into the subject -- as the result of particular circumstances of special intensity, or because of a more perfect analogy with the unconscious image -- even the normal example of this type is induced to *act* in accordance with his unconscious model. Such action has an illusory quality in relation to objective reality, and therefore has a very odd and strange character. It instantly reveals the anti-real subjectivity of the type, But, where the influence of the object does not entirely succeed, it encounters a benevolent neutrality, disclosing little sympathy, yet constantly striving to reassure and adjust. The too-low is raised a little, the too-high is made a little lower; the enthusiastic is damped, the [p. 503] extravagant restrained; and the unusual brought within the 'correct' formula: all this in order to keep the influence of the object within the necessary bounds. Thus, this type becomes an affliction to his circle, just in so far as his entire harmlessness is no longer above suspicion. But, if the latter should be the case, the individual readily becomes a victim to the aggressiveness and ambitions of others. Such men allow themselves to be abused, for which they usually take vengeance at the most unsuitable occasions with redoubled stubbornness and resistance. When there exists no capacity for artistic expression, all impressions sink into the inner depths, whence they hold consciousness under a spell, removing any possibility it might have had of mastering the fascinating impression by means of conscious expression. Relatively speaking, this type has only archaic possibilities of expression for the disposal of his impressions; thought and feeling are relatively unconscious, and, in so far as they have a certain consciousness, they only serve in the necessary, banal, every-day expressions. Hence as conscious functions, they are wholly unfitted to give any adequate rendering of the subjective perceptions. This type, therefore, is uncommonly inaccessible to an objective understanding and he fares no better in the understanding of himself.

Above all, his development estranges him from the reality of the object, handing him over to his subjective perceptions, which orientate his consciousness in accordance with an archaic reality, although his deficiency in comparative judgment keeps him wholly unaware of this fact. Actually he moves in a mythological world, where men animals, railways, houses, rivers, and mountains appear partly as benevolent deities and partly as malevolent demons. That thus they, appear to him never enters his mind, although their effect upon his judgments and acts can bear no other interpretation. He judges and acts as [p. 504] though he had such powers to deal with; but this begins to strike him only when he discovers that his sensations are totally different from reality. If his tendency is to reason objectively, he will sense this difference as morbid; but if, on the other hand, he remains faithful to his irrationality, and is prepared to grant his sensation reality value, the objective world will appear a mere make-belief and a comedy. Only in extreme cases, however, is this dilemma reached. As a rule, the individual acquiesces in his isolation and in the banality of the reality, which, however, he unconsciously treats archaically.

PSYCHOANALYSIS   441

His unconscious is distinguished chiefly by the repression of intuition, which thereby acquires an extraverted and archaic character. Whereas true extraverted intuition has a characteristic resourcefulness, and a 'good nose' for every possibility in objective reality, this archaic, extraverted intuition has an amazing flair for every ambiguous, gloomy, dirty, and dangerous possibility in the background of reality. In the presence of this intuition the real and conscious intention of the object has no significance; it will peer behind every possible archaic antecedent of such an intention. It possesses, therefore, something dangerous, something actually undermining, which often stands in most vivid contrast to the gentle benevolence of consciousness. So long as the individual is not too aloof from the object, the unconscious intuition effects a wholesome compensation to the rather fantastic and over credulous attitude of consciousness. But as soon as the unconscious becomes antagonistic to consciousness, such intuitions come to the surface and expand their nefarious influence: they force themselves compellingly upon the individual, releasing compulsive ideas about objects of the most perverse kind. The neurosis arising from this sequence of events is usually a compulsion neurosis, in which the hysterical characters recede and are obscured by symptoms of exhaustion. [p. 505]

8. Intuition

Intuition, in the introverted attitude, is directed upon the inner object, a term we might justly apply to the elements of the unconscious. For the relation of inner objects to consciousness is entirely analogous to that of outer objects, although theirs is a psychological and not a physical reality. Inner objects appear to the intuitive perception as subjective images of things, which, though not met with in external experience, really determine the contents of the unconscious, i.e. the collective unconscious, in the last resort. Naturally, in their per se character, these contents are, not accessible to experience, a quality which they have in common with the outer object. For just as outer objects correspond only relatively with our perceptions of them, so the phenomenal forms of the inner object are also relative; products of their (to us) inaccessible essence and of the peculiar nature of the intuitive function. Like sensation, intuition also has its subjective factor, which is suppressed to the farthest limit in the extraverted intuition, but which becomes the decisive factor in the intuition of the introvert. Although this intuition may receive its impetus from outer objects, it is never arrested by the external possibilities, but stays with that factor which the outer object releases within.

Whereas introverted sensation is mainly confined to the perception of particular innervation phenomena by way of the unconscious, and does not go beyond them, intuition represses this side of the subjective factor and perceives the image which has really occasioned the innervation. Supposing, for instance, a man is overtaken by a psychogenic attack of giddiness. Sensation is arrested by the peculiar character of this innervationdisturbance, perceiving all its qualities, its intensity, its transient course, the nature of its origin and disappearance [p. 506] in their every detail, without raising the smallest inquiry concerning the nature of the thing which produced the disturbance, or advancing anything as to its content. Intuition, on the other hand, receives from the sensation only the impetus to immediate activity; it peers behind the scenes, quickly

442   THE MEANING OF LIFE

perceiving the inner image that gave rise to the specific phenomenon, i.e. the attack of vertigo, in the present case. It sees the image of a tottering man pierced through the heart by an arrow. This image fascinates the intuitive activity; it is arrested by it, and seeks to explore every detail of it. It holds fast to the vision, observing with the liveliest interest how the picture changes, unfolds further, and finally fades. In this way introverted intuition perceives all the background processes of consciousness with almost the same distinctness as extraverted sensation senses outer objects. For intuition, therefore, the unconscious images attain to the dignity of things or objects. But, because intuition excludes the co-operation of sensation, it obtains either no knowledge at all or at the best a very inadequate awareness of the innervation-disturbances or of the physical effects produced by the unconscious images. Accordingly, the images appear as though detached from the subject, as though existing in themselves without relation to the person.

Consequently, in the above-mentioned example, the introverted intuitive, when affected by the giddiness, would not imagine that the perceived image might also in some way refer to himself. Naturally, to one who is rationally orientated, such a thing seems almost unthinkable, but it is none the less a fact, and I have often experienced it in my dealings with this type.

The remarkable indifference of the extraverted intuitive in respect to outer objects is shared by the introverted intuitive in relation to the inner objects. Just as the extraverted intuitive is continually scenting out new [p. 507] possibilities, which he pursues with an equal unconcern both for his own welfare and for that of others, pressing on quite heedless of human considerations, tearing down what has only just been established in his everlasting search for change, so the introverted intuitive moves from image to image, chasing after every possibility in the teeming womb of the unconscious, without establishing any connection between the phenomenon and himself. Just as the world can never become a moral problem for the man who merely senses it, so the world of images is never a moral problem to the intuitive. To the one just as much as to the other, it is an ae[]sthenic problem, a question of perception, a 'sensation'. In this way, the consciousness of his own bodily existence fades from the introverted intuitive's view, as does its effect upon others. The extraverted standpoint would say of him: 'Reality has no existence for him; he gives himself up to fruitless phantasies'. A perception of the unconscious images, produced in such inexhaustible abundance by the creative energy of life, is of course fruitless from the standpoint of immediate utility. But, since these images represent possible ways of viewing life, which in given circumstances have the power to provide a new energic potential, this function, which to the outer world is the strangest of all, is as indispensable to the total psychic economy as is the corresponding human type to the psychic life of a people. Had this type not existed, there would have been no prophets in Israel.

Introverted intuition apprehends the images which arise from the a priori, i.e. the inherited foundations of the unconscious mind. These archetypes, whose innermost nature is inaccessible to experience, represent the precipitate of psychic functioning of the whole ancestral line, i.e. the heaped-up, or pooled, experiences of organic existence in general, a million times repeated, and condensed into types. Hence, in these archetypes all experiences are [p. 508] represented which since primeval time have happened on this planet. Their archetypal distinctness is the more

PSYCHOANALYSIS   443

marked, the more frequently and intensely they have been experienced. The archetype would be -
- to borrow from Kant -- the noumenon of the image which intuition perceives and, in perceiving,
creates.

Since the unconscious is not just something that lies there, like a psychic caput mortuum, but
is something that coexists and experiences inner transformations which are inherently related to
general events, introverted intuition, through its perception of inner processes, gives certain data
which may possess supreme importance for the comprehension of general occurrences: it can
even foresee new possibilities in more or less clear outline, as well as the event which later
actually transpires. Its prophetic prevision is to be explained from its relation to the archetypes
which represent the law-determined course of all experienceable things.

9. The Introverted Intuitive Type

The peculiar nature of introverted intuition, when given the priority, also produces a peculiar
type of man, viz. the mystical dreamer and seer on the one hand, or the fantastical crank and artist
on the other. The latter might be regarded as the normal case, since there is a general tendency of
this type to confine himself to the perceptive character of intuition. As a rule, the intuitive stops at
perception; perception is his principal problem, and -- in the case of a productive artist-the
shaping of perception. But the crank contents himself with the intuition by which he himself is
shaped and determined. Intensification of intuition naturally often results in an extraordinary
aloofness of the individual from tangible reality; he may even become a complete enigma to his
own immediate circle. [p. 509]

If an artist, he reveals extraordinary, remote things in his art, which in iridescent profusion
embrace both the significant and the banal, the lovely and the grotesque, the whimsical and the
sublime. If not an artist, he is frequently an unappreciated genius, a great man 'gone wrong', a sort
of wise simpleton, a figure for 'psychological' novels.

Although it is not altogether in the line of the introverted intuitive type to make of perception
a moral problem, since a certain reinforcement of the rational functions is required for this, yet
even a relatively slight differentiation of judgment would suffice to transfer intuitive perception
from the purely æsthetic into the moral sphere. A variety of this type is thus produced which
differs essentially from its æsthetic form, although none the less characteristic of the introverted
intuitive. The moral problem comes into being when the intuitive tries to relate himself to his
vision, when he is no longer satisfied with mere perception and its æsthetic shaping and
estimation, but confronts the question: What does this mean for me and for the world? What
emerges from this vision in the way of a duty or task, either for me or for the world? The pure
intuitive who represses judgment or possesses it only under the spell of perception never meets
this question fundamentally, since his only problem is the How of perception. He, therefore, finds
the moral problem unintelligible, even absurd, and as far as possible forbids his thoughts to dwell
upon the disconcerting vision. It is different with the morally orientated intuitive. He concerns
himself with the meaning of his vision; he troubles less about its further æsthetic possibilities than
about the possible moral effects which emerge from its intrinsic significance. His judgment

444 THE MEANING OF LIFE

allows him to discern, though often only darkly, that he, as a man and as a totality, is in some way inter-related with his vision, that [p. 510] it is something which cannot just be perceived but which also would fain become the life of the subject. Through this realization he feels bound to transform his vision into his own life. But, since he tends to rely exclusively upon his vision, his moral effort becomes one-sided; he makes himself and his life symbolic, adapted, it is true, to the inner and eternal meaning of events, but unadapted to the actual present-day reality. Therewith he also deprives himself of any influence upon it, because he remains unintelligible. His language is not that which is commonly spoken -- it becomes too subjective. His argument lacks convincing reason. He can only confess or pronounce. His is the 'voice of one crying in the wilderness'.

The introverted intuitive's chief repression falls upon the sensation of the object. His unconscious is characterized by this fact. For we find in his unconscious a compensatory extraverted sensation function of an archaic character. The unconscious personality may, therefore, best be described as an extraverted sensation-type of a rather low and primitive order. Impulsiveness and unrestraint are the characters of this sensation, combined with an extraordinary dependence upon the sense impression. This latter quality is a compensation to the thin upper air of the conscious attitude, giving it a certain weight, so that complete 'sublimation' is prevented. But if, through a forced exaggeration of the conscious attitude, a complete subordination to the inner perception should develop, the unconscious becomes an opposition, giving rise to compulsive sensations whose excessive dependence upon the object is in frank conflict with the conscious attitude. The form of neurosis is a compulsion-neurosis, exhibiting symptoms that are partly hypochondriacal manifestations, partly hypersensibility of the sense organs and partly compulsive ties to definite persons or other objects. [p. 511]

10. Recapitulation of Introverted Irrational Types

The two types just depicted are almost inaccessible to external judgment. Because they are introverted and have in consequence a somewhat meagre capacity or willingness for expression, they offer but a frail handle for a telling criticism. Since their main activity is directed within, nothing is outwardly visible but reserve, secretiveness, lack of sympathy, or uncertainty, and an apparently groundless perplexity. When anything does come to the surface, it usually consists in indirect manifestations of inferior and relatively unconscious functions. Manifestations of such a nature naturally excite a certain environmental prejudice against these types. Accordingly they are mostly underestimated, or at least misunderstood. To the same degree as they fail to understand themselves -- because they very largely lack judgment -- they are also powerless to understand why they are so constantly undervalued by public opinion. They cannot see that their outward-going expression is, as a matter of fact, also of an inferior character. Their vision is enchanted by the abundance of subjective events. What happens there is so captivating, and of such inexhaustible attraction, that they do not appreciate the fact that their habitual communications to their circle express very, little of that real experience in which they themselves are, as it were, caught up. The fragmentary and, as a rule, quite episodic character of their communications make too great a demand upon the understanding and good will of their circle; furthermore, their mode of expression lacks that flowing warmth to the object which alone can have convincing force. On the contrary, these types show very often a brusque, repelling demeanour towards the outer world, although of this they are quite unaware, and have not the least intention of showing it. We shall form a [p. 512] fairer judgment of such men and grant them a greater indulgence, when we begin to realize how hard it is to translate into intelligible language what is perceived within. Yet this indulgence must not be so liberal as to exempt them altogether from the necessity of such expression. This could be only detrimental for such types. Fate itself prepares for them, perhaps even more than for other men, overwhelming external difficulties, which have a very sobering effect upon the intoxication of the inner vision. But frequently only an intense personal need can wring from them a human expression.

From an extraverted and rationalistic standpoint, such types are indeed the most fruitless of men. But, viewed from a higher standpoint, such men are living evidence of the fact that this rich and varied world with its overflowing and intoxicating life is not purely external, but also exists within. These types are admittedly one sided demonstrations of Nature, but they are an educational experience for the man who refuses to be blinded by the intellectual mode of the day. In their own way, men with such an attitude are educators and promoters of culture. Their life teaches more than their words. From their lives, and not the least from what is just their greatest fault, viz. their incommunicability, we may understand one of the greatest errors of our civilization, that is, the superstitious belief in statement and presentation, the immoderate overprizing of instruction by means of word and method. A child certainly allows himself to be impressed by the grand talk of its parents. But is it really imagined that the child is thereby educated? Actually it is the parents' lives that educate the child -- what they add thereto by word and gesture at best serves only to confuse him. The same holds good for the teacher. But we have such a belief in method that, if only the method be good, the practice of it seems to hallow the teacher. An inferior [p. 513] man is never. a good teacher. But he can conceal his injurious inferiority, which secretly poisons the pupil, behind an excellent method or, an equally brilliant intellectual capacity. Naturally the pupil of riper years desires nothing better than the knowledge of useful methods, because he is already defeated by the general attitude, which believes in the victorious method. He has already learnt that the emptiest head, correctly echoing a method, is the best pupil. His whole environment not only urges but exemplifies the doctrine that all success and happiness are external, and that only the right method is needed to attain the haven of one's desires. Or is the life of his religious instructor likely to demonstrate that happiness which radiates from the treasure of the inner vision? The irrational introverted types are certainly no instructors of a more complete humanity. They lack reason and the ethics of reason, but their lives teach the other possibility, in which our civilization is so deplorably wanting.

11. The Principal and Auxiliary Functions

In the foregoing descriptions I have no desire to give my readers the impression that such pure types occur at all frequently in actual practice. The are, as it were, only Galtonesque family-portraits, which sum up in a cumulative image the common and therefore typical characters,

446   THE MEANING OF LIFE

stressing these disproportionately, while the individual features are just as disproportionately effaced. Accurate investigation of the individual case consistently reveals the fact that, in conjunction with the most differentiated function, another function of secondary importance, and therefore of inferior differentiation in consciousness, is constantly present, and is a -- relatively determining factor. [p. 514]

For the sake of clarity let us again recapitulate: The products of all the functions can be conscious, but we speak of the consciousness of a function only when not merely its application is at the disposal of the will, but when at the same time its principle is decisive for the orientation of consciousness. The latter event is true when, for instance, thinking is not a mere esprit de l'escalier, or rumination, but when its decisions possess an absolute validity, so that the logical conclusion in a given case holds good, whether as motive or as guarantee of practical action, without the backing of any further evidence. This absolute sovereignty always belongs, empirically, to one function alone, and can belong only to one function, since the equally independent intervention of another function would necessarily yield a different orientation, which would at least partially contradict the first. But, since it is a vital condition for the conscious adaptation-process that constantly clear and unambiguous aims should be in evidence, the presence of a second function of equivalent power is naturally forbidden' This other function, therefore, can have only a secondary importance, a fact which is also established empirically. Its secondary importance consists in the fact that, in a given case, it is not valid in its own right, as is the primary function, as an absolutely reliable and decisive factor, but comes into play more as an auxiliary or complementary function. Naturally only those functions can appear as auxiliary whose nature is not opposed to the leading function. For instance, feeling can never act as the second function by the side of thinking, because its nature stands in too strong a contrast to thinking. Thinking, if it is to be real thinking and true to its own principle, must scrupulously exclude feeling. This, of course, does not exclude the fact that individuals certainly exist in whom thinking and feeling stand upon the same [p. 515] level, whereby both have equal motive power in con~sdousness. But, in such a case, there is also no question of a differentiated type, but merely of a relatively undeveloped thinking and feeling. Uniform consciousness and unconsciousness of functions is, therefore, a distinguishing mark of a primitive mentality

Experience shows that the secondary function is always one whose nature is different from, though not antagonistic to, the leading function : thus, for example, thinking, as primary function, can readily pair with intuition as auxiliary, or indeed equally well with sensation, but, as already observed, never with feeling. Neither intuition nor sensation are antagonistic to thinking, i.e. they have not to be unconditionally excluded, since they are not, like feeling, of similar nature, though of opposite purpose, to thinking -- for as a judging function feeling successfully competes with thinking -- but are functions of perception, affording welcome assistance to thought. As soon as they reached the same level of differentiation as thinking, they would cause a change of attitude, which would contradict the tendency of thinking. For they would convert the judging attitude into a perceiving one; whereupon the principle of rationality indispensable to thought would be suppressed in favour of the irrationality of mere perception. Hence the auxiliary function is

PSYCHOANALYSIS 447

possible and useful only in so far as it serves the leading function, without making any claim to the autonomy of its own principle.

For all the types appearing in practice, the principle holds good that besides the conscious main function there is also a relatively unconscious, auxiliary function which is in every respect different from the nature of the main function. From these combinations well-known pictures arise, the practical intellect for instance paired with sensation, the speculative intellect breaking through [p. 516] with intuition, the artistic intuition which selects. and presents its images by means of feeling judgment, the philosophical intuition which, in league with a vigorous intellect, translates its vision into the sphere of comprehensible thought, and so forth.

A grouping of the unconscious functions also takes place in accordance with the relationship of the conscious functions. Thus, for instance, an unconscious intuitive feeling attitude may correspond with a conscious practical intellect, whereby the function of feeling suffers a relatively stronger inhibition than intuition. This peculiarity, however, is of interest only for one who is concerned with the practical psychological treatment of such cases. But for such a man it is important to know about it. For I have frequently observed the way in which a physician, in the case for instance of an exclusively intellectual subject, will do his utmost to develop the feeling function directly out of the unconscious. This attempt must always come to grief, since it involves too great a violation of the conscious standpoint. Should such a violation succeed, there ensues a really compulsive dependence of the patient upon the physician, a 'transference' which can be amputated only by brutality, because such a violation robs the patient of a standpoint -- his physician becomes his standpoint. But the approach to the unconscious and to the most repressed function is disclosed, as it were, of itself, and with more adequate protection of the conscious standpoint, when the way of development is via the secondary function-thus in the case of a rational type by way of the irrational function. For this lends the conscious standpoint such a range and prospect over what is possible and imminent that consciousness gains an adequate protection against the destructive effect of the unconscious. Conversely, an irrational type demands a stronger development of the rational auxiliary function [p. 517] represented in consciousness, in order to be sufficiently prepared to receive the impact of the unconscious.

The unconscious functions are in an archaic, animal state. Their symbolical appearances in dreams and phantasies usually represent the battle or coming encounter of two animals or monsters.

[1] William Blake, Marriage of Heaven and Hell
[2] Semon, Mneme, translated by Louis Simon (London: Allen & Unwin).

CHAPTER 11

HUMANISTIC PSYCHOLOGY

In response to the reductionism of behaviourism and the psychodynamic principles of psychoanalysis, a large movement of psychologists wanted to recapture the humanness of therapy. Drawing largely upon the intellectual traditions of phenomenology and existentialism, a strong movement began to take shape, forming a new movement of psychology. This *third force* is in many ways a loosely knit group and at times many existential therapists are included within this group simply because they are not clearly behaviouristic or psychoanalytic. There is, however, one main figure that has come to typify this movement, Carl R. Rogers (1902-1987).

The founder of a new approach to therapy (first called nondirective, then client-centered, and finally person-centered), Carl Rogers was one of the most innovative figures of the third force movement. Foremost in Rogers' contribution to the field of therapy was his stance on the role of diagnosis in the treatment of emotional problems. In the usual medical model, diagnosis precedes treatment, yet in person-centred therapy there is a backlash against negative labels for clients. Rather, Rogers argued that the therapist must not be so narrow as to fixate upon a diagnosis, but embrace the full and complex life of the client and all the ways that the client defines him/herself.

Central to Rogers' therapeutic process was the notion of *unconditional positive regard* (in contrast to conditional love that often typifies a household). The notion of *unconditional positive regard* is so central to therapy because it begins to give people a sense of self worth bolstered by the affirmation by the therapist that they have intrinsic worth. This positive view of humanity has significant implications for the practice of therapy. With its implicit view that people have the capacity to move themselves if given support, the therapist plays the role of supporter and encourager rather than detached healer.

The mythopoeic focus of Rogerian therapy focuses therefore on the how clients act in their mythopoeically constructed world with others, how they can move forward in constructive directions, and how they can successfully encounter obstacles (both real and perceived) that block their growth. The implication is that therapy is more than making someone *normal* or simply *solving problems.* Therapy is rather seen as going in a direction towards growth and self-actualization (always striving for the impossible goal of full health and full actualization). In essence the therapist, then, is to live by the sentence: "If I can provide a certain type of relationship, the other person will discover within himself or herself the capacity to use that relationship for growth and change, and personal development will occur." (Rogers 1961).

READ AND DECIDE FOR YOURSELF:

Excerpts from:

SIGNIFICANT ASPECTS OF CLIENT-CENTERED THERAPY
(CARL R. ROGERS)

A THEORY OF HUMAN MOTIVATION
(A. H. MASLOW)

SIGNIFICANT ASPECTS OF CLIENT-CENTERED THERAPY [1]

Carl R. Rogers (1946)

University of Chicago

First published in *American Psychologist, 1*, 415-422[72]

In planning to address this group, I have considered and discarded several possible topics. I was tempted to describe the process of non-directive therapy and the counselor techniques and procedures which seem most useful in bringing about this process. But much of this material is now in writing. My own book on counseling and psychotherapy contains much of the basic material, and my recent more popular book on counseling with returning servicemen tends to supplement it. The philosophy of the client-centered approach and its application to work with children is persuasively presented by Allen. The application to counseling of industrial employees is discussed in the volume by Cantor. Curran has now published in book form one of the several research studies which are throwing new light on both process and procedure. Axline is publishing a book on play and group therapy. Snyder is bringing out a book of cases. So it seems unnecessary to come a long distance to summarize material which is, or soon ·n-ill be. obtainable in written form.

Another tempting possibility, particularly in this setting, was to discuss some of the roots from which the client-centered approach has sprung. It would have been interesting to show how in its concepts of repression and release, in its stress upon catharsis and insight, it has many roots in Freudian thinking, and to acknowledge that indebtedness. Such an analysis could also have shown that in its concept of the individual's ability to organize his own experience there is an even deeper indebtedness to the work of Rank, Taft, and Allen. In its stress upon objective research, the subjecting of fluid attitudes to scientific investigation, the willingness to submit all hypotheses to a verification or disproof by research methods, the debt is obviously to the whole field of American psychology, with its genius for scientific methodology. It could also have been pointed out that although everyone in the clinical field has been heavily exposed to the eclectic "team" approach to therapy of the child guidance movement, and the somewhat similar eclecticism of the Adolf Meyers -- Hopkins school of thought, these eclectic viewpoint have perhaps not been so fruitful in therapy and that little from these sources has been retained in the non-directive approach. It might also have been pointed out that in its basic trend away from

---

72 http://psychclassics.yorku.ca/Rogers/therapy.htm

452   THE MEANING OF LIFE

guiding and directing the client. the non-directive approach is deeply rooted in practical clinical experience, and is in accord with the experience of most clinical workers, so much so that one of the commonest reactions of experienced therapists is that "You have crystallized and put into words something that I have been groping toward in my own experience for a long time.'

Such an analysis, such a tracing or root ideas, needs to be made, but I doubt my own ability to make it. I am also doubtful that anyone who is deeply concerned with a new development knows with any degree of accuracy where his ideas came from.

Consequently I am, in this presentation. Adopting a third pathway. While I shall bring in a brief description of process and procedure. and while I shall acknowledge in a general way our indebtedness to many root sources, and shall recognize the many common elements shared by client-centered therapy and other approaches, I believe it will be to our mutual advantage if I stress primarily those aspects in which nondirective[*] therapy differs most sharply and deeply from other therapeutic procedures. I hope to point out some of the basically significant ways in which the client-centered viewpoint differs from others, not only in its present principles, but in the wider divergencies which are implied by the projection of its central principles. [p. 416]

THE PREDICTABLE PROCESS OF CLIENT-CENTERED THERAPY

The first of the three distinctive elements of client-centered therapy to which I wish to call your attention is the predictability of the therapeutic process in this approach. We find, both clinically and statistically, that a predictable pattern of therapeutic development takes place. The assurance which we feel about this was brought home to me recently when I played a recorded first interview for the graduate students in our practicum immediately after it was recorded, pointing out the characteristic aspects, and agreeing to play later interviews for them to let them see the later phases of the counseling process. The fact that I knew with assurance what the later pattern would be before it had occurred only struck me as I thought about the incident. We have become clinically so accustomed to this predictable quality that we take it for granted. Perhaps a brief summarized description of this therapeutic process will indicate those elements of which we feel sure.

It may be said that we now know how to initiate a complex and predictable chain of events in dealing with the maladjusted individual, a chain of events which is therapeutic, and which operates effectively in problem situations of the most diverse type. This predictable chain of events may come about through the use of language as in counseling, through symbolic language, as in play therapy, through disguised language as in drama or puppet therapy. It is effective in dealing with individual situations, and also in small group situations.

It is possible to state with some exactness the conditions which must be met in order to initiate and carry through this releasing therapeutic experience. Below are listed in brief form the conditions which seem to be necessary, and the therapeutic results which occur.

This experience which releases the growth forces within the individual will come about in most cases if the following elements are present.

(1) If the counselor operates on the principle that the individual is basically responsible for himself, and is willing for the individual to keep that responsibility.

(2) If the counselor operates on the principle that the client has a strong drive to become mature, socially adjusted. independent, productive, and relies on this force, not on his own powers, for therapeutic change.

(3) If the counselor creates a warm and permissive atmosphere in which the individual is free to bring out any attitudes and feelings which he may have, no matter how unconventional, absurd, or contradictory these attitudes may be. The client is as free to withhold expression as he is to give expression to his feelings.

(4) If the limits which are set are simple limits set on behavior, and not limits set on attitudes. (This applies mostly to children. The child may not be permitted to break a window or leave the room. but he is free to feel like breaking a window, and the feeling is fully accepted. The adult client may not be permitted more than an hour for an interview, but there is full acceptance of his desire to claim more time.)

(5) If the therapist uses only those procedures and techniques in the interview which convey his deep understanding of the emotionalized attitudes expressed and his acceptance of them. This under standing is perhaps best conveyed by a sensitive reflection and clarification of the client's attitudes. The counselor's acceptance involves neither approval nor disapproval.

(6) If the counselor refrains from any expression or action which is contrary to the preceding principles. This means reframing from questioning, probing, blame, interpretation, advice, suggestion, persuasion, reassurance.

If these conditions are met. then it may be said with assurance that in the great majority of cases the following results will take place.

(1) The client will express deep and motivating attitudes.

(2) The client will explore his own attitudes and reactions more fully than he has previously done and will come to be aware of aspects of his attitudes which he has previously denied.

(3) He will arrive at a clearer conscious realization of his motivating attitudes and will accept himself more completely. This realization and this acceptance will include attitudes previously denied. He may or may not verbalize this clearer conscious understanding of himself and his behavior.

(4) In the light of his clearer perception of himself he will choose, on his own initiative and on his own [p. 417] responsibility, new goal which are more satisfying than his maladjusted goals.

(5) He will choose to behave in a different fashion in order to reach these goals, and this new behavior will be in the direction of greater psychological growth and maturity. It will also be more spontaneous and less tense, more in harmony with social needs of others, will represent a more realistic and more comfortable adjustment to life. It will be more integrated than his former behavior. It will be a step forward in the life of the individual.

The best scientific description of this process is that supplied by Snyder. Analyzing a number of cases with strictly objective research techniques, Snyder has discovered that the

454   THE MEANING OF LIFE

development in these cases is roughly parallel, that the initial phase of catharsis is replaced by a phase in which insight becomes the most significant element, and this in turn by a phase marked by the increase in positive choice and action

Clinically, we know that sometimes this process is relatively shallow, involving primarily a fresh reorientation to an immediate problem, and in other instances so deep as to involve a complete reorientation of personality. It is recognizably the same process whether it involves a girl who is unhappy in a dormitory and is able in three interviews to see something of her childishness and dependence, and to take steps in a mature direction, or whether it involves a young man who is on the edge of a schizophrenic break, and who in thirty interviews works out deep insights in relation to his desire for his father's death, and his possessive and incestuous impulses toward is mother, and who not only takes new steps but rebuilds his whole personality in the process. Whether shallow or deep, it is basically the same.

We are coming to recognize with assurance characteristic aspects of each phase of the process. We know that the catharsis involves a gradual and more complete expression of emotionalized attitudes. We know that characteristically the conversation goes from superficial problems and attitudes to deeper problems and attitudes. We know that this process of exploration gradually unearths relevant attitudes which have been denied to consciousness. We recognize too that the process of achieving insight is likely to involve more adequate facing of reality as it exists within the self, as well as external reality; that it involves the relating of problems to each other, the perception of patterns of behavior; that it involves the acceptance of hitherto denied elements of the self, and a reformulating of the self-concept; and that it involves the making of new plans.

In the final phase we know that the choice of new ways of behaving will be in conformity with the newly organized concept of the self; that first steps in putting these plans into action will be small but symbolic; that the individual will feel only a minimum degree of confidence that he can put his plans into effect, that later steps implement more and more completely the new concept of self, and that this process continues beyond the conclusion of the therapeutic interviews.

If these statements seem to contain too much assurance, to sound "too good to be true," I can only say that for many of them we now have research backing, and that as rapidly as possible we are developing our research to bring all phases of the process under objective scrutiny. Those of us working clinically with client-centered therapy regard this predictability as a settled characteristic, even though we recognize that additional research will be necessary to fill out the picture more completely.

It is the implication of this predictability which is startling. Whenever, in science, a predictable process has been discovered, it has been found possible to use it as a starting point for a whole chain of discoveries. We regard this as not only entirely possible, but inevitable, with regard to this predictable process in therapy. Hence, we regard this orderly and predictable nature of nondirective therapy as one of its most distinctive and significant points of difference from other approaches. Its importance lies not only in the fact that it is a present difference. but in the

HUMANISTIC PSYCHOLOGY   455

fact that it points toward a sharply different future, in which scientific exploration of this known chain of events should lead to many new discoveries, developments. and applications.

THE DISCOVERY OF THE CAPACITY OF THE CLIENT

Naturally the question is raised, what is the reason for this predictability in a type of therapeutic procedure in which the therapist serves only a catalytic function? Basically the reason for the predictability [p. 418] of the therapeutic process lies in the discovery -- and I use that word intentionally -- that within the client reside constructive forces whose strength and uniformity have been either entirely unrecognized or grossly underestimated. It is the clearcut and disciplined reliance by the therapist upon those forces within the client, which seems to account for the orderliness of the therapeutic process, and its consistency from one client to the next.

I mentioned that I regarded this as a discovery. I would like to amplify that statement. We have known for centuries that catharsis and emotional release were helpful. Many new methods have been and are being developed to bring about release, but the principle is not new. Likewise, we have known since Freud's time that insight, if it is accepted and assimilated by the client, is therapeutic. The principle is not new. Likewise we have realized that revised action patterns, new ways of behaving, may come about as a result of insight. The principle is not new.

But we have not known or recognized that in most if not all individuals there exist growth forces, tendencies toward self-actualization, which may act as the sole motivation for therapy. We have not realized that under suitable psychological conditions these forces bring about emotional release in those areas and at those rates which are most beneficial to the individual. These forces drive the individual to explore his own attitudes and his relationship to reality. and to explore these areas effectively. We have not realized that the individual is capable of exploring his attitudes and feelings, including those which have been denied to consciousness, at a rate which does not cause panic, and to the depth required for comfortable adjustment. The individual is capable of discovering and perceiving, truly and spontaneously, the interrelationships between his own attitudes, and the relationship of himself to reality. The individual has the capacity and the strength to devise, quite unguided, the steps which will lead him to a more mature and more comfortable relationship to his reality. It is the gradual and increasing recognition of these capacities within the individual by the client-centered therapist that rates, I believe, the term discovery. All of these capacities I have described are released in the individual if a suitable psychological atmosphere is provided.

There has, of course, been lip service paid to the strength of the client, and the need of utilizing the urge toward independence which exists in the client. Psychiatrists, analysts, and especially social case workers have stressed this point. Yet it is clear from what is said, and even more clear from the case material cited. that this confidence is a very limited confidence. It is a confidence that the client can take over, if guided by the expert, a confidence that the client can assimilate insight if it is first, given to him by the expert, can make choices providing guidance is given at crucial points. It is, in short, the same sort of attitude which the mother has toward the

456   THE MEANING OF LIFE

adolescent. that she believes in his capacity to make his own decisions and guide his own life, providing he takes the directions of which she approves.

This is very evident in the latest book on psychoanalysis by Alexander and French. Although many of the former views and practices of psychoanalysis are discarded, and the procedures are far more nearly in line with those of nondirective therapy, it is still the therapist who is definitely in control. He gives the insights. he is ready to guide at crucial points. Thus while the authors state that the aim of the therapist is to free the patient to develop his capacities, and to increase his ability to satisfy his needs in ways acceptable to himself and society; and while they speak of the basic conflict between competition and cooperation as one which the individual must settle for himself; and speak of the integration of new insight as a normal function of the ego, it is clear when they speak of procedures that they have no confidence that the client has the capacity to do any of these things. For in practice, "As soon as the therapist takes the more active role we advocate, systematic planning becomes imperative. In addition to the original decision as to the particular sort of strategy to be employed in the treatment of any case, we recommend the conscious use of various techniques in a flexible manner, shifting tactics to fit the particular needs of the moment. Among these modifications of the standard technique are; using not only the method of free association but interviews of a more direct character, manipulating the frequency of the interviews, giving [p. 419] directives to the patient concerning his daily life, employing interruptions of long or short duration in preparation for ending the treatment, regulating the transference relation-hip to meet the specific needs of the case, and making use of real-life experiences as an integral part of therapy" (1). At least this leaves no doubt as to whether it is the client's or the therapist's hour; it is clearly the latter. The capacities which the client is to develop are clearly not to be developed in the therapeutic sessions.

The client-centered therapist stands at an opposite pole, both theoretically and practically. He has learned that the constructive forces in the individual can be trusted. and that the more deeply they are relied upon, the more deeply they are released. He has come to build his procedures upon these hypotheses, which are rapidly becoming established as facts; that the client knows the areas of concern which he is ready to explore; that the client is the best judge as to the most desirable frequency of interviews; that the client can lead the way more efficiently than the therapist into deeper concerns; that the client will protect himself from panic by ceasing to explore an area which is becoming too painful; that the client can and will uncover all the repressed elements which it is necessary to uncover in order to build a comfortable adjustment; that the client can achieve for himself far truer and more sensitive and accurate insights than can possibly be given to him; that the client is capable of translating these insights into constructive behavior which weigh his own needs and desires realistically against the demands of society; that the client knows when therapy is completed and he is ready to cope with life independently. Only one condition is necessary for all these forces to be released, and that is the proper psychological atmosphere between client and therapist.

Our case records and increasingly our research bear out these statements. One might suppose that there would be a generally favorable reaction to this discovery, since it amounts in effect to tapping great reservoirs of hitherto little-used energy. Quite the contrary is true, however, in professional groups. There is no other aspect of client-centered therapy which comes under such vigorous attack. It seems to be genuinely disturbing to many professional people to entertain the thought that this client upon whom they have been exercising their professional skill actually knows more about his inner psychological self than they can possibly know, and that he possesses constructive strengths which make the constructive push by the therapist seem puny indeed by comparison. The willingness fully to accept this strength of the client, with all the re-orientation of therapeutic procedure which it implies, is one of the ways in which client-centered therapy differs most sharply from other therapeutic approaches.

THE CLIENT-CENTERED NATURE OF THE THERAPEUTIC RELATIONSHIP

The third distinctive feature of this type of therapy is the character of the relationship between therapist and client. Unlike other therapies in which the skills of the therapist are to be exercised upon the client. in this approach the skills of the therapist are focussed upon creating a psychological atmosphere in which the client can work. If the counselor can create a relationship permeated by warmth, understanding, safety from any type of attack, no matter how trivial, and basic acceptance of the person as he is, then the client will drop his natural defensiveness and use the situation. As we have puzzled over the characteristics of a successful therapeutic relationship, we have come to feel that the sense of communication is very important. If the client feels that he is actually communicating his present attitudes, superficial, confused, or conflicted as they may be, and that his communication is understood rather than evaluated in any way, then he is freed to communicate more deeply. A relationship in which the client thus feels that he is communicating is almost certain to be fruitful.

All of this means a drastic reorganization in the counselor's thinking, particularly if he has previously utilized other approaches. He gradually learns that the statement that the time is to be "the client's hour" means just that, and that his biggest task is to make it more and more deeply true.

Perhaps something of the characteristics of the relationship may be suggested by excerpts from a paper written by a young minister who has spent several months learning client-centered counseling procedures. [p. 420]

"Because the client-centered, nondirective counseling approach has been rather carefully defined and clearly illustrated, it gives the "Illusion of Simplicity." The technique seems deceptively easy to master. Then you begin to practice. A word is wrong here and there. You don't quite reflect feeling, but reflect content instead. It is difficult to handle questions; you are tempted to interpret. Nothing seems so serious that further practice won't correct it. Perhaps you are having trouble playing two roles -- that of minister and that of counselor. Bring up the question in class and the matter is solved again with a deceptive ease. But these apparently minor errors and a certain woodenness of response seem exceedingly persistent.

"Only gradually does it dawn that if the technique is true it demands a feeling of warmth. You begin to feel that the attitude is the thing. Every little word is not so important if you have

458   THE MEANING OF LIFE

the correct accepting and permissive attitude toward the client. So you bear down on the permissiveness and acceptance. You will permiss[sic] and accept and reflect the client, if it kills you!

[§]'But you still have those troublesome questions from the client. He simply doesn't know the next step. He asks you to give him a hint, some possibilities, after all you are expected to know something, else why is he here! As a minister, you ought to have some convictions about what people should believe, how they should act. As a counselor, you should know something about removing this obstacle -- you ought to have the equivalent of the surgeon's knife and use it. Then you begin to wonder. The technique is good, *but* ... does it go *far* enough! does it really work on clients? is it *right* to leave a person helpless, when you might show him the way out?

"Here it seems to me is the crucial point. "Narrow is the gate" and hard the path from here on. So one else can give satisfying answers and even the instructors seem frustrating because they appear not to be helpful in your specific case. For here is demanded of you what no other person can do or point out -- and that is to rigorously scrutinize yourself and your attitudes towards others. Do you believe that all people truly have a creative potential in them? That each person is a unique individual and that he alone can work out his own individuality? Or do you really believe that some persons are of "negative value" and others are weak and must be led and taught by "wiser," "stronger" people.

"You begin to see that there is nothing compartmentalized about this method of counseling. It is not just counseling, because it demands the most exhaustive, penetrating, and comprehensive consistency. In other methods you can shape tools, pick them up for use when you will. But when genuine acceptance and permissiveness are your tools it requires nothing less than the whole complete personality. And to grow oneself is the most demanding of all."

He goes on to discuss the notion that the counselor must be restrained and "self-denying." He concludes that this is a mistaken notion.

"Instead of demanding less of the counselor's personality in the situation, client-centered counseling in some ways demands more. It demands discipline, not restraint. It calls for the utmost in sensitivity, appreciative awareness. channeled and disciplined. It demands that the counselor put all he has of these precious qualities into the situation, but in a disciplined, resfined manner. It is restraint only in the sense that the counselor does not express himself in certain areas that he may use himself in others.

"Even this is deceptive, however. It is not so much restraint in any area as it is a focusing, sensitizing one's energies and personality in the direction of an appreciative and understanding attitude."

As time has gone by we have come to put increasing stress upon the "client-centeredness" of the relationship, because it is more effective the more completely the counselor concentrates upon trying to understand the client as the client seems to himself. As I look back upon some of our earlier published cases -- the case of Herbert Bryan in my book, or Snyder's case of Mr. M. -- I realize that we have gradually dropped the vestiges of subtle directiveness which are all too evident in those cases. We [p. 421] have come to recognize that if we can provide understanding of the way the client seems to himself at this moment, he can do the rest. The therapist must lay aside his preoccupation with diagnosis and his diagnostic shrewdness, must discard his tendency to make professional evaluations, must cease his endeavors to formulate an accurate prognosis, must give up the temptation subtly to guide the individual, and must concentrate on one purpose only; that of providing deep understanding and acceptance of the attitudes consciously held at this moment by the client as he explores step by step into the dangerous areas which he has been denying to consciousness.

I trust it is evident from this description that this type of relationship can exist only if the counselor is deeply and genuinely able to adopt these attitudes. Client-centered counseling, if it is to be effective, cannot be a trick or a tool. It is not a subtle way of guiding the client while pretending to let him guide himself. To be effective, it must be genuine. It is this sensitive and sincere "client-centeredness" in the therapeutic relationship that I regard as the third characteristic of nondirective therapy which sets it distinctively apart from other approaches.

SOME IMPLICATIONS

Although the client-centered approach had its origin purely within the limits of the psychological clinic, it is proving to have implications, often of a startling nature, for very diverse fields of effort. I should like to suggest a few of these present and potential implications.

In the field of psychotherapy itself, it leads to conclusions that seem distinctly heretical. It appears evident that training and practice in therapy should probably precede training in the field of diagnosis. Diagnostic knowledge and skill is not necessary for good therapy, a statement which sounds like blasphemy to many, and if the professional worker, whether psychiatrist, psychologist or caseworker, received training in therapy first he would learn psychological dynamics in a truly dynamic fashion, and would acquire a professional humility and willingness to learn from his client which is today all too rare.

The viewpoint appears to have implications for medicine. It has fascinated me to observe that when a prominent allergist began to use client-centered therapy for the treatment of non-specific allergies, he found not only very good therapeutic results, but the experience began to affect his whole medical practice. It has gradually meant the reorganization of his office procedure. He has given his nurses a new type of training in understanding the patient. He has decided to have all medical histories taken by a nonmedical person trained in nondirective techniques, in order to get a true picture of the client's feelings and attitudes toward himself and his health, uncluttered by the bias and diagnostic evaluation which is almost inevitable when a medical person takes the history and unintentionally distorts the material by his premature judgments. He has found these histories much more helpful to the physicians than those taken by physicians.

The client-centered viewpoint has already been shown to have significant implications for the field of survey interviewing and public opinion study. Use of such techniques by Likert, Lazarsfeld, and others has meant the elimination of much of the factor of bias in such studies.

460 THE MEANING OF LIFE

This approach has also, we believe, deep implications for the handling of social and group conflicts, as I have pointed out in another paper (9). Our work in applying a client-centered viewpoint to group therapy situations, while still in its early stages, leads us to feel that a significant clue to the constructive solution of interpersonal and intercultural frictions in the group may be in our hands. Application of these procedures to staff groups, to inter-racial groups, to groups with personal problems and tensions, is under way.

In the field of education, too, the client-centered approach is finding significant application. The work of Cantor, a description of which will soon be published, is outstanding in this connection, but a number of teachers are finding that these methods, designed for therapy, produce a new type of educational process, an independent learning which is highly desirable, and even a reorientation of individual direction which is very similar to the results of individual or group therapy.

Even in the realm of our philosophical orientation, the client-centered approach has its deep implications. I should like to indicate this by quoting briefly from a previous paper.

As we examine and try to evaluate our clinical experience with client-centered therapy, the [p. 422] phenomenon of the reorganization of attitudes and the redirection of behavior by the individual assumes greater and greater importance. This phenomenon seems to find inadequate explanation in terms of the determinism which is the predominant philosophical background of most psychological work. The capacity of the individual to reorganize his attitudes and behavior in ways not determined by external factors nor by previous elements in his own experience, but determined by his own insight into those factors, is an impressive capacity. It involves a basic spontaneity which we have been loathe to admit into our scientific thinking.

The clinical experience could be summarized by saying that the behavior of the human organism may be determined by the influences to which it has been exposed, but it may also be determined by the creative and integrative insight of the organism itself. This ability of the person to discover new meaning in the forces which impinge upon him and in the past experiences which have been controlling him, and the ability to alter consciously his behavior in the light of this new meaning, has a profound significance for our thinking which has not been fully realized. We need to revise the philosophical basis of our work to a point where it can admit that forces exist within the individual which can exercise a spontaneous and significant influence upon behavior which is not predictable through knowledge of prior influences and conditionings. The forces released through a catalytic process of therapy are not adequately accounted for by a knowledge of the individual's previous conditionings, but only if we grant the presence of a spontaneous force within the organism which has the capacity of integration and redirection. This capacity for volitional control is a force which we must take into account in any psychological equation (9).

So we find an approach which began merely as a way of dealing with problems of human maladjustment forcing us into a revaluation of our basic philosophical concepts.

SUMMARY

I hope that throughout this paper I have managed to convey what is my own conviction, that what we now know or think we know about a client-centered approach is only a beginning, only the opening of a door beyond which we are beginning to see some very challenging roads, some fields rich with opportunity. It is the facts of our clinical and research experience which keep pointing forward into new and exciting possibilities. Yet whatever the future may hold, it appears already clear that we are dealing with materials of a new and significant nature, which demand the most openminded[sic] and thorough exploration. If our present formulations of those facts are correct, then we would say that some important elements already stand out; that certain basic attitudes and skills can create a psychological atmosphere which releases, frees, and utilizes deep strengths in the client; that these strengths and capacities are more sensitive and more rugged than hitherto supposed; and that they are released in an orderly and predictable process which may prove as significant a basic fact in social science as some of the laws and predictable processes in the physical sciences.

SELECTED REFERENCES

1. ALEXANDER, F. AND FRENCH, T. *Psychoanalytic Therapy.* New York: Ronald Press, 1946.
2. ALLEN, F. *Psychotherapy with Children.* New York: Norton, 1942.
3. CANTOR, N. *Employee Counseling.* New York: McGraw-Hill Book Company.
4. CANTOR, N. *The Dynamics of Learning.* (unpublished mss.) University of Buffalo, 1943.
5. CURRAN, C. A. *Personality Factors in Counseling.* New York: Grune and Stratton, 1945.
6. RANK, O. *Will Therapy.* New York: Alfred A. Knopf 1936.
7. ROGERS, C. R. "Counseling", *Review of Educational Research.* April 1945 (Vol. 15), pp. 135-163.
8. ROGERS, C. R. *Counseling and Psychotherapy.* New York: Houghton Mifflin Co., 1942.
9. ROGERS, C`. R. *The implications of nondirective therapy for the handling of social conflicts.* Paper given to a seminar of the Bureau of Intercultural Education, New York City, Feb. 18, 1946.
10. ROGERS. C. R. AND WALLEN, J. L. *Counseling with Returned Servicemen.* New York: McGraw-Hill, 1946.
11. SNYDER, W. U. "An Investigation of the Nature of Non-Directive Psychotherapy." *Journal of General Psychology.* Vol. 33, 1945. pp.193-223.
12. TAFT, J. The Dynamics of Therapy in a Controlled Relationship. New York: Macmillan, 1933.

Footnote
[1] Paper given at a seminar of the staffs of the Menninger Clinic and the Topeka Veteran's Hospital, Topeka, Kansas, May 15, 1946.
[*] *Classics Editor's note*: Sometimes Rogers hyphenates this term, and sometimes not. I have rendered it as he does at each instance.
[§] *Classics Editor's note:* Rogers is inconsistent in his use of quotation marks in this passage.

462   THE MEANING OF LIFE

A Theory of Human Motivation

A. H. Maslow (1943)

Originally Published in *Psychological Review*, 50, 370-396.

[p. 370] I. INTRODUCTION

In a previous paper (*13*) various propositions were presented which would have to be included in any theory of human motivation that could lay claim to being definitive. These conclusions may be briefly summarized as follows:

1. The integrated wholeness of the organism must be one of the foundation stones of motivation theory.

2. The hunger drive (or any other physiological drive) was rejected as a centering point or model for a definitive theory of motivation. Any drive that is somatically based and localizable was shown to be atypical rather than typical in human motivation.

3. Such a theory should stress and center itself upon ultimate or basic goals rather than partial or superficial ones, upon ends rather than means to these ends. Such a stress would imply a more central place for unconscious than for conscious motivations.

4. There are usually available various cultural paths to the same goal. Therefore conscious, specific, local-cultural desires are not as fundamental in motivation theory as the more basic, unconscious goals.

5. Any motivated behavior, either preparatory or consummatory, must be understood to be a channel through which many basic needs may be simultaneously expressed or satisfied. Typically an act has more than one motivation.

6. Practically all organismic states are to be understood as motivated and as motivating.

7. Human needs arrange themselves in hierarchies of pre-potency. That is to say, the appearance of one need usually rests on the prior satisfaction of another, more

HUMANISTIC PSYCHOLOGY   463

pre-potent need. Man is a perpetually wanting animal. Also no need or drive can be treated as if it were isolated or discrete; every drive is related to the state of satisfaction or dissatisfaction of other drives.

8. *Lists* of drives will get us nowhere for various theoretical and practical reasons. Furthermore any classification of motivations [p. 371] must deal with the problem of levels of specificity or generalization the motives to be classified.

9. Classifications of motivations must be based upon goals rather than upon instigating drives or motivated behavior.

10. Motivation theory should be human-centered rather than animal-centered.

11. The situation or the field in which the organism reacts must be taken into account but the field alone can rarely serve as an exclusive explanation for behavior. Furthermore the field itself must be interpreted in terms of the organism. Field theory cannot be a substitute for motivation theory.

12. Not only the integration of the organism must be taken into account, but also the possibility of isolated, specific, partial or segmental reactions. It has since become necessary to add to these another affirmation.

13. Motivation theory is not synonymous with behavior theory. The motivations are only one class of determinants of behavior. While behavior is almost always motivated, it is also almost always biologically, culturally and situationally determined as well.

The present paper is an attempt to formulate a positive theory of motivation which will satisfy these theoretical demands and at the same time conform to the known facts, clinical and observational as well as experimental. It derives most directly, however, from clinical experience. This theory is, I think, in the functionalist tradition of James and Dewey, and is fused with the holism of Wertheimer (*19*), Goldstein (*6*), and Gestalt Psychology, and with the dynamicism of Freud (*4*) and Adler (*1*). This fusion or synthesis may arbitrarily be called a 'general-dynamic' theory.

It is far easier to perceive and to criticize the aspects in motivation theory than to remedy them. Mostly this is because of the very serious lack of sound data in this area. I conceive this lack of sound facts to be due primarily to the absence of a valid theory of motivation. The present theory then must be considered to be a suggested program or framework for future research and must stand or fall, not so much on facts available or evidence presented, as upon researches to be done, researches suggested perhaps, by the questions raised in this paper.[p. 372]

464   THE MEANING OF LIFE

II. THE BASIC NEEDS

The 'physiological' needs. -- The needs that are usually taken as the starting point for motivation theory are the so-called physiological drives. Two recent lines of research make it necessary to revise our customary notions about these needs, first, the development of the concept of homeostasis, and second, the finding that appetites (preferential choices among foods) are a fairly efficient indication of actual needs or lacks in the body.

Homeostasis refers to the body's automatic efforts to maintain a constant, normal state of the blood stream. Cannon (2) has described this process for (1) the water content of the blood, (2) salt content, (3) sugar content, (4) protein content, (5) fat content, (6) calcium content, (7) oxygen content, (8) constant hydrogen-ion level (acid-base balance) and (9) constant temperature of the blood. Obviously this list can be extended to include other minerals, the hormones, vitamins, etc.

Young in a recent article (21) has summarized the work on appetite in its relation to body needs. If the body lacks some chemical, the individual will tend to develop a specific appetite or partial hunger for that food element.

Thus it seems impossible as well as useless to make any list of fundamental physiological needs for they can come to almost any number one might wish, depending on the degree of specificity of description. We can not identify all physiological needs as homeostatic. That sexual desire, sleepiness, sheer activity and maternal behavior in animals, are homeostatic, has not yet been demonstrated. Furthermore, this list would not include the various sensory pleasures (tastes, smells, tickling, stroking) which are probably physiological and which may become the goals of motivated behavior.

In a previous paper (13) it has been pointed out that these physiological drives or needs are to be considered unusual rather than typical because they are isolable, and because they are localizable somatically. That is to say, they are relatively independent of each other, of other motivations [p. 373] and of the organism as a whole, and secondly, in many cases, it is possible to demonstrate a localized, underlying somatic base for the drive. This is true less generally than has been thought (exceptions are fatigue, sleepiness, maternal responses) but it is still true in the classic instances of hunger, sex, and thirst.

It should be pointed out again that any of the physiological needs and the consummatory behavior involved with them serve as channels for all sorts of other needs as well. That is to say, the person who thinks he is hungry may actually be seeking more for comfort, or dependence, than for vitamins or proteins. Conversely, it is possible to satisfy the hunger need in part by other activities such as drinking water or smoking cigarettes. In other words, relatively isolable as these physiological needs are, they are not completely so.

Undoubtedly these physiological needs are the most pre-potent of all needs. What this means specifically is, that in the human being who is missing everything in life in an extreme fashion, it is most likely that the major motivation would be the physiological needs rather than any others. A person who is lacking food, safety, love, and esteem would most probably hunger for food more strongly than for anything else.

If all the needs are unsatisfied, and the organism is then dominated by the physiological needs, all other needs may become simply non-existent or be pushed into the background. It is then fair to characterize the whole organism by saying simply that it is hungry, for consciousness is almost completely preempted by hunger. All capacities are put into the service of hunger-satisfaction, and the organization of these capacities is almost entirely determined by the one purpose of satisfying hunger. The receptors and effectors, the intelligence, memory, habits, all may now be defined simply as hunger-gratifying tools. Capacities that are not useful for this purpose lie dormant, or are pushed into the background. The urge to write poetry, the desire to acquire an automobile, the interest in American history, the desire for a new pair of shoes are, in the extreme case, forgotten or become of sec-[p.374]ondary importance. For the man who is extremely and dangerously hungry, no other interests exist but food. He dreams food, he remembers food, he thinks about food, he emotes only about food, he perceives only food and he wants only food. The more subtle determinants that ordinarily fuse with the physiological drives in organizing even feeding, drinking or sexual behavior, may now be so completely overwhelmed as to allow us to speak at this time (but only at this time) of pure hunger drive and behavior, with the one unqualified aim of relief.

Another peculiar characteristic of the human organism when it is dominated by a certain need is that the whole philosophy of the future tends also to change. For our chronically and extremely hungry man, Utopia can be defined very simply as a place where there is plenty of food. He tends to think that, if only he is guaranteed food for the rest of his life, he will be perfectly happy and will never want anything more. Life itself tends to be defined in terms of eating. Anything else will be defined as unimportant. Freedom, love, community feeling, respect, philosophy, may all be waved aside as fripperies which are useless since they fail to fill the stomach. Such a man may fairly be said to live by bread alone.

It cannot possibly be denied that such things are true but their generality can be denied. Emergency conditions are, almost by definition, rare in the normally functioning peaceful society. That this truism can be forgotten is due mainly to two reasons. First, rats have few motivations other than physiological ones, and since so much of the research upon motivation has been made with these animals, it is easy to carry the rat-picture over to the human being. Secondly, it is too often not realized that culture itself is an adaptive tool, one of whose main functions is to make the physiological emergencies come less and less often. In most of the known societies, chronic extreme hunger of the emergency type is rare, rather than common. In any case, this is still true in the United States. The average American citizen is experiencing appetite rather than hunger when he says "I am [p. 375] hungry." He is apt to experience sheer life-and-death hunger only by accident and then only a few times through his entire life.

Obviously a good way to obscure the 'higher' motivations, and to get a lopsided view of human capacities and human nature, is to make the organism extremely and chronically hungry or thirsty. Anyone who attempts to make an emergency picture into a typical one, and who will measure all of man's goals and desires by his behavior during extreme physiological deprivation is certainly being blind to many things. It is quite true that man lives by bread alone -- when there

466 THE MEANING OF LIFE

is no bread. But what happens to man's desires when there is plenty of bread and when his belly is chronically filled?

At once other (and 'higher') needs emerge and these, rather than physiological hungers, dominate the organism. And when these in turn are satisfied, again new (and still 'higher') needs emerge and so on. This is what we mean by saying that the basic human needs are organized into a hierarchy of relative prepotency.

One main implication of this phrasing is that gratification becomes as important a concept as deprivation in motivation theory, for it releases the organism from the domination of a relatively more physiological need, permitting thereby the emergence of other more social goals. The physiological needs, along with their partial goals, when chronically gratified cease to exist as active determinants or organizers of behavior. They now exist only in a potential fashion in the sense that they may emerge again to dominate the organism if they are thwarted. But a want that is satisfied is no longer a want. The organism is dominated and its behavior organized only by unsatisfied needs. If hunger is satisfied, it becomes unimportant in the current dynamics of the individual.

This statement is somewhat qualified by a hypothesis to be discussed more fully later, namely that it is precisely those individuals in whom a certain need has always been satisfied who are best equipped to tolerate deprivation of that need in the future, and that furthermore, those who have been de-[p. 376]prived in the past will react differently to current satisfactions than the one who has never been deprived.

The safety needs. -- If the physiological needs are relatively well gratified, there then emerges a new set of needs, which we may categorize roughly as the safety needs. All that has been said of the physiological needs is equally true, although in lesser degree, of these desires. The organism may equally well be wholly dominated by them. They may serve as the almost exclusive organizers of behavior, recruiting all the capacities of the organism in their service, and we may then fairly describe the whole organism as a safety-seeking mechanism. Again we may say of the receptors, the effectors, of the intellect and the other capacities that they are primarily safety-seeking tools. Again, as in the hungry man, we find that the dominating goal is a strong determinant not only of his current world-outlook and philosophy but also of his philosophy of the future. Practically everything looks less important than safety, (even sometimes the physiological needs which being satisfied, are now underestimated). A man, in this state, if it is extreme enough and chronic enough, may be characterized as living almost for safety alone.

Although in this paper we are interested primarily in the needs of the adult, we can approach an understanding of his safety needs perhaps more efficiently by observation of infants and children, in whom these needs are much more simple and obvious. One reason for the clearer appearance of the threat or danger reaction in infants, is that they do not inhibit this reaction at all, whereas adults in our society have been taught to inhibit it at all costs. Thus even when adults do feel their safety to be threatened we may not be able to see this on the surface. Infants will react in a total fashion and as if they were endangered, if they are disturbed or dropped suddenly, startled by loud noises, flashing light, or other unusual sensory stimulation, by rough handling, by general loss of support in the mother's arms, or by inadequate support.[1][p. 377]

In infants we can also see a much more direct reaction to bodily illnesses of various kinds. Sometimes these illnesses seem to be immediately and per se threatening and seem to make the child feel unsafe. For instance, vomiting, colic or other sharp pains seem to make the child look at the whole world in a different way. At such a moment of pain, it may be postulated that, for the child, the appearance of the whole world suddenly changes from sunniness to darkness, so to speak, and becomes a place in which anything at all might happen, in which previously stable things have suddenly become unstable. Thus a child who because of some bad food is taken ill may, for a day or two, develop fear, nightmares, and a need for protection and reassurance never seen in him before his illness.

Another indication of the child's need for safety is his preference for some kind of undisrupted routine or rhythm. He seems to want a predictable, orderly world. For instance, injustice, unfairness, or inconsistency in the parents seems to make a child feel anxious and unsafe. This attitude may be not so much because of the injustice per se or any particular pains involved, but rather because this treatment threatens to make the world look unreliable, or unsafe, or unpredictable. Young children seem to thrive better under a system which has at least a skeletal outline of rigidity, In which there is a schedule of a kind, some sort of routine, something that can be counted upon, not only for the present but also far into the future. Perhaps one could express this more accurately by saying that the child needs an organized world rather than an unorganized or unstructured one.

The central role of the parents and the normal family setup are indisputable. Quarreling, physical assault, separation, divorce or death within the family may be particularly terrifying. Also parental outbursts of rage or threats of punishment directed to the child, calling him names, speaking to him harshly, shaking him, handling him roughly, or actual [p. 378] physical punishment sometimes elicit such total panic and terror in the child that we must assume more is involved than the physical pain alone. While it is true that in some children this terror may represent also a fear of loss of parental love, it can also occur in completely rejected children, who seem to cling to the hating parents more for sheer safety and protection than because of hope of love.

Confronting the average child with new, unfamiliar, strange, unmanageable stimuli or situations will too frequently elicit the danger or terror reaction, as for example, getting lost or even being separated from the parents for a short time, being confronted with new faces, new situations or new tasks, the sight of strange, unfamiliar or uncontrollable objects, illness or death. Particularly at such times, the child's frantic clinging to his parents is eloquent testimony to their role as protectors (quite apart from their roles as food-givers and love-givers).

From these and similar observations, we may generalize and say that the average child in our society generally prefers a safe, orderly, predictable, organized world, which he can count, on, and in which unexpected, unmanageable or other dangerous things do not happen, and in which, in any case, he has all-powerful parents who protect and shield him from harm.

468   THE MEANING OF LIFE

That these reactions may so easily be observed in children is in a way a proof of the fact that children in our society, feel too unsafe (or, in a word, are badly brought up). Children who are reared in an unthreatening, loving family do not ordinarily react as we have described above (17). In such children the danger reactions are apt to come mostly to objects or situations that adults too would consider dangerous.[2]

The healthy, normal, fortunate adult in our culture is largely satisfied in his safety needs. The peaceful, smoothly [p. 379] running, 'good' society ordinarily makes its members feel safe enough from wild animals, extremes of temperature, criminals, assault and murder, tyranny, etc. Therefore, in a very real sense, he no longer has any safety needs as active motivators. Just as a sated man no longer feels hungry, a safe man no longer feels endangered. If we wish to see these needs directly and clearly we must turn to neurotic or near-neurotic individuals, and to the economic and social underdogs. In between these extremes, we can perceive the expressions of safety needs only in such phenomena as, for instance, the common preference for a job with tenure and protection, the desire for a savings account, and for insurance of various kinds (medical, dental, unemployment, disability, old age).

Other broader aspects of the attempt to seek safety and stability in the world are seen in the very common preference for familiar rather than unfamiliar things, or for the known rather than the unknown. The tendency to have some religion or world-philosophy that organizes the universe and the men in it into some sort of satisfactorily coherent, meaningful whole is also in part motivated by safety-seeking. Here too we may list science and philosophy in general as partially motivated by the safety needs (we shall see later that there are also other motivations to scientific, philosophical or religious endeavor).

Otherwise the need for safety is seen as an active and dominant mobilizer of the organism's resources only in emergencies, e. g., war, disease, natural catastrophes, crime waves, societal disorganization, neurosis, brain injury, chronically bad situation.

Some neurotic adults in our society are, in many ways, like the unsafe child in their desire for safety, although in the former it takes on a somewhat special appearance. Their reaction is often to unknown, psychological dangers in a world that is perceived to be hostile, overwhelming and threatening. Such a person behaves as if a great catastrophe were almost always impending, i.e., he is usually responding as if to an emergency. His safety needs often find specific [p. 380] expression in a search for a protector, or a stronger person on whom he may depend, or perhaps, a Fuehrer.

The neurotic individual may be described in a slightly different way with some usefulness as a grown-up person who retains his childish attitudes toward the world. That is to say, a neurotic adult may be said to behave 'as if' he were actually afraid of a spanking, or of his mother's disapproval, or of being abandoned by his parents, or having his food taken away from him. It is as if his childish attitudes of fear and threat reaction to a dangerous world had gone underground, and untouched by the growing up and learning processes, were now ready to be called out by any stimulus that would make a child feel endangered and threatened.[3]

The neurosis in which the search for safety takes its dearest form is in the compulsive-obsessive neurosis. Compulsive-obsessives try frantically to order and stabilize the world so that no unmanageable, unexpected or unfamiliar dangers will ever appear (14); They hedge themselves about with all sorts of ceremonials, rules and formulas so that every possible contingency may be provided for and so that no new contingencies may appear. They are much like the brain injured cases, described by Goldstein (6), who manage to maintain their equilibrium by avoiding everything unfamiliar and strange and by ordering their restricted world in such a neat, disciplined, orderly fashion that everything in the world can be counted upon. They try to arrange the world so that anything unexpected (dangers) cannot possibly occur. If, through no fault of their own, something unexpected does occur, they go into a panic reaction as if this unexpected occurrence constituted a grave danger. What we can see only as a none-too-strong preference in the healthy person, e. g., preference for the familiar, becomes a life-and-death. necessity in abnormal cases.

The love *needs*. -- If both the physiological and the safety needs are fairly well gratified, then there will emerge the love and affection and belongingness needs, and the whole cycle [p. 381] already described will repeat itself with this new center. Now the person will feel keenly, as never before, the absence of friends, or a sweetheart, or a wife, or children. He will hunger for affectionate relations with people in general, namely, for a place in his group, and he will strive with great intensity to achieve this goal. He will want to attain such a place more than anything else in the world and may even forget that once, when he was hungry, he sneered at love.

In our society the thwarting of these needs is the most commonly found core in cases of maladjustment and more severe psychopathology. Love and affection, as well as their possible expression in sexuality, are generally looked upon with ambivalence and are customarily hedged about with many restrictions and inhibitions. Practically all theorists of psychopathology have stressed thwarting of the love needs as basic in the picture of maladjustment. Many clinical studies have therefore been made of this need and we know more about it perhaps than any of the other needs except the physiological ones (14).

One thing that must be stressed at this point is that love is not synonymous with sex. Sex may be studied as a purely physiological need. Ordinarily sexual behavior is multi-determined, that is to say, determined not only by sexual but also by other needs, chief among which are the love and affection needs. Also not to be overlooked is the fact that the love needs involve both giving and receiving love.[4]

The esteem needs. -- All people in our society (with a few pathological exceptions) have a need or desire for a stable, firmly based, (usually) high evaluation of themselves, for self-respect, or self-esteem, and for the esteem of others. By firmly based self-esteem, we mean that which is soundly based upon real capacity, achievement and respect from others. These needs may be classified into two subsidiary sets. These are, first, the desire for strength, for achievement, for adequacy, for confidence in the face of the world, and for independence and freedom.[5] Secondly, we have what [p. 382] we may call the desire for reputation or prestige (defining it as respect or esteem from other people), recognition, attention, importance or appreciation.[6] These

470 THE MEANING OF LIFE

needs have been relatively stressed by Alfred Adler and his followers, and have been relatively neglected by Freud and the psychoanalysts. More and more today however there is appearing widespread appreciation of their central importance.

Satisfaction of the self-esteem need leads to feelings of self-confidence, worth, strength, capability and adequacy of being useful and necessary in the world. But thwarting of these needs produces feelings of inferiority, of weakness and of helplessness. These feelings in turn give rise to either basic discouragement or else compensatory or neurotic trends. An appreciation of the necessity of basic self-confidence and an understanding of how helpless people are without it, can be easily gained from a study of severe traumatic neurosis (8).[7]

The need for self-actualization. -- Even if all these needs are satisfied, we may still often (if not always) expect that a new discontent and restlessness will soon develop, unless the individual is doing what he is fitted for. A musician must make music, an artist must paint, a poet must write, if he is to be ultimately happy. What a man can be, he must be. This need we may call self-actualization.

This term, first coined by Kurt Goldstein, is being used in this paper in a much more specific and limited fashion. It refers to the desire for self-fulfillment, namely, to the tendency for him to become actualized in what he is potentially. This tendency might be phrased as the desire to become more and more what one is, to become everything that one is capable of becoming.[p. 383]

The specific form that these needs will take will of course vary greatly from person to person. In one individual it may take the form of the desire to be an ideal mother, in another it may be expressed athletically, and in still another it may be expressed in painting pictures or in inventions. It is not necessarily a creative urge although in people who have any capacities for creation it will take this form.

The clear emergence of these needs rests upon prior satisfaction of the physiological, safety, love and esteem needs. We shall call people who are satisfied in these needs, basically satisfied people, and it is from these that we may expect the fullest (and healthiest) creativeness.[8] Since, in our society, basically satisfied people are the exception, we do not know much about self-actualization, either experimentally or clinically. It remains a challenging problem for research.

The preconditions for the basic need satisfactions. -- There are certain conditions which are immediate prerequisites for the basic need satisfactions. Danger to these is reacted to almost as if it were a direct danger to the basic needs themselves. Such conditions as freedom to speak, freedom to do what one wishes so long as no harm is done to others, freedom to express one's self, freedom to investigate and seek for information, freedom to defend one's self, justice, fairness, honesty, orderliness in the group are examples of such preconditions for basic need satisfactions. Thwarting in these freedoms will be reacted to with a threat or emergency response. These conditions are not ends in themselves but they are *almost* so since they are so closely related to the basic needs, which are apparently the only ends in themselves. These conditions are defended because without them the basic satisfactions are quite impossible, or at least, very severely endangered.[p. 384]

HUMANISTIC PSYCHOLOGY   471

If we remember that the cognitive capacities (perceptual, intellectual, learning) are a set of adjustive tools, which have, among other functions, that of satisfaction of our basic needs, then it is clear that any danger to them, any deprivation or blocking of their free use, must also be indirectly threatening to the basic needs themselves. Such a statement is a partial solution of the general problems of curiosity, the search for knowledge, truth and wisdom, and the ever-persistent urge to solve the cosmic mysteries.

We must therefore introduce another hypothesis and speak of degrees of closeness to the basic needs, for we have already pointed out that any conscious desires (partial goals) are more or less important as they are more or less close to the basic needs. The same statement may be made for various behavior acts. An act is psychologically important if it contributes directly to satisfaction of basic needs. The less directly it so contributes, or the weaker this contribution is, the less important this act must be conceived to be from the point of view of dynamic psychology. A similar statement may be made for the various defense or coping mechanisms. Some are very directly related to the protection or attainment of the basic needs, others are only weakly and distantly related. Indeed if we wished, we could speak of more basic and less basic defense mechanisms, and then affirm that danger to the more basic defenses is more threatening than danger to less basic defenses (always remembering that this is so only because of their relationship to the basic needs).

The desires to know and to understand. -- So far, we have mentioned the cognitive needs only in passing. Acquiring knowledge and systematizing the universe have been considered as, in part, techniques for the achievement of basic safety in the world, or, for the intelligent man, expressions of self-actualization. Also freedom of inquiry and expression have been discussed as preconditions of satisfactions of the basic needs. True though these formulations may be, they do not constitute definitive answers to the question as to the motivation role of curiosity, learning, philosophizing, experimenting, etc. They are, at best, no more than partial answers.[p. 385]

This question is especially difficult because we know so little about the facts. Curiosity, exploration, desire for the facts, desire to know may certainly be observed easily enough. The fact that they often are pursued even at great cost to the individual's safety is an earnest of the partial character of our previous discussion. In addition, the writer must admit that, though he has sufficient clinical evidence to postulate the desire to know as a very strong drive in intelligent people, no data are available for unintelligent people. It may then be largely a function of relatively high intelligence. Rather tentatively, then, and largely in the hope of stimulating discussion and research, we shall postulate a basic desire to know, to be aware of reality, to get the facts, to satisfy curiosity, or as Wertheimer phrases it, to see rather than to be blind.

This postulation, however, is not enough. Even after we know, we are impelled to know more and more minutely and microscopically on the one hand, and on the other, more and more extensively in the direction of a world philosophy, religion, etc. The facts that we acquire, if they are isolated or atomistic, inevitably get theorized about, and either analyzed or organized or both. This process has been phrased by some as the search for 'meaning.' We shall then postulate a desire to understand, to systematize, to organize, to analyze, to look for relations and meanings.

472   THE MEANING OF LIFE

Once these desires are accepted for discussion, we see that they too form themselves into a small hierarchy in which the desire to know is prepotent over the desire to understand. All the characteristics of a hierarchy of prepotency that we have described above, seem to hold for this one as well.

We must guard ourselves against the too easy tendency to separate these desires from the basic needs we have discussed above, i.e., to make a sharp dichotomy between 'cognitive' and 'conative' needs. The desire to know and to understand are themselves conative, i.e., have a striving character, and are as much personality needs as the 'basic needs' we have already discussed (19).[p. 386]

III. FURTHER CHARACTERISTICS OF THE BASIC NEEDS

The degree of fixity of the hierarchy of basic needs. -- We have spoken so far as if this hierarchy were a fixed order but actually it is not nearly as rigid as we may have implied. It is true that most of the people with whom we have worked have seemed to have these basic needs in about the order that has been indicated. However, there have been a number of exceptions.

(1) There are some people in whom, for instance, self-esteem seems to be more important than love. This most common reversal in the hierarchy is usually due to the development of the notion that the person who is most likely to be loved is a strong or powerful person, one who inspires respect or fear, and who is self confident or aggressive. Therefore such people who lack love and seek it, may try hard to put on a front of aggressive, confident behavior. But essentially they seek high self-esteem and its behavior expressions more as a means-to-an-end than for its own sake; they seek self-assertion for the sake of love rather than for self-esteem itself.

(2) There are other, apparently innately creative people in whom the drive to creativeness seems to be more important than any other counter-determinant. Their creativeness might appear not as self-actualization released by basic satisfaction, but in spite of lack of basic satisfaction.

(3) In certain people the level of aspiration may be permanently deadened or lowered. That is to say, the less pre-potent goals may simply be lost, and may disappear forever, so that the person who has experienced life at a very low level, i. e., chronic unemployment, may continue to be satisfied for the rest of his life if only he can get enough food.

(4) The so-called 'psychopathic personality' is another example of permanent loss of the love needs. These are people who, according to the best data available (9), have been starved for love in the earliest months of their lives and have simply lost forever the desire and the ability to give and to receive affection (as animals lose sucking or pecking reflexes that are not exercised soon enough after birth).[p. 387]

(5) Another cause of reversal of the hierarchy is that when a need has been satisfied for a long time, this need may be underevaluated. People who have never experienced chronic hunger are apt to underestimate its effects and to look upon food as a rather unimportant thing. If they are dominated by a higher need, this higher need will seem to be the most important of all. It then becomes possible, and indeed does actually happen, that they may, for the sake of this higher need, put themselves into the position of being deprived in a more basic need. We may expect

that after a long-time deprivation of the more basic need there will be a tendency to reevaluate both needs so that the more pre-potent need will actually become consciously prepotent for the individual who may have given it up very lightly. Thus, a man who has given up his job rather than lose his self-respect, and who then starves for six months or so, may be willing to take his job back even at the price of losing his a self-respect.

(6) Another partial explanation of apparent reversals is seen in the fact that we have been talking about the hierarchy of prepotency in terms of consciously felt wants or desires rather than of behavior. Looking at behavior itself may give us the wrong impression. What we have claimed is that the person will want the more basic of two needs when deprived in both. There is no necessary implication here that he will act upon his desires. Let us say again that there are many determinants of behavior other than the needs and desires.

(7) Perhaps more important than all these exceptions are the ones that involve ideals, high social standards, high values and the like. With such values people become martyrs; they give up everything for the sake of a particular ideal, or value. These people may be understood, at least in part, by reference to one basic concept (or hypothesis) which may be called 'increased frustration-tolerance through early gratification'. People who have been satisfied in their basic needs throughout their lives, particularly in their earlier years, seem to develop exceptional power to withstand present or future thwarting of these needs simply because they have strong,[p. 388] healthy character structure as a result of basic satisfaction. They are the 'strong' people who can easily weather disagreement or opposition, who can swim against the stream of public opinion and who can stand up for the truth at great personal cost. It is just the ones who have loved and been well loved, and who have had many deep friendships who can hold out against hatred, rejection or persecution.

I say all this in spite of the fact that there is a certain amount of sheer habituation which is also involved in any full discussion of frustration tolerance. For instance, it is likely that those persons who have been accustomed to relative starvation for a long time, are partially enabled thereby to withstand food deprivation. What sort of balance must be made between these two tendencies, of habituation on the one hand, and of past satisfaction breeding present frustration tolerance on the other hand, remains to be worked out by further research. Meanwhile we may assume that they are both operative, side by side, since they do not contradict each other, In respect to this phenomenon of increased frustration tolerance, it seems probable that the most important gratifications come in the first two years of life. That is to say, people who have been made secure and strong in the earliest years, tend to remain secure and strong thereafter in the face of whatever threatens.

Degree of relative satisfaction. -- So far, our theoretical discussion may have given the impression that these five sets of needs are somehow in a step-wise, all-or-none relationships to each other. We have spoken in such terms as the following: "If one need is satisfied, then another emerges." This statement might give the false impression that a need must be satisfied 100 per cent before the next need emerges. In actual fact, most members of our society who are normal, are partially satisfied in all their basic needs and partially unsatisfied in all their basic needs at the

474   THE MEANING OF LIFE

same time. A more realistic description of the hierarchy would be in terms of decreasing percentages of satisfaction as we go up the hierarchy of prepotency, For instance, if I may assign arbitrary figures for the sake of illustration, it is as if the average citizen [p. 389] is satisfied perhaps 85 per cent in his physiological needs, 70 per cent in his safety needs, 50 per cent in his love needs, 40 per cent in his self-esteem needs, and 10 per cent in his self-actualization needs.

As for the concept of emergence of a new need after satisfaction of the prepotent need, this emergence is not a sudden, saltatory phenomenon but rather a gradual emergence by slow degrees from nothingness. For instance, if prepotent need A is satisfied only 10 per cent: then need B may not be visible at all. However, as this need A becomes satisfied 25 per cent, need B may emerge 5 per cent, as need A becomes satisfied 75 per cent need B may emerge go per cent, and so on.

Unconscious character of needs. -- These needs are neither necessarily conscious nor unconscious. On the whole, however, in the average person, they are more often unconscious rather than conscious. It is not necessary at this point to overhaul the tremendous mass of evidence which indicates the crucial importance of unconscious motivation. It would by now be expected, on a priori grounds alone, that unconscious motivations would on the whole be rather more important than the conscious motivations. What we have called the basic needs are very often largely unconscious although they may, with suitable techniques, and with sophisticated people become conscious.

Cultural specificity and generality of needs. -- This classification of basic needs makes some attempt to take account of the relative unity behind the superficial differences in specific desires from one culture to another. Certainly in any particular culture an individual's conscious motivational content will usually be extremely different from the conscious motivational content of an individual in another society. However, it is the common experience of anthropologists that people, even in different societies, are much more alike than we would think from our first contact with them, and that as we know them better we seem to find more and more of this commonness, We then recognize the most startling differences to be superficial rather than basic, e. g., differences in style of hair-dress, clothes, tastes in food, etc. Our classification of basic [p. 390] needs is in part an attempt to account for this unity behind the apparent diversity from culture to culture. No claim is made that it is ultimate or universal for all cultures. The claim is made only that it is relatively more ultimate, more universal, more basic, than the superficial conscious desires from culture to culture, and makes a somewhat closer approach to common-human characteristics, Basic needs are more common-human than superficial desires or behaviors.

Multiple motivations of behavior. -- These needs must be understood not to be exclusive or single determiners of certain kinds of behavior. An example may be found in any behavior that seems to be physiologically motivated, such as eating, or sexual play or the like. The clinical psychologists have long since found that any behavior may be a channel through which flow various determinants. Or to say it in another way, most behavior is multi-motivated. Within the sphere of motivational determinants any behavior tends to be determined by several or all of the basic needs simultaneously rather than by only one of them. The latter would be more an exception than the former. Eating may be partially for the sake of filling the stomach, and partially for the sake of comfort and amelioration of other needs. One may make love not only for pure sexual release, but also to convince one's self of one's masculinity, or to make a conquest, to feel powerful, or to win more basic affection. As an illustration, I may point out that it would be possible (theoretically if not practically) to analyze a single act of an individual and see in it the expression of his physiological needs, his safety needs, his love needs, his esteem needs and self-actualization. This contrasts sharply with the more naive brand of trait psychology in which one trait or one motive accounts for a certain kind of act, i. e., an aggressive act is traced solely to a trait of aggressiveness.

Multiple determinants of behavior. -- Not all behavior is determined by the basic needs. We might even say that not all behavior is motivated. There are many determinants of behavior other than motives.[9] For instance, one other im-[p. 391]portant class of determinants is the so-called 'field' determinants. Theoretically, at least, behavior may be determined completely by the field, or even by specific isolated external stimuli, as in association of ideas, or certain conditioned reflexes. If in response to the stimulus word 'table' I immediately perceive a memory image of a table, this response certainly has nothing to do with my basic needs.

Secondly, we may call attention again to the concept of 'degree of closeness to the basic needs' or 'degree of motivation.' Some behavior is highly motivated, other behavior is only weakly motivated. Some is not motivated at all (but all behavior is determined).

Another important point [10] is that there is a basic difference between expressive behavior and coping behavior (functional striving, purposive goal seeking). An expressive behavior does not try to do anything; it is simply a reflection of the personality. A stupid man behaves stupidly, not because he wants to, or tries to, or is motivated to, but simply because he is what he is. The same is true when I speak in a bass voice rather than tenor or soprano. The random movements of a healthy child, the smile on the face of a happy man even when he is alone, the springiness of the healthy man's walk, and the erectness of his carriage are other examples of expressive, non-functional behavior. Also the style in which a man carries out almost all his behavior, motivated as well as unmotivated, is often expressive.

We may then ask, is all behavior expressive or reflective of the character structure? The answer is 'No.' Rote, habitual, automatized, or conventional behavior may or may not be expressive. The same is true for most 'stimulus-bound' behaviors. It is finally necessary to stress that expressiveness of behavior, and goal-directedness of behavior are not mutually exclusive categories. Average behavior is usually both.

Goals as centering principle in motivation theory. -- It will be observed that the basic principle in our classification has [p. 392] been neither the instigation nor the motivated behavior but rather the functions, effects, purposes, or goals of the behavior. It has been proven sufficiently by various people that this is the most suitable point for centering in any motivation theory.[11]

Animal- and human-centering. -- This theory starts with the human being rather than any lower and presumably 'simpler' animal. Too many of the findings that have been made in animals have been proven to be true for animals but not for the human being. There is no reason

476   THE MEANING OF LIFE

whatsoever why we should start with animals in order to study human motivation. The logic or rather illogic behind this general fallacy of 'pseudo-simplicity' has been exposed often enough by philosophers and logicians as well as by scientists in each of the various fields. It is no more necessary to study animals before one can study man than it is to study mathematics before one can study geology or psychology or biology.

We may also reject the old, naive, behaviorism which assumed that it was somehow necessary, or at least more 'scientific' to judge human beings by animal standards. One consequence of this belief was that the whole notion of purpose and goal was excluded from motivational psychology simply because one could not ask a white rat about his purposes. Tolman (18) has long since proven in animal studies themselves that this exclusion was not necessary.

Motivation and the theory of psychopathogenesis. -- The conscious motivational content of everyday life has, according to the foregoing, been conceived to be relatively important or unimportant accordingly as it is more or less closely related to the basic goals. A desire for an ice cream cone might actually be an indirect expression of a desire for love. If it is, then this desire for the ice cream cone becomes extremely important motivation. If however the ice cream is simply something to cool the mouth with, or a casual appetitive reaction, then the desire is relatively unimportant. Everyday conscious desires are to be regarded as symptoms, as [p. 393] surface indicators of more basic needs. If we were to take these superficial desires at their face value me would find ourselves in a state of complete confusion which could never be resolved, since we would be dealing seriously with symptoms rather than with what lay behind the symptoms.

Thwarting of unimportant desires produces no psychopathological results; thwarting of a basically important need does produce such results. Any theory of psychopathogenesis must then be based on a sound theory of motivation. A conflict or a frustration is not necessarily pathogenic. It becomes so only when it threatens or thwarts the basic needs, or partial needs that are closely related to the basic needs (10).

The role of gratified needs. -- It has been pointed out above several times that our needs usually emerge only when more prepotent needs have been gratified. Thus gratification has an important role in motivation theory. Apart from this, however, needs cease to play an active determining or organizing role as soon as they are gratified.

What this means is that, e. g., a basically satisfied person no longer has the needs for esteem, love, safety, etc. The only sense in which he might be said to have them is in the almost metaphysical sense that a sated man has hunger, or a filled bottle has emptiness. If we are interested in what actually motivates us, and not in what has, will, or might motivate us, then a satisfied need is not a motivator. It must be considered for all practical purposes simply not to exist, to have disappeared. This point should be emphasized because it has been either overlooked or contradicted in every theory of motivation I know.[12] The perfectly healthy, normal, fortunate man has no sex needs or hunger needs, or needs for safety, or for love, or for prestige, or self-esteem, except in stray moments of quickly passing threat. If we were to say otherwise, we should also have to aver that every man had all the pathological reflexes, e. g., Babinski, etc., because if his nervous system were damaged, these would appear.

It is such considerations as these that suggest the bold [p. 394] postulation that a man who is thwarted in any of his basic needs may fairly be envisaged simply as a sick man. This is a fair parallel to our designation as 'sick' of the man who lacks vitamins or minerals. Who is to say that a lack of love is less important than a lack of vitamins? Since we know the pathogenic effects of love starvation, who is to say that we are invoking value-questions in an unscientific or illegitimate way, any more than the physician does who diagnoses and treats pellagra or scurvy? If I were permitted this usage, I should then say simply that a healthy man is primarily motivated by his needs to develop and actualize his fullest potentialities and capacities. If a man has any other basic needs in any active, chronic sense, then he is simply an unhealthy man. He is as surely sick as if he had suddenly developed a strong salt-hunger or calcium hunger.[13]

If this statement seems unusual or paradoxical the reader may be assured that this is only one among many such paradoxes that will appear as we revise our ways of looking at man's deeper motivations. When we ask what man wants of life, we deal with his very essence.

IV. SUMMARY

(1) There are at least five sets of goals, which we may call basic needs. These are briefly physiological, safety, love, 'esteem, and self-actualization. In addition, we are motivated by the desire to achieve or maintain the various conditions upon which these basic satisfactions rest and by certain more intellectual desires.

(2) These basic goals are related to each other, being arranged in a hierarchy of prepotency. This means that the most prepotent goal will monopolize consciousness and will tend of itself to organize the recruitment of the various capacities of the organism. The less prepotent needs are [p. 395] minimized, even forgotten or denied. But when a need is fairly well satisfied, the next prepotent ('higher') need emerges, in turn to dominate the conscious life and to serve as the center of organization of behavior, since gratified needs are not active motivators.

Thus man is a perpetually wanting animal. Ordinarily the satisfaction of these wants is not altogether mutually exclusive, but only tends to be. The average member of our society is most often partially satisfied and partially unsatisfied in all of his wants. The hierarchy principle is usually empirically observed in terms of increasing percentages of non-satisfaction as we go up the hierarchy. Reversals of the average order of the hierarchy are sometimes observed. Also it has been observed that an individual may permanently lose the higher wants in the hierarchy under special conditions. There are not only ordinarily multiple motivations for usual behavior, but in addition many determinants other than motives.

(3) Any thwarting or possibility of thwarting of these basic human goals, or danger to the defenses which protect them, or to the conditions upon which they rest, is considered to be a psychological threat. With a few exceptions, all psychopathology may be partially traced to such threats. A basically thwarted man may actually be defined as a 'sick' man, if we wish.

(4) It is such basic threats which bring about the general emergency reactions.

478   THE MEANING OF LIFE

(5) Certain other basic problems have not been dealt with because of limitations of space. Among these are (a) the problem of values in any definitive motivation theory, (b) the relation between appetites, desires, needs and what is 'good' for the organism, (c) the etiology of the basic needs and their possible derivation in early childhood, (d) redefinition of motivational concepts, i. e., drive, desire, wish, need, goal, (e) implication of our theory for hedonistic theory, (f) the nature of the uncompleted act, of success and failure, and of aspiration-level, (g) the role of association, habit and conditioning, (h) relation to the [p. 396] theory of inter-personal relations, (i) implications for psychotherapy, (j) implication for theory of society, (k) the theory of selfishness, (l) the relation between needs and cultural patterns, (m) the relation between this theory and Alport's theory of functional autonomy. These as well as certain other less important questions must be considered as motivation theory attempts to become definitive.

Notes

[1] As the child grows up, sheer knowledge and familiarity as well as better motor development make these 'dangers' less and less dangerous and more and more manageable. Throughout life it may be said that one of the main conative functions of education is this neutralizing of apparent dangers through knowledge, e. g., I am not afraid of thunder because I know something about it.

[2] A 'test battery' for safety might be confronting the child with a small exploding firecracker, or with a bewhiskered face; having the mother leave the room, putting him upon a high ladder, a hypodermic injection, having a mouse crawl up to him, etc. Of course I cannot seriously recommend the deliberate use of such 'tests' for they might very well harm the child being tested. But these and similar situations come up by the score in the child's ordinary day-to-day living and may be observed. There is no reason why those stimuli should not be used with, far example, young chimpanzees.

[3] Not all neurotic individuals feel unsafe. Neurosis may have at its core a thwarting of the affection and esteem needs in a person who is generally safe.

[4] For further details see (12) and (16, Chap. 5).

[5] Whether or not this particular desire is universal we do not know. The crucial question, especially important today, is "Will men who are enslaved and dominated inevitably feel dissatisfied and rebellious?" We may assume on the basis of commonly known clinical data that a man who has known true freedom (not paid for by giving up safety and security but rather built on the basis of adequate safety and security) will not willingly or easily allow his freedom to be taken away from him. But we do not know that this is true for the person born into slavery. The events of the next decade should give us our answer. See discussion of this problem in (*5*).

[6] Perhaps the desire for prestige and respect from others is subsidiary to the desire for self-esteem or confidence in oneself. Observation of children seems to indicate that this is so, but clinical data give no clear support for such a conclusion.

[7] For more extensive discussion of normal self-esteem, as well as for reports of various researches, see (11).

HUMANISTIC PSYCHOLOGY **479**

[8] Clearly creative behavior, like painting, is like any other behavior in having multiple, determinants. It may be seen in 'innately creative' people whether they are satisfied or not, happy or unhappy, hungry or sated. Also it is clear that creative activity may be compensatory, ameliorative or purely economic. It is my impression (as yet unconfirmed) that it is possible to distinguish the artistic and intellectual products of basically satisfied people from those of basically unsatisfied people by inspection alone. In any case, here too we must distinguish, in a dynamic fashion, the overt behavior itself from its various motivations or purposes.

[9] I am aware that many psychologists md psychoanalysts use the term 'motivated' and 'determined' synonymously, e. g., Freud. But I consider this an obfuscating usage. Sharp distinctions are necessary for clarity of thought, and precision in experimentation.

[10] To be discussed fully in a subsequent publication.

[11] The interested reader is referred to the very excellent discussion of this point in Murray's Explorations in Personality (15).

[12] Note that acceptance of this theory necessitates basic revision of the Freudian theory.

[13] If we were to use the word 'sick' in this way, we should then also have to face squarely the relations of man to his society. One clear implication of our definition would be that (1) since a man is to be called sick who is basically thwarted, and (2) since such basic thwarting is made possible ultimately only by forces outside the individual, then (3) sickness in the individual must come ultimately from sickness in the society. The 'good' or healthy society would then be defined as one that permitted man's highest purposes to emerge by satisfying all his prepotent basic needs.

References
1. ADLER, A. Social interest. London: Faber & Faber, 1938.
2. CANNON, W. B. Wisdom of the body. New York: Norton, 1932.
3. FREUD, A. The ego and the mechanisms of defense. London: Hogarth, 1937.
4. FREUD, S. New introductory lectures on psychoanalysis. New York: Norton, 1933.
5. FROMM, E. Escape from freedom. New York: Farrar and Rinehart, 1941.
6. GOLDSTEIN, K. The organism. New York: American Book Co., 1939.
7. HORNEY, K. The neurotic personality of our time. New York: Norton, 1937.
8. KARDINER, A. The traumatic neuroses of war. New York: Hoeber, 1941.
9. LEVY, D. M. Primary affect hunger. *Amer. J. Psychiat.*, 1937, 94, 643-652.
10. MASLOW, A. H. Conflict, frustration, and the theory of threat. *J. abnorm. (soc.) Psychol.*, 1943, 38, 81-86.
11. ----------. Dominance, personality and social behavior in women. *J. soc. Psychol.*, 1939, 10, 3-39.
12. ----------. The dynamics of psychological security-insecurity. *Character & Pers.*, 1942, 10, 331-344.
13. ----------. A preface to motivation theory. *Psychosomatic Med.*, 1943, 5, 85-92.
14. ----------. & MITTLEMANN, B. *Principles of abnormal psychology*. New York: Harper & Bros., 1941.
15. MURRAY, H. A., *et al. Explorations in Personality*. New York: Oxford University Press, 1938.
16. PLANT, J. *Personality and the cultural pattern*. New York: Commonwealth Fund, 1937.
17. SHIRLEY, M. Children's adjustments to a strange situation. *J. abrnorm. (soc.) Psychol.*, 1942, 37, 201-217.
18. TOLMAN, E. C. *Purposive behavior in animals and men*. New York: Century, 1932.
19. WERTHEIMER, M. Unpublished lectures at the New School for Social Research.
20. YOUNG, P. T. *Motivation of behavior*. New York: John Wiley & Sons, 1936.
21. ----------. The experimental analysis of appetite. *Psychol. Bull.*, 1941, 38, 129-164.

480   THE MEANING OF LIFE

<u>REVIEW/ DISCUSSION QUESTIONS</u>

1.   How do you perceive that thinkers like Sechenov, Pavlov and Watson believe we find meaning in our life?

2.   What limits does Freud see in the psychology's ability (as a science) to provide meaning in life?

3.   Which approach would you use (Watson, Freud or Rogers) to care for the psychological wellbeing of a cancer patient? Why?

SECTION FOUR

THE FLAVOURING MOVEMENTS

CHAPTER 12:

PHENOMENOLOGICAL EXISTENTIAL PSYCHOLOGY

While existential psychology is often lumped into the category of *third force humanism,* it is in fact a movement that is intended to flavour all approaches to psychology. The benefit of this flavouring approach is that it contributes to the reflective mythopoeic component that is often lacking in the main schools of psychology. The philosophical fields of existentialism and phenomenology also connect the modern science of psychology with a framework for meaning making that is essential to human life. Therefore the existential approach allows psychology to contribute what the ancient religions used to provide to humanity.

As a general movement, phenomenology is interested with the understanding and description of existence without the aid of a biased construct. As such, it is an idealized attempt to understand the universe through the basic Socratic model of acknowledging our ignorance and building knowledge from a better foundation (Solomon, 1962). In essence, it acknowledges that what we consider to be *truth* is simply a story of our own construction.

In contrast to phenomenology, existentialism is concerned with human actions and meaning in life. When one views the historical relationship between the mythic construct of life as a context for meaning making in human action[73] it should not be surprising to see a marriage between these two philosophical movements (Solomon, 1962). With the long list of Phenomenological Existential thinkers, this book must limit its focus, however, it will review some ideas intrinsic to the key leaders: Kierkegaard, Heidegger, Sartre and Husserl. This will provide a foundation for the discussion of the psychological implications of this broad philosophical movement and its therapeutic implications.

Modern Phenomenological Existentialism

Existentialism as a philosophical movement really came into its own in the 19th and 20th centuries. Because of the diversity of positions associated with existentialism, a precise definition

---

73 A predecessor to the marriage of these schools was Fyodor Dostoyevsky who in 1864 published, *Notes From the Underground.* The main theme of Dostoyevsky was that a mythic pattern is needed in order to find peace in life, because the world itself is not patterned but chaotic. Therefore, if one followed Dostoyevsky's logic, the whole notion of phenomenology and the rebuilding of a mythic structure on the basis of reason and clear observation is absurd. Indeed the notion of the absurdity of life is the idea most often associated with Dostoyevsky. One can argue that his conclusion leads to the end statement that the content or organization of the mythic structure of ones life is not important (as far as any connection with reality), as long as it serves to give life meaning (for without it there is no hope for meaning in life and life is found to be utterly absurd) (Owen, 1994). In spite of Dostoyevsky's work, modern philosophy does find a marriage between phenomenology and existentialism.

484   THE MEANING OF LIFE

is impossible; however, it suggests one major theme—a stress on individual existence and, consequently, on subjectivity, individual freedom, and choice.

While most philosophers since Plato have held that the highest ethical good is universal, Soren Kierkegaard reacted against this tradition[74], insisting that the individual's highest good is to find his or her own unique vocation (Evans, 1990). Kierkegaard's conviction about individual choice as the basis of finding meaning in existence therefore brings an ancient concept into the modern age, clearly following the old model for life meaning as professed by the 20th - 5th centuries B.C.E. near eastern thinkers.

As a father of modern existentialism, Kierkegaard and those who have followed him have argued that there is no objective, rational basis for logical decisions (Solomon 1962). However, while Kierkegaard was himself influenced strongly by Christian thought and literature (and therefore recognized the role of "faith" as a basis of making such choices), his more atheistic disciples stress the importance of individualism in deciding questions of morality and truth. Most existentialists have therefore followed the clear Socratic model and held that rational clarity is desirable wherever possible. Yet, as good existentialists, they also acknowledged that life's most important questions are not accessible to reason or science, implicitly acknowledging the importance of a mythic construct in everyday living, and emphasizing the role of existential psychology in the study of the human psyche (Evans, 1990).

In contrast to Soren Kierkegaard, the eclectic German philosophy professor Edmund Husserl took the Socratic notion of recognizing our ignorance and rebuilding our mythic construct to the level of a fine art (Solomon 1962). In his often confusing and contradictory manner Husserl has succeeded formulating the basic movement known as phenomenology. Phenomenology holds as its principal purpose to study the phenomena, or appearances, of human experience while attempting to suspend all consideration of their objective reality or subjective association (Solomon 1962). The phenomena studied are those experienced in various acts of consciousness, mainly cognitive or perceptual acts, but also in such acts as valuation and aesthetic appreciation. Husserl intended to develop a philosophical method that was devoid of all presuppositions and that would describe phenomena by focusing exclusively on them, to the exclusion of all questions of their causal origins and their status outside the act of consciousness itself (Owen, 1994). His aim was to discover the essential structures and relationships of the phenomena as well as the acts of consciousness in which the phenomena appeared, and to do this by as faithful an exploration as possible, uncluttered by scientific or cultural presuppositions (Solomon, 1962). Husserl wished to

---

74 Kierkegaard argues that the beginning to discovering our unique and good existence is through the existential anxiety (dread or fear). Kierkegaard theorized that people are driven to discover their own responsibility for their choices and actions by this "dread". However, this driving force of dread can also be skewed to cause us to live inauthentic lives by not allowing us to think about such ideas as our own mortality. Therefore, reflection upon ones' own death is an important counterbalance to the use of the driving force of anxiety. Each person then has the responsibility to choose his or her direction and meaning in life, driven on by that unsettling force of "fear" (Owen, 1994).

PHENOMENOLOGICAL EXISTENTIAL PSYCHOLOGY   485

rebuild a purely logical and totally factual mythic structure in the great Socratic tradition. (For further readings on Husserl see Read For Yourself Section, this chapter.)

In his original conception of phenomenology, Husserl's idea of a presuppositionless science amounted to rejecting all antecedent commitments to theories of knowledge and following the Socratic notion of our own ignorance. This meant rejecting our social and individual mythic constructions that to this point in our existence have formulated and guided our sense of meaning and purpose (Husserl, 1962). He intended by this suspension, or bracketing, of extraneous commitments to go beyond the usual choices of Idealism and Realism, to "the things themselves" (Husserl, 1962). While Husserl was primarily interested in the difference between human knowledge (in the phenomenological sense) and belief (in the mythic psychological construct sense), his teachings had a profound effect on the philosophy of human behaviour.

Heidegger (as with J.P. Sartre) turned the phenomenological attention towards the problems of human practice, which was essentially the problem that "tripped up" Husserl (as he began to blur the notion of pure phenomenological knowledge in his later writings)(Solomon, 1972). For Heidegger, following also the line of Kiekegaard, the notion of freedom of choice, through which each human being creates his or her own meaning, is primary (Solomon). Because individuals are free to choose their own path, they must accept the risk and responsibility of their actions. Kierkegaard (in his Christian model) held that a feeling of general apprehension, which he called dread, is God's way of calling each individual to commit to a personally valid way of life.[75] Relatedly, Martin Heidegger felt that anxiety leads to the individual's confrontation with the impossibility of finding ultimate justification for his or her choices (Solomon). (For further information on Heidegger's perspective on Phenomenology see Read For Yourself Section, this chapter).

It is within this marriage of Kierkegaardian and Heidegger philosophies that the modern notion of Phenomenological Existentialism stems (Solomon, 1962) (Owen, 1994). However, this combination of ideas is not a new one, but indeed a marriage of ancient Near-Eastern and Socratic ideologies in the very human search for meaning.

Meaning in Psychology

This reunion of the phenomenological and existential in the twentieth century was inevitably linked with the new role of psychology. During this time a whole series of psychologists immersed themselves in the issue of human meaning, and while these scholars often did not draw upon the sharp philosophical insights of Heidegger, Sartre and Kierkegaard, they often held a clear sense of how one forms meaning in existence. It is therefore important to review those who

---

75 Through this model of "dread" or "fear" it is clear that Kiekegaard was strongly influenced by the 10th century B.C.E. thinkers, for the Semitic proverb, "The fear of the Lord is the beginning of wisdom" (Prov. 1:7) was clearly at the heart of Kiekegaard's writing about the concept of fear and dread. Indeed, the Kiekegaardian model of "a student of reality" vs. "a student of possibility" affirms that Kierkegaard had this ancient proverb in mind while reflecting upon the function of dread.

486 THE MEANING OF LIFE

have influenced this line of inquiry from the perspective of self-actualisation to transcendence of the self.

In general, most early psychologists dealing with the issue of "meaning" fell into one of the two main camps of either self-actualisation or self-transcendence. While each is of course not totally mutually exclusive, and it is clear that both are existential (to some extent) in nature, the philosophical structure of each camp is very different.

The self-actualisation psychologists are those that are the least existential, as their basic philosophy is derived from the notion that essence precedes existence (in contrast to the essential existential idea of existence preceding essence). Such psychologists are primarily concerned with identifying one's essence potentials and actualising them within a mythic structure. Eric Fromm, for example, contends that the meaningful life arises from productivity, which is clearly in line with the ancient notion of "there is nothing better than for a person to find satisfaction in work"[76] (MacCoby, 2002). Abraham Maslow also emphasizes discovering one's needs and powers and developing oneself (Annlson, 2000), (essence preceding existence). For self-actualisation psychologists, "meaning" is experienced when one is doing what one is meant to do (Kiel, 1999).

Rollo May represents a psychological step towards the core notion of existentialism in existence preceding essence and the role of mythic structures (May, 1991). However, May does retain the idea that a minor essence (in bodily experience) is the basis of existence (in choice) that leads to essence (in human meaning and self definition). For May (1991), meaning is experienced by a person centered in him/herself, who is able to live by his/her highest values, who knows his own mythic structure and who will choose a direction and stance in life (Rabinowitz, Good, & Cozad, 1989).

In a different vein altogether, James Fowler examined the development and structure of personal mythopoeics and their role in the meaning making process. Fowler's approach is unique in the realm of existential psychology since he borrows the developmental pattern of Kholberg[77], and the childhood insights of Piaget (Fowler, 1981). In this thorough examination Fowler argues that there is a predictable pattern of mythic structural formation prior to age 12. Then, once *formal operations* emerges within adolescence, the existential development of the person is largely up to the individual (Fowler). Interestingly, Fowler (1981) does note that the highest level of meaning making actually requires a Socratic- or Husserlian-style revisiting and recreation of childhood mythic structures (Fowler).

In taking another step towards the prime existential credo we find the Viennese psychiatrist Viktor Frankl. For Frankl, meaning only comes by responding to the demands of the situation at hand, discovering and committing oneself to one's own unique task in life, and by allowing

---

76 Author's translation of Quoheleth 3:13. Snaith, N.H. ed. *Biblia Hebraica*. London: British and Foreign Bible Society.

77 See Read For Yourself Section, this chapter– Stages of Existential Development, for a full description of Fowler's theories, combined with other areas of research relating to identity theory.

oneself to experience or trust in an ultimate meaning (within a mythic structure) (Lantz, 2000). Frankl therefore combines both the personal and logical recreation of a mythic structure (which is the natural growth of the phenomenological foundation) and the existential task of choosing to dedicate oneself to an end outside the self. In a sense, then, we see the emergence of phenomenological existentialism forming into a specific psychological model for human experience (Lantz). Such a birth then leads us to the present age and the two leading phenomenological/ existential thinkers in psychology: Emmy van Deurzen-Smith and Ernesto Spinelli.

Emmy van Deurzen-Smith is in many ways the instigator and formalizing drive behind the professional movement of existential psychoanalysis (Taylor, 1995). Until the late 20th century there was really no one bastion of knowledge about existential psychotherapy within the Anglo-American world, but rather there was the smattering of intellectuals and authors honest enough to delve into the issues relating to existentialism, the mind and phenomenology. However, through Van Deurzen-Smith's work with Antioch University and eventually the emergence of the Regent's College school of Psychotherapy all that was changed. Through the strong influence of Van Deurzen-Smith there is now a formal program for doing what psychology set out to do in the first place, "understand how people function in themselves, in the world, in relationship, and how one can enable people to do it better" (Taylor). If Van Deurzen-Smith is the modern political engine for existential psychotherapy, then Ernesto Spinelli is the prime international theorist.

While Ernesto Spinelli notes that existential psychotherapy flourished in Continental Europe during the 20th century (Spinelli, 2003), it is truly his work that lays the foundation for its rising influence on the Anglo-American scene. Undoubtedly Spinelli is influenced by the Continental work of Ludwig Binswanger and Medard Boss (Spinelli, 2003). At the same time, Spinelli's insights from his own professional experience and his encyclopaedic knowledge of Heidegger's philosophy are merged to further the field.

Foremost in Spinelli is the relational emphasis of human experience and self-definition. In addition, Spinelli reflects modern neuroscience's understanding of memory to assert that an individual's past is not so much a "causal agent" as it is an "interpretive means by which one's present is validated and one's future ... orientations are clarified" (Spinelli, 2003). Spinelli's insights into the interpretive aspects of human experience clearly display his agreement with the prominent ancient models and the contributions of modern science and philosophy. Through his insightful synthesis of all these areas of human knowledge the formation of a phenomenological existential psychotherapy is taking hold across the Anglo-American world.

READ AND DECIDE FOR YOURSELF:

Excerpts from:

THE CRISIS OF EUROPEAN SCIENCES
(EDMUND HUSSERL)

THE BASIC PROBLEMS OF PHENOMENOLOGY
(MARTIN HEIDEGGER)

EXCERPTS FROM VICTOR FRANKL

QUOTATIONS FROM ROLLO MAY

EXISTENTIAL DEVELOPMENT OF JAMES FOWLER

THE CRISIS OF EUROPEAN SCIENCES

Edmund Husserl (1937)

Source: The Crisis of European Sciences and Transcendental Phenomenology (1954).

Sections 22 - 25 and 57 – 68. [78]

Part II: Clarification of the Origin of the Modern Opposition between Physicalistic Objectivism and Transcendental Subjectivism. ...

§ 22. Locke's naturalistic-epistemological psychology.

IT IS IN THE EMPIRICIST development, as we know, that the new psychology, which was required as a correlate to pure natural science when the latter was separated off, is brought to its first concrete execution, Thus it is concerned with investigations of introspective psychology in the field of the soul, which has now been separated from the body, as well as with physiological and psychophysical explanations. On the other hand, this psychology is of service to a theory of knowledge which, compared with the Cartesian one, is completely new and very differently worked out. In Locke's great work this is the actual intent from the start. It offers itself as a new attempt to accomplish precisely what Descartes's Meditations intended to accomplish: an epistemological grounding of the objectivity of the objective sciences. The sceptical posture of this intent is evident from the beginning in questions like those of the scope, the extent, and the degrees of certainty of human knowledge. Locke senses nothing of the depths of the Cartesian epoche [critique] and of the reduction to the ego. He simply takes over the ego as soul, which becomes acquainted, in the self-evidence of self-experience, with its inner states, acts, and capacities. Only what inner self-experience shows, only our own "ideas," are immediately, self-evidently given. Everything in the external world is inferred.

What comes first, then, is the internal-psychological analysis purely on the basis of the inner experience - whereby use is made, quite naively, of the experiences of other human beings and of the conception of self experience as what belongs to me one human being among human beings; that is, the objective validity of inferences to others is used; just as, in general, the whole investigation proceeds as an objective psychological one, indeed even has recourse to the physiological - when it is precisely all this objectivity, after all, which is in question.

The actual problem of Descartes, that of transcending egological (interpreted as internal-psychological) validities, including all manners of inference pertaining to the external world, the

---

78 Accessed: http://www.marxists.org/reference/subject/philosophy/works/ge/husserl.htm

490 THE MEANING OF LIFE

question of how these, which are, after all, themselves cogitationes in the encapsuled soul, are able to justify assertions about extrapsychic being - these problems disappear in Locke or turn into the problem of the psychological genesis of the real experiences of validity or of the faculties belonging to them. That sense-data, extracted from the arbitrariness of their production, are affections from the outside and announce bodies in the external world, is not a problem for him but something taken for granted.

Especially portentous for future psychology and theory of knowledge is the fact that Locke makes no use of the Cartesian first introduction of the cogitatio as cogitatio of cogitata - that is, intentionality; he does not recognise it as a subject of investigation (indeed the most authentic subject of the foundation-laying investigations) . He is blind to the whole distinction. The soul is something self-contained and real by itself, as is a body; in naive naturalism the soul is now taken to be like an isolated space, like a writing tablet, in his famous simile, on which psychic data come and go. This data-sensationalism, together with the doctrine of outer and inner sense, dominates psychology and the theory of knowledge for centuries, even up to the present day; and in spite of the familiar struggle against "psychic atomism," the basic sense of this doctrine does not change. Of course one speaks quite unavoidably, even in the Lockean terminology, of perceptions, representations "of" things, or of believing "in something," willing "something," and the like. But no consideration is given to the fact that in the perceptions, in the experiences of consciousness themselves, that of which we are conscious is included as such - that the perception is in itself a perception of something, of "this tree."

How is the life of the soul, which is through and through a life of consciousness, the intentional life of the ego, which has objects of which it is conscious, deals with them through knowing, valuing, etc. - how is it supposed to be seriously investigated if intentionality is overlooked? How can the problems of reason be attacked at all? Can they be attacked at all as psychological problems? In the end, behind the psychological-epistemological problems, do we not find the problems of the "ego" of the Cartesian epoche, touched upon but not grasped by Descartes? Perhaps these are not unimportant questions, which give a direction in advance to the reader who thinks for himself. In any case they are an indication of what will become a serious problem in later parts of this work, or rather will serve as a way to a philosophy which can really be carried through "without prejudice," a philosophy with the most radical grounding in its setting of problems, in its method, and in work which is systematically accomplished.

It is also of interest that the Lockean scepticism in respect to the rational ideal of science, and its limitation of the scope of the new sciences (which are supposed to retain their validity), leads to a new sort of agnosticism. It is not that the possibility of science is completely denied, as in ancient scepticism, although again unknowable things-in-themselves are assumed. But our human science depends exclusively on our representations and concept-formations; by means of these we may, of course, make inferences extending to what is transcendent; but in principle we cannot obtain actual representations of the things-in-themselves, representations which adequately express the proper essence of these things. We have adequate representations and knowledge only of what is in our own soul.

PHENOMENOLOGICAL EXISTENTIAL PSYCHOLOGY 491

§ 23. Berkeley. David Hume's psychology as fictionalistic theory of knowledge: the "bankruptcy" of philosophy and science.

LOCKE'S NAÏVETÉS and inconsistencies lead to a rapid further development of his empiricism, which pushes toward a paradoxical idealism and finally ends in a consummated absurdity. The foundation continues to be sensationalism and what appears to be obvious, i.e., that the sole indubitable ground of all knowledge is self-experience and its realm of immanent data. Starting from here, Berkeley reduces the bodily things which appear in natural experience to the complexes of sense-data themselves through which they appear. No inference is thinkable, according to Berkeley, through which conclusions could be drawn from these sense-data about anything but other such data. It could only be inductive inference, i.e., inference growing out of the association of ideas. Matter existing in itself, a je ne sais quoi, according to Locke, is for Berkeley a philosophical invention. It is also significant that at the same time he dissolves the manner in which rational natural science builds concepts and transforms it into a sensationalistic critique of knowledge.

In this direction, Hume goes on to the end. All categories of objectivity - the scientific ones through which an objective, extrapsychic world is thought in scientific life, and the prescientific ones through which it is thought in everyday life - are fictions. First come the mathematical concepts: number, magnitude, continuum, geometrical figure, etc. We would say that they are methodically necessary idealisations of what is given intuitively. For Hume, however, they are fictions; and the same is true, accordingly, of the whole of supposedly apodictic mathematics. The origin of these fictions can be explained perfectly well psychologically (i.e., in terms of immanent sensationalism), namely, through the immanent lawfulness of the associations and the relations between ideas. But even the categories of the prescientific world, of the straightforwardly intuited world - those of corporeity (i.e., the identity of persisting bodies supposedly found in immediate, experiencing intuition), as well as the supposedly experienced identity of the person - are nothing but fictions. We say, for example, "that" tree over there, and distinguish from it its changing manners of appearing. But immanently, psychically, there is nothing there but these "manners of appearing." These are complexes of data, and again and again other complexes of data - "bound together," regulated, to be sure, by association, which explains the illusion of experiencing something identical. The same is true of the person: an identical "I" is not a datum but a ceaselessly changing bundle of data. Identity is a psychological fiction. To the fictions of this sort also belongs causality, or necessary succession. Immanent experience exhibits only a post hoc. The propter hoc, the necessity of the succession, is a fictive misconstruction. Thus, in Hume's Treatise, the world in general, nature, the universe of identical bodies, the world of identical persons, and accordingly also objective science, which knows these in their objective truth, are transformed into fiction. To be consistent, we must say: reason, knowledge, including that of true values, of pure ideals of every sort, including the ethical - all this is fiction. This is indeed, then, a bankruptcy of objective knowledge. Hume ends up, basically, in a solipsism. For how could inferences from data to other data ever reach beyond the immanent sphere? Of course, Hume did not ask the question, or at least did not say a word, about the status of the reason -

492   THE MEANING OF LIFE

Hume's - which established this theory as truth, which carried out these analyses of the soul and demonstrated these laws of association. How do rules of associative ordering "bind"? Even if we knew about them, would not that knowledge itself be another datum on the tablet?

Like all scepticism, all irrationalism, the Humean sort cancels itself out. Astounding as Hume's genius is, it is the more regrettable that a correspondingly great philosophical ethos is not joined with it. This is evident in the fact that Hume takes care, throughout his whole presentation, blandly to disguise or interpret as harmless his absurd results, though he does paint a picture (in the final chapter of Volume I of the Treatise) of the immense embarrassment in which the consistent theoretical philosopher gets involved. Instead of taking up the struggle against absurdity, instead of unmasking those supposedly obvious views upon which this sensationalism, and psychologism in general, rests, in order to penetrate to a coherent self-understanding and a genuine theory of knowledge, he remains in the comfortable and very impressive role of academic scepticism. Through this attitude he has become the father of a still effective, unhealthy positivism which hedges before philosophical abysses, or covers them over on the surface, and comforts itself with the successes of the positive sciences and their psychologistic elucidation.

§ 24. The genuine philosophical motif hidden in the absurdity of Hume's scepticism: the shaking of objectivism.

LET US STOP FOR A MOMENT. Why does Hume's Treatise (in comparison to which the Essay Concerning Human Understanding is badly watered down) represent such a great historical event? What happened there? The Cartesian radicalism of presuppositionlessness, with the goal of tracing genuine scientific knowledge back to the ultimate sources of validity and of grounding it absolutely upon them, required reflections directed toward the subject, required the regression to the knowing ego in his immanence. No matter how little one may have approved of Descartes's epistemological procedure, one could no longer escape the necessity of this requirement. But was it possible to improve upon Descartes's procedure? Was his goal, that of grounding absolutely the new philosophical rationalism, still attainable after the sceptical attacks? Speaking in favour of this from the start was the immense force of discoveries in mathematics and natural science that were proceeding at breakneck speed. And so all who themselves took part in these sciences through research or study were already certain that its truth, its method, bore the stamp of finality and exemplariness. And now empiricist scepticism brings to light what was already present in the Cartesian fundamental investigation but was not worked out, namely, that all knowledge of the world, the prescientific as well as the scientific, is an enormous enigma. It was easy to follow Descartes, when he went back to the apodictic ego, in interpreting the latter as soul, in taking the primal self-evidence to be the self-evidence of "inner perception." And what was more plausible than the way in which Locke illustrated the reality of the detached soul and the history running its course within it, its internal genesis, by means of the "white paper" and thus naturalised this reality? But now, could the "idealism" of Berkeley and Hume, and finally scepticism with all its absurdity, be avoided? What a paradox! Nothing could cripple the peculiar force of the rapidly growing and, in their own accomplishments, unassailable exact sciences or the belief in their truth. And yet, as soon as one took into account that they are the accomplishments of the consciousness of knowing subjects, their self-evidence and clarity were transformed into incomprehensible absurdity. No offence was taken if, in Descartes, immanent sensibility engendered pictures of the world; but in Berkeley this sensibility engendered the world of bodies itself; and in Hume the entire soul, with its "impressions" and "ideas," the forces belonging to it, conceived of by analogy to physical forces, its laws of association (as parallels to the law of gravity!), engendered the whole world, the world itself, not merely something like a picture - though, to be sure, this product was merely a fiction, a representation put together inwardly which was actually quite vague. And this is true of the world of the rational sciences as well as that of experientia vaga.

Was there not, here, in spite of the absurdity which may have been due to particular aspects of the presuppositions, a hidden and unavoidable truth to be felt? Was this not the revelation of a completely new way of assessing the objectivity of the world and its whole ontic meaning and, correlatively, that of the objective sciences, a way which did not attack their own validity but did attack their philosophical or metaphysical claim, that of absolute truth? Now at last it was possible and necessary to become aware of the fact - which had remained completely unconsidered in these sciences - that the life of consciousness is a life of accomplishment: the accomplishment, right or wrong, of ontic meaning, even sensibly intuited meaning, and all the more of scientific meaning. Descartes had not pondered the fact that, just as the sensible world, that of everyday life, is the cogitatum of sensing cogitationes, so the scientific world is the cogitatum of scientific cogitationes; and he had not noticed the circle in which he was involved when he presupposed, in his proof of the existence of God, the possibility of inferences transcending the ego, when this possibility, after all, was supposed to be established only through this proof. The thought was quite remote from him that the whole world could itself be a cogitatum arising out of the universal synthesis of the variously flowing cogitationes and that, on a higher level, the rational accomplishment of the scientific cogitationes, built upon the former ones, could be constitutive of the scientific world. But was this thought not suggested, now, by Berkeley and Hume - under the presupposition that the absurdity of their empiricism lay only in a belief that was supposedly obvious, through which immanent reason had been driven out in advance? Through Berkeley's and Hume's revival and radicalisation of the Cartesian fundamental problem, "dogmatic" objectivism was, from the point of view of our critical presentation, shaken to the foundations. This is true not only of the mathematising objectivism, so inspiring to people of the time, which actually ascribed to the world itself a mathematical-rational in-itself (which we copy, so to speak, better and better in our more or less perfect theories); it was also true of the general objectivism which had been dominant for millennia.

§ 25. The "transcendental" motif in rationalism: Kant's conception of a transcendental philosophy.

AS IS KNOWN, Hume has a particular place in history also because of the turn he brought about in the development of Kant's thinking. Kant himself says, in the much-quoted words, that Hume roused him from his dogmatic slumbers and gave his investigations in the field of speculative philosophy a different direction. Was it, then, the historical mission of Kant to

494   THE MEANING OF LIFE

experience the shaking of objectivism, of which I just spoke, and to undertake in his transcendental philosophy the solution of the task before which Hume drew back? The answer must be negative. It is a new sort of transcendental subjectivism which begins with Kant and changes into new forms in the systems of German idealism. Kant does not belong to the development which expands in a continuous line from Descartes through Locke, and he is not the successor of Hume. His interpretation of the Humean scepticism and the way in which he reacts against it are determined by his own provenance in the Wolffian school. The "revolution of the way of thinking" motivated by Hume's impulse is not directed against empiricism but against post-Cartesian rationalism's way of thinking, whose great consummator was Leibniz and which was given its systematic textbook-like presentation, its most effective and by far most convincing form, by Christian Wolff.

First of all, what is the meaning of the "dogmatism," taken quite generally, that Kant uproots? Although the Meditations continued to have their effect on post-Cartesian philosophy, the passionate radicalism which drove them was not passed on to Descartes's successors. They were quite prepared to accept what Descartes only wished to establish, and found so hard to establish, by inquiring back into the ultimate source of all knowledge: namely, the absolute metaphysical validity of the objective sciences, or, taking these together, of philosophy as the one objective universal science; or, what comes to the same thing, the right of the knowing ego to let its rational constructs, in virtue of the self-evidences occurring in its mens, count as nature with a meaning transcending this ego. The new conception of the world of bodies, self-enclosed as nature, and the natural sciences related to them, the correlative conception of the self-enclosed souls and the task, related to them, of a new psychology with a rational method according to the mathematical model - all this had established itself. In every direction rational philosophy was under construction; of primary interest were discoveries, theories, the rigour of their inferences, and correspondingly the general problem of method and its perfection. Thus knowledge was very much discussed, and from a scientifically general point of view. This reflection on knowledge, however, was not transcendental reflection but rather a reflection on the praxis of knowledge and was thus similar to the reflection carried out by one who works in any other practical sphere of interest, the kind which is expressed in the general propositions of a technology. It is a matter of what we are accustomed to call logic, though in a traditional, very narrow, and limited sense. Thus we can say quite correctly (broadening the meaning): it is a matter of a logic as a theory of norms and a technology with the fullest universality, to the end of attaining a universal philosophy.

The thematic direction was thus twofold: on the one hand, toward a systematic universe of "logical laws," the theoretical totality of the truths destined to function as norms for all judgments which shall be capable of being objectively true - and to this belongs, in addition to the old formal logic, also arithmetic, all of pure analytic mathematics, i.e., the mathesis universalis of Leibniz, and in general everything that is purely a priori.

On the other hand, the thematic direction was toward general considerations about those who make judgments as those striving for objective truth: how they are to make normative use of those

PHENOMENOLOGICAL EXISTENTIAL PSYCHOLOGY   495

laws so that the self-evidence through which a judgment is certified as objectively true can appear, and similarly about the ways and temptations of failure, etc.

Now clearly, in all the laws which are in the broader sense "logical," beginning with the principle of non-contradiction, metaphysical truth was contained eo ipso. The systematically worked-out theory of these laws had, of itself, the meaning of a general ontology. What happened here scientifically was the work of pure reason operating exclusively with concepts innate in the knowing soul. That these concepts, that logical laws, that pure rational lawfulness in general contained metaphysical-objective truth was "obvious." Occasionally appeal was made to God as a guarantee, in remembrance of Descartes, with little concern for the fact that it was rational metaphysics which first had to establish God's existence.

Over against the faculty of pure a priori thinking, that of pure reason, stood that of sensibility, the faculty of outer and inner experience. The subject, affected in outer experience from "outside," thereby becomes certain of affecting objects, but in order to know them in their truth he needs pure reason, i.e., the system of norms in which reason displays itself, as the 'logic" for all true knowledge of the objective world. Such is the typical rationalist conception.

As for Kant, who had been influenced by empiricist psychology: Hume had made him sensitive to the fact that between the pure truths of reason and metaphysical objectivity there remained a gulf of incomprehensibility, namely, as to how precisely these truths of reason could really guarantee the knowledge of things. Even the model rationality of the mathematical natural sciences was transformed into an enigma. That it owed its rationality, which was in fact quite indubitable - that is, its method - to the normative a priori of pure logico-mathematical reason, and that the latter, in its disciplines, exhibited an unassailable pure rationality, remained unquestioned. Natural science is, to be sure, not purely rational insofar as it has need of outer experience, sensibility; but everything in it that is rational it owes to pure reason and its setting of norms; only through them can there be rationalised experience. As for sensibility, on the other hand, it had generally been assumed that it gives rise to the merely sensible data, precisely as a result of affection from the outside. And yet one acted as if the experiential world of the prescientific man - the world not yet logicised by mathematics - was the world pre-given by mere sensibility.

Hume had shown that we naively read causality into this world and think that we grasp necessary succession in intuition. The same is true of everything that makes the body of the everyday surrounding world into an identical thing with identical properties, relations, etc. (and Hume had in fact worked this out in detail in the Treatise, which was unknown to Kant). Data and complexes of data come and go, but the thing, presumed to be simply experienced sensibly, is not something sensible which persists through this alteration. The sensationalist thus declares it to be a fiction.

He is substituting, we shall say, mere sense-data for perception, which after all places things (everyday things) before our eyes. In other words, he overlooks the fact that mere sensibility, related to mere data of sense, cannot account for objects of experience. Thus he overlooks the fact that these objects of experience point to a hidden mental accomplishment and to the problem of

496   THE MEANING OF LIFE

what kind of an accomplishment this can be. From the very start, after all, it must be a kind which enables the objects of prescientific experience, through logic, mathematics, mathematical natural science, to be knowable with objective validity, i.e., with a necessity which can be accepted by and is binding for everyone.

But Kant says to himself: undoubtedly things appear, but only because the sense-data, already brought together in certain ways, in concealment, through a priori forms, are made logical in the course of their alteration - without any appeal to reason as manifested in logic and mathematics, without its being brought into normative function. Now is this quasi-logical function something that is psychologically accidental? If we think of it as absent, can a mathematics, a logic of nature, ever have the possibility of knowing objects through mere sense-data?

These are, if I am not mistaken, the inwardly guiding thoughts of Kant. Kant now undertakes, in fact, to show, through a regressive procedure, that if common experience is really to be experience of objects of nature, objects which can really be knowable with objective truth, i.e., scientifically, in respect to their being and non-being, their being-such and being-otherwise, then the intuitively appearing world must already be a construct of the faculties of "pure intuition" and "pure reason," the same faculties that express themselves in explicit thinking in mathematics and logic.

In other words, reason has a twofold way of functioning and showing itself. One way is its systematic self-exposition, self-revelation in free and pure mathematising, in the practice of the pure mathematical sciences. Here it presupposes the forming character of "pure intuition," which belongs to sensibility itself. The objective result of both faculties is pure mathematics as theory. The other way is that of reason constantly functioning in concealment, reason ceaselessly rationalising sense-data and always having them as already rationalised. Its objective result is the sensibly intuited world of objects - the empirical presupposition of all natural-scientific thinking, i.e., the thinking which, through manifest mathematical reason, consciously gives norms to the experience of the surrounding world. Like the intuited world of bodies, the whole world of natural science (and with it the dualistic world which can be known scientifically) is a subjective construct of our intellect, only the material of the sense-data arises from a transcendent affection by "things in themselves." The latter are in principle inaccessible to objective scientific knowledge. For according to this theory, man's science, as an accomplishment bound by the interplay of the subjective faculties "sensibility" and "reason" (or, as Kant says here, "understanding"), cannot explain the origin, the "cause," of the factual manifolds of sense-data. The ultimate presuppositions of the possibility and actuality of objective knowledge cannot be objectively knowable.

Whereas natural science had pretended to be a branch of philosophy, the ultimate science of what is, and had believed itself capable of knowing, through its rationality, what is in itself, beyond the subjectivity of the factualities of knowledge, for Kant, now, objective science, as an accomplishment remaining within subjectivity, is separated off from his philosophical theory. The latter, as a theory of the accomplishments necessarily carried out within subjectivity, and thus as a theory of the possibility and scope of objective knowledge, reveals the naivete of the supposed rational philosophy of nature-in-itself.

We know how this critique is for Kant nevertheless the beginning of a philosophy in the old sense, for the universe of being, thus extending even to the rationally unknowable in-itself - how, under the titles "critique of practical reason" and "critique of judgment," he not only limits philosophical claims but also believes he is capable of opening ways toward the "scientifically" unknowable in-itself. Here we shall not go into this. What interests us now is - speaking in formal generality - that Kant, reacting against the data-positivism of Hume (as he understands it) outlines a great, systematically constructed, and in a new way still scientific philosophy in which the Cartesian turn to conscious subjectivity works itself out in the form of a transcendental subjectivism.

Irrespective of the truth of the Kantian philosophy, about which we need not pass judgment here, we must not pass over the fact that Hume, as he is understood by Kant, is not the real Hume.

Kant speaks of the "Humean problem." What is the actual problem, the one which drives Hume himself? We find it when we transform Hume's sceptical theory, his total claim, back into his problem, extending it to those consequences which do not quite find their complete expression in the theory - although it is difficult to suppose that a genius with a spirit like Hume's did not see these consequences, which are not expressly drawn and not theoretically treated. If we proceed in this way, we find nothing less than this universal problem:

How is the naive obviousness of the certainty of the world, the certainty in which we live - and, what is more, the certainty of the everyday world as well as that of the sophisticated theoretical constructions built upon this everyday world - to be made comprehensible?

What is, in respect to sense and validity, the "objective world," objectively true being, and also the objective truth of science, once we have seen universally with Hume (and in respect to nature even with Berkeley) that "world" is a validity which has sprung up within subjectivity, indeed - speaking from my point of view, who am now philosophising - one which has sprung up within my subjectivity, with all the content it ever counts as having for me?

The naivete of speaking about "objectivity" without ever considering subjectivity as experiencing, knowing, and actually concretely accomplishing, the naivete of the scientist of nature or of the world in general, who is blind to the fact that all the truths he attains as objective truths and the objective world itself as the substratum of his formulae (the everyday world of experience as well as the higher-level conceptual world of knowledge) are his own life-construct developed within himself - this naivete is naturally no longer possible as soon as life becomes the point of focus. And must this liberation not come to anyone who seriously immerses himself in the Treatise and, after unmasking Hume's naturalistic presuppositions, becomes conscious of the power of his motivation?

But how is this most radical subjectivism, which subjectivises the world itself, comprehensible? The world-enigma in the deepest and most ultimate sense, the enigma of a world whose being is being through subjective accomplishment, and this with the self-evidence that another world cannot be at all conceivable - that, and nothing else, is Hume's problem.

498   THE MEANING OF LIFE

Kant, however, for whom, as can easily be seen, so many presuppositions are "obviously" valid, presuppositions which in the Humean sense are included within this world-enigma, never penetrated to the enigma itself. For his set of problems stands on the ground of the rationalism extending from Descartes through Leibniz to Wolff.

In this way, through the problem of rational natural science which primarily guides and determines Kant's thinking, we seek to make understandable Kant's position, so difficult to interpret, in relation to his historical setting. What particularly interests us now - speaking first in formal generality - is the fact that in reaction to the Humean data-positivism, which in his fictionalism gives up philosophy as a science, a great and systematically constructed scientific philosophy appears for the first time since Descartes - a philosophy which must be called transcendental subjectivism.

§ 26. Preliminary discussion of the concept of the "transcendental" which guides us here.

I SHOULD LIKE TO NOTE the following right away: the expression "transcendental philosophy" has been much used since Kant, even as a general title for universal philosophies whose concepts are oriented toward those of the Kantian type. I myself use the word "transcendental" in the broadest sense for the original motif, discussed in detail above, which through Descartes confers meaning upon all modern philosophies, the motif which, in all of them, seeks to come to itself, so to speak - seeks to attain the genuine and pure form of its task and its systematic development. It is the motif of inquiring back into the ultimate source of all the formations of knowledge, the motif of the knower's reflecting upon himself and his knowing life in which all the scientific structures that are valid for him occur purposefully, are stored up as acquisitions, and have become and continue to become freely available. Working itself out radically, it is the motif of a universal philosophy which is grounded purely in this source and thus ultimately grounded. This source bears the title I-myself, with all of my actual and possible knowing life and, ultimately, my concrete life in general. The whole transcendental set of problems circles around the relation of this, my "I" - the "ego" - to what it is at first taken for granted to be - my soul - and, again, around the relation of this ego and my conscious life to the world of which I am conscious and whose true being I know through my own cognitive structures.

Of course this most general concept of the "transcendental" cannot be supported by documents; it is not to be gained through the internal exposition and comparison of the individual systems. Rather, it is a concept acquired by pondering the coherent history of the entire philosophical modern period: the concept of its task which is demonstrable only in this way, lying within it as the driving force of its development, striving forward from vague dynamis towards its energeia.

This is only a preliminary indication, which has already been prepared to a certain extent by our historical analysis up to this point; our subsequent presentations are to establish the justification for our kind of "teleological" approach to history and its methodical function for the definitive construction of a transcendental philosophy which satisfies its most proper meaning. This preliminary indication of a radical transcendental subjectivism will naturally seem strange and arouse scepticism. I welcome this, if this scepticism bespeaks, not the prior resolve of rejection, but rather a free withholding of any judgment.

§ 27. The philosophy of Kant and his followers seen from the perspective of our guiding concept of the "transcendental." The task of taking a critical position.

RETURNING AGAIN TO KANT: his system can certainly be characterised, in the general sense defined, as one of "transcendental philosophy," although it is far from accomplishing a truly radical grounding of philosophy, the totality of all sciences. Kant never permitted himself to enter the vast depths of the Cartesian fundamental investigation, and his own set of problems never caused him to seek in these depths for ultimate groundings and decisions. Should I, in the following presentations, succeed - as I hope - in awakening the insight that a transcendental philosophy is the more genuine, and better fulfils its vocation as philosophy, the more radical it is and, finally, that it comes to its actual and true existence, to its actual and true beginning, only when the philosopher has penetrated to a clear understanding of himself as the subjectivity functioning as primal source, we should still have to recognise, on the other hand, that Kant's philosophy is on the way to this, that it is in accord with the formal, general sense of a transcendental philosophy in our definition. It is a philosophy which, in opposition to prescientific and scientific objectivism, goes back to knowing subjectivity as the primal locus of all objective formations of sense and ontic validities, undertakes to understand the existing world as a structure of sense and validity, and in this way seeks to set in motion an essentially new type of scientific attitude and a new type of philosophy. In fact, if we do not count the negativistic, sceptical philosophy of a Hume, the Kantian system is the first attempt, and one carried out with impressive scientific seriousness, at a truly universal transcendental philosophy meant to be a rigorous science in a sense of scientific rigour which has only now been discovered and which is the only genuine sense.

Something similar holds, we can say in advance, for the great continuations and revisions of Kantian transcendentalism in the great systems of German Idealism. They all share the basic conviction that the objective sciences (no matter how much they, and particularly the exact sciences, may consider themselves, in virtue of their obvious theoretical and practical accomplishments, to be in possession of the only true method and to be treasure houses of ultimate truths) are not seriously sciences at all, not cognitions ultimately grounded, i.e., not ultimately, theoretically responsible for themselves - and that they are not, then, cognitions of what exists in ultimate truth. This can be accomplished according to German Idealism only by a transcendental-subjective method and, carried through as a system, transcendental philosophy. As was already the case with Kant, the opinion is not that the self-evidence of the positive-scientific method is an illusion and its accomplishment an illusory accomplishment but rather that this self-evidence is itself a problem; that the objective-scientific method rests upon a never questioned, deeply concealed subjective ground whose philosophical elucidation will for the first time reveal the true meaning of the accomplishments of positive science and, correlatively, the true ontic meaning of the objective world - precisely as a transcendental-subjective meaning.

500   THE MEANING OF LIFE

Now in order to be able to understand the position of Kant and of the systems of transcendental idealism proceeding from him, within modern philosophy's teleological unity of meaning, and thus to make progress in our own self-understanding, it is necessary to critically get closer to the style of Kant's scientific attitude and to clarify the lack of radicalism we are attacking in his philosophising. It is with good reason that we pause over Kant, a significant turning point in modern history. The critique to be directed against him will reflect back and elucidate all earlier philosophical history, namely, in respect to the general meaning of scientific discipline which all earlier philosophies strove to realize - as the only meaning which lay and could possibly lie within their spiritual horizon. Precisely in this way a more profound concept - the most important of all - of "objectivism" will come to the fore (more important than the one we were able to define earlier), and with it the genuinely radical meaning of the opposition between objectivism and transcendentalism.

Yet, over and above this, the more concrete critical analyses of the conceptual structures of the Kantian turn, and the contrast between it and the Cartesian turn, will set in motion our own concurrent thinking in such a way as to place us, gradually and of its own accord, before the final turn and the final decisions. We ourselves shall be drawn into an inner transformation through which we shall come face to face with, to direct experience of, the long-felt but constantly concealed dimension of the "transcendental." The ground of experience, opened up in its infinity, will then become the fertile soil of a methodical working philosophy, with the self-evidence, furthermore, that all conceivable philosophical and scientific problems of the past are to be posed and decided by starting from this ground.

PHENOMENOLOGICAL EXISTENTIAL PSYCHOLOGY   501

THE BASIC PROBLEMS OF PHENOMENOLOGY

Martin Heidegger (1927)

Introduction

Source: The Basic Problems of Phenomenology (1954) Published by Indiana University Press, 1975. Introduction, p 1 - 23 reproduced here.

---

§ 1. Exposition and general division of the theme

This course sets for itself the task of posing the basic problems of phenomenology, elaborating them, and proceeding to some extent toward their solution. Phenomenology must develop its concept out of what it takes as its theme and how it investigates its object. Our considerations are aimed at the inherent content and inner systematic relationships of the basic problems. The goal is to achieve a fundamental illumination of these problems.

In negative terms this means that our purpose is not to acquire historical knowledge about the circumstances of the modern movement in philosophy called phenomenology. We shall be dealing not with phenomenology but with what phenomenology itself deals with. And, again, we do not wish merely to take note of it so as to be able to report then that phenomenology deals with this or that subject; instead, the course deals with the subject itself, and you yourself are supposed to deal with it, or learn how to do so, as the course proceeds. The point is not to gain some knowledge about philosophy but to be able to philosophise. An introduction to the basic problems could lead to that end.

And these basic problems themselves? Are we to take it on trust that the ones we discuss do in fact constitute the inventory of the basic problems? How shall we arrive at these basic problems? Not directly but by the roundabout way of a discussion of certain individual problems. From these we shall sift out the basic problems and determine their systematic interconnection. Such an understanding of the basic problems should yield insight into the degree to which philosophy as a science is necessarily demanded by them.

The course accordingly divides into three parts. At the outset we may outline them roughly as follows:

1. Concrete phenomenological inquiry leading to the basic problems

2. The basic problems of phenomenology in their systematic order and foundation

3. The scientific way of treating these problems and the idea of phenomenology

502   THE MEANING OF LIFE

The path of our reflections will take us from certain individual problems to the basic problems. The question therefore arises, How are we to gain the starting point of our considerations? How shall we select and circumscribe the individual problems? Is this to be left to chance and arbitrary choice? In order to avoid the appearance that we have simply assembled a few problems at random, an introduction leading up to the individual problems is required.

It might be thought that the simplest and surest way would be to derive the concrete individual phenomenological problems from the concept of phenomenology. Phenomenology is essentially such and such; hence it encompasses such and such problems. But we have first of all to arrive at the concept of phenomenology. This route is accordingly closed to us. But to circumscribe the concrete problems we do not ultimately need a clear-cut and fully validated concept of phenomenology. Instead it might be enough to have some acquaintance with what is nowadays familiarly known by the name "phenomenology." Admittedly, within phenomenological inquiry there are again differing definitions of its nature and tasks. But, even if these differences in defining the nature of phenomenology could be brought to a consensus, it would remain doubtful whether the concept of phenomenology thus attained, a sort of average concept, could direct us toward the concrete problems to be chosen. For we should have to be certain beforehand that phenomenological inquiry today has reached the center of philosophy's problems and has defined its own nature by way of their possibilities. As we shall see, however, this is not the case - and so little is it the case that one of the main purposes of this course is to show that conceived in its basic tendency, phenomenological research can represent nothing less than the more explicit and more radical understanding of the idea of a scientific philosophy which philosophers from ancient times to Hegel sought to realize time and again in a variety of internally coherent endeavours.

Hitherto, phenomenology has been understood, even within that discipline itself, as a science propaedeutic to philosophy, preparing the ground for the proper philosophical disciplines of logic, ethics, aesthetics, and philosophy of religion. But in this definition of phenomenology as a preparatory science the traditional stock of philosophical disciplines is taken over without asking whether that same stock is not called in question and eliminated precisely by phenomenology itself. Does not phenomenology contain within itself the possibility of reversing the alienation of philosophy into these disciplines and of revitalising and reappropriating in its basic tendencies the great tradition of philosophy with its essential answers? We shall maintain that phenomenology is not just one philosophical science among others, nor is it the science preparatory to the rest of them; rather, the expression "phenomenology" is the name for the method of scientific philosophy in general.

Clarification of the idea of phenomenology is equivalent to exposition of the concept of scientific philosophy. To be sure, this does not yet tell us what phenomenology means as far as its content is concerned, and it tells us even less about how this method is to be put into practice. But it does indicate how and why we must avoid aligning ourselves with any contemporary tendency in phenomenology.

We shall not deduce the concrete phenomenological problems from some dogmatically proposed concept of phenomenology; on the contrary, we shall allow ourselves to be led to them by a more general and preparatory discussion of the concept of scientific philosophy in general. We shall conduct this discussion in tacit apposition to the basic tendencies of Western philosophy from antiquity to Hegel.

In the early period of ancient thought philosophia means the same as science in general. Later, individual philosophies, that is to say, individual sciences - medicine, for instance, and mathematics - become detached from philosophy. The term philosophia then refers to a science which underlies and encompasses all the other particular sciences. Philosophy becomes science pure and simple. More and more it takes itself to be the first and highest science or, as it was called during the period of German idealism, absolute science. If philosophy is absolute science, then the expression "scientific philosophy" contains a pleonasm. It then means scientific absolute science. It suffices simply to say "philosophy." This already implies science pure and simple. Why then do we still add the adjective "scientific" to the expression "philosophy"? A science, not to speak of absolute science, is scientific by the very meaning of the term. We speak of "scientific philosophy" principally because conceptions of philosophy prevail which not only imperil but even negate its character as science pure and simple. These conceptions of philosophy are not just contemporary but accompany the development of scientific philosophy throughout the time philosophy has existed as a science. On this view philosophy is supposed not only, and not in the first place, to be a theoretical science, but to give practical guidance to our view of things and their interconnection and our attitudes toward them, and to regulate and direct our interpretation of existence and its meaning. Philosophy is wisdom of the world and of life, or, to use an expression current nowadays, philosophy is supposed to provide a Weltanschauung, a world-view. Scientific philosophy can thus be set off against philosophy as world-view.

We shall try to examine this distinction more critically and to decide whether it is valid or whether it has to be absorbed into one of its members. In this way the concept of philosophy should become clear to us and put us in a position to justify the selection of the individual problems to be dealt with in the first part. It should be borne in mind here that these discussions concerning the concept of philosophy can be only provisional - provisional not just in regard to the course as a whole but provisional in general. For the concept of philosophy is the most proper and highest result of philosophy itself. Similarly, the question whether philosophy is at all possible or not can be decided only by philosophy itself.

§ 2. The concept of philosophy
Philosophy and world-view

In discussing the difference between scientific philosophy and philosophy as world-view, we may fittingly start from the latter notion and begin with the term "Weltanschauung," "world-view." This expression is not a translation from Greek, say, or Latin. There is no such expression as kosmotheoria. The word "Weltanschauung" is of specifically German coinage; it was in fact coined within philosophy. It first turns up in its natural meaning in Kant's Critique of Judgment -

504 THE MEANING OF LIFE

world-intuition in the sense of contemplation of the world given to the senses or, as Kant says, the mundus sensibilis - a beholding of the world as simple apprehension of nature in the broadest sense. Goethe and Alexander von Humboldt thereupon use the word in this way. This usage dies out in the thirties of the last century under the influence of a new meaning given to the expression "Weltanschauung" by the Romantics and principally by Schelling. In the Introduction to the draft of a System of Philosophy of Nature, (1799), Schelling says: "Intelligence is productive in a double manner, either blindly and unconsciously or freely and consciously; it is unconsciously productive in Weltanschauung and consciously productive in the creation of an ideal world." Here Weltanschauung is directly assigned not to sense-observation but to intelligence, albeit to unconscious intelligence. Moreover, the factor of productivity, the independent formative process of intuition, is emphasised. Thus the word approaches the meaning we are familiar with today, a self-realised, productive as well as conscious way of apprehending and interpreting the universe of beings. Schelling speaks of a schematism of Weltanschauung, a schematised form for the different possible world-views which appear and take shape in fact. A view of the world, understood in this way, does not have to be produced with a theoretical intention and with the means of theoretical science. In his Phenomenology of Spirit, Hegel speaks of a "moral world-view." Görres makes use of the expression "poetic world-view." Ranke speaks of the "religious and Christian world-view." Mention is made sometimes of the democratic, sometimes of the pessimistic world-view or even of the medieval world-view. Schleiermacher says: "It is only our world-view that makes our knowledge of God complete." Bismarck at one point writes to his bride: "What strange views of the world there are among clever people!" From the forms and possibilities of world-view thus enumerated it becomes clear that what is meant by this term is not only a conception of the contexture of natural things but at the same time an interpretation of the sense and purpose of the human Dasein [the being that we are ourselves] and hence of history. A world-view always includes a view of life. A world-view grows out of an all-inclusive reflection on the world and the human Dasein, and this again happens in different ways, explicitly and consciously in individuals or by appropriating an already prevalent world-view. We grow up within such a world-view and gradually become accustomed to it. Our world-view is determined by environment - people, race, class, developmental stage of culture. Every world-view thus individually formed arises out of a natural world-view, out of a range of conceptions of the world and determinations of the human Dasein which are at any particular time given more or less explicitly with each such Dasein. We must distinguish the individually formed world-view or the cultural world-view from the natural world-view.

A world-view is not a matter of theoretical knowledge, either in respect of its origin or in relation to its use. It is not simply retained in memory like a parcel of cognitive property. Rather, it is a matter of a coherent conviction which determines the current affairs of life more or less expressly and directly. A world-view is related in its meaning to the particular contemporary Dasein at any given time. In this relationship to the Dasein the world-view is a guide to it and a source of strength under pressure. Whether the world-view is determined by superstitions and prejudices or is based purely on scientific knowledge and experience or even, as is usually the case, is a mixture of superstition and knowledge, prejudice and sober reason it all comes to the same thing; nothing essential is changed.

This indication of the characteristic traits of what we mean by the term "world-view" may suffice here. A rigorous definition of it would have to be gained in another way, as we shall see. In his Psychologie der Weltanschauungen, Jaspers says that "when we speak of world-views we mean Ideas, what is ultimate and total in man, both subjectively, as life-experience and power and character, and objectively, as a world having objective shape." For our purpose of distinguishing between philosophy as world-view and scientific philosophy, it is above all important to see that the world-view, in its meaning, always arises out of the particular factical existence of the human being in accordance with his factical possibilities of thoughtful reflection and attitude-formation, and it arises thus for this factical Dasein. The world-view is something that in each case exists historically from, with, and for the factical Dasein. A philosophical world-view is one that expressly and explicitly or at any rate preponderantly has to be worked out and brought about by philosophy, that is to say, by theoretical speculation, to the exclusion of artistic and religious interpretations of the world and the Dasein. This world-view is not a by-product of philosophy; its cultivation, rather, is the proper goal and nature of philosophy itself. In its very concept philosophy is world-view philosophy, philosophy as world-view. If philosophy in the form of theoretical knowledge of the world aims at what is universal in the world and ultimate for the Dasein - the whence, the whither, and the wherefore of the world and life - then this differentiates it from the particular sciences, which always consider only a particular region of the world and the Dasein, as well as from the artistic and religious attitudes, which are not based primarily on the theoretical attitude. It seems to be without question that philosophy has as its goal the formation of a world-view. This task must define the nature and concept of philosophy. Philosophy, it appears, is so essentially world-view philosophy that it would be preferable to reject this latter expression as an unnecessary overstatement. And what is even more, to propose to strive for a scientific philosophy is a misunderstanding. For the philosophical world-view, it is said, naturally ought to be scientific. By this is meant: first, that it should take cognisance of the results of the different sciences and use them in constructing the world-picture and the interpretation of the Dasein; secondly, that it ought to be scientific by forming the world-view in strict conformity with the rules of scientific thought. This conception of philosophy as the formation of a world-view in a theoretical way is so much taken for granted that it commonly and widely defines the concept of philosophy and consequently also prescribes for the popular mind what is to be and what ought to be expected of philosophy. Conversely, if philosophy does not give satisfactory answers to the questions of world-view, the popular mind regards it as insignificant. Demands made on philosophy and attitudes taken toward it are governed by this notion of it as the scientific construction of a world-view. To determine whether philosophy succeeds or fails in this task, its history is examined for unequivocal confirmation that it deals knowingly with the ultimate questions - of nature, of the soul, that is to say, of the freedom and history of man, of God.

506 THE MEANING OF LIFE

If philosophy is the scientific construction of a world-view, then the: distinction between "scientific philosophy" and "philosophy as world-view" vanishes. The two together constitute the essence of philosophy, so that what is really emphasised ultimately is the task of the world-view. This seems also to be the view of Kant, who put the scientific character of philosophy on a new basis. We need only recall the distinction he drew in the introduction to the Logic between the academic and the cosmic conceptions of philosophy. Here we turn to an oft-quoted Kantian distinction which apparently supports the distinction between scientific philosophy and philosophy as world-view or, more exactly, serves as evidence for the fact that Kant himself, for whom the scientific character of philosophy was central, likewise conceives of philosophy as philosophical world-view.

According to the academic concept or, as Kant also says, in the scholastic sense, philosophy is the doctrine of the skill of reason and includes two parts: "first, a sufficient stock of rational cognitions from concepts; and, secondly, a systematic interconnection of these cognitions or a combination of them in the idea of a whole." Kant is here thinking of the fact that philosophy in the scholastic sense includes the interconnection of the formal principles of thought and of reason in general as well as the discussion and determination of those concepts which, as a necessary presupposition, underlie our apprehension of the world, that is to say, for Kant, of nature. According to the academic concept, philosophy is the whole of all the formal and material fundamental concepts and principles of rational knowledge.

Kant defines the cosmic concept of philosophy or, as he also says, philosophy in the cosmopolitan sense, as follows: "But as regards philosophy in the cosmic sense (in sensu cosmico), it can also be called a science of the supreme maxims of the use of our reason, understanding by 'maxim' the inner principle of choice among diverse ends." Philosophy in the cosmic sense deals with that for the sake of which all use of reason, including that of philosophy itself, is what it is. "For philosophy in the latter sense is indeed the science of the relation of every use of knowledge and reason to the final purpose of human reason, under which, as the supreme end, all other ends are subordinated and must come together into unity in it. In this cosmopolitan sense the field of philosophy can be defined by the following questions: 1) What can I know? 2) What should I do? 3) What may I hope? 4) What is man?" At bottom, says Kant, the first three questions are concentrated in the fourth, "What is man?" For the determination of the final ends of human reason results from the explanation of what man is. It is to these ends that philosophy in the academic sense also must relate.

Does this Kantian separation between philosophy in the scholastic sense and philosophy in the cosmopolitan sense coincide with the distinction between scientific philosophy and philosophy as world-view? Yes and no. Yes, since Kant after all makes a distinction within the concept of philosophy and, on the basis of this distinction, makes the questions of the end and limits of human existence central. No, since philosophy in the cosmic sense does not have the task of developing a world-view in the designated sense. What Kant ultimately has in mind as the task of philosophy in the cosmic sense, without being able to say so explicitly, is nothing but the a priori and therefore ontological circumscription of the characteristics which belong to the

PHENOMENOLOGICAL EXISTENTIAL PSYCHOLOGY 507

essential nature of the human Dasein and which also generally determine the concept of a world-view. As the most fundamental a priori determination of the essential nature of the human Dasein Kant recognises the proposition: Man is a being which exists as its own end. Philosophy in the cosmic sense, as Kant understands it, also has to do with determinations of essential nature. It does not seek a specific factual account of the merely factually known world and the merely factually lived life; rather, it seeks to delimit what belongs to world in general, to the Dasein in general, and thus to world-view in general. Philosophy in the cosmic sense has for Kant exactly the same methodological character as philosophy in the academic sense, except that for reasons which we shall not discuss here in further detail Kant does not see the connection between the two. More precisely, he does not see the basis for establishing both concepts on a common original ground. We shall deal with this later on. For the present it is clear only that, if philosophy is viewed as being the scientific construction of a world-view, appeal should not be made to Kant. Fundamentally, Kant recognises only philosophy as science.

A world-view, as we saw, springs in every case from a factical Dasein in accordance with its factical possibilities, and it is what it is always for this particular Dasein. This in no way asserts a relativism of world-views. What a world-view fashioned in this way says can be formulated in propositions and rules which are related in their meaning to a specific really existing world, to the particular factically existing Dasein. Every world-view and life-view posits; that is to say, it is related being-ly to some being or beings. It posits a being, something that is; it is positive. A world-view belongs to each Dasein and, like this Dasein, it is always in fact determined historically. To the world-view there belongs this multiple positivity that it is always rooted in a Dasein which is in such and such a way; that as such it relates to the existing world and points to the factically existent Dasein. It is just because this positivity - that is, the relatedness to beings, to world that is, Dasein that is - belongs to the essence of the world-view, and thus in general to the formation of the world-view, that the formation of a world-view cannot be the task of philosophy. To say this is not to exclude but to include the idea that philosophy itself is a distinctive primal form of world-view. Philosophy can and perhaps must show, among many other things, that something like a world-view belongs to the essential nature of the Dasein. Philosophy can and must define what in general constitutes the structure of a world-view. But it can never develop and posit some specific world-view qua just this or that particular one. Philosophy is not essentially the formation of a world-view; but perhaps just on this account it has an elementary and fundamental relation to all world-view formation, even to that which is not theoretical but factually historical.

The thesis that world-view formation does not belong to the task of philosophy is valid, of course, only on the presupposition that philosophy does not relate in a positive manner to some being qua this or that particular being, that it does not posit a being. Can this presupposition that philosophy does not relate positively to beings, as the sciences do, be justified? What then is philosophy supposed to concern itself with if not with beings, with that which is, as well as with the whole of what is? What is not, is surely the nothing. Should philosophy, then, as absolute science, have the nothing as its theme? What can there be apart from nature, history, God, space,

508 THE MEANING OF LIFE

number? We say of each of these, even though in a different sense, that it is. We call it a being. In relating to it, whether theoretically or practically, we are comporting ourselves toward a being. Beyond all these beings there is nothing. Perhaps there is no other being beyond what has been enumerated, but perhaps, as in the German idiom for "there is," es gibt [literally, it gives], still something else is given, something else which indeed is not but which nevertheless, in a sense yet to be determined, is given. Even more. In the end something is given which must be given if we are to be able to make beings accessible to us as beings and comport ourselves toward them, something which, to be sure, is not but which must be given if we are to experience and understand any beings at all. We are able to grasp beings as such, as beings, only if we understand something like being. If we did not understand, even though at first roughly and without conceptual comprehension, what actuality signifies, then the actual would remain hidden from us. If we did not understand what reality means, then the real would remain inaccessible. If we did not understand what life and vitality signify, then we would not be able to comport ourselves toward living beings. If we did not understand what existence and existentiality signify, then we ourselves would not be able to exist as Dasein. If we did not understand what permanence and constancy signify, then constant geometric relations or numerical proportions would remain a secret to us. We must understand actuality, reality, vitality, existentiality, constancy in order to be able to comport ourselves positively toward specifically actual, real, living, existing, constant beings. We must understand being so that we may be able to be given over to a world that is, so that we can exist in it and be our own Dasein itself as a being. We must be able to understand actuality before all factual experience of actual beings. This understanding of actuality or of being in the widest sense as over against the experience of beings is in a certain sense earlier than the experience of beings. To say that the understanding of being precedes all factual experience of beings does not mean that we would first need to have an explicit concept of being in order to experience beings theoretically or practically. We must understand being - being, which may no longer itself be called a being, being, which does not occur as a being among other beings but which nevertheless must be given and in fact is given in the understanding of being.

§ 3. Philosophy as science of being

We assert now that being is the proper and sole theme of philosophy. This is not our own invention; it is a way of putting the theme which comes to life at the beginning of philosophy in antiquity, and it assumes its most grandiose form in Hegel's logic. At present we are merely asserting that being is the proper and sole theme of philosophy. Negatively, this means that philosophy is not a science of beings but of being or, as the Greek expression goes, ontology. We take this expression in the widest possible sense and not in the narrower one it has, say, in Scholasticism or in modern philosophy in Descartes and Leibniz.

A discussion of the basic problems of phenomenology then is tantamount to providing fundamental substantiation for this assertion that philosophy is the science of being and establishing how it is such. The discussion should show the possibility and necessity of the absolute science of being and demonstrate its character in the very process of the inquiry. Philosophy is the theoretical conceptual interpretation of being, of being's structure and its possibilities. Philosophy is ontological. In contrast, a world-view is a positing knowledge of beings and a positing attitude toward beings; it is not ontological but ontical. The formation of a world-view falls outside the range of philosophy's tasks, but not because philosophy is in an incomplete condition and does not yet suffice to give a unanimous and universally cogent answer to the questions pertinent to world-views; rather, the formation of a world-view falls outside the range of philosophy's tasks because philosophy in principle does not relate to beings. It is not because of a defect that philosophy renounces the task of forming a world-view but because of a distinctive priority: it deals with what every positing of beings, even the positing done by a world-view, must already presuppose essentially. The distinction between philosophy as science and philosophy as world-view is untenable, not - as it seemed earlier - because scientific philosophy has as its chief end the formation of a world-view and thus would have to be elevated to the level of a world-view philosophy, but because the notion of a world-view philosophy is simply inconceivable. For it implies that philosophy, as science of being, is supposed to adopt specific attitudes toward and posit specific things about beings. To anyone who has even an approximate understanding of the concept of philosophy and its history, the notion of a world-view philosophy is an absurdity. If one term of the distinction between scientific philosophy and world-view philosophy is inconceivable, then the other, too, must be inappropriately conceived. Once it has been seen that world-view philosophy is impossible in principle if it is supposed to be philosophy, then the differentiating adjective "scientific" is no longer necessary for characterising philosophy. That philosophy is scientific is implied in its very concept. It can be shown historically that at bottom all the great philosophies since antiquity more or less explicitly took themselves to be, and as such sought to be, ontology. In a similar way, however, it can also be shown that these attempts failed over and over again and why they had to fail. I gave the historical proof of this in my courses of the last two semesters, one on ancient philosophy and the other on the history of philosophy from Thomas Aquinas to Kant. We shall not now refer to this historical demonstration of the nature of philosophy, a demonstration having its own peculiar character. Let us rather in the whole of the present course try to establish philosophy on its own basis, so far as it is a work of human freedom. Philosophy must legitimate by its own resources its claim to be universal ontology.

In the meantime, however, the statement that philosophy is the science of being remains a pure assertion. Correspondingly, the elimination of world-view formation from the range of philosophical tasks has not yet been warranted. We raised this distinction between scientific philosophy and world-view philosophy in order to give a provisional clarification of the concept of philosophy and to demarcate it from the popular concept. The clarification and demarcation, again, were provided in order to account for the selection of the concrete phenomenological problems to be dealt with next and to remove from the choice the appearance of complete arbitrariness.

Philosophy is the science of being. For the future we shall mean by "philosophy" scientific philosophy and nothing else. In conformity with this usage, all non-philosophical sciences have as their theme some being or beings, and indeed in such a way that they are in every case antecedently given as beings to those sciences. They are posited by them in advance; they are a positum for them. All the propositions of the non-philosophical sciences, including those of mathematics, are positive propositions. Hence, to distinguish them from philosophy, we shall call all non-philosophical sciences positive sciences. Positive sciences deal with that which is, with beings; that is to say, they always deal with specific domains, for instance, nature. Within a given domain scientific research again cuts out particular spheres: nature as physically material lifeless nature and nature as living nature. It divides the sphere of the living into individual fields: the plant world, the animal world. Another domain of beings is history; its spheres are art history, political history, history of science, and history of religion. Still another domain of beings is the pure space of geometry, which is abstracted from space pre-theoretically uncovered in the environing world. The beings of these domains are familiar to us even if at first and for the most part we are not in a position to delimit them sharply and clearly from one another. We can, of course, always name, as a provisional description which satisfies practically the purpose of positive science, some being that falls within the domain. We can always bring before ourselves, as it were, a particular being from a particular domain as an example. Historically, the actual partitioning of domains comes about not according to some preconceived plan of a system of science but in conformity with the current research problems of the positive sciences.

We can always easily bring forward and picture to ourselves some being belonging to any given domain. As we are accustomed to say, we are able to think something about it. What is the situation here with philosophy's object? Can something like being be imagined? If we try to do this, doesn't our head start to swim? Indeed, at first we are baffled and find ourselves clutching at thin air A being - that's something, a table, a chair, a tree, the sky, a body, some words, an action. A being, yes, indeed - but being? It looks like nothing - and no less a thinker than Hegel said that being and nothing are the same. Is philosophy as science of being the science of nothing? At the outset of our considerations, without raising any false hopes and without mincing matters, we must confess that under the heading of being we can at first think to ourselves nothing. On the other hand, it is just as certain that we are constantly thinking being. We think being just as often as, daily, on innumerable occasions, whether aloud or silently, we say "This is such and such," "That other is not so," "That was," "It will be." In each use of a verb we have already thought, and have always in some way understood, being. We understand immediately "Today is Saturday; the sun is up." We understand the "is" we use in speaking, although we do not comprehend it conceptually. The meaning of this "is" remains closed to us. This understanding of the "is" and of being in general is so much a matter of course that it was possible for the dogma to spread in philosophy uncontested to the present day that being is the simplest and most self-evident concept, that it is neither susceptible of nor in need of definition. Appeal is made to common sense. But wherever common sense is taken to be philosophy's highest court of appeal, philosophy must become suspicious. In On the Essence of Philosophical Criticism, Hegel says:

PHENOMENOLOGICAL EXISTENTIAL PSYCHOLOGY   511

"Philosophy by its very nature is esoteric; for itself it is neither made for the masses nor is it susceptible of being cooked up for them. It is philosophy only because it goes exactly contrary to the understanding and thus even more so to 'sound common sense,' the so-called healthy human understanding, which actually means the local and temporary vision of some limited generation of human beings. To that generation the world of philosophy is in and for itself a topsy-turvy, an inverted, world. The demands and standards of common sense have no right to claim any validity or to represent any authority in regard to what philosophy is and what it is not.

What if being were the most complex and most obscure concept? What f arriving at the concept of being were the most urgent task of philosophy, the task which has to be taken up ever anew? Today, when philosophising is so barbarous, so much like a St. Vitus' dance, as perhaps in no other period of the cultural history of the West, and when nevertheless the resurrection of metaphysics is hawked up and down all the streets, what Aristotle says on one of his most important investigations in the Metaphysics has been completely forgotten. "That which has been sought for from of old and now and in the future and constantly, and that on which inquiry founders over and over again, is the problem What is being?" If philosophy is the science of being, then the first and last and basic problem of philosophy must be, What does being signify? Whence can something like being in general be understood? How is understanding of being at all possible?

§ 4. The four theses about being and the basic problems of phenomenology

Before we broach these fundamental questions, it will be worthwhile first to make ourselves familiar for once with discussions about being. To this end we shall deal in the first part of the course with some characteristic theses about being as individual concrete phenomenological problems, theses that have been advocated in the course of the history of Western philosophy since antiquity. In this connection we are interested, not in the historical contexts of the philosophical inquiries within which these theses about being make their appearance, but in their specifically inherent content. This content is to be discussed critically, so that we may make the transition from it to the above-mentioned basic problems of the science of being. The discussion of these theses should at the same time render us familiar with the phenomenological way of dealing with problems relating to being. We choose four such theses:

1. Kant's thesis: Being is not a real predicate.

2. The thesis of medieval ontology (Scholasticism) which goes back to Aristotle: To the constitution of the being of a being there belong (a) whatness, essence (Was-sein, essentia), and (b) existence or extantness (existentia, Vorhandensein).

3. The thesis of modern ontology: The basic ways of being are the being of nature (res extensa) and the being of mind (res cogitans).

4. The thesis of logic in the broadest sense: Every being, regardless of its particular way of being, can be addressed and talked about by means of the "is." The being of the copula.

512 THE MEANING OF LIFE

These theses seem at first to have been gathered together arbitrarily. Looked at more closely, however, they are interconnected in a most intimate way. Attention to what is denoted in these theses leads to the insight that they cannot be brought up adequately - not even as problems - as long as the fundamental question of the whole science of being has not been put and answered: the question of the meaning of being in general. The second part of our course will deal with this question. Discussion of the basic question of the meaning of being in general and of the problems arising from that question constitutes the entire stock of basic problems of phenomenology in their systematic order and their foundation. For the present we delineate the range of these problems only roughly.

On what path can we advance toward the meaning of being in general? Is not the question of the meaning of being and the task of an elucidation of this concept a pseudo-problem if, as usual, the opinion is held dogmatically that being is the most general and simplest concept? What is the source for defining this concept and in what direction is it to be resolved?

Something like being reveals itself to us in the understanding of being, an understanding that lies at the root of all comportment toward beings. Comportment toward beings belongs, on its part, to a definite being, the being which we ourselves are, the human Dasein. It is to the human Dasein that there belongs the understanding of being which first of all makes possible every comportment toward beings. The understanding of being has itself the mode of being of the human Dasein. The more originally and appropriately we define this being in regard to the structure of its being, that is to say, ontologically, the more securely we are placed in a position to comprehend in its structure the understanding of being that belongs to the Dasein, and the more clearly and unequivocally the question can then be posed, What is it that makes this understanding of being possible at all? Whence - that is, from which antecedently given horizon - do we understand the like of being?

The analysis of the understanding of being in regard to what is specific to this understanding and what is understood in it or its intelligibility presupposes an analytic of the Dasein ordered to that end. This analytic has the task of exhibiting the basic constitution of the human Dasein and of characterising the meaning of the Dasein's being. In this ontological analytic of the Dasein, the original constitution of the Dasein's being is revealed to be temporality. The interpretation of temporality leads to a more radical understanding and conceptual comprehension of time than has been possible hitherto in philosophy. The familiar concept of time as traditionally treated in philosophy is only an offshoot of temporality as the original meaning of the Dasein. If temporality constitutes the meaning of the being of the human Dasein and if understanding of being belongs to the constitution of the Dasein's being, then this understanding of being, too, must be possible only on the basis of temporality. Hence there arises the prospect of a possible confirmation of the thesis that time is the horizon from which something like being becomes at all intelligible. We interpret being by way of time (tempus). The interpretation is a Temporal one. The fundamental subject of research in ontology, as determination of the meaning of being by way of time, is Temporality.

PHENOMENOLOGICAL EXISTENTIAL PSYCHOLOGY 513

We said that ontology is the science of being. But being is always the being of a being. Being is essentially different from a being, from beings. How is the distinction between being and beings to be grasped? How can its possibility be explained? If being is not itself a being, how then does it nevertheless belong to beings, since, after all, beings and only beings are? What does it mean to say that being belongs to beings? The correct answer to this question is the basic presupposition needed to set about the problems of ontology regarded as the science of being. We must be able to bring out clearly the difference between being and beings in order to make something like being the theme of inquiry. This distinction is not arbitrary; rather, it is the one by which the theme of ontology and thus of philosophy itself is first of all attained. It is a distinction which is first and foremost constitutive for ontology. We call it the ontological difference - the differentiation between being and beings. Only by making this distinction - krinein in Greek - not between one being and another being but between being and beings do we first enter the field of philosophical research. Only by taking this critical stance do we keep our own standing inside the field of philosophy. Therefore, in distinction from the sciences of the things that are, of beings, ontology, or philosophy in general, is the critical science, or the science of the inverted world, With this distinction between being and beings and that selection of being as theme we depart in principle from the domain of beings. We surmount it, transcend it. We can also call the science of being, a critical science, transcendental science. In doing so we are not simply taking over unaltered the concept of the transcendental in Kant, although we are indeed adopting its original sense and its true tendency, perhaps still concealed from Kant. We are surmounting beings in order to reach being. Once having made the ascent we shall not again descend to a being, which, say, might lie like another world behind the familiar beings. The transcendental science of being has nothing to do with popular metaphysics, which deals with some being behind the known beings; rather, the scientific concept of metaphysics is identical with the concept of philosophy in general - critically transcendental science of being, ontology. It is easily seen that the ontological difference can be cleared up and carried out unambiguously for ontological inquiry only if and when the meaning of being in general has been explicitly brought to light, that is to say, only when it has been shown how temporality makes possible the distinguishability between being and beings. Only on the basis of this consideration can the Kantian thesis that being is not a real predicate be given its original sense and adequately explained.

Every being is something, it has its what and as such has a specific possible mode of being. In the first part of our course, while discussing the second thesis, we shall show that ancient as well as medieval ontology dogmatically enunciated this proposition - that to each being there belongs a what and way of being, essentia and existentia - as if it were self-evident. For us the question arises, Can the reason every being must and can have a what, a ti, and a possible way of being be grounded in the meaning of being itself, that is to say, Temporally? Do these characteristics, whatness and way of being, taken with sufficient breadth, belong to being itself? "Is" being articulated by means of these characteristics in accordance with its essential nature? With this we are now confronted by the problem of the basic articulation of being, the question of

514 THE MEANING OF LIFE

the necessary belonging-together of whatness and way-of-being and of the belonging of the two of them in their unity to the idea of being in general.

Every being has a way-of-being. The question is whether this way-of-being has the same character in every being - as ancient ontology believed and subsequent periods have basically had to maintain even down to the present - or whether individual ways-of-being are mutually distinct. Which are the basic ways of being? Is there a multiplicity? How is the variety of ways-of-being possible and how is it at all intelligible, given the meaning of being? How can we speak at all of a unitary concept of being despite the variety of ways-of-being? These questions can be consolidated into the problem of the possible modifications of being and the unity of being's variety.

Every being with which we have any dealings can be addressed and spoken of by saying "it is" thus and so, regardless of its specific mode of being. We meet with a being's being in the understanding of being. It is understanding that first of all opens up or, as we say, discloses or reveals something like being. Being is given only in the specific disclosedness that characterises the understanding of being. But we call the disclosedness of something truth. That is the proper concept of truth, as it already begins to dawn in antiquity. Being is given only if there is disclosure, that is to say, if there is truth. But there is truth only if a being exists which opens up, which discloses, and indeed in such a way that disclosure itself belongs to the mode of being of this being. We ourselves are such a being. The Dasein Itself exists in the truth. To the Dasein there belongs essentially a disclosed world and with that the disclosedness of the Dasein itself. The Dasein, by the nature of its existence, is "in" truth, and only because it is "in" truth does it have the possibility of being "in" untruth. Being is given only if truth, hence if the Dasein, exists. And only for this reason is it not merely possible to address beings but within certain limits sometimes - presupposing that the Dasein exists - necessary. We shall consolidate these problems of the interconnectedness between being and truth into the problem of the truth-character of being (veritas transcendentalis).

We have thus identified four groups of problems that constitute the content of the second part of the course: the problem of the ontological difference, the problem of the basic articulation of being, the problem of the possible modifications of being in its ways of being, the problem of the truth-character of being. The four theses treated provisionally in the first part correspond to these four basic problems. More precisely, looking backward from the discussion of the basic problems in the second half, we see that the problems with which we are provisionally occupied in the first part, following the lead of these theses, are not accidental but grow out of the inner systematic coherence of the general problem of being.

§ 5. The character of ontological method
The three basic components of Phenomenological method

Our conduct of the ontological investigation in the first and second parts opens up for us at the same time a view of the way in which these phenomenological investigations proceed. This raises the question of the character of method in ontology. Thus we come to the third part of the course: the scientific method of ontology and the idea of phenomenology.

The method of ontology, that is, of philosophy in general, is distinguished by the fact that ontology has nothing in common with any method of any of the other sciences, all of which as positive sciences deal with beings. On the other hand, it is precisely the analysis of the truth-character of being which shows that being also is, as it were, based in a being, namely, in the Dasein. Being is given only if the understanding of being, hence the Dasein, exists. This being accordingly lays claim to a distinctive priority in ontological inquiry. It makes itself manifest in all discussions of the basic problems of ontology and above all in the fundamental question of the meaning of being in general. The elaboration of this question and its answer requires a general analytic of the Dasein. Ontology has for its fundamental discipline the analytic of the Dasein. This implies at the same time that ontology cannot be established in a purely ontological manner. Its possibility is referred back to a being, that is, to something ontical - the Dasein. Ontology has an ontical foundation, a fact which is manifest over and over again in the history of philosophy down to the present. For example, it is expressed as early as Aristotle's dictum that the first science, the science of being, is theology. As the work of the freedom of the human Dasein, the possibilities and destinies of philosophy are bound up with man's existence, and thus with temporality and with historicality, and indeed in a more original sense than is any other science. Consequently, in clarifying the scientific character of ontology, the first task is the demonstration of its ontical foundation and the characterisation of this foundation itself.

The second task consists in distinguishing the mode of knowing operative in ontology as science of being, and this requires us to work out the methodological structure of ontological-transcendental differentiation. In early antiquity it was already seen that being and its attributes in a certain way underlie beings and precede them and so are a proteron, an earlier. The term denoting this character by which being precedes beings is the expression a priori, apriority, being earlier or prior. As a priori, being is earlier than beings. The meaning of this a priori, the sense of the earlier and its possibility, has never been cleared up. The question has not even once been raised as to why the determinations of being and being itself must have is character of priority and how such priority is possible. To be earlier is a determination of time, but it does not pertain to the temporal order of the time that we measure by the clock; rather, it is an earlier that belongs to the "inverted world." Therefore, this earlier which characterises being is taken by the popular understanding to be the later. Only the interpretation of being by way of temporality can make clear why and how this feature of being earlier, apriority, goes together with being. The a priori character of being and of all the structures of being accordingly calls for a specific kind of approach and way of apprehending being - a priori cognition.

The basic components of a priori cognition constitute what we call phenomenology. Phenomenology is the name for the method of ontology, that is, of scientific philosophy. Rightly conceived, phenomenology is the concept of a method. It is therefore precluded from the start that phenomenology should pronounce any theses about being which have specific content, thus adopting a so-called standpoint.

516   THE MEANING OF LIFE

We shall not enter into detail concerning which ideas about phenomenology are current today, instigated in part by phenomenology itself. We shall touch briefly on just one example. It has been said that my work is Catholic phenomenology - presumably because it is my conviction that thinkers like Thomas Aquinas and Duns Scotus also understood something of philosophy, perhaps more than the moderns. But the concept of a Catholic phenomenology is even more absurd than the concept of a Protestant mathematics. Philosophy as science of being is fundamentally distinct in method from any other science. The distinction in method between, say, mathematics and classical philology is not as great as the difference between mathematics and philosophy or between philology and philosophy. The breadth of the difference between philosophy and the positive sciences, to which mathematics and philology belong, cannot at all be estimated quantitatively. In ontology, being is supposed to be grasped and comprehended conceptually by way of the phenomenological method, in connection with which we may observe that, while phenomenology certainly arouses lively interest today, what it seeks and aims at was already vigorously pursued in Western philosophy from the very beginning.

Being is to be laid hold of and made our theme. Being is always being of beings and accordingly it becomes accessible at first only by starting with some being. Here the phenomenological vision which does the apprehending must indeed direct itself toward a being, but it has to do so in such a way that the being of this being is thereby brought out so that it may be possible to mathematise it. Apprehension of being, ontological investigation, always turns, at first and necessarily, to some being; but then, in a precise way, it is led away from that being and led back to its being. We call this basic component of phenomenological method - the leading back or reduction of investigative vision from a naively apprehended being to being phenomenological reduction. We are thus adopting a central term of Husserl's phenomenology in its literal wording though not in its substantive intent. For Husserl the phenomenological reduction, which he worked out for the first time expressly in the Ideas Toward a Pure Phenomenology and Phenomenological Philosophy (1913), is the method of leading phenomenological vision from the natural attitude of the human being whose life is involved in the world of things and persons back to the transcendental life of consciousness and its noetic-noematic experiences, in which objects are constituted as correlates of consciousness. For us phenomenological reduction means leading phenomenological vision back from the apprehension of a being, whatever may be the character of that apprehension, to the understanding of the being of this being (projecting upon the way it is unconcealed). Like every other scientific method, phenomenological method grows and changes due to the progress made precisely with its help into the subjects under investigation. Scientific method is never a technique. As soon as it becomes one it has fallen away from its own proper nature.

Phenomenological reduction as the leading of our vision from beings to being nevertheless is not the only basic component of phenomenological method; in fact, it is not even the central component. For this guidance of vision back from beings to being requires at the same time that we should bring ourselves forward toward being itself. Pure aversion from beings is a merely negative methodological measure which not only needs to be supplemented by a positive one but expressly requires us to be led toward being; it thus requires guidance. Being does not become accessible like a being. We do not simply find it in front of us. As is to be shown, it must always be brought to view in a free projection. This projecting of the antecedently given being upon its being and the structures of its being we call phenomenological construction.

But the method of phenomenology is likewise not exhausted by phenomenological construction. We have heard that every projection of being occurs in a reductive recursion from beings. The consideration of being takes its start from beings. This commencement is obviously always determined by the factual experience of beings and the range of possibilities of experience that at any time are peculiar to a factical Dasein, and hence to the historical situation of a philosophical investigation. It is not the case that at all times and for everyone all beings and all specific domains of beings are accessible in the same way; and, even if beings are accessible inside the range of experience, the question still remains whether, within naive and common experience, they are already suitably understood in their specific mode of being. Because the Dasein is historical in its own existence, possibilities of access and modes of interpretation of beings are themselves diverse, varying in different historical circumstances. A glance at the history of philosophy shows that many domains of beings were discovered very early - nature, space, the soul - but that, nevertheless, they could not yet be comprehended in their specific being. As early as antiquity a common or average concept of being came to light, which was employed for the interpretation of all the beings of the various domains of being and their modes of being, although their specific being itself, taken expressly in its structure, was not made into a problem and could not be defined. Thus Plato saw quite well that the soul, with its logos, is a being different from sensible being. But he was not in a position to demarcate the specific mode of being of this being from the mode of being of any other being or non-being. Instead, for him as well as for Aristotle and subsequent thinkers down to Hegel, and all the more so for their successors, all ontological investigations proceed within an average concept of being in general. Even the ontological investigation which we are now conducting is determined by its historical situation and, therewith, by certain possibilities of approaching beings and by the preceding philosophical tradition. The store of basic philosophical concepts derived from the philosophical tradition is still so influential today that this effect of tradition can hardly be overestimated. It is for this reason that all philosophical discussion, even the most radical attempt to begin all over again, is pervaded by traditional concepts and thus by traditional horizons and traditional angles of approach, which we cannot assume with unquestionable certainty to have arisen originally and genuinely from the domain of being and the constitution of being they claim to comprehend. It is for this reason that there necessarily belongs to the conceptual interpretation of being and its structures, that is, to the reductive construction of being, a destruction - a critical process in which the traditional concepts, which at first must necessarily be employed, are de-constructed down to the sources from which they were drawn. Only by means of this destruction can ontology fully assure itself in a phenomenological way of the genuine character of its concepts.

These three basic components of phenomenological metho - reduction, construction, destruction - belong together in their content and must receive grounding in their mutual

518   THE MEANING OF LIFE

pertinence. Construction in philosophy is necessarily destruction, that is to say, a de-constructing of traditional concepts carried out in a historical recursion to the tradition. And this is not a negation of the tradition or a condemnation of it as worthless; quite the reverse, it signifies precisely a positive appropriation of tradition. Because destruction belongs to construction, philosophical cognition is essentially at the same time, in a certain sense, historical cognition. History of philosophy, as it is called, belongs to the concept of philosophy as science, to the concept of phenomenological investigation. The history of philosophy is not an arbitrary appendage to the business of teaching philosophy, which provides an occasion for picking up some convenient and easy theme for passing an examination or even for just looking around to see how things were in earlier times. Knowledge of the history of philosophy is intrinsically unitary on its own account, and the specific mode of historical cognition in philosophy differs in its object from all other scientific knowledge of history.

The method of ontology thus delineated makes it possible to characterise the idea of phenomenology distinctively as the scientific procedure of philosophy. We therewith gain the possibility of defining the concept of philosophy more concretely. Thus our considerations in the third part lead back again to the starting point of the course.

SARTRE'S EXISTENTIAL VIEW

(Banach, 2003)

Existentialism is defined by the slogan <u>Existence precedes Essence</u> (Banach).

EXISTENCE PRECEDES ESSENCE[79] (Banach, 2003)

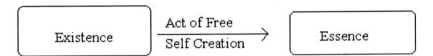

The Traditional View (which Sartre argues against):

ESSENCE PRECEDES EXISTENCE[80] (Banach)

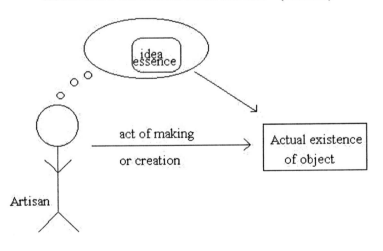

---

[79] Image from Banach, 2003.

References

Banach, D. (n.d.). Existentialism. Retrieved June 11, 2003, from http://www.anselm.edu/homepage/dbanach/sartreol.htm

[80] Ibid.

520 THE MEANING OF LIFE

EXERPTS FROM VIKTOR FRANKL:[81]

From The Doctor and the Soul: Man lives in three dimensions: the somatic, the mental, and the spiritual. The spiritual dimension cannot be ignored, for it is what makes us human. To be concerned about the meaning of life is not necessarily a sign of disease or of neurosis. It may be; but then again, spiritual agony may have very little connection with a disease of the psyche. The proper diagnosis can be made only by someone who can see the spiritual side of man.

Psychoanalysis speaks of the *pleasure principle*, individual psychology of *status drive*. The pleasure principle might be termed the *will-to-pleasure* the status drive is equivalent to the *will-to power*. But where do we hear of that which most deeply inspires man; where is the innate desire to give as much meaning as possible to one's life, to actualized as many values as possible--what I should like to call the will-to-meaning?

This will-to-meaning is the most human phenomenon of all, since an animal certainly never worries about the meaning of its existence. Yet psychotherapy would turn this will-to-meaning into a human frailty neurotic complex. A therapist who ignores man's spiritual side, and is thus forced to ignore the will-to-meaning, is giving away one of his most valuable assets. For it is to this will that a psychotherapist should appeal. Again and again we have seen that an appeal to continue life, to survive the most unfavorable conditions, can be made only when such survival appears to have a meaning. That meaning must be specific and personal, a meaning which can be realized by this one person alone. For we must never forget that every man is unique in the universe. (p xvi)

Men can give meaning to their lives by realizing what I call creative values, by achieving task. But they can also give meaning to their live by realizing experiential values, by experiencing the Good, the True, and the Beautiful, or by knowing one single human being in all his uniqueness. And to experience one human being as unique means to love him.

But even a man who finds himself in the greatest distress, in which neither activity nor creativity can bring values to life, nor experience give meaning to it - even such a man can still give his life a meaning by the way he faces his fate, his distress. By taking his unavoidable suffering upon himself he may yet realize values.

Thus, life has a meaning to the last breath. For the possibility of realizing values by the very attitude with which we face our unchangeable suffering - this possibility exists to the very last moment. I call such values attitudinal values. (p xix)

---

81 http://www.durbinhypnosis.com/frankl.htm#VIKTOR%20FRANKL:%20CHAPTER%207:

When it comes to evaluating people, collectivism leads us astray. For in place of responsible persons, the collectivist idea substitutes a mere type, and in place of personal responsibility, substitutes conformity to norms. (p 73)

Destiny appears to man in three principal forms: (1) natural disposition or endowment, what Tandler has called "somatic fate"; (2) as his situation, the total of his external environment; (3) disposition and situation together make up man's position. Toward this he "takes a position"--that is, he form an attitude. This "position taken" or attitude is - in contrast I basically destined "position given" matter of free choice. Proof of this is the fact that man can "change his position," take a attitude (as soon as we include the time dimension in our scheme, since a change of position means an alteration of attitude course of time). Included under change of position in this is, for example, everything we call education, learning and self-improvement, but also psychotherapy in the broadest sense of the word, and such inner revolutions as religious conversion. (p 80)

From The Will to Meaning: A person is free to shape his own character, and man is responsible for what he may have made of himself. What matters is not the features of our character or the drives and instincts per es, but rather the stand we take toward them. And the capacity t take such a stand is what makes us human beings. (p 17)

Suffering is only one aspect of what I call "The Tragic Triad" of human existence. This triad is made up of pain, guilt, and death. There is no human being who may say that he has not failed, that he does not suffer, and that he will not die.

The reader may notice that here the third "triad" is introduced. The first triad is constituted by freedom of will, will to meaning, and meaning to life. Meaning of life is composed of the second triad - creative , experiential, and attitudinal values. And attitudinal values are subdivided into the third triad - meaningful attitudes to pain, guilt, and death.

Speaking of the "tragic triad" should not mislead the reader to assume that logotherapy is as pessimistic as existentialism is said to be. Rather logotherapy is an optimistic approach to life, for it teaches that there are no tragic and negative aspects which could not be by the stand one takes to them transmuted into a positive accomplishment. (p 73)

From Psychotherapy and existentialism: Logotherapy exceeds and surpasses existential analysis, ...to the extent that it is essentially more than analysis of existence, of being, and involves more than a mere analysis of its subject. Logotherapy is concerned not only with being but also with meaning; not only with ontos but also with logos; and this feature may well account for the activistic, therapeutic orientation of logotherapy. In other words, logotherapy is not only analysis but also therapy. (p 1)

A good sense of humor is inherent in this technique. This is understandable since we know that humor is a paramount way of putting distance between something and oneself. One might say as well, that humor helps man to rise above his own predicament by allowing him to look at himself

522 THE MEANING OF LIFE

in a more detached way. So humor would also have to located in the noetic dimension. After all, no animal is able to laugh, least of all at himself.. (p 4)

In fact, it is my conviction that man should not, indeed cannot, struggle for identity in a direct way; he rather finds identity to the extent to which he commits himself to something beyond himself. No one has put it as cogently as Karl Jaspers did when he said, "What man is, he ultimately becomes through the cause which he made his own." (p 9)

Man is ultimately self-determining. What he becomes - within limits of endowment and environment - he has made himself. In the living laboratories of the concentration camps we watched comrades behaving like swine while others like saints. Man has both these potentialities within himself. Which one he actualizes depends on decision, not on conditions. It is time that this decision quality of human existence be included in our definition man. Our generation has come to know man as he really is: the being that has invented the gas chambers of Auschwitz, and also the being who entered those gas chambers upright, the Lord's Prayer or the Shema Yisrael on his lips. (p 35)

To this extent man is not only responsible for what he does but also for what is, inasmuch as man does not only behave according to what he is but also becomes what he is according to how he behaves. In the last analysis, man has become what he has made of himself. Instead of being fully conditioned by any conditions, he is constructing himself. (p 61)

QUOTATIONS FROM ROLLO MAY:[82]

"Lacking positive myths to guide him, many a sensitive contemporary man finds only the model of the machine beckoning him from every side to make himself over into its image."

■ (Psychology and the Human Dilemma, 1967, p. 30)

"...when people feel their insignificance as individual persons, they also suffer an undermining of their sense of human responsibility."

■ (Psychology and the Human Dilemma, 1967, p. 31)

"Increasingly in our time--this is an inevitable result of collectivization--it is the organization man who succeeds. And he is characterized by the fact that he has significance only if he gives up his significance."

■ (Psychology and the Human Dilemma, 1967, p. 37)

"Anxiety occurs because of a threat to the values a person identifies with his existence as a self...most anxiety comes from a threat to social, emotional and moral values the person identifies with himself. And here we find that a main source of anxiety, particularly in the younger generation, is that they do not have viable values available in the culture on the basis of which they can relate to their world. The anxiety which is inescapable in an age in which values are so radically in transition is a central cause of apathy..., such prolonged anxiety tends to develop into lack of feeling and the experience of depersonalization."

■ (Psychology and the Human Dilemma, 1967, p. 42)

"...the overemphasis on the Baconian doctrine of knowledge as power, and the accompanying concern with gaining power over nature as well as over ourselves in the sense of treating ourself as objects to be manipulated rather than human beings whose aim is to expand in meaningful living, have resulted in the invalidation of the self. This tends to shrink the individual's consciousness, to block off his awareness, and thus play into...unconstructive anxiety...I propose that the aim of education is exactly the opposite, namely, the widening and deepening of consciousness. To the extent that education can help the student develop sensitivity, depth of perception, and above all the capacity to perceive significant forms in what he is studying, it will be developing at the same time the student's capacity to deal with anxiety constructively."

■ (Psychology and the Human Dilemma, 1967, p. 50)

---

[82] http://www.mythosandlogos.com/May.html

524   THE MEANING OF LIFE

"a person can meet anxiety to the extent that his values are stronger than the threat."

■ (Psychology and the Human Dilemma, 1967, p. 51)

"Now it is no longer a matter of deciding what to do, but of deciding how to decide."

■ (Love and Will, 1969, p. 15)

"The schizoid man is the natural product of the technological man. It is one way to live and is increasingly utilized--and it may explode into violence."

■ (Love and Will, 1969, p. 17)

"Our patients are the ones who express and live out the subconscious and unconscious tendencies in the culture. The neurotic, or person suffering from what we now call character disorder, is characterized by the fact that the usual defenses of the culture do not work for him--a generally painful situation of which he is more or less aware..."

■ (Love and Will, 1969, p. 20)

"Both artists and neurotics speak and live from the subconscious and unconscious depths of their society. The artist does this positively, communicating what he experiences to his fellow men. The neurotic does this negatively."

■ (Love and Will, 1969, p. 21)

"When inward life dries up, when feeling decreases and apathy increases, when one cannot affect or even genuinely touch another person, violence flares up as a daimonic necessity for contact, a mad drive forcing touch in the most direct way possible."

■ (Love and Will, 1969, p. 31)

"In a world where numbers inexorably take over as our means of identification, like flowing lava threatening to suffocate and fosilize all breathing life in its path; in a world where 'normality' is defined as keeping your cool; where sex is so available that the only way to preserve any inner center is to have intercourse without committing yourself--in such a schizoid world, which young people experience more directly since they have not had time to build up the defenses which dull the senses of their elders, it is not surprising that will and love have become increasingly problematic and even, as some people believe, impossible of achievement."

■ (Love and Will, 1969, p. 32)

"The constructive schizoid person stands against the spiritual emptiness of encroaching technology and does not let himself be emptied by it. He lives and works with the machine without becoming a machine. He finds it necessary to remain detached enough to get meaning from the experience, but in doing so, to protect his own inner life from impoverishment."

■ (Love and Will, 1969, p. 32)

526   THE MEANING OF LIFE

EXISTENTIAL DEVELOPMENT OF JAMES FOWLER

This section is designed to integrate the basic psychological process of identity formation with the developmental model of meaning making as elaborated by James A. Fowler. Within Fowler's (1981) work, "Stages of Faith", there is a developmental process that incorporates the works of Erikson, Piaget and Kohlberg. Fowler's developmental structure essentially acknowledges that there are prerequisite cognitive developmental stages that must occur before the existential pilgrimage can proceed. Fowler also acknowledges[1] that each developmental stage has a unique method of contributing to an individual's existential identity. Therefore, this unique method of contribution must be considered in the psychoanalytic process and understanding a person's existential maturity.

Within this developmental review, this project shall summarize Fowler's view of development at each stage of growth. For there exists an ongoing existential tension between beliefs that serve personal well-being and beliefs that reflect external circumstances and social evaluators. Besides, developmental changes are part of this tension, defining what is an appropriate existential outlook with each stage of growth. For instance the belief of a 3 year old in his/her omnipotence may enable the child to reduce anxieties. Yet, if those same ideas are present in adolescence one will inevitably express concern for the child's mental status. Old beliefs and processes must be revised in development and Fowler's work provides an adequate outline of the process. According to Fowler,[2] at the age from birth to one and a half years, Eric Erikson views the formation of the value of "basic trust vs. mistrust" at the core of existence.[3] This value formation is in turn associated with Piaget's sensorimotor stage of the basic coordination of hands, arms, mouth etc.[4] From the ages of two to six Erikson[5] identified the formative period of two values: Autonomy vs. Shame and Doubt (the will) and Initiative vs. Guilt (purpose).[6]

Preoperational Stage and Intuitive-Projective Existentialism (Stage One)

At the age period between two and six Piaget identifies the cognitive developmental stage of "preoperations". Within the preoperational stage a child thinks by way of mental pictures that imitate visual reality. Within this stage the child is unable to reverse this picture or understand how reality works.[7] If one agrees that Fowler's definition of "faith" as "meaning making" is equivalent to an "existential world view" then one begins to see how Fowler's stage theory will influence the clarification of existential development.[8]

At the pre-operations stage of psychological development, Fowler[9] identifies the intuitive - projective stage of existentialism. This stage of existential development is the cognitive inability to compare two different perspectives on the same object and by that simply assume without question that the perceptions they have are the only available perspective. This stage is important for the therapist because it dominates the child's view of the world and "God" (essentially the child's rudimentary existential system). All concepts are concrete and find expression in anthropomorphic terms. This stage forms an existential system that reflects the attitudes of others around the child. Therefore parables, stories, myths and attitudes that dominate the child's atmosphere, with significant elders, form the basis of his/her existential foundation.[10]

Concrete Operations and Mythic-Literal Existentialism (Stage Two)

The subsequent stage of life transition takes place at approximately the age of seven. Piaget characterizes this age as the "concrete - operational" stage. For the child, thinking becomes more practical as the child learns to take account of differences of perspective between the self and others. This "Mythic - Literal" stage[11] of existential development is the stage when the person takes on the stories, beliefs and observances that symbolize belonging to his or her community. The symbols and rituals of one's community are interpreted in the new linear fashion of concrete operations, making coherence and meaning out of life. Within this stage, the socialization process has a major influence upon one's development of an existential framework.

Synthetic - Conventional Existentialism (Stage Three).

The next stage of development, namely adolescence, is the most traumatic in many respects. Erikson indicates[12] that the values of "identity vs. role confusion" find expression during this critical stage. The ability to think about what others think about oneself causes the adolescent to suddenly become self-conscious. This stage also brings with it what Piaget terms "formal operations" thinking, which is the ability to think abstractly. Fowler identifies the[13] "Synthetic - Conventional" stage of existential development to occur with formal operations. This "synthetic - conventional" stage of existential development is more personal and abstract than the previous stage and essentially makes the development of "personal myths". Such myths are beliefs about the uniqueness of self and how the self relates with others.

Review of childhood existentialism

This paper will now summarize the process of existential identity development from childhood to the synthetic - conventional stage. This summary provides the reader with a clarification of the process. We must realize that along with the adolescent's sense of identity, there is also the struggle to discover a sense of meaning[14]. For as the child emerges into adolescence, his/her cognitive abilities change and increase, allowing the individual to pass beyond the concrete reasoning and enable him/her to grasp what is "possible". This level of "formal operations" reasoning lends the child to a certain level of existential emptiness, since this new found reasoning ability lacks practice.

Ideally this existential emptiness fills through the child's safe exploration of his/her personal and family faith history. However, this existential filling is hindered by the mobility of modern society. That is, the mobility of the modern family robs the child of the dramatic impact of the resources that tells one what to do, or to invest certain acts with significance, or to model meaningful engagement in life. The result is a lack of a sturdy existential framework, for the

528 THE MEANING OF LIFE

adolescent, within which to understand life.[15] This existential emptiness often manifests itself in a vague sense of boredom that often typifies the stage of adolescence.[16]

Adult Existentialism

Intuitive - Reflective Existentialism (stage four)

In the fourth stage of development, an adult is at some time forced by circumstance to clarify his/her values and assert individual control and responsibility for his/her direction in life. The two essential features17 of the emergence of stage four, then, are the critical distancing from one's previous support of his/her existential system to encourage the emergence of stage four, then, are the critical distancing from one's previous support of his/her existential system to encourage the emergence of an "executive ego". That is, to take control and responsibility for the direction and meaning of one's life. As these two critical features occur a person is forming a new identity. This new identity is the enacting of ones life theory in the shaping of a "lifestyle" apart from familial or contextual influences.

As an individual leaves home and becomes responsible for his/her own actions he/she enters the stage that Levinson calls the "novice adult" and views the person as forming his/her first adult life structures.18 Erikson identifies the crisis19of Intimacy vs. Isolation with this period.20 Intimacy requires the ability to stand alone, and to risk one's forming self and sense of identity in close engagement with other persons and with ideological commitments that define the individual's refines existential system.

While the emergence of stage four usually occurs in the mid-twenties, it may be delayed in some individuals until the mid thirties or forties.21 The transition that forces an adult into stage four is usually life events that would typify a mid-life crisis. Changes in primary relationships such as divorce, death of spouses, parent; child or children simply growing up and leaving home. A minister should be aware that late stage transition in one's life may be extended five to ten years.22 From a developmental perspective therefore one hopes that this transition would be made in early adulthood.

Identity Issues in Early Existential Development

This author will now further clarify the previous existential stages through discussion on the relationship between identity formation and existential maturity. The reason that further clarification is necessary is because developmental aspects that occur at this stage are critical to existential development and identity formation and subsequent ego strength for moral reasoning. The redefining of one's self is finally possible with the abstract thinking of formal operations. A complete restructuring of the self may occur, where old beliefs, perceptions and values are replaced by new ones. In some instances however, the individual may choose to experiment with various identities and frameworks of existence.

At some point an adolescent will be pressured to choose an identity23and to use the existential framework chosen to define how he/she will act in society. If however the adolescent does not choose a clear identity and their existential framework remains fluid or poorly defined, existential development halts.

As Marcia indicates24 mature identity occurs when an individual experiences pressure from some outward circumstance to commit to a clear existential framework and expression (ideology and occupation). When an individual succeeds (or fails) at defining a basic existential framework that is committed to in action, they pass into one of four identity statuses:[25] diffusion; foreclosure; moratorium; identity achieved.

Identity Diffusion and Existential Stages Two and Three

The status that has the most vaguely defined existential world view is the status of identity diffusion. In this case the individual is not aware of, or significantly influenced by, pressure to choose an identity and occupation.26 The lack of pressure may also mean that the individual has not gone through the process of searching out new identities or existential frameworks. This lack of searching means that the individual has not defined his/her life theory and is therefore operating with a vague and rudimentary apparatus for making life meaningful. Due to the rudimentary apparatus for functioning the individual will likely respond to increased social pressure with anger and defiance or withdraw in apathy (which may lead to personality disintegration, perhaps even schizophrenia or suicide). The danger of this identity status, in the view of this student, is the abuse of substances that inhibits cognitive functioning and reduces the chance of defining a personal existential framework. This status most closely fits Frankl's noogenic neurosis or "existential vacuum".[27] In addition the individual in identity diffusion is "functionally" at stage two existentialism, although abstract thinking is possible. Yet since the individual is not actively concerned about defining an abstract life theory the individual does not truly mature to the third stage of existentialism known as synthetic-conventional.[28]

Foreclosure and Stage Three in Transition.

The second potential status of identity formation is known as foreclosure. This study views foreclosure as indicative of stage three existential development, or of an inflexible and immature stage four. As Celia, Dewolfe and Fitzgibbon indicate29 individuals in foreclosure do commit to an existential framework and expression (ideology and occupation). Yet the individual has not experienced the existential searching normally necessary to reach a commitment to such an existential framework. In essence the individual stays within the defining parameters and expectations of the peer, family and/ or mythic (faith) community. The benefit of this status is that the individual has a readily defined epistemological / theological framework and a somewhat defined personal existential framework within which to live.30The detrimental aspect of this status (in not experiencing a crisis) is that the individual does not develop the skills to clearly define a personal existential framework. Thereby the individual will have a rigid and inflexible (stage three existential) outlook on life that may cause problems when personal supports are lost. The loss of a support structure, such as the death of a parent or spouse or the loss of a job, can be particularly devastating.

530   THE MEANING OF LIFE

Moratorium and Existential Stages Three and Four.

A typical identity status for college students is known as Moratorium. In this status the individual actively involves him/herself in evaluating various systems of understanding the world and finding a role within it without yet making a commitment.31 Due to the nature of this status an individual will often appear unstable and discontented. The apparent instability of the individual is because a clearly defined set of "personal rules and outlook" are not yet established.

The individual within moratorium may appear to have the existential flexibility to be categorized above the fourth stage of existential development. Yet, since the individual has not yet made a commitment to a life direction and existential framework they cannot be classified at even stage four. Therefore the individual experiencing identity moratorium should actually be categorized as in the third existential stage and approaching (or in active transition to) stage four existentialism.

Identity Achieved and Existential Stages Three and Four

When an individual has an opportunity to evaluate various world-views and life direction options (moratorium) and actually makes a personalized decision one is on his/her way to achieving a personal existential framework. With a commitment to a personal life theory into action as a life direction one may be said to be at the identity status of identity achieved.32

From an existential development perspective one may view the "identity achieved" status as the satisfaction of stage four and the movement towards stage five. The critical factor of those who go through the process of moratorium, life crisis and decision, life theory development and making a life direction commitment to it is they have the intra-psychic experience of choosing and defining a comprehensive existential framework. This intra-psychic experience thereby allows for the higher levels of intra-psychic integration, self-definition, commitment and social adaptation necessary for Stage Five Existentialism. That is, the fine tuning of one's world -view and coping mechanisms.

Existential Achievement and Moral Maturity

Conjunctive - Meaning Existentialism - Stage Five

With the movement into Fowler's fifth stage we move into the centre of existential analysis. Stage Five is the stage of "conjunctive meaning"33 and is different in character and form from the previous existential stages. The difference lies in that it involves the individual re-examining the previous stages to integrate the whole. Stage five, as a way of seeing, of knowing, of committing, moves beyond the dichotomizing logic of stage four's either/or toward a dialectical knowing. That is, one's perspectives are examined and evaluated in light of the world and the infinite possibilities of existence.34 In essence it is the active harmonizing use of the two existential systems.

The two existential systems are the epistemological system of one's view of the universe and the personal existential system. An individual uses the first system as a compass to find his/her

PHENOMENOLOGICAL EXISTENTIAL PSYCHOLOGY   531

place in the world. Between these two systems, for the individual in stage five, there is a relativity that one acknowledges and owns. It is the recognition of personal weaknesses yet responsibility, of independence and dependence.35   It is the acknowledgment of relativity in existence and that one's life and understanding is fragile and only a dim reflection of the reality to which it mediates.

The Character of Stage Five Existentialism - Maturity

As Fowler indicates36, stage five is the ability of an individual to actively reshape and restructure his/her existential framework (the goal of therapy). This restructuring process comes through a new reclaiming and reworking of one's past. There is a critical recognition of one's unconscious - the myths, ideal images, and prejudices built deeply into one's existential identity by virtue of one's particular history. Yet it not only recognizes them but actively reshapes them. On a social level37as well, the individual is ready to help others cultivate and generate identity and meaning.

Stage Six Existentialism

Ideally, an individual should be able to recognize his/her identity status and role in the world, and express this through his/her efforts and actions. As a developmental stage it is beyond stage five for the simple reason38 that it is the actual ideal expression of one's existential status. This is in contrast to stage five that still clings to the very human tendency of being caught between the desire to serve the ultimate reality and the need and will to preserve one's well-being. Yet theoretically at least, for an individual at stage six, life is both loved and held loosely. At this stage an individual becomes open to die at the hands of those whom they hope to change.39

Within this stage Fowler alludes to the character of hope that springs from the past and into the future, leaving the present to be an open expression of this hope. Herein lies the ability of a stage six individual to hold life loosely.

Developmental Summary

The importance of identity development to the existential and moral development process is two fold. First, it provides a basis upon which one may ensure that appropriate steps occur to ensure existential growth through the normal life processes of the first four stages. The encouragement of existential identity development then, is the training for stage five, where an individual can revisit his/her childhood and adult interests, occupations etc. This revisiting will then enable the individual to evaluate, reinvent and reintegrate positive views and moral choices at the previous stages. From the view of the ego psychologist[40] the existential component of identity development and moral reasoning is stage "regression in the service of the ego". That is, a process of self analysis where an individual returns from present levels of existential and ego functioning to earlier ones in order to rework and refine certain aspects of his/her identity formation. Such a pattern therefore leads to release from earlier dysfunctional patterns and formation of a more integrated existential system. The resulting ego integrity and positive coping mechanisms facilitate higher levels of living and personal meaning.

PHENOMENOLOGICAL EXISTENTIAL PSYCHOLOGY   533

<u>REVIEW / DISCUSSION QUESTIONS</u>

1. Summarize the philosophies of Husserl, Heidegger and Sartre as they apply to psychology.

2. What is the mythic basis of Kierkegaard's existentialism and why is it different from most existential philosophers? What is its value?

3. What are the main differences between the ways of discovering meaning according to Rollo May, Viktor Frankl and Abraham Maslow?

534   THE MEANING OF LIFE

4. What stage of existential development are you in (according to Fowler's model)? Why do you place yourself at this stage?

CHAPTER 13

REDISCOVERING A LOST HERITAGE: UNDERSTANDING THE VALUE OF A TRADITIONAL CHRISTIAN APPROACH

INTRODUCTION

At times we as individuals (especially at the age of college students) want to reject our traditions in order to "understand" who we are. This very natural process, however, often results in a detrimental effect in that what we reject is of much value for creating order and meaning within our life. I would therefore like to take some time to talk about the issue of overall individual *(moral and ethical)* development and maturity within the *Christian* community. It is the premise of this book that the Christian message and community have much to offer in the realm of human wellness and psychological understanding. Therefore we must seek to understand its value and not dismiss it as "non-scientific" when it is the basic mythic structure needed for our very human narrative.

In essence, I suggest that the disintegration of traditional worship and socialization processes within the *Christian* community influences the level of ethical and existential maturity of its parishioners (and therefore the ability of those individuals to cope psychologically with life's issues). That is, from a theoretical standpoint there is benefit in combining innovation and tradition in the life of the church. Conversely, a lack of understanding about the nature of psychological development leads to two equally destructive directions within Christian ministry: 1. Rigid, inflexible traditionalism; 2. Anti-liturgical, non-traditional churches.

It is the premise of this chapter that the church plays an integral role in the development and maturity of ethics, values and morals in society. Some church leaders do not understand the essential prerequisites to moral reasoning and maturity. Therefore, many aspects of the Christian church come under undue criticism. This criticism often takes the form of "denomination bashing".

The blame for the churches' inability to produce "well rounded individuals" is often placed on the traditional liturgy of the worship community. As a result, churches often adopt the "community church" model. This model usually emphasizes socialization with contemporary non-traditional worship services and an almost anti-liturgical, anti-tradition mentality. At the other end of the pendulum swing is the extreme traditionalist position. Such traditionalist churches become inflexible in style and form and are ineffective at outreach or ministry to those outside its walls.

The goal is to clarify what is essential to ethical development and existential maturity. This chapter will deal with the psychological, philosophical, developmental and theological issues essential to a ministry toward ethical development, for there is a time and place for both

536   THE MEANING OF LIFE

traditional and non-traditional ministries. It is important to understand when a certain type of ministry is appropriate. Without an understanding of moral development, ministry philosophies will continue to polarize. What Christian ministry as a whole needs is a proper use of tradition and flexibility within the worship life of the church.

A considerable amount of research has been done in the area of ethical and moral development and behavior. The following are the primary theories that dominate the field: the psychoanalytic approach; the behavioral modification approach and the cognitive moral reasoning approach.

Psychodynamics as Moral Development

The most penetrating sub-structural ontology of psychology and the human character was fostered and popularized by the illustrious views of Sigmund Freud. It is, however, difficult to establish a clear and precise format for personality development based on his work. Throughout his extensive work he was continually developing, elaborating and revising his perspective on human nature. It is thus the view of this writer that we survey the primary characteristic views of human personality and then touch on the psychoanalytical approach to moral development.

A chief notion set forth by Freudian theory about personality is that all humans, regardless of age, possess a foundational energy or tendency, called libido, directed at maximizing pleasure. However, many of the acts and motives arising from the libido cause conflict. This conflict is primarily the result of a myriad of tensions between the three primary segments of the human personality within Freudian theory. Those major parts to which Freud conceived are what is known as the id, ego and superego.[41]

The Id

The id, or most fundamental and primeval of the three parts, springs from what Freudian theory holds to be two innate drives that all people possess. One of these drives is the libido, consisting of sexual urges and such associated aspirations as being well fed, warm and comfortable. The other is a drive toward aggression to overcome anyone or anything that impedes gratification.[42]

The drives incite the id to a condition of exhilaration and tension. In seeking to relieve the tension, the id operates on what Freudian theory identifies as the "pleasure principle", imperiously pursuing results and tolerating no delay. To gratify the libido, the id seeks undivided possession of everything coveted and loved. To quench the urge for aggression, it wants to devastate everything that gets in the way. As we grow up, we learn to regulate the demands of the id to some extent, but it remains active and powerful throughout life. Although it is unconscious and we are not aware of its workings, it continues to strive to relieve its tensions and find instant gratification.[43]

Freud, who was uncertain about the specific nature of the instinctual drive called it the *id*, from the Latin word for "it". Many biopsychologists picture these drives as mediated by the lower centers of the brain, such as the limbic system and the hypothalamus. As such, the id is at the deepest level of your unconscious mind, far removed from conscious reality. Freudian theory describes the id as a "caldron of excitement" that lacks inner structure or organization, which operates in illogical ways, and that seeks only the pleasure that comes from discharging its pent-up energies.[44]

The Ego

The id helps the infant survive because it is selfish and impulsive. Yet, as the infant matures, the "real world" begins to make demands on the child and punishes it severely if the child does not respond in socially appropriate ways. As the infant begins to detain gratification of some of its instinctual needs, it gradually becomes conscious that there is a difference between its own yearnings and those of other people. Once the child begins to differentiate between itself and the outer world, its "ego", or conscious self, comes into being.[45]

This is the "real" us as we prefer to think of ourselves, including our knowledge, skills, beliefs, and deliberate motives. The ego operates on the "reality principle". It does our logical thinking and helps us get along in the world. Freudian theory hypothesizes that the intellectual and social skills that everyone uses daily are due to the ability to deal with the demands of the id. To the extent that these demands can be appeased in some rational manner, the ego permits satisfaction. Yet when the id's demands threaten to get us rejected by society, the ego represses them or tries to furnish alternatives that are socially tolerable. The ego, thus, has to pacify not only the id but the rules of society that we incorporate in our sense of what is acceptable behavior.[46]

The Superego

It is indeed true that the Freudian personality model is not complete with just the id and ego, for personality is more than the pleasure principle and reality principle. As a person grows, the people around oneself demand that one adopt society's rules and regulations. To do so, one must build up a conscience, or as this writer prefers, to be socialized and psychologically enculturated in a way that prevents the person from violating rules. Freudian theory labels this portion of the personality structure the "superego" and regards it as a part of one's ego that disjoins and commences to act on its own.[47] One's superego is therefore one's unconscious voice that helps an individual discriminate social rights from wrongs without the individual being aware of why he/she does so.

The Internal Personality Conflicts

Unfortunately, basic need (id), reason (ego), morality (superego), and the demands of the environment are often at odds, thus creating inner turmoil known as intrapsychic or psychodynamic conflict, which the ego must try to resolve. Freudian theory views the number and outcome of intrapsychic conflicts as important factors that shape each individual's

538   THE MEANING OF LIFE

personality and determine aspects of behavior. Thus, normal, adaptive behavior is associated with having relatively few conflicts or with resolving them effectively.[48]

In a sense, the conscious ego is engaged in a constant struggle to satisfy the insatiable demands of the unconscious id without incurring the wrath of the largely unconscious superego. To the extent that the ego controls one's behavior, it is realistic and socially acceptable. To the extent that one's behavior is ruled by the passions of the id and the unrelenting disapproval of the superego, it tends to be maladjusted and neurotic.[49]

Freudian theory also addresses these continual conflicts as the ego learns to resolve the conflicting demands made by the id, superego and the external environment. The ego has several "defense mechanisms" at its disposal to protect itself from these conflicts. Yet the ego is not always aware of what the needs of the id and superego are, because many of these needs are unconscious. The occurrence of signal anxiety warns the ego that intrapsychic tensions have become so strong that they threaten to disable the individual.

Psychodynamics Expressed as Moral Behavior

With the vast array of different mechanisms within Freudian theory it is clear that the average individual cannot employ psychoanalytic techniques to overcome the intrapsychic conflicts. Still, the essence of the Freudian approach to moral development is clear. That is, the goal of moral development is to strengthen the ego's defense system. In supporting the ego it becomes the victor over both the sexual urges of the id and the idealistic but impossible demands of the superego. Within this, Freudian theory views the analyst as coming to the aid of the client: "Our knowledge shall compensate for his ignorance and shall give his ego more mastery over the lost provinces of his mental life. The pact constitutes the analytic situation."[50]

A difficulty with the Freudian understanding of moral development is that it emphasizes the unconscious and affective components of the personality. With the elemental disregard for the cognitive, the client is helpless, becoming essentially dependent upon the psychoanalyst.[51]

In summary, while this approach is not readily available to most people it does provide a legacy of significant insight into the structure of moral development; that is, an understanding of the early (Freudian) stages of childhood and the inherent needs of each stage. Within the recognition of each stage, then, comes the ability to formulate the child's personality at the base level of ego formation. Therefore the eventual internalization of social and parental standards results in a child's ability to monitor his/her own behavior and to experience feelings of guilt when that behavior is not in conformity with expected demands.

Behavior Modification as Moral Development

According to the behavioral approach, that which is of primary relevance is what the individual does. As such, the behavioral approach considers human nature as an outgrowth of social learning, conditioning and past experience.[52] The primary emphasis of behavior modification therefore is to get rid of the problem through shaping or fading certain behaviors.

For example, if a child stops lying and speaks the truth one can assume that the problem no longer exists.

With the assumption that moral behavior does not just happen, but is the product of social conditioning, comes several basic paradigms. While more elaborate approaches such as behavior chaining and stimulus control may be used, two basic approaches are Classical and Instrumental conditioning.

The first paradigm is the Pavlovian Respondent/Classical Conditioning paradigm. In simple terms this paradigm may be summarized as: "The learned association between the weak and strong signal which transfers sufficient power to the weaker stimulus so that it comes to elicit the same response originally controlled only by the stronger one."[53] Within this basic method of behavior modification the affective attachments form for or against any perceptible stimulus, resulting in a reflex that elicits a certain response. As such, with classical conditioning applied to an individual, the individual will clearly learn to fear situations associated with negative experience. Such pain associated with the situation produces a natural response of avoidance.

The second basic method within the behavior modification model is the theory of Instrumental Conditioning. The difference between instrumental and classical conditioning is essentially that instrumental conditioning forms upon what follows the response rather than what preceded it. In such cases the major difference is that instrumental conditioning forms on the classical affective reflex responses, that is, the consequences of the behavior rather than a prior stimulus determine its continuance.[54]

Both classical and instrumental conditioning are very effective tools when one can effectively manipulate the environment. This is particularly noteworthy for schools, especially those within a residential context. The behavior paradigm demands the manipulation of environmental conditions so that good things happen after certain behaviors. Through such environmental manipulation proper moral living results.

Within the ministry context these various conditioning responses have significant effects (if not unusual methodologies). Entertainment, gifts and food are often part of a strategy to boost church attendance.[55] While the methodology may seem unorthodox, Clouse points to historical classical/instrumental conditioning regarding worship:

Learning about God relates both to the everyday activities in the home (Dt. 6:7) and to those special times when the people of God gather together to worship and praise their redeemer. In the Old Testament we read that these special occasions meant a break from the regular duties of the week (Lv. 23:3-4) and an opportunity for feasting (Ex. 12:14) and for storytelling (Jos. 4: 21-24) - events that all children enjoy ... But twentieth century America is different. Times have changed, and going to the place of worship may not be the high point of a person's week ...".[56]

It is for this very reason that I support the efforts of such specialized ministries as, summer camps, sporting events, Christian concerts and youth field trips. When positive, exciting activities can be paired with worship and the Christian community, the likelihood of continued worship and Christian identity formation increases.

540 THE MEANING OF LIFE

Kohlberg's Cognitive Moral Reasoning

The most interesting perspective of moral development is the work of L. Kohlberg and his cognitive approach. Such a perspective centers upon the mental/super-ego processes to view and understand moral development. At times such a view is misleading, since the emphasis is upon "psychic" (that is, cognitive) reasoning rather than behavioral outcomes.[57]

Cognitive psychologists view morality as primarily developmental in nature. Of chief importance in cognitive theory is that morality is due to intrapsychic conditions, not an outside source. Yet while the environment may encourage morality or may produce conditions that impede it, the dynamics of morality are still intra-psychic.[58]

Such an intrapsychic structure, as understood for reasons of cognitive reasoning theory, may be established through Freudian psychology. Such Freudian theory is comprehensive in its description of this intrapsychic structure as we have already discussed. Within cognitive theory then, is the use of the Freudian defined psychic structures. Therefore, when a difficulty arises between experiences and perceptions, an individual must adjust the use of psychic structures in order to resolve the conflict. The ability to manipulate the structures intrapsychically is the basis for movement from one moral reasoning stage to a higher stage.[59]

According to Freudian theory, and as experimental research suggests, self-awareness is vital to moral reasoning, yet one must be aware that such self-awareness is <u>not</u> totally uninfluenced by the environment and socialization (behavior modification).[60] In accordance with Freudian theory, self-awareness allows an individual to have the "ego strength" necessary to use his/her psychic structures in the appropriate manner to produce moral reasoning. By that, it may be considered a philosophical morality.

Within this general outline of cognitive moral reasoning Lawrence Kohlberg outlines a structure of moral reasoning into three basic levels: Preconventional, Conventional and Postconventional.[61] Within these three levels are six stages of Kohlberg's construct of cognitive reasoning (two stages for each level). Within the preconventional individual there is really no standard of morality. The preconventional individual simply interprets labels such as "good" and "bad" in terms of their physical consequences (punishment or reward) or in terms of the power of those who make the rules.[62] Within this preconventional level are two stages: Stage one is the morality of self preservation and avoidance of punishment, and stage two is the morality of the exchange of favors.[63]

The second level of cognitive moral reasoning is the Conventional level. Within this level are two stages, known as stages three and four. Stage three is moral reasoning based on the approval or disapproval in one's peer group. Stage four in moral reasoning incorporates societal values along with peer group values.[64]

The final and highest level of moral cognitive reasoning within the Kohlberg construct is Postconventional reasoning. This level also has two stages, known generically as stages five and six. The Postconventional level uses moral principles that have validity apart from the authority of groups to which one belongs. Stage five, the "morality of societal consensus"[65] is the tendency to reason in terms of societal rights and standards. Stage six is similar, except it utilizes ethical principles that tend to transcend societal rules and laws.[66]

While the practical aspects of cognitive moral reasoning may not be readily apparent, especially in terms of Kohlberg's theory, one must remain mindful of the benefit of such a structural theory. To understand a structure of thought is the first step toward influencing the development and maturity of that thought structure. The hope is, therefore, that the ministry of the Christian church could be geared to gradually foster higher levels of moral reasoning, for with each graduation in the hierarchy is a greater integration of the individual's thinking, problem solving and relating to the world.

CHRISTIAN EXISTENTIAL DEVELOPMENT

Existential Development

To understand the process of existential identity development as the basis of moral reasoning one must first examine the development process that contributes to existential well-being. We shal now therefore review the developmental integration process as elaborated by James A. Fowler. Within Fowler's (1981) work, <u>Stages of Faith</u>, is a developmental process that incorporates the works of Erikson, Piaget and Kohlberg. Fowler's developmental structure essentially acknowledges that there are prerequisite cognitive developmental stages that must occur before the existential faith pilgrimage can proceed. Fowler also acknowledges[67] that each developmental stage has a unique method of contributing to an individual's existential identity. Therefore, this unique method of contribution must be considered in the psychoanalytic process and understanding of moral maturity.

Within this developmental review, I shall summarize Fowler's view of development at each stage of growth for there exists an ongoing existential tension between beliefs that serve personal well-being and beliefs that reflect external circumstances and social evaluators. Furthermore, developmental changes are part of this tension, defining what is an appropriate existential outlook with each stage of growth. For instance, the belief of a 3-year-old in his/her omnipotence may enable the child to reduce anxieties. Yet, if those same ideas are present in adolescence one will inevitably express concern for the child's mental status. Old beliefs and processes must be revised in development and Fowler's work provides an adequate outline of the process. According to Fowler,[68] from birth to one-and-a-half years, Eric Erikson views the formation of the value of "basic trust vs. mistrust" at the core of existence.[69] This value formation is in turn associated with Piaget's sensorimotor stage of the basic coordination of hands, arms, mouth etc.[70] From the ages of two to six Erikson[71] identified the formative period of two values: Autonomy vs. Shame and Doubt (the will) and Initiative vs. Guilt (purpose).[72]

542 THE MEANING OF LIFE

Preoperational Stage and Intuitive-Projective Existentialism (Stage One)

At the age period between two and six Piaget identifies the cognitive developmental stage of "preoperations". Within the preoperational stage a child thinks by way of mental pictures that imitate visual reality. Within this stage the child is unable to reverse this picture or understand how reality works.[73] If one agrees that Fowler's definition of faith as "meaning making" is equivalent to an "existential worldview" one begins to see how Fowler's stage theory will influence the clarification of existential and moral development.[74]

At the preoperations stage of psychological development Fowler[75] identifies the intuitive-projective stage of existentialism. This stage of existential development is the individual's cognitive inability to compare two different perspectives on the same object and by that simply assume without question that the perception he/she has is the only available perspective. This stage is important for the therapist because it dominates the child's view of the world and God (essentially the child's rudimentary existential system). All concepts are concrete and find expression in anthropomorphic terms. This stage forms an existential system that reflects the attitudes of others around the child. Therefore parables, stories, myths and attitudes that dominate the child's atmosphere, with significant elders, form the basis of his/her existential foundation.[76]

Concrete Operations and Mythic-Literal Existentialism (Stage Two)

The subsequent stage of life transition takes place at approximately the age of seven. Piaget characterizes this age as the "concrete-operational" stage. For the child, thinking becomes more practical as the child learns to take account of differences of perspective between the self and others. This "Mythic-Literal" stage[77] of existential development is the stage when the person takes on the stories, beliefs and observances that symbolize belonging to his or her community. The symbols and rituals of one's community are interpreted in the new linear fashion of concrete operations, making coherence and meaning out of life. Within this stage, the socialization process has a major influence upon one's development of an existential framework.

Synthetic-Conventional Existentialism (Stage Three).

The next stage of development, namely adolescence, is the most traumatic in many respects. Erikson indicates[78] that the values of "identity vs. role confusion" find expression during this critical stage. The ability to think about what others think about oneself causes the adolescent to suddenly become self-conscious. This stage also brings with it what Piaget terms "formal operations" thinking, which is the ability to think abstractly. Fowler identifies the[79] "Synthetic-Conventional" stage of existential development to occur with formal operations. This "synthetic - conventional" stage of existential development is more personal and abstract than the previous stage and essentially makes the development of "personal myths". Such myths are beliefs about the uniqueness of self and how the self relates with others.

Review of childhood existentialism

We will now summarize the process of existential identity development from childhood to the synthetic-conventional stage to provide a clarification of the process. We must realize that along with the adolescent's burgeoning sense of identity there is also a struggle to discover a sense of meaning[80]. As the child emerges into adolescence, his/her cognitive abilities change and increase, allowing the individual to pass beyond concrete reasoning and enabling him/her to grasp what is "possible". This level of "formal operations" reasoning lends the child to a certain level of existential emptiness since this newly found reasoning ability lacks practice.

Ideally this existential emptiness fills through the child's safe exploration of his/her personal and family faith history. However, this existential filling is hindered by the mobility of modern society. That is, the mobility of the modern family robs the child of the dramatic impact of the resources that tells one what to do, or how to invest certain acts with significance, or to model meaningful engagement in life, and the result is a lack of a sturdy existential framework for the adolescent within which to understand life.[81] This existential emptiness often manifests itself in a vague sense of boredom that often typifies the stage of adolescence.[82]

Adult Existentialism
Intuitive - Reflective Existentialism (stage four)

In the fourth stage of development, an adult is at some time forced by circumstance to clarify his/her values and assert individual control and responsibility for his/her direction in life. The essential feature[83] of the emergence of stage four, then, is the critical distancing from one's previous support of his/her existential system to encourage the emergence of stage four. This occurs through the critical distancing from one's previous support of his/her existential system to encourage the emergence of an "executive ego". That is, to take control and responsibility for the direction and meaning of one's life. As this critical feature occurs a person is forming a new identity. This new identity is the enacting of one's life theory in the shaping of a "lifestyle" apart from familial or contextual influences.

As an individual leaves home and becomes responsible for his/her own actions he/she enters the stage that Levinson calls the "novice adult" where the person is forming his/her first adult life structures.[84] Erikson identifies the crisis[85] of Intimacy vs. Isolation with this period.[86] Intimacy requires the ability to stand alone and to risk one's forming self and sense of identity in close engagement with other persons and with ideological commitments that define the individual's refined existential system.

While the emergence of stage four usually occurs in the mid-twenties, it may be delayed in some individuals until the mid thirties or forties.[87] The transition that forces an adult into stage four is usually a life event that would typify a mid-life crisis such as changes in primary relationships such as divorce; the death of spouse, parent, or child; or children simply growing up and leaving home. A minister should be aware that late stage transition in an individual's life may

544   THE MEANING OF LIFE

be extended five to ten years.[88] From a developmental perspective therefore one hopes that this transition would be made in early adulthood.

Identity Issues in Early Existential Development

It seems logical to now clarify the previous existential stages through discussion on the relationship between identity formation and existential maturity. The reason that further clarification is necessary is that developmental aspects that occur at this stage are critical to existential development and identity formation and subsequent ego strength for moral reasoning. The redefining of one's self is finally possible with the abstract thinking of formal operations. A complete restructuring of the self may occur, where old beliefs and values are replaced by new ones. In some instances, however, the individual may choose to experiment with various identities and frameworks of existence.

At some point an adolescent will be pressured to choose an identity[89] and to use the existential framework chosen to define how he/she will act in society. If, however, the adolescent does not choose a clear identity and their existential framework remains fluid or poorly defined, existential development halts.

As Marcia indicates,[90] mature identity occurs when an individual experiences pressure from some outward circumstance to commit to a clear existential framework and expression (ideology and occupation). When an individual succeeds (or fails) at defining a basic existential framework that is committed to in action, he/she passes into one of four identity statuses:[91] diffusion; foreclosure; moratorium; or identity achieved.

Identity Diffusion and Existential Stages Two and Three

The status that has the most vaguely defined existential world view is the status of identity diffusion. In this case the individual is either not aware of, nor significantly influenced by, pressure to choose an identity and occupation.[92] The lack of pressure may also mean that the individual has not gone through the process of searching out new identities or existential frameworks. This lack of searching means that the individual has not defined his/her life theory and is therefore operating with a vague and rudimentary apparatus for making life meaningful. Due to the rudimentary apparatus for functioning the individual will likely respond to increased social pressure with anger and defiance or withdraw in apathy (which may lead to personality disintegration, perhaps even schizophrenia or suicide). The danger of this identity status, in the view of this writer, is the potential for abuse of substances that inhibits cognitive functioning and reduces the chance of defining a personal existential framework. This status most closely fits Frankl's noogenic neurosis or "existential vacuum".[93] In addition, the individual in identity diffusion is "functionally" at stage two existentialism, although abstract thinking is possible. Yet since the individual is not actively concerned about defining an abstract life theory the individual does not truly mature to the third stage of existentialism known as synthetic-conventional.[94]

Foreclosure and Stage Three in Transition.

The second potential status of identity formation is known as foreclosure. This study views foreclosure as indicative of stage three existential development, or of an inflexible and immature stage four. As Celia, DeWolfe and Fitzgibbon indicate,[95] individuals in foreclosure do commit to an existential framework and expression (ideology and occupation). Yet the individual has not experienced the existential searching normally necessary to reach a commitment to such an existential framework. In essence the individual stays within the defining parameters and expectations of the peer; family and/or faith community. The benefit of this status is that the individual has a readily defined epistemological/theological framework and a somewhat defined personal existential framework within which to live.[96] The detrimental aspect of this status (in not experiencing a crisis) is that the individual does not develop the skills to clearly define a personal existential framework. Thereby the individual will have a rigid and inflexible (stage three existential) outlook on life that may cause problems when personal supports are lost. The loss of a support structure, such as the death of a parent or spouse (as mentioned previously) or the loss of a job, can be particularly devastating.

Moratorium and Existential Stages Three and Four.

A typical identity status for college students is known as Moratorium. In this status the individual actively involves him/herself in evaluating various systems of understanding the world and finding a role within it without yet making a commitment.[97] Due to the nature of this status an individual will often appear unstable and discontented. The apparent instability of the individual is because a clearly-defined set of "personal rules and outlook" are not yet established.

The individual within moratorium may appear to have the existential flexibility to be categorized above the fourth stage of existential development. Yet, since the individual has not yet made a commitment to a life direction and existential framework he/she cannot be classified at even stage four. Therefore the individual experiencing identity moratorium should actually be categorized as in the third existential stage and approaching (or in active transition to) stage four existentialism.

Identity Achieved and Existential Stages Three and Four

When an individual has an opportunity to evaluate various worldviews and life direction options (moratorium) and actually makes a personalized decision, he/she is on his/her way to achieving a personal existential framework. With a commitment to a personal-life-theory-into-action-as-a life-direction, one may be said to be at the identity status of identity achieved.[98]

From an existential development perspective one may view the "identity achieved" status as the fulfillment of stage four and the movement towards stage five. The critical factor of those who go through the process of moratorium, life crisis and decision, life theory development and making a life direction commitment to it is the intrapsychic experience of choosing and defining a comprehensive existential framework. This intrapsychic experience thereby allows for the higher

546 THE MEANING OF LIFE

levels of intrapsychic integration, self definition, commitment and social adaptation necessary for stage five existentialism; that is, the fine-tuning of one's world view and coping mechanisms.

Existential Achievement and Moral Maturity
Conjunctive-Meaning Existentialism - Stage Five

In Fowler's fifth stage we move into the center of existential analysis. Stage five, the stage of "conjunctive meaning"[99] is different in character and form from the previous existential stages. The difference lies in that it involves the individual's reexamining the previous stages to integrate the whole. Stage five, as a way of seeing, of knowing, of committing, moves beyond the dichotomizing logic of stage four's "either/or" toward a dialectical knowing. That is, one's perspectives are examined and evaluated in light of the world and the infinite possibilities of existence.[100] In essence it is the active harmonizing use of the two existential systems (epistemological/theological and personal/practical).

The two existential systems are the epistemological system of one's view of the universe and one's personal existential system. An individual uses the first system as a compass to find his/her place in the world. Between these two systems, for the individual in stage five, there is a relativity that one acknowledges and owns. It is the recognition of personal weaknesses yet responsibility, of independence and dependence.[101] It is the acknowledgment of relativity in existence and that one's life and understanding are fragile and only a dim reflection of the reality to which it mediates.

The Character of Stage Five Existentialism - Moral Maturity

As Fowler indicates[102], stage five is the ability of an individual to actively reshape and restructure his/her existential framework (the goal of therapy). This restructuring process comes through a new reclaiming and reworking of one's past. There is a critical recognition of one's unconscious—the myths, ideal images, and prejudices built deeply into one's existential identity by virtue of one's particular history. Yet it not only recognizes them but actively reshapes them. On a social level[103] as well, the individual is ready to help others cultivate and generate identity and meaning.

Stage Six Existentialism

Ideally, an individual should be able to recognize his/her identity status and role in the world, and express this through his/her efforts and actions. For the Christian, this statement is often set in the phrase "to be like Christ" and is presented as the ultimate goal of the actions of life.

As a developmental stage it is beyond stage five for the simple reason[104] that stage six is the actual ideal expression of one's existential status. This is in contrast to stage five which still clings to the very human tendency of being caught between the desire to serve the ultimate reality and the need and will to preserve one's well-being. Yet, theoretically at least, for an individual at stage six, life is both loved and held loosely. At this stage an individual becomes open and willing to die at the hands of those whom he/she hopes to change.[105]

Within this stage Fowler alludes to the eschatological character of the Kingdom of God, and I would like to reinterpret it as a "theology of hope". That is, stage six is the experience of hope that springs from the past and into the future, leaving the present to be an open expression of this future hope. Herein lies the ability of a stage six individual to hold life loosely. An individual in stage six existentialism views the role of humanity as an existential expression of the ultimate existential framework of God's promises, in essence, that humans are to live in oneness and love and mutual service and fulfill their role as caretakers of creation. To this end one may think of Martin Luther King's statement that "segregation is nothing but the existential expression of the state of humanity".

Developmental Summary

The importance of identity development to the existential and moral development process is twofold. First, it provides a basis upon which one may ensure that appropriate steps occur to ensure existential growth through the normal life processes of the first four stages. The encouragement of existential identity development then, is the training for stage five, whereby an individual can revisit his/her childhood and adult interests, occupations etc.. This revisiting will then enable the individual to evaluate, reinvent and reintegrate positive views and moral choices formed at the previous stages. From the view of the ego psychologist[106] the existential component of identity development and moral reasoning is stage "regression in the service of the ego". That is, a process of self analysis where an individual returns from present levels of existential and ego functioning to earlier ones in order to rework and refine certain aspects of his/her identity formation. Such a pattern therefore leads to release from earlier dysfunctional patterns and formation of better integrated existential systems. The resulting ego integrity and positive coping mechanisms facilitate higher levels of moral reasoning and behavior.

THE PSYCHOLOGICAL VALUE OF WORSHIP AND CHRISTIAN LITURGICAL CULTURE

"RITES AND RITUALS"

Defining Rites and Rituals

A ritual is a set of words or actions or an event that is central to the identity of the community.[107] A rite or ritual has a central core or theme that defines the character of the event.[108] Such a common action or ritual invites individuals to engage fully in the meanings, feelings and

548 THE MEANING OF LIFE

identity that accompany the occasion. It supports the individual and shapes both individual and corporate identities, meanings and values.

Within the catholic Christian community an individual's process of identity formation and existential and moral development generally forms through the rituals of the community known as "christening" and "catecheses". The first formative ritual significant in identity formation then is christening.[109] Christening is the process a person goes through within a Christian community of being formed and transformed into a new being, modeled after the likeness of Christ.[110]

Catecheses, then, is the support, encouragement and maturity of this transformed identity and status. It requires three deliberate, or intentional, systematic and interrelated lifelong processes that are essential to the maturity of faith and morals. Catecheses is therefore a support network of three basic components of Christian ministry: Instruction, Education and Identity Formation.[111]

Catecheses traditionally places an emphasis upon the instructional aspect. The instructional aspect is important since it helps a person acquire a knowledge of Christian theology. A secondary benefit is the ability to think theologically and to make moral decisions. However, instruction does little for laying the foundation of existential identity formation in the child. The limitation of instruction is that the mental processes required are limited developmentally until early adolescence. This instructional component also relates to the educational component of Catecheses, which is limited in childhood due to the developmental issues. Education is the critical reflection in practice and experience in light the Christian faith.

The aspect of catecheses known as "formation" is important for identity and moral development, yet is poorly understood. In essence, formation is a use of rituals and experiences with the intentional process of acculturation for children within a Christian faith community and assimilation with adults. If the formation process in Christian ministry is done poorly, persons may be assimilated into the society. This societal assimilation implies losing one's sense of self-identity as believers in Jesus Christ and members in His church.[112]

The Role of Rituals in Existential Moral Development

How then does this relate to the development of an individual's identity and moral growth (both overall development and cognitive reasoning skills)? Let us begin with the onset of Piaget's stage of concrete operations. Piaget characterizes the ages of seven to approximately twelve as the stage of concrete operations. For the child in this stage, thinking becomes more practical as the child learns that things are "stable". This new mode of reasoning enables the child to take account of differences of perspective between the self and others. This age is concurrent with the Mythic-Literal stage of Fowler's existential identity development. It is within this mythic-literal stage that the person begins to take on for him/herself the stories, beliefs and observances that symbolize belonging to his or her community. The symbols and rituals of one's community are understood in the new linear fashion of concrete operations, making coherence and meaning out of life. Within this stage, the socialization process has a major influence upon one's development of an existential and moral framework.

Westerhoff identifies the essential components of this developmental stage. Westerhoff notes that communal rites are essential in identity formation. Such communal rites take the form of repetitive, symbolic and social acts. The cultic life of the community is therefore the method of identity formation or catecheses at this developmental stage. The cultic life of a church may therefore be summarized as:

1. Ceremonial acts - prescribed behaviors.
2. Ritual acts - prescribed words.
3. Rites of intensification that follow the calendar (once a week, month, year etc.) and that shape, sustain and enhance the community's existential identity as well as increase group solidarity.
4. Rites of passage that follow the life cycle and promote meaningful passage for persons and the community from one stage of life to another.
5. Rites of initiation that induct people into the community.

The role of these rites in the existential development of a child between the ages of seven and twelve is important to developing an existential framework of time.[113] The rites and rituals in this process cause an orientation toward past, present and future, and structure time in terms of particular events. The ordering of time in terms of the calendar and activities provides a structure for understanding the meaning and purpose of one's behavior.[114]

Due to the vast interrelationship between church life and existential and moral development this chapter will limit itself to a summary of each stage. Within this, this author would like to mention that the goal of the minister is to enable the individual to embark on the journey of understanding his/her universe and how he/she fits within this universe. The goal of the existential aspect of Christian ministry and worship therefore is to enable an individual to develop two existential systems. The primary role of the minister, therefore is to enable the individual to develop the theological/ontological/epistemological structure of God and His creation in a mythical manner (stage 1); an anthropological manner (stage 2); and a synthetic manner (stage 3).

Such an epistemological existential system of one's identity comes into formation through the process mentioned previously as the Catecheses (identity) formation. Therefore the formation of the first stage of existential and moral identity formation is through the formative process of "being in the presence of believers".[115] The first stage of existential identity (Intuitive - Projective Faith)[116] is marked by imitation and fantasy where examples, stories, moods and actions are the central items in forming long-lasting images and feelings.[117] In essence this phase is the first stage of self-awareness that exists in an intuitive understanding of the world.[118]

The second stage of existential development (mythic - literal) is more linear and narrative in construction. In addition, the symbols of the community greatly influence perceptions that form within this stage.[119] As I have already mentioned, rituals of the community serve to mark out time and provide meanings to the occasions of the community. Therefore within this stage the

550 THE MEANING OF LIFE

formation process of rituals is the primary force for developing the existential and moral systems of an individual.

The third stage of development, known as "synthetic-conventional" existentialism, is the stage of being partially conformist and partially individualistic. What this means is that an individual begins to develop a personalized myth and identity yet wants to conform to significant others because one is unsure of his/her own personal identity.[120] The formation process within this phase is the invitation to express one's beliefs and begin the process of clarification, autonomy and personal definition of identity and values.[121]

A portion of the formative process of stage four (Intuitive - Reflective) is also to express one's belief. However, this expression goes beyond the defining and clarification of one's beliefs. It is the demythologizing of symbols[122] that form the basis of one's identity and values. It is at this point that the true understanding of community symbols begins to relate to personal identity and ideology.

The final formative process of Christian ministry then is the call to personal responsibility and leadership.[123] This formative process relates to the maturation of stage four existentialism. In addition, personal responsibility relates to the onset of the conjunctive identity of stage five (conjunctive faith) existentialism.[124] The maturity of stage four is the commitment of personal responsibility. The transition to stage five is the willed return to previous stages of development to shore-up the ideas and images of these stages. It relates to the desire to help others to grow. It is the understanding of principles, post conventional moral reasoning, and the application of these principles in a life direction:

> "Conjunctive faith cannot live with the demythologizing strategy of stage 4 as regards to symbols and liturgy ... [rather] it is the veteran of critical reflection [stage 4] and the effort to "reduce" the symbolic, the liturgical and the mythical to conceptual meanings. ... [then] to resubmit to the intuitive [symbolism] of life with [a deeper understanding] ... It carries forward the critical capacities and methods of the previous stages, but it no longer trusts them except as tools to avoid self-deception and to order truths encountered in other ways."[125]

Ritual Summary

The rituals which are appropriate and important for each stage therefore are as follows:

- Stories, attitudes and community atmosphere is of essential importance for the pre-schooler.

- Rituals that mark out time, such as Advent, Christmas, Lent, Easter and Pentecost celebrations are important for elementary school age children.

- Transition rituals and celebrations such as baptism birthdays, confirmation, marriage and funerals are important to adolescents.

In addition, participation in proclaiming aspects of worship and investigation of the background of celebrations is important. For the young adult what is important is the clarification of life living issues and life theories (the enacting of their existential identity systems). In this respect then intergenerational events and mentoring (such as Promise Keepers) is essential for existential identity development. To take a role of proclaiming one's faith is important and therefore a minister should involve young adults in Sunday school teaching and fun activities with the children of the congregation as well as serving as acolytes and ushers. As the individual matures and defines him/herself, he/she develops the cognitive flexibility (depending on life experiences mentioned in chapter two) to understand the intricacies of faith and life. At this stage of adult maturity the individual will return to the importance of rituals and symbols, for all the rituals and symbols of the Christian community summarize, express and validate an older individual's existential identity and life theory.

Therefore, the finest sense of worship and involvement in rituals is its significant impact on the process of existential formation. For when worship is "the to adoring of man to the one eternal God, self-revealed in time" it seems to subsume the totality of the Christian life.[126]

THE PSYCHOLOGICAL VALUE OF THEOLOGICAL THINKING

As the previous sections suggest, we are not primarily concerned with information as the process for moral development. Rather, what is essential is to be forming a clear identity that supports the ego enough to allow moral choices to be made.

Of course, church leaders are also involved in the teaching of Biblical content and of materials phrased in dogmative categories. However, since church leaders are to be concerned about being in on the formation that the Spirit is achieving, they are to be chiefly teaching Biblical content as the confirming witness to the action of the Spirit. Thereby, theological teaching is a confirmation of the action which is already going on in the lives of the baptized community. There will never be a time when the Spirit does not stand ready to use the Scriptures in the process of identity formation that creates, sustains, and intensifies the new life. We must therefore avoid the stance of simply imparting information because it may obscure the real objective by permitting the community of faith to rest content with an inferior objective.[127]

Theism as the Basis of Formation

The existential psychology and moral development theories presented thus far fit into an area of psychology known as humanistic psychology. This movement of humanistic psychology sees a great deal of value in a study of subjective experiences. A definition of a humanistic psychologist therefore begins with the proposition that humanity is essentially good, and the highest of all beings.[128] This definition may continue to encompass those psychologists who believe that will, reason and purpose are real and significant and not merely illusory creations of the mind.[129] Existential psychology views humanity as the central source of meaning and significance. This

552   THE MEANING OF LIFE

anthropocentric view causes the existential psychologist to define three patterns for discovering meaning in life: (1) doing a deed; (2) experiencing a value; and (3) suffering.[130]

The Problem with and strictly agnostic/atheistic Humanism

The humanistic premise of existential identity formation is inadequate for the task of discovering meaning and providing a basis for moral reasoning and action. Life meaning and morality require a context and understanding of reality that goes beyond the anthropocentric basis of humanism. In addition, this project asserts that the humanistic basis of some existential and moral theories is simply a diversionary approach to enable the individual to ignore his/her inauthentic mode of living (essentially immaturity).

The foundational difference between the humanistic basis of identity formation and moral reasoning and this study's proposed alternative substructure within Christianity is the view of humanity. While the humanist views humanity as essentially "good" and the "highest of all beings", the Christian holds the broad view of humanity as the bearer of God's image, yet also of sin, human depravity, and the object of both divine judgment and salvation. The humanistic denial of the biblical God makes the humanistic existential view of life to be faulty and inadequate as the foundation of a meaning and a process for moral development based upon self. The faultiness of the humanistic perspective will be further explained throughout this chapter.

The validity of a theistic perspective of reality must be discussed, contrasting Theism with Humanism with the goal of determining the logical basis for existential identity and moral formation. The implications of the Genesis discourse are necessary for arriving at a proper anthropology that in turn brings us to a true philosophy of life. Let us evaluate the humanistic perspective as a source and context of meaning and morality in life.

This discussion must certainly begin at the point of the origin of humanity. The Christian theistic view obviously claims that God is the Creator of the universe and creation is accountable to God. In contrast, the humanistic view incorporates the view of evolution that skews a "proper" anthropology and passes the Genesis narrative off as the foolish folklore of an ancient, primitive culture.[131] Moreover, the concept of divine judgment is cast aside in favor of a thought pattern that declares that "there is no God".[132] The humanistic perspective therefore states that humanity is accountable to no one but itself.

With the absence of an ultimate being or Creator, God, the humanistic perspective fosters a relativism in understanding life. Relativism is an essential part of most moral development approaches. Since there are no absolutes, humanistic relativism encourages an individualized cosmology without giving thought to frames of reference within reality. However, if there are no absolutes, how can anyone understand anything? Indeed, the declaration that there are no absolutes and everything is relative is in itself an absolute statement and therefore inconsistent with humanistic relativism.[133]

Unlike the humanistic accusation that truth is relative, the Christian presupposes that truth is truth, while recognizing that individual perceptions are but a portion of this truth. Moreover, God

REDISCOVERING A LOST HERITAGE... TRADITIONAL CHRISTIAN APPROACH   553

(as revealed in Scripture) is truth and it is from Him that all truth springs: "No one can blame us for we base our position on the Word of God as the eternal truth."[134]

Yet the school of humanism responds to theism by stating that it is a blind leap of faith.[135] In counter to the humanistic response the Christian clarifies faith as a rational dependence on a dependable and trustworthy God who has revealed himself to humankind.[136] In addition, a vast expanse of scientific evidence supports the Christian's perspective.

True Life or Simple Diversions?

From the developmental psychology standpoint, the discussion of the benefit of humanism or theism may seem moot. Yet in the final analysis, the faultiness of the humanistic perspective displays itself in a true vista of life, for a life theory that incorporates death is essential in existential identity formation and subsequent moral reasoning and behavior. Yet death is the very issue which humanism ignores.

Death is a deciding point for determining which existential identities are sufficient. In the topic of death the weaknesses of humanism become apparent, because humanism is an inadequate method for dealing with the subject. Indeed the Humanistic Manifesto of 1973 simply says: "Humanism can provide the purpose and inspiration that so many seek; it can give personal meaning and significance to human life."[137] However, this episode is faulty, for the Manifesto also states, "No deity will save us, we must save ourselves."[138] Yet such a statement begs the question, "In the face of death, how will they save themselves?"

According to the humanistic worldview the answer to the question of death is to "find meaning in an action". Therefore this study must conclude that due to its humanistic foundation, the common view of identity formation must deal with death by diverting one's attention away from the inevitability of it. Such a view follows a long and hopeless tradition that has plagued people down through the ages. Even the ancient "pagans" would not ignore this topic. Yet, they too found the answer to be the same as the humanist, for without God and His grace there is no hope.

Within the ancient Babylonian Epic of Gilgamesh, Siduru tells Gilgamesh that his search for everlasting life is hopeless:

Gilgamesh, where are you hurrying to? You will never find that life for which you are looking. When the gods created man they allotted to him death, but life they retained in their own keeping. As for you Gilgamesh, fill your belly with good things; day and night, dance and be merry, feast and rejoice. Let your clothes be fresh, bathe yourself in water, cherish the little child that holds your hand, and make your wife happy in your embrace; for this too is the lot of man.[139]

It is therefore this "loss of being" or realization of death which then may be one of the most important aspects for overcoming modern humanistic thought, for one characteristic of death will inevitably emerge:

554 THE MEANING OF LIFE

That death is always someone's own death, and cannot be experienced vicariously. There are innumerable ways in which one person can represent or stand in for another, and we utilize these ways every day. But nothing of the kind is possible in the case of death. Death shares one of the characteristics that belong to all human existence; it is always someone's own.140 Death is the mark of human finitude and we are bound by it.141

It is at this point that this study must conclude the humanistic vista to be questionable. For in response to the biblical/theistic view the humanist may simply ignore it and declare "Who knows?". However, in the face of death, all diversions from this question fade away, and the humanist must deal with an authentic existence that realizes death.

Unfortunately, identity development, in the tradition of humanism, tends to adopt an inauthentic mode of being. That is, it exists to "cover up death" or to relegate it to an infinite future as something that will happen "one day":[142]

Religious humanism considers the complete realization of human personality to be the end of man's life and seeks its development and fulfillment in the here and   now... we strive for the good life, here and now ... The quest for the good life is still the central task   of mankind.[143]

The Superiority of Faith Based Mythopoeics

The humanistic presupposition is an inauthentic mode of living and moral behavior. While the humanistic movement simply declares that "the quest for the good life is ... the central task of mankind", [144] the Christian can take the meaningful, ethical and true perspective of life based on a hope in God and his promises. When faced with the inevitable question of death the humanist is left hopeless. The theistic view is therefore held as the only source of adequate meaning and hope and the foundation of the formation and discovery of both meaning and hope, and as the basis of proper identity formation.

Moral Reasoning Based In Theism
The Formative Aspect of Fear

This study shall now clarify how moral reasoning arises from the theistic basis. The humanistic world view lacks an adequate philosophical context for understanding life and developing a hardy identity. This is dangerous since an experience or action without a "reason" or context is meaningless, for it is the context of reality that gives the action or service meaning. The theistic epistemological view therefore provides a new perspective of life and impetus for action, as Frankl states: "The crowning experience of all, for the homecoming man, is the wonderful feeling that, after all he has suffered, there is nothing that need be feared any more - except his God."[145] To act morally and to find a meaningful life, fear is central. As Kierkegaard has said:

The adventure that every human being must go through - to learn to be anxious [in dread] in order that he may not perish ... whoever has learned to be [in dread] in the right way has learned the ultimate.[146]

Yet what is the significance of fear and the meaning of it? The interpretation that seems to best suit this statement is to "fear the Lord, and to learn from that fear."[147] That is, the fear of the Lord is to recognize his character, statutes, love and judgment in all that we do. The fear of the Lord is to be what Kierkegaard terms "to be a student of possibility", for by recognizing the possibility of divine judgment one goes beyond the realm of visible human reality to an existential understanding.

In contrast, humanistic theories (without a proper substructure of meaning) cause one to be a "student of reality" and therefore one who identifies only human judgment. In doing so the individual calculates the odds of "getting away" with destructive behavior without getting caught. Such a student of reality is thus the antithesis of the student of possibility, for the student of possibility recognizes the fact that, if he/she is not caught by the human systems of judgment, the divine is unavoidable.[148] Therefore it is evident that two individuals may think at the same cognitive moral reasoning levels (according to Kohlberg theory discussed in chapter 1), yet their respective existential outlooks on life will cause them to act in completely different ways.

A Context for Meaning and Morality

Thus it can be recognized that the humanist is like the Kierkegaardian "student of reality" (mentioned in the previous paragraph) who will struggle to find a framework of morality since the only understanding of guilt is from the finite, and hence the understanding of existence and meaning is lost in the finite. Indeed, the reality that the humanist perceives is finite, and finitely the question of an individual's meaning in life or even whether he is "guilty" cannot be determined except in an external and most imperfect sense:

Whoever learns to know his [meaning or] guilt only by analogy to judgment of the police court and the supreme court never really understands that he is guilty, for if a man is guilty, he is infinitely guilty.[149]

Hence, the antithesis to the humanist and student of reality is that individual who learns from the "possibility" of the divine. Such fear of the inevitable possibility of divine authority and judgment is absolutely educative.[150] Particularly educative is the fear that is through faith, for this fear also allows the possibility of grace. Such fear consumes all finite ends and discovers all their deceptions.[151] For while the humanist may attempt to evade the consequences of his actions, the "fear of the Lord" causes the student of possibility to know no such evasion.

The central importance of this fear is that it is set in the character, teaching, judgment and love of the Lord. Fear that is not rooted in such divine things is therefore finite, which is thereby deceptive and improper in guiding one to the proper understanding of life: "If at the beginning of his education he misunderstands the anxiety [dread], so that it does not lead him to faith but away

556 THE MEANING OF LIFE

from faith, then he is lost."[152] Without faith, fear is not proper, hence an individual cannot be directed to an adequate meaning for life and will eventually end up in an existential crisis.

Indeed, the individual whose existential identity is formed upon visible human finitude, as the humanist would like, does not understand how to live in fear of God and his authority. Thereby a meaning for life with God is lacking, and meaning and morality are not found, except in a very mediocre and fragile sense.

In contrast, the Christian "student of possibility" has a view of reality that is not only an infinite, abstract possibility of divine judgment but of grace as well. Thus, for the Christian there is present a substructural framework that provides significance and meaning to the finite experiences of life. That is, the recognition of the infinite "theological" aspects of life provide a context for finding meaning and expressing moral imperatives in everyday activities. Indeed, without the consideration of the infinite there is no context or occasion for meaning in the finite.

Testing the Formation Structure - Death Issues

As was discussed previously, the ultimate test of identity formation is how it deals with death. Thereby this study shall examine the proposed foundation of theism and the consideration of the infinite aspects of life, namely God, as the context for meaning in life. In this issue of death the study has already determined the limits of current humanism since it is confined (at present) to finite experiences. In this finiteness the meaning would most certainly be lost, for death is where the finite ends and the infinite begins. Thus that which is merely finite will be lost within death.

When both the infinite and finite are considered, life and the meaning to be found within it takes on a whole new texture in the face of death; death becomes integrative rather than destructive for existence. An authentic existence which anticipates death and understands all living to be also dying will then transcend the triviality of everyday existence and achieved meaning and unity. It is through laying hold of and appropriating this untransferable and intrinsic possibility of self that "genuine unified selfhood is attained".[153]

Therefore this study acknowledges that the unity of the finite and infinite is not only beneficial for finding meaning in the face of death, but in everyday existence as well. Death, or rather anxiety in the face of death, has the role of causing individuals to remember to live a meaningful and moral life, as well as awakening the mind to the wonder of living under the authority of God.[154]

The teaching of Scripture must therefore end in the following goals: a clear existential worldview, a clear life theory and a clear structure for making moral decisions. All of these structures are part and parcel of Christian formation and the goal of the hearing of Scripture. We as church leaders therefore must shatter the "inferior objective" of "just providing information", in our own minds, lest by stress we tend to obscure the dramatic identity formation that occurs in the people of God. Only by participation with the Spirit in the identity formation of God's people are we working at the task God assigned to us. We are to assist in the process of "making disciples"—"making learners" is quite another matter. We make disciples by equipping people with information <u>and</u> involving them in the existential formation activity of the Spirit.

CONCLUSION

Psychological and Existential Aspects

Essentially, the educative goal of ministry is to assist in the Christian Identity Formation process. The ideal goal of existential and moral development is to reach Stage 5 maturity. In Stage 5 existential identity an individual has the tools to actively reshape their views and approaches to living. The Stage 5 level of moral reasoning is the clarification and utilization of the universal principles inherent in the individual's existential identity.

The achievement of Stage 5 existentialism is dependent upon certain life experiences in the identity formation process. Such experiences essential for stage 5 are identity moratorium and then the status of identity achieved, along with commitment to a life direction. A lesser achievement, yet one which is a realistic goal of the church community, is the individual member's achievement of the identity status of foreclosure, for such a status still provides an existential identity, a faith framework and a context for moral reasoning and behavior.

Christian ministry for moral development should not center on simply teaching facts. Rather, the primary goal and intent is to be in on the identity formation of the people of God (through the use of worship, rituals, stories, inter-generational interaction and theological teachings), a formation that is underway through the Spirit's power. Although Christian ministry holds the goal of formation, it also acknowledges and accepts as a part of its confession that nothing we do toward formation of the family of God is really done by us.

The Christian existential identity formation process, then, is the assisting in the formation of the existential structures that frame one's thoughts and moral reasoning. The evidence from research points to the formation process of faith and existential well-being as a very high correlate to moral behavior.[155] As such, when one is considering the value of the Christian Community in psychological formation the benefits must not be dismissed.

POST-SCRIPT

PERVERSIONS OF THE HELPING PROFESSION

"Persuasive efforts are labeled *propagandistic* when someone judges that the action which is the goal of the persuasive effort will be advantageous to the persuader but not in the best interests of the persuadee. There are no objective techniques for determining the best interests of the persons involved in a persuasive effort. Consequently the social psychologist does not decide whether or not a given effort is propagandistic. Propaganda comes into psychology as a judgment made by others. We can study propaganda as we can study good and evil. *We don't make the judgments but we can study the phenomena so judged.*"

■ Roger Brown, *Words and Things* (1958)

Psychological Warfare

A credo that seems to typify humanity is "The greatest things are also the worst things." For example, the greatest technical achievement of the modern age must surely be harnessing the power of the atom, and yet this same achievement has held its masters in fear because of its awesome destructive power. It seems our fate that whenever we do something great it is inevitably turned into something sinister.

Sadly this credo has also been true of the field of psychology. While its goal was to better understand humanity in order to help, heal and comfort, that same knowledge has also been applied to pervert, twist and break the human spirit. Nowhere is this twist of power more formalized that in the industrial military complexes of the western world. Despite the lessons we should have learned from the rise of such maniacal leaders as Adolph Hitler, the same techniques that dragged Germany into the pit of Nazism has been embraced by governments around the world including our own.

One only has to look at pictures of what are called "unlawful combatants" held at the US Marine base in Guantanamo Bay, Cuba to recognize that considerable psychological abuse is taking place. Indeed the techniques used and even the execution facilities announced in May of 2003 are all frighteningly similar to the Nazi controlled camps of W.W.II. One only has to note the seemingly innocent practice of shining halogen lights down on the prisoners 24 hours a day (thereby disrupting their sleep pattern and throwing all neurochemicals into disarray) to recognize that even the simplest and subtlest of techniques are designed to maximize the psychological torture.

Without going into any great detail I wish to simply highlight the primary techniques that have been used throughout the last century relating to psychological warfare. It is my hope that this simple survey will help the reader to better question the attitudes and practices that are used

562 THE MEANING OF LIFE

by politicians. Indeed, the reason I wish to emphasize this is because I am concerned about the dramatic rise in psychological warfare techniques since the beginning of the twenty first century. Such a drastic change can only have devastating results on the world as people's attitudes are shaped to accept policies that strip people of their rights and their human dignity leading people to even accept unjust killings all for the sake of "security".

Of the most popular of propaganda techniques are the simple word games that pollute the airways and have become a mainstay of politicians and their military associates. The simplest and most effective technique is the simple (and though childish, frighteningly effective) practice of *Name-calling*. The name-calling technique links a person or idea to a negative symbol. The propagandist who uses this technique hopes that the audience will reject the person or the idea on the basis of the negative symbol, instead of looking at the available evidence.

> *"Bad names have played a tremendously powerful role in the history of the world and in our own individual development. They have ruined reputations, stirred men and women to outstanding accomplishments, sent others to prison cells, and made men mad enough to enter battle and slaughter their fellowmen. They have been and are applied to other people, groups, gangs, tribes, colleges, political parties, neighborhoods, states, sections of the country, nations, and races."*
>
> ■ (Institute for Propaganda Analysis, 1938)

The most obvious type of name-calling is very simple in that it automatically devalues the individual as a person and strips them of all identity except for those negative aspects that foster ire in the eyes of the public. Obviously the post 9/11 attitude is to brand someone as a *terrorist* or *Islamic extremist* while in the generation previous the term *commie* was the byword. In the movie *Blackhawk Down* the public was exposed to the current use of name-calling in the military when Somalians were referred to as *Skinnys*.[83] Other names have also typified the formal psychological

---

[83] Whether we are willing to admit it or not, this simple practice of name-calling allows a person (whether a soldier or not) to kill with frightening efficiency (and often to their own psychological detriment). One of the best examples in recent American history involved a company of U.S. Army Rangers who were ambushed and trapped while attempting to capture Mohammed Aidid, a Somali paramilitary/political leader. In this circumstance no artillery or air strikes were used, and no tanks or other armored vehicles or heavy weapons were available to American forces. The firefights were close quarters small arms fire accounting for 18 U.S. troops killed and 26 wounded. In contrast the troops were so well trained (and so desensitized to the whole notion of killing) that 364 Somali were killed and another 1400 were seriously wounded (1/3 of them being women and children). While some may argue that it is a testament to the excellent training of the soldiers it is also frightening reality that we are far more comfortable with killing (and the glorification of killing) than were the previous generations. This vast expanse between our sense of entertainment and what the rest of the world considers perverse sadism was clearly made when movies like *Blackhawk Down* and later the Bruce Willis movie *Tears of the Sun* had to be pulled from theatres across Europe and Africa after very public protests against their callous and dehumanizing themes.

warfare strategies of the past two generations: Fascist, Pig, Yuppie, Bum and Queer just to name a few.[84]

Further examples of psychological warfare include the emphasis of false connections and special appeals to special fears within the culture. Nowhere has this been more clear in recent years than in the Al-Queda/Hussein connections. While every expert agreed that Sadaam Hussein's secular regime in Iraq would have nothing to do with the Islamic Al-Queda movement it was nevertheless a central theme of US and UK politicians in their lead up to the 2003 invasion of Iraq. Only after the invasion did questions start to arise about the validity of such claims.

Creating a Killing Soldier

Another example of what I consider to be a perversion of psychology is the application of behaviour modification and desensitization strategies to overcome the logical human aversion to kill another human being. According to a famous study on military practices by S.L. Marshall (during W.W.II) it was concluded that virtually all people have a natural aversion toward killing. It is indeed part of our mythopoeic construct that killing is bad, that fighting is bad and that we must neither fight or kill. As the Marshall report states it, "the average and healthy individual ... has such an inner and usually unrealized resistance toward killing a fellow man that he will not of his own volition take life if it is possible to turn away from that responsibility." (Grossman 1996).[85]

The difference today is that we have a whole culture of desensitization to violence and killing. As our cultural myths are transformed we are slowly having our own mythopoeic processes that say "killing is bad" hijacked with a more callous notion. The notion that killing is somehow easy begins to seep into our consciousness as we are entertained by the casual killing by such *innocent* movies as James Bond, the Star Wars series and even my personal favourite Indiana Jones. The general trend towards misinformation about the ease of killing (to kill and not suffer the serious mental consequences) creates a society that is predisposed to being transformed to be efficient and cold-blooded killers (or at least passive participants/observers).[86]

---

84 A most current example of the use of name-calling as a way to form people's attitudes within psychological warfare is in the CNN announcement of the killing of Udai and Qusai Hussein in Mosul, Iraq on July 23, 2003. The announcer started off the run-down of the days news with the statement, "We have a theme in our news today, as we learn more about the deaths of the *mutant spawn* of Sadaam Hussein ... and how our troops rid the world of this filth."

85 The U.S. Army Air Corps (now the U.S. Air Force) decided in the 1950's to incorporate a "psychological formation of a killer" strategy into their basic and advanced training programs after reviewing their W.W. II experiences. Those experiences showed that only 1% of their fighter pilots accounted for 30-40% of all enemy aircraft destroyed in the air. This strategy included pairing the concept of violence and killing with sexual thought in order to elicit a sort of sexual euphoria from the experience of "the kill".

86 To be sure not all Hollywood movies portray the ease of killing, indeed Gene Hackman's movie *BAT 21* is an excellent example of the exception. In this movie an Air Force officer has to kill people up close and personal for a change and is horrified by what he has done.

564 THE MEANING OF LIFE

To be sure, our militaries are more efficient, especially as we perfect the technique of psychologically transforming our sons and daughters into efficient killing machines. Nations that are supposedly the symbols of peace and freedom are slowly having their international reputation eroded by training soldiers that may be "too efficient". In Canada the basic programming strategies have long been recognized as some of the best in the world, followed by Israel and the U.S. (and to a lesser extent the U.K.). However, the result is also disturbing as Canadian peacekeepers in Africa (including an Armed Forces chaplain) were tried and convicted of torturing and killing civilians. Likewise during the 2002 U.S. campaign in Afghanistan over 1600 *prisoners of war* died after being locked in steal containers (and then after begging for ventilation their captors simply shot into the containers "to allow them to breathe"). While this atrocity was technically carried out by *Afghan Northern Alliance* soldiers, they were with (and under the control of) the U.S. Special Forces.

Despite the atrocities, the argument is made that such training makes sense since a nation will then require fewer soldiers in their military. This is most certainly true as later studies by Marshall and Watson clearly note that the firing rate (to kill the enemy) has steadily increased. The result is that in the Korean War a full 55% of U.S. Soldiers shot to kill. With further pairing of violence and sexuality, along with name calling strategies this level hit a peak of 95% of soldiers shooting to kill in the Vietnam War.

To be sure all of our knowledge of psychology has lead us to the goals we have set for ourselves (at least as a military power). However it is now time to step back and look at our selves as a society from the phenomenological and existential perspective. What have we become and what are the dangers of how we have conditioned ourselves? In particular we must remember that the psychological strategies to sway our opinions have been well thought out and are now deeply engrained into our North American society. It is therefore our responsibility as citizens to identify these strategies and dig beneath their influences to uncover how they sway our own constructed reality of the world, for only in so doing will we be able to call our governments to account.

I retain a stark image of the burning of some peasant huts in Russia, their owners still inside them. We saw the children and the women with their babies and then I heard the poouff – the flame had broken through the thatched roof and there was yellow-brown smoke column going up into the air. It didn't hit me all that much then, but when I think of it now – I slaughtered those people. I murdered them.

■ R. Holmes (Nazi Soldier)

REVIEW / DISCUSSION QUESTIONS

1. The name-calling technique was first identified by the Institute for Propaganda Analysis (IPA) in 1938. When we spot an example of name-calling we should stop and ask. "What does the name mean?" Give an example of name-calling that you are familiar with and describe its emotional attachments and meaning.

2. Does the idea in question have a legitimate connection with the real meaning of the name?

3. Can you give an example of an idea that serves your best interests being dismissed through giving it a name you don't like? Leaving the name out of consideration, what are the merits of the idea itself?

References

Adams, W. (1999). The interpretation of self and world: Empirical research, existential phenomenology and transpersonal psychology. *Journal of Phenomenological Psychology*, 30(2), 27-44.

Adams, W. W. (1999). The interpermeation of self and world: Empirical research, existential phenomenology and transpersonal psychology. *Journal of Phenomenological Psychology*, 30(2), 39-67.

Adkins, A. J. (1985). Cosmogony and Order in Ancient Greece. In R, Lovin (Ed.), *Cosmogony and Ethical Order* (pp. 39-66). Chicago: Chicago University.

Annlson, J. (2000). Towards a clearer understanding of the meaning of "home". *Journal of Intellectual and Developmental Disabilities*, 25(4), 251-263.

Aristotle, & Editor: Bambrough (1969). *Politics*. New York: Penguin.

Barash, D. P. (2000). Evolutionary Existentialism, Sociobiology, and the Meaning of Life. *BioScience*, 50(11), 1012-1017.

Barton, E. R. (2000). Parallels between mythopoetic men's work/ men's peer group support and selected feminists theories. In Barton, E.R. (Ed.), *Mythopoetic perspectives of men's healing work: An anthology for therapists and others.* (1 ed., pp. 3-20). Detroit: University of Michigan.

Bernstein, A. (2001). Freud and Oedipus: A new look at the Oedipus complex in the light of Freud's life. *Modern Psychoanalysis*, 26(2), 269-283.

Bonvecchi, O. C. (1999). Sophia-analysis and the existential unconscious. *International Journal of Psychotherapy*, 4(1), 79-85.

Campion, N., & Rossi, JP (2001). Associative and Causal Constraints in the Process of Generating Predictive Inference. *Discourse Processes*, 31(2), 263-291.

Caveny, C. M. (2003). *Wholesomeness, Holiness and Hairspray*. America, 188(7), 15-19.

Cenkner, W. (1997). *Evil and the response of world religions* (1 ed.). New York: Paragon.

Chung, M. C. (1999). Revisiting and contrasting thought between Descartes and Spinoza in the light of psychotherapy. *Counseling Psychology Quarterly*, 12(1), 49-56.

Cooper, L. (2001). Beyond the Tripartite Soul: The Dynamic Psychology of the Republic. *Review of Politics*, 63(2), 341-360.

Cottingham, J. (2002). Descartes and the Voluntariness of Belief. *Monist*, 85(3), 343-360.

Cropsey, J. (1995). *Plato's World: Man's Place in the Cosmos*. Chicago: Chicago University .

568 THE MEANING OF LIFE

Curley, E. (1985). *The Collected Works of Spinoza* (1 ed.). New York: Princeton Press.

De Andrade, C. E. (2000). Becoming the wise woman: A study of women's journey through midlife transformation. *University microfilms international - Dissertation*, 61, 1109.

Descartes, Rene' (). *Meditatio on First Philosophy*. New York: .

Dillon, M. (2000). Dialogues with Death: The Last Days of Socrates and the Buddha. *Philosophy East and West*, 50(4), 525-560.

Dorsa, D. (1995). The importance of ritual to children. *Dissertation International*: US Microfiles.

Edwards, A. (1991). Clipping the wings off the Enneagram: A study of people's perceptions of a ninefold personality typology. *Social Behavior and Personality*, 19, 11-20.

Evans, S. C. (1990). *Soren Kiekegaard's Christian Psychology*. Vancouver: Regent College .

Fowler, J. (1981). *Stages of Faith: The Psychology of Human Development and the Quest for Meaning*. San Francisco: HarperCollins.

Gaultieri, A. (1968). The Resurrection: An Existential Verification. *Christian Century*, 85, 451-453.

Gill, D. (1991). Socrates and Jesus in non-retaliation and love of enemies. *Horizons*, 18, 246-262.

Hamel, S., LeClerc, G., & LeFrancois, R. (2003). A psychological outlook on the concept of transcendent actualization. *International Journal for the Psychology of Religion*, 13(1), 3-15.

Hermanson, M. (2000). Hybrid Identity Formations in Muslim America. *Muslim World*, 90, 148-190.

Hill, W. (1975). Does God know the future:Aquinas and some moderns. *Theological Studies*, 35, 3-18.

Husserl, E. (1962). The Thesis of the Natural Standpoint and Its Suspension. In R. Solomon (Ed.), *Phenomenology and Existentialism* (pp. 112-117). New York: Harper and Row.

Jacob, A. (1999). Cosmology and Ethics in the Religions of the Peoples of the Ancient Near East. *The Mankind Quarterly*, XL(1), 95-119.

Jeffs, T. (2003). Quest for knowledge begins with a recognition of shared ignorance. *Adults Learning*, 14(6), 28.

Johnson, L. D. (1975). *Israel's Wisdom - Live and Learn*. Nashville: Broadman.

Kaiser, W. C. (1979). *Ecclesiastes: Total Life*. Chicago: Moody.

Keeler, M. L., & Swanson, H. L. (2001). Does Strategy Knowledge Influence Working Memory in Children with Mathematical Disabilities? *Journal of Learning Disabilities*, 34(5), 418-435.

Keijzer, F. A. (2000). Modeling human experience?! *Philosophical Psychology*, 13(2), 239-245.

Kiel, J. (1999). Reshaping Maslow's hierarchy of needs to reflect today's educational and managerial philosophies. *Journal of Instructional Psychology*, 26(3), 167-168.

Kushner , H. (1986). *When all you've ever wanted isn't enough*. New York: Summit Books.

Languilla, N. T. (1993). On location at Socrates feet or the immanence of transcendence. *Telos*, 96, 143-147.

Lantz, J. (2000). Phenomenological Reflection and time in Viktor Frankl's Existential Psychotherapy. *Journal of Phenomenological Psychology*, 31(2), 220-232.

Lasky, E. (1975). *Humanness and Exploration into Mythologies about Women and Men*. New York: MSS Information Corp..

Levenson, M. R., & Khilwati, A. H. (1999). Mystical self-annihilation: Method and meaning. *International Journal for the Psychology of Religion*, 9(4), 251-258.

Lillegard, N. (2000). Passion and Reason: Artistotelian Strategies in Kierkegaard's Ethics. *Journal of Religious Ethics*, 30(2), 251-273.

MacCoby, M. (2002). Towards a Science of Social Character. *International Forum on Psychoanalysis*, 11(1), 33-45.

MacHovec, F. J. (1984). Current Therapies and the Ancient East. *American Journal of Psychotherapy*, 38(1), 87-96.

Mageo, J. M. (2002). Intertextual interpretation, fantasy and Samoan dreams. *Culture and Psychology*, 8(4), 417-448.

May, R. (1991). *Cry for Myth*. New York: W W Norton.

McDowell, M. J. (2001). Principles of Organization: A dynamic systems view of the archetype as such. *Journal of Analytical Psychology*, 46(4), 637-654.

McPherson, C. W. (2000). Augustine our Contemporary. *CrossCurrents*, 50, 170-177.

McWilliam, J. (1995). Language and Love: Introducing Augustine's Religious Thought through the Confessions Story. *Theological Studies*, 56, 814-815.

Michalon, M. (2001). "Selflessness" in the service of the Ego: Contributions, Limitations and Dangers of Buddhist Psychology for Western Psychology. *Journal of Psychotherapy*, 55(2), 202-219.

Montana, C. (2002). Schizophrenia and Story: Intimate threads weaving psyche's fabric. *Dissertations International*, 63, 2013.

Najman, H. (2000). The writings and reception of Philo of Alexandria. In L. Johnson (Ed.), *Christianity in Jewish Terms* (pp. 99-106 & 378-397). Boulder: Westview.

Olson, C. (1977). Existential, Social and Cosmic significance fo the Upanayana rite. *Numen*, 24, 152-160.

Owen, I. R. (1994). Introducing an Existential-Phenomenological Approach Part 2 - Theory for Practice. *Counselling Psychology Quarterly*, 7(4), 347-359.

Pekarsky, D. (1994). Socratic Teaching: A Critical Assessment. *Journal of Moral Education*, 23(2), 119-133.

Penticoff, J. (2002). A personal journey through the Mosaic of Thought. *Journal of Adolescent and Adult Literacy*, 45(7), 634-670.

Rabinowitz, F., Good, G., & Cozad, L. (1989). Rollo May: A Man of Myth and Meaning. *Journal of Counselling and Development*, 67(8), 436-442.

Richards, J. (1978). Early Indo-Aryan Social Structure. *Mankind Quarterly*, 19(2), 129-150.

Samons, L. J. (2000). Socrates, Virtue and the Modern Professor. *Journal of Education*, 182(2), 19-28.

Sanders, N. K. (1987). *The Epic of Gilgamesh*. New York: Penguin.

Sartorius, T. C. (2003). Myth, meaning and mystery. *Arts and Activities*, 132(5), 32-36.

Sartre, J. P. (1956). *Being and Nothingness* : Translation by Barnes, H.. New York: Philosophical Library.

Segal, G. (2000). Beyond Subjectivity: Spinoza's Cognitivism of the Emotions. *British Journal for the History of Philosophy*, 8(1), 1-19.

Solomon, R. C. (1972). *Phenomenology and Existentialism*. New York: Harper and Row.

Spinelli, E. (n.d.). Existential Psychotherapy - A Personal View. Retrieved June 12, 2003, from *http://www.alanmiles.net/old800/psychotherapy/psyexistential.htm*

Stein, M. (1987). Looking Backward: Archetypes in reconstruction. In Schwartz-Salant (Ed.), *Archetypal process in psychotherapy* (pp. 57-74). : .

Steinberg, D. (1998). The Method and Structure of Knowledge in Spinoza. *Pacific Philsophical Quarterly*, 79(2), 158-176.

Tamas, R. (2002). Is the modern Psyche undergoing a Rite of Passage? *ReVision*, 24(3), 2-9.

Taylor, M. (1995). Tuning In: An Interview with Emmy Van Deurzen-Smith. *Journal of Guidance and Counseling*, 23(1), .

Teeter, E. (1997). *The Presentation of MAAT*. Chicago: Oriental Institute - University of Chicago.

van Neikerk, A. (1999). Death, Meaning and Tragedy. *South African Journal of Philosophy*, 18(4), 408-426.

Wamble, M. (2002). *St Augustine's Confessions*. U.S. Catholic, 67, 17.

Williams, A. (1994). Clinical sociometry to define space in family systems. *Journal of Group Psychotherapy, Psychodrama and Sociometry*, 47(3), 126-144.

Wood , L. (2003). Living by the Word. *Christian Century*, 120(10), 20-22.

Zuroff, D. (1982). Person, situation and person by situation interaction components in person perception. *Journal of Personality*, 50(1), 1-14.

APPENDIX A

THE GREEK ALPHABET

The Greek Alphabet

	Letter	Name & Sound	Modern Greek Pronunciation	Classic Greek Pronunciation
1	Α α	*Alpha*	[a], as in "father". Same like [a] in Spanish and Italian. Phonetically, this sound is: open, central, and unrounded.	As in Modern Greek
2	Β β	*Beta*	[v], as in "vet".	[b], as in "bet". *Evidence*
3	Γ γ	*Gamma*	[gh], a sound that does not exist in English. If followed by the sound [u] then it sounds almost like the initial sound in "woman".	[g], as in "got". Evidence
4	Δ δ	*Delta*	[th], as in "this".	[d], as in "do". Evidence
5	Ε ε	*Epsilon*	[e] as in "pet", except that the [e] in "pet" (and in most other English words) is lax, while in Greek it is tense.	As in Modern Greek
6	Ζ ζ	*Zeta*	[z], as in "zone". Actually, the remark for sigma (see below) applies to zeta as well (it is shifted a bit towards [Z], as in "pleasure").	[zd], as in "Mazda". Evidence
7	Η η	*Eta*	[i], as in "meet", but shorter, not so long. This is one of the three [i] in the Greek alphabet.	long open mid-[e], as in French "κtre". Evidence
8	Θ θ	*Theta*	[th], as in "think".	[t^h], as in "top", but more aspirated. Evidence
9	Ι ι	*Iota*	[i], exactly like eta (see above). The name of the letter is pronounced "yota" in Modern Greek	As in Modern Greek

576 THE MEANING OF LIFE

	Letter	Name & Sound	Modern Greek Pronunciation	Classic Greek Pronunciation
10	Κ κ	*Kappa*	[k], as in "pack".	As in Modern Greek
11	Λ λ	*Lambda*	[l] as in "lap".	As in Modern Greek
12	Μ μ	*Mu*	[m], as in "map".	As in Modern Greek
13	Ν ν	*Nu*	[n], as in "noble".	As in Modern Greek
14	Ξ ξ	*Ksi*	[ks] as in "fox". Contrary to the English "x", the letter ksi does not change pronunciation in the beginning of a word.	As in Modern Greek
15	Ο ο	*Omicron*	[o] as in "hop", except that the [o] in "hop" (and in most other English words).	As in Modern Greek
16	Π π	*Pi*	[p], as in "top"..	As in Modern Greek
17	Ρ ρ	*Rho*	[rh], a sound that does not exist in English (but exists in Scottish).	Probably as in Modern Greek
18	Σ σ ς	*Sigma*	[s], as is "sit". The last form of sigma is used exclusively when the letter appears at the end of a word (there is only one capital form); this rule has no exceptions.	Probably as in Modern Greek

APPENDIX A – THE GREEK ALPHABET   **577**

	Letter	Name & Sound	Modern Greek Pronunciation	Classic Greek Pronunciation
19	Τ τ	*Tau*	[t], as in "pot". Notice that in English [t] is aspirated if it is at the beginning of a word; Greek makes no such distinction.	As in Modern Greek
20	Υ υ	*Upsilon*	[i], exactly like eta and iota.	Rounded [i], as in French "une". Evidence
21	Φ φ	*Phi*	[f] as in "fat".	[p^h], as in "pit", but more aspirated. Evidence
22	Χ χ	*Chi*	[ch], a sound that does not exist in English (but exists in Scottish, as in "loch").	[k^h], as in "cut", but more aspirated. Evidence
23	Ψ ψ	*Psi*	[ps] as in "lopsided".	As in Modern Greek
24	Ω ω	*Omega*	[o], exactly like omicron.	Long open mid-back [o], as in "law". Evidence

APPENDIX B

HISTORY OF PSYCHOLOGY

History Timeline[87]

PART ONE: Year 600 before our era to 1899

600 YEARS BEFORE OUR TIME

The cosmogonic hypotheses of Greek mathematician and philosopher Thales of Miletus

500 YEARS BEFORE OUR TIME

- **580** The Greek philosopher Anaximander organizes a world map
- **550** Pythagoras of Samos enunciates his famous theorem
- **500 to -428** Life of Greek philosopher Anaxagoras

400 YEARS BEFORE OUR TIME

- **474** Parmenides of Elea writes On Nature
- **460 a -370** Life of Greek philosopher Democritus
- **427 a -348** Life of Greek philosopher Plato

300 YEARS BEFORE OUR TIME

- **399** Socrates dies
- **384 a -322** Life of Greek philosopher Aristotle
- **367** Plato founds the Academy
- **360** Plato writes Timaeus
- **350** Aristotle writes The Anima
- Aristotle writes On memory and reminiscence
- **347** Plato dies
- **335** Aristotle founds the Lyceum

---

87 http://www.geocities.com/Athens/Delphi/6061/en_linha.htm#-600

582 THE MEANING OF LIFE

100

- **170** Claudius Galeno describes the anatomy of the brain and its ventricles

400

- **406** Augustine finishes Confessions
- **426** Augustine finishes City of God

1000

- **1020** Avicenna suggests that the three ventricles of the brain perform five distinct cognitives processes: common sense, imagination, cogitation, estimation and memory

1200

- **1264** Thomas Aquinas publishes SummaTheologica
- **1253** Robert Grosseteste dies
- **1294** Roger Bacon dies

1300

- **1308** Duns Scotus dies
- **1349** William of Ockham dies

1400

- **1473** Polish astronomer Nicolau Copernicus refutes the geocentric theory of the universe
- **1462** Marsilio Ficino establishes Platonic Academy in Florence

1500

- **1506** The Croatian humanist Marco Marulic employs the term psichiologia
- **1508** Dutch humanist Erasmus publishes the The Praise of Folly

APPENDIX B – HISTORY TIMELINE   583

- **1513** Italian humanist Nicolau Maquiavel publishes The Prince
- **1516** English writer Thomas Morus publishes The Utopia
- **1524** Marco Marulik publishes The Psychology of Human Thought volume 1
- **1540** Phillip Melanchton publishes Commentary about the Soul
- **1543** Belgian physiologist Vesalius practices the dissection of cadavers
- **1557** Alonso de la Veracruz publishes in Mexico the book Physica Speculatio
- **1566** Bernardino Alvarez establishes in Mexico the Hospital de San Hipolito,the firstin the Americas dedicated to serving patients with psychological problems
- **1575** Johannes Thomas Freigius uses the term psychologia in the book Catalogueof Common Places
- **1579** Johannes Thomas Freigius re-utilizes the term psychologia in the latin bookQuaestiones Physicae 1586 Giovanni Battista della Porta publishes a body morphology book De Humana Physiognomonia
- **1588** The french theologist Noel Taillepied use the French word psichologie in the book Psychology. The book is about the realities of spirits, knoledge of erring souls, phantoms, miracles and strange happenings, which at times precede the death of important personalities, or announces that affairs of state are falling apart.
- **1590** Rudolphus Goclenius writes a treatise under the title Psychology
- **1594** Otto Cassman, a student of Glocenius, writes Psychologia Anthropologica, or Animae Humanae Doctrina

1600

- **1605** Francis Bacon publishes The Proficiency and Advancement of Learning
- **1616** English physiologist William Harvey explains the blood's circulation
- **1624** Pierre Gassendi publishes Paradoxes Against the Aristotelian
- **1632** Galilei Galileo publishes Dialogue on the Two Great Systems of the World
- **1635** E. Neuhaus, a student of Cassman, publishes a book that summarizes the reason for studying psychology
- **1637** French philosopher Renê Descartes publishes Discourse on Method
- **1649** René Descartes postulates the total separation of body and soul in the book Passions of the Soul

584   THE MEANING OF LIFE

- **1651** Thomas Hobbes publishes Leviathan

- **1677** Benedict de Spinoza dies

- **1690** English philosopher John Locke publishes An Essay Concerning Human Understanding

- **1692** Christian Thomasius publishes in Germany the book Further Elucidation by DifferentExamples of the recent Proposals for a New Science for Discerning the Nature of Other Men's Mind

---

1700

- **1709** George Berkeley publishes An Essay Toward a New Theory of Vision

- **1732** Christian von Wolff publishes a treatise of empirical psychology

- **1734** Christian von Wolff publishes a treatise of rational psychology

- **1745** Julien Offray de La Mettrie publishes The Natural History of the Soul

- **1748** David Hume publishes An Inquiry Concerning Human Understanding

- Julien Offray de La Mettrie publishes Edward Tolman publishes Purposive Behavior in man and in animals

- Rensis Likert emploies an empirical aproach to the measurement of attitude

- Frederick Bartlett publishes Remembering: A study in experimental and social psychology

- **1751** Robert Whytt, in the book, On the Vital and Other Involuntary Motionsof Animals summarizes the physiology of reflex

- **1752** Mathias Ayres Ramos da Silva de Eça publishes Reflections on the the men's vanity or Moral speeches on the effects of the vanity

- **1754** E. Condillac, in his Treatise on Sensation, maintained that sensations are the only source of knowledge

- The Swiss scientist and philosopher Charles Bonnet publishes Essay about Psychology

- **1764** After publishing Inquiry into the Human Mind on the Principles of Common Sense, Thomas Reid accepted the Chair of Moral Philosophy at Glasgow

- **1765** Gottfried Wilhelm von Leibniz publishes New Essays on the Human Understanding

- **1768** The Scottish physiologist Robert Whytt uses the expression motion from a stimulus

APPENDIX B – HISTORY TIMELINE   585

- **1771** Johann August Unzer uses the term reflex to distinguish this kind of action from that carried out volitionally
- **1774** Franz Mesmer performed his first supposed cure using "animal magnetism"
- **1775** The Swiss minister Johann Caspar Lavater publishes Essays on the Physiognomony Designated to promote the knowledge and Love of Mankind
- **1777** A Scottish physician, William Cullen, publishes First Line in the practice of Physic in which he uses the term neurosis to define mental illness
- **1782** German philosopher Immanuel Kant publishes The Critic of the Pure Reason
- **1785** Thomas Reid publishes Essay in the Intellectual Powers of Man
- Johann Jakob Emgel distinguishes the expressive and representational behavior of the actor in the book Ideas for a Mimic
- **1786** Established in Ecuador the Hospital San Lazaro
- Luigi Galvani reports the results of experiments on the stimulation of the muscles of the frog by application of an electric pulse
- **1788** Thomas Reid publishes Essay on the Active Powers of the Human Mind
- **1789** Thomas Malthus publishes Essays on the progress of the population
- Jerome Bentham publishes Principles of Morals and Legislation
- **1790** Erasmus Darwin produces a theory of human behavior and experience in terms of three fundamental categories: stimulation, muscular contraction and a central sensory power
- **1794** French philosopher Denis Diderot publishes Essays on the Progress of the Human Spirit
- Francisco de Mello Franco publishes Theological Medicine
- **1797** Joaquín Millás publishes in Argentina the book Instituiciones psicológicas

---

1800

- **1802** Pierre Jean Georges Cabanis publishes Traité du Physique et du Moral de l'Homme
- Thomas Young publishes A Theory of Color Vision in which he postulate that the retina is equipped with three kinds of color-sensitive points
- **1805** Franz Joseph Gall and Johann Kaspar Spurzheim left Vienna motivated by the Austrian government's displeasure with Gall's doctrine

586   THE MEANING OF LIFE

- **1809** Gall and Spurzheim publish a book on descriptive anatomy of brain, Recherches sur le Systèm Nerveux

1810

- **1810** Gall publishes the first volume of Anatomie et Physionomie du Systèm Nerveux
- **1811** Sir Charles Bell reports to associates at a dinner party the anatomical separation of sensory and motor function of spinal cord
- **1813** Francisco de Mello Franco publishes Elements of Hygiene or Theoretical and Practical Precepts to Conserve Health and to Prolong Life
- **1815** J. K. Surzheim publishes The Phisiognonimal System of Drs.Gall and Spurzheim
- **1816** Johann Friedrich Herbart publishes Lehrbuch zur Psychologie
- **1817** Ernst Weber was appointed Dozent in physiology at the University of Leipzig
- **1818** Spurzheim publishes Observations sur la phrénologie, ou la Naissance de l'Homme

1820

- **1820** German philosopher Friedrich Eduard Beneke publishes On the Relationship between the Soul and the Body
- **1821** Rudolphi Burdach defines the task of physiology as including the study of psychological matter
- **1822** Phrenological doctrines was available in America when George Combe publishes Essays on Phrenology, Or An Inquiry into the Principles and Utility of the Systemof Drs. Gall and Spurzheim, and into the objections Made Against It.
- Francis Magendie publishes an article which postulates the separation of sensory and motor function of the spinal cord
- Baron Cuvier postulates the use of the term l'intelligence , rather than reason, in the context of discussion about intelligent behavior of animals

1830

- **1832** Johann Kaspar Spurzheim suggests 35 special faculties of the mind
- **1834** Johannes Müller publishes Handbüch des Physiologie des Menschen
- **1836** Manuel Inácio de Figueiredo defends in Rio of Janeiro the thesis Passions and Affections of the Soul
- **1838** Johannes Müller publishes Elements of Physiology

APPENDIX B – HISTORY TIMELINE   587

1840

- **1840** Friedrich August Rauch publishes in America the book Psychology, or A View of the Human Soul; including Anthropology
- **1842** Samuel Schmuker publishes in America the book Psychology: Elementsof a New System of mental Philosophy or The Basis of Consciousness and Common Sense
- **1843** José Augusto Menezes defends in Rio de Cesar de Janeiro the thesis Propositions regarding the Intelligence John Stuart Mill publishes A system of Logic
- **1848** The french neurologist Jean-Baptiste Bouillard offered 500 francs to anyone who could show him a brain from an individual who had suffered from speech disturbance and did not have damage to the left frontal lobe

1850

- **1851** Francisco Tavares da Cunha defends in Salvador the thesis Psychophysiologyconcerning the Man
- Manuel Ancizar publishes Lecciones de Psicología , the first psychological book published in Colombia
- **1852** Sir Henry Holland publishes Chapters on Mental Physiology
- **1853** The first program in mental health, The Casa de Orates is established in Chile
- **1855** Herbert Spencer publishes the two volumes of the Principles of Psychology
- Alexander Bain publishes the first psychological textbook: The senses and the intellect
- **1856** Hermann Ludwig Ferdinand von Helmholtz publishes the first volume of the Handbuch der physiologischen Optik
- **1858** Wilhelm Wundt becomes assistant of Hermann von Helmholtz
- **1859** Charles Darwin publishes The origin of the species
- Alexander Bain publishes The Emotions and the Will

1860

- **1860** Gustav Fechner publishes The Elements of Psychophysics
- Thomas Laycock publishes Mind and Brain
- **1861** Paul Broca shows that the loss of speech in one individual is due to a lesion in third convolution of the left frontal lobe
- **1862** Wundt teaches a summer course entitled Psychology as a Natural Science

588   THE MEANING OF LIFE

- **1863** Wundt publishes Lectures on Human and Animal Psychology
- I. M. Sechenov publishes a monograph Reflexes of the Brain , in whichhe attempted to analyze the higher order functions in terms of the reflex schema
- **1865** F. Galton publishes Hereditary talent and character
- **1864** Ernesto Carneiro Ribeiro defends in Salvador the thesis Relationship of the Medicine with the Philosophical Sciences: Legitimacy of Psychology
- **1867** Henry Maudsley publishes Physiology and Pathology of the Mind
- Theodor Piderit, a critic of phrenology, publishes Scientific System of Mimics and Physiognomy
- **1868** Dutch physiologist F. C. Donders publishes Over den snelheid van psychische processen
- **1869** Francis Galton publishes Hereditary Genius
- Francis Galton uses the normal distribution for purposes of classification

1870

- **1870** G. Fritsch and E. Hitzig realize the first direct electric stimulation of the brain
- **1871** Charles Darwin publishes The descent of man
- **1872** French neurologist Jean Marie Charcot begins to teach in La Salpêtrière
- Charles Darwin publishes The Expression of the Emotions in the Man and in the Animals
- **1873** Wundt publishes Principles of Physiological Psychology
- **1874** Franz Brentano publishes Psychology from an Empirical Standpoint
- Wundt left Heidelberg for a position at the University of Zurich
- William Benjamin Carpenter publishes Principles of Mental Physiology, a book which was extensively cited by William James
- **1875** William James taught the course The relationships among the Physiology and the Psychology
- Francis Galton publishes History of twins
- Wundt leaves Zurich and goes to University of Leipzig
- **1876** Guedes Cabral defends in Rio de Janeiro the thesis Functions of the Brain
- Francis Galton uses the method of twin comparisons

APPENDIX B – HISTORY TIMELINE **589**

- Alexander Bain establishes Mind, the first journal devoted to psychological research
- Théodule Ribot establishes the Revue Philosophique in which psychologicalwork frequently appears
- **1877** Charles Darwin publishes A biographical sketch of a infant
- 1879 Wilhelm Wundt establishes the first psychological laboratory at the University of Leipzig in Germany
- Francis Galton utilizes the method of word association
- Lightner Witmer uses for the first time the term clinical psychology

1880

- **1880** F. Galton publishes Statistics of mental imagery Francis Galton makes systematic use of questionaries
- **1881** Max Friedrich becomes the recipient of first doctoral degree in experimental psychology
- **1882** George Romanes develops his anedoctal method in the book Animal Inteligence
- William T. Preyer publishes the first volume of The Mind of the Children
- **1883** Francis Galton publishes Inquiries into Human Faculty and Its Development
- The first laboratory of psychology in America is established at Johns Hopkins University
- University authorities gave Wundt's Leipzig laboratory formal recognition
- Wilhelm Wundt establishes Philosophische Studien to publish the results of his laboratory research
- **1884** William James publishes What is an emotion ?
- John Dewey publishes The new psychology
- French doctor Hipollyte Bernheim publishes On the Suggestion in the   hypnotic state
- **1885** Herman Ebbinghaus publishes Memory: A contribution to experimental Psychology
- The first laboratory of psychology in Italy is established at the University of Rome
- Francis Galton introduces tests batteries to arrive at a manysided assessment of abilities for a given person
- **1886** James McKeen Cattell publishes The time taken up by cerebral operations
- Ernst Mach publishes The Analysis of Sensations

590 THE MEANING OF LIFE

- V. Betcherev founds the first laboratory of psychology in Russian territory
- Victor Horsley described early successful surgery for epilepsy to the Sectionon Surgery of the British Medical Association
- **1887** The Journal of American Psychology publishes the article "Dermal Sensitiveness to Gradual Presure Changes" written by Hall and the pioneer of psychology in Japan, Yuzero Motora
- **1888** J. McKeen Cattell becomes America's first professor of psychology at the University of Pennsylvania
- Yuzero Motora earns the first PhD degree in japanese with the thesis "Exchange: Considered as the Principles of Social Life"
- **1889** The first laboratory of psychology in Canada is established at the University of Toronto
- First International Congress of Psychology
- The first laboratory of psychology in France is established at the Sorbonne
- Theodule Ribot is appointed Professor of Experimental Psychology at the College of France
- First Chinese translation of a western psychology book, Mental Philosophy , of Joseph Raven, by Yan Yougjing

1890

- **1890** José Estelita Rodrigues inaugurates research about cognition with the work Psychology of thePerception and Representations
- Veríssimo Dias de Castro publishes On Emotions
- Benjamim Constant Reform introduces the notions of psychology in the curricula of the Normal Schools
- William James publishes Principles of Psychology
- J. M. Cattell publishes Mental tests and measurements.
- Christian von Ehrenfels publishes About the qualities of the gestalt
- Pierre Janet succeeds Charcot as head of the Psychological Laboratoryat the Salpètriere
- Gabriel Tarde publishes The Laws of imitation
- Yuzero Motora becomes Professor of Psychology at The Imperial University of Tokio

APPENDIX B – HISTORY TIMELINE 591

- **1891** Odilon Goulart writes Psychoclinical studies of Aphasia
- James M. Cattell moves to Columbia University as Professor of Psychology and administrative head of the department
- The first laboratory of psychology in Belgium is established in Louvain
- **1892** William James writes The stream of consciousness
- The American Psychological Association is founded, having 42 members
- Edward Titchener introduces structuralism in America.
- Christine Ladd Franklin completes the doctoral program in psychology, no degree granted due to prohibition against womem
- J. M. Baldwin publishes The psychological laboratory in the University of Toronto
- **1893** Ezequiel Cháves was named the first professor of psychology in Mexico
- Oswald Külpe publishes Outline of Psychology
- The first laboratory of psychology in Holland is established in Gronigen
- The Laboratory of Experimental Psychology is established at the University of Iassy, Romania
- **1894** Alberto Seabra publishes the first brazilian psychological study about memory: The Memory and the Personality
- John Dewey publica The ego as cause
- Cattell and Baldwin found Psychological Review, Psychological Index and Psychological Monographs
- Margaret Floy Washburn becomes the first woman to receive a PhD in psychology
- The first laboratory of psychology in Austria is established at the University of Graaz
- Philippe Tessié publishes an article in which he discusses the psychologicaland physiological aspects of bicycle racing
- C. Lloyd Morgan develops his famous canon in the book Introduction to Comparative Psychology
- **1895** Mary Whiton Calkins receives a doctoral degree in psychology
- J. M. Baldwin publishes Types of reaction
- Josef Breuer and Sigmund Freud publish Studies on Hystery
- Gustave Le Bon publishes Psychologie de Foules

THE MEANING OF LIFE

- **1896** John Dewey publishes in the Psychological Review his famous article The Reflex Arc Concept in Psychology
- Lightner Witmer establishes at the University of Pennsylvania a clinic of psychology, the first psychological clinic in America and perhaps in the world
- Benjamin Bourdon establishes the Laboratory of Experimental Psychology and Linguistics at the University of Rennes
- **1897** Julio Afrânio Peixoto publishes Epilepsy and Crime
- Norman Tripllet publishes The dynamogenic factors in pacemaking and competition.
- William Wundt publishes Outlines of Psychology
- Laboratories of psychology are established at the Universities of Cambridge and of London
- The first laboratory of psychology in Poland is established at the University of Cracow
- Angelo Mosso publishes the book Physiology of Man in the Alps , in which he studies the psychological and physiological effects of mountain climb
- **1898** Franco da Rocha establishes new services at the Central Asylum of Juqueri
- Edward Titchener publishes The postulates of a Structural Psychology
- E. L. Thorndike publishes Animal Inteligence
- Baldin, Cattel & Jastrow publish Physical and mental tests.
- Horacio Pinero establishes a psychology laboratory in Buenos Aires
- Norman Triplett conducts at the Indiana University the first experiment in sport psychology
- Emile Durkheim publishes Représentations individuelles et représentations collectives
- **1899** H. S. Jennings publishes The Psychology of a Protozoan, later The Behaviorof Paramecium
- Helen Bradford Thompson receives a doctoral degree in psychology
- W. Caldwell publishes The postulates of a structural psychology

PART TWO: 1900 to 2000

1900

- **1900** Henrique Roxo, under Teixera Brandão's orientation, writes Duration of the Elementary Psychic Acts
- Sigmund Freud publishes The Interpretation of Dreams
- The first volume of Wundt's Völkerpsychologie appears
- William Stern publishes On the Psychology of the Individual Differences
- Carl G. Jung is appointed Bleuler's assistant
- Pierre de Coubertin, the man who created the modern olympic games, coins the term sport psychology in his articleThePsychology of Sport
- **1901** Edward Titchener publishes between 1901 and 1905 the four volumes of his Manual of Experimental Psychology
- Sigmund Freud publishes The psychopathology of everyday life
- James Baldwin publishes the first edition of the Dictionary of Philosophy and Psychology
- Pierre Janet and George Dumas found the French Psychological Society
- Gabriel Tarde publishes L'Opinion de la Foule
- **1902** Ebbinghaus states the famous sentence "Psychology has a long past, but onlya short story"
- The physician Luis Simarro becomes the first professor of psychology in Spain
- **1903** William Stern uses the term Psychotechnique
- First laboratory of psychology of Japan is established at the Tokyo University
- **1904** Willliam James publishes Does consciousness exist? and A world of pure experience
- Cattell and Baldwin found Psychological Bulletin
- James R. Angell publishes Psychology: An Introductory Study of the Structure and Function of Human Consciousness
- Ezequiel Chaves translates to spanish Titchener's Elements of Psychology

594 THE MEANING OF LIFE

- Karl Pearson publishes a study on the inheritance of human mental characteristics
- Charles Spearman publishes his first paper on general intelligence
- James Ward and W. H. Rivers launch the British Journal of Psychology
- Established in France the Journal de Psychologie Normale et Pathologique
- Established the German Psychology Society (Deutsche Gesellschaft fürPsychologie - D.G.f Ps)
- **1905** Alfred Binet publishes New methods for the diagnosis of the intellectuallevel of subnormals.
- **1906** Medeiros e Albuquerque organizes a laboratory of educational psychology
- H. S. Jennings publishes Behavior of the Lower Organisms
- James McKeen Cattell publish the first edition of American Men of Science
- Ivan Pavlov publishes his findings regarding classical conditioning
- The Institute of Applied Psychology is established in Berlin
- Psychology appears in the teacher-training college curriculum in the Egyptian educational system
- **1907** Maurício de Campos defends the thesis Methods in Psychology
- James R. Angell publishes The province of functional psychology
- Lightner Witmer publishes Clinical psychology
- Carl G. Jung publishes The Psychology of Dementia Praecox
- Alfred Adler publishes his main work: A Study of Organic Inferiority and Its Psychical Compensation
- Russian physiologist and psychiatrist Vladimir Betcherev publishes Objective Psychology
- William Stern establishes the Zeitschrift für Angewandte Psychologie (Journal of Applied Psychology) , the first psychological journal devoted to applied psychology
- **1908** William McDougall publishes An Introduction to Social Psychology
- Edward Ross publishes Social Psychology: an outline and source book
- Walter Dill Scott publishes Psychology of Advertising
- Hugo Munsterberg attempts in his book On The Witness Sand to apply psychology to legal problems

APPENDIX B – HISTORY TIMELINE   595

- The Sociedad Argentina de Psicologia (Argentine Psychology Society) is established
- The first laboratory of psychology in Chile is established at the Universidad de Chile
- Alfred Binet and Theodor Simon begin to develop tests for measurement of children intelligence
- T. A. Hunter establishes a psychological laboratory at the University of New Zealand
- **1909** Robert Yerkes and Sergius Morgulis publish The method of Pavlov in animalpsychology
- Freud and Jung visit the United States during the twentieth anniversary of Clark University
- W. Healy establishes in Chicago the first psychological clinic attached to a juvenile court
- Maria Montessori publishes Corso di pedagogia cientifica (The method of scientific pedagogy applied to child education)

1910

- **1910** The Journal of Educational Psychology is founded
- Hugo Munsterberg develops attitude test for streetcar drivers
- Sigmund Freud publishes The origin and development of psychoanalysis
- Carl G. Jung publish The association method
- Elton Mayo was appointed to lectureship in philosophy at the University of Queensland, Australia
- **1911** Plinio Olinto publishes Association of Ideas
- A. A. Brill founds the Psychoanalytical Association of New York
- Edward Thorndike publishes Animal intelligence
- The Journal of Animal Behavior is established
- José Ingenieros publishes in Argentina Psicologia Genética , later Principios de psicologia biológica
- **1912** E. B. Titchener publishes The schema of introspection
- Max Wertheimer publishes the paper Experimental Studies of the Perception of Movement
- Edouard Claparède establishes in Geneva the Jean Jacques Rousseau Institute, dedicated to educational investigation

596   THE MEANING OF LIFE

- George Brett publishes A History of Psychology
- The first text which announces in its title that psychology was the study of behaviour, by William McDougall, appears
- **1913** John Watson publishes Psychology as the Behaviorist Views It
- Hugo Münsterberg publishes Psychology and industrial efficiency
- George H. Mead publishes The social self.
- Wolfgang Köhler initiates his studies at the Anthropoid Station in Tenerife
- Carl G. Jung departs from freudian views and develops his own theories
- **1914** Aragão de Souza Pinto defends the thesis Of Psychoanalysis: the Sexuality of the Neuroses
- Italian psychologist Ugo Pizzoli inaugurates in the Escola Normal de São Paulo an experimental psychology laboratory
- Edward Titchener publishes On "Psychology as the behaviorist views it, the official reply to Watson
- Hugo Munsterberg uses the term Psychotechnics
- **1915** Honorio Delgado introduces psychoanalysis in Peru
- W. Healy publishes Honesty: A Study of the Causes and Treatment of Disonesty Among Children
- Sigmund Freud publishes the metapsychological work On repression
- First department of psychology in India is established at Calcutta University
- **1916** Lewis M. Terman publishes The measurement of intelligence
- The Journal of Experimental Psychology is established
- The Division of Applied Psychology is established at the Carnegie Institute of Technology
- Wilson and Wilson publishThe Motivation of School Work, the first book to have the word motivation in its title
- Margaret Floy Washburn publishes Movement and mental imagery: outline of a motor theory of the complexes mental process
- Enrique Arágon establishes the first psychological laboratory in the Mexico
- A complete account of E. Thorndike's studies is published in the Egyptian journal Al-Muktataf

APPENDIX B – HISTORY TIMELINE   597

- **1917** Manuel Bonfim publishes Notions of Psychology
- The Journal of Applied Psychology is established
- Kurt Lewin publishes his first professional work: Kriegslandchaft
- In Dresden, Germany, a psychotechnical laboratory for training of railroad engineers is established
- Cai Yuanpei establishes at Beijing University the first psychological laboratory in China
- **1918** Fernandes Figueira begins to work in the National Hospice with psychological tests, using Binet-Simon's tests.
- Franco da Rocha begins to spread psychoanalysis through courses taught at the Faculdade de Medicina de São Paulo
- Robert S. Woodworth publishes Dynamic Psychology, in which introduces the concept of drive
- **1919** Franco da Rocha publishes Freud's Doctrine
- Knight Dunlap publishes Are they any instincts?
- Karl Bühler is apointed professor of philosophy and psychology at the Technical Academy in Dresden
- Held in the Swiss city of Lausanne, the First Congress of Sport Psychology and Physiology

1920

- **1920** E. Frost publishes in the Journal of Applied Psychology the article What industry wants and does not want from the psychologists
- John B. Watson & Rosalie Rayner publish Conditioned emotional reactions.
- William McDougal publishes The group mind
- The first Spanish journal partly dedicated to psychology is established: Archivos de Neurobiología, Psicología,Histología, Fisiología, Neurología y Psiquiatría
- The first Chinese psychology independent department, at Nanjing University
- **1921** Köhler, Koffka and Wertheimer establish the journal Psychologische Forschung to give exposure to the Gestalt viewpoints on psychological problems
- The first psychology department in Australia is established at the University of Sydney
- **1922** The Brazilian League of Mental Hygieneis established

598 THE MEANING OF LIFE

- Edward C. Tolman publishes A new formula for behaviorism.
- John Dewey publishes The Human Nature and the Conduct
- Koffka writes in the Psychological Bulletin the introductory statement of the Gestalt position for American psychologists
- Walter Lippman publishes Public Opinion
- J. M. Cattell states: "The army intelligence tests have put psychology on the map of United States"
- Levy-Bruhl publishes La mentalité primitive
- **1923** Waclaw Radecki arrives in Brazil
- The Laboratory of Psychology of Engenho de Dentro is established
- Sigmund Freud publishes The Ego and the Id
- Max Wertheimer publishes Laws of organization in perceptual forms
- **1924** Medeiros e Albuquerque publishes the first brazilian book on psychological tests, The Tests
- Isaias Alves works in the Brazilian adaptation of Binet-Simon's scale
- Floyd Allport publishes Social Psychology
- L.L.Thurstone publishes The nature of intelligence
- Max Wertheimer publishes Gestalt theory
- The Indian Psychological Association is established
- **1925** Ulisses Pernambuco establishes in Recife the Selection and Professional Orientation Institute of Pernambuco
- Lourenço Filho assumes the chair of Psychology at the Escola Normal de São Paulo
- Harvey Carr publishes Psychology: a study of the mental activity
- E. K. Strong publishes The Psychology of Selling and Advertising
- Viennese psychoanalyst Karl Abraham publishes Psychoanalytical studies about the Character Formation
- **1926** The first works in the Institute of Hygiene, located in São Paulo, appears
- Florence L. Goodenough's Measurement of Intelligence by Drawings was published, describing Goodenough's Draw-A-Man Test .

- Thophilos Voréas, a Wundt' student, teaches a course in psychology at the school of philosophy at the University of Athens
- A psychology laboratory is established in the University of Athens
- The Indian Journal of Psychology is founded
- **1927** Lourenço Filho publishes Contribution to the Experimental Study of the Habit
- Henri Pieron arrives in São Paulo to teach experimental psychology and psychometrics
- Hugo Münsterberger publishes On the witness stand
- Edward Titchener dies
- First edition of Psychological Abstracts
- First edition of Journal General of Psychology
- The International Association of Applied Psychology is established
- Kurt Koffka emigrates to America
- Gestalt psychologist Wolfgang Kohler publishes The mentality of apes
- Psychology examination of officer candidates becomes obligatory in German army
- All-Union Society for Psychology Engineering and Applied Psychophysiology is founded in the U.S.S.R.
- Research Center for Economic Psychology is founded in Vienna
- **1928** L. T. Troland publishes the first general text featuring the word motivation in the main title, The Fundamentals of Human Motivation
- Ezequiel Chaves publishes in Mexico Ensayo de psicologia de la adolescencia (Essay on adolescency psychology)
- In the U.S.S.R. the journal Psikhofiziologia truda i psikhotekhnika, later Sovetskaia psikhotekhnika, is established
- A research institute for psychology is opened at the Chinese Academy of Sciences
- The Egyptian psychologist El-Kabbani conducts the first empirical psychological research on 4,000 school children
- **1929** Waclaw Radecki publishes Tratado de Psicologia
- Edward Boring publishes the first edition of A History of Experimental Psychology
- Thurstone and Chaves publish The Measurement of Attitude

600 THE MEANING OF LIFE

- Carl Murchison publishes The Psychological Register
- First edition of Journal of Social Psychology
- Karl Lashley publishes Brain Mechanisms and Intelligence
- W. B. Cannon introduces the modern concept of homeostasis in the book Bodily Changes in Pain, Hunger, Fear and Rage
- The Yale' s Institute of Human Relations is established
- Wolfgang Köhler publishes An old pseudoproblem
- The College of Arts of University of Cairo and Higher Institute of Education sent their best graduates to study psychology in Europe
- Mohhamed M. Said is appointed the first professor of Psychology in Higher Institute of Education of Cairo

1930

- **1930** B. F. Skinner publishes his first experimental paper, On The Conditions of Eliciation of certain Eating Reflexes
- Karl Lashley publishes Basic neural mechanisms in behavior
- Enrique Mouchet reorganizes the Buenos Aires Society of Psychology
- The first psychological laboratory at theHigherInstituteof Education of Cairo is established
- Henri Ferguson becomes the first to hold the title of Lecturer in Experimental Psychology at the University of Dunedin, New Zealand
- **1931** Enrique Mouchet founded the Institute of Psychology at the Universidad deBuenos Aires
- The Japanese Applied Psychological Association is founded
- **1932** José Leme Lopes, in Rio and Sylvio Rabello, in São Paulo, introduce the Rorschach in Brazil
- Edward Tolman publishes Purposive Behavior in man and in animals
- Rensis Likert emploies an empirical aproach to the measurement of attitude
- Frederick Bartlett publishes Remembering: A study in experimental and social psychology
- **1933** Floyd H. Allport publishes Institutional behavior
- Dorothy Thomas attempts to sistematize and quantify the observation of social behavior

APPENDIX B – HISTORY TIMELINE **601**

- Waclaw Radecki arrives in Uruguay and teach a course of General Psychology
- Alfred Adler publishes On the Sense of the Life
- C. G. Jung becomes professor at the Federal Polytechnical University in Zurich
- Max Wertheimer and Kurt Lewin emigrate to America
- The British Union of Practical Psychologist is established
- The Psychological Engineering Section of the State Institute for Experimental Psychology is abolished in U.S.S.R.
- The Japanese Society for Animal Psychology is established
- **1934** Plinio Olinto publishes Psychology
- The discipline psychology becomes obligatory in some undergraduate courses
- Alfred Adler emigrates to America
- The American Institute of Public Opinion is established
- Jacob Moreno introduces the sociometric measurement technique
- Jacob Moreno publishes Who Shall Survive?
- The Norwegian Psychological Association (Norsk Psykologforening) was established
- The first psychological clinical in Egypt founded at the Higher Institute of Education
- **1935** Sylvio Rabello publishes Psychology of the Infantile Drawing
- Jean Maugué begins to teach Psychology in Bachelor in Philosophy, staying until 1944
- B. F. Skinner distinguishes pavlovian conditioning and operant conditioning in the paper Two Types of Conditioned Reflex and a Pseudo-Type
- Wolfgang Kohler and Kurt Goldstein emigrate to America
- Carl Murchison publishes Handbook of Social Psychology
- Egon Brunswik is invited by Edward Tolman to spend a year as a visiting lecturer at research fellow at the University of California, Berkeley
- Alfred Adler establishes the International Journal of Individual Psychology
- Christiana Morgan e Henry Murray develop TAT - Test of Thematic Apperception
- Walter Blumenfeld arrives in Peru and works at Institute of Psychology at Universidad San Marcos
- Wolfgang Köhler leaves his chair in Berlin

602   THE MEANING OF LIFE

- Kurt Koffka publishes Principles of Gestalt Psychology
- **1936** Noemi Silveira assumes the teaching of educational psychology at the Faculdade de Filosofia Ciências e Letras de São Paulo
- The Society for the Psychological Study Social of Issues is founded
- Muzafer Sherif publishes The psychology of social norms
- Erwin Levy publishes A case of mania with its social implications
- Founded the first independent chair of psychology in Finland
- **1937** Psychological laboratory do Engenho de Dentro was incorporated by the University of Brazil
- Gordon Allport publishes his most significant work: Personality: psychological interpretation
- B. F. Skinner uses the term operant for the first time and applies the term respondent to the pavlovian type of reflex
- Donald O. Hebb returns to Canada as fellow of the Neurological Institute of Montreal
- First psychology program in School of Philosophy and Literature of the National Autonomous University of Mexico (UNAM)
- Anna Freud publishes The Ego and the Mechanisms of Defense
- Karen Horney publishes The neurotic personality of our time
- **1938** Sylvio Rabello publishes The representation of the time in the child
- Djacir Menezes publishes in Fortaleza the Dictionary of Pedagogical Psychology
- B. F.Skinner publishes The Behavior of the Organisms
- Henry Murray publishes Explorations in Personality
- D. Katz and R. L. Schank publish Social Psychology
- The Romanian psychologist Florian Stefanescu-Goanga establishes the Revista de Psichologie
- M. B. Hushiyar establishes the first psychological laboratory and publishes the first Iranian experimental psychology textbook (Experimental Psychology)
- **1939** Arthur Ramos publishes The problem children
- John Dollard, Neal Miller and collaborators present the hypothesis of frustration - aggression, in the book Frustration and Aggression

APPENDIX B – HISTORY TIMELINE **603**

- The Canadian Psychological Association was established by 38 founding members
- The Spanish psychologist Mercedes Rodrigo arrives in Colombia
- Emilio Mira y Lopez presents in Royal Society of Medicine in London the Test depsicodiagnostico miokinetico PMK
- A psychology course is taught at the University of Hong Kong

1940

- **1941** B. Moore & B. Fine publish A History of Medical Psychology
- The Instituto de Psicologia is establishedat the Universidad de Chile
- The experimental psychological school in Peru is established at the Instituto Psicopedagogico Nacional
- The first German diploma examination and professional university training in psychology is established in Germany
- **1942** S.R.Hathaway e McKinley publish Minnesota Multiphasic Personality Inventory - MMPI
- Carl Rogers develops the therapy centered on the patient
- The Sociedad de Estudios Psicológicos,Psiquiátricos y Disciplinas Conexas is established in Ecuador
- **1943** Clark L. Hull publishes Principles of Behavior
- Clifford Morgan publishes Physiological Psychology, a standard text for decades
- Enrique Mouchet publishes Percepcion, instinto y razon
- Bruno Bettelheim publishes Individual and mass behavior in extreme situations
- Erwin Levy publishes Some Aspects of the Schizophrenic Formal Disturbance of Thought.
- **1944** Plinio Olinto traces an inclusive panorama of the experimentation in The Experimental Psychology in Brazil
- Donald O. Hebb postulates the cell assembly theory
- **1945** Annita Marcondes de Cabral and Otto Klineberg create the Society of Psychology of São Paulo
- Kurt Lewin organizes the Research Center for Group Dynamics in the Massachussets Institute of Technology

604   THE MEANING OF LIFE

- The first U.S. state law for certification or licensure of psychologists was signed by Governor Raymond Baldwin of Connecticut.

- Otto Fenichel publishes Psychoanalytical Theories of Neuroses

- K. Duncker publishes in the periodic Psychological Monographs the famous article On problem solving

- The Journal of Clinical Psychology is founded

- The journal Egyptian Journal of Psychology, edited by Yousif Mourad and Mustapha Ziwar, is established

- The Australian branch of the British Psychological Society is established

- **1946** Fritz Heider publishes Attitudes and cognitive organization

- The first number of American Psychologist is published

- Bela Székely publishes Los tests

- The Decree 1023 regulates the formation of psychologists in Chile

- Psychology as profession begins in Guatemala

- The journal Revista de Psicología General y Aplicada is established in Spain

- The Korean Psychological Association is established

- **1947** Jerome Bruner and Cecile Goodman publish Value and need as organizing factors in perception

- Gardner Murphy publishesPersonality: a biosocial approach to origin and structure

- Kurt Goldstein publishes The Organism: A holistic approach to biology derived from pathology data in men

- Roger Barker and Herbert Wright establish the Midwest Psychological Field Station dedicated to study of ecological psychology

- The Faculdad de Filosofia de la Universidad de Chile initiates the professionalization of psychologists

- Psychology as profession begins in Colombia

- Established in France a university degree (licence de psychologie) in psychology

- The Belgian Psychological Society is established

- Jaime Zaguirre establishes the first Philipino neuropsychological services unit at the V. Luna General Hospital

APPENDIX B – HISTORY TIMELINE   605

- **1948** B. F. Skinner publishes Walden Two
- E. C. Tolman publish the paper Cognitive Maps in Rats and Man
- Keneth MacCorquodale and Paul Meehl publish On a distinction between hypothetical constructs and intervening variables
- Established the Instituto de Psicologia y Investigaciones Psicologicas in the Faculdad de Humanidades de La Universidad San Carlos, in Guatemala
- The C. G. Jung Institute is established in Zurich
- Psychology as an independent university subject begins to be studied in Czechoslovakia
- The Egyptian Association for Psychological Societies (EAPS) is established
- **1949** The journal Arquivos Brasileiros de Psicotécnica, later Arquivos Brasileirosde Psicologia is founded
- Jerome Bruner and Leo Postman publish On the perception of incongruity: a paradigm
- Donald O. Hebb publishes The Organization of Behavior
- George Miller and Frederick Frick publishes Statistical Behavioristics and Sequences of Responses
- The Wechsler Intelligence Scale for Children was first published
- Gilbert Ryle publishes The concept of mind
- Shannon and Weaver publish The mathematical theory of the communication
- A conference about scientific and professional formation in psychology is held in Boulder, Colorado
- The Japanese Group Dynamics Association is established

1950

- **1950** Second edition of Boring's A History of Experimental Psychology
- Adorno, Frenkel-Brunswick, Levinson & Sanford publish The Authoritarian Personality
- Theodor Newcomb publishes Social Psychology
- George Homans publishes The Human Group
- Alan Turing publishes Computing machinery and intelligence
- Robert Bales introduces the Interactional Process Analysis

606   THE MEANING OF LIFE

- Established the Mexican Society of Psychology
- Established at the Central University of Ecuador the Institute of Psychology
- The Israel Psychological Association is established
- **1951** The International Union of Psychological Science (IUPS), later International Union of Psychological Sciences (IUPsyS) is founded
- The Interamerican Society of Psychology is founded in Mexico
- The Institute of Psychology Chinese Academy of Science is founded
- **1952** Egon Brunswick publishes The conceptual framework of psychology
- Salomon Asch publishes Social Psychology
- Frederic Bartlett publishes Think and to Conceive: Experiments of Practical psychology
- The Spanish Psychological Society is established
- The Japanese Educational Psychology Association is established
- **1953** The American Association of Psychology publishes the first Code of Ethics of Psychologists
- B. F. Skinner publishes Science and Human Behavior
- Leon Festinger and Daniel Katz publish Research methods in the behavioral sciences
- C. Hovland, I. Janis and H. Kelley publish Communication and persuasion: psychological studies of opinion change
- The Sociedad de Psicologia del Uruguai is established
- A postgraduate school of psychology at theUniversity of Madrid is established
- Iraj Ayman establishes the Testing and Vocational Guidance Unit at the U.S. Technical Operation Mission in Tehran
- **1954** The Brazilian Association of the Psychologists is established
- In the journal Arquivos Brasileiros de Psicotécnica a law project about the formation and the regulation of the psychologist's profession is published
- Gordon Allport publishes The nature of prejudice
- Leon Festinger postulates the theory of social comparison process
- Abraham Maslow develops a hierarquical theory of human personality in the book Motivation and Personality

APPENDIX B – HISTORY TIMELINE **607**

- B. F. Skinner demonstrates at the University of Pittsburgh a machine designed to teach arithmetic, using an instructional program
- The journal Acta Psiquiatrica y Psicologicade America Latina is established in Argentina
- The Sociedad Peruana de Psicologia is established
- **1955** Social psychologist Richard Crutchfield publishes the article Conformity and Character
- George Kelly publishes Psychology of Personal Constructs
- Lee J. Cronbach and Paul E. Meehl's article Construct Validity in Psychological Tests was published
- Established the Federacion Colombiana de Psicologia (Colombian Federation of Psychology)
- Established the formation in psychology at the Universidad SanMarcos at Peru
- The Journal of Analytical Psychology is established in London
- South-African psychiatrist David Cooper arrives in England
- A psychology department is established at the University of Queensland, Australia
- **1956** Jerome Bruner and collaborators publish A study of thinking
- George A. Miller publishes in Psychological Review his famous articleon the magic number seven
- Salomon Asch publishes his studies about conformity
- U. T. Place postulates in the article Is Consciousness a Brain Process?, the first modern statement of the identity theory
- Swiss psychiatrist Ludwig Biswanger publishes Three Forms of Frustrated existence: Extravagance, Idiosyncrasy and Affectation
- The journal CeskolovenskaPsychologie (Czechoslovak Psychology) is founded
- Law No. 198 regulates the clinical practice of psychologists in Egypt
- **1957** Leon Festinger publishes Theory of the Cognitive Dissonance
- B.F. Skinner and Charles B. Ferster publish, after five years of collaboration, the book Schedules of Reinforcement
- B. F. Skinner publishes Verbal behavior
- H. J. Eysenck publishes The effects of psychotherapy: an evaluation

608 THE MEANING OF LIFE

- L. Cronbach publishes The two disciplines of scientific psychology

- The Instituto deInvestigaciones Psicologicas is founded at the Universidad de Costa Rica

- The Finnish Psychological Society is established

- **1958** Allen Newell, Marvin E. Shaw, and Herbert A. Simon's article Elements of a Theory of Human Problem Solving, the first exposition of the information-processing approach in psychology

- Herbert Feigl publishes The 'Mental' and the 'Physical'

- Howard A. Rusk publishes Rehabilitation Medicine, in which his suggests that approximately one-half of physically disabled adults would require psychological services to attain a reasonable adaptation

- Donald Broadbent publishes Perception and Communication

- Offered in France a doctorate with an option in psychology

- The Czechoslovak Psychological Society and the Slovak Psychological Society were founded

- The Pattern Completion Test (PATCO), devised by the South African National Institute of Personal Research, is applied to nomadic Bushmen during the first and second(1959) Kalahari expeditions

- **1959** Wolfgang Köhler publishes Gestalt psychology today

- John W. Thibaut and Harold H. Kelley's book The Social Psychology of Groups was published

- J. P. Guilford's article The three faces of intellect was published in the American Psychologist

- Noam Chomsky publishes his revision of the book Verbal Behavior previously published by B. F. Skinner

- J. J. C. Smart publishes the article Sensations and Brain Process

- Iraj Ayman establishes the Iran's first psychological department at the National Teacher's College in Tehran

- In Tananarive, Madagascar, the C.C.T.A/C.S.A. Meeting of Specialists of the Basic Psychology of Africanand Madagascan Populations is held

1960

- **1960** G. Sperling publishes its famous article about the sensorial memory
- Robert Watson publishes the article History of Psychology: a Neglected Area
- Milton Rokeach publishes The open and the closed mind
- First school of professional psychology is established in Mexico
- The Japanese Social Psychology Association is established
- **1961** First edition of Journal of Humanistic Psychology
- Carl Rogers publishes On becoming a person
- The Handbook of Clinical Psychology, edited by Benjamin Wolman, was first published
- Rensis Likert's book New Patterns of Management , a landmark in organizational psychology, was published.
- Michael Argyle and Janet Dean's article Eye-Contact, Distance, and Affiliation was published in Sociometry.
- Hans Toch publishes Legal and Criminal Psychology , the first psycholegal textbook
- A psychology program is established at the University of las Villas, Cuba
- **1962** Creation of bachelor courses and the profession of psychologist
- The University of São Paulo hires Fred Keller
- Michael Murphy and Richard Price found the Esalen Institute at Big Sur, in California
- The Psychological Association of the Philipinnes is established
- **1963** Pedro Parafita Bessa creates the course of Psychology at the Universidade Federal de Minas Gerais
- Sigmund Koch publishes Psychology: a Study of a Science
- Neil Smelser publishes Theory of Collective Behavior
- J. A. Ritchie publishes in Wellington, New Zealand the book The Making of a Maori: A case study of a changing country
- **1964** Fred Keller, Carolina M. Bori, Rodolpho Azzi e J. G. Sherman install the Department of Psychology of the Universidade de Brasília
- Stanley Milgram publishes Obedience to authority

610 THE MEANING OF LIFE

- Emergence of humanistic psychology as "third force" in psychology
- T. W.Wann edits Behaviorism and Phenomenology: contrasting bases for modern psychology
- The Union Cubana de Psicologia is established
- The Sociedad Salvadorena de Psicologia is established
- The yugoslav historian of psychology Kruno Kristic publishes in the journal Acta Instituti Psychologici Universitatis Zagabrensis the article Marko Marulik. The autor of the term "psychology"
- The Association of Romanian Psychologists is established
- **1965** The military regime dissolves the Department of Psychology of the Universidade de Brasília
- Roger Brown publishes Social Psychology
- Robert Zajonc analises the process of social facilitation
- The Journal for the History of Behavioural Sciences is founded
- A conference held in Swampscott, Massachusetts,establishes the field of community psychology
- The Asociación Panameña de Psicologos is established
- T'Sao Jih-chang translate Woodward and Schlossberg's Experimental Psychology into Chinese
- The Pakistan Journal of Psychology is established
- The first laboratory of experimental psychology in independent sub-saarian Africa is established in Zambia
- **1966** J. J. Gibson publishes The senses considered as perceptual system
- Jerome S. Bruner's book Studies in Cognitive Growth was published.
- Saul Sternberg's article High Speed Scanning in Human Memory was published in Science
- First master's program in humanistic psychology is established in the psychology department of the Sonoma State College
- The first federal legislation to protect animal research subjects, The Animal Welfare Act, was enacted
- Established the Sociedad Paraguaya de Psicologia

APPENDIX B – HISTORY TIMELINE **611**

- Psychology as banned as a university subject, the Institute of Psychology in Chinese Academic of Sciences is closed and the publication of psychology journals and books is ceased in China
- The iranian psychologist A. A. Siyassi publishes in Persian the book Science of Mind or Psychology from the standpoint of education
- The Australian Psychological Society is established
- **1967** The journal Revista Interamericana de Psicologia/Interamerican Journal of Psychology is established
- Rollo May publishes Psychology and the Human Dillema
- Hilary Putnam suggests the idea of multiple realizability of mental properties
- Robert Watson establishes the first history of psychology PHD program in the world
- The department of psychology at the Universidad Autonoma de Santo Domingo in Dominican Republic is established
- Ulric Neisser publishes Cognitive Psychology
- **1968** Abraham Maslow publishes Toward a Psychology of Being
- The International Encyclopedia of the Social Sciences is published
- Established the Colegio de Psicólogos de Chile (union of psychologists)
- Lourdes García-Averasturi establishes in Cuba the National Group of Psychology
- David Armstrong publishes A Materialistic Theory of Mind
- Cheiron, the International Organizations for the History of the Behavioral and Social Sciences is established
- The Department of Psychology at the University of Hong Kong and the Hong Kong Psychological Society is established
- The Psychological Association of Iran is established
- The Korean Journal of Psychology is established
- The Pakistan Psychological Association held its first meeting in Dhaka
- A department of psychology is established in the University of Zambia
- **1969** Gregory Bateson publishes Schizophrenia and Family
- Albert Bandura publishes Principles of Modification of the Behavior

612 THE MEANING OF LIFE

- Gardner Lindzey & Elliot Aronson publishes the second edition of the Handbook of Social Psychology
- Joseph Wolpe publishes The practice of behavior therapy
- Elizabeth Kubler-Ross publishes On the Death and Dying
- Ruben Ardila founds in Colombia the Latin American Journal of Psychology
- The Revista Argentina de Psicologia is established
- Lewis Brandt and Wolfgang Metzer publish 'Reality,' What does it mean?

1970

- **1970** The Association Humanistic Psychology creates the Humanistic Psychology Institute as an educational and research institute
- The french psychologist Francois Lapointe publishes in the journal American Psychologist the article Origins and evolutions of the term psychology
- First International Invitation Conference on Humanistic Psychology in Amsterdam
- Stanislav Kratochvil publishes in Czechoslovakia Psychotherapy: Approaches, Methods and research
- **1971** R. Shepard & J.Metzler publishes the article Mental rotation of three-dimensional objects
- B. F. Skinner publishes Beyond Freedom and Dignity
- H. Rimoldi establishes the Interdisciplinary Center of Research in Mathematical and Experimental Psychology
- Italian psychiatrist Franco Basaglia publishes The Denied Institution
- The Psychological Practices Act governs the psychological practice in Zimbabwe
- **1972** A. Newell & H. Simon publish Human Problem Solving
- Ron Harré and Paul Secord publish The Explanation of Social Behavior
- R. A. LeVine and D. T. Campbell publish Ethnocentrism
- J. Israel and H. Tajfel publish The context of social psychology
- J. R. Eiser and W. Stroebe publish Categorization and social judgment
- The Swiss psychiatrist Medard Boss founds in Zurich the Institute Analytic Existential of Psychotherapy and Psychosomatic

APPENDIX B – HISTORY TIMELINE 613

- **1973** Established the Faculty of Psychology at the National University of Mexico (UNAM)
- Karl von Frisch, Konrad Lorenz and Nikollaas Tinbergen receive the Nobel Prize in recognition of their studies on the behavior of the animals
- A psychological licensing law was adopted in Norway
- **1974** The First Annual Convention of the American Psychology-Law Society is held
- The Journal of Black Psychology was first published by the Association of Black Psychologists.
- The Egyptian Association for Psychological Societies publishes the first volume of the Egyptian Yearbook of Psychology
- The Medical, Dental , and Supplementary Health Service Professions Act governs the profession of psychologist in South Africa
- **1975** Paul Feyerabend publishes Against the Method: Outline of an anarchist theory of knowledge
- Mary Henle publishes Gestalt psychology and gestalt therapy
- The Center for Advanced Study in Theoretical Psychology is established at the Alberta University , Canada
- The first college program in Community Psychology is offered by the psychology department of the University of Puerto Rico at Rio Piedras
- The Associacion Dominicana de Psicologia (Dominican Association of Psychology) is established
- William Sahakian publishes History of Psychology
- **1976** The Latin American Association of Social Psychology (ALAPSO) is established
- V. Sexton and H. Misiak publish Psychology Around the World
- J. Ehrenwald publishes A History of Psychotherapy
- Psychology is recognized as a independent school at the University of Havana
- The Colegio de Psicólogos de Bolivia is established
- Ulric Neisser publishes Cognition and Reality
- M. Billig publishes Social psychology and intergroup relations
- **1977** R. Schank & R. Abelson publish Scripts, Plans, Goals and Understanding
- Alan Gauld & John Shotter publish Human action and its psychological investigation

614   THE MEANING OF LIFE

- Joseph Rychlak publishes Psychology of Rigorous Humanism
- Sheldon Stryker distinguishes between psychological and sociological social psychology
- An article by a group of psychologist at Beijing University suggest the revival of psychology as an academic discipline
- The Law of Psychologists regulates the profession of psychologist in Israel
- Nixon and Taft publish Psychology in Australia: Achievements and Prospects
- **1978** Kelley and Thibaut publish Interpersonal relations: A theory of interdependence
- The Laboratorio de Psicologia at the Universidad de Los Andes , Merida, Venezuela is founded
- The journal Boletin de Psicologia is founded in La Habana, Cuba
- The Federacion de Psicólogos de Venezuela is established
- The Columbian Society of Psychology is established
- A new universitary law reduces the time of study of psychology in Czechoslovakia from 5 to 4 years
- The Chinese Society of Psychology is refounded
- **1979** J.J. Gibson publishes The ecological approach to visual perception
- Lachman, Lachman & Butterfield publish Cognitive psychology and information processing: An introduction
- The journal Revista Chilena de Psicologia is founded
- The journal Psychologie und Gesellschaftskritik published two issues (1979/1980) on Psychology and Fascism containing several studies on psychology in Nazi Germany
- The Belgian Federations of Psychologists is established
- The Greek Parliament promulges a law specifying the qualifications for the profession of psychologist

1980

- **1980** M. J. Lerner publishes The belief in a just world
- It is estimated that one out of ten doctorates granted in the United States in psychology
- John Searle presents in the article Minds, Brain, and Programs   the Chinese room argument

- Ned Block publishes the first volume of Readings in Philosophy of Psychology
- The Colegio Oficial de Psicólogos (Union of Psychologist) is established in Spain
- The Institute of Psychology of Bucharest and the official teaching of psychology are abolished in Romaniabetween 1980 and 1989
- The Belgian Federation of Psychologist publishes its Code of Ethics
- **1981** M. Rosenzweig estimates the total number of psychologist in the world to be 260,000
- American Psychological Association has approximately 50,500 members
- The journal Revista de la Association Latinoamericana de Psicologia Social is established in Mexico
- J. C. Turner and H. Giles publish Intergroup behavior
- Estabelecida a Federação Européia das Associações Profissionais de Psicólogos
- **1982** D. Kahneman, P. Slovic and A. Tversky publish Judgment under Uncertainty: Heuristics and Biases
- David Marr publishes Vision: an investigation computational on the human representation and the processing of the visual information
- The Humanistic Psychology Institute changes its name to the Saybrook Institute
- The journal Revista de Historia de la Psicología is established in Spain
- The Academy of Arabic Language in Cairo approves a dictionary of psychological terms
- **1983** John R. Anderson publishes The Architecture of Cognition
- Jerry Fodor publishes The Modularity of the Mind
- Law 58 legalizes the profession of psychologist in Colombia
- The journal New Ideas in Psychology is established
- The Japonese Journal of Clinical Psychology is established
- Established the Psychological Association of South Africa (PASA)
- **1984** Helmuth Krüger publishes Introduction to Social Psychology
- S. T. Fiske and S. E. Taylor publish Social Cognition
- Zenon Pylyshyn publishes Computation and Cognition
- The journal Revista Cubana de Psicologia is esblished in La Habana, Cuba

616   THE MEANING OF LIFE

- Robert Farr and Serge Moscovici publish Social representations
- Over 400 students are reported to receive doctoral degree in psychology in India
- **1985** Gardner Lindzey & Elliot Aronson publish the third edition of Handbook of Social Psychology
- Howard Gardner publishes The new mind's science
- Petr Rezek publishes anonymously in Prague Lectures on Phenomenological Psychology
- Law n. 85-772 defines the professional regulation of psychologists in France
- The Japanese Industrial and Organizational Association is established
- There are an estimated 58 academic psychologist in Nigeria and 22 in Cameroon
- **1986** McClelland, J. L. & Rumelhart, D. E. publish the series of books Parallel Distributed Processing
- A. Paivio publishes Mental Representations: a dual code approach
- Robert Wyer, Jr. & Thomas Srull publish the article Human cognition in its social context
- Willem Doise publishes Levels of explanation in social psychology
- Psychological consultation becomes popular in China
- China's "Humanistic Psychology Craze", especially its "Maslow Craze" gradually took shape, and through 1989 Maslow's books sell 557,900 copies
- A. A. Shoarinejad publishes in Tehran A Dictionary of behavioral sciences
- **1987** An estimated 18,000 psychologists in France
- The Pakistan Psychological Association publishes a report on the standard for the practice of psychotherapy in Pakistan
- Janak Pandey publishes the three volume book Psychology in India: The State of the Art
- 815 people have professional register to work as psychologists in New Zealand
- **1988** An estimated 5,000 psychologists in Germany and 2,160 in Norway
- Published in Hebrew language the journal Israel Quarterly of Psychology
- **1989** I. Altman publishes the article Centripetal and centrifugal trends in psychology
- John Searle publishes Minds, brains, and science
- A group of experimental psychologists establishes the Canadian Society for Brain, Behaviour and Cognitive Sciences

- Diaz-Guerrero developes one of the most significant psychological projects of Mexico - Mexican Ethnopsychology
- State Law No. 56 regulates the profession of psychologist in the Italy
- The journal Psychology and Developing Societies at the University of Alahhabad, India is established

---

1990

- **1990** Established the Union Peruvian of Psychologists
- 15,000 licensed psychologist in Mexico
- Dalal estimates between 4,000 and 4,500 psychologists in India
- An estimated 5,000 clinical psychologist in Japan
- **1991** There are 27,000 registered students of psychology in Mexico
- The Association of Academic Unities in Psychology is established in Argentina
- Law 360/1990 regulates the profession of psychologist in Austria
- **1992** Aproximately 10,000 people are working as psychologists in Argentina and 8,000 in Canada
- The Law 30 regulates the graduate study in psychology in Colombia
- Aproximately 6,000 people are working as psychologists in Polland, 1,350 in Austria and 6,000 in Belgium
- Aproximately 600 people are working as psychologists in the Pakistan, 5,000 in India and 2,500 in Israel
- International Workshop on "Child Development and National Development" was organized in Yaounde,Cameroon
- An estimated 5,000 to 6,000 people are working as psychologists in Australia
- **1993** A. H. Eagly and S. Chaiken publish The psychology of attitudes
- Roger Sperry publishes in American Psychologist the article The Impact and Promise of the Cognitive Revolution
- Beijing Research Association of Healthy Personalities (BRAHP) and Beijing People's Radio Station launched a radio program, "Healthy Personalities and Life"
- **1994** A total of 111 Brazilian Universities have psychology programs

618 THE MEANING OF LIFE

- The first National PsychologyCongress is held in Campos do Jordão
- M. P. Zanna and J. M. Olson publish The psychology of prejudice: The Ontario Symposium, vol. 7
- The first Encontros Integradores de Psicologos del Mercosur is held in Montevideo
- Roger Sperry dies
- J. P. Leyens, V. Yzerbyt and G. Schadron publish Stereotypes and social cognition
- The Decree concerning Health Care Professional regulates the title of psychotherapist in Finland
- **1995** The second Encontros Integradores de Psicologos del Mercosur is held in Buenos Ayres
- First issue of Psychology, Public Policy, And Law
- Aproximately 1,200 people are working as psychologists in Colombia
- The European Federation of Professional Psychologists Associaciation accepts the Meta-Code of Ethics
- **1996** Jaegwon Kin publishes Philosophy of Mind
- Established the Guatemalan Association of Psychology
- A total of 59 Canadian Universities have psychology programs and approximately 10,000 psychologists are legally recognized to practice psychology in Canada.
- Approximately 3,600 psychologists are legally recognized to practice psychology in Cuba
- **1997** The IV Encontro Integrador dos Psicólogos do Mercosul is held in Montevideo with participants of Federación de Psicologos de la Republica Argentina, Conselho Federal de Psicologia (Brasil), Colegio de Psicologos de Chile, Sociedad Paraguaya de Psicologia and Coordinadoria de Psicologos del Uruguay
- Established the Union of Psychologists of Costa Rica
- Joseph Wolpe and Hans Eysenck die
- S. Russel, P. Oakes, N. Ellemers e S. A. Haslam publish The Social Psychology of Stereotyping and Group Life
- **1998** Approximately 3,700 psychologists are legally recognized to practice psychology in Chile
- An estimated 1,200 people are working as psychologists in Bolivia

APPENDIX B – HISTORY TIMELINE   619

- An estimated 1,700 people are legally recognized to practice psychology in Paraguay
- Dies M. T. Bazany, one of the most important psychologist of Czechoslovakia
- **1999** Approximately 100,000 psychologists are legally recognized to practice psychology in Brazil.
- Nise da Silveira, one of the most important brazilian junguian psychologist dies
- Psychology in the Americas, edited by Modesto Alonso and Alice Eagly, was published by Interamerican Society of Psychology (SIP)

2000

- **2000** Held in Stockholm, Sweden, The XXVII International Congress of Psychology

ENDNOTES

[1] Fowler, J. W. (1981) Stages of Faith (New York: Harper Collins, 44-234.

[2] Fowler, 46.

[3] Fowler, 89.

[4] Fowler, 91.

[5] Fowler, 93.

[6] Erikson, E. H. (1950) Childhood and Society New York: W.W. Norton. 21-38.

[7] Fowler, 91.
[8] Fowler, 86.

[9] Fowler, 123.

[10] Fowler, 110-125.

[11] Fowler, 149.

[12] See: Erikson, E. H. (1968) Identity, Youth and Crisis New York: W.W. Norton.

[13] Fowler, J. W. 151.

[14] Fowler, 150 - 163.

[15] Marquarrie, (1965) Studies in Christian Existentialism (Philadelphia: 58.

[16] Frankl, V. E. Man's Search for Meaning New York: Pocket Books, 89-91.

[17] Fowler, 179.

[18] Fowler, 181.

[19] Erikson, E. H. (1959) Identity and the Life Cycle New York; International University Press.

[20] Erikson, E. H. (1968) Identity, Youth and Crisis New York: W.W. Norton Co..

[21] Fowler, J. W. Stages of Faith (New York: Harper Collins, 1981).

[22] Fowler, 123- 160.

ENDNOTES **621**

[23] Rotherham, B. "Ethnic Difference in Adolescent's Identity Status and Associated Behavior Problems" Journal of Adolescence v.12, 361-374.

[24] Marcia, J. E. "Development and Validation of Ego Identity Status" Journal of Personality and Social Psychology 3, 551-558.

[25] Marcia, J.E. "Identity in Adolescence" IN: Handbook of Adolescent Psychology New York: Wiley, 1980, 159-187.

[26] Archer, S. L. & Waterman, A.S. "Varieties of Identity Differences and Foreclosure" Journal of Adolescent Research, 5, 96-111.

[27] Frankl, V.E. Man's Search for Meaning New York, Pocket Books, 120-134.

[28] Fowler, J. W. (1981)
[29] Celia, D.F.; DeWolfe, A.S. and Fitzgibbon, M. "Ego Identity Status, Identification and Decision - Making Style in Late Adolescence" Adolescence, 22, 851-860.

[30] Fowler, J. W.(1981) 165-172.

[31] Toder, N.L. and Marcia, J.E. "Ego Identity Status and Response to Conformity Pressure in College Women" Journal of Personality and Social Psychology, 26, 290-294.

[32] Marcia, J.E. "Development and Validation of Ego Identity Status" Journal of Personality and Social Psychology, 3, 355.

[33] Fowler, J. W (1981), 166-189.

[34] Fowler, 163.

[35] Fowler, 164-166.

[36] Fowler, 161-168.

[37] Fowler, 160 - 169.

[38] Fowler, 170 - 174.

[39] Fowler, 173 - 175.

[40] Fowler, 284.

[41] Kagan and Segal Psychology (New York: Harcourt, Brace and Jovanovich, 1988), 352.

[42] Kagan and Segal, 353.

[43] McConnel, J. V. Understanding Human Behavior (Ann Arbour: Concept Press, 1982), 485.

44 McConnel, 485.

45 McConnel, 485.

46 Kagan and Segal Psychology (New York: Harcourt, Brace and Jovanovich Publishers, 1988), 354.

47 McConnel, J. V. Understanding Human Behavior (Ann Arbour: Concept Press, 1982), 485.

48 Bernstein, D.A. Psychology (Boston: Houghton Mifflin Co.l, 1988), 512.
49 Kagan and Segal Psychology (New York: Harcourt, Brace Jovanovich Publishers, 1988), 356.

50 Freud, S. A General Introduction to Psychoanalysis (New York: Prema Giants, 1949), 430.

51 Clouse, B. Moral Development (Grand Rapids: Baker, 1985), 225.

52 Bernstein, D.A. Psychology (Geneva: Houghton Mifflin Co., 1988), 607.

53 Zimbardo, P.G. Psychology and Life (London: Scott, Foreman and Co., 1979), 67.

54 Clouse, B. Moral Development (Grand Rapids: Baker, 1985), 41.

55 Wilson, B. Buses, Bibles and Banana Splits (Grand Rapids: Baker, 1977)

56 Clouse, B. Moral Development (Grand Rapids: Baker, 1985), 86.
57 Clouse, 24.

58 Zimbardo, P. G. Psychology and Life (Glenview: Scott, Foreman and Co., 1979)

59 Kohlberg, L. "The Contribution of Developmental Psychology to Education" Educational Psychology V. 10, 13.

60 Liebert, R.M; Wicks - Nelson, R.; Kail, R.V. Developmental Psychology (New Jersey; Prentice - Hall, 1986), 312.

61 Kohlberg, L. "A cognitive - developmental analysis of Children's sex-role concepts and attitudes" IN: Mussen, P.H. (Ed.) Handbook of Child Psychology (New York, Wiley Press, 1966)

62 Liebert, R.M.; Wicks-Nelson, R.; Kail, R. V. Developmental Psychology (New Jersey: Prentice - Hall, 1986), 336

63 Clouse, B. Moral Development (Grand Rapids, Baker, 1985), 108.

64 Clouse, 109.

65 Clouse, 110.

66 Clouse, 110.

67 Fowler, J. W. Stages of Faith (New York: Harper Collins, 1981), 44-234.

ENDNOTES   623

[68] Fowler, 46.

[69] Fowler, 89.

[70] Fowler, 91.

[71] Fowler, 93.

[72] Erikson, E. H. Childhood and Society (New York: W.W. Norton, 1950) 21-38.

[73] Fowler, 91.
[74] Fowler, 86.

[75] Fowler, 123.

[76] Fowler, 110-125.

[77] Fowler, 149.

[78] See: Erikson, E. H. Identity, Youth and Crisis (New York: W.W. Norton, 1968).

[79] Fowler, J. W. Stages of Faith (New York: Harper Collins, 1981), 151.

[80] Fowler, 150 - 163.

[81] Marquarrie, Studies in Christian Existentialism (Philadelphia:, 1965), 58.

[82] Frankl, V. E. Man's Search for Meaning (New York: Pocket Books), 89-91.

[83] Fowler, 179.

[84] Fowler, 181.

[85] Erikson, E. H. Identity and the Life Cycle (New York; International University Press, 1959).

[86] Erikson, E. H. Identity, Youth and Crisis (New York: W.W. Norton Co., 1968).

[87] Fowler, J. W. Stages of Faith (New York: Harper Collins, 1981).

[88] Fowler, 123- 160.

[89] Rotherham, B. "Ethnic Difference in Adolescent's Identity Status and Associated Behavior Problems" Journal of Adolescence v.12, 361-374.

[90] Marcia, J. E. "Development and Validation of Ego Identity Status" Journal of Personality and Social Psychology 3, 551-558.

624   THE MEANING OF LIFE

---

[91] Marcia, J.E. "Identity in Adolescence" IN: <u>Handbook of Adolescent Psychology</u> (New York: Wiley, 1980), 159-187.

[92] Archer, S. L. & Waterman, A.S. "Varieties of Identity Differences and Foreclosure" <u>Journal of Adolescent Research</u>, 5, 96-111.

[93] Frankl, V.E. <u>Man's Search for Meaning</u> (New York, Pocket Books), 120-134.

[94] Fowler, J. W. <u>Stages of Faith</u> (New York; Harper Collins).

[95] Celia, D.F.; DeWolfe, A.S. and Fitzgibbon, M. "Ego Identity Status, Identification and Decision - Making Style in Late Adolescence" <u>Adolescence</u>, 22, 851-860.

[96] Fowler, J. W. <u>Stages of Faith</u> (New York, Harper Collins, 1981), 165-172.

[97] Toder, N.L. and Marcia, J.E. "Ego Identity Status and Response to Conformity Pressure in College Women" <u>Journal of Personality and Social Psychology</u>, 26, 290-294.

[98] Marcia, J.E. "Development and Validation of Ego Identity Status" <u>Journal of Personality and Social Psychology</u>, 3, 355.

[99] Fowler, J. W. <u>Stages of Faith</u> (New York: Harper Collins, 1981), 166-189.

[100] Fowler, 163.

[101] Fowler, 164-166.

[102] Fowler, 161-168.

[103] Fowler, 160 - 169.

[104] Fowler, 170 - 174.

[105] Fowler, 173 - 175.

[106] Fowler, 284.

[107] Westerhoff, J.H. <u>Today's Church</u> (Waco: Word Book, 1976).

[108] Nelson, G. M. <u>To Dance with God</u> (New York: Paulist Press, 1986), 47.

[109] Westerhoff, J. H. <u>Living the Faith Community</u> (New York: Harper & Row, 1985).

[110] See: Westerhoff, J. H. <u>Will Our Children Have Faith?</u> (New York: Seabury Press, 1976).

[111] Westerhoff, J.H. "Formation, Education and Instruction" <u>Religious Education</u> (82, 1987), 578-581.

[112] Westerhoff, 583-590.

ENDNOTES   625

[113] See Fowler.

[114] See: Marthaler, B. "Socialization as a Model for Catechizes" IN: <u>Foundations of Religious Education</u> (New York: Paulist Press, 1978).

[115] See Evenson, R. <u>Nurturing the Maturity of Faith</u> (St. Louis: Concordia/ Project Serve, 1985).

[116] Fowler, J. W. <u>Stages of Faith</u> (New York: Harper Collins, 1981), 133.

[117] Fowler, 133- 135.

[118] Fowler, 134.

[119] Fowler, 149.

[120] Fowler, 149.

[121] See: Evenson, R. <u>Nurturing the Maturity of Faith</u> (St. Louis: Concordia/ Project Serve, 1985).

[122] Fowler, J. W. <u>Stages of Faith</u> (New York: Harper Collins, 1981), 180- 183.

[123] See: Evenson, R. <u>Nurturing the Maturity of Faith</u> (St. Louis: Concordia/ Project Serve, 1985).

[124] Fowler, J. W. <u>Stages of Faith</u> (New York: Harper Collins, 1981), 183.

[125] Fowler, 187-188.

[126] See: Hoyer, G.W. "Worship and Teaching of the Faith" <u>Lutheran Education</u> (v.101, 1966), 242 - 249.

[127] Hoyer, G. W. "Worship and the Teaching of Faith" <u>Lutheran Education</u> (101, 1996), 242-249.

[128] <u>Humanistic Manifesto I & II</u> (London: Prometheus Books, 1985), 9.

[129] Collins, G. R. <u>The Rebuilding of Psychology</u> (Wheaton: Tyndale, 1989), 57.

[130] Frankl, V. E. <u>Man's Search for Meaning</u> (New York: Pocket Books), 174.

[131] <u>Humanistic Manifesto I & II</u> (New York: Prometheus Books, 1985) Article #6 of "Humanistic Manifesto I" 1933.

[132] Article 4 of "Humanistic Manifesto I" (1933).

[133] Collins, G. R. <u>The Rebuilding of Psychology</u> (Wheaton: Tyndale House, 1989), 83.

[134] Tappert, T. G. (Gen. Ed.) <u>The Book of Concord: The Confessions of the Evangelical Lutheran Church</u> (Philadelphia: Fortress Press, 1989): 506.

135 Humanistic Manifesto I & II
　　　Article 4 & 5 of "Humanistic Manifesto I"

136 Collins, G. R. The Rebuilding of Psychology (Wheaton, 1985), 125.

137 Humanistic Manifesto I & II (New York: Prometheus Books), 15.

138 Humanistic Manifesto , 15.

139 Sandars, N.K. The Epic of Gilgamesh (Middlesex: Penguin Books, 1987), 102.

140 MacQuarrie, J. Studies in Christian Existentialism, 52.

141 MacQuarrie, 53.

142 Maquarrie, 55.

143 Humanistic Manifesto I & II - The ethics declaration of Manifesto II.

144 Ethics Declaration Humanistic Manifesto I & II.

145 Frankl, V.E. Man's Search for Meaning, 148.

146 Kierkegaard, S. The Concept of Anxiety [Dread] (Princeton: Princeton University Press, 1980), 159.

147 The author's paraphrase of Proverbs 1:7 "the fear of the Lord is the beginning of knowledge."

148 Kierkegaard, 155.

149 Kierkegaard, 155 -156.

150 Kierkegaard, 152.

151 Kierkegaard, 155.

152 Kierkegaard, 159.

153 MacQuarrie, J. Studies in Christian Existentialism, 56.

154 MacQuarrie, 156.

155 Strommen, M.P. Four Imperatives: Youth and Family Ministry (Minneapolis: Augsburg, 1991), 4.

Printed in the United States
20621LVS00003B/25-102